PATTON'S 1996

PREDICTIONS FOR ROTISSERIE

Baseball

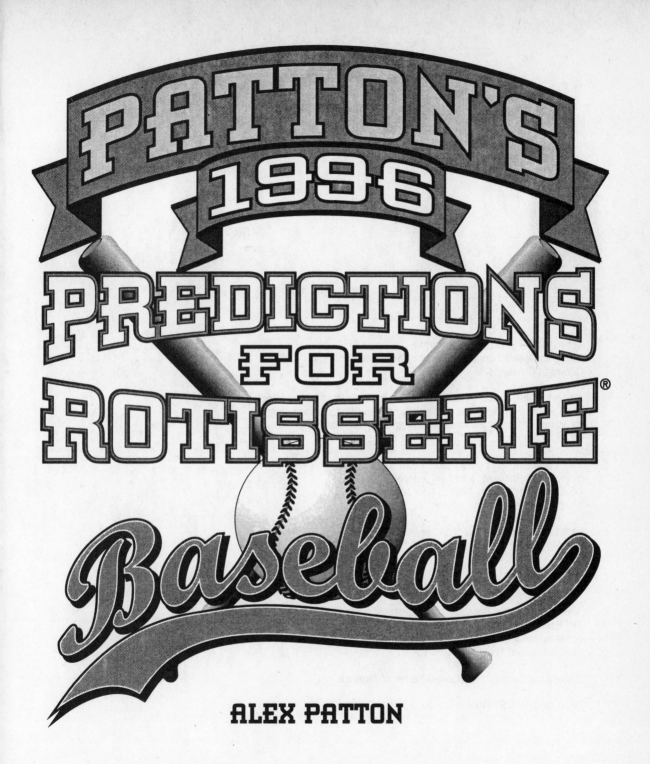

PATTON'S 1996 PREDICTIONS FOR ROTISSERIE® Baseball

ALEX PATTON

Park Lane Press
New York • New Jersey

This 1996 edition is published by Park Lane Press,
a division of Random House Value Publishing, Inc.,
40 Engelhard Avenue, Avenel, New Jersey 07001
by arrangement with the author.

Park Lane Press and colophon are trademarks of
Random House Value Publishing, Inc.

Random House
New York • Toronto • London • Sydney • Auckland

"Rotisserie League Baseball" is a registered trademark of
The Rotisserie League Baseball Association, Inc.
For information contact RLBA at 370 Seventh Avenue,
Suite 312, New York, New York 10001.

Printed and bound in the United States of America

Cover design by Bill Akunevicz Jr.

8 7 6 5 4 3 2 1

Table of Contents

Acknowledgments

Samuel Beckett, I trust, is no longer a baseball fan. It seems that all that's left are the owners, the players, and you and I. But the great thing is, you can sit anywhere now. And on we go, into another season.

To review last season, I still rely on the three terrific Stats Inc. books that come out in early November; the *Major League Handbook*, *Minor League Handbook*, and *Player Profiles*. They are the red, the green and the blue pillars of the player comments.

To find out what's going on in Rotisserie baseball, I continue to delve into the massive amount of material that Jerry Heath sends me. Anyone who uses his stat service can get it. If yours is less than perfect, you should call Jerry at (804) 498-8197 or write to Heath Data Services, 228 N. Lynhaven Rd. #106, Virginia Beach VA 23452 for information.

All of last year's predictions and theories were put to the acid test by, in the AL: Bruce Buschel, Chris Connelly, Larry Fine, Ron Givens, Peter Golenbock, Mark Goodman, Mark Jurkowitz, Peter Kreutzer, Mark Leibovich, Les Leopold, Steven Levy, Tony Lucas, Jeff Mitchell, Walter Shapiro, Mark Starr, Steve Stoneburn and Michael Walsh. Not necessarily in that order. In the NL: Susan Ashmore, Stu Baron, Al Chaby, Jim Dressel, Dottie Enrico, John Hunt, Michael Laub, Scott Newman, Steve Mann, Ron Shandler, John Snider, Mike Vogel and Rick Wilton.

It was a pleasure, for the second time, to join forces with Peter Golenbock in the Baseball Weekly league, while Dollar Bill Berensmann, for the umpteenth year, supported every bad move I made in the American Dreams, and added a few of his own.

Eric Lindow provided all the necessities, which otherwise would have been lacking, for generating the predictions.

At Random House Value Publishing, Kate Hartson, above all, gets credit for daring to play three. Pat LoBrutto stepped forward as the team's GM. Simon Tasker remained head of scouting. Yvette Romero handled the press, Bill Akunevicz Jr. designed the uniforms, Baman Motival was the trainer, and Michael Siebert made sure the team got out on the field.

The MVP again was Adam Summers, who had less than a week to turn a fistful of disks into what you are holding in your hands. Thank you, Adam; may you never get your PhD.

Thanks also to Pam Kwiatkowski for proof reading, as well as looking after of both of us during the crunch.

For providing a place to work all fall, not to mention live, heartfelt thanks go to Tiny and Rene Carrillo.

As always, I depended on Peg Summers for food and clean clothing and so much else.

Chapter 1
Player Profiles

American League Hitters

MIKE ALDRETE   OF   Age 35   Bid: R3

Year	Team	G	AB	R	H	BB	SO	D	T	HR	RBI	SB	CS	BA	$
1991	SD/CLE	97	198	24	48	39	41	6	1	1	20	1	3	.242	1
1993	OAK	95	255	40	68	34	45	13	1	10	33	1	1	.267	8
1994	OAK	76	178	23	43	20	35	5	0	4	18	2	0	.242	2
1995	CAL	78	149	19	40	19	31	8	0	4	24	0	0	.268	4

There are five types of reserve picks. R3, the middle classification, is for players on opening day rosters that you sort of hope you don't find on your own opening rosters, not even for $1. The most that is expected of minor league R3's is that they will be major league R3's.

R1's are the prospects who don't make opening day rosters but figure to be brought up quickly and have a significant impact; depending on league rules, they could well be keepers next year and should be grabbed quickly in the reserve draft. R2's have a good chance of being September call-ups and a few might even be keepers; they have brighter futures than major league R3's, certainly, but seldom are as productive this year.

R5's have the highest long-range hopes, and virtually no chance of making a contribution this season. They are the prizes that eventually pay off big in leagues with carry-over farm systems. R4's are a bit closer to the majors than R5's and less prized.

MANNY ALEXANDER   2B   Age 26   Bid: $3

Year	Team	G	AB	R	H	BB	SO	D	T	HR	RBI	SB	CS	BA	$
1992	BAL	4	5	1	1	0	3	0	0	0	0	0	0	.200	0
1993	BAL	3	0	1	0	0	0	0	0	0	0	0	0	.000	0
1995	BAL	94	242	35	57	20	30	9	1	3	23	11	4	.236	5

Bid limits aren't the same as predicted earnings. A total of 168 American League hitters have bids adding up to $2,100; 108 pitchers have bids adding up to $1,020. The $3,120 total is the amount standard 12-team Rotisserie leagues have to spend.

Bids are able to take into account all sorts of things that are beyond the scope of any formula that is generated by predicted stats. Many, many factors — such as position scarcity and reliability — come into play, but there's one basic rule of life: the big guys get paid at least in full, the little guys get cheated.

LUIS ALICEA
2B   Age 30   Bid: $5

Year	Team	G	AB	R	H	BB	SO	D	T	HR	RBI	SB	CS	BA	$
1991	STL	56	68	5	13	8	19	3	0	0	0	0	1	.191	-2
1992	STL	85	265	26	65	27	40	9	11	2	32	2	5	.245	4
1993	STL	115	362	50	101	47	54	19	3	3	46	11	1	.279	11
1994	STL	88	205	32	57	30	38	12	5	5	29	4	5	.278	9
1995	BOS	132	419	64	113	63	61	20	3	6	44	13	10	.270	13

A little guy who becomes an R3 if the Red Sox win the bidding war for either Roberto Alomar or Craig Biggio.

ROBERTO ALOMAR
2B   Age 28   Bid: $31

Year	Team	G	AB	R	H	BB	SO	D	T	HR	RBI	SB	CS	BA	$
1991	TOR	161	637	88	188	57	86	41	11	9	69	53	11	.295	42
1992	TOR	152	571	105	177	87	52	27	8	8	76	49	9	.310	40
1993	TOR	153	589	109	192	80	67	35	6	17	93	55	15	.326	51
1994	TOR	107	392	78	120	51	41	25	4	8	38	19	8	.306	24
1995	TOR	130	517	71	155	47	45	24	7	13	66	30	3	.300	32

Now, if *Cleveland* wins the bidding war, raise the bid you see here at least $5. They won't let him jake in the Jake.

I won't be shocked if he re-signs with the Blue Jays, though. There's some sort of odd but definitely intense connection between Roberto Alomar and Canada. During the season, he literally sleeps in the clubhouse; he lives in the Skydome. Women adore him — they screech, Canadian style, when he comes on the field — but the extent that he reciprocates is a subject the Toronto tabloids won't go near. One unfortunate woman made a very feeble threat against his life this summer, because he wouldn't answer her letters, and he took it seriously. So did the tabloids.

When Cone was traded, Alomar removed himself from the line-up. The real reason was that the Blue Jays wouldn't renegotiate his contract during the season. This caused such a stir — half of the fans outraged, the better half pleading with the Blue Jays to start negotiating — that Alomar agreed to play a game or two to quiet everyone down. He chose, however, to be a stationary object in the field, which brought shocked silence to the Skydome. His teammates — the once proud likes of Molitor and Carter and Devo — also had nothing to say.

Gaston stood for this. He apparently hasn't worn out his welcome either.

The more I think about it, the more I feel like moving this bid for Alomar $5 in the other direction, if he stays.

SANDY ALOMAR
C   Age 30   Bid: $10

Year	Team	G	AB	R	H	BB	SO	D	T	HR	RBI	SB	CS	BA	$
1991	CLE	51	184	10	40	8	24	9	0	0	7	0	4	.217	-2

Year	Team	G	AB	R	H	BB	SO	D	T	HR	RBI	SB	CS	BA	$
1992	CLE	89	299	22	75	13	32	16	0	2	26	3	3	.251	**4**
1993	CLE	64	215	24	58	11	28	7	1	6	32	3	1	.270	**7**
1994	CLE	80	292	44	84	25	31	15	1	14	43	8	4	.288	**18**
1995	CLE	66	203	32	61	7	26	6	0	10	35	3	1	.300	**12**

Appendix A shows what three veteran leagues that didn't have freezes paid for the Alomars: the Baseball Weekly AL league, the American Dreams League in New York and Cowtown in Texas. The fourth league, Ashpole in North Carolina, did have freezes, and so isn't counted in computing the average salary.

The "touts" are John Hunt and myself. At about the same time in mid-April, we produced last-minute, strike-adjusted, roster-updated, mind-altered — if not altering — price recommendations: John's were published in Baseball Weekly on April 19; mine went out two days before as the Free Spring Training Update (although many people, due to some foolish wording of mine in the postscript, sent 58 cents).

John got a 100% similarity score for Roberto Alomar, and I would have gotten him in the auction. I got a 92% similarity score for his brother, and John would have gotten him.

The last column in Appendix A shows what each player earned in 1994. Hunt and I both thought Roberto would go up, Sandy would go down. So, in fact, did the market. Ashpole paid more than any of the start-up leagues for Roberto — indicative of inflation. Ashpole froze Sandy at well under his free-market price — indicative of what causes inflation.

RICH AMARAL   OF   Age 34   Bid: $2

Year	Team	G	AB	R	H	BB	SO	D	T	HR	RBI	SB	CS	BA	$
1991	SEA	14	16	2	1	1	5	0	0	0	0	0	0	.063	**-1**
1992	SEA	35	100	9	24	5	16	3	0	1	7	4	2	.240	**2**
1993	SEA	110	373	53	108	33	54	24	1	1	44	19	11	.290	**16**
1994	SEA	77	228	37	60	24	28	10	2	4	18	5	1	.263	**5**
1995	SEA	90	238	45	67	21	33	14	2	2	19	21	2	.282	**13**
1995	CLE	28	60	5	12	4	6	3	0	1	7	1	3	.200	**0**

A bid limit is partly a prediction, of course, but it's more precisely a way of establishing a hierarchy. Rich Amaral is close to the bottom of the barrel of fifth outfielders, but he's not quite there. Late in the game, if someone says $1, you might say $2. However, if he's nominated early, you don't say $2 just because that's what's written on a sheet of paper. Nor do you nominate him yourself unless you're prepared to have him on your team.

BRADY ANDERSON   OF   Age 32   Bid: $22

Year	Team	G	AB	R	H	BB	SO	D	T	HR	RBI	SB	CS	BA	$
1991	BAL	113	256	40	59	38	44	12	3	2	27	12	5	.230	**6**

Year	Team	G	AB	R	H	BB	SO	D	T	HR	RBI	SB	CS	BA	$
1992	BAL	159	623	100	169	98	98	28	10	21	80	53	16	.271	**41**
1993	BAL	142	560	87	147	82	99	36	8	13	66	24	12	.263	**21**
1994	BAL	111	453	78	119	57	75	25	5	12	48	31	1	.263	**26**
1995	BAL	143	554	108	145	87	111	33	10	16	64	26	7	.262	**23**

Price predictions are fuzzy; they don't even need stats to go with them. Retrospective prices are exact; they tell how big a bite out of the total pie a player took that year.

Since the pie changes each year, so must the formulas for determining the bite size. At a glance we can see that Brady Anderson's 1992 season wasn't nearly twice as good as 1993, if the stats have no context. But 1993 was the expansion year, the beginning of the hitting explosion. Brady dropped off relative to the average player as well as to himself.

To everyone's surprise, 1994 saw even more hitting. So how does Brady get a $5 bigger bite with more or less the same stats?

The strike. Last year's book had an ugly line that no one ever wants to see again: "1994 proj." In a full season, Brady would have had cumulative stats of 17-67-43, to go with the .263 batting average.

Stats Inc. and Bill James dealt with this problem by playing out the season on a computer. It was a noble effort, I guess, that I didn't look at until just a minute ago. Brady's projected 1994 stats: 18-64-38, and a .248 batting average. He evidently was on the verge of one of his baffling slumps.

All slumps are baffling, but Brady's are especially so, since he has speed, and when the highs have been mixed in with the lows (.318 in April, .205 in August), he's about as steady as anybody.

Would Brady have earned more than $23 last year if the full 162 games had been played?

No. Cumulative stats of 18-72-29, and the same .262 batting average, would have still been worth $23, if the pie also grew by 12.5% (162/144).

So even though his stats last year look very much like his stats in 1993, they actually were better. But they weren't much better, because there was more hitting last year than there was in 1993. Or would have been, if they had started on time. Even if they had, there wasn't going to be quite as much hitting as there would have been in 1994, if they hadn't quit early.

GARRET ANDERSON   OF Age 24   Bid: $25

Year	Team	G	AB	R	H	BB	SO	D	T	HR	RBI	SB	CS	BA	$
1993	(AAA)	124	467	57	137	31	95	31	8	4	71	3	4	.293	x
1994	(AAA)	123	505	75	162	28	93	42	6	12	102	3	3	.321	x
1994	CAL	5	13	0	5	0	2	0	0	0	1	0	0	.385	1
1995	CAL	106	374	50	120	19	65	19	1	16	69	6	2	.321	**24**

In Stage Two of Rotisserie baseball, Garret Anderson would cost more this year than you care to pay. But this is Stage Three, there's an incredible wealth of information available — such as that his batting averages by month last year were: .000 in April and May (8 AB!), .313 in June, .410 in July, .308 in August, .269 in September/October — and this bid price will get him.

CARLOS BAERGA

2B   Age 27   Bid: $29

Year	Team	G	AB	R	H	BB	SO	D	T	HR	RBI	SB	CS	BA	$
1991	CLE	158	593	80	171	48	74	28	2	11	69	3	2	.288	18
1992	CLE	161	657	92	205	35	76	32	1	20	105	10	2	.312	35
1993	CLE	154	624	105	200	34	68	28	6	21	114	15	4	.321	38
1994	CLE	103	442	81	139	10	45	32	2	19	80	8	2	.314	31
1995	CLE	135	557	87	175	35	31	28	2	15	90	11	2	.314	30

Was on a 17-homer pace, as opposed to 27 the year before. A little of the magic has gone out of his wand.

HAROLD BAINES

DH   Age 36   1995: $17

Year	Team	G	AB	R	H	BB	SO	D	T	HR	RBI	SB	CS	BA	$
1991	OAK	141	488	76	144	72	67	25	1	20	90	0	3	.295	23
1992	OAK	140	478	58	121	59	61	18	0	16	76	1	1	.253	15
1993	BAL	118	416	64	130	57	52	22	0	20	78	0	0	.313	23
1994	BAL	94	326	44	96	30	49	12	1	16	54	0	0	.294	17
1995	BAL	127	385	60	115	70	45	19	1	24	63	0	2	.299	21

For the first time in many years, there is an abundance of DH-onlies; the last couple will cost no more than $2. Harold's price perhaps should come down further.

BRET BARBERIE

2B   Age 28   Bid: $1

Year	Team	G	AB	R	H	BB	SO	D	T	HR	RBI	SB	CS	BA	$
1991	MTL	57	136	16	48	20	22	12	2	2	18	0	0	.353	7
1992	MTL	111	285	26	66	47	62	11	0	1	24	9	5	.232	3
1993	FLA	99	375	45	104	33	58	16	2	5	33	2	4	.277	7
1994	FLA	107	372	40	112	23	65	20	2	5	31	2	0	.301	13
1995	BAL	90	237	32	57	36	50	14	0	2	25	3	3	.241	2

He's not as bad as last year but may not get a chance to prove it.

KIMERA BARTEE

OF   Age 23   Bid: R4

Year	Team	G	AB	R	H	BB	SO	D	T	HR	RBI	SB	CS	BA	$
1993	(R)	66	264	59	65	44	66	15	2	4	37	27	6	.246	x

Year	Team	G	AB	R	H	BB	SO	D	T	HR	RBI	SB	CS	BA	$
1994	(A)	130	514	97	150	56	117	22	4	10	57	44	9	.292	x
1995	(AA)	53	218	45	62	23	45	9	1	3	19	22	7	.284	x
1995	(AAA)	15	52	5	8	0	16	2	1	0	3	0	0	.154	x

A phenom one year ago, the Orioles were all too happy to trade him to the Twins after his 15 games as Rochester (AAA), even if it meant they had to take Scott Erickson

HOWARD BATTLE 3B   Age 24   Bid: R3

Year	Team	G	AB	R	H	BB	SO	D	T	HR	RBI	SB	CS	BA	$
1994	(AAA)	139	517	72	143	40	82	26	8	14	75	26	2	.277	x
1995	(AAA)	118	443	43	111	39	73	17	4	8	48	10	11	.251	x
1995	TOR	9	15	3	3	4	8	0	0	0	0	1	0	.200	0

After seeing Battle play a bit in September, I'm reluctant to consign Battle to R3 oblivion; he looked great in the field and held his own at the plate. But he's a crucial year older than Bartee, with *much* more Triple-A experience, and is obviously not improving.

DANNY BAUTISTA OF   Age 24   Bid: $2

Year	Team	G	AB	R	H	BB	SO	D	T	HR	RBI	SB	CS	BA	$
1993	DET	17	61	6	19	1	10	3	0	1	9	3	1	.311	4
1994	DET	31	99	12	23	3	18	4	1	4	15	1	2	.232	2
1995	DET	89	271	28	55	12	68	9	0	7	27	4	1	.203	0

Sent to Toledo, Bautista had no homers, one walk and ten strikeouts in 58 at-bats. Brought back to the Tigers in late September — because why not — he went on a tear. About a .250 tear, but several shots into the upper deck. He's a killer in BP. If he's in next year's profiles, which is highly unlikely, there will be a two-digit bid for him.

RICH BECKER OF   Age 24   Bid: $2

Year	Team	G	AB	R	H	BB	SO	D	T	HR	RBI	SB	CS	BA	$
1993	MIN	3	7	3	2	5	4	2	0	0	0	1	1	.286	0
1994	MIN	28	98	12	26	13	25	3	0	1	8	6	1	.265	4
1995	MIN	106	392	45	93	34	95	15	1	2	33	8	9	.237	3

Becker is a bigger bum (an inch shorter but 19 pounds heavier than Bautista) who now is trying his luck batting left only. I saw him a Florida, when he was still a switch-hitter, and he was not at all what I expected: choppy, almost ponderous, even chasing flyballs.

In 87 AB against lefties, he hit .149 with one double. He hit .282 against right-handers.

ALBERT BELLE OF   Age 29   Bid: $43

Year	Team	G	AB	R	H	BB	SO	D	T	HR	RBI	SB	CS	BA	$
1991	CLE	123	461	60	130	25	99	31	2	28	95	3	1	.282	26
1992	CLE	153	585	81	152	52	128	23	1	34	112	8	2	.260	31
1993	CLE	159	594	93	172	76	96	36	3	38	129	23	12	.290	43
1994	CLE	106	412	90	147	58	71	35	2	36	101	9	6	.357	50
1995	CLE	143	546	121	173	73	80	52	1	50	126	5	2	.317	46

After two years of serious hitting, not just by Albert but the league, we would expect all 1995 forecasts, even the most mechanical, to be on the robust side for Belle, and they were.

1995 Predictions: BELLE

	AB	HR	RBI	SB	BA
Patton	575	47	130	9	.315
James	594	40	126	15	.298
Benson	553	45	125	13	.307
Shandler	600	45	139	10	.313
Mann	606	42	132	13	.300

These were the forecasters that were tracked in last year's book; we'd all get excellent similarity scores, if we weren't banking on 162 games. Cut down to 144 games, this is what we predicted:

1995 Predictions Scaled: BELLE

	AB	HR	RBI	SB	BA
Patton	511	42	116	8	.315
James	528	36	112	13	.298
Benson	492	40	111	12	.307
Shandler	533	40	124	9	.313
Mann	539	37	117	12	.300

When the strike was settled, almost everybody in the business scrambled to put out revised forecasts. Clearly, to simply chop everything down by 11 percent wouldn't do; the abbreviated spring training had to be taken into account. Now, I never did see the new predictions that Bill James, John Benson, Ron Shandler and Steve Mann most likely generated, but John Hunt's were in the April 19 issue of Baseball Weekly, and Peter Kreutzer, who is doing the predictions in Peter Golenbock's book this year, and who is also in my league, the American Dreams, posted updated numbers on the ESPNet SportZone a week before the start of the season . My own revised stat forecasts were contained on the update disk that went in mid-April to buyers of the software program (details in the PS).

Strike-adjusted Predictions: BELLE

	AB	HR	RBI	SB	BA
Patton	525	45	124	11	.324
Hunt	500	39	142	7	.328
Kreutzer	523	37	118	12	.306

Hunt and I could hardly jam more hitting into 500+ AB, and we still fell short. Kreutzer falls way short; heck, Albert had 26 home runs in 192 AB after Peter traded for him.

```
Top 10 AL hitters
            earned  avg          Heath Data    - touts -
Name         1995   sal  +/-  |  Pts    Rk  |  AP   JH  |  $94
BELLE,A        46    45    1  |  52.5   85  |  48   41  |   50
KNOBLAUCH,C    44    31   13  |  56.9   13  |  32   32  |   35
MARTINEZ,E     42    17   26  |  59.0    4  |  21   22  |   17
VAUGHN,M       41    33    8  |  57.8    8  |  35   31  |   31
LOFTON,K       40    49   -9  |  56.9   14  |  51   49  |   61
SALMON,T       39    30    9  |  57.5    9  |  32   22  |   22
THOMAS,F       37    45   -8  |  52.9   73  |  50   39  |   46
PALMEIRO,R     37    32    5  |  49.6  148  |  34   28  |   33
VALENTIN,JOH   37    15   22  |  61.6    1  |  20   17  |   18
JOHNSON,L      36    24   12  |  53.8   55  |  21   19  |   23
    average    40    32    8  |  55.9   41  |  34   30  |   34
```

This is the MVP voting for hitters in the league last year. Belle finished second in 1994, after Lofton. He finished fifth in 1993. Roberto Alomar was first that year; Frank Thomas was sixth, so his losing streak against Belle has reached three.

Repeats on the list above from 1994: Belle, Knoblauch, Lofton and Thomas. Repeats from the 1993 list: Belle, Lofton, Thomas and Palmeiro.

The average salaries are derived from the three non-freeze leagues that are shown in Appendix A (Baseball Weekly, the American Dreams and Cowtown). Albert just about broke even. The next two columns show how he fared in leagues whose stats are kept by Heath Data Services. The point totals are the average of the points in the final standings of the teams that drafted him. Since 52 is the middle, a .500 team, his teams just about broke even.

Jerry Heath, who runs Heath Data Services, tracks all players that were drafted by at least ten teams in his leagues; there were 195 such players, and Belle, by ranking eighty-fifth, finished just above the halfway point.

Notice, though, that most of the players on this top-10 earnings list ranked much higher. Thomas lost $8, theoretically, and ranked seventy-third. Lofton lost $9, but the teams that drafted him did just fine (in effect, finished fourteenth in a mammoth pennant race involving 195 teams). Only one player on this list, Palmeiro, is associated with teams that finished below .500 in their leagues (that is, averaged fewer than 52 points).

These players as a group, even though they were very expensive (cost an average of $32), finished forty-first out of 195 in the mega-competition. In a 12-team race, that would be either second or third.

The next two columns are my dollar predictions in the update that I mailed to readers on April 18 and those that John Hunt published in Baseball Weekly on April 19. The final column is what the players earned in 1994.

In a three-way battle between Hunt, myself and the average league, I would get Belle, Vaughn, Lofton, Salmon, Thomas, Palmeiro and Valentin; Hunt would get Martinez; and the league would get Johnson. Hunt would win the tie-breaker for Knoblauch, since I'd be broke.

But in a two-way battle between myself and 1994, 1994 would get five of these great hitters (Belle, Knoblauch, Lofton, Thomas and Johnson). We don't just tie head-to-head, we tie overall: the 10 top performers last year earned an average of $34 in 1994, which happens to be the average of what I predicted they would earn last year. It could be said that both 1994 and I had an 85% success rate (34/40) at predicting how much the 10 best hitters in 1995 would earn. It could further be said that, depending on who or what you use as a yardstick, the best hitters in 1995 were between 85% predictable (myself and 1994) and 75% predictable (Hunt).

In baseball that's very, very predictable.

GERONIMO BERROA   OF   Age 31   Bid: $20

Year	Team	G	AB	R	H	BB	SO	D	T	HR	RBI	SB	CS	BA	$
1992	CIN	13	15	2	4	2	1	1	0	0	0	0	1	.267	0
1993	FLA	14	34	3	4	2	7	1	0	0	0	0	0	.118	-2
1994	OAK	96	340	55	104	41	62	18	2	13	65	7	2	.306	23
1995	OAK	141	546	87	152	63	98	22	3	22	88	7	4	.278	23

Solid hitter who was probably at his peak in the minors.

MIKE BLOWERS   3B   Age 31   Bid: $14

Year	Team	G	AB	R	H	BB	SO	D	T	HR	RBI	SB	CS	BA	$
1991	NYY/SE	15	35	3	7	4	3	0	0	1	1	0	0	.200	0
1992	SEA	31	73	7	14	6	20	3	0	1	2	0	0	.192	-1
1993	SEA	127	379	55	106	44	98	23	3	15	57	1	5	.280	14
1994	SEA	85	270	37	78	25	60	13	0	9	49	2	2	.289	13
1995	SEA	134	439	59	113	53	128	24	1	23	96	2	1	.257	19

Would you rather have had Blowers or Boggs?

Appendix B shows the way that they came out tied. Blowers earned $9 with his homers, $11 with his ribbies, $1 with his stolen bases, and lost $3 with his batting average. Boggs earned $2 with his homers, $7 with his ribbies, 0 dollars (45 cents) with his stolen base, and $9 with his batting average. The idea is that 96 RBIs help a team as much in the standings as a .324 batting average in 460 AB. Well, a little more ($9.22 versus $8.71). To be really finicky, Blowers earned $18.64 and Boggs earned $18.57. You've just read the masochist chapter.

Why is Boggs just a tick higher on my wish list than Blowers? Aren't the twin pillars of Rotisserie baseball the power categories? (In fact, they are the second two, behind ERA and ratio; Okrent really should get some credit for the kind of bizarre harmonies that he created.) And didn't Blowers hit 17 home runs after the All-Star break? And isn't Boggs an old fart?

The most important point is that I think we've just seen Blowers' career year, and a wonderful one it was. However, he struck out once every 3.4 AB last year, which is almost Benji Gil territory.

The second point is that you can get what Blowers gives from all sorts of people; Wade's specialty is more unusual.

WADE BOGGS   3B   Age 38   Bid: $15

Year	Team	G	AB	R	H	BB	SO	D	T	HR	RBI	SB	CS	BA	$
1991	BOS	144	546	93	181	89	32	42	2	8	51	1	2	.332	21
1992	BOS	143	514	62	133	74	31	22	4	7	50	1	3	.259	9
1993	NYY	143	560	83	169	74	49	26	1	2	59	0	1	.302	14
1994	NYY	97	366	61	125	61	29	19	1	11	55	2	1	.342	25

Year	Team	G	AB	R	H	BB	SO	D	T	HR	RBI	SB	CS	BA	$
1995	NYY	126	460	76	149	74	50	22	4	5	63	1	1	.324	**19**

He did get old in a hurry, but he seems to have gotten over it. The unbelievably potent Runs Created Days are far in the past — off the screen — but he could keep poking out singles, coupled with the odd home run, for several more years. Grounders that come to him are pieces of cake. He should be able to keep it up until he gets 3,000 hits.

BOBBY BONILLA   3B,OF   Age 33   Bid: $35

Year	Team	G	AB	R	H	BB	SO	D	T	HR	RBI	SB	CS	BA	$
1991	PIT	157	577	112	174	90	67	44	6	18	100	2	4	.302	**28**
1992	NYM	128	438	102	109	66	73	23	0	19	70	4	3	.249	**19**
1993	NYM	139	502	81	133	72	96	21	3	34	87	3	3	.265	**24**
1994	NYM	108	403	60	117	55	101	24	1	20	67	1	3	.290	**24**
1995	NYM	80	317	49	103	31	48	25	4	18	53	0	3	.325	**22**
1995	BAL	61	237	47	79	23	31	12	4	10	46	0	2	.333	**15**

Counting both leagues, Bonilla earned an astonishing $12 with his batting average. He hit .378 in the last month. He was terrible at third base, but he had a shortstop who could cover for him. The clubhouse was said to be better for his presence, which may say more about the Orioles than Bobby Bo.

MIKE BORDICK   SS   Age 30   Bid: $4

Year	Team	G	AB	R	H	BB	SO	D	T	HR	RBI	SB	CS	BA	$
1991	OAK	90	235	21	56	14	37	5	1	0	21	3	4	.238	**2**
1992	OAK	154	504	62	151	40	59	19	4	3	48	12	6	.300	**18**
1993	OAK	159	546	60	136	60	58	21	2	3	48	10	10	.249	**7**
1994	OAK	114	391	38	99	38	44	18	4	2	37	7	2	.253	**5**
1995	OAK	126	428	46	113	35	48	13	0	8	44	11	3	.264	**12**

They aren't called bid limits for nothing, but just *suppose* I spent $36 for Bonilla — what would I do?

Right away, pencil in $3 next to Bordick.

DOUG BRADY   2B   Age 26   Bid: R2

Year	Team	G	AB	R	H	BB	SO	D	T	HR	RBI	SB	CS	BA	$
1994	(AA)	127	516	38	128	38	59	18	8	4	59	34	12	.248	**x**
1995	(AAA)	125	450	71	134	31	76	15	6	5	31	32	6	.298	**x**

Year	Team	G	AB	R	H	BB	SO	D	T	HR	RBI	SB	CS	BA	$
1995	CHW	12	21	4	4	2	4	1	0	0	3	0	1	.190	0

His best year by far since becoming a pro in 1991. Has R3 written all over him, but for his speed. And it probably isn't enough speed for the majors. Maybe he's just an R2 to Ray Durham owners.

DARREN BRAGG   OF   Age 26   Bid: R3

Year	Team	G	AB	R	H	BB	SO	D	T	HR	RBI	SB	CS	BA	$
1994	SEA	8	19	4	3	2	5	1	0	0	2	0	0	.158	-1
1995	SEA	52	145	20	34	18	37	5	1	3	12	9	0	.234	4

Had the speed, but no bat. Hit .307 back at Tacoma, which is not nearby.

SCOTT BROSIUS   3B,OF,1B   Age 29   Bid: $5

Year	Team	G	AB	R	H	BB	SO	D	T	HR	RBI	SB	CS	BA	$
1991	OAK	36	68	9	16	3	11	5	0	2	4	3	1	.235	2
1992	OAK	38	87	13	19	3	13	2	0	4	13	3	0	.218	3
1993	OAK	70	213	26	53	14	37	10	1	6	25	6	0	.249	6
1994	OAK	96	324	31	77	24	57	14	1	14	49	2	6	.238	8
1995	OAK	123	388	69	102	41	67	19	2	17	46	4	2	.263	12

The bids can and should be endlessly tweaked. Brosius should be perhaps $6. Pencil in $3 next to Bordick.

JAY BUHNER   OF   Age 31   Bid: $27

Year	Team	G	AB	R	H	BB	SO	D	T	HR	RBI	SB	CS	BA	$
1991	SEA	137	406	64	99	53	117	14	4	27	77	0	1	.244	17
1992	SEA	152	543	69	132	71	146	16	3	25	79	0	6	.243	17
1993	SEA	158	563	91	153	100	144	28	3	27	98	2	5	.272	23
1994	SEA	101	358	74	100	66	63	23	4	21	68	0	1	.279	19
1995	SEA	126	470	86	123	60	120	23	0	40	121	0	1	.262	28

There's a bias in the formulas in favor of power to begin with; the bids take it further. Buhner's 29 home runs in the second half were accompanied by a .253 batting average. This is as good as it gets for him. But if he just slides back a little, overpaying by a little is fine.

JEROMY BURNITZ OF   Age 27   Bid: R2

Year	Team	G	AB	R	H	BB	SO	D	T	HR	RBI	SB	CS	BA	$
1993	NYM	86	263	49	64	38	66	10	6	13	38	3	6	.243	8
1994	NYM	45	143	26	34	23	45	4	0	3	15	1	1	.238	2
1995	CLE	9	7	4	4	0	0	1	0	0	0	0	0	.571	1

Hit .284-19-85 in 128 games at Buffalo, stole a few bases. Got a good shot with the Mets, deserves another one now, and of course won't get it with Cleveland.

JOSE CANSECO DH   Age 31   Bid: $23

Year	Team	G	AB	R	H	BB	SO	D	T	HR	RBI	SB	CS	BA	$
1991	OAK	154	572	115	152	78	152	32	1	44	122	26	6	.266	44
1992	OAK	119	439	74	107	63	128	15	0	26	87	6	7	.244	21
1993	TEX	60	231	30	59	16	62	14	1	10	46	6	6	.255	10
1994	TEX	111	429	88	121	69	114	19	2	31	90	15	8	.282	35
1995	BOS	102	396	64	121	42	93	25	1	24	81	4	0	.306	26

The fact that he qualifies at DH only, together with the fact that he's bound to miss a portion of the season, is what keeps my bid for him this low. It means he won't be on my team.

```
        Top 10 salaries, AL hitters
                earned  avg              Heath Data      - touts -
        Name      1995   sal   +/-   |   Pts    Rk   |   AP    JH  |  $94
        LOFTON,K    40    49    -9   |  56.9    15   |   51    49  |   61
        GRIFFEY,KJR 12    45   -33   |  47.1   179   |   52    41  |   45
        THOMAS,F    37    45    -8   |  52.9    73   |   50    39  |   46
        BELLE,A     46    45     1   |  52.5    85   |   48    41  |   50
        ALOMAR,R    32    37    -6   |  52.7    77   |   38    32  |   24
        CANSECO,J   26    36   -10   |  53.6    59   |   33    32  |   35
        BAERGA,C    30    35    -5   |  54.1    46   |   36    31  |   31
        VAUGHN,M    41    33     8   |  57.8     8   |   35    31  |   31
        PALMEIRO,R  37    32     5   |  49.6   148   |   34    28  |   33
        CARTER,J    20    31   -11   |  51.4   115   |   33    26  |   31
          average   32    39    -7   |  52.9    81   |   41    35  |   39
```

Did the three non-freeze leagues in Appendix A actually pay $3 more for Jose Canseco than Mo Vaughn? They must have thought he was going to go bonkers in Fenway (where no right-handed hitter has gone bonkers since Jim Rice). But — here's something interesting — the freeze-list league that is shown for comparison purposes in Appendix A *really* believed Mo would go bonkers; at least the team that owned him the year before did: he was frozen for $46!

It often happens, as a matter of fact, that frozen players are no bargains. Here's the breakdown of what was paid in each league for the 10 most expensive hitters:

AL hitters	BW	ADL	COW	ASH	f
LOFTON,K	46	55	45	55	
GRIFFEY,KJR	42	51	42	51	
THOMAS,F	43	50	42	50	
BELLE,A	40	48	46	46	f
ALOMAR,R	36	36	40	43	
CANSECO,J	36	31	41	35	f
BAERGA,C	35	34	36	32	f
VAUGHN,M	31	34	33	46	f
PALMEIRO,R	30	36	30	27	f
CARTER,J	26	32	36	43	f
average	37	41	39	43	

Ashpole spent more than anyone else for these players, which wouldn't be surprising at all if most of them were free agents, but only four of them were. Based on the prices that Griffey and Thomas fetched on the open market, you have to wonder if Vaughn would have gone to $46, no matter how bad the inflation was in that league (which can't be determined from what we see here). The team that froze Joe Carter at $43 was probably wasting even more money.

It might be worth looking at the 10 best hitters in 1995 (shown in the Belle comment) from this perspective:

AL hitters	BW	ADL	COW	ASH	f
BELLE,A	40	48	46	46	f
KNOBLAUCH,C	27	38	28	14	f
MARTINEZ,E	16	18	16	32	
VAUGHN,M	31	34	33	46	f
LOFTON,K	46	55	45	55	
SALMON,T	26	30	34	20	f
THOMAS,F	43	50	42	50	
PALMEIRO,R	30	36	30	27	f
VALENTIN,JOH	16	17	12	24	
JOHNSON,L	20	29	22	20	f
average	30	36	31	33	

Knoblauch was an excellent freeze and some of the others weren't bad, but the seven freezes here as a group really aren't causing the inflation. On the other hand, that there is strong inflation can be inferred from the prices for Edgar Martinez and John Valentin.

Another thing worth noting is that the three non-freeze leagues seem to have quite different personalities. The Dreamers (ADL), even with 276 players to buy, are free spenders. Cowtown and particularly Baseball Weekly guard their pennies.

And, although I've tried to lose sight of the fact by all sorts of diversionary tactics, fairness insists I point out that John Hunt gets his revenge in this group. As long as the money lasted, I would have snatched every one of these players from him in an auction, and only two (Vaughn and Palmeiro) would earn more than I paid for them.

But how many of these hitters would I have been unhappy with? I've long contended you're not really expecting profits on the high-ticket items; you're just looking for a reasonably safe place to put your money. The only truly unsafe place here was (wince) Griffey, and Joe Carter wasn't his usual self. Everyone else ranged from a solid $26 return to a delightful $41 return.

The Heath data supports the notion that this group, even though it loses money, is a good investment. In 45 leagues, all but three of these players are drafted by teams that finish in the first division. The teams ended up with 52.9 points, on average, which may not seem much above .500; however, using the same logic as in the Belle comment, to rank eighty-fifth out of 195 works out to a fifth place finish in a twelve-team league. The 10 most expensive players in 1995 lost an average of $7, and their teams ended up just out of the money.

The ten most expensive hitters in 1994 cost $36. The $3 pay raise is significant. Last year I counted the Heath "won-lost" record — the number of first-place teams in 1994 that drafted a player versus the number of last — and it averaged out to 15-8 for the most expensive hitters.

AL hitters

Kind of ridiculous. Clearly, bettors were being too conservative. Last year they opened up their purse strings a bit. But it would appear they have a tad further to go. A $40 average salary for the 10 best hitters, the expected 10 best hitters, would probably neutralize their impact.

JOE CARTER OF Age 36 Bid: $24

Year	Team	G	AB	R	H	BB	SO	D	T	HR	RBI	SB	CS	BA	$
1991	TOR	162	638	89	174	49	112	42	3	33	108	20	9	.273	**36**
1992	TOR	158	622	97	164	36	109	30	7	34	119	12	5	.264	**34**
1993	TOR	155	603	92	153	47	113	33	5	33	121	8	3	.254	**27**
1994	TOR	111	435	70	118	33	64	25	2	27	103	11	0	.271	**31**
1995	TOR	139	558	70	141	37	87	23	0	25	76	12	1	.253	**20**

Hit .228 in the second half. Doesn't have the kind of swing that's built to last. Even so, he could drive in 100 runs again if he has the same three hitters in front of him and they play the way they used to.

JEFF CIRILLO 2B,3B Age 26 Bid: $5

Year	Team	G	AB	R	H	BB	SO	D	T	HR	RBI	SB	CS	BA	$
1994	(AAA)	61	236	45	73	28	39	18	2	10	46	4	0	.309	**x**
1994	MIL	39	126	17	30	11	16	9	0	3	12	0	1	.238	**1**
1995	MIL	125	328	57	91	47	42	19	4	9	39	7	2	.277	**12**

More walks than strikeouts is not always a good sign.

JERALD CLARK OF Age 32 Bid: $2

Year	Team	G	AB	R	H	BB	SO	D	T	HR	RBI	SB	CS	BA	$
1994	JPN	—	376	61	110	—	—	15	1	20	53	3	—	.293	**x**
1995	MIN	36	109	17	37	2	11	8	3	3	15	3	0	.339	**7**

Not to be discounted. He wasn't *that* bad for the Rockies their first year (.282-13-67 in 478 AB), while he was he was one of the better foreign hitters in Japan in 1994. If he's healthy and makes the Twins, to get him as your fifth outfielder, you might have to push the limit to $3.

TONY CLARK 1B Age 24 Bid: R1

Year	Team	G	AB	R	H	BB	SO	D	T	HR	RBI	SB	CS	BA	$
1994	(AA)	107	394	25	110	40	113	25	0	21	86	0	4	.279	**x**
1994	(AAA)	25	92	4	24	12	25	4	0	2	13	2	0	.261	**x**
1995	(AAA)	110	405	50	98	52	129	17	2	14	63	0	2	.242	**x**

Year	Team	G	AB	R	H	BB	SO	D	T	HR	RBI	SB	CS	BA	$
1995	DET	27	101	10	24	8	30	5	1	3	11	0	0	.238	1

A beautiful if somewhat long swing from both sides of the plate. Home runs that don't come down. Liability in the field. Tigers would be fools to start him in the majors before he's had some decent success at Toledo.

WILL CLARK 1B Age 32

Bid: $18

Year	Team	G	AB	R	H	BB	SO	D	T	HR	RBI	SB	CS	BA	$
1991	SF	148	565	84	170	51	91	32	7	29	116	4	2	.301	36
1992	SF	144	513	69	154	73	82	40	1	16	73	12	7	.300	29
1993	SF	132	491	82	139	63	68	27	2	14	73	2	2	.283	17
1994	TEX	110	389	73	128	71	59	24	2	13	80	5	1	.329	29
1995	TEX	123	454	85	137	68	50	27	3	16	92	0	1	.302	22

A minimal Bid: someone else will get him.

ALEX COLE OF Age 29

Bid: $2

Year	Team	G	AB	R	H	BB	SO	D	T	HR	RBI	SB	CS	BA	$
1991	CLE	122	387	58	114	58	47	17	3	0	21	27	17	.295	19
1992	PIT	64	205	44	57	18	46	3	7	0	10	7	4	.278	5
1993	COL	126	348	50	89	43	58	9	4	0	24	30	13	.256	11
1994	MIN	105	345	68	102	44	60	15	5	4	23	29	8	.296	24
1995	MIN	28	79	10	27	8	15	3	2	1	14	1	3	.342	5

Hit .365 against the pitchers Rich Becker plans to face.

MICHAEL COLEMAN OF Age 20

Bid: R4

Year	Team	G	AB	R	H	BB	SO	D	T	HR	RBI	SB	CS	BA	$
1994	(R)	25	95	15	26	10	20	6	1	3	15	5	3	.274	x
1994	(A)	23	65	16	11	14	21	2	0	1	3	11	1	.169	x
1995	(A)	112	422	70	113	40	93	16	2	11	61	29	5	.268	x

Minor league Player of the Year for the Red Sox. In other words, he beat out Trot Nixon. Nothing wrong with his stats for a first full professional season.

VINCE COLEMAN   OF   Age 34   Bid: $17

Year	Team	G	AB	R	H	BB	SO	D	T	HR	RBI	SB	CS	BA	$
1991	NYM	72	278	45	71	39	47	7	5	1	17	37	14	.255	15
1992	NYM	71	229	37	63	27	41	11	1	2	21	24	9	.275	13
1993	NYM	92	373	64	104	21	58	14	8	2	25	38	13	.279	18
1994	KC	104	438	61	105	29	72	14	12	2	33	50	8	.240	25
1995	KC/SE	115	455	66	131	37	80	23	6	5	29	42	16	.288	27

Lit a firecracker under the Mariners when they desperately needed one. You'll like him well enough if you get him at this price.

BRENT COOKSON   OF   Age 26   Bid: R2

Year	Team	G	AB	R	H	BB	SO	D	T	HR	RBI	SB	CS	BA	$
1994	(AA)	62	207	32	67	18	57	21	3	11	41	4	1	.324	x
1994	(AAA)	14	43	7	12	5	14	0	1	1	6	0	1	.279	x
1995	(AAA)	40	137	28	55	17	24	13	0	4	20	0	0	.401	x
1995	KC	22	35	2	5	2	7	1	0	0	5	1	0	.143	-1

Anyone who hits .401 at Omaha, then gets released (he's now with the Red Sox), is worth keeping an eye on, as Mazeroski used to say.

RON COOMER   1B   Age 28   Bid: R2

Year	Team	G	AB	R	H	BB	SO	D	T	HR	RBI	SB	CS	BA	$
1993	(AA)	69	262	44	85	15	43	18	0	13	50	1	1	.324	x
1993	(AAA)	59	211	34	66	10	29	19	0	13	51	1	2	.313	x
1994	(AAA)	127	535	89	181	26	62	34	6	22	123	4	3	.338	x
1995	(AAA)	85	323	54	104	18	28	23	2	16	76	5	2	.322	x
1995	MIN	37	101	15	26	9	11	3	1	5	19	0	1	.257	4

Was sitting behind Scott Leius at the end, which may have been his final insult.

JOEY CORA   2B   Age 31   Bid: $8

Year	Team	G	AB	R	H	BB	SO	D	T	HR	RBI	SB	CS	BA	$
1991	CHW	100	228	37	55	20	21	2	3	0	18	11	6	.241	5
1992	CHW	68	122	27	30	22	13	7	1	0	9	10	3	.246	4

Year	Team	G	AB	R	H	BB	SO	D	T	HR	RBI	SB	CS	BA	$
1993	CHW	153	579	95	155	67	63	15	13	2	51	20	8	.268	14
1994	CHW	90	312	55	86	38	32	13	4	2	30	8	4	.276	9
1995	SEA	120	427	64	127	37	31	19	2	3	39	18	7	.297	18

Our last image was of him weeping in the arms of Alex Rodriguez in the Seattle dugout, but he was a winner.

```
Top 10 profits, AL hitters
                        earned    avg Heath Data    - touts -
Name          1995 sal  +/-      Pts    Rk  | AP   JH  | $94
MARTINEZ,E     42   17   26     59.0     4  | 21   22  | 17
EDMONDS,J      30    6   24     56.2    19  |  7    5  |  9
ANDERSON,G     24    1   23     48.8   159  |  2    3  |  1
VALENTIN,JO    37   15   22     61.6     1  | 20   17  | 18
SNOW,JT        25    4   21     54.4    43  |  4   10  |  1
GAETTI,G       24    4   20     57.9     7  |  5    4  | 15
GOODWIN,T      30   10   20     53.1    71  |  6   11  |  0
SURHOFF,B      24    5   19     51.5   110  |  4    6  |  4
O'LEARY,T      17    1   16     53.5    62  | R3       |  2
CORA,J         18    3   15     55.4    28  |  2   10  |  9
     average   27    7   21     55.1    50  |  7    9  |  8
```

John Valentin was a *bigger* winner, but it's a long way to the V's.

In any event, Joey Cora ranked twenty-eighth out of 195 in a tracking of how the teams that drafted players did in 45 Heath leagues. Quite wonderful, really. The crapshoot lives.

What was up with Garret Anderson?

In the Baseball Weekly league, Greg Ambrosius got him for $1 and finished eleventh. In the American Dreams, the Palukas paid $2 for him — which is twice as much to their credit — and finished last. In Cowtown, the Heroes spent $1 on Garret Anderson and finished last.

Must be the curse of Gene Autry.

Despite this anomaly, the group performs well enough: ranking 50th out of 195 is the equivalent of finishing third in a twelve-team league. What's interesting, though, is that it doesn't perform as well as the group of top 10 hitters overall (Belle comment). In that group there is also an anomaly — Palmeiro, even harder to explain — and it still has a higher average point total, even though the $8 profit is much smaller than the $21 profit that we see here.

MARTY CORDOVA OF Age 26 Bid: $26

Year	Team	G	AB	R	H	BB	SO	D	T	HR	RBI	SB	CS	BA	$
1993	(AA)	138	508	83	127	64	153	30	5	19	77	10	5	.250	x
1994	(AAA)	103	385	69	138	39	63	25	4	19	66	17	6	.358	x
1995	MIN	137	512	81	142	52	111	27	4	24	84	20	7	.277	29

Speed was one of those you're–only–rookie–of–the–year–once things; power will grow.

STEVE COX   1B   Age 21   Bid: R4

Year	Team	G	AB	R	H	BB	SO	D	T	HR	RBI	SB	CS	BA	$
1994	(A)	99	311	37	75	41	95	19	2	6	32	2	6	.241	x
1995	(A)	132	483	95	144	84	88	29	3	30	110	5	4	.298	x

Plans to be paired up with, or replacing, Mark McGwire in a few years. Excellent BB and SO for so much power. According to *Baseball America*, "he hit 30 home runs to all fields." Is 6'4", 200; bats left.

JOSE CRUZ JR   OF   Age 22   Bid: R4

Year	Team	G	AB	R	H	BB	SO	D	T	HR	RBI	SB	CS	BA	$
1995	(A)	3	11	6	5	3	3	0	0	0	2	1	0	.455	x
1995	(A)	35	144	34	37	24	50	7	1	7	29	3	1	.257	x

As the college-bred son of Jose Cruz, he was used to aluminum bats. That's the standard explanation, anyway, for a poor debut. He was nonetheless BA's number three prospect in the California League (the second one shown here, an advanced A league). He's 6'0", 190; bats both; gets faint praise for his defense.

CHAD CURTIS   OF   Age 27   Bid: $24

Year	Team	G	AB	R	H	BB	SO	D	T	HR	RBI	SB	CS	BA	$
1992	CAL	138	441	59	114	51	71	16	2	10	46	43	18	.259	26
1993	CAL	152	583	94	166	70	89	25	3	6	59	48	24	.285	32
1994	CAL	114	453	67	116	37	69	23	4	11	50	25	11	.256	21
1995	DET	144	586	96	157	70	93	29	3	21	67	27	15	.268	27

Chad was worth $15 without his steals (Appendix B). I figure he'll do about what he did last year but chop a few dollars off his running game so I can have more money to spend on the power game.

JOHNNY DAMON   OF   Age 21   Bid: $25

Year	Team	G	AB	R	H	BB	SO	D	T	HR	RBI	SB	CS	BA	$
1993	(A)	127	511	82	148	51	83	25	13	5	50	59	18	.290	x
1994	(A)	119	472	96	149	62	55	25	13	5	75	44	9	.316	x
1995	(AA)	111	423	83	145	67	35	15	9	16	54	26	15	.343	x
1995	KC	47	188	32	53	12	22	11	5	3	23	7	0	.282	8

The real deal — Grade A and Blue Chip. Skipped Triple-A, which means less and less these days. Nabbed at second a few too many times at Wichita, but has to be full of baserunning confidence after his seven swipes in the majors. Swings a little bit down on the ball. Caught everything in center field. Rookie of the Year, except he no longer qualifies.

CHILI DAVIS   DH   Age 35

Bid: $23

Year	Team	G	AB	R	H	BB	SO	D	T	HR	RBI	SB	CS	BA	$
1991	MIN	153	534	84	148	95	117	34	1	29	93	5	6	.277	27
1992	MIN	138	444	63	128	73	76	27	2	12	66	4	5	.288	18
1993	CAL	153	573	74	139	71	135	32	0	27	112	4	1	.243	20
1994	CAL	108	392	72	122	69	84	18	1	26	84	3	2	.311	31
1995	CAL	119	424	81	135	89	79	23	0	20	86	3	3	.318	27

The only reason he earns less than in 1994 is that the season was even shorter then. Doesn't get a higher bid because of the DH glut.

RUSS DAVIS   3B   Age 25

Bid: $5

Year	Team	G	AB	R	H	BB	SO	D	T	HR	RBI	SB	CS	BA	$
1994	(AAA)	117	416	76	115	62	93	30	2	25	69	3	7	.276	x
1994	NYY	4	14	0	2	0	4	0	0	0	1	0	0	.143	-1
1995	(AAA)	20	76	12	19	17	23	4	1	2	15	0	0	.250	x
1995	NYY	40	98	14	27	10	26	5	2	2	12	0	0	.276	2

Basically, collected rust last year. Nevertheless, if a spot has been cleared, either on the Yankees or anywhere else, raise the bid to around $10. He looks like he can hit.

CARLOS DELGADO   OF   Age 24

Bid: R1

Year	Team	G	AB	R	H	BB	SO	D	T	HR	RBI	SB	CS	BA	$
1992	(A)	133	485	83	157	59	91	30	2	30	100	2	5	.324	x
1993	(AA)	140	468	91	142	102	98	28	0	25	102	10	3	.303	x
1993	TOR	2	1	0	0	1	0	0	0	0	0	0	0	.000	0
1994	TOR	43	130	17	28	25	46	2	0	9	24	1	1	.215	4
1994	(AAA)	85	307	52	98	42	58	11	0	19	58	1	0	.319	x
1995	TOR	37	91	7	15	6	26	3	0	3	11	0	0	.165	-2
1995	(AAA)	91	333	59	106	45	78	23	4	22	74	0	4	.318	x

No one could figure out *what* Delgado was going to do last spring. Catch? Play left field? DH? Play some first base? We just thought he'd do it.

```
Top 10 losses, AL hitters
          earned avg   Heath Data    - touts -
Name       1995  sal   +/- |  Pts   Rk  | AP   JH | $94

GRIFFEY,KJR  12   45   -33 |  47.1  179 | 52   41 |  45
HAMELIN,B    -3   22   -25 |  48.7  164 | 19   24 |  23
WHITEN,M     -2   23   -25 |  48.2  174 | 21   24 |  23
DELGADO,C    -2   18   -19 |  51.8  100 | 14   14 |   4
TARTABULL,D   3   18   -15 |  51.6  105 | 15   16 |  14
OLERUD,J     13   27   -14 |  48.7  163 | 31   25 |  19
MOLITOR,P    18   31   -14 |  53.6   60 | 37   29 |  41
POLONIA,L     6   18   -13 |  46.7  186 | 13   17 |  22
CARTER,J     20   31   -11 |  51.4  115 | 33   26 |  31
JOSE,F       -2   10   -11 |  44.8  125 | R1      |  22
  average     6   24   -18 |  49.3  137 | 24   22 |  24
```

It's sort of surprising that Delgado didn't do more damage in Heath leagues. His teams came within two tenths of a point of playing .500. Olrerud, bad as he was, wasn't as big a bust, but his teams did worse; maybe carrying a dud on your roster all year is more harmful than having a player bomb so badly that have to replace him with someone else.

Look at the number of Blue Jays here. There are five, because you have to count Whiten.

Think of how many human beings had their summers ruined when they watched Griffey's arm disappear into the padding, again and again and again, on Baseball Tonight.

What *do* we do about trades to the other league? In the Baseball Weekly leagues, John Hunt decided to award the traded-away player's salary to his ex-owner's free-agent acquisition budget. Since the initial budget was $100, it made a certain amount of sense. The refinement I would propose is to scale the compensation down by however much of the season remains to be played. Polonia was traded after week 15; there were eight more weeks to go. Polonia's owners should have received 35% of what they paid for him in compensation. For Bill Kulik in the BWAL league, that would have meant $6.

Half of the player's on this biggest busts list were frozen in Ashpole:

```
— leagues —
AL hitters    BW   ADL  COW  ASH f
GRIFFEY,KJR   42   51   42   51
HAMELIN,B     21   23   22   12 f
WHITEN,M      25   21   23   25
DELGADO,C     19   24   10   10 f
TARTABULL,D   16   17   22   34
OLERUD,J      29   28   23   31
MOLITOR,P     28   35   31   30 f
POLONIA,L     18   17   20    9
CARTER,J      26   32   36   43 f
JOSE,F         1   18   10   19 f
    Average   23   27   24   26
```

Even with all the keepers, Ashpole spends almost as much as the American Dreams on these flops.

Good old Molly is the only player who's teams finished above .500. The overall damage is 137/195 x 12: an eighth place finish, on average, for any team that bought one of these players.

As for Delgado, of course he's an R1 if he starts out in Syracuse again. How much will I pay for him if he's the Blue Jays' first baseman?

More than for Olerud if he's the Blue Jay's first baseman.

ALEX DIAZ
OF   Age 27   Bid: $2

Year	Team	G	AB	R	H	BB	SO	D	T	HR	RBI	SB	CS	BA	$
1993	MIL	32	69	9	22	10	19	2	0	0	1	5	3	.319	3
1994	MIL	79	187	17	47	10	19	5	7	1	17	5	5	.251	3
1995	SEA	103	270	44	67	13	27	14	0	3	27	18	8	.248	10

There are lots and lots of worse fifth outfielders.

EDWIN DIAZ
2B   Age 21   Bid: R4

Year	Team	G	AB	R	H	BB	SO	D	T	HR	RBI	SB	CS	BA	$
1994	(A)	122	413	52	109	22	107	22	7	11	60	11	14	.264	x
1995	(A)	115	450	48	128	33	94	26	5	8	56	8	13	.284	x

He's 5'11", 170, bats right, and was the Rangers' Minor League Player of the Year. Rangers aren't long on prospects and need one at his position.

GARY DISARCINA
SS   Age 28   Bid: $9

Year	Team	G	AB	R	H	BB	SO	D	T	HR	RBI	SB	CS	BA	$
1991	CAL	18	57	5	12	3	4	2	0	0	3	0	0	.211	-1
1992	CAL	157	518	48	128	20	50	19	0	3	42	9	7	.247	7
1993	CAL	126	416	44	99	15	38	20	1	3	45	5	7	.238	4
1994	CAL	112	389	53	101	18	28	14	2	3	33	3	7	.260	4
1995	CAL	99	362	61	111	20	25	28	6	5	41	7	4	.307	15

The magic year for DiSarcina, while it lasted, was 27 indeed. (Ages in this book are baseball standard time: July 1 of the upcoming season.) His slugging average rose from .329 to .459. He was wearing down a bit in July (.287), and that was still 55 points above his lifetime batting average. Not only did he have a career two-thirds year, but his team fell apart without him. They both have unfinished business.

STEVE DUNN
1B   Age 26   Bid: R3

Year	Team	G	AB	R	H	BB	SO	D	T	HR	RBI	SB	CS	BA	$
1994	(AAA)	90	330	61	102	24	75	21	2	15	73	0	0	.309	x
1994	MIN	14	35	2	8	1	12	5	0	0	4	0	0	.229	0
1995	(AAA)	109	402	57	127	30	63	31	1	12	83	3	2	.316	x
1995	MIN	5	6	0	0	1	3	0	0	0	0	0	0	.000	-1

The team's batting average at Salt Lake City (AAA) was .304. He's not a prospect, but he's worth keeping an eye on because of the Twins' gaping hole at first base.

RAY DURHAM 2B Age 23 Bid: $16

Year	Team	G	AB	R	H	BB	SO	D	T	HR	RBI	SB	CS	BA	$
1993	(AA)	137	528	83	143	42	100	22	10	3	37	39	25	.271	x
1994	(AAA)	133	527	89	156	46	91	33	12	16	66	34	11	.296	x
1995	CHW	125	471	68	121	31	83	27	6	7	51	18	5	.257	**14**

He seemed to be sort of in the doghouse at the end of the season. Could be he played himself there by batting .175 in the last month. Could be he was tired. In the shortened first month, he hit .174. Without those bookends, Durham did about as well as could be expected. The fact remains, though, he fell short of them (Appendix A), and many leagues will be cutting him loose.

He won't come back much cheaper.

DAMION EASLEY 2B,SS Age 26 Bid: $1

Year	Team	G	AB	R	H	BB	SO	D	T	HR	RBI	SB	CS	BA	$
1992	CAL	47	151	14	39	8	26	5	0	1	12	9	5	.258	**5**
1993	CAL	73	230	33	72	28	35	13	2	2	22	6	6	.313	**9**
1994	CAL	88	316	41	68	29	48	16	1	6	30	4	5	.215	**0**
1995	CAL	114	357	35	77	32	47	14	2	4	35	5	2	.216	**0**

The one Angel who didn't get with the program.

JIM EDMONDS OF Age 26 Bid: $28

Year	Team	G	AB	R	H	BB	SO	D	T	HR	RBI	SB	CS	BA	$
1993	(AAA)	95	356	59	112	41	81	28	4	9	74	6	8	.315	x
1993	CAL	18	61	5	15	2	16	4	1	0	4	0	2	.246	**0**
1994	CAL	94	289	35	79	30	72	13	1	5	37	4	2	.273	**9**
1995	CAL	141	558	120	162	51	130	30	4	33	107	1	4	.290	**30**

Comment in last year's book: "Not enough upside to bid his full predicted value," which was $12.

DARIN ERSTAD OF Age 22 Bid: R1

Year	Team	G	AB	R	H	BB	SO	D	T	HR	RBI	SB	CS	BA	$
1995	(A)	4	18	2	10	1	1	1	0	0	1	1	0	.556	x
1995	(A)	25	113	24	41	6	22	7	3	5	24	3	0	.363	x

Ultra leagues probably picked him while he was still punting at Nebraska. Good idea, unless you have the first farm pick this year. Was continuing to find the pitching thoroughly to his liking in the Arizona Fall League.

TONY FERNANDEZ
3B   Age 35   Bid: $2

Year	Team	G	AB	R	H	BB	SO	D	T	HR	RBI	SB	CS	BA	$
1991	SD	145	558	81	152	55	74	27	5	4	38	23	9	.272	16
1992	SD	155	622	84	171	56	62	32	4	4	37	20	20	.275	16
1993	NY/TO	142	526	65	147	56	45	23	11	5	64	21	10	.279	19
1994	CIN	104	366	50	102	44	40	18	6	8	50	12	7	.279	18
1995	NYY	108	384	57	94	42	40	20	2	5	45	6	6	.245	6

Ranked twenty-fourth in fielding range among regular shortstops. Yankee fans are nodding their heads.

CECIL FIELDER
1B   Age 32   Bid: $19

Year	Team	G	AB	R	H	BB	SO	D	T	HR	RBI	SB	CS	BA	$
1991	DET	162	624	102	163	78	151	25	0	44	133	0	0	.261	32
1992	DET	155	594	80	145	73	151	22	0	35	124	0	0	.244	27
1993	DET	154	573	80	153	90	125	23	0	30	117	0	1	.267	25
1994	DET	109	425	67	110	50	110	16	2	28	90	0	0	.259	21
1995	DET	136	494	70	120	75	116	18	1	31	82	0	1	.243	16

To say that he's far from finished is an overstatement; he's getting there. But he can easily come back to his 1994 level.

JOHN FLAHERTY
C   Age 28   Bid: $1

Year	Team	G	AB	R	H	BB	SO	D	T	HR	RBI	SB	CS	BA	$
1994	DET	34	40	2	6	1	11	1	0	0	4	0	1	.150	-2
1995	DET	112	354	39	86	18	47	22	1	11	40	0	0	.243	5

Flaherty's 1993 and 1994 seasons with the Red Sox look almost exactly like his 1994 season, and there's enough ugliness in the world. There's a slight chance he'll shed his past and repeat 1995.

JULIO FRANCO   DH   Age 33   Bid: R4

Year	Team	G	AB	R	H	BB	SO	D	T	HR	RBI	SB	CS	BA	$
1991	TEX	146	589	108	201	65	78	27	3	15	78	36	9	.341	46

Year	Team	G	AB	R	H	BB	SO	D	T	HR	RBI	SB	CS	BA	$
1992	TEX	35	107	19	25	15	17	7	0	2	8	1	1	.234	1
1993	TEX	144	532	85	154	62	95	31	3	14	84	9	3	.289	22
1994	CHW	112	433	72	138	62	75	19	2	20	98	8	1	.319	35

It's time Bill James produced an MLE for Japan. Julio only hit .306 for the Lotte Lions. Now that *was* third in the league, but doesn't that just lend more support to the possibility that there are a bunch of good pitchers over there?

Ichiro of Orix is the only clearly outstanding Japanese hitter. He hit .342-25-80. Kokubo of Daiei won the home run crown with 28, and hit .286.

Troy Neel finished one behind him in homers but only hit .244.

Irabu of Lotte led the league in ERA with 2.53 and struck out 239 batters in 203 innings.

That's all in the Pacific League. In the Central League, Alonzo Powell won the batting crown with .355, but, like Franco, doesn't rank among the home run leaders. The best power hitter was Etoh of Hiroshima (39), followed by Nomura of Hiroshima (32), followed by O'Malley of Yakult (31). Tom hit .304. Bobby Rose, playing for Yokohama, hit .319-22-97. He's the only other American in the top ten in batting average. (Darin Jackson, .289, was the only American besides Franco in the Central League top ten.) Kevin Mitchell at least had the good grace to hit .300 during his limited stay. Shane Mack hit .275. Mel Hall hit .236.

LOU FRAZIER   OF   Age 31   Bid: $1

Year	Team	G	AB	R	H	BB	SO	D	T	HR	RBI	SB	CS	BA	$
1993	MTL	112	189	27	54	16	24	7	1	1	16	17	2	.286	9
1994	MTL	76	140	25	38	18	23	3	1	0	14	20	4	.271	12
1995	MTL	35	63	6	12	8	12	2	0	0	3	4	0	.190	-1
1995	TEX	49	99	19	21	7	20	2	0	0	8	9	1	.212	2

A useless pick-up in the crapshoot or potentially a quite valuable one, depending where you are in the speed hunt.

JEFF FRYE   2B   Age 29   Bid: $2

Year	Team	G	AB	R	H	BB	SO	D	T	HR	RBI	SB	CS	BA	$
1992	TEX	67	199	24	51	16	27	9	1	1	12	1	3	.256	2
1994	TEX	57	205	37	67	29	23	20	3	0	18	6	1	.327	11
1995	TEX	90	313	38	87	24	45	15	2	4	29	3	3	.278	7

His range factor was well above average, McLemore's well below. He won't hit below the league average, and we, like the Rangers, have to have a second baseman.

TRAVIS FRYMAN

3B   Age 27   Bid: $21

Year	Team	G	AB	R	H	BB	SO	D	T	HR	RBI	SB	CS	BA	$
1991	DET	149	557	65	144	40	149	36	3	21	91	12	5	.259	**23**
1992	DET	161	659	87	175	45	144	31	4	20	96	8	4	.266	**24**
1993	DET	151	607	98	182	77	128	37	5	22	97	9	4	.300	**30**
1994	DET	114	464	66	122	45	128	34	5	18	85	2	2	.263	**18**
1995	DET	144	567	79	156	63	100	21	5	15	81	4	2	.275	**18**

Seems to have made a conscious effort to make better contact at the expense of power. If I were him, looking at these numbers over the winter, I'd try to go back to what I was doing before.

GARY GAETTI

3B   Age 37   Bid: $18

Year	Team	G	AB	R	H	BB	SO	D	T	HR	RBI	SB	CS	BA	$
1991	CAL	152	586	58	144	33	104	22	1	18	66	5	5	.246	**14**
1992	CAL	130	456	41	103	21	79	13	2	12	48	3	1	.226	**7**
1993	KC	102	331	40	81	21	87	20	1	14	50	1	3	.245	**9**
1994	KC	90	327	53	94	19	63	15	3	12	57	0	2	.287	**15**
1995	KC	137	514	76	134	47	91	27	0	35	96	3	3	.261	**24**

Now has gone over the 1,000 RBI mark; what were the odds of that a few years ago?

The mystery of Gaetti's career is less how it came back than why it collapsed? Did religion do it both times? The only reason to tread lightly in his direction is the not knowing. He's not too old.

GREG GAGNE

SS   Age 34   Bid: $5

Year	Team	G	AB	R	H	BB	SO	D	T	HR	RBI	SB	CS	BA	$
1991	MIN	139	408	52	108	26	72	23	3	8	42	11	9	.265	**13**
1992	MIN	146	439	53	108	19	83	23	0	7	39	6	7	.246	**8**
1993	KC	159	540	66	151	33	93	32	3	10	57	10	12	.280	**16**
1994	KC	107	375	39	97	27	79	23	3	7	51	10	17	.259	**12**
1995	KC	120	430	58	110	38	60	25	4	6	49	3	5	.256	**7**

Third best range factor in the majors. The year before, on the old carpet, he ranked fourth.

He only hit .272 at home last year, compared to .313 the year before, but he still hit better than on the road. The Royals as a team hit .268 at home, .252 on the road, compared to .297 at home, .239 on the road in 1994. They traded a 35-24 home won-lost record for a 35-37 record in their new stadium. Planting grass probably cost them the wild card spot in the play-offs.

MIKE GALLEGO

2B   Age 35   Bid: R3

Year	Team	G	AB	R	H	BB	SO	D	T	HR	RBI	SB	CS	BA	$
1991	OAK	159	482	67	119	67	84	15	4	12	49	6	9	.247	10
1992	NYY	53	173	24	44	20	22	7	1	3	14	0	1	.254	3
1993	NYY	119	403	63	114	50	65	20	1	10	54	3	2	.283	13
1994	NYY	89	306	39	73	38	46	17	1	6	41	0	1	.239	3
1995	OAK	43	120	11	28	9	24	0	0	0	8	0	1	.233	-1

His slugging percentage was the same as his batting average! Isolated Power of zero. In well over 100 at-bats — has it ever been done?

Last year, in the American League, his closest competition was Shannon Stewart, with 38 AB. Others who had 20 or more cracks at an extra-base hit without getting one, in descending order of chances: Damon Buford, Duane Singleton, Chris Tremie, Steve Buechele, Fausto Cruz, Orlando Palmeiro, Dick Schofield and Scooter Tucker. Ten hitters who between them played in 163 games. These are their stats:

G	AB	R	H	BB	SO	D	T	HR	RBI	SB	CS	BA	$
163	352	25	64	39	63	0	0	0	19	7	3	.182	-8

Slow little devils.

BRENT GATES

2B   Age 26   Bid: $12

Year	Team	G	AB	R	H	BB	SO	D	T	HR	RBI	SB	CS	BA	$
1993	OAK	139	535	64	155	56	75	29	2	7	69	7	3	.290	17
1994	OAK	64	233	29	66	21	32	11	1	2	24	3	0	.283	7
1995	OAK	136	524	60	133	46	84	24	4	5	56	3	3	.254	6

The bid you see here is $1 more than his average salary last year. It should be more than enough to get him, in other words, without going too far out on a limb if Brent Gates fails again.

For fail he did. This is a player who many of us thought had batting title potential. I went so far as to say his set-back in 1994 would work to his advantage. After finally seeming to get his game on track in August, when he hit .316, he hit .243 over the last month. He didn't distinguish himself at second. If he has to move to third, suddenly his career takes on a whole different appearance; it's in jeopardy.

JASON GIAMBI

3B,1B Age 25   Bid: $2

Year	Team	G	AB	R	H	BB	SO	D	T	HR	RBI	SB	CS	BA	$
1994	(AA)	56	193	31	43	27	31	9	0	6	30	0	0	.223	10
1994	(AAA)	52	176	28	56	25	32	20	0	4	38	1	0	.318	10
1995	(AAA)	55	190	34	65	34	26	26	1	3	41	0	0	.342	10
1995	OAK	54	176	27	45	28	31	7	0	6	25	2	1	.256	5

Has the look of a professional hitter in the making. Depending on how spring training goes, might want to borrow a dollar or two from Gates to get him.

BENJI GIL   SS   Age 23   Bid: $3

Year	Team	G	AB	R	H	BB	SO	D	T	HR	RBI	SB	CS	BA	$
1993	(AA)	101	342	45	94	35	89	9	1	17	59	20	12	.275	x
1993	TEX	22	57	3	7	5	22	0	0	0	2	1	2	.123	-3
1995	TEX	130	415	36	91	26	147	20	3	9	46	2	4	.219	1

Was as good as advertised in the field. Better. Led the majors, by a lot, in range factor. Led the league in assists (two more than Vizquel) and was second to Ripken in DPs. Tied for the third most errors in the league, with 17, but was involved in so many plays that even his fielding percentage was above average.

This while striking out more frequently than anyone else in the game. In July he hit .157, in August .159. It must have been getting to be pure hell for him. But he came through it. He's shown he's tough. He's still very young. The sort of player who, if he can just improve a little bit, might improve a lot.

BRIAN GILES   OF   Age 25   Bid: R2

Year	Team	G	AB	R	H	BB	SO	D	T	HR	RBI	SB	CS	BA	$
1994	(AAA)	128	434	74	136	55	61	18	3	16	58	8	5	.313	x
1995	(AAA)	123	413	67	128	54	40	18	8	15	67	7	3	.310	x
1995	CLE	6	9	6	5	0	1	0	0	1	3	0	0	.556	2

I got to see him get his first major league hit, a home run, and nearly kill the Indians' second baseman in the same game; he didn't play a whole lot after that. But a .556 batting average is a .556 batting average, and the Indians put him on their 40-man roster to forestall his becoming a six-year free agent. They don't ask much for him.

CHRIS GOMEZ   SS   Age 25   Bid: $6

Year	Team	G	AB	R	H	BB	SO	D	T	HR	RBI	SB	CS	BA	$
1993	DET	46	128	11	32	9	17	7	1	0	11	2	2	.250	1
1994	DET	84	296	32	76	33	64	19	0	8	53	5	3	.257	11
1995	DET	123	431	49	96	41	96	20	2	11	50	4	1	.223	4

Good player. Will hit for more power and should climb back to the .250 level.

ALEX GONZALEZ   SS   Age 23   Bid: $9

Year	Team	G	AB	R	H	BB	SO	D	T	HR	RBI	SB	CS	BA	$
1992	(A)	134	535	83	145	38	119	22	9	10	62	26	14	.271	x

Year	Team	G	AB	R	H	BB	SO	D	T	HR	RBI	SB	CS	BA	$
1993	(AA)	142	561	93	162	39	110	29	7	16	69	38	13	.289	x
1994	(AAA)	110	437	69	124	53	92	22	4	12	57	23	6	.284	x
1994	TOR	15	53	7	8	4	17	3	1	0	1	3	0	.151	-2
1995	TOR	111	367	51	89	44	114	19	4	10	42	4	4	.243	6

He may have had a worse season, in real baseball, than Benji Gil. His range factor was last in the league. In 25 fewer games, he committed as many errors. If he had played as many innings as Gil, he would have had a hundred fewer assists. He didn't click on even half as many double plays, and his partner wasn't named Jeff Frye or Mark McLemore.

At the plate, he struck out at an alarming rate also. His offense was a little better across the board, while still far below the average player's.

Nor, perhaps, did he come through it. He sat out many a game in September. They hit for almost identical averages (Gil .237, Gonzalez .238), but Gil's at least was going up.

So why am I willing to pay three times as much for Gonzalez anyway?

First, I have every confidence I won't get him at that price.

Second, I don't want anyone else to get him for less, because I could be very wrong.

JUAN GONZALEZ   DH   Age 26   Bid: $26

Year	Team	G	AB	R	H	BB	SO	D	T	HR	RBI	SB	CS	BA	$
1991	TEX	142	545	78	144	42	118	34	1	27	102	4	4	.264	24
1992	TEX	155	584	77	152	35	143	24	2	43	109	0	1	.260	32
1993	TEX	140	536	105	166	37	99	33	1	46	118	4	1	.310	41
1994	TEX	107	422	57	116	30	66	18	4	19	85	6	4	.275	23
1995	TEX	90	352	57	104	17	66	20	2	27	82	0	0	.295	23

The back problem, a DH — unlike Canseco, not much fun — but man can he hit.

CURTIS GOODWIN   OF   Age 23   Bid: $13

Year	Team	G	AB	R	H	BB	SO	D	T	HR	RBI	SB	CS	BA	$
1993	(A)	138	555	98	156	52	90	15	10	2	42	61	15	.281	x
1994	(AA)	142	597	105	171	40	78	18	8	2	37	59	10	.286	x
1995	(AAA)	36	140	24	37	12	15	3	3	0	7	17	3	.264	x
1995	BAL	87	289	40	76	15	53	11	3	1	24	22	4	.263	12

More downside but as much upside as Tom Goodwin.

TOM GOODWIN   OF   Age 27   Bid: $21

Year	Team	G	AB	R	H	BB	SO	D	T	HR	RBI	SB	CS	BA	$
1991	LA	16	7	3	1	0	0	0	0	0	0	1	1	.143	0
1992	LA	57	73	15	17	6	10	1	1	0	3	7	3	.233	2
1993	LA	30	17	6	5	1	4	1	0	0	1	1	2	.294	1
1994	KC	2	2	0	0	0	1	0	0	0	0	0	0	.000	0
1995	KC	133	480	72	138	38	72	16	3	4	28	50	18	.288	30

The assumption is he hangs onto left field and bats in front of Damon. It would be exciting, and great for Damon. On the other hand, if they do that, the Royals will once again be punting the home run category.

SHAWN GREEN   OF   Age 22   Bid: $26

Year	Team	G	AB	R	H	BB	SO	D	T	HR	RBI	SB	CS	BA	$
1993	(AA)	99	360	40	102	26	72	14	2	4	34	4	9	.283	x
1993	TOR	3	6	0	0	0	1	0	0	0	0	0	0	.000	-1
1994	(AAA)	109	433	82	149	40	54	27	3	13	61	19	7	.344	x
1994	TOR	14	33	1	3	1	8	1	0	0	1	1	0	.091	-2
1995	TOR	121	379	52	109	20	68	31	4	15	54	1	2	.288	15

He was fine last year. In fact, he led the Blue Jays in slugging average — by 50 points. In the last two months, he hit .317. There were some embarrassing moments in the outfield, but scrambling after his goofs, he showed speed that could yet translate into a few steals. He'll be on enough sleeper lists to make you scream.

TODD GREENE   C   Age 25   Bid: R1

Year	Team	G	AB	R	H	BB	SO	D	T	HR	RBI	SB	CS	BA	$
1993	(A)	76	305	55	82	34	44	15	3	15	71	4	3	.269	x
1994	(A)	133	524	98	158	64	96	39	2	35	124	10	3	.302	x
1995	(AA)	82	318	59	104	17	55	19	1	26	57	3	5	.327	x
1995	(AAA)	43	168	28	42	11	36	3	1	14	35	1	0	.250	x

He can hit 'em but can he catch 'em? If he can't, can the Angels find somebody to pick up Chile's contract, because he sure can hit 'em. The numbers at Vancouver (AAA) may not be pretty, but the ball went over the fence every three games. Baseball Weekly actually made Greene their Minor League Player of the Year, while Baseball America picked 18-year-old Andruw Jones. The editors at BW are like you and I: they don't give a damn about posterity, they want to win every year.

MIKE GREENWELL   OF   Age 32   Bid: $18

Year	Team	G	AB	R	H	BB	SO	D	T	HR	RBI	SB	CS	BA	$
1991	BOS	147	544	76	163	43	35	26	6	9	83	15	5	.300	26
1992	BOS	49	180	16	42	18	19	2	0	2	18	2	3	.233	2
1993	BOS	146	540	77	170	54	46	38	6	13	72	5	4	.315	24
1994	BOS	95	327	60	88	38	26	25	1	11	45	2	2	.269	11
1995	BOS	120	481	67	143	38	35	25	4	15	76	9	5	.297	23

Hit eight homers in the last two months — while his batting average sagged.

RUSTY GREER   OF   Age 27   Bid: $8

Year	Team	G	AB	R	H	BB	SO	D	T	HR	RBI	SB	CS	BA	$
1994	TEX	80	277	36	87	46	46	16	1	10	46	0	0	.314	16
1995	TEX	131	417	58	113	55	66	21	2	13	61	3	1	.271	13

Trim a little power, add some speed, and you have the stats of the average hitter.

BEN GRIEVE OF   Age 20   Bid: R4

Year	Team	G	AB	R	H	BB	SO	D	T	HR	RBI	SB	CS	BA	$
1994	(A)	72	252	44	83	51	48	13	0	7	50	2	2	.329	x
1995	(A)	102	371	53	97	60	75	16	1	4	62	11	3	.261	x
1995	(A)	28	107	17	28	15	22	5	0	2	14	2	0	.262	x

So he hit .262, .261, whatever. He's just a kid, for heaven's sake. Two Junes ago he was the second pick in the draft right out of high school; did so well in the college-dominated Northwest League that he was Baseball America's number one prospect. And now he's dumped. Not a prospect in the Midwest League, not a prospect in the California League.

Buncha front-runners. I'm sticking with this guy. Years from now I'll remind you if I was right and won't if I was wrong.

KEN GRIFFEY JR   OF   Age 26   Bid: $45

Year	Team	G	AB	R	H	BB	SO	D	T	HR	RBI	SB	CS	BA	$
1991	SEA	154	548	76	179	71	82	42	1	22	100	18	6	.327	39
1992	SEA	142	565	83	174	44	67	39	4	27	103	10	5	.308	36
1993	SEA	156	582	113	180	96	91	38	3	45	109	17	9	.309	45
1994	SEA	111	433	94	140	56	73	24	4	40	90	11	3	.323	45

Year	Team	G	AB	R	H	BB	SO	D	T	HR	RBI	SB	CS	BA	$
1995	SEA	72	260	52	67	52	53	7	0	17	42	4	2	.258	**12**

Quite a contrast between his home-run trots and Sierra's as things came down to the wire last season. Sierra's was so thoroughly nauseating that any neutral fan wanted to throw the ball back onto the field. Griffey just got into his glide. He rounded first, rounded second, rounded third, and stepped on home — serene, as Tom Wolfe would say.

Baseball, a sign in the Kingdome said, doesn't make character; it reveals it. While Griffey was hitting nothing but pitiful dribblers to second, he never made excuses. Never said his timing was off, never pointed out he had heavy metal still in his wrist. His teammates didn't just say they had to step up in his absence, they did.

Gee, you don't seem too excited, one of the announcers said to Edgar Martinez, after he beat the Yankees. I guess I'm hiding my emotions, he answered. He knew that the game humbles you when you open your yap, and even when you don't.

Other Mariners just couldn't stop laughing over the way Griffey motored on Edgar's double. They *knew* he was fast, they did! Has there ever been a more satisfying end to a deciding game? To a neutral fan. (I admit to hating the Yankees when I was a kid, Sierra, when they were worth it, so nothing will ever compare to Mazeroski's home run.) For game-long drama, the standard remains the sixth game in 1986 between the Mets and the Astros. The sixth game of the next series (technically not decisive) exceeded the wildest nightmare that any losing side could ever have, but nightmares aren't all that satisfying. The only way reality might have fallen short of the wildest dreams of Mariner fans, as they waited for their half of the ninth inning, is that there wasn't enough time to bite their nails. After one pitch, Cora on first. After another (so it seemed), Cora on third, Griffey on first. Edgar Martinez at the plate. Tie game for sure, tie game for sure, tie game for — before they could say it a third time, much less start chewing, it wasn't a tie game.

The replay showed Cora desperately signaling, Slide, Griffey, slide! He slid, and was there easily.

The replay showed Fernandez taking the throw from Gerald Williams, and making a nice relay: no fuss, no muss, and no mustard. Tony Fernandez to the end.

The replay showed teammates piling high on top of Griffey. All except one. Who was it? I knew what he was doing, but who was it? Luckily, you got to see the replay again and again, and it was Cora, flashing off the top of the screen, heading for Edgar.

OZZIE GUILLEN   SS   Age 33   Bid: $5

Year	Team	G	AB	R	H	BB	SO	D	T	HR	RBI	SB	CS	BA	$
1991	CHW	154	524	52	143	11	38	20	3	3	49	21	15	.273	**18**
1992	CHW	12	40	5	8	1	5	4	0	0	7	1	0	.200	**0**
1993	CHW	134	457	44	128	10	41	23	4	4	50	5	4	.280	**11**
1994	CHW	100	365	46	105	14	35	9	5	1	39	5	4	.288	**10**
1995	CHW	122	415	50	103	13	25	20	3	1	41	6	7	.248	**4**

Winning is infectious, and so is losing.

BOB HAMELIN DH Age 28   Bid: $2

Year	Team	G	AB	R	H	BB	SO	D	T	HR	RBI	SB	CS	BA	$
1993	KC	16	49	2	11	6	15	3	0	2	5	0	0	.224	1
1994	KC	101	312	64	88	56	62	25	1	24	65	4	3	.282	23
1995	KC	72	208	20	35	26	56	7	1	7	25	0	1	.168	-3

Stick a forklift in him.

DARYL HAMILTON OF Age 31   Bid: $3

Year	Team	G	AB	R	H	BB	SO	D	T	HR	RBI	SB	CS	BA	$
1991	MIL	122	405	64	126	33	38	15	6	1	57	16	6	.311	20
1992	MIL	127	470	67	140	45	42	19	7	5	62	41	14	.298	31
1993	MIL	135	520	74	161	45	62	21	1	9	48	21	13	.310	25
1994	MIL	36	141	23	37	15	17	10	1	1	13	3	0	.262	3
1995	MIL	112	398	54	108	47	35	20	6	5	44	11	1	.271	12

His 1995 stats actually aren't all that bad for a lead-off or number 2 hitter. His .350 on-base average was better than Devon White's or Vince Coleman's — or just about anybody on the Brewers (team OBA .336, eleventh in the league). His range factor in center field was much better than Hulse's. He's as good as anyone the Brewers have, which makes him an extremely attractive fifth outfielder.

JEFFREY HAMMONDS OF Age 25   Bid: $8

Year	Team	G	AB	R	H	BB	SO	D	T	HR	RBI	SB	CS	BA	$
1993	(AA)	24	92	13	26	9	18	3	0	3	10	4	3	.283	x
1993	(AAA)	36	151	25	47	5	27	9	1	5	23	6	3	.311	x
1993	BAL	33	105	10	32	2	16	8	0	3	19	4	0	.305	6
1994	BAL	68	250	45	74	17	39	18	2	8	31	5	0	.296	13
1995	BAL	57	178	18	43	9	30	9	1	4	23	4	2	.242	4

For the first time, he wasn't just brittle, he was bad. Nevertheless, at Double-A Bowie briefly (nine games), he hit .387, slugged .645. If Bonilla plays third, he gets one more chance.

BRIAN HARPER C Age 35   Bid: Adieu

Year	Team	G	AB	R	H	BB	SO	D	T	HR	RBI	SB	CS	BA	$
1991	MIN	123	441	54	137	14	22	28	1	10	69	1	2	.311	19

Year	Team	G	AB	R	H	BB	SO	D	T	HR	RBI	SB	CS	BA	$
1992	MIN	140	502	58	154	26	22	25	0	9	73	0	1	.307	**20**
1993	MIN	147	530	52	161	29	29	26	1	12	73	1	3	.304	**20**
1994	MIL	64	251	23	73	9	18	15	0	4	32	0	2	.291	**8**
1995	OAK	2	7	0	0	0	1	0	0	0	0	0	0	.000	**-1**

Came to The Show late, left early. And I bet good money he was a movie junkie.

RICKEY HENDERSON OF Age 37 Bid: $20

Year	Team	G	AB	R	H	BB	SO	D	T	HR	RBI	SB	CS	BA	$
1991	OAK	134	470	105	126	98	73	17	1	18	57	58	18	.268	**41**
1992	OAK	117	396	77	112	95	56	18	3	15	46	48	11	.283	**33**
1993	TOR	134	481	114	139	120	65	22	2	21	59	53	8	.289	**40**
1994	OAK	87	296	66	77	72	45	13	0	6	20	22	7	.260	**15**
1995	OAK	112	407	67	122	72	66	31	1	9	54	32	10	.300	**28**

Hit .419 with runners in scoring position, so maybe Art Howe will do something I've long proposed: bat him third. Then again, in 1994 he hit .196 with runners in scoring position. Rickey's Rickey, which doesn't play well as you approach 40.

JOSE HERRERA OF Age 23 Bid: R2

Year	Team	G	AB	R	H	BB	SO	D	T	HR	RBI	SB	CS	BA	$
1993	(A)	95	388	60	123	26	63	22	5	5	42	36	20	.317	**x**
1994	(A)	103	370	59	106	38	76	20	3	11	56	21	12	.286	**x**
1995	(AA)	92	358	37	101	27	58	11	4	6	45	9	8	.282	**x**
1995	OAK	33	70	9	17	6	11	1	2	0	2	1	3	.243	**0**

Jose is not Rickey. For one thing, he's got a strong throwing arm. Where he hit in the line-up at Double-A Huntsville is not known, but one hopes it wasn't first, second *or* third, based on the number of runs he scored.

PHIL HIATT OF Age 27 Bid: 0

Year	Team	G	AB	R	H	BB	SO	D	T	HR	RBI	SB	CS	BA	$
1993	KC	81	238	30	52	16	82	12	1	7	36	6	3	.218	**5**
1995	KC	52	113	11	23	9	37	6	0	4	12	1	0	.204	**0**

It's true that Hiatt never had Hamelin's, or even Hammonds', success in the majors, but it's worth noting that not everyone thrives when they're demoted to the bushes. Hiatt hit .182, walked twice and struck out 25 times in 20 games back at Omaha. What that means, besides that he's through, is that there are some good pitchers coming along.

BOBBY HIGGINSON OF Age 25   Bid: $8

Year	Team	G	AB	R	H	BB	SO	D	T	HR	RBI	SB	CS	BA	$
1994	(AAA)	137	476	81	131	46	99	28	3	23	67	16	8	.275	x
1995	DET	131	410	61	92	62	107	17	5	14	43	6	4	.224	6

Will play in at least 131 games again and must get more than 92 hits.

DENNY HOCKING SS Age 26   Bid: R3

Year	Team	G	AB	R	H	BB	SO	D	T	HR	RBI	SB	CS	BA	$
1993	MIN	15	36	7	5	6	8	1	0	0	0	1	0	.139	-1
1994	MIN	11	31	3	10	0	4	3	0	0	2	2	0	.323	2
1995	MIN	9	25	4	5	2	2	0	2	0	3	1	0	.200	0

Hit .282-8-75, stole 12 bases, at Salt Lake City; team hit .304.

CHRIS HOILES C Age 31   Bid: $14

Year	Team	G	AB	R	H	BB	SO	D	T	HR	RBI	SB	CS	BA	$
1991	BAL	107	341	36	83	29	61	15	0	11	31	0	2	.243	6
1992	BAL	96	310	49	85	55	60	10	1	20	40	0	2	.274	15
1993	BAL	126	419	80	130	69	94	28	0	29	82	1	1	.310	27
1994	BAL	99	332	45	82	63	73	10	0	19	53	2	0	.247	12
1995	BAL	114	352	53	88	67	80	15	1	19	58	1	0	.250	12

There are more misprints in this book than there should be, far more, but Hoiles really is 31. It is not unusual for him to play fewer than 100 games in a full season. He had a fine second half (.519 SA), but chase with care.

DAVE HOLLINS 1B Age 30   Bid: R2

Year	Team	G	AB	R	H	BB	SO	D	T	HR	RBI	SB	CS	BA	$
1991	PHI	56	151	18	45	17	26	10	2	6	21	1	1	.298	7
1992	PHI	156	586	104	158	76	110	28	4	27	93	9	6	.270	32
1993	PHI	143	543	104	148	85	109	30	4	18	93	2	3	.273	19
1994	PHI	44	162	28	36	23	32	7	1	4	26	1	0	.222	2

Year	Team	G	AB	R	H	BB	SO	D	T	HR	RBI	SB	CS	BA	$
1995	PHI	65	205	46	47	53	38	12	2	7	25	1	1	.229	3
1995	BOS	5	13	2	2	4	7	0	0	0	1	0	0	.154	-1

Healthy,with Canseco elsewhere, he becomes interesting.

DWAYNE HOSEY   OF   Age 29   Bid: $12

Year	Team	G	AB	R	H	BB	SO	D	T	HR	RBI	SB	CS	BA	$
1994	(AAA)	112	406	95	135	61	85	23	8	27	80	27	12	.333	x
1995	(AAA)	75	271	59	80	29	45	21	4	12	50	15	6	.295	x
1995	BOS	24	68	20	23	8	16	8	1	3	7	6	0	.338	7

In addition to Hiatt, Felix Jose, Les Norman and Keith Miller were given a chance or two in the Royals' outfield. Baffling. The cautious souls in Baseball Weekly pushed him to $5 on April 18, when he was still in training camp. He got off to a rough start, understandably, back at Omaha, where he had been the American Association MVP in 1994, but Hosey was coming on strong when the Royals released him.

They loved him in Boston. The Globe ran Hosey's picture on the front page the day after the Red Sox clinched. He's crossing home plate, looking — not too different than Ken Griffey. I won't predict better things for Hosey than Greenwell with the bid, but I might in the next chapter.

REX HUDLER   2B,OF   Age 35   Bid: $2

Year	Team	G	AB	R	H	BB	SO	D	T	HR	RBI	SB	CS	BA	$
1991	STL	101	207	21	47	10	29	10	2	1	15	12	10	.227	2
1992	STL	61	98	17	24	2	23	4	0	3	5	2	8	.245	4
1994	CAL	56	124	17	37	6	28	8	0	8	20	2	2	.298	9
1995	CAL	84	223	30	59	10	48	16	0	6	27	12	0	.265	10

He's already forgiven Langston. He wants to play on a winner before he's through, and the Angels are going to win the division this year.

DAVID HULSE   OF   Age 28   Bid: $3

Year	Team	G	AB	R	H	BB	SO	D	T	HR	RBI	SB	CS	BA	$
1992	TEX	32	92	14	28	3	18	4	0	0	2	3	1	.304	3
1993	TEX	114	407	71	118	26	57	9	10	1	29	29	9	.290	18
1994	TEX	77	310	58	79	21	53	8	4	1	19	18	2	.255	10
1995	MIL	119	339	46	85	18	60	11	6	3	47	15	3	.251	10

Cheap speed, might hit .275.

JEFF HUSON

JEFF HUSON 2B,3B Age 31 Bid: $1

Year	Team	G	AB	R	H	BB	SO	D	T	HR	RBI	SB	CS	BA	$
1991	TEX	119	268	36	57	39	32	8	3	2	26	8	3	.213	3
1992	TEX	123	318	49	83	41	43	14	3	4	24	18	6	.261	11
1993	TEX	23	45	3	6	0	10	1	1	0	2	0	0	.133	-2
1995	BAL	66	161	24	40	15	20	4	2	1	19	5	4	.248	3

Qualifying at two weak positions, both of which are unsettled on the Orioles, is the most you can say for him.

RAUL IBANEZ

RAUL IBANEZ C Age 24 Bid: R4

Year	Team	G	AB	R	H	BB	SO	D	T	HR	RBI	SB	CS	BA	$
1994	(A)	91	327	55	102	32	37	30	3	7	59	10	5	.312	x
1995	(A)	95	361	59	120	41	49	23	9	20	108	4	3	.332	x

Too old to be an R5, Ibanez is far too green and too positionless to be an R1. He might be an R2 as a DH, but not as a catcher. Was an outfielder in junior college. The Mariners drafted him in the thirty-sixth round in 1992. He started doing a bit of catching in 1994. Baseball America doesn't even rate him as a top 10 prospect in the California League. Nevertheless, playing in a very tough home run park (Riverside), he had a .612 slugging average. The jump in power over the previous season is noteworthy also. The last person to be drafted so low, suddenly blossom after a few years in the minors, and end up catching and doing some hitting in the majors was Mike Piazza.

JOHN JAHA

JOHN JAHA 1B Age 30 Bid: $18

Year	Team	G	AB	R	H	BB	SO	D	T	HR	RBI	SB	CS	BA	$
1992	MIL	47	133	17	30	12	30	3	1	2	10	10	0	.226	4
1993	MIL	153	515	78	136	51	109	21	0	19	70	13	9	.264	20
1994	MIL	84	291	45	70	32	75	14	0	12	39	3	3	.241	7
1995	MIL	88	316	59	99	36	66	20	2	20	65	2	1	.313	21

Has to be a head case. No other explanation for taking *this* long to blossom. Head cases make bettors nervous. Talent turns them on.

STAN JAVIER

STAN JAVIER OF Age 32 Bid: $20

Year	Team	G	AB	R	H	BB	SO	D	T	HR	RBI	SB	CS	BA	$
1991	LA	121	176	21	36	16	36	5	3	1	11	7	1	.205	1
1992	LA/PH	130	334	42	83	37	54	17	1	1	29	18	3	.249	9

Year	Team	G	AB	R	H	BB	SO	D	T	HR	RBI	SB	CS	BA	$
1993	CAL	92	237	33	69	27	33	10	4	3	28	12	2	.291	**11**
1994	OAK	109	419	75	114	49	76	23	0	10	44	24	7	.272	**23**
1995	OAK	130	442	81	123	49	63	20	2	8	56	36	5	.278	**27**

The only reason not to pay him more is that you also believe in shortchanging the running game.

REGGIE JEFFERSON DH Age 27 1995:$1

Year	Team	G	AB	R	H	BB	SO	D	T	HR	RBI	SB	CS	BA	$
1991	CIN/CL	31	108	11	21	4	24	3	0	3	13	0	0	.194	**0**
1992	CLE	24	89	8	30	1	17	6	2	1	6	0	0	.337	**4**
1993	CLE	113	366	35	91	28	78	11	2	10	34	1	3	.249	**6**
1994	SEA	63	162	24	53	17	32	11	0	8	32	0	0	.327	**12**
1995	BOS	46	121	21	35	9	24	8	0	5	26	0	0	.289	**6**

What to bid if Canseco moves on and it appears that Jefferson will the DH against righthanders?
  Not more than $5, due to the DH glut.

DEREK JETER SS Age 22 Bid: R1

Year	Team	G	AB	R	H	BB	SO	D	T	HR	RBI	SB	CS	BA	$
1993	(A)	128	515	85	152	58	95	14	11	5	71	18	9	.295	x
1994	(A)	69	292	61	96	23	30	13	8	0	39	28	2	.329	x
1994	(AA)	34	122	17	46	15	16	7	2	2	13	12	2	.377	x
1994	(AAA)	35	126	25	44	20	15	7	1	3	16	10	4	.349	x
1995	(AAA)	123	486	96	154	61	56	27	9	2	45	20	12	.317	x
1995	NYY	15	48	5	12	3	11	4	1	0	7	0	0	.250	**0**

What to bid if Fernandez has moved on?
  Hmm, a tough one.
  $15?
  $17?

LANCE JOHNSON OF Age 32 Bid: $26

Year	Team	G	AB	R	H	BB	SO	D	T	HR	RBI	SB	CS	BA	$
1991	CHW	159	588	72	161	26	58	14	13	0	49	26	11	.274	**19**
1992	CHW	157	567	67	158	34	33	15	12	3	47	41	14	.279	**26**

Year	Team	G	AB	R	H	BB	SO	D	T	HR	RBI	SB	CS	BA	$
1993	CHW	147	540	75	168	36	33	18	14	0	47	35	7	.311	**27**
1994	CHW	106	412	56	114	26	23	11	14	3	54	26	6	.277	**23**
1995	CHW	142	607	98	186	32	31	18	12	10	57	40	6	.306	**36**

Split the difference between '94 and "95, then nick him a bit for the running game.

WALLY JOYNER   1B   Age 34   Bid: $18

Year	Team	G	AB	R	H	BB	SO	D	T	HR	RBI	SB	CS	BA	$
1991	CAL	143	551	79	166	52	66	34	3	21	96	2	0	.301	**27**
1992	KC	149	572	66	154	55	50	36	2	9	66	11	5	.269	**17**
1993	KC	141	497	83	145	66	67	36	3	15	65	5	9	.292	**19**
1994	KC	97	363	52	113	47	43	20	3	8	57	3	2	.311	**19**
1995	KC	131	465	69	144	69	65	28	0	12	83	3	2	.310	**22**

Hit .336 at home, so he loved that grass.

RON KARKOVICE   C   Age 32   Bid: $2

Year	Team	G	AB	R	H	BB	SO	D	T	HR	RBI	SB	CS	BA	$
1991	CHW	75	167	25	41	15	42	13	0	5	22	0	0	.246	**3**
1992	CHW	123	342	39	81	30	89	12	1	13	50	10	4	.237	**13**
1993	CHW	128	403	60	92	29	126	17	1	20	54	2	2	.228	**9**
1994	CHW	77	207	33	44	36	68	9	1	11	29	0	3	.213	**2**
1995	CHW	113	323	44	70	39	84	14	1	13	51	2	3	.217	**5**

Easy to picture the 1995 line again, just with more at-bats.

PAT KELLY   2B   Age 28   Bid: $3

Year	Team	G	AB	R	H	BB	SO	D	T	HR	RBI	SB	CS	BA	$
1991	NYY	96	298	35	72	15	52	12	4	3	23	12	1	.242	**7**
1992	NYY	106	318	38	72	25	72	22	2	7	27	8	5	.226	**6**
1993	NYY	127	406	49	111	24	68	24	1	7	51	14	11	.273	**15**
1994	NYY	93	286	35	80	19	51	21	2	3	41	6	5	.280	**11**
1995	NYY	89	270	32	64	23	65	12	1	4	29	8	3	.237	**5**

If he's lost his job to Velarde, it's about time.

WAYNE KIRBY   OF   Age 32   Bid: R3

Year	Team	G	AB	R	H	BB	SO	D	T	HR	RBI	SB	CS	BA	$
1991	CLE	21	43	4	9	2	6	2	0	0	5	1	2	.209	1
1992	CLE	21	18	9	3	3	2	1	0	1	1	0	3	.167	0
1993	CLE	131	458	71	123	37	58	19	5	6	60	17	5	.269	16
1994	CLE	78	191	33	56	13	30	6	0	5	23	11	4	.293	13
1995	CLE	101	188	29	39	13	32	10	2	1	14	10	3	.207	2

Knows where he sits.

CHUCK KNOBLAUCH   2B   Age 27   Bid: $35

Year	Team	G	AB	R	H	BB	SO	D	T	HR	RBI	SB	CS	BA	$
1991	MIN	151	565	78	159	59	40	24	6	1	50	25	5	.281	21
1992	MIN	155	600	104	178	88	60	19	6	2	56	34	13	.297	27
1993	MIN	153	602	82	167	65	44	27	4	2	41	29	11	.277	19
1994	MIN	109	445	85	139	41	56	45	3	5	51	35	6	.312	35
1995	MIN	136	538	107	179	78	95	34	8	11	63	46	18	.333	44

The formula also cheats the running game, although not nearly as much as the bids. And still Knoblauch beat out Edgar Martinez. In Appendix B, he's as far ahead of the second base pack as Roberto Alomar used to be. A weak position, a strong track record, about to hit the magic age (although I don't really subscribe to that theory) — how come I can't find more money for Chuck Knoblauch?

Chastened perhaps by my $40 bid in last year's book for Alomar?

Not all. It's deep-seated prejudice. I mean, I can look for evidence to support it, anyone can. The 18 CS last year. But you know what Vince Scully says: statistics are the hobgoblins of small minds. Something like that. No, it has nothing to do with stats. It's prejudice, pure and simple, I admit it.

His name is Chuck.

RANDY KNORR   C   Age 27   Bid: $1

Year	Team	G	AB	R	H	BB	SO	D	T	HR	RBI	SB	CS	BA	$
1992	TOR	8	19	1	5	1	5	0	0	1	2	0	0	.263	1
1993	TOR	39	101	11	25	9	29	3	2	4	20	0	0	.248	3
1994	TOR	40	124	20	30	10	35	2	0	7	19	0	0	.242	4
1995	TOR	45	132	18	28	11	28	8	0	3	16	0	0	.212	0

Sandy Martinez hit .229 at Knoxville.

JEFF LADD   C,DH   Age 25   Bid: R2

Year	Team	G	AB	R	H	BB	SO	D	T	HR	RBI	SB	CS	BA	$
1994	(A)	59	203	43	66	44	60	13	0	12	44	4	1	.325	x
1994	(A)	41	140	20	37	21	48	4	0	8	25	3	1	.264	x
1995	(A)	94	311	54	95	78	94	17	3	19	58	6	3	.305	x
1995	(AA)	9	24	1	7	5	8	1	1	0	2	0	0	.292	x

Jeff Ladd hit .292 at Knoxville. The good numbers (.563 SA, .454 OBA) were posted at Single-A Hagerstown, where you're not meant to be 24.

Like Ibanez, he was a DH wearing a catcher's mitt (occasionally). Unlike Ibanez, he really didn't improve much over the year before (split between St. Catherines and Hagerstown). R2 could be as good as it gets, but for one year, anyway, he's lifted himself above R3.

MIKE LAVALLIERE   C   Age 35   Bid: $1

Year	Team	G	AB	R	H	BB	SO	D	T	HR	RBI	SB	CS	BA	$
1991	PIT	108	336	25	97	33	27	11	2	3	41	2	1	.289	10
1992	PIT	95	293	22	75	44	21	13	1	2	29	0	3	.256	4
1993	CHW	37	97	6	25	4	14	2	0	0	8	0	1	.258	0
1994	CHW	59	139	6	39	20	15	4	0	1	24	0	2	.281	4
1995	CHW	46	98	7	24	9	15	6	0	1	19	0	0	.245	1

And not a penny more.

MATT LAWTON   OF   Age 24   Bid: R1

Year	Team	G	AB	R	H	BB	SO	D	T	HR	RBI	SB	CS	BA	$
1994	(A)	122	446	79	134	80	64	30	1	7	51	42	19	.300	x
1995	(AA)	114	412	75	111	56	70	19	5	13	54	26	9	.269	x
1995	MIN	21	60	11	19	7	11	4	1	1	12	1	1	.317	3

Is there a difference these days between Double-A and Triple-A?

Some observers argue that the better prospects are actually in Double-A; Triple-A is the gym that Lavalliere goes to when the White Sox don't need him.

Lawton still must be listed below Becker and Cole on the Twins' depth chart, but he undoubtedly figures more prominently in there plans. He's 5'10", 196, so he's not to be confused with Cole. The 13 home runs at New Britain were his first time in double figures, however, and his best base-stealing season was whichever one you see here that you like better.

SCOTT LEIUS

3B　Age 30　　　　　　　　　　　Bid: $1

Year	Team	G	AB	R	H	BB	SO	D	T	HR	RBI	SB	CS	BA	$
1991	MIN	109	199	35	57	30	35	7	2	5	20	5	5	.286	8
1992	MIN	129	409	50	102	34	61	18	2	2	35	0	5	.249	6
1993	MIN	10	18	4	3	2	4	0	0	0	2	0	0	.167	0
1994	MIN	97	350	57	86	37	58	16	1	14	49	2	4	.246	9
1995	MIN	117	372	51	92	49	54	16	5	4	45	2	1	.247	4

Leius has filled out to 6'3", 200, which seems to have fatally affected his bat.

JIM LEYRITZ

C,1B　Age 32　　　　　　　　　　Bid: $5

Year	Team	G	AB	R	H	BB	SO	D	T	HR	RBI	SB	CS	BA	$
1991	NY	A	32	77	8	14	13	15	3	0	0	4	0	.182	-2
1992	NYY	63	144	17	37	14	22	6	0	7	26	0	1	.257	6
1993	NYY	95	259	43	80	37	59	14	0	14	53	0	0	.309	15
1994	NYY	75	249	47	66	35	61	12	0	17	58	0	0	.265	14
1995	NYY	77	264	37	71	37	73	12	0	7	37	1	1	.269	7

Depending on who the first baseman is, might get some more playing time.

PAT LISTACH

SS　Age 29　　　　　　　　　　Bid: $1

Year	Team	G	AB	R	H	BB	SO	D	T	HR	RBI	SB	CS	BA	$
1992	MIL	149	579	93	168	55	124	19	6	1	47	54	18	.290	32
1993	MIL	98	356	50	87	37	70	15	1	3	30	18	9	.244	9
1994	MIL	16	54	8	16	3	8	3	0	0	2	2	1	.296	2
1995	MIL	101	334	35	73	25	61	8	2	0	25	13	3	.219	2

Four years after his freshman year, he might not find a job

KEITH LOCKHART

2B　Age 31　　　　　　　　　　Bid: $4

Year	Team	G	AB	R	H	BB	SO	D	T	HR	RBI	SB	CS	BA	$
1994	SD	27	43	4	9	4	10	0	0	2	6	1	0	.209	1
1995	KC	94	274	41	88	14	21	19	3	6	33	8	1	.321	15

The poor showing at San Diego in 1994 was an I-told-you-so after he hit .320 at Las Vegas in his sixth year in Triple-A. The superb showing at KC last year after hitting .378 in 44 games at

Omaha was his in-your-face.

Do it again, Spider. For my team.

KENNY LOFTON   OF   Age 29   Bid: $46

Year	Team	G	AB	R	H	BB	SO	D	T	HR	RBI	SB	CS	BA	$
1991	HOU	20	74	9	15	5	19	1	0	0	0	0	2	.203	-1
1992	CLE	148	576	96	164	68	54	15	8	5	42	66	12	.285	37
1993	CLE	148	569	116	185	81	83	28	8	1	42	70	14	.325	45
1994	CLE	112	459	105	160	52	56	32	9	12	57	60	12	.349	61
1995	CLE	118	481	93	149	40	49	22	13	7	53	54	15	.310	40

Most of us were unaware of his intensity until the play-offs. Dan Wilson clearly didn't watch him catch the last out of the game before, or he would have known full well that Lofton, too, was coming home on the passed ball.

On the season, Lofton hit .274 against lefties. In his career, though, there is no differential whatsoever: .310 may be as low as Lofton hits in the next ten seasons. Just at the point that Rickey becomes eligible for the Hall of Fame (and there will be a lot of foolish talk on *that* subject) the best part of Lofton's career will be in full view. The comparisons will be interesting.

MARK LORETTA   SS   Age 24   Bid: R2

Year	Team	G	AB	R	H	BB	SO	D	T	HR	RBI	SB	CS	BA	$
1994	(AA)	77	302	50	95	27	33	13	6	0	38	8	5	.315	x
1994	(AAA)	43	138	16	29	12	13	7	0	1	14	2	1	.210	x
1995	(AAA)	127	479	48	137	34	47	22	5	7	79	8	9	.286	x
1995	MIL	19	50	13	13	4	7	3	0	1	3	1	1	.260	1

Loretta's first season was 1993; he hit .321 in Rookie ball and .363 in a slow A league. The only glitch is his first stop at New Orleans (AAA).

It's been a mercurial rise, with absolutely no fanfare, which is the way it is when you don't have power and you don't have speed.

MIKE MACFARLANE   C   Age 32   Bid: $5

Year	Team	G	AB	R	H	BB	SO	D	T	HR	RBI	SB	CS	BA	$
1991	KC	84	267	34	74	17	52	18	2	13	41	1	0	.277	12
1992	KC	129	402	51	94	30	89	28	3	17	48	1	5	.234	10
1993	KC	117	388	55	106	40	83	27	0	20	67	2	5	.273	17
1994	KC	92	314	53	80	35	71	17	3	14	47	1	0	.255	10
1995	BOS	115	364	45	82	38	78	18	1	15	51	2	1	.225	6

Led the majors, by a wide margin, in passed balls. Red Sox pitchers were fourth in the league in wild pitches. Hit .201 against righthanders, .162 with runners in scoring position, and put only seven balls onto the screen.

SHANE MACK   OF   Age 32   Bid: R4

Year	Team	G	AB	R	H	BB	SO	D	T	HR	RBI	SB	CS	BA	$
1991	MIN	143	442	79	137	34	79	27	8	18	74	13	9	.310	28
1992	MIN	156	600	101	189	64	106	31	6	16	75	26	14	.315	36
1993	MIN	128	503	66	139	41	76	30	4	10	61	15	5	.276	18
1994	MIN	81	303	55	101	32	51	21	2	15	61	4	1	.333	25

Hit .278-20-52 for the Yomiuri Giants. Fellow could get discouraged if that keeps up. Won't come back this year — not exactly the right job climate — but why not pick him for next year?

JOSE MALAVE   OF   Age 25   Bid: R1

Year	Team	G	AB	R	H	BB	SO	D	T	HR	RBI	SB	CS	BA	$
1993	(A)	82	312	42	94	36	54	27	1	8	54	2	3	.301	x
1994	(AA)	122	465	87	139	52	81	37	7	24	92	4	7	.299	x
1995	(AAA)	91	318	55	86	30	67	12	1	23	57	0	1	.270	x

With each step up, his batting average dips, but there's still a lot to like in this resume. Last year, a .523 slugging average and — well, that's what counts.

In truth, the Red Sox don't seem to think he's an R1 anymore (there was talk of trading him) and he was dropped from Baseball America's top 10 prospects..

JEFF MANTO   3B   Age 31   Bid: R3

Year	Team	G	AB	R	H	BB	SO	D	T	HR	RBI	SB	CS	BA	$
1994	(AAA)	37	115	20	30	27	28	6	0	4	17	1	0	.261	x
1994	(AAA)	94	329	61	102	43	47	25	2	27	83	2	2	.310	x
1995	BAL	89	254	31	65	24	69	9	0	17	38	0	3	.256	9

Came, saw, conquered briefly.

DAVE MARTINEZ   OF,1B   Age 31   Bid: $3

Year	Team	G	AB	R	H	BB	SO	D	T	HR	RBI	SB	CS	BA	$
1991	MTL	124	396	47	117	20	54	18	5	7	42	16	7	.295	18
1992	CIN	135	393	47	100	42	54	20	5	3	31	12	8	.254	8
1993	SF	91	241	28	58	27	39	12	1	5	27	6	3	.241	4

Year	Team	G	AB	R	H	BB	SO	D	T	HR	RBI	SB	CS	BA	$
1994	SF	97	235	23	58	21	22	9	3	4	27	3	4	.247	**4**
1995	CHW	119	303	49	93	32	41	16	4	5	37	8	2	.307	**14**

Got better as the season progressed. Ended up hitting .348 in his stints in the number 3 spot (92 AB), which was better than the other fellow who hit there. Stole the odd base. Qualified at two positions. And now reverts to form.

EDGAR MARTINEZ DH   Age 33   Bid: $31

Year	Team	G	AB	R	H	BB	SO	D	T	HR	RBI	SB	CS	BA	$
1991	SEA	150	544	98	167	84	72	35	1	14	52	0	3	.307	**19**
1992	SEA	135	528	100	181	54	61	46	3	18	73	14	4	.343	**36**
1993	SEA	42	135	20	32	28	19	7	0	4	13	0	0	.237	**1**
1994	SEA	89	326	47	93	53	42	23	1	13	51	6	2	.285	**17**
1995	SEA	145	511	121	182	116	87	52	0	29	113	4	3	.356	**42**

Even though I think that batting titles with lots of run production are very much Edgar's form, he doesn't qualify in the field and there's the back worry — which is less of a worry as long as he doesn't play in the field.

TINO MARTINEZ   1B   Age 28   Bid: $28

Year	Team	G	AB	R	H	BB	SO	D	T	HR	RBI	SB	CS	BA	$
1991	SEA	36	112	1	23	11	24	2	0	4	9	0	0	.205	**0**
1992	SEA	136	460	53	118	42	77	19	2	16	66	2	1	.257	**15**
1993	SEA	109	408	48	108	45	56	25	1	17	60	0	3	.265	**13**
1994	SEA	97	329	42	86	29	52	21	0	20	61	1	2	.261	**15**
1995	SEA	141	519	92	152	62	91	35	3	31	111	0	0	.293	**29**

Last year was the time to hitch onto his rising star.

JOHN MARZANO   C   Age 33   Bid: R3

Year	Team	G	AB	R	H	BB	SO	D	T	HR	RBI	SB	CS	BA	$
1995	(AAA)	120	427	55	132	33	54	41	3	9	56	3	4	.309	**x**
1995	TEX	2	6	1	2	0	0	0	0	0	0	0	0	.333	**0**

He was the All-Star catcher in the American Association, deservedly so. Now he joins the 504 six-year minor league free agents who are contributing to the buyer's market.

DAN MASTELLER
OF,1B   Age 28   Bid: R3

Year	Team	G	AB	R	H	BB	SO	D	T	HR	RBI	SB	CS	BA	$
1994	(AAA)	98	338	53	102	21	27	26	3	8	27	4	1	.302	x
1995	(AAA)	48	152	25	46	15	17	10	7	4	18	4	1	.303	x
1995	MIN	71	198	21	47	18	19	12	0	3	21	1	2	.237	1

Andres Duncan, Ricardo Ingram, Patrick Lennon, Tim Moore, Scott Pose, Carlos Pulido, Bubba Smith and Van Snider are the Twins' contribution to the minor league pool.

DON MATTINGLY
1B   Age 35   Bid: $9

Year	Team	G	AB	R	H	BB	SO	D	T	HR	RBI	SB	CS	BA	$
1991	NYY	152	587	64	169	46	42	35	0	9	68	2	0	.288	17
1992	NYY	156	640	89	184	39	43	40	0	14	86	3	0	.288	23
1993	NYY	134	530	78	154	61	42	27	2	17	86	0	0	.291	20
1994	NYY	97	372	62	113	60	24	20	1	6	51	0	0	.304	14
1995	NYY	128	458	59	132	40	35	32	2	7	49	0	2	.288	11

The Yankees are offering Joe Ausanio and 18 other minor leaguers to the free agent pool, plus Wade Boggs, David Cone, Rick Honeycutt, Steve Howe, Dion James, Jack McDowell, Mike Stanley, Darryl Strawberry, Randy Velarde and the once unthinkable; Baseball himself is a free agent.

BRENT MAYNE
C   Age 28   Bid: $1

Year	Team	G	AB	R	H	BB	SO	D	T	HR	RBI	SB	CS	BA	$
1991	KC	85	231	22	58	23	42	8	0	3	31	2	4	.251	5
1992	KC	82	213	16	48	11	26	10	0	0	18	0	4	.225	-1
1993	KC	71	205	22	52	18	31	9	1	2	22	3	2	.254	3
1994	KC	46	144	19	37	14	27	5	1	2	20	1	0	.257	3
1995	KC	110	307	23	77	25	41	18	1	1	27	0	1	.251	1

Loves his job.

WILLIE MCGEE
OF   Age 37   Bid: R3

Year	Team	G	AB	R	H	BB	SO	D	T	HR	RBI	SB	CS	BA	$
1991	SF	131	497	67	155	34	74	30	3	4	43	17	9	.312	21
1992	SF	138	474	56	141	29	88	20	2	1	36	13	4	.297	15

Year	Team	G	AB	R	H	BB	SO	D	T	HR	RBI	SB	CS	BA	$
1993	SF	130	475	53	143	38	67	28	1	4	46	10	9	.301	15
1994	SF	45	156	19	44	15	24	3	0	5	23	3	0	.282	8
1995	BOS	67	200	32	57	9	41	11	3	2	15	5	2	.285	6

In last year's book, I proposed that Willie McGee, who had played for $3.5 million in 1994, would sign for $300,000. He signed for $200,000. Pretty good prediction, come on. It's like saying a $35 player this year will earn $3 next year and he ends up earning $2.

RYAN MCGUIRE   1B   Age 24   Bid: R2

Year	Team	G	AB	R	H	BB	SO	D	T	HR	RBI	SB	CS	BA	$
1993	(R)	58	213	23	69	27	34	12	2	4	38	2	4	.324	x
1994	(A)	137	489	70	133	79	77	29	0	10	73	10	9	.272	x
1995	(AA)	109	414	59	138	58	51	29	1	7	59	11	8	.333	x

He's only 6'1", 195; if only he played second base, people would stop bugging him.

But he's a lefty all the way, and it's his fate to play first base in the Red Sox organization. Furthermore, if he's asked one more time if he's Mark's brother, he tells you, he's going to...

The R2 designation is based on the Red Sox contribution to the free agent pool: Jose Canseco among six others.

MARK MCGWIRE   1B   Age 32   Bid: $28

Year	Team	G	AB	R	H	BB	SO	D	T	HR	RBI	SB	CS	BA	$
1991	OAK	154	483	62	97	93	116	22	0	22	75	2	1	.201	8
1992	OAK	139	467	87	125	90	105	22	0	42	104	0	1	.268	32
1993	OAK	27	84	16	28	21	19	6	0	9	24	0	1	.333	8
1994	OAK	47	135	26	34	37	40	3	0	9	25	0	0	.252	6
1995	OAK	104	317	75	87	88	77	13	0	39	90	1	1	.274	27

You're looking at him. As a place to salt away money, he doesn't compare to Griffey, Thomas or Belle, but he's the one who could surpass Maris this year.

You won't find McGwire's name among the top 10 slugging averages, because he didn't qualify, and even so, with one more home run he would have tied for second! His rate of homers, one per 8.1 AB, was the best in history. (Minimum 300 AB.) He must stop walking so much, though, because if he had played in 154 games, he would have only had 58 home runs.

He was on schedule to play only 117 games.

1995 proj.	G	AB	HR	RBI	SB	BA
BELLE,A	161	614	56	142	6	.317
BUHNER,J	142	529	45	136	0	.262
THOMAS,F	163	555	45	125	3	.308
PALMEIRO,R	161	623	44	117	3	.310
VAUGHN,M	158	619	44	142	12	.300
MCGWIRE,M	117	357	44	101	1	.274

With the season expanded out to 162 games, McGwire doesn't even reach 50 home runs.

The only one who was going to challenge Maris last year was Belle. Given how hot he was, it could have been very close.

Expanding 1994 out is more problematic, since so much more of it is missing; however, as many as three hitters could have reached 50 home runs, and all you need is a hot spell...

1994 proj.	G	AB	HR	RBI	SB	BA
GRIFFEY,K	155	606	56	126	15	.323
THOMAS,F	158	558	53	141	3	.353
BELLE,A	148	577	50	141	13	.357
CANSECO,J	155	600	43	126	21	.282
FIELDER,C	153	595	39	126	0	.259

It's interesting to note, on the other hand, that more hitters were going to reach the mid-40's last year.

How much hitting to expect overall this time is a subject for the next chapter. But there can be no question that Roger Maris, and Babe Ruth, have dodged bullets in each of the last two seasons. Several of the gunslingers that you see above are in their absolute, absolute primes.

Mark McGwire's the Doc Holiday in the group.

MARK MCLEMORE 2B,OF   Age 31   Bid: $6

Year	Team	G	AB	R	H	BB	SO	D	T	HR	RBI	SB	CS	BA	$
1991	HOU	21	61	6	9	6	13	1	0	0	2	11	5	.148	3
1992	BAL	101	228	40	56	21	26	7	2	0	27	11	5	.246	6
1993	BAL	148	581	81	165	64	92	27	5	4	72	21	15	.284	21
1994	BAL	104	343	44	88	51	50	11	1	3	29	20	5	.257	13
1995	TEX	129	467	73	122	59	71	20	5	5	41	21	11	.261	14

You'll use him just the opposite of the way the Rangers use him; he'll start in your infield and end up subbing in your outfield.

PAT MEARES   SS   Age 27   Bid: $10

Year	Team	G	AB	R	H	BB	SO	D	T	HR	RBI	SB	CS	BA	$
1993	MIN	111	346	33	87	7	52	14	3	0	33	4	5	.251	3
1994	MIN	80	229	29	61	14	50	12	1	2	24	5	1	.266	6
1995	MIN	116	390	57	105	15	68	19	4	12	49	10	4	.269	14

After hitting .250, .307 and .289 in the first three months, Meares hit .174 in July. The pitchers figuring out what he had figured out?

Maybe, but he figured again, if so, and hit .274 and .294 during the last two months.

MATT MIESKE   OF   Age 28   Bid: $3

Year	Team	G	AB	R	H	BB	SO	D	T	HR	RBI	SB	CS	BA	$
1993	MIL	23	58	9	14	4	14	0	0	3	7	0	2	.241	1
1994	MIL	84	259	39	67	21	62	13	1	10	38	3	5	.259	9
1995	MIL	117	267	42	67	27	45	13	1	12	48	2	4	.251	9

Once again, thumped lefties (.306, 9 HR), flailed against righties. Gives him a better future than if he hit .251 against both of them.

PAUL MOLITOR   DH   Age 39   1995: $21

Year	Team	G	AB	R	H	BB	SO	D	T	HR	RBI	SB	CS	BA	$
1991	MIL	158	665	133	216	77	62	32	13	17	75	19	8	.325	37
1992	MIL	158	609	89	195	73	66	36	7	12	89	31	6	.320	39
1993	TOR	160	636	121	211	77	71	37	5	22	111	22	4	.332	44
1994	TOR	115	454	86	155	55	48	30	4	14	75	20	0	.341	41
1995	TOR	130	525	63	142	61	57	31	2	15	60	12	0	.270	18

No sign of decay in the interior stats. Could have been the strike activity, could have been some mechanical flaw. Hit .331 in August. But Molly's suddenly 39 going on 40.

LYLE MOUTON   OF   Age 27   Bid: $11

Year	Team	G	AB	R	H	BB	SO	D	T	HR	RBI	SB	CS	BA	$
1993	(AA)	135	491	74	125	74	76	22	3	16	76	19	13	.255	x
1994	(AA)	74	274	42	84	42	42	23	1	12	42	7	6	.307	x
1994	(AAA)	59	204	26	64	26	32	14	5	4	32	5	1	.314	x
1995	(AAA)	71	267	40	79	23	58	17	0	8	41	10	4	.296	x
1995	CHW	58	179	23	54	19	46	16	0	5	27	1	0	.302	8

When I saw him in September, he was on fire. Outside pitches hit on the nose to right field, inside pitches smashed over the third base bag. Swing was a little long, ball wasn't carrying into the stands, but still, very impressive.

Ended the season on a one-for-17 note.

Bid is predicated on his winning the right field job this spring.

PEDRO MUNOZ   OF   Age 27   Bid: $14

Year	Team	G	AB	R	H	BB	SO	D	T	HR	RBI	SB	CS	BA	$
1991	MIN	51	138	15	39	9	31	7	1	7	26	3	0	.283	8

Year	Team	G	AB	R	H	BB	SO	D	T	HR	RBI	SB	CS	BA	$
1992	MIN	127	418	44	113	17	90	16	3	12	71	4	5	.270	16
1993	MIN	104	326	34	76	25	97	11	1	13	38	1	2	.233	6
1994	MIN	75	244	35	72	19	67	15	2	11	36	0	0	.295	12
1995	MIN	104	376	45	113	19	86	17	0	18	58	0	3	.301	18

There was a grand total of 59 .300 hitters in the league last year. (An all-time record?) Even though he just missed this group in 1994, Munoz is perhaps the oddest hitter in it. His Isolated Power (SA minus BA) was .188, right behind Murray's. His Isolated Free Passes (OBA minus BA) was .037, just ahead of Baerga's. His ratio of whiffs to walks, 4.5, was far and away the worst of any .300 hitter who came to the plate 300 times last year. The next is Garret Anderson, 3.4, and the average .300 hitter struck out 1.7 times for each walk.

EDDIE MURRAY   1B   Age 40   Bid: $23

Year	Team	G	AB	R	H	BB	SO	D	T	HR	RBI	SB	CS	BA	$
1991	LA	153	576	69	150	55	74	23	1	19	96	10	3	.260	23
1992	NYM	156	551	64	144	66	74	37	2	16	93	4	2	.261	22
1993	NYM	154	610	77	174	40	61	28	1	27	100	2	2	.285	26
1994	CLE	108	433	57	110	31	53	21	1	17	76	8	4	.254	18
1995	CLE	113	436	68	141	39	65	21	0	21	82	5	1	.323	29

Most leagues have set a minimum of 20 games to qualify at a position. Strike-adjusted, that's 18 (the number being used in this book). Getting ready to flash the leather against Atlanta, Murray played two games at first in the last week, ended up at exactly 18, and raised his value to the hundreds of owners who were going to keep him anyway (average salary $14) by at least $5.

GLENN MURRAY   OF   Age 25   Bid: R3

Year	Team	G	AB	R	H	BB	SO	D	T	HR	RBI	SB	CS	BA	$
1993	(AA)	127	475	82	120	56	111	21	4	26	96	16	7	.253	x
1994	(AAA)	130	465	74	104	55	134	17	1	25	64	9	3	.224	x
1995	(AAA)	104	336	66	82	34	109	15	0	25	66	5	6	.244	x

Jose Malave probably still has some pretty good trade value; Glenn Murray probably doesn't. Dan Duquette, who was called a clever if dirty dog when he brought Murray along with him from Montreal, will most likely keep Murray at Pawtuckett. Nobody paid any attention when Duquette picked up Troy O'Leary, and, as he'd be the first to say, you never know.

GREG MYERS C Age 30 Bid: $2

Year	Team	G	AB	R	H	BB	SO	D	T	HR	RBI	SB	CS	BA	$
1991	TOR	107	309	25	81	21	45	22	0	8	36	0	0	.262	7
1992	TOR/CA	30	78	4	18	5	11	7	0	1	13	0	0	.231	1
1993	CAL	108	290	27	74	17	47	10	0	7	40	3	3	.255	7
1994	CAL	45	126	10	31	10	27	6	0	2	8	0	2	.246	0
1995	CAL	85	273	35	71	17	49	12	2	9	38	0	1	.260	7

He's the lefty catcher who can hit lefties a little bit — Fabreags can't at all — so is that good or bad?

TIM NAEHRING 3B Age 29 Bid: $9

Year	Team	G	AB	R	H	BB	SO	D	T	HR	RBI	SB	CS	BA	$
1991	BOS	20	55	1	6	6	15	1	0	0	3	0	0	.109	-3
1992	BOS	72	186	12	43	18	31	8	0	3	14	0	0	.231	1
1993	BOS	39	127	14	42	10	26	10	0	1	17	1	0	.331	6
1994	BOS	80	297	41	82	30	56	18	1	7	42	1	3	.276	9
1995	BOS	126	433	61	133	77	66	27	2	10	57	0	2	.307	16

The reason not to put a two-digit bid on Naehring is you won't need that much. He's a fine hitter, worth more than Ripken last year, but he's not quite cut from the same cloth as Cal, which is what everyone else is thinking; if you put, say, a $13 bid limit on Naehring, you have to shave $4 from other hitters (or pitchers). For players that you like, you want prices that are only a notch better than the room's. Two notches gives you a false sense of security, and you don't want that.

TROY NEEL 1B Age 30 Bid: R3

Year	Team	G	AB	R	H	BB	SO	D	T	HR	RBI	SB	CS	BA	$
1992	OAK	24	53	8	14	5	15	3	0	3	9	0	1	.264	2
1993	OAK	123	427	59	124	49	101	21	0	19	63	3	5	.290	19
1994	OAK	83	278	43	74	38	61	13	0	15	48	2	3	.266	13

The same as the Shane Mack thinking. The R3 designation means you're really grabbing at straws now, late in an ultra draft.

PHIL NEVIN 3B,OF Age 25 Bid: $2

Year	Team	G	AB	R	H	BB	SO	D	T	HR	RBI	SB	CS	BA	$
1993	(AAA)	123	448	67	128	52	99	21	3	10	93	8	1	.286	x

Year	Team	G	AB	R	H	BB	SO	D	T	HR	RBI	SB	CS	BA	$
1994	(AAA)	118	445	67	117	55	101	20	1	12	79	3	2	.263	x
1995	(AAA)	62	223	31	65	27	39	16	0	7	41	2	3	.291	x
1995	HOU	18	60	4	7	7	13	1	0	0	1	1	0	.117	-4
1995	(AAA)	7	23	3	7	1	5	2	0	1	3	0	0	.304	x
1995	DET	29	96	9	21	11	27	3	1	2	12	0	0	.219	0

Flat out can't hit. No way. Not a prospect.
   But worth a shot.

DAVE NILSSON OF   Age 26   Bid: $17

Year	Team	G	AB	R	H	BB	SO	D	T	HR	RBI	SB	CS	BA	$
1992	MIL	51	164	15	38	17	18	8	0	4	25	2	2	.232	4
1993	MIL	100	296	35	76	37	36	10	2	7	40	3	6	.257	7
1994	MIL	109	397	51	109	34	61	28	3	12	69	1	0	.275	15
1995	MIL	81	263	41	73	24	41	12	1	12	53	2	0	.278	12

Might be a sleeper. He probably felt like hell all year. There was a huge home/away differential (.317/.234), which may mean nothing at all and may mean he's still capable of being a very good hitter.

OTIS NIXON OF   Age 37   Bid: $24

Year	Team	G	AB	R	H	BB	SO	D	T	HR	RBI	SB	CS	BA	$
1991	ATL	124	401	81	119	47	40	10	1	0	26	72	21	.297	33
1992	ATL	120	456	79	134	39	54	14	2	2	22	41	18	.294	22
1993	ATL	134	461	77	124	61	63	12	3	1	24	47	13	.269	19
1994	BOS	103	398	60	109	55	65	15	1	0	25	42	10	.274	26
1995	TEX	139	589	87	174	58	85	21	2	0	45	50	21	.295	33

League differences have been narrowed down considerably in recent seasons, but remember when Whitey Ball was the rage in the National League? Even the Braves got into it. The more there is, though, the less it's worth. That's how come Otis doesn't get paid more in 1991 than he earned last year. In our game. In their game, he's earning about half as much.

TROT NIXON OF   Age 22   Bid: R4

Year	Team	G	AB	R	H	BB	SO	D	T	HR	RBI	SB	CS	BA	$
1994	(A)	71	264	33	65	44	53	12	0	12	53	10	3	.246	x

Year	Team	G	AB	R	H	BB	SO	D	T	HR	RBI	SB	CS	BA	$
1995	(A)	73	264	43	80	45	46	11	4	5	39	7	5	.303	x
1995	(AA)	25	94	9	15	7	20	3	1	2	8	2	1	.160	x

He did well in the Florida State League (A), where the dimensions of the parks are major league, then had back problem and possibly Double-A problems at Trenton. ETA in Boston has been pushed back at least a year.

JON NUNNALLY   OF   Age 24   Bid: $7

Year	Team	G	AB	R	H	BB	SO	D	T	HR	RBI	SB	CS	BA	$
1994	(A)	132	483	70	129	64	125	29	2	22	74	23	11	.267	x
1995	KC	119	303	51	74	51	86	15	6	14	42	6	4	.244	10

Is it really worth buying 15 different publications, hoping one of them will tell you about Jon Nunnally?

```
1995 Rookie Contributions, AL hitters
                                           - AP -
AL 1995       Age Team   AB  HR  RBI  SB   BA   $  Bk  Up
NUNNALLY,J     23 KCR    303  14   42   6  .244  10      R4
DAMON,J        21 KCR    188   3   23   7  .282   8  R5  R5
MOUTON,L       27 CHW    179   5   27   1  .302   8  R3  R3
GIAMBI,J       24 OAK    176   6   25   2  .256   5      R2
WILLIAMS,Geo   25 OAK     79   3   14   0  .291   3
LAWTON,Mat     23 MIN     60   1   12   1  .317   3
SNOPEK,C       24 CHW     68   1    7   1  .324   3      R3
ZAUN,Gregg     24 BAL    104   3   14   1  .260   3
STEVERSON      23 DET     42   2    6   2  .262   2      R3
GILES,B        24 CLE      9   1    3   0  .556   2      R1
CACERES,E      31 KCR    117   1   17   2  .239   2
MASTELLER      27 MIN    198   3   21   1  .237   1
GROTEWALD,J    29 KCR     36   1    6   0  .278   1
LORETTA,Ma     23 MIL     50   1    3   1  .260   1
PALMEIRO,O     26 CAL     20   0    1   0  .350   1
average (15)   25        109   3   15   2  .269   3
```

Not included are rookies who made opening day rosters (like Garret Anderson) or who auditioned last year (like Herbert Perry); you're not looking for 15 different opinions about them. You're looking for Jon Nunnally.

He's hard to find. Not mentioned in my book last year (he did make it into the update). Mazeroski didn't think he was Worth Watching. The Bill James *Player Ratings* skips from Matt Nokes to Edwin Nunez. Benson's *A to Z* has him; he follows Tom Nuneviller and Ramon Nunez.

And then again, what's to see? A grand total of 15 Nunnallies came along from God knows where to earn $1 or more. Between them they hit 45 home runs in 1,629 at-bats. Their average is shown.

That's one way of looking at it. The other is, if you had Nunnally, Damon, Mouton or even Gambi on your reserve list, it might have made all the difference. And if you had all four...

No harm in trying. I'm certainly not trying to put myself and 14 others out of business. Nor am I completely discouraged by my own performance. Two of the top four hitters I did at least mention in the book; by the time of the update, I'm four for four. In the update, I get seven of the top ten.

What it means is, it's easier to see the season as it gets closer to you.

Not seeing things — there's something to be said for that. From Caceres down, there's nothing to be proud of. I had Masteller for a while on my team, a waiver pick-up, and I'm not boasting.

SERGIO NUNEZ 2B   Age 21   Bid: R4

Year	Team	G	AB	R	H	BB	SO	D	T	HR	RBI	SB	CS	BA	$
1994	(R)	59	232	64	92	32	17	9	7	5	24	37	12	.397	x
1995	(A)	124	460	63	109	51	66	10	2	4	25	33	19	.237	x

It was speculated last year that he was lucky that he didn't hit .400 in the short-season Gulf Coast League; now it just looks like he was lucky. His teammate Mendy Lopez, who hit .362 in 1994, dropped to .272 at Single-A Wilmington in the Royals organization. They both are worth continuing to watch, because it's fun.

SHERMAN OBANDO   OF,DH   Age 26   Bid: R3

Year	Team	G	AB	R	H	BB	SO	D	T	HR	RBI	SB	CS	BA	$
1992	(AA)	109	381	71	107	32	67	19	3	17	56	3	1	.281	x
1993	BAL	31	92	8	25	4	26	2	0	3	15	0	0	.272	3
1993	(AA)	19	58	8	14	9	11	2	0	3	12	1	0	.241	x
1994	(AAA)	109	403	67	133	30	53	36	7	20	69	1	1	.330	x
1995	BAL	16	38	0	10	2	12	1	0	0	3	1	0	.263	1
1995	(AAA)	85	324	42	96	29	57	26	6	9	53	1	1	.296	x

While working on his fielding at Triple-A, his slugging average dropped from .603 to .497.

JOHN OLERUD   1B   Age 27   Bid: $17

Year	Team	G	AB	R	H	BB	SO	D	T	HR	RBI	SB	CS	BA	$
1991	TOR	139	454	64	116	68	84	30	1	17	68	0	2	.256	13
1992	TOR	138	458	68	130	70	61	28	0	16	66	1	0	.284	19
1993	TOR	158	551	109	200	114	65	54	2	24	107	0	2	.363	39
1994	TOR	108	384	47	114	61	53	29	2	12	67	1	2	.297	19
1995	TOR	135	492	72	143	84	54	32	0	8	54	0	0	.291	13

Apparently, just can't pull the ball anymore. If he's playing somewhere else this spring, which would seem like an excellent idea for both sides, he did hit .310 and get all but one of his home runs away from the Skydome. At this point, if he can just get back to *1994*, he'll be happy; he could stay in the majors another five years.

JOE OLIVER C Age 30   Bid: $3

Year	Team	G	AB	R	H	BB	SO	D	T	HR	RBI	SB	CS	BA	$
1991	CIN	94	269	21	58	18	53	11	0	11	41	0	0	.216	6
1992	CIN	143	485	42	131	35	75	25	1	10	57	2	3	.270	15
1993	CIN	139	482	40	115	27	91	28	0	14	75	0	0	.239	9
1994	CIN	6	19	1	4	2	3	0	0	1	5	0	0	.211	1
1995	MIL	97	337	43	92	27	66	20	0	12	51	2	4	.273	12

Terrible August slump (.185) took some of the luster off his come-back season. Hit .341 with runners in scoring position.

LUIS ORTIZ 3B Age 26   Bid: R3

Year	Team	G	AB	R	H	BB	SO	D	T	HR	RBI	SB	CS	BA	$
1993	BOS	9	12	0	3	0	2	0	0	0	1	0	0	.250	0
1994	BOS	7	18	3	3	1	5	2	0	0	6	0	0	.167	0
1995	TEX	41	108	10	25	6	18	5	2	1	18	0	1	.231	1

Hit .306 in 47 games at Oklahoma City. Will play more there this year.

SPIKE OWEN SS Age 35   Bid: R3

Year	Team	G	AB	R	H	BB	SO	D	T	HR	RBI	SB	CS	BA	$
1991	MON	139	424	39	108	42	61	22	8	3	26	2	6	.255	4
1992	MON	122	386	52	104	50	30	16	3	7	40	9	4	.269	13
1993	NYY	103	334	41	78	29	30	16	2	2	20	3	2	.234	0
1994	CAL	82	268	30	83	49	17	17	2	3	37	2	8	.310	12
1995	CAL	82	218	17	50	18	22	9	3	1	28	3	2	.229	1

It's all Whitey's fault, as I've been saying for several years. He's the one who should have figured out, when he was the Angels' GM, that he didn't have to pay Spike Owen dink, no matter what any arbiter said if you asked him.

Spike's salary in the last year of his contract was $3.5 million.

TROY O'LEARY OF Age 26   Bid: $14

Year	Team	G	AB	R	H	BB	SO	D	T	HR	RBI	SB	CS	BA	$
1993	MIL	19	41	3	12	5	9	3	0	0	3	0	0	.293	1
1994	MIL	27	66	9	18	5	12	1	1	2	7	1	1	.273	2

Year	Team	G	AB	R	H	BB	SO	D	T	HR	RBI	SB	CS	BA	$
1995	BOS	112	399	60	123	29	64	31	6	10	49	5	3	.308	17

He can hit this well or better as the regular Red Sox right fielder, but did not field well enough to nail down the position.

PAUL O'NEILL   OF   Age 33

Bid: $29

Year	Team	G	AB	R	H	BB	SO	D	T	HR	RBI	SB	CS	BA	$
1991	CIN	152	532	71	136	73	107	36	0	28	91	12	7	.256	27
1992	CIN	148	496	59	122	77	85	19	1	14	66	6	3	.246	16
1993	NYY	141	498	71	155	44	69	34	1	20	75	2	4	.311	24
1994	NYY	103	368	68	132	72	56	25	1	21	83	5	4	.359	37
1995	NYY	127	460	82	138	71	76	30	4	22	96	1	2	.300	25

Pretty good year for someone who never really got going.

RAFAEL PALMEIRO   1B   Age 31

Bid: $38

Year	Team	G	AB	R	H	BB	SO	D	T	HR	RBI	SB	CS	BA	$
1991	TEX	159	631	115	203	68	72	49	3	26	88	4	3	.322	34
1992	TEX	159	608	84	163	72	83	27	4	22	85	2	3	.268	22
1993	TEX	160	597	124	176	73	85	40	2	37	105	22	3	.295	41
1994	BAL	111	436	82	139	54	63	32	0	23	76	7	3	.319	33
1995	BAL	143	554	89	172	62	65	30	2	39	104	3	1	.310	37

He's not going to join the Big Three, but he's so clearly the cream of the next crop that he'll cost almost as much if you don't watch out.

DEAN PALMER   3B   Age 27

Bid: $22

Year	Team	G	AB	R	H	BB	SO	D	T	HR	RBI	SB	CS	BA	$
1991	TEX	81	268	38	50	32	98	9	2	15	37	0	2	.187	3
1992	TEX	152	541	74	124	62	154	25	0	26	72	10	4	.229	18
1993	TEX	148	519	88	127	53	154	31	2	33	96	11	10	.245	24
1994	TEX	93	342	50	84	26	89	14	2	19	59	3	4	.246	13
1995	TEX	36	119	30	40	21	21	6	0	9	24	1	1	.336	10

Was on a pace to strike out 95 times in 541 AB — and, of course, walk 95 times. Would have had 41 homers, 109 ribbies, and would have earned $45. He's the Magic Age. Can't imagine anyone

I'd rather get for $22.

CRAIG PAQUETTE 3B,OF   Age 27   Bid: $1

Year	Team	G	AB	R	H	BB	SO	D	T	HR	RBI	SB	CS	BA	$
1993	OAK	105	393	35	86	14	108	20	4	12	46	4	2	.219	5
1993	(AAA)	50	183	29	49	14	54	8	0	8	29	3	3	.268	x
1994	(AAA)	65	245	39	70	14	48	12	3	17	48	3	3	.286	x
1994	OAK	14	49	0	7	0	14	2	0	0	0	1	0	.143	-3
1995	OAK	105	283	42	64	12	88	13	1	13	49	5	2	.226	8

You can buy both Brosius and Paquette for peanuts.

RUDY PEMBERTON   OF   Age 26   Bid: R2

Year	Team	G	AB	R	H	BB	SO	D	T	HR	RBI	SB	CS	BA	$
1994	(AAA)	99	360	49	109	18	62	113	3	12	58	30	9	.303	x
1995	DET	12	30	3	9	1	5	3	1	0	3	0	0	.300	1
1995	(AAA)	67	224	31	77	15	36	15	3	7	23	8	4	.344	x

Not on the Tiger's 40-man. Must not be very good in BP.

SHANNON PENN   OF   Age 26   Bid: R3

Year	Team	G	AB	R	H	BB	SO	D	T	HR	RBI	SB	CS	BA	$
1994	(AAA)	114	444	63	126	30	96	14	6	2	33	45	16	.284	x
1995	DET	3	9	0	3	1	2	0	0	0	0	0	0	.333	0
1995	(AAA)	63	218	41	54	17	40	4	1	1	15	15	9	.248	x

The Tigers' second baseman at Jacksonville (AA), Frank Catalanotto, hit .226.

EDUARDO PEREZ 3B   Age 26   Bid: R2

Year	Team	G	AB	R	H	BB	SO	D	T	HR	RBI	SB	CS	BA	$
1993	CAL	52	180	16	45	9	39	6	2	4	30	5	4	.250	6
1994	CAL	38	129	10	27	12	29	7	0	5	16	3	0	.209	2
1995	CAL	29	71	9	12	12	9	4	1	1	7	0	2	.169	-2

Hit .325 in 69 games at Vancouver, one of the few parks in the PCL where the hitting's not easy. Needs a new major league venue.

ROBERT PEREZ   OF   Age 27   Bid: R3

Year	Team	G	AB	R	H	BB	SO	D	T	HR	RBI	SB	CS	BA	$
1994	(AAA)	128	510	63	155	27	76	28	3	10	65	4	7	.304	x
1994	TOR	4	8	0	1	0	1	0	0	0	0	0	0	.125	-1
1995	(AAA)	122	502	70	172	13	60	38	6	9	66	7	5	.343	x
1995	TOR	17	48	2	9	0	5	2	0	1	3	0	0	.188	-1

Would seem to have done enough to chase Mike Huff away.

HERBERT PERRY   1B   Age 26   Bid: $6

Year	Team	G	AB	R	H	BB	SO	D	T	HR	RBI	SB	CS	BA	$
1993	(AA)	89	327	52	88	37	47	21	1	9	55	7	4	.269	x
1994	(AAA)	102	376	67	123	41	56	20	4	13	70	9	4	.327	x
1994	CLE	4	9	1	1	3	1	0	0	0	1	0	0	.111	-1
1995	(AAA)	49	180	27	57	15	18	14	1	2	17	1	0	.317	x
1995	CLE	52	162	23	51	13	28	13	1	3	23	1	3	.315	7

If he wasn't considered an integral part of the team before, he is after the play-offs.

TONY PHILLIPS   3B,OF   Age 37   Bid: $19

Year	Team	G	AB	R	H	BB	SO	D	T	HR	RBI	SB	CS	BA	$
1991	DET	146	564	97	160	79	95	28	4	17	72	10	5	.284	23
1992	DET	159	606	114	167	114	93	32	3	10	64	12	10	.276	19
1993	DET	151	566	113	177	132	102	27	0	7	57	16	11	.313	24
1994	DET	114	438	91	123	95	105	19	3	19	61	13	5	.281	25
1995	CAL	139	525	119	137	113	135	21	1	27	61	13	10	.261	21

With Philips on the team, the Tigers scored 5.66 runs per game in 1994. The Angels scored 4.72 runs per game with Chad Curtis on their team.

Last year the Angels scored 5.52 runs per game, the Tigers scored 4.54 runs per game.

Had Phillips not hit .188 August and .210 in September/October, there's no way the Angel's would have collapsed. His intensity may have done them in.

GREG PIRKL   1B   Age 25   Bid: R3

Year	Team	G	AB	R	H	BB	SO	D	T	HR	RBI	SB	CS	BA	$
1993	SEA	7	23	1	4	0	4	0	0	1	4	0	0	.174	0

Year	Team	G	AB	R	H	BB	SO	D	T	HR	RBI	SB	CS	BA	$
1994	SEA	19	53	7	14	1	12	3	0	6	11	0	0	.264	4
1995	SEA	10	17	2	4	1	7	0	0	0	0	0	0	.235	0

A .621 slugging average at Tacoma (174 AB). A .235 slugging average in the majors.

PORK CHOP POUGH   1B,DH   Age 26   Bid: R3

Year	Team	G	AB	R	H	BB	SO	D	T	HR	RBI	SB	CS	BA	$
1993	(A)	120	418	59	113	66	57	18	1	12	57	8	3	.270	x
1994	(AA)	105	379	69	113	43	86	24	3	20	66	3	2	.298	x
1994	(AAA)	16	42	1	9	6	13	4	0	0	4	0	0	.214	x
1995	(AA)	97	363	68	101	50	101	23	5	21	69	11	5	.278	x
1995	(AAA)	30	99	12	23	7	27	8	1	5	23	0	0	.232	x

Now in the Red Sox organization, he got off to a fast start at Double-A Trenton, then faded. The Stats Inc. Green Book calls him Chop Pough, which could be less PC.

ARQUIMEDES POZO   2B   Age 22   Bid: R2

Year	Team	G	AB	R	H	BB	SO	D	T	HR	RBI	SB	CS	BA	$
1993	(A)	127	515	98	176	56	56	44	6	13	83	10	10	.342	x
1994	(AA)	119	447	70	129	32	43	31	1	14	54	11	8	.289	x
1995	(AAA)	122	450	57	135	26	31	19	6	10	62	3	3	.300	x
1995	SEA	1	1	0	0	0	0	0	0	0	0	0	0	.000	0

Bats right; might work his way into a platoon with Cora.

KIRBY PUCKETT   OF   Age 35   Bid: $33

Year	Team	G	AB	R	H	BB	SO	D	T	HR	RBI	SB	CS	BA	$
1991	MIN	152	611	92	195	31	78	29	6	15	89	11	5	.319	32
1992	MIN	160	639	104	210	44	97	38	4	19	110	17	7	.329	41
1993	MIN	156	622	89	184	47	93	39	3	22	89	8	6	.296	28
1994	MIN	108	439	79	139	28	47	32	3	20	112	6	3	.317	35
1995	MIN	137	538	83	169	56	89	39	0	23	99	3	2	.314	30

Hit .347 in the second half, had his best on-base average ever.

TIM RAINES OF   Age 36   Bid: $16

Year	Team	G	AB	R	H	BB	SO	D	T	HR	RBI	SB	CS	BA	$
1991	CHW	155	609	102	163	83	68	20	6	5	50	51	15	.268	31
1992	CHW	144	551	102	162	81	48	22	9	7	54	45	6	.294	32
1993	CHW	115	415	75	127	64	35	16	4	16	54	21	7	.306	26
1994	CHW	101	384	80	102	61	43	15	5	10	52	13	0	.266	17
1995	CHW	133	502	81	143	70	52	25	4	12	67	13	2	.285	21

A player for whom I've always set a bid price just a notch below what I think will get him.

MANNY RAMIREZ   OF   Age 24   Bid: $36

Year	Team	G	AB	R	H	BB	SO	D	T	HR	RBI	SB	CS	BA	$
1993	(AAA)	40	145	38	46	27	35	12	0	14	36	1	1	.317	x
1993	CLE	22	53	5	9	2	8	1	0	2	5	0	0	.170	-1
1993	(AA)	89	344	67	117	45	68	32	0	17	79	2	2	.340	x
1994	CLE	91	290	51	78	42	72	22	0	17	60	4	2	.269	17
1995	CLE	137	484	85	149	75	112	26	1	31	107	6	6	.308	34

Everyone will bid $36 for Manny; how much further is up to you.

JEFF REBOULET   SS,3B   Age 26   Bid: $1

Year	Team	G	AB	R	H	BB	SO	D	T	HR	RBI	SB	CS	BA	$
1992	MIN	73	137	15	26	23	26	7	1	1	16	3	2	.190	-1
1993	MIN	109	240	33	62	35	37	8	0	1	15	5	5	.258	4
1994	MIN	74	189	28	49	18	23	11	1	3	23	0	0	.259	3
1995	MIN	87	216	39	63	27	34	11	0	4	23	1	2	.292	6

No denying he's getting better. Qualifies at two weak positions.

DESI RELAFORD   SS   Age 22   Bid: R4

Year	Team	G	AB	R	H	BB	SO	D	T	HR	RBI	SB	CS	BA	$
1993	(AA)	133	472	49	115	50	103	16	4	8	47	16	12	.244	x
1994	(AA)	37	143	24	29	22	28	7	3	3	11	10	1	.203	x
1994	(A)	99	374	95	116	78	78	27	5	5	59	27	6	.310	x

Year	Team	G	AB	R	H	BB	SO	D	T	HR	RBI	SB	CS	BA	$
1995	(AA)	90	352	51	101	41	58	11	2	7	27	25	9	.287	x
1995	(AAA)	30	113	20	27	13	24	5	1	2	7	6	0	.239	x

Will be at Tacoma, once again the Alex Rodriguez understudy, hoping for the flu.

BILLY RIPKEN 2B   Age 31   Bid: R3

Year	Team	G	AB	R	H	BB	SO	D	T	HR	RBI	SB	CS	BA	$
1991	BAL	104	287	24	62	15	31	11	1	0	14	0	1	.216	-3
1992	BAL	111	330	35	76	18	26	15	0	4	36	2	3	.230	3
1993	TEX	50	132	12	25	11	19	4	0	0	11	0	2	.189	-3
1994	TEX	32	81	9	25	3	11	5	0	0	6	2	0	.309	3
1995	CLE	8	17	4	7	0	3	0	0	2	3	0	0	.412	2

Hangs in there too; hit .292 with 34 doubles at Buffalo.

CAL RIPKEN SS   Age 35   Bid: $20

Year	Team	G	AB	R	H	BB	SO	D	T	HR	RBI	SB	CS	BA	$
1991	BAL	162	650	99	210	53	46	46	5	34	114	6	1	.323	42
1992	BAL	162	637	73	160	64	50	29	1	14	72	4	3	.251	14
1993	BAL	162	641	87	165	65	58	26	3	24	90	1	4	.257	17
1994	BAL	112	444	71	140	32	41	19	3	13	75	1	0	.315	24
1995	BAL	144	550	71	144	52	59	33	2	17	88	0	1	.262	15

His average salary was $15; that is, not one penny extra to tag along with him. Maybe the contrary: there would be a lot of pressure.

That's okay. It's the way to play in Stage Three, and there is no Stage Four. The bid for Cal is based on position scarcity, injury risk, and the feeling he'll hit about .275; not sentiment, I promise.

RUBEN RIVERA   OF   Age 22   Bid: R1

Year	Team	G	AB	R	H	BB	SO	D	T	HR	RBI	SB	CS	BA	$
1993	(A)	55	199	45	55	32	66	7	6	13	47	11	5	.276	x
1994	(A)	105	400	83	115	47	125	24	3	28	81	36	5	.288	x
1994	(A)	34	134	18	35	8	38	4	3	5	20	12	5	.261	x
1995	(AA)	71	256	49	75	37	77	16	8	9	39	15	8	.293	x

Year	Team	G	AB	R	H	BB	SO	D	T	HR	RBI	SB	CS	BA	$
1995	(AAA)	48	174	37	47	26	62	8	2	15	35	8	4	.270	x
1995	NYY	5	1	0	0	0	1	0	0	0	0	0	0	.000	0

Nothing wrong with his Columbus stats (AAA); he slugged .598. Dropped from Baseball America's Minor League Player of the Year to number 5 in the International League, but because for them the magic age is 18. For us, he's moved from the R1 of R5's to the R1 or R1's.

ALEX RODRIGUEZ SS Age 20 Bid: $17

Year	Team	G	AB	R	H	BB	SO	D	T	HR	RBI	SB	CS	BA	$
1994	(A)	65	248	49	79	24	44	17	6	14	55	16	5	.319	x
1994	(AA)	17	59	7	17	10	13	4	1	1	8	2	1	.288	x
1994	(AAA)	32	119	22	37	8	25	7	4	6	21	2	4	.311	x
1994	SEA	17	54	4	11	3	20	0	0	0	2	3	0	.204	0
1995	(AAA)	54	214	37	77	18	44	12	3	15	45	2	4	.360	x
1995	SEA	48	142	15	33	6	42	6	2	5	19	4	2	.232	4

Let's see, 356 AB last year? Bad management.

Bad managing by Piniella had Rodriguez playing shortstop, after pinch-running for Tino Martinez, in the ninth inning of the deciding play-off game against the Yankees. Had Edgar's double been a little less resounding, the score would have been tied, no outs, Ken Griffey on third, Alex Rodriguez at the plate.

IVAN RODRIGUEZ C Age 24 Bid: $16

Year	Team	G	AB	R	H	BB	SO	D	T	HR	RBI	SB	CS	BA	$
1991	TEX	88	280	24	74	5	42	16	0	3	27	0	1	.264	4
1992	TEX	123	420	39	109	24	73	16	1	8	37	0	0	.260	8
1993	TEX	137	473	56	129	29	70	28	4	10	66	8	7	.273	15
1994	TEX	99	363	56	108	31	42	19	1	16	57	6	3	.298	22
1995	TEX	130	492	56	149	16	48	32	2	12	67	0	2	.303	18

In 127 games, base runners attempted to run on him 77 times, by far the lowest rate of stolen bases attempted against any regular catcher. Some other G/SBA rates: Piazza 112/116, Manwaring 118/98, Charles Johnson 97/89 (that will change), Karkovice 113/101, Flaherty 112/104, Oliver 91/99, Stanley 107/103. Now, going the other way, the percent of failed attempts (CS/SBA): Stanley 28%, Oliver 27%, Flaherty 24%, Karkovice 34%, Johnson 43%, Manwaring 29%, Piazza 25%, Rodriguez 48%.

Rodriguez caught 1,065 innings last year, over 200 more than the average starting catcher. He got to DH once; that is, had one opportunity to post some stats on a rest day. (Stanley had 10.) The Rangers rely on his defense more than his owners would like to see.

DONNIE SADLER
SS Age 21 Bid: R4

Year	Team	G	AB	R	H	BB	SO	D	T	HR	RBI	SB	CS	BA	$
1994	(R)	53	206	52	56	23	27	8	6	1	16	32	8	.272	x
1995	(A)	118	438	103	124	79	85	25	8	9	55	41	13	.283	x

The No. 3 prospect in the Midwest League, he's 5'6", 165. Plays for the Red Sox.
A Gammons favorite.

TIM SALMON
OF Age 27 Bid: $36

Year	Team	G	AB	R	H	BB	SO	D	T	HR	RBI	SB	CS	BA	$
1992	CAL	23	79	8	14	11	23	1	0	2	6	1	1	.177	0
1993	CAL	142	515	93	146	82	135	35	1	31	95	5	6	.283	28
1994	CAL	100	373	67	107	54	102	18	2	23	70	1	3	.287	22
1995	CAL	143	537	111	177	91	111	34	3	34	105	5	5	.330	39

Great camera-work in the play-offs, terrible announcing. In game 145 of the regular season, with the score 10 Mariners, in the innocent words of the USA Today scoring summary: "Blowers singled to left. Martinez safe on fielder's choice to pitcher, Blowers to second."

The announcers, Jon Miller and Joe Morgan, like us, were a little puzzled by Langston's choice, since he didn't throw to either second or first; he held the ball.

Then the camera showed why. On a replay, we see that Hudler's back was turned at first base, as he looked for the relay from second.

The announcers can hardly be faulted for missing this the first time — what's amazing is that Langston saw it — and they certainly explained it as best they could, watching the replay.

Next: "Wilson sacrificed Blowers to third, Martinez to second." Perfect bunt.

Next: "Cora hit by pitch." Bases loaded. One out.

Next: "Coleman lined to shallow right." Blowers didn't tag and try to go home.

Both Miller and Morgan were beside themselves. Miller in particular was unforgiving, sure the Mariners would live to regret "the bone-headed base running by Blowers."

Sounds good. But there was a problem. Not only was it shallow right, but Salmon made a sliding catch, came up throwing — and Allanson didn't have to move his mitt. Darn good catch, nifty recovery, and one of the great clutch throws of all time!

The replay showed this over and over, the ball lasering to Allanson, who doesn't move half a step in any direction. Blowers, for his part, does seem a little lost as to what to do; and with one out and the right fielder down, it is indeed a no-brainer, he goes. But he would have been dead meat. Vince Coleman would have been.

Next: "Sojo doubled to right, Blowers, Martinez and Cora scored. Sojo to third advancing on the throw. Sojo scored on Langston's throwing error," and it's all academic.

JUAN SAMUEL
1B Age 35 Bid: $1

Year	Team	G	AB	R	H	BB	SO	D	T	HR	RBI	SB	CS	BA	$
1991	LA	153	594	62	161	49	133	22	6	12	58	23	8	.271	22
1992	LA/KC	76	224	22	61	14	49	2	4	2	23	8	3	.262	7

Year	Team	G	AB	R	H	BB	SO	D	T	HR	RBI	SB	CS	BA	$
1993	CIN	103	261	31	60	23	53	10	4	4	26	9	7	.230	**4**
1994	DET	59	136	32	42	10	26	9	5	5	21	5	2	.309	**10**
1995	KC	91	205	31	54	29	49	10	1	12	39	6	4	.263	**11**

Check out Appendix B; the bid perhaps should be $2.

KEVIN SEITZER   3B,1B   Age 34   Bid: $11

Year	Team	G	AB	R	H	BB	SO	D	T	HR	RBI	SB	CS	BA	$
1991	KC	85	234	28	62	29	21	11	3	1	25	4	1	.265	**5**
1992	MIL	148	540	74	146	57	44	35	1	5	71	13	11	.270	**17**
1993	MIL	120	417	45	112	44	48	16	2	11	57	7	7	.269	**13**
1994	MIL	80	309	44	97	30	38	24	2	5	49	2	1	.314	**15**
1995	MIL	132	492	56	153	64	57	33	3	5	69	2	0	.311	**18**

Seitzer, who ranks seventh among third basemen in Appendix B, would be eleventh if he were listed among first basemen. The 18 best first basemen earned an average of $21, the 18 best third basemen earned $15. First is clearly a stronger position, in other words. But they're both shallow. It's a fitting accident that the eighteenth first baseman is Ron Coomer, the eighteenth third baseman Scott Leius.

RICHIE SEXSON   1B   Age 21   Bid: R5

Year	Team	G	AB	R	H	BB	SO	D	T	HR	RBI	SB	CS	BA	$
1994	(A)	130	488	88	133	37	87	25	2	14	77	7	3	.273	x
1995	(A)	131	494	80	151	43	115	34	0	22	85	4	6	.306	x

A shortstop in high school, Sexon is now 6'6", 200. He did a lot better at fast-A Kinston (Indians) last year than he did at slow-A Columbus the year before. The year before that, when he was a 24th-round draft pick, he hit .186 in Rookie ball. A right-handed batter, "the lanky Sexon showed excellent range at first base," according to Baseball America, which ranked him third in the Carolina League. He was in triple-crown contention until slowed down by nagging injuries. "He's got power," says his manager, Gordy MacKenzie. "And he can stay inside the fastball. He can keep those inside pitches fair." Worth watching, and if that's not possible, keeping an eye on.

TERRY SHUMPERT   2B,3B   Age 29   Bid: R3

Year	Team	G	AB	R	H	BB	SO	D	T	HR	RBI	SB	CS	BA	$
1991	KC	144	369	45	80	30	75	16	4	5	34	17	11	.217	**8**
1992	KC	35	94	6	14	3	17	5	1	1	11	2	2	.149	**-1**

Year	Team	G	AB	R	H	BB	SO	D	T	HR	RBI	SB	CS	BA	$
1993	KC	8	10	0	1	2	2	0	0	0	0	1	0	.100	0
1994	KC	64	183	28	44	13	39	6	2	8	24	18	3	.240	13
1995	BOS	21	47	6	11	4	13	3	0	0	3	3	1	.234	1

Shumpy's average salary was $7, Alicea's $4. Doesn't mean anyone thought he was a shoe-in to beat Alicea out; just that if he did, there'd be a big pay-off.

RUBEN SIERRA OF   Age 30   Bid: $15

Year	Team	G	AB	R	H	BB	SO	D	T	HR	RBI	SB	CS	BA	$
1991	TEX	161	661	110	203	56	91	44	5	25	116	16	4	.307	39
1992	TEX	151	601	83	167	45	68	34	7	17	87	14	4	.278	26
1993	OAK	158	630	77	147	52	97	23	5	22	101	25	5	.233	23
1994	OAK	110	426	71	114	23	64	21	1	23	92	8	5	.268	25
1995	NYY	126	479	73	126	46	76	32	0	19	86	5	4	.263	18

Whereas sentiment is not supposed to add to a player's price, there's nothing wrong with putting a low price on player's you don't like. And you don't even have to bid to it. But I'd learn to like Ruben at $15.

CHRIS SNOPEK 3B   Age 25   Bid: R1

Year	Team	G	AB	R	H	BB	SO	D	T	HR	RBI	SB	CS	BA	$
1994	(AA)	106	365	58	96	58	49	25	3	6	54	9	4	.263	x
1995	(AAA)	113	393	56	127	50	72	23	4	12	55	2	5	.323	x
1995	CHW	22	68	12	22	9	12	4	0	1	7	1	0	.324	3

He hit .245 at Sarasota (A) in 1993, so with each step up, he's increased his batting average. If he can bat .325 this year, he really might force Ventura off of third.

Eddie Epstein in *The Scouting Notebook* last year: "Snopek's season might not look impressive, but it is. Birmingham is a tough park in which to hit, and it's especially tough on home-run production. The Barons' leading home-run hitter hit seven... Snopek has doubles power and good strike-zone judgement; that combination plus maturity and an easier park could mean home-run power in the future. He is also a very good defensive third baseman with good hands and a good arm."

I've quoted about half of the comment. There's a lot of technical stuff having to with Snopek's EPS. An EPS is an "Epstein Average," something that looks like a batting average but "correlates much better with team run production than batting average." He gives a long but rather vague explanation at the beginning of the book; I wouldn't be surprised if EPS in the end is OBS (on-base + slugging) boiled down to batting average size. Whatever it is, Epstein constantly tells us how much better or worse a player's was than his league's, which is all that counts. He gave Snopek a B for a grade.

J.T. SNOW 1B Age 28   Bid: $19

Year	Team	G	AB	R	H	BB	SO	D	T	HR	RBI	SB	CS	BA	$
1992	NYY	7	14	1	2	5	5	1	0	0	2	0	0	.143	0
1993	CAL	129	419	60	101	55	88	18	2	16	57	3	0	.241	10
1994	CAL	61	223	22	49	19	48	4	0	8	30	0	1	.220	1
1995	CAL	143	544	80	157	52	91	22	1	24	102	2	1	.289	25

In Appendix A, doesn't it look like the four leagues are getting steadily smarter about J.T. Snow?
   They are.
   Baseball Weekly drafted on April 18 and the American Dreams on April 23, before a game had been played. When Cowtown drafted, a week into the season, Snow was hitting .313. By the time Ashpole convened on May 9, Snow had two homers to go with a .320 batting average.
   As Ron Shandler observes in his *Baseball Forecaster*, projecting a player's stats is a process that changes daily.

LUIS SOJO SS,2B Age 31   Bid: $2

Year	Team	G	AB	R	H	BB	SO	D	T	HR	RBI	SB	CS	BA	$
1991	CAL	113	364	38	94	14	26	14	1	3	20	4	2	.258	5
1992	CAL	106	368	37	100	14	24	12	3	7	43	7	11	.272	12
1993	TOR	19	47	5	8	4	2	2	0	0	6	0	0	.170	-1
1994	SEA	63	213	32	59	8	25	9	2	6	22	2	1	.277	7
1995	SEA	102	339	50	98	23	19	18	2	7	39	4	2	.289	11

The wonderful 1995 stat line is not a fluke, but neither is the competition.

PAUL SORRENTO 1B Age 30   Bid: $18

Year	Team	G	AB	R	H	BB	SO	D	T	HR	RBI	SB	CS	BA	$
1991	MIN	26	47	6	12	4	11	2	0	4	13	0	0	.255	3
1992	CLE	140	458	52	123	51	89	24	1	18	60	0	3	.269	16
1993	CLE	148	463	75	119	58	121	26	1	18	65	3	1	.257	14
1994	CLE	95	322	43	90	34	68	14	0	14	62	0	1	.280	15
1995	CLE	104	323	50	76	51	71	14	0	25	79	1	1	.235	15

Qualitative can't be that bad again; quantitatives should be about the same.

SCOTT SPIEZIO   3B   Age 23   Bid: R2

Year	Team	G	AB	R	H	BB	SO	D	T	HR	RBI	SB	CS	BA	$
1993	(A)	31	125	32	41	16	18	10	2	3	19	0	5	.328	x
1993	(A)	32	110	12	28	23	19	9	1	1	13	1	3	.255	x
1994	(A)	127	453	84	127	88	72	32	5	14	68	5	0	.280	x
1995	(AA)	141	528	78	149	67	78	33	8	13	86	10	3	.282	x

"Yes, he is Ed Spiezio's son," says Eddie Epstein (said in last year's book). This year's book, which is available in mid-January, won't give Scott a lower grade than last year (B-), I'm sure of that.

Double-A is often the step that prospects trip on, but Spiezio took Huntsville in stride. He goes to Edmonton this year, hopes he hits better than .280 — because that will be lower than the team average and he'll get a bad EPS next year — and keeps an eye on Brosius and Paquette down in Oakland.

ED SPRAGUE   3B   Age 28   Bid: $7

Year	Team	G	AB	R	H	BB	SO	D	T	HR	RBI	SB	CS	BA	$
1991	TOR	61	160	17	44	19	43	7	0	4	20	0	3	.275	4
1992	TOR	22	47	6	11	3	7	2	0	1	7	0	0	.234	1
1993	TOR	150	546	50	142	32	85	31	1	12	73	1	0	.260	12
1994	TOR	109	405	38	97	23	95	19	1	11	44	1	0	.240	5
1995	TOR	144	521	77	127	58	96	27	2	18	74	0	0	.244	10

A long, slow fade in the second half is nothing to be too afraid of.

SCOTT STAHOVIAK   3B,1B   Age 26   Bid: R3

Year	Team	G	AB	R	H	BB	SO	D	T	HR	RBI	SB	CS	BA	$
1993	(AA)	93	331	40	90	56	95	25	1	12	56	10	2	.272	x
1993	MIN	20	57	1	11	3	22	4	0	0	1	0	2	.193	-2
1994	(AAA)	123	437	96	139	70	90	41	6	13	94	6	8	.318	x
1995	(AAA)	9	33	6	10	6	3	1	0	0	5	2	0	.303	x
1995	MIN	94	263	28	70	30	61	19	0	3	23	5	1	.266	5

Eddie Epstein in his 1995 book: "Offensively, *just* offensively, Stahoviak could be a Keith Hernandez-type player."

He'll eat those words. We all eat some.

MATT STAIRS OF Age 27   Bid: R3

Year	Team	G	AB	R	H	BB	SO	D	T	HR	RBI	SB	CS	BA	$
1994	(AA)	93	317	44	98	53	38	25	2	9	61	10	7	.309	x
1995	(AAA)	75	271	40	77	29	41	17	0	13	56	3	3	.284	x
1995	BOS	39	88	8	23	4	14	7	1	1	17	0	1	.261	2

Oddly enough, he has a better future in the National League (where he played briefly in '92 and '93), because pinch-hitters are used there more often. That was basically his role on the Red Sox — he was not a defensive replacement — and he hit .355 with runners in scoring position, .313 Close & Late.

MIKE STANLEY C Age 33   Bid: $17

Year	Team	G	AB	R	H	BB	SO	D	T	HR	RBI	SB	CS	BA	$
1991	TEX	95	181	25	45	34	44	13	1	3	25	0	0	.249	3
1992	TEX/NY	68	173	24	43	27	33	7	0	8	27	0	0	.249	6
1993	NYY	130	423	70	129	57	85	17	1	26	84	1	1	.305	25
1994	NYY	82	290	54	87	39	56	20	0	17	57	0	0	.300	19
1995	NYY	118	399	63	107	57	106	29	1	18	83	1	1	.268	17

Hit .320 with runners in scoring position, .367 Close & Late, and seemingly, about half of his home runs with the bases loaded.

TERRY STEINBACH C Age 34   Bid: $12

Year	Team	G	AB	R	H	BB	SO	D	T	HR	RBI	SB	CS	BA	$
1991	OAK	129	456	50	125	22	70	31	1	6	67	2	2	.274	12
1992	OAK	128	438	48	122	45	58	20	1	12	53	2	3	.279	15
1993	OAK	104	389	47	111	25	65	19	1	10	43	3	3	.285	12
1994	OAK	103	369	51	105	26	62	21	2	11	57	2	1	.285	15
1995	OAK	114	406	43	113	25	74	26	1	15	65	1	3	.278	15

The steadiest catcher who ever lived, but that means he's getting on.

SHANNON STEWART OF Age 22 R1

Year	Team	G	AB	R	H	BB	SO	D	T	HR	RBI	SB	CS	BA	$
1994	(A)	56	225	39	73	23	39	10	5	4	25	15	11	.324	x
1995	(AA)	138	498	89	143	89	61	24	6	5	55	42	16	.287	x

AL hitters

Year	Team	G	AB	R	H	BB	SO	D	T	HR	RBI	SB	CS	BA	$
1995	TOR	12	38	2	8	5	5	0	0	0	1	2	0	.211	0

The jump from 15 SB to 42 SB is especially nice when that's what you've got to do to climb to the majors.

DARRYL STRAWBERRY   DH   Age 34   Bid: $7

Year	Team	G	AB	R	H	BB	SO	D	T	HR	RBI	SB	CS	BA	$
1991	LA	139	505	86	134	75	125	22	4	28	99	10	8	.265	29
1992	LA	43	156	20	37	19	34	8	0	5	25	3	1	.237	6
1993	LA	32	100	12	14	16	19	2	0	5	12	1	0	.140	-1
1994	SF	29	92	13	22	19	22	3	1	4	17	0	3	.239	3
1995	DET	62	116	13	29	19	27	11	0	2	19	0	1	.250	2

Will be flying back and forth between playing winter ball in Puerto Rico and testifying against his agent for falsifying his taxes. Has to play well enough in Puerto Rico to get a contract to pay what he owes. Can't make a tenth what he used to make at card shows. Better not take it out on his girlfriends. Must remain sober.

B.J. SURHOFF   C,OF,1B   Age 31   Bid: $16

Year	Team	G	AB	R	H	BB	SO	D	T	HR	RBI	SB	CS	BA	$
1991	MIL	143	505	27	146	26	33	19	4	5	68	5	8	.289	16
1992	MIL	139	480	63	121	46	41	19	1	4	62	14	8	.252	13
1993	MIL	148	552	66	151	36	47	38	3	7	79	12	9	.274	17
1994	MIL	40	134	20	35	16	14	11	2	5	22	0	1	.261	4
1995	MIL	117	415	72	133	37	43	26	3	13	73	7	3	.320	24

Delighted people who paid $5 for him by the way he played and where he played (exactly 18 games at catcher).

MIKE SWEENEY   C   Age 22   Bid: R4

Year	Team	G	AB	R	H	BB	SO	D	T	HR	RBI	SB	CS	BA	$
1994	(A)	86	276	47	83	55	43	20	3	10	52	0	1	.301	x
1995	(A)	99	332	61	103	60	39	23	1	18	53	6	1	.310	x
1995	KC	4	4	1	1	0	0	0	0	0	0	0	0	.250	0

This top 10 prospect in the Carolina League is 6'1", 195, bats right. But you already know that, because he's played four games in the majors.

DANNY TARTABULL
OF Age 33   Bid: $7

Year	Team	G	AB	R	H	BB	SO	D	T	HR	RBI	SB	CS	BA	$
1991	KC	132	484	78	153	65	121	35	3	31	100	6	3	.316	35
1992	NYY	123	421	72	112	103	115	19	0	25	85	2	2	.266	22
1993	NYY	138	513	87	128	92	156	33	2	31	102	0	0	.250	20
1994	NYY	104	399	68	102	66	111	24	1	19	67	1	1	.256	14
1995	OAK	83	280	34	66	43	82	16	0	8	35	0	2	.236	3

His reflexes have gone.

MICKEY TETTLETON
C Age 35   Bid: $14

Year	Team	G	AB	R	H	BB	SO	D	T	HR	RBI	SB	CS	BA	$
1991	DET	154	501	85	132	101	131	17	2	31	89	3	3	.263	24
1992	DET	157	525	82	125	122	137	25	0	32	83	0	6	.238	20
1993	DET	152	522	79	128	109	139	25	4	32	110	3	7	.245	22
1994	DET	107	339	57	84	97	98	18	2	17	51	0	1	.248	10
1995	TEX	134	429	76	102	107	110	19	1	32	78	0	0	.238	16

Since he did not qualify at catcher, it's a tough call whether to freeze him at $15, as I can (hardly a surprise to many readers). Freezing players because of the inflation brings the inflation down.

FRANK THOMAS
1B Age 28   Bid: $45

Year	Team	G	AB	R	H	BB	SO	D	T	HR	RBI	SB	CS	BA	$
1991	CHW	158	573	107	183	141	115	32	2	33	112	1	2	.318	35
1992	CHW	160	580	109	187	124	89	47	2	24	116	6	3	.323	37
1993	CHW	153	581	112	184	119	57	38	0	43	136	4	2	.317	41
1994	CHW	113	572	152	202	156	87	49	1	54	145	3	4	.353	46
1995	CHW	145	551	114	170	152	83	30	0	45	124	3	2	.308	37

The ingredients needed to challenge Maris are good health, a hot streak and plate discipline. And lots of power helps, especially power to all fields. So Frank Thomas is as good a candidate as anybody, of course. If he does get hot and finds himself with 40 home runs in August, the question is, will he expand his strike zone? And if he does, can he stay hot?

There may never have been a more consistently productive hitter — or do I mean more productively consistent? His BB/SO ratios for the last two years could hardly be closer: the across-the-board drop-off of his other stats makes you wonder if we don't have evidence right here that the ball was juiced in 1994. Take a good look.

Have you figured out yet that not one of these stat lines is real?

Even 1991 through 1993 are fake. What we have is Frank Thomas's stats if he had played every game in the last five years, and every game had been played. In other words, under G should be 162 in each case; the numbers under G here are the only true stats for Thomas, then each stat to the right is multiplied by 162 over it (162/158 x the number of AB Thomas really had in 1991 = 573).

In case your eyes dropped down to it, I gave the real Frank Thomas, shown in the next box, an alias.

JOHN THOMPSON   1B   Age 24   Bid: R2

Year Team	G	AB	R	H	BB	SO	D	T	HR	RBI	SB	CS	BA	$
1991 (R)	158	559	104	178	138	112	31	2	32	109	1	2	.318	**35**
1992 (A)	160	573	108	185	122	88	46	2	24	115	6	3	.323	**37**
1993 (A)	153	549	106	174	112	54	36	0	41	128	4	2	.317	**41**
1994 (AA)	113	399	106	141	109	61	34	1	38	101	2	3	.353	**46**
1995 (AAA)	145	493	102	152	136	74	27	0	40	111	3	2	.308	**37**

Probably didn't work. Your eyes probably dropped down anyway — ever on the look for prospects — and you said, My God!

Is that John Thompson's son? How come I've never heard of him? Why isn't he an R1?

JIM THOME   3B   Age 25   Bid: $29

Year Team	G	AB	R	H	BB	SO	D	T	HR	RBI	SB	CS	BA	$
1991 CLE	27	98	12	25	5	16	4	2	1	9	1	1	.255	**2**
1992 CLE	40	117	8	24	10	34	3	1	2	12	2	0	.205	**1**
1993 CLE	47	154	28	41	29	36	11	0	7	22	2	1	.266	**6**
1994 CLE	98	321	58	86	46	84	20	1	20	52	3	3	.268	**16**
1995 CLE	137	452	92	142	97	113	29	3	25	73	4	3	.314	**27**

Hit .275 against lefties, .242 with runners in scoring position, .361 Close & Late; he'll drive in more runs.

LEE TINSLEY   OF   Age 27   Bid: $4

Year Team	G	AB	R	H	BB	SO	D	T	HR	RBI	SB	CS	BA	$
1993 SEA	11	19	2	3	2	9	1	0	1	2	0	0	.158	**-1**
1994 BOS	78	144	27	32	19	36	4	0	2	14	13	0	.222	**6**
1995 BOS	100	341	61	97	39	74	17	1	7	41	18	8	.284	**17**

What I'm paid to do: make calls on Lee Tinsley.

He's toast.

ALAN TRAMMELL SS Age 38   Bid: R3

Year	Team	G	AB	R	H	BB	SO	D	T	HR	RBI	SB	CS	BA	$
1991	DET	101	375	57	93	37	39	20	0	9	55	11	2	.248	13
1992	DET	29	102	11	28	15	4	7	1	1	11	2	2	.275	3
1993	DET	112	401	72	132	38	38	25	3	12	60	12	8	.329	25
1994	DET	76	292	38	78	16	35	17	1	8	28	3	0	.267	8
1995	DET	74	223	28	60	27	19	12	0	2	23	3	1	.269	4

Great career. Better than Whitaker's? You could debate that all winter.

MICHAEL TUCKER OF Age 25   Bid: $5

Year	Team	G	AB	R	H	BB	SO	D	T	HR	RBI	SB	CS	BA	$
1993	(A)	61	239	42	73	34	49	14	2	6	44	12	2	.305	x
1993	(AA)	72	244	38	68	42	31	7	4	9	35	12	5	.279	x
1994	(AA)	132	485	75	134	69	111	16	7	21	77	11	3	.276	x
1995	KC	62	177	23	46	18	51	10	0	4	17	2	3	.260	3
1995	(AAA)	71	275	37	84	24	39	18	4	4	28	11	4	.305	x

I've been down on Tucker for a while now, and have been right. Now I could be wrong.

JOHN VALENTIN SS Age 29   Bid: $28

Year	Team	G	AB	R	H	BB	SO	D	T	HR	RBI	SB	CS	BA	$
1992	BOS	58	185	21	51	20	17	13	0	5	25	1	0	.276	6
1993	BOS	144	468	50	130	49	77	40	3	11	66	3	4	.278	14
1994	BOS	84	301	53	95	42	38	26	2	9	49	3	1	.316	18
1995	BOS	135	520	108	155	81	67	37	2	27	102	20	5	.298	37

His steals were worth $5, and it seems like he'll bat second again.

JOSE VALENTIN SS Age 26   Bid: $11

Year	Team	G	AB	R	H	BB	SO	D	T	HR	RBI	SB	CS	BA	$
1992	MIL	4	3	1	0	0	0	0	0	0	1	0	0	.000	0
1993	MIL	19	53	10	13	7	16	1	2	1	7	1	0	.245	1

Year	Team	G	AB	R	H	BB	SO	D	T	HR	RBI	SB	CS	BA	$
1994	MIL	97	285	47	68	38	75	19	0	11	46	12	3	.239	**12**
1995	MIL	112	338	62	74	37	83	23	3	11	49	16	8	.219	**10**

Expectancies were high enough last year that a lot of people won't want him this year.

JOSE VALENTIN   C   Age 20   Bid: R5

Year	Team	G	AB	R	H	BB	SO	D	T	HR	RBI	SB	CS	BA	$
1994	(R)	54	210	23	44	15	44	5	0	9	27	0	1	.210	**x**
1995	(A)	112	383	59	124	47	75	26	5	19	65	0	5	.324	**x**

The No. 1 prospect in the Midwest League is 5'10", 191; bats both; was a third-round pick by the Twins in '93. Don't know what he did in '93, but it can't be too good, since he played in Rookie ball in '94. Improved by leaps last year. Believe it or not, he's the previous player's younger brother.

GREG VAUGHN   DH   Age 30   Bid: $5

Year	Team	G	AB	R	H	BB	SO	D	T	HR	RBI	SB	CS	BA	$
1991	MIL	145	542	81	132	62	125	24	5	27	98	2	2	.244	**19**
1992	MIL	141	501	77	114	60	123	18	2	23	78	15	15	.228	**20**
1993	MIL	154	569	97	152	89	118	28	2	30	97	10	7	.267	**26**
1994	MIL	95	370	59	94	51	93	24	1	19	55	9	5	.254	**17**
1995	MIL	108	392	67	88	55	89	19	1	17	59	10	4	.224	**11**

A battered and beaten mighty warrior.

MO VAUGHN   1B   Age 28   Bid: $36

Year	Team	G	AB	R	H	BB	SO	D	T	HR	RBI	SB	CS	BA	$
1991	BOS	74	219	21	57	26	43	12	0	4	32	2	1	.260	**6**
1992	BOS	113	355	42	83	47	67	16	2	13	57	3	3	.234	**10**
1993	BOS	152	539	86	160	79	130	34	1	29	101	4	3	.297	**30**
1994	BOS	111	394	65	122	57	112	25	1	26	82	4	4	.310	**31**
1995	BOS	140	550	98	165	68	150	28	3	39	126	11	4	.300	**41**

The only thing pitchers learned from his failure in the play-off is that they're in trouble.

RANDY VELARDE   INF,OF   Age 33   Bid: $6

Year	Team	G	AB	R	H	BB	SO	D	T	HR	RBI	SB	CS	BA	$
1991	NYY	80	184	19	45	18	43	11	1	1	15	3	1	.245	2
1992	NYY	120	412	57	112	38	78	24	1	7	46	7	2	.272	13
1993	NYY	85	226	28	68	18	39	13	2	7	24	2	2	.301	9
1994	NYY	77	280	47	78	22	61	16	1	9	34	4	2	.279	11
1995	NYY	111	367	60	102	55	64	19	1	7	46	5	1	.278	11

Batting Other was rough for Velarde; he hit .237. But in the No. 2 slot — an underappreciated place in the batting order, I think — he hit .305, and, fittingly, he hit .323 in the No. 9 slot to lead the majors.

ROBIN VENTURA   3B,1B   Age 28   Bid: $26

Year	Team	G	AB	R	H	BB	SO	D	T	HR	RBI	SB	CS	BA	$
1991	CHW	157	606	92	172	80	67	25	1	23	100	2	4	.284	25
1992	CHW	157	592	85	167	93	71	38	1	16	93	2	4	.282	23
1993	CHW	157	554	85	145	105	82	27	1	22	94	1	6	.262	18
1994	CHW	109	401	57	113	61	69	15	1	18	78	3	1	.282	21
1995	CHW	135	492	79	145	75	98	22	0	26	93	4	3	.295	27

Ventura should not move to first; Appendix B has relevance to big league teams.

JOE VITIELLO   DH   Age 26   Bid: $2

Year	Team	G	AB	R	H	BB	SO	D	T	HR	RBI	SB	CS	BA	$
1993	(AA)	117	413	62	119	57	95	25	2	15	95	2	0	.288	x
1994	(AAA)	98	352	46	121	56	63	25	3	10	63	3	2	.344	x
1995	KC	53	130	13	33	8	25	4	0	7	21	0	0	.254	4

Solid against lefties (.569 SA), he has no value as a DH-only unless he also plays against righties.

OMAR VIZQUEL   SS   Age 29   Bid: $11

Year	Team	G	AB	R	H	BB	SO	D	T	HR	RBI	SB	CS	BA	$
1991	SEA	142	426	42	98	45	37	16	4	1	41	7	2	.230	3
1992	SEA	136	483	49	142	32	38	20	4	0	21	15	13	.294	13
1993	SEA	158	560	68	143	50	71	14	2	2	31	12	14	.255	6

Year	Team	G	AB	R	H	BB	SO	D	T	HR	RBI	SB	CS	BA	$
1994	CLE	69	286	39	78	23	23	10	1	1	33	13	4	.273	**11**
1995	CLE	136	542	87	144	59	59	28	0	6	56	29	11	.266	**20**

If he bats ninth this year, he could actually do more running.

MATT WALBECK C Age 26 Bid: $2

Year	Team	G	AB	R	H	BB	SO	D	T	HR	RBI	SB	CS	BA	$
1993	CHC	11	30	2	6	1	6	2	0	1	6	0	0	.200	**0**
1994	MIN	97	338	31	69	17	37	12	0	5	35	1	1	.204	**-4**
1995	MIN	115	393	40	101	25	71	18	1	1	44	3	1	.257	**4**

Pay less than what he earned for what you hope is a little more.

TODD WALKER 2B Age 23 Bid: R1

Year	Team	G	AB	R	H	BB	SO	D	T	HR	RBI	SB	CS	BA	$
1994	(A)	46	171	29	52	32	15	5	2	10	34	6	3	.304	**x**
1995	(AA)	137	513	83	149	63	101	27	3	21	85	23	9	.290	**x**

He's interesting. The Twins's No.1 pick out of LSU in '94, he's 6'0", 170, bats left. In his first pro year, he had an amazing ratio of walks-to-K's-to-doubles-to homers. Last year looks normal, except he's 6-feet, 170, and bats left. And plays second base. If the Twins decide to fire-sale Knoblauch (he's coming up on his free-agent year), he makes the Twins this season.

LOU WHITAKER 2B Age 39 Bid: $6

Year	Team	G	AB	R	H	BB	SO	D	T	HR	RBI	SB	CS	BA	$
1991	DET	138	470	94	131	90	45	26	2	23	78	4	2	.279	**22**
1992	DET	130	453	77	126	81	46	26	0	19	71	6	4	.278	**22**
1993	DET	119	383	72	111	78	46	32	1	9	67	3	3	.290	**15**
1994	DET	92	322	67	97	41	47	21	2	12	43	2	0	.301	**16**
1995	DET	84	249	36	73	31	41	14	0	14	44	4	0	.293	**14**

Worth betting more on? You could debate that all winter.

DEVON WHITE OF Age 33 Bid: $19

Year	Team	G	AB	R	H	BB	SO	D	T	HR	RBI	SB	CS	BA	$
1991	TOR	156	642	110	181	55	135	40	10	17	60	33	10	.282	**32**

Year	Team	G	AB	R	H	BB	SO	D	T	HR	RBI	SB	CS	BA	$
1992	TOR	153	641	98	159	47	133	26	7	17	60	37	4	.248	26
1993	TOR	146	598	116	163	57	127	42	6	15	52	34	4	.273	26
1994	TOR	100	403	67	109	21	80	24	6	13	49	11	3	.270	17
1995	TOR	101	427	61	121	29	97	23	5	10	53	11	2	.283	17

The trouble with the range factor is that if they don't hit 'em to your vicinity, you have a poor range factor. Zone rating, a somewhat new stat from Stats Inc., attempts to correct that.

Stats Inc. scorers are left to determine the number of "balls hit in the area where a fielder can reasonably be expected to record an out." Zone rating divides that number into the number of outs that are recorded, by put-out or assist.

Devo's zone rating was .803 — four out of five balls that came into his area with a "reasonable expectation" of being caught he caught.

Is that a lot or a little?

The major league zone rating for center fielders was .811 last year. They all catch four out of five. So the next question is, is catching .803 significantly worse than catching .811?

Who else has a great reputation in center field?

Lofton's zone rating was .828.

Griffey's was .785.

Nixon's was .787.

Johnson's was .814.

Kennedy's was...

No, he was a catcher.

Grissom's was .846.

McRae's was .830.

Some center fielders with less than sterling reputations: Lankford .757, Curtis .810, Edmonds .879, Tinsley .817.

A few others: Finley .867, Carr .822, Deion .842, Bernie .871.

Almost all of these outfielders played enough to have had 400 balls hit "In Zone." That would be enough AB to be statistically relevant. The Outs for each outfielder, which aren't a judgement call at all, can be considered as Hits: the zone rating can be thought of as a batting average, except the average is much higher.

Of the players in this sample, Edmonds, surprisingly enough, wins the batting title. He was 8% above average. A hitter who was 8% above average last year hit .292. By the same reasoning, the worst player in this sample, Lankford, hit .252 in center field last year.

Does that mean that Devo hit .267 patrolling the outfield last year? Lofton hit .276? Griffey hit .261?

It seems to.

The catch, of course, is the number of balls hit In Zone. Someone is sitting in the stands, making this call. Where does he or she draw the line of "reasonably expectations," and doesn't the area shrink and expand according to how the ball is hit?

Clearly, there's something in this stat that Stats Inc. labors so hard over. Both Lofton and Finley are found near the bottom of the heap, judging by range factor. They simply didn't make many putouts, probably because they played behind groundball pitchers. Griffey and Devo are found near the top; they had a lot of balls hit to them.

It just doesn't seem possible that they let more drop than Tinsley would have. There's almost no point in going to the game and savoring the action, if that's the case. Ken Griffey Jr. and Devon White are as good is gets in center field.

Aren't they?

I sometimes wonder if we would know how good certain hitters are, if we didn't record batting averages. Or how bad. Without the numbers, would even Brewers fans have noticed B.J. Surhoff this year — which only seems like the riddle, if a tree falls in the forest.

No, Griffey and White are great center fielders, I'll swear by that. There's got to be some other explanation for their zone ratings. It could be that the scorers in Seattle and Toronto just have greater expectations than anyone else, a wider strike zone, so to speak. There's a home disadvantage. Zone rating sounds good, but it's a tough call, and different people make the calls.

Just like balls and strikes.

BERNIE WILLIAMS   OF   Age 27   Bid: $29

Year	Team	G	AB	R	H	BB	SO	D	T	HR	RBI	SB	CS	BA	$
1991	NYY	85	320	43	76	48	57	19	4	3	34	10	5	.238	7
1992	NYY	62	261	39	73	29	36	14	2	5	26	7	6	.280	10
1993	NYY	139	567	67	152	53	106	31	4	12	68	9	9	.268	16
1994	NYY	108	408	80	118	61	54	29	1	12	57	16	9	.289	24
1995	NYY	144	563	93	173	75	98	29	9	18	82	8	6	.307	27

Hit .350 in the second half, Torre might ask him to try to steal again; he very well could go into the 30's.

GEORGE WILLIAMS   C   Age 27   Bid: $3

Year	Team	G	AB	R	H	BB	SO	D	T	HR	RBI	SB	CS	BA	$
1994	(A)	63	221	40	67	44	47	20	1	8	48	3	3	.303	x
1995	(AAA)	81	290	53	90	50	52	20	0	13	55	0	4	.310	x
1995	OAK	29	79	13	23	11	21	5	1	3	14	0	0	.291	3

Seems to be a good hitter, particularly batting right-handed (.310 for the A's, .347 at Edmonton).

GERALD WILLIAMS   OF   Age 29   Bid: $1

Year	Team	G	AB	R	H	BB	SO	D	T	HR	RBI	SB	CS	BA	$
1992	NYY	15	27	7	8	0	3	2	0	3	6	2	0	.296	3
1993	NYY	42	67	11	10	1	14	2	3	0	6	2	0	.149	-2
1994	NYY	57	86	19	25	4	17	8	0	4	13	1	3	.291	5
1995	NYY	100	182	33	45	22	34	18	2	6	28	4	2	.247	6

May be asked to run more under Torre.

DAN WILSON
C   Age 27   Bid: $4

Year	Team	G	AB	R	H	BB	SO	D	T	HR	RBI	SB	CS	BA	$
1992	CIN	12	25	2	9	3	8	1	0	0	3	0	0	.360	1
1993	CIN	36	76	6	17	9	16	3	0	0	8	0	0	.224	-1
1994	SEA	91	282	24	61	10	57	14	2	3	27	1	2	.216	-3
1995	SEA	119	399	40	111	33	63	22	3	9	51	2	1	.278	11

Had a year to dream about, although Lofton must jar him awake a few times.

ERNIE YOUNG
OF   Age 26   Bid: R3

Year	Team	G	AB	R	H	BB	SO	D	T	HR	RBI	SB	CS	BA	$
1994	(AA)	72	257	45	89	37	45	19	4	14	55	5	6	.346	x
1994	(AAA)	29	102	19	29	13	27	4	0	6	16	0	5	.284	x
1994	OAK	11	30	2	2	1	8	1	0	0	3	0	0	.067	-3
1995	(AAA)	95	347	70	96	49	73	21	4	15	72	2	2	.277	x
1995	OAK	26	50	9	10	8	12	3	0	2	5	0	0	.200	0

Huntsville in 1994 must have been a hot streak.

GREG ZAUN
C   Age 25   Bid: $1

Year	Team	G	AB	R	H	BB	SO	D	T	HR	RBI	SB	CS	BA	$
1994	(AAA)	123	388	61	92	56	72	16	4	7	43	4	2	.237	x
1995	(AAA)	42	140	26	41	14	21	13	1	6	18	0	3	.293	x
1995	BAL	40	104	18	27	16	14	5	0	3	14	1	1	.260	3

His slugging average at Rochester rose from .353 to .529. Good enough glove to take some playing time from Hoiles.

AL hitters

JIM ABBOTT Age 28

Bid: $10

Year	Team	G	GS	IP	H	HR	BB	SO	W	L	ERA	Ratio	Sv	$
1991	CAL	34	34	243	222	14	73	158	18	11	2.89	10.93	0	31
1992	CAL	29	29	211	208	12	68	130	7	15	2.77	11.77	0	16
1993	NYY	32	32	214	221	22	73	95	11	14	4.37	12.36	0	8
1994	NYY	24	24	160	167	24	64	90	9	8	4.55	12.97	0	11
1995	CH/CA	30	30	197	209	14	64	86	11	8	3.70	12.47	0	20

The bid limits for hitters can easily stand as predictions. The differences between them and the predicted earnings for hitters that you see in the next chapter are often negligible and are seldom dramatic. That's not the case with pitchers.

For one thing, there are no predicted earnings. The next chapter ranks the pitchers in descending order of what I *think* they will earn, I guess, but really it just ranks them in descending order of preference. In case you thought the bid price above was low, Jim Abbott is my 36th favorite pitcher for next season. Actually, it's a six-way tie between him, Jason Bere, Roger Pavlik, Andy Pettite, Jeff Russel and Aaron Sele.

What a crew... Who would you take? They earned, respectively, $20, ($26), $14, $16, $19 and $6 last year. (I know: You're all saying Pettite.) If they earn an average of $10 next year, even that will be a surprise; the one sure thing is that they aren't going to earn anything near $10 each.

The pitching bids add up to $1,020. The hitting bids added up to $2,100. They're meant to be just starting points for figuring out your own preferences. If you like the fact that Abbott became an extreme ground ball pitcher last year and don't mind the fact that his K-rate reached a career low, bid more for him. As Bill James would say, some lefties make that transition. And some don't.

Just make sure you take the money from somewhere else.

MARK ACRE Age 27

Bid: $2

Year	Team	G	GS	IP	H	HR	BB	SO	W	L	ERA	Ratio	Sv	$
1993	(A)	26	0	31	9	1	13	41	0	0	.29	6.39	20	x
1993	(AA)	19	0	22	22	2	3	21	1	1	2.42	10.23	10	x
1994	OAK	34	0	34	24	4	23	21	5	1	3.41	12.32	0	9
1994	(AAA)	20	0	29	24	1	11	31	1	1	1.88	10.86	6	x
1995	OAK	43	0	52	52	7	28	47	1	2	5.71	13.85	0	-4

The $2 bid limit on Mark Acre permits me to say something when Mark Acre's name is nominated. I'm not obligated to by any means. It all depends on what else is left to buy.

RICK AGUILERA

Age 34   Bid: $35

Year	Team	G	GS	IP	H	HR	BB	SO	W	L	ERA	Ratio	Sv	$
1991	MIN	63	0	69	44	3	30	61	4	5	2.35	9.65	42	38
1992	MIN	64	0	67	60	7	17	52	2	6	2.84	10.40	41	32
1993	MIN	65	0	72	60	9	14	59	4	3	3.11	9.21	34	34
1994	MIN	44	0	45	57	7	10	46	1	4	3.63	13.50	23	23
1995	MN/BOS	52	0	55	46	6	13	52	3	3	2.60	9.60	32	39

The price for Aguilera is contingent on his *not* going back to Minnesota. The fact that he would even want to makes me wonder about him.

In any event, he is clearly one of the very best relievers in baseball and is my fourth favorite pitcher overall. There was a time when $35 might not be enough for him, but I'm pretty sure it would get him now. Closers have gone out of vogue, and this is why:

```
Top 10 AL pitchers
                earned avg            Heath Data      - touts -
Name            1995   sal   +/-      Pts    Rk      AP    JH    $94
JOHNSON,R         58    26    31      57.6   10      28    26     41
MESA,J            57     3    54      62.2    2       4     8     16
MUSSINA,M         50    30    20      56.3   19      28    27     48
WAKEFIELD         42
WETTELAND,J       39    38     1      50.6   85      42    28     37
AGUILERA,R        39    29    10      57.4   11      25    24     23
CONE,D            38    27    11      56.4   18      26    33     53
MARTINEZ,De       36    20    16      52.8   54      18    19     36
ROGERS,K          35    12    23      57.8    9       9    16     20
SMITH,L           32    26     7      48.6  100      24    20     37
    average       43    21    22      55.5   34      20    20     31
```

Only three clearly defined closers at the start of the season — out of a possible 14 — are among the 10 most valuable pitchers at the finish. There was no scarcity of saves last year, relative to other years, but it was hard to identify where they would come from.

Mesa?

Can't be Jose Mesa, you would be saying, if you had carried out your threat to avoid baseball entirely and now were getting reacclimated. When you realized it was Jose Mesa, you'd be no more shocked than seeing Wakefield there, because that's the way starters are.

But then — how shocking is this group? Despite Mesa and Wakefield, they did not come cheap. Quickly name the number of pitchers you would spend $21 for? That's what these pitchers cost on average (counting Wakefield). The ten best pitchers last year combined to earn an average of $31 in 1994.

John Hunt and I both discount that to $20. In a three-way battle with the average league, the league gets Mussina, Aguilera, Dennis Martinez and Lee Smith; Hunt gets Mesa, Cone and Rogers; and I get Johnson and Wetteland. So I'll get Wakefield on waivers.

In a four-way battle, the only one 1994 doesn't get is Aguilera.

The corresponding group of pitchers in last year's book earned $21 the year before; I was blown away by that. They cost $18, making them a group for whom the expectations were high indeed. But this group above is the most predictable bunch of pitchers since I, or you, started doing this for money.

Which is precisely why the impact in 45 Heath leagues isn't greater. The 55.5 points, on average, that the teams that drafted them finished with happens to match exactly what the teams that bought the 10 best hitters (Belle comment) finished with. The pitchers rank higher, thirty-fourth instead of thirty-ninth, but a total of 129 pitchers qualify for this "competition," as against 195 hitters. The conversion to a twelve-team race (34/129 x 12) comes out to roughly the same: a third-place finish for the teams that bought any of these pitchers.

Why does Lee Smith rank 100 out of 129?

He played on the same team with Garret Anderson.

WILSON ALVAREZ Age 26   Bid: $14

Year	Team	G	GS	IP	H	HR	BB	SO	W	L	ERA	Ratio	Sv	$
1991	CHW	10	9	56	47	9	29	32	3	2	3.51	12.14	0	3
1992	CHW	34	9	100	103	12	65	66	5	3	5.20	15.07	1	-9
1993	CHW	31	31	208	168	14	122	155	15	8	2.95	12.57	0	23
1994	CHW	24	24	162	147	16	62	108	12	8	3.45	11.64	0	31
1995	CHW	29	29	175	171	21	93	118	8	11	4.32	13.58	0	6

Lefties somehow hit .296 against Wilson Alvarez. But that wasn't his problem, since he faced so few; his problem was he was out of shape. In the second half, he had a 3.49 ERA and struck out 73 batters. Control was marginally better. He's a good excuse all by himself for going to Sarasota this spring.

BRIAN ANDERSON Age 25   Bid: R2

Year	Team	G	GS	IP	H	HR	BB	SO	W	L	ERA	Ratio	Sv	$
1993	CAL	4	1	11	11	1	2	4	0	0	3.97	10.32	0	1
1994	CAL	18	18	102	120	13	27	47	7	5	5.22	13.01	0	4
1995	CAL	18	17	100	110	24	30	45	6	8	5.87	12.64	0	0

Lefties hit .342 against Brian Anderson, slugged .633. Righties slugged almost .500. His G/F ratio (grounders-to-flies) was .94, and every fourth inning saw a long fly.

But R2 means take him fairly quickly in the reserve rounds, because he's had moments of brilliance and he's a lefty.

LUIS ANDULAR Age 23   Bid: $3

Year	Team	G	GS	IP	H	HR	BB	SO	W	L	ERA	Ratio	Sv	$
1994	(AA)	15	15	77	90	5	25	64	3	7	5.05	13.50	0	x
1995	(AA)	27	27	167	147	10	44	146	14	8	2.85	10.29	0	x
1995	CHW	5	5	30	26	4	14	9	2	1	3.26	11.87	0	5

At Double-A Birmingham in 1993, Andujar started six games, won five, had a 1.82 ERA and plain blew everybody away. Back with the Barons in '94, he posted the numbers that you see here and blew out his arm. Trying again with the Barons last year, he lost six of his first seven decisions. Then his arm came back with a vengeance, as we see.

It's possible he was wearing down again by the time he was called up by the White Sox; that's what the dearth of strikeouts suggests, even though he was successful. If the box scores don't show prettier BB/SO ratios in spring training, steer clear, because he's an extreme flyball pitcher (G/F .63 in the majors).

KEVIN APPIER Age 28   Bid: $25

Year	Team	G	GS	IP	H	HR	BB	SO	W	L	ERA	Ratio	Sv	$
1991	KC	34	31	208	205	13	61	158	13	10	3.42	11.53	0	17
1992	KC	30	30	208	167	10	68	150	15	8	2.46	10.15	0	33
1993	KC	34	34	239	183	8	81	186	18	8	2.56	9.96	0	46
1994	KC	23	23	155	137	11	63	145	7	6	3.83	11.61	0	22
1995	KC	31	31	201	163	14	80	185	15	10	3.89	10.86	0	31

Was heading for a $60 season, easily, through June, by which time he had won 11 games and had an ERA near 2.00. He still ranked as the 22nd "winningest" pitcher in Heath Leagues. Teams that drafted him finished, on average, with 55.6 points, showing that they simply couldn't bring themselves to trade him.

PAUL ASSENMACHER Age 35   Bid: $1

Year	Team	G	GS	IP	H	HR	BB	SO	W	L	ERA	Ratio	Sv	$
1992	CHC	70	0	68	72	6	26	67	4	4	4.10	12.97	8	4
1993	CHC	46	0	39	44	5	13	34	2	1	3.49	13.27	0	1
1993	NYY	26	0	17	10	0	9	11	2	2	3.12	9.87	0	4
1994	CHW	44	0	33	26	2	13	29	1	2	3.55	10.64	1	7
1995	CLE	47	0	38	32	3	12	40	6	2	2.82	10.33	0	13

Good fifth outfielders are hard to find, and so, in fact, are good ninth pitchers.

BOBBY AYALA Age 26   Bid: $6

Year	Team	G	GS	IP	H	HR	BB	SO	W	L	ERA	Ratio	Sv	$
1992	CIN	5	5	29	33	1	13	23	2	1	4.34	14.28	0	-2
1993	CIN	43	9	98	106	16	45	65	7	10	5.60	13.87	3	-5
1994	SEA	46	0	57	42	2	26	76	4	3	2.86	10.80	18	31
1995	SEA	63	0	71	73	9	30	77	6	5	4.44	13.06	19	20

The interior stats aren't *that* bad. Became more hittable, but the batting average against Ayala (.262) was eight points better than the league average. The problem was the home runs, even though he remained an extreme ground ball pitcher (G/F 1.61).

Strong comeback as set-up man foreseen; with the Mariners could mean 10 wins.

TIM BELCHER   Age 34   Bid: $2

Year	Team	G	GS	IP	H	HR	BB	SO	W	L	ERA	Ratio	Sv	$
1991	LA	33	33	209	189	10	75	156	10	9	2.62	11.35	0	16
1992	CIN	35	34	228	201	17	80	149	15	14	3.91	11.11	0	8
1993	CIN/CH	34	33	209	198	19	74	135	12	11	4.44	11.73	0	8
1994	DET	25	25	162	192	21	78	76	7	15	5.89	15.00	0	-15
1995	SEA	28	28	179	188	19	88	96	10	12	4.52	13.85	0	5

His G/F ratio last year was 1.00. That often can mean — and in his case does — that he's an extreme line-drive pitcher.

STAN BELINDA   Age 29   Bid: $4

Year	Team	G	GS	IP	H	HR	BB	SO	W	L	ERA	Ratio	Sv	$
1991	PIT	60	0	78	50	10	35	71	7	5	3.45	9.77	16	20
1992	PIT	59	0	71	58	8	29	57	6	4	3.15	10.98	18	20
1993	PIT/KC	63	0	70	65	6	17	55	4	2	3.88	10.59	19	18
1994	KC	37	0	49	47	6	24	37	2	2	5.14	13.04	1	1
1995	BOS	63	0	70	51	5	28	57	8	1	3.10	10.21	10	26

Perhaps more responsible than any other cast-off for Boston's success, Belinda was feeling it at the end (only 8 games in the last month).

ANDY BENES   Age 28   Bid: $14

Year	Team	G	GS	IP	H	HR	BB	SO	W	L	ERA	Ratio	Sv	$
1991	SD	33	33	223	194	23	59	167	15	11	3.03	10.21	0	23
1992	SD	34	34	231	230	14	61	169	13	14	3.35	11.32	0	11
1993	SD	34	34	231	200	23	86	179	15	15	3.78	11.16	0	18
1994	SD	25	25	172	155	20	51	189	6	14	3.86	10.76	0	16
1995	SD	19	19	119	121	10	45	126	4	7	4.17	12.59	0	1
1995	SEA	12	12	63	72	8	33	45	7	2	5.86	15.00	0	-2

To win seven games in 12 starts and lose money takes a lot of run support. On the season, counting the Padres, Benes got 6.04 runs each start, so he should have won more than he did.

A hard-thrower who still hasn't learned to pitch, even though he's been at it long enough for a PhD, will always get the big salary.

ARMANDO BENITEZ

Age 23   Bid: R1

Year	Team	G	GS	IP	H	HR	BB	SO	W	L	ERA	Ratio	Sv	$
1993	(A)	12	0	14	7	0	4	29	3	0	.66	7.07	4	x
1993	(A)	40	0	53	31	2	19	83	5	1	1.52	8.49	14	x
1994	(AA)	53	0	72	41	6	39	106	8	4	3.14	10.00	16	x
1994	BAL	3	0	10	8	0	4	14	0	0	.90	10.80	0	3
1995	BAL	44	0	48	37	8	37	56	1	5	5.66	13.97	2	-2
1995	(AAA)	17	0	22	10	2	7	37	2	2	1.25	6.95	8	x

Armando Benitez is living, breathing, sometimes weeping proof of something I've long suspected: the minor league managers and scouts who vote for Baseball America's top 10 prospects are front runners. Are you going to seriously tell me that Rey Ordonez (8) and Butch Huskey (10) belong ahead of Benitez in the International League? Look at that ratio! He had a 4-to-1 K's to *hits* rate.

    It's true that he threatened to quit the game after his rude treatment at the previous level. He was only 22. No one — not anybody — had shown him bad manners in the past. Don't you remember how you behaved the first time you were humiliated?

    I say: He'll be back. Unless he doesn't grow up.

JASON BERE

Age 25   Bid: $10

Year	Team	G	GS	IP	H	HR	BB	SO	W	L	ERA	Ratio	Sv	$
1993	(AAA)	8	8	49	36	1	25	52	5	1	2.37	11.20	0	x
1993	CHW	24	24	143	109	12	81	129	12	5	3.47	11.99	0	16
1994	CHW	24	24	142	119	17	80	127	12	2	3.81	12.64	0	22
1995	CHW	27	27	138	151	21	106	110	8	15	7.19	16.80	0	-26

Every outing was Friday the Thirteenth, you won't get to fully experience the sequel for much under $10.

SEAN BERGMAN

Age 26   Bid: R3

Year	Team	G	GS	IP	H	HR	BB	SO	W	L	ERA	Ratio	Sv	$
1993	DET	9	6	40	47	6	23	19	1	4	5.67	15.88	0	-6
1994	DET	3	3	18	22	2	7	12	2	1	5.60	14.77	0	0
1995	DET	28	28	135	169	19	67	86	7	10	5.12	15.69	0	-8

He had his problems, but the Tigers had more (5.49 team ERA).

JOE BOEVER   Age 35   Bid: R3

Year	Team	G	GS	IP	H	HR	BB	SO	W	L	ERA	Ratio	Sv	$
1991	PHI	68	0	98	90	10	54	89	3	5	3.84	13.18	0	-3
1992	HOU	81	0	111	103	3	45	67	3	6	2.51	11.96	2	6
1993	DET	61	0	102	101	9	44	63	6	3	3.61	12.75	3	9
1994	DET	46	0	81	80	12	37	49	9	2	3.98	12.95	3	16
1995	DET	60	0	99	128	17	44	71	5	7	6.39	15.69	3	-11

Buddy Bell will take any saver.

RODNEY BOLTON   Age 27   Bid: R3

Year	Team	G	GS	IP	H	HR	BB	SO	W	L	ERA	Ratio	Sv	$
1993	CHW	9	8	42	55	4	16	17	2	6	7.44	15.09	0	-8
1995	CHW	8	3	22	33	4	14	10	0	2	8.18	19.23	0	-9

One again, was very tough at Triple-A (14-3, 2.88 at Nashville). He never walks *anybody* in the minors, which could be the tip-off.

RICKEY BONES   Age 27   Bid: $2

Year	Team	G	GS	IP	H	HR	BB	SO	W	L	ERA	Ratio	Sv	$
1991	SD	11	11	54	57	3	18	31	4	6	4.83	12.50	0	-2
1992	MIL	31	28	163	169	27	48	65	9	10	4.57	11.96	0	2
1993	MIL	32	31	204	222	28	63	63	11	11	4.86	12.59	0	3
1994	MIL	24	24	171	166	17	45	57	10	9	3.43	11.13	0	33
1995	MIL	32	31	200	218	26	83	77	10	12	4.63	13.52	0	5

Bettors knocked his pay down to $9 last year, and may have been lucky to get $5 out of him. Truly alarming interior stats.

CHRIS BOSIO   Age 33   Bid: $2

Year	Team	G	GS	IP	H	HR	BB	SO	W	L	ERA	Ratio	Sv	$
1991	MIL	32	32	205	187	15	58	117	14	10	3.25	10.77	0	23
1992	MIL	33	33	231	223	21	44	120	16	6	3.62	10.39	0	24
1993	SEA	29	24	164	138	14	59	119	9	9	3.45	10.79	1	21
1994	SEA	19	19	125	137	15	40	67	4	10	4.32	12.74	0	8

Year	Team	G	GS	IP	H	HR	BB	SO	W	L	ERA	Ratio	Sv	$
1995	SEA	31	31	170	211	18	69	85	10	8	4.92	14.82	0	-3

I've been afraid of Bosio so long that he doesn't seem to frighten me anymore. On my preference list, I guess decimals will put him ahead of Bones.

SEAN BOSKIE   Age 29   Bid: $1

Year	Team	G	GS	IP	H	HR	BB	SO	W	L	ERA	Ratio	Sv	$
1991	CHC	28	20	129	150	14	52	62	4	9	5.23	14.09	0	-9
1992	CHC	23	18	92	96	14	36	39	5	11	5.01	12.91	0	-6
1993	CHC	39	2	66	63	7	21	39	5	3	3.43	11.51	0	6
1994	3 tms	22	15	91	92	15	30	61	4	7	5.06	12.03	0	-1
1995	CAL	20	20	112	127	16	25	51	7	7	5.64	12.25	0	2

The reason he gets a dollar bid instead of the much more prudent R3 is that he was 5-3 with a 3.72 ERA in April.
    You get the plan.

BILLY BREWER Age 28   Bid: R2

Year	Team	G	GS	IP	H	HR	BB	SO	W	L	ERA	Ratio	Sv	$
1993	KC	46	0	39	31	6	20	28	2	2	3.46	11.77	0	4
1994	KC	50	0	39	28	4	16	25	4	1	2.56	10.24	3	16
1995	KC	48	0	45	54	9	20	31	2	4	5.56	14.69	0	-3

What happened to him? Set-up men are out of vogue, with good reason.

KEVIN BROWN   Age 31   Bid: $19

Year	Team	G	GS	IP	H	HR	BB	SO	W	L	ERA	Ratio	Sv	$
1991	TEX	33	33	211	233	17	90	96	9	12	4.40	13.80	0	-5
1992	TEX	35	35	266	262	11	76	173	21	11	3.32	11.45	0	26
1993	TEX	34	34	233	228	14	74	142	15	12	3.59	11.67	0	23
1994	TEX	26	25	170	218	18	50	123	7	9	4.82	14.19	0	-1
1995	BAL	26	26	172	155	10	48	117	10	9	3.60	10.60	0	28

He and Erickson kept Cal busy: they were one, two in the league in G/F ratio (2.68 and 2.59 — phenomenal). They both were in the top five in GDP per 9 IP. You'd think, against those odds, managers would send base runners frequently, but only seven bases were stolen against Brown all year. Only Randy Johnson gave up fewer home runs per IP. Brown, as usual, had trouble getting started (7.11 ERA in April) and finished strong (2.42 the last month). The Orioles should do much better this year.

With all theses pluses, there are still too many minuses in his five-year scan to break the $20 barrier.

RAFAEL CARMONA   Age 23   Bid: R2

Year	Team	G	GS	IP	H	HR	BB	SO	W	L	ERA	Ratio	Sv	$
1994	(A)	50	0	67	48	3	19	63	8	2	2.81	9.00	21	x
1995	(AA)	15	0	15	11	0	3	17	0	1	1.80	8.40	4	x
1995	SEA	15	3	48	55	9	34	28	2	4	5.66	16.80	1	-6
1995	(AAA)	8	8	48	52	6	19	37	4	3	5.06	13.31	0	x

Terrific arm. Nothing goes straight. If he makes the team (as a reliever; experiment back in Triple-A was a bust), definitely worth a flyer.

TONY CASTILLO   Age 33   Bid: $3

Year	Team	G	GS	IP	H	HR	BB	SO	W	L	ERA	Ratio	Sv	$
1991	ATL/NY	17	3	32	40	4	11	18	2	1	3.34	14.20	0	-1
1993	TOR	51	0	51	44	4	22	28	3	2	3.38	11.72	0	6
1994	TOR	41	0	68	66	7	28	43	5	2	2.51	12.44	1	17
1995	TOR	55	0	73	64	7	24	38	1	5	3.22	10.90	13	20

Cito wore him out (4.38 ERA in August, 6.00 in September). Think set-up man, even if you're secretly thinking closer by default.

NORM CHARLTON   Age 33   Bid: $33

Year	Team	G	GS	IP	H	HR	BB	SO	W	L	ERA	Ratio	Sv	$
1991	CIN	39	11	108	92	6	34	77	3	5	2.91	10.47	1	9
1992	CIN	64	0	81	79	7	26	90	4	2	2.99	11.62	26	24
1993	SEA	34	0	35	22	4	17	48	1	3	2.34	10.13	18	17
1995	PHI	25	0	22	23	2	15	12	2	5	7.36	15.55	0	-5
1995	SEA	30	0	48	23	2	16	58	2	1	1.51	7.36	14	29

Closer big-time!

I saw him in Florida. He looked great. Got pounded right out of Philly. What do I know?

It must have been control — or command, as they say now.

It's not possible to be any better than he was at Seattle; it's really not. Even Eckerlsey was never any better than that. You can see it, just looking at the interior stats.

Counting Philly, the batting average against him was .189, the slugging average .263.

MIKE CHRISTOPHER Age 32   Bid: R2

Year	Team	G	GS	IP	H	HR	BB	SO	W	L	ERA	Ratio	Sv	$
1991	LA	3	0	4	2	0	3	2	0	0	.00	11.25	0	1
1992	CLE	10	0	18	17	2	10	13	0	0	3.00	13.50	0	0
1993	CLE	9	0	12	14	3	2	8	0	0	3.86	12.34	0	0
1995	DET	36	0	61	71	8	14	34	4	0	3.82	12.47	1	8

Everyone will say: Don't pay any attention to his minor league record (2.23 ERA, 21 saves at Toledo); journeymen often are closers in Triple-A. I don't disagree — that's why he's an R2.

But perhaps we should pay attention to his major league record. He actually pitched enough for the Tigers to qualify in the various categories: no one allowed fewer inherited runners to score.

MARK CLARK Age 28   Bid: $7

Year	Team	G	GS	IP	H	HR	BB	SO	W	L	ERA	Ratio	Sv	$
1991	STL	7	2	22	17	3	11	13	1	1	4.03	11.29	0	0
1992	STL	20	20	113	117	12	36	44	3	10	4.45	12.15	0	-5
1993	CLE	26	15	109	119	18	25	57	7	5	4.28	11.85	0	7
1994	CLE	20	20	127	133	14	40	60	11	3	3.82	12.23	0	22
1995	CLE	22	21	125	143	13	42	68	9	7	5.27	13.36	0	2

His only sin, really, was to give up 10more hits than last year, for which he seems to have been unduly punished.

ROGER CLEMENS Age 33   Bid: $23

Year	Team	G	GS	IP	H	HR	BB	SO	W	L	ERA	Ratio	Sv	$
1991	BOS	35	35	271	219	15	65	241	18	10	2.62	9.42	0	44
1992	BOS	32	32	247	203	11	62	208	18	11	2.41	9.67	0	42
1993	BOS	29	29	192	175	17	67	160	11	14	4.46	11.36	0	12
1994	BOS	24	24	171	124	15	71	168	9	7	2.85	10.28	0	42
1995	BOS	23	23	140	141	15	60	132	10	5	4.18	12.92	0	12

Thanks to the pricing system, Hall of Fame numbers are still clearly there in three of the last five years. He can earn $30 again.

DAVID CONE   Age 33   Bid: $27

Year	Team	G	GS	IP	H	HR	BB	SO	W	L	ERA	Ratio	Sv	$
1991	NYM	34	34	233	204	13	73	241	14	14	3.29	10.72	0	17
1992	NY/TOR	35	34	250	201	15	111	261	17	10	2.81	11.25	0	22
1993	KC	34	34	254	205	20	114	191	11	14	3.33	11.30	0	25
1994	KC	23	23	172	130	15	54	132	16	5	2.94	9.65	0	53
1995	TOR/NY	30	30	229	195	24	88	191	18	8	3.57	11.11	0	38

The 10 pitchers who were expected to be the best last year weren't quite as good as the 10 who were in fact the best (Aguilera comment), but they still earned more than the market paid for them!

Top 10 salaries, AL pitchers

Name	earned 1995	avg sal	+/-	Heath Data Pts	Rk	- touts - AP	JH	$94
WETTELAND,J	39	38	1	50.6	85	42	28	37
HERNANDEZ,R	28	34	-6	59.7	3	31	32	18
AYALA,B	20	32	-12	55.2	24	33	25	31
MONTGOMERY,J	32	31	1	54.4	32	37	26	28
MUSSINA,M	50	30	20	56.3	19	28	27	48
AGUILERA,R	39	29	10	57.4	11	25	24	23
CONE,D	38	27	11	56.4	18	26	33	53
RYAN,K	1	27	-25	52.2	62	29	23	22
JOHNSON,R	58	26	31	57.6	10	28	26	41
SMITH,L	32	26	7	48.6	100	24	20	37
average	34	30	4	54.8	36	30	26	34

These are all the pitchers that the three leagues in Appendix A saw fit to pay at least $26 for. That they earned $34 the year before is not at all surprising; the market always bets against stellar repeat performances, even by hitters, and where pitchers are involved, the betting can get downright disrespectful. Cone earned $53 with the Royals and is now playing for the Blue Jays? Bully for him. He'll probably get traded to the Yankees.

In 1994 auctions, the 10 most expensive hitters also happened to earn $34 the year before. They cost an average of $29 in the auctions and earned an average of $23. We can infer that the market wasn't sorry about that result from the fact that it managed to pay just a little bit more for the expected 10 best pitchers last year.

The "won-lost" measurement that was used in last year's book (too few leagues for that this year; ah, the strike) showed eight of the 10 most expensive pitchers with winning records, Aguilera breaking even, and only Duane Ward dragging his teams down into the depths of the second division.

The break-even point in the current tracking method is 52 points; only Wetteland and Autry's Angel fall below it. Somehow, Ken Ryan's owners managed to finish in the first division. The group all told ranked only two places lower than the 10 best actual pitchers, and teams that were willing to pay the price for at least one of these pitchers finished no worse than fourth (36/129 x 12).

RHEAL CORMIER   Age 29   Bid: $1

Year	Team	G	GS	IP	H	HR	BB	SO	W	L	ERA	Ratio	Sv	$
1991	STL	11	10	68	74	5	8	38	4	5	4.12	10.91	0	2
1992	STL	31	30	186	194	15	33	117	10	10	3.68	10.98	0	7
1993	STL	38	21	145	163	18	27	75	7	6	4.33	11.77	0	4
1994	STL	7	7	40	40	6	7	26	3	2	5.45	10.66	0	2
1995	BOS	48	12	115	131	12	31	69	7	5	4.07	12.68	0	10

Right-handed batters hit .305 against him, which equates into a 4.86 ERA in his 12 starts (lucky at that). But Cormier earned his play-off ring if only for coming into 8 games on 0 Days rest — no doubt to deal with a succession of left-handed batters in a desperate situation — and giving up 8 hits, 2 walks and 0 earned runs in 13.2 IP. For that he got no saves and one loss.

DANNY COX   Age 36   Bid: R3

Year	Team	G	GS	IP	H	HR	BB	SO	W	L	ERA	Ratio	Sv	$
1991	PHI	23	17	102	98	14	39	46	4	6	4.57	12.05	0	-3
1992	PIT	25	7	63	66	5	27	48	5	3	4.60	13.36	3	-1
1993	TOR	44	0	84	73	8	29	84	7	6	3.12	10.97	2	15
1994	TOR	10	0	19	7	0	7	14	1	1	1.45	6.75	3	12
1995	TOR	24	0	45	57	4	33	38	1	3	7.40	18.00	0	-13

If he hasn't packed it in, he's worth a stab in Ultra leagues.

ROB DIBBLE   Age 32   Bid: R3

Year	Team	G	GS	IP	H	HR	BB	SO	W	L	ERA	Ratio	Sv	$
1991	CIN	67	0	82	67	5	25	124	3	5	3.17	10.06	31	27
1992	CIN	63	0	70	48	3	31	110	3	5	3.07	10.11	25	25
1993	CIN	45	0	42	34	8	42	49	1	4	6.48	16.42	19	1
1995	MIL	31	0	26	16	2	46	26	1	2	7.18	21.19	1	-9

In Rob Dibble's mind, he's no R3. He doesn't understand that I'm saying he's still got a chance.

So do lots of pitchers, so there are just a ton of R3's in the next chapter, many more than are profiled. Do you like Cox's chances better than Dibble's?

No problem, then, because the R3's are listed alphabetically. The software program (details in the PS) allows more refined secondary sorts. You can, in effect, give the R categories decimals.

You can give the bids decimals. Even the zero bids (a few of which are listed in the next chapter; there are plenty in the software) can have decimals. Both categories, the R3's and zero bids, are so large that maybe the best thing to do is list them alphabetically — so you can find them — then have a preference stated in the comment field that can be printed with your lists. A comment such as, "1993 Cox?" Can't make it too long.

The only preference that can't be expressed is your preference for players that aren't listed at all.

JOHN DOHERTY   Age 29   Bid: $2

Year	Team	G	GS	IP	H	HR	BB	SO	W	L	ERA	Ratio	Sv	$
1992	SD	15	15	96	92	6	33	46	4	7	3.28	11.72	0	3
1992	DET	47	11	116	131	4	25	37	7	4	3.88	12.10	3	7
1993	DET	32	31	185	205	19	48	63	14	11	4.44	12.33	0	10
1994	DET	18	17	101	139	13	26	28	6	7	6.48	14.65	0	-11
1995	DET	48	2	113	130	10	37	46	5	9	5.10	13.30	6	5

Was 6-for-9 in save opportunities. Came right at them: first-batter on-base percentage was lowest in the league, .049.

The second batter must have seen something.

DENNIS ECKERSLEY   Age 40   Bid: $22

Year	Team	G	GS	IP	H	HR	BB	SO	W	L	ERA	Ratio	Sv	$
1991	OAK	67	0	76	60	11	9	87	5	4	2.96	8.17	43	41
1992	OAK	69	0	80	62	5	11	93	7	1	1.91	8.21	51	51
1993	OAK	64	0	67	67	7	13	80	2	4	4.16	10.75	36	27
1994	OAK	45	0	44	49	5	13	47	5	4	4.26	12.59	19	24
1995	OAK	52	0	50	53	5	11	40	4	6	4.83	11.44	29	28

Had nine blown saves (second to Roberto Hernandez). Left-handed batters slugged .504. Was all over the place, month by month (1.93 ERA in August, 11.05 in September). LaRussa's gone.

And he's still the Eck.

CAL ELDRED   Age 28   Bid: $6

Year	Team	G	GS	IP	H	HR	BB	SO	W	L	ERA	Ratio	Sv	$
1991	MIL	3	3	16	20	2	6	10	2	0	4.50	14.63	0	0
1992	MIL	14	14	100	76	4	23	62	11	2	1.79	8.88	0	26
1993	MIL	36	36	258	232	32	91	180	16	16	4.01	11.27	0	23
1994	MIL	25	25	179	158	23	84	98	11	11	4.68	12.17	0	16
1995	MIL	4	4	24	24	4	10	18	1	1	3.42	12.93	0	2

"Torn ligament in right elbow" doesn't mean curtains anymore.

ALAN EMBREE   Age 26   Bid: $4

Year	Team	G	GS	IP	H	HR	BB	SO	W	L	ERA	Ratio	Sv	$
1992	CLE	4	4	18	19	3	8	12	0	2	7.00	13.50	0	-3
1995	CLE	23	0	25	23	2	16	23	3	2	5.11	14.23	1	2

His stats were ruined by an atrocious tune-up for the play-offs (6 ER in two-thirds of an inning against the Twins, in case you didn't have him). Hard-throwing lefties out of the pen are almost an extinct species.

SCOTT ERICKSON   Age 28   Bid: $8

Year	Team	G	GS	IP	H	HR	BB	SO	W	L	ERA	Ratio	Sv	$
1991	MIN	32	32	204	189	13	71	108	20	8	3.18	11.47	0	25
1992	MIN	32	32	212	197	18	83	101	13	12	3.40	11.89	0	15
1993	MIN	34	34	219	266	17	71	116	8	19	5.19	13.87	0	-10
1994	MIN	23	23	144	173	15	59	104	8	11	5.44	14.50	0	-5
1995	BAL	32	31	196	213	18	67	106	13	10	4.81	12.84	0	10

Was 9-4 with a 3.89 ERA with the Orioles; 4-0, 1.47 ERA the last month. Completed a career-high 7 games. As the pitch count went up, the batting average against him went down (.230 after 91 pitches, .217 after 106). Like Brown, he was hard to run on (only 10 SB), even though there was plenty of incentive to try (third highest GDP rate in the league).

Bid might go higher in the update, once I've had a chance to absorb all this.

VAUGN ESHELMAN   Age 28   Bid: R1

Year	Team	G	GS	IP	H	HR	BB	SO	W	L	ERA	Ratio	Sv	$
1994	(AA)	27	25	166	175	13	60	133	11	9	4.00	12.72	0	x
1995	BOS	23	14	82	86	3	36	41	6	3	4.85	13.44	0	3
1995	(AA)	2	2	7	3	0	0	7	0	1	.00	3.86	0	x

He was so good when he was good — and wasn't all that bad when he came back to the Red Sox (3.19 ERA in 12 games) — that I'd take maybe a $3 shot at him if he makes the team.

ALEX FERNANDEZ   Age 26   Bid: $25

Year	Team	G	GS	IP	H	HR	BB	SO	W	L	ERA	Ratio	Sv	$
1991	CHW	34	32	192	186	16	88	145	9	13	4.51	12.87	0	-1
1992	CHW	29	29	188	199	21	50	95	8	11	4.27	11.94	0	3
1993	CHW	34	34	247	221	27	67	169	18	9	3.13	10.48	0	38

Year	Team	G	GS	IP	H	HR	BB	SO	W	L	ERA	Ratio	Sv	$
1994	CHW	24	24	170	163	25	50	122	11	7	3.86	11.25	0	**29**
1995	CHW	30	30	204	200	19	65	159	12	8	3.80	11.71	0	**25**

How many teams owned both Appier and Fernandez? I'd love to know. Did anyone trade Appier *for* Fernandez? Say, at the All-Star break? Puckett and give me Alex Fernandez for Appier.

It happened somewhere. It's not a fantasy.

MIKE FETTERS Age 31

Bid: $12

Year	Team	G	GS	IP	H	HR	BB	SO	W	L	ERA	Ratio	Sv	$
1991	CAL	19	4	45	53	4	28	24	2	5	4.84	16.32	0	**-5**
1992	MIL	50	0	63	38	3	24	43	5	1	1.87	8.90	2	**16**
1993	MIL	45	0	59	59	4	22	23	3	3	3.34	12.29	0	**5**
1994	MIL	42	0	46	41	0	27	31	1	4	2.54	13.30	17	**22**
1995	MIL	40	0	35	40	3	20	33	0	3	3.38	15.58	22	**16**

Before the All-Star break, a 1.72 ERA and 10 saves; after it, a 4.74 ERA and 12 saves. Push the bid up if he looks good in spring training, but don't forget.

CHUCK FINLEY Age 33

Bid: $17

Year	Team	G	GS	IP	H	HR	BB	SO	W	L	ERA	Ratio	Sv	$
1991	CAL	34	34	227	205	23	101	171	18	9	3.80	12.11	0	**15**
1992	CAL	31	31	204	212	24	98	124	7	12	3.96	13.65	0	**-3**
1993	CAL	35	35	251	243	22	82	187	16	14	3.15	11.64	0	**29**
1994	CAL	25	25	183	178	21	71	148	10	10	4.32	12.22	0	**19**
1995	CAL	32	32	203	192	20	93	195	15	12	4.21	12.64	0	**19**

Besides the last week, when he won two games in five days to get the Angels into the playoff, there were three other games in which he started with less than four days rest. In the four combined, allowed 14 hits and 11 walks in 23 innings, and gave up 2 earned runs.

The run-support for Finley was an Angelic 6.65, and yet he still managed to get pinned with 4 Tough Losses, second in the league behind Jack McDowell. On 5/23 against the Yankees, he produced the Top Game Score of the Year, according to Bill James, meaning on that day he was so hot he would have beaten Randy Johnson.

BRIAN GIVENS Age 30

Bid: R1

Year	Team	G	GS	IP	H	HR	BB	SO	W	L	ERA	Ratio	Sv	$
1994	(AA)	36	13	110	103	8	52	111	4	7	3.68	12.68	1	**x**

Year	Team	G	GS	IP	H	HR	BB	SO	W	L	ERA	Ratio	Sv	$
1995	(AAA)	16	11	78	67	2	33	75	7	4	2.55	11.54	0	x
1995	MIL	19	19	107	116	11	54	73	5	7	4.95	14.25	0	-2

Hitting R1's are studs. The problem is, they're not in the majors.

Pitching R1's are many times pitchers that you can buy for $1 at the auction, but you don't dare. As soon as you can tuck them safely away on your reserve list, that's what you should do.

Tell yourself to lay off the hitting R1's, even though it's hard.

TOM GORDON   Age 28   Bid: $6

Year	Team	G	GS	IP	H	HR	BB	SO	W	L	ERA	Ratio	Sv	$
1991	KC	45	14	158	129	16	87	167	9	14	3.87	12.30	1	7
1992	KC	40	11	118	116	9	55	98	6	10	4.59	13.08	0	-2
1993	KC	48	14	156	125	11	77	143	12	6	3.58	11.68	1	18
1994	KC	24	24	155	136	15	87	126	11	7	4.35	12.92	0	15
1995	KC	31	31	189	204	12	89	119	12	12	4.43	13.95	0	7

The best tip in the book: drop Flash Gordon before the final week. This time he had a 3.97 ERA going into it.

JEFF GRANGER   Age 24   Bid: R2

Year	Team	G	GS	IP	H	HR	BB	SO	W	L	ERA	Ratio	Sv	$
1993	(A)	8	7	36	28	2	10	56	3	3	3.00	9.50	0	x
1993	KC	1	0	1	3	0	2	1	0	0	27.00	45.00	0	-2
1994	(AA)	25	25	140	155	8	61	112	7	7	3.87	13.89	0	x
1994	KC	2	2	9	13	2	6	3	0	1	6.75	18.32	0	-3
1995	(AA)	18	18	96	122	9	40	81	4	7	5.93	15.19	0	x

Pitched in Wichita last season; as we see, with miserable results. But he's young and a lefty.

KEVIN GROSS   Age 35   Bid: $4

Year	Team	G	GS	IP	H	HR	BB	SO	W	L	ERA	Ratio	Sv	$
1991	LA	46	10	116	123	10	50	95	10	11	3.58	13.46	3	4
1992	LA	34	30	205	182	11	77	158	8	13	3.17	11.39	0	8
1993	LA	33	32	202	224	15	74	150	13	13	4.14	13.26	0	2
1994	LA	25	23	157	162	11	43	124	9	7	3.60	11.73	1	17

Year	Team	G	GS	IP	H	HR	BB	SO	W	L	ERA	Ratio	Sv	$
1995	TEX	31	30	184	200	27	89	106	9	15	5.54	14.16	0	-7

The average pitcher is worth $8.67. Gross seems bound and determined to be worth about that, on average, when his career is over.

EDDIE GUARDADO Age 25 Bid: R3

Year	Team	G	GS	IP	H	HR	BB	SO	W	L	ERA	Ratio	Sv	$
1993	MIN	19	16	95	123	13	36	46	3	8	6.18	15.12	0	-13
1994	MIN	4	4	17	26	3	4	8	0	2	8.47	15.88	0	-6
1995	MIN	51	5	91	99	13	45	71	4	9	5.12	14.19	2	-1

Has some hope as a reliever (3.86 ERA) but not as Aguilera.

MARK GUBICZA Age 33 Bid: $5

Year	Team	G	GS	IP	H	HR	BB	SO	W	L	ERA	Ratio	Sv	$
1991	KC	26	26	133	168	10	42	89	9	12	5.68	14.21	0	-10
1992	KC	18	18	111	110	8	36	81	7	6	3.72	11.80	0	7
1993	KC	49	6	104	128	2	43	80	5	8	4.66	14.75	2	-3
1994	KC	22	22	130	158	11	26	59	7	9	4.50	12.74	0	10
1995	KC	33	33	213	222	21	62	81	12	14	3.75	11.98	0	24

Does Mark Gubicza still play for the Royals? Is he only 33?

The Baseball Weekly league rescued him from the Rotisserie version of the Homestead Homeless, paying $1 for him on April 18. When the American Dreams convened on April 23, just before the start of the season, Gubicza was ignored. When Cowtown met on April 29, even though Gubicza started the Royals' second game and only gave up two runs in four innings, he was overlooked. By the time Ashpole met on May 9, he had a 1-2 record and 5.27 ERA; Ashpole forked out a dollar.

```
            Top 10 profits, AL pitchers
                  earned avg          Heath Data    - touts -
      Name        1995   sal  +/-      Pts    Rk    AP   JH   | $94
      MESA,J        57     3   54      62.2    2     4    8   |  16
      JOHNSON,R     58    26   31      57.6   10    28   26   |  41
      BELINDA,S     26     0   26      58.7    7     1    6   |   1
      TAVAREZ,J     26     1   25      54.2   36    R1        |  -4
      GUBICZA,M     24     0   24      53.8   42     1    4   |  10
      NELSON,J      26     2   24      52.7   56     3    6   |   7
      ROGERS,K      35    12   23      57.8    9     9   16   |  20
      WELLS,D       27     4   23      59.1    6     9   14   |  17
      PERCIVAL,T    27     4   23      56.5   15    R1        |
      HERSHISER,O   30     8   22      53.6   46     7   12   |   7
        average     34     6   28      56.6   23     6    9   |  12
```

Stan Belinda also had an average salary of 33 cents (rescued again by Baseball Weekly). By May 9, however, he was a hot property and Ashpole ran him up to $10.

Interestingly, the three non-freeze leagues each pay the same amount for these sleepers, even though they pick different ones:

AL pitchers	— leagues —				
	BW	ADL	COW	ASH	f
MESA,J	1	5	2	1	f
JOHNSON,R	20	31	28	15	f
BELINDA,S	1			10	
TAVAREZ,J		2		1	
GUBICZA,M	1			1	
NELSON,J	3		3	4	f
ROGERS,K	12	10	13	1	f
WELLS,D	3	3	6	1	f
PERCIVAL,T	4	3	5		
HERSHISER,O	10	9	5	4	
average	6	6	6	4	

The freeze lists in Ashpole finally start to kick in.

John Hunt absolutely cleans house here. Head-to-head with me, he gets every pitcher except Randy Johnson. In fact, in a six-way competition that includes all four leagues, the only other pitchers he loses out on are Belinda (to Ashpole), Tavarez (to the ADL) and Percival (to Cowtown). Hunt even outbids 1994 for one of these pitchers (Hershiser), which is really letting it hang out.

Can he afford them? Well, since he's been taking a pass on virtually all of the high-priced players so far, he's got plenty of money left. If these are his first six purchases, his pitching staff so far looks like this (topping the next highest bid): Rogers $14, Hershiser $11, Wells $10, Gubicza $2, Nelson $4 and Mesa $6. Total: $47.

Wow!

JUAN GUZMAN   Age 29   Bid: $4

Year	Team	G	GS	IP	H	HR	BB	SO	W	L	ERA	Ratio	Sv	$
1991	TOR	23	23	139	98	6	66	123	10	3	2.99	10.64	0	19
1992	TOR	28	28	181	135	6	72	165	16	5	2.64	10.31	0	29
1993	TOR	33	33	221	211	17	110	194	14	3	3.99	13.07	0	10
1994	TOR	25	25	147	165	20	76	124	12	11	5.68	14.72	0	-4
1995	TOR	24	24	135	151	13	73	94	4	14	6.32	14.90	0	-16

Trouble is, John's also got a few pitchers from this group:

Top 10 losses, AL pitchers

Name	earned 1995	avg sal	+/-	Heath Data Pts	Rk	— touts — AP	JH	$94
KEY,J	-2	25	-27	49.1	96	22	23	36
GUZMAN,Ju	-16	10	-26	43.1	128	5	24	-4
RYAN,K	1	27	-25	52.2	62	29	23	22
HENTGEN,P	-5	19	-25	50.6	87	24	20	37
WARD,D	-7	13	-20	49.8	94	12	18	
BENITEZ,A	-2	17	-19	47.4	108	12	9	3
DARWIN,D	-18	0	-18	45.4	121	R3	3	-5
BALDWIN,J	-13	3	-16	51.5	76	R1		
ALVAREZ,W	6	21	-15	52.2	61	21	19	31
FERNANDEZ,S	-8	7	-15	50.0	92	9	13	7
average	-6	14	-21	49.1	93	13	15	13

Head-to-head, he gets Key, Guzman, Ward, Darwin and Sid. And he's even willing to pay $2 more for this group, on average, than it earned the previous year.

The leagues that he would be battling in the six-way competition:

		— leagues —			
AL pitchers	BW	ADL	COW	ASH	f
KEY,J	22	29	25	25	
GUZMAN,Ju	10	8	11	17	f
RYAN,K	22	27	31	8	f
HENTGEN,P	17	25	16	11	f
WARD,D	9	15	14	17	f
BENITEZ,A	11	18	22	6	f
DARWIN,D	1				
BALDWIN,J		2	8		
ALVAREZ,W	17	23	23	13	
FERNANDEZ,S	7	9	4	10	f
average	13	17	17	13	

So he would have gotten Guzman and Ward, both for $18, and Sid for $14. Nine pitchers, $97. It's still a good staff.

The 10 biggest bargains shown in the previous comment have their hitting counterparts in the Cora comment. The comparisons are interesting. The pitchers cost only a dollar less, so from that standpoint they were only slightly bigger surprises. However, they earned $7 more each — making them much more pleasant surprises to the people who bought them — and had a bigger impact, as a result, on the standings. Teams that drafted even one of these pitchers finished second (23/129 x 12).

The corresponding hitter flops were seen in the Delgado comment. Costing a full $10 more than the pitcher flops, they softened the blow considerably by earning $12 more than the pitchers did.

That's not to say the pitchers earned ($6) for each team that bought them; a guess would be they earned ($2) or even ($3) as free agents, after they were fired. They had done their damage already, though. Teams that drafted even one of *these* pitchers finished ninth (93/129 x 12).

DARREN HALL   Age 31   Bid: R1

Year	Team	G	GS	IP	H	HR	BB	SO	W	L	ERA	Ratio	Sv	$
1993	(AAA)	60	0	79	75	10	31	68	6	7	5.33	12.03	13	x
1994	TOR	30	0	32	26	3	14	28	2	3	3.41	11.37	17	21
1994	(AAA)	6	0	6	5	0	2	7	1	0	1.59	11.12	3	x
1995	TOR	17	0	16	21	2	9	11	0	2	4.41	16.53	3	0

Clearly, he's not an R1 if he's healthy, because he'll make the team. Then we'll have to bid on him, which will be painful.

I'll take him to $7, making sure Castillo, Timlin and others pay for it.

CHRIS HANEY   Age 27   Bid: R3

Year	Team	G	GS	IP	H	HR	BB	SO	W	L	ERA	Ratio	Sv	$
1991	MON	16	16	85	94	6	43	51	3	7	4.04	14.56	0	-6
1992	MON/KC	16	13	80	75	11	26	54	4	6	4.61	11.36	2	0

Year	Team	G	GS	IP	H	HR	BB	SO	W	L	ERA	Ratio	Sv	$
1993	KC	23	23	124	141	13	53	65	9	9	6.02	14.08	0	-8
1994	KC	6	6	28	36	2	11	18	2	2	7.31	14.93	0	-5
1995	KC	16	13	81	78	7	33	31	3	4	3.65	12.28	0	8

Item by item comparison of his 1995 stats with his 1992 combined stats shows how fortunate he was last year, how hopeless he is now. He does get lefties out (.184 batting average against) and he did give up no runs in his three relief appearances (7 innings), so that's where his future lies.

ERIK HANSON   Age 31   Bid: $14

Year	Team	G	GS	IP	H	HR	BB	SO	W	L	ERA	Ratio	Sv	$
1991	SEA	27	27	175	182	16	56	143	8	8	3.81	12.26	0	6
1992	SEA	31	30	187	209	14	57	112	8	17	4.82	12.83	0	-5
1993	SEA	31	30	215	215	17	60	163	11	12	3.47	11.51	0	21
1994	CIN	22	21	123	137	10	23	101	5	5	4.11	11.74	0	7
1995	BOS	29	29	187	187	17	59	139	15	5	4.24	11.86	0	22

Without being able to throw his vaunted curve ball in the second half, he still won eight games. Price assumes his curve will be back in the repertoire.

LATROY HAWKINS Age 23   Bid: $1

Year	Team	G	GS	IP	H	HR	BB	SO	W	L	ERA	Ratio	Sv	$
1993	(A)	26	23	157	110	5	41	179	15	5	2.06	8.66	0	x
1994	(A)	6	6	39	32	1	6	36	4	0	2.33	8.77	0	x
1994	(AA)	11	11	73	50	2	28	53	9	2	2.33	9.62	0	x
1994	(AAA)	12	12	82	92	8	33	37	5	4	4.08	13.72	0	x
1995	MIN	6	6	27	39	3	12	9	2	3	8.67	17.00	0	-8
1995	(AAA)	22	22	144	150	7	40	74	9	7	3.55	11.88	0	x

Youth is on his side. Aspirin will be at ours.

JIMMY HAYNES   Age 23   Bid: $7

Year	Team	G	GS	IP	H	HR	BB	SO	W	L	ERA	Ratio	Sv	$
1993	(A)	27	27	172	139	13	61	174	12	8	3.03	10.47	0	x
1994	(AA)	25	25	174	154	16	46	177	13	8	2.90	10.34	0	x
1994	(AAA)	3	3	13	20	3	6	14	1	0	6.75	18.00	0	x

Year	Team	G	GS	IP	H	HR	BB	SO	W	L	ERA	Ratio	Sv	$
1995	(AAA)	26	25	167	162	16	49	140	12	8	3.29	11.37	0	x
1995	BAL	4	3	24	11	2	12	22	2	1	2.25	8.63	0	8

Might well be seven times better than Latroy, and still be a minus.

DWAYNE HENRY   Age 34   Bid: R3

Year	Team	G	GS	IP	H	HR	BB	SO	W	L	ERA	Ratio	Sv	$
1991	HOU	52	0	68	51	7	39	51	3	2	3.19	11.97	2	4
1992	CIN	60	0	84	59	4	44	72	3	3	3.33	11.08	0	3
1993	SEA	31	1	55	56	6	35	35	2	1	6.67	14.89	2	6
1993	CIN	3	0	5	6	0	4	2	0	1	3.86	19.29	0	-1
1995	DET	10	0	9	11	0	10	9	1	0	6.23	21.81	5	2

Only Sparky could talk a player like this into being 5-for-5 in save opportunities. Plus Dwayne won one game.

Those other four games counted in stat leagues.

PAT HENTGEN   Age 27   Bid: $13

Year	Team	G	GS	IP	H	HR	BB	SO	W	L	ERA	Ratio	Sv	$
1991	TOR	3	1	7	5	1	3	3	0	0	2.46	9.82	0	1
1992	TOR	28	2	50	49	7	32	39	5	2	5.36	14.48	0	-3
1993	TOR	34	32	216	215	27	74	122	19	9	3.87	12.02	0	21
1994	TOR	24	24	175	158	21	59	147	13	8	3.40	11.18	0	37
1995	TOR	30	30	201	236	24	90	135	10	14	5.11	14.62	0	-5

Dollar Bill Berensmann and I first went to Florida in 1982 to find some players for a paper team we were already calling Moose Factory — after a town on James Bay that was the birthplace of Bill's dog — which would be our entry in some sort of gambling game that had been partially explained to us by near-total strangers who called themselves the American Dreams and who were somewhat candid about the fact that the first season of this game had been so vicious that there were a number of openings. Dollar and I didn't even know each other that well, but we became familiar with each others quirks as we drove all over Florida, buying ticket at the gate, settling in among the old-timers in perfect seats, sun or shade, and watching more live baseball in a week than either of us had in a decade.

We bought George Wright for $1 in the auction, which was then misnamed a draft, and triggered a stampede of Dreamers to Florida the following spring. For several years after that, we could spot each other easily and even sit together, if we wanted to. However, by 1994 even Dollar's organizational skills were being put to the test, just getting us to and into the ball games that we wanted to see.

Last-year was a throw-back to the early 80's. Hardly any traffic; tickets at the gate; any seat in the house after the first inning. We saw pitcher after pitcher from right behind the screen — could see the spin, hear it even, and track the movement on the fastball, the break on the slider, etc. Nobody impressed us more than Pat Hentgen.

I put a $24 bid on him in the update (two critical dollars more than the price in the book) and, son of a gun, if he didn't go for $25 in the American Dreams League. He threw 8 shutout innings in his first start and the team that bought him — our old and staunch rivals, the Tooners —commenced its fire sale in June.

ROBERTO HERNANDEZ   Age 31   Bid: $28

Year	Team	G	GS	IP	H	HR	BB	SO	W	L	ERA	Ratio	Sv	$
1991	CHW	9	3	15	18	1	7	6	1	0	7.80	15.00	0	-3
1992	CHW	43	0	71	45	4	20	68	7	3	1.65	8.24	12	27
1993	CHW	70	0	79	66	6	20	71	3	4	2.29	9.84	38	38
1994	CHW	45	0	48	44	5	19	50	4	4	4.91	11.90	14	18
1995	CHW	60	0	60	63	9	28	84	3	7	3.92	13.73	32	28

Won't be the same as last year; it's 50-50 he'll go $10 in either direction.

OREL HERSHISER   Age 37   Bid: $20

Year	Team	G	GS	IP	H	HR	BB	SO	W	L	ERA	Ratio	Sv	$
1991	LA	21	21	112	112	3	32	73	7	2	3.46	11.57	0	6
1992	LA	33	33	211	209	15	69	130	10	15	3.67	11.88	0	3
1993	LA	33	33	216	201	17	72	141	12	14	3.59	11.39	0	16
1994	LA	21	21	135	146	15	42	72	6	6	3.79	12.50	0	7
1995	CLE	26	26	167	151	21	51	111	16	6	3.87	10.86	0	30

It's now an argument whether he or Bob Gibson has been the greatest post-season pitcher ever. Did Orel look fit or what? It was as if he had run up to have his picture taken behind one of those cardboard cut-outs at a fair. When Eddie Murray pointed his finger at Greg Maddux after some chin music and benches cleared, Orel climbed the mound to share a laugh with Maddux: two choir boys snickering.

KEN HILL Age 30   Bid: $12

Year	Team	G	GS	IP	H	HR	BB	SO	W	L	ERA	Ratio	Sv	$
1991	STL	30	30	181	147	15	67	121	11	10	3.57	10.62	0	12
1992	MON	33	33	218	187	9	75	150	16	9	2.68	10.82	0	22
1993	MON	28	28	184	163	7	74	90	9	7	3.23	11.61	0	14
1994	MTL	23	23	155	145	12	44	85	16	5	3.32	11.00	0	31

Year	Team	G	GS	IP	H	HR	BB	SO	W	L	ERA	Ratio	Sv	$
1995	STL	18	18	110	125	16	45	50	6	7	5.06	13.87	0	-6
1995	CLE	12	11	75	77	5	32	48	4	1	3.98	13.14	0	5

Gave the Indians a boost, and the other way around, but remained far off form, even allowing for the DH.

STERLING HITCHCOCK   Age 25   Bid: $5

Year	Team	G	GS	IP	H	HR	BB	SO	W	L	ERA	Ratio	Sv	$
1992	NYY	3	3	13	23	2	6	6	0	2	8.31	20.08	0	-6
1993	NYY	6	6	31	32	4	14	26	1	2	4.65	13.35	0	-1
1994	NYY	23	5	49	48	3	29	37	4	1	4.20	14.05	2	6
1995	NYY	27	27	168	155	22	68	121	11	10	4.70	11.92	0	14

The difference between Hitchcock and Pettite, according to one of the Yankee co-owners, is that when Darryl Strawberry or Ruben Sierra butchers a ball in the outfield, Hitchcock despairs and Pettite says, "I shouldn't have let them hit it that hard."

RICK HONEYCUTT   Age 42   Bid: R3

Year	Team	G	GS	IP	H	HR	BB	SO	W	L	ERA	Ratio	Sv	$
1991	OAK	43	0	38	37	3	20	26	2	4	3.58	13.62	0	1
1992	OAK	54	0	39	41	2	10	32	1	4	3.69	11.77	3	3
1993	OAK	52	0	42	30	2	20	21	1	4	2.81	10.80	1	6
1994	TEX	42	0	25	37	4	9	18	1	2	7.20	16.56	1	-6
1995	OAK/NY	52	0	46	39	6	10	21	5	1	2.96	9.66	2	15

Did his job: lefties slugged .202 against him. Should not have tried to do someone else's: righties slugged .531.

STEVE HOWE   Age 38   Bid: R3

Year	Team	G	GS	IP	H	HR	BB	SO	W	L	ERA	Ratio	Sv	$
1991	NYY	37	0	48	39	1	7	34	3	1	1.68	8.57	3	14
1992	NYY	20	0	22	9	1	3	12	3	0	2.45	4.91	6	12
1993	NYY	51	0	51	58	7	10	19	3	5	4.97	12.08	4	4
1994	NYY	40	0	40	28	2	7	18	3	0	1.80	7.88	15	32
1995	NYY	56	0	49	66	7	17	28	6	3	4.96	15.24	2	3

The main difference between Howe and Honeycutt is that Howe tried to do someone else's job much more often: he faced 141 righthanded batters, Honeycutt 86, in about the same number of innings.

The result is that Howe was not even a two-category pitcher. As can be seen in Appendix B, his two bad qualitative categories almost cancel out his best quantitative category; his two saves were about all he contributed to a Rotisserie team.

Honeycutt not only was a four category-pitcher, his 49 innings were more helpful to a Rotisserie team's ERA and ratio than Nagy's 178, Pettite's 175, Langston's 200, Leiter's 183 or Finley's 203. The first starting pitcher above Honeycutt in Appendix B who contributes more in the qualitative categories is Abbott.

JASON JACOMBE   Age 25   Bid: R2

Year	Team	G	GS	IP	H	HR	BB	SO	W	L	ERA	Ratio	Sv	$
1994	NYM	8	8	54	54	3	17	30	4	3	2.67	11.83	0	10
1995	NYM	5	5	21	33	3	15	11	0	4	10.29	20.57	0	-13
1995	KC	15	14	84	101	15	21	39	4	6	5.36	13.07	0	0

He fooled no one, not even National League bettors, who spent $5 for a pitcher with a 2.67 lifetime ERA.

DOUG JOHNS   Age 28   Bid: R2

Year	Team	G	GS	IP	H	HR	BB	SO	W	L	ERA	Ratio	Sv	$
1994	(AA)	9	0	15	16	1	12	9	3	0	1.20	16.80	0	x
1994	(AAA)	22	19	134	114	10	48	65	9	8	2.89	10.88	0	x
1995	(AAA)	23	21	132	148	8	43	70	9	5	3.41	13.02	0	x
1995	OAK	11	9	55	44	5	26	25	5	3	4.61	11.52	0	7

Was quoted in the paper over the winter as saying he wasn't at all surprised by how he had done so far in the majors.

So he will be.

RANDY JOHNSON   Age 32   Bid: $37

Year	Team	G	GS	IP	H	HR	BB	SO	W	L	ERA	Ratio	Sv	$
1991	SEA	33	33	201	151	15	152	228	13	10	3.98	13.54	0	3
1992	SEA	31	31	210	154	13	144	241	12	14	3.77	12.75	0	7
1993	SEA	35	34	255	185	22	99	308	19	8	3.24	10.01	1	41
1994	SEA	23	23	172	132	14	72	204	13	6	3.19	10.67	0	41
1995	SEA	30	30	214	159	12	65	294	18	2	2.48	9.41	0	58

Was he better than Mesa last year?

A question only a masochist would try to answer, so we'll save it for chapter 3.
Will he be better than Mesa this year?
Yes. I predict.
But I still won't pay more for him.

DOUG JONES　　Age　39　　　　　　　　　Bid: $11

Year	Team	G	GS	IP	H	HR	BB	SO	W	L	ERA	Ratio	Sv	$
1991	CLE	36	0	63	87	7	17	48	4	8	5.54	14.78	7	-2
1992	HOU	80	0	112	96	5	17	93	11	8	1.85	9.11	36	50
1993	HOU	71	0	85	102	7	21	66	4	10	4.54	12.97	26	14
1994	PHI	47	0	54	55	2	6	38	2	4	2.17	10.17	27	35
1995	BAL	52	0	47	55	6	16	42	0	4	5.01	13.69	22	15

Behind Fetters on my wish list. That is *all* the $11 means.

SCOTT KAMIENIECKI　　Age　32　　　　　　　Bid: $3

Year	Team	G	GS	IP	H	HR	BB	SO	W	L	ERA	Ratio	Sv	$
1991	NYY	9	9	55	54	8	22	34	4	4	3.90	12.36	0	3
1992	NYY	28	28	188	193	13	74	88	6	14	4.36	12.78	0	-3
1993	NYY	30	20	154	163	17	59	72	10	7	4.08	12.95	1	8
1994	NYY	22	16	117	115	13	59	71	8	6	3.76	13.35	0	14
1995	NYY	17	16	90	83	8	49	43	7	6	4.01	13.25	0	8

Don't ever bid $3 for anyone who walks more than he fans; except, possibly, when you get to see him pitch a lot.

MATT KARCHNER　　Age　29　　　　　　　　Bid: $2

Year	Team	G	GS	IP	H	HR	BB	SO	W	L	ERA	Ratio	Sv	$
1994	(AA)	39	0	43	36	0	14	29	5	2	1.26	10.47	6	x
1994	(AAA)	17	0	26	18	0	7	19	4	2	1.37	8.54	2	x
1995	(AAA)	28	0	37	39	3	10	29	3	3	1.45	11.92	9	x
1995	CHW	31	0	32	33	2	12	24	4	2	1.69	12.66	0	9

Doesn't let many people score. That's the point, isn't it?

SCOTT KARL Age 24

Bid: $2

Year	Team	G	GS	IP	H	HR	BB	SO	W	L	ERA	Ratio	Sv	$
1994	(AA)	8	8	55	44	2	15	51	5	1	2.96	9.65	0	x
1994	(AAA)	15	13	89	92	10	33	54	5	5	3.84	12.64	0	x
1995	(AAA)	8	6	46	47	3	12	29	3	4	3.30	11.54	0	x
1995	MIL	25	18	124	141	10	50	59	6	7	4.14	13.86	0	5

Completely different from Jacome, Johns, et al.
No, a little bit different, and that may be enough.

JIMMY KEY Age 35

Bid: $14

Year	Team	G	GS	IP	H	HR	BB	SO	W	L	ERA	Ratio	Sv	$
1991	TOR	33	33	209	207	12	44	125	16	12	3.05	10.79	0	27
1992	TOR	33	33	217	205	24	59	117	13	13	3.53	10.97	0	18
1993	NYY	34	34	237	219	26	43	173	18	6	3.00	9.96	0	41
1994	NYY	25	25	168	177	10	52	97	17	4	3.27	12.27	0	36
1995	NYY	5	5	30	40	3	6	14	1	2	5.64	13.65	0	-2

You can do it, Jimmy!
Steve Karsay did not pitch anywhere last year, but he is on the Oakland 40-Man.

MARK KIEFER Age 27

Bid: $1

Year	Team	G	GS	IP	H	HR	BB	SO	W	L	ERA	Ratio	Sv	$
1993	MIL	6	0	9	3	0	5	7	0	0	.00	7.71	1	4
1994	MIL	7	0	11	15	4	8	8	1	0	8.44	19.41	0	-4
1995	MIL	24	0	50	37	6	27	41	4	1	3.44	11.60	0	9

Take a chance on anyone who holds major league hitters to a .203 batting average in 24 ballgames.

RICK KRIVDA Age 26

Bid: $2

Year	Team	G	GS	IP	H	HR	BB	SO	W	L	ERA	Ratio	Sv	$
1994	(AA)	28	26	163	149	12	73	122	9	10	3.53	12.26	0	x
1994	(AAA)	28	26	163	149	12	73	122	9	10	3.53	12.26	0	x
1995	(AAA)	16	13	102	96	11	32	74	6	5	3.19	11.29	0	x

Year	Team	G	GS	IP	H	HR	BB	SO	W	L	ERA	Ratio	Sv	$
1995	BAL	13	13	75	76	9	25	53	2	7	4.54	12.07	0	4

Decimals put him ahead of Karl.

MARK LANGSTON   Age 35   Bid: $17

Year	Team	G	GS	IP	H	HR	BB	SO	W	L	ERA	Ratio	Sv	$
1991	CAL	34	34	246	190	30	96	183	19	8	3.00	10.45	0	33
1992	CAL	32	32	229	206	14	74	174	13	14	3.66	11.00	0	17
1993	CAL	35	35	256	220	22	85	196	16	11	3.20	10.71	0	35
1994	CAL	18	18	119	121	19	54	109	7	8	4.68	13.20	0	7
1995	CAL	31	31	200	212	21	64	142	15	7	4.63	12.40	0	16

I'll take Rex Hudler in my foxhole any day.

AL LEITER   Age 30   Bid: $6

Year	Team	G	GS	IP	H	HR	BB	SO	W	L	ERA	Ratio	Sv	$
1993	TOR	34	12	105	93	8	56	66	9	6	4.11	12.77	2	8
1994	TOR	20	20	112	125	6	65	100	6	7	5.08	15.31	0	-5
1995	TOR	28	28	183	162	15	108	153	11	11	3.64	13.28	0	16

Bid's much too low for anyone who holds opponents to a .238 BA these days. Much too high for someone who walks that many batters.

JOSE LIMA   Age 23   Bid: $5

Year	Team	G	GS	IP	H	HR	BB	SO	W	L	ERA	Ratio	Sv	$
1994	DET	3	1	7	11	2	3	7	0	1	13.50	18.90	0	-6
1995	DET	15	15	74	85	10	18	37	3	9	6.11	12.58	0	-3

Ended strong.

FELIPE LIRA   Age 24   Bid: $2

Year	Team	G	GS	IP	H	HR	BB	SO	W	L	ERA	Ratio	Sv	$
1994	(AAA)	26	26	151	171	19	45	110	7	12	4.7	12.85	0	x
1995	DET	37	22	146	151	17	56	89	9	13	4.31	12.73	1	12

His girlfriend was down in Florida, talking to him through the screen before the game; I watched her watching him while he pitched, which no doubt was well enough to get into the update if I'd watched him.

ALBIE LOPEZ   Age 24   Bid: R2

Year	Team	G	GS	IP	H	HR	BB	SO	W	L	ERA	Ratio	Sv	$
1993	CLE	9	9	50	49	7	32	25	3	1	5.98	14.68	0	-5
1994	CLE	4	4	17	20	3	6	18	1	2	4.24	13.76	0	1
1995	CLE	6	2	23	17	4	7	22	0	0	3.13	9.39	0	4

The numbers at Buffalo last year: 101 H, 10 HR, 51 BB, 82 K in 101 IP. 4.44 ERA. Won 5, lost 10. An R3 who's an R2 based on the 23 IP at Cleveland.

MIKE MADDUX   Age 34   Bid: $3

Year	Team	G	GS	IP	H	HR	BB	SO	W	L	ERA	Ratio	Sv	$
1991	SD	64	1	99	78	4	27	57	7	2	2.46	9.58	5	18
1992	SD	50	1	80	71	2	24	60	2	2	2.37	10.73	5	10
1993	NYM	58	0	75	67	3	27	57	3	8	3.60	11.28	5	8
1994	NYM	27	0	44	45	7	13	32	2	1	5.11	11.86	2	1
1995	PIT	8	0	9	14	0	3	4	1	0	9.00	17.00	0	-3
1995	BOS	36	4	90	86	5	15	65	4	1	3.61	10.14	1	16

The Madduxes were 24-3 with one save, had a 2.42 ERA and 8.11 ratio, and earned $81.

DENNIS MARTINEZ   Age 41   Bid: $17

Year	Team	G	GS	IP	H	HR	BB	SO	W	L	ERA	Ratio	Sv	$
1991	MON	31	31	222	187	9	62	123	14	11	2.39	10.09	0	28
1992	MON	32	32	226	172	12	60	147	16	11	2.47	9.23	0	32
1993	MON	35	34	225	211	27	64	138	15	9	3.85	11.02	1	19
1994	CLE	24	24	177	166	14	44	92	11	6	3.52	10.70	0	36
1995	CLE	28	28	187	174	17	46	99	12	5	3.08	10.59	0	36

A great pitcher who was put on this earth to illustrate that 1995, when the dust had settled, was a somewhat longer (much less dramatic) replay of 1994.

KIRK MCCASKILL   Age 35   Bid: R3

Year	Team	G	GS	IP	H	HR	BB	SO	W	L	ERA	Ratio	Sv	$
1991	CHW	30	30	178	193	19	66	71	10	19	4.26	13.12	0	1

Year	Team	G	GS	IP	H	HR	BB	SO	W	L	ERA	Ratio	Sv	$
1992	CHW	34	34	209	193	11	95	109	12	13	4.18	12.40	0	5
1993	CHW	30	14	114	144	12	36	65	4	8	5.23	14.25	2	-6
1994	CHW	40	0	53	51	6	22	37	1	4	3.42	12.47	3	9
1995	CHW	55	1	81	97	10	33	50	6	4	4.89	14.44	2	2

There are goals left for him to shoot for but not in baseball.

BEN MCDONALD   Age 28   Bid: $13

Year	Team	G	GS	IP	H	HR	BB	SO	W	L	ERA	Ratio	Sv	$
1991	BAL	21	21	126	126	16	43	85	6	8	4.84	12.04	0	0
1992	BAL	35	35	227	213	32	74	158	13	13	4.24	11.38	0	10
1993	BAL	34	34	220	185	17	86	171	13	14	3.39	11.07	0	26
1994	BAL	24	24	157	151	14	54	94	14	7	4.06	11.73	0	27
1995	BAL	14	13	80	67	10	38	62	3	6	4.16	11.81	0	7

Didn't want to pitch in relief, didn't want to go to Rochester (did for one game); basically, didn't react well to adversity. Only athletes manage not to have to face it until they're 27.

JACK MCDOWELL   Age 30   Bid: $21

Year	Team	G	GS	IP	H	HR	BB	SO	W	L	ERA	Ratio	Sv	$
1991	CHW	35	35	254	212	19	82	191	17	10	3.41	10.43	0	28
1992	CHW	34	34	261	247	21	75	178	20	10	3.18	11.12	0	28
1993	CHW	34	34	257	261	20	69	158	22	10	3.37	11.57	0	33
1994	CHW	25	25	181	186	12	42	127	10	9	3.73	11.34	0	30
1995	NYY	30	30	218	211	25	78	157	15	10	3.93	11.95	0	26

If he's not with the Yankees when you read this, it means they have reason to believe the knot in his back is serious, and take my bet down $10.

ROGER MCDOWELL   Age 35   Bid: $3

Year	Team	G	GS	IP	H	HR	BB	SO	W	L	ERA	Ratio	Sv	$
1991	LA	71	0	101	100	4	48	50	9	9	2.93	13.15	10	12
1992	LA	65	0	84	103	3	42	50	6	10	4.09	15.60	14	4
1993	LA	54	0	68	76	2	30	27	5	3	2.25	14.03	2	7

Year	Team	G	GS	IP	H	HR	BB	SO	W	L	ERA	Ratio	Sv	$
1994	LA	32	0	41	50	3	22	29	0	3	5.23	15.68	0	-9
1995	TEX	64	0	85	86	5	34	49	7	4	4.02	12.71	4	13

Will have an even better year.

JOSE MESA   Age 30   Bid: $41

Year	Team	G	GS	IP	H	HR	BB	SO	W	L	ERA	Ratio	Sv	$
1991	BAL	23	23	124	151	11	62	64	6	11	5.97	15.50	0	-17
1992	BAL/CL	28	27	161	169	14	70	62	7	12	4.59	13.39	0	-5
1993	CLE	34	33	209	232	21	62	118	10	12	4.92	12.68	0	1
1994	CLE	51	0	73	71	3	26	63	7	5	3.82	11.96	2	16
1995	CLE	62	0	64	49	3	17	58	3	0	1.13	9.28	46	57

Dollar Bill, while we were driving around Florida, proposed the following:

Buy all Cleveland pitchers.

Good idea, I thought. Only trouble might be that they would come too expensive.

So we devised two strategies, one with an all-Indian pitching staff, one without. And into the auction we went.

Price enforcing, just price enforcing (we should have at least waited until we could nominate an Indian!), we bought Wetteland as the second player in the draft — $38 — so the strategy was shot to hell.

Anyway, the first Cleveland pitcher came up five pitchers later: Eric Plunk.

Peter Golenbock nominated him, and Peter Golenbock bought him, for $12.

Excellent move. He had who everyone thought would be the Cleveland closer (his average salary is lower than that in Appendix A only because Cowtown drafted a week later) for dirt. Our "straight" price for Plunk was $20; we'd have had no trouble topping Peter, *if* we hadn't already bought Wetteland. But we had.

In the might-have-been scenario, give us Plunk for $13, assuming Peter would have cooled his jets.

The next Indian nominated was Mark Clark, in the fourth round. The Easy Marks added him to their ranks for $12.

The Hackers nominated Clark, so maybe the EZ's would have backed off when we went one more knock for him. (On our sheet he was $9, but once we have Plunk, that's out the window.) Give us Clark for $13.

The next Cleveland pitcher was Paul Shuey in the sixth round.

Laugh now, but we would have paid $15 for Shuey. At least.

Three pitchers for $41, and they're named Clark, Shuey and Plunk. Hang in there, Moose; a plan's a plan.

The next Indian nominated was Dennis Martinez, in the eighth round. The Nova paid $23 for him. Give us Martinez for $24, best case.

Orel Hershiser came up next, five players later. He went to the Nabobs for $9. This might be one of those Bermuda Triangles, so grant us Orel for $10.

There's a lull in the Indian pitchers market until Bud Black is nominated late in the tenth round. He goes to the Hackers for $5. Give us Bud Black for $6 (we even had the last bid on him).

Now our staff consists of Dennis Martinez $24, Charels Nagy $17. Mark Clark $13, Orel

Hershiser $10, Bud Black $6, Eric Plunk $13, and Paul Shuey $15. We've spent $98 — $20 more than I think is prudent — and have two slots left.

Now there's a big lull, until finally, in the 18th round, we get impatient and nominate Gregg Olson.

The Nova bid $3 — just before we do — so we get Olson for $4.

One slot left.

The *ninth* Indian pitcher was Jason Grimsley. Tooners nominate him for $1; we look at each other — a plan's a plan — and say $2 just before the gavel sounds.

ANGEL MIRANDA   Age 26   Bid: $1

Year	Team	G	GS	IP	H	HR	BB	SO	W	L	ERA	Ratio	Sv	$
1993	MIL	22	17	120	100	12	52	88	4	5	3.30	11.40	0	12
1994	MIL	8	8	46	39	8	27	24	2	5	5.28	12.91	0	0
1995	MIL	30	10	74	83	8	49	45	4	5	5.23	16.05	1	-5

Is acceptable only as a reliever and only vaguely.

JEFF MONTGOMERY   Age 34   Bid: $29

Year	Team	G	GS	IP	H	HR	BB	SO	W	L	ERA	Ratio	Sv	$
1991	KC	67	0	90	83	6	28	77	4	4	2.90	11.10	33	29
1992	KC	65	0	83	61	5	27	69	1	6	2.18	9.58	39	36
1993	KC	69	0	87	65	3	23	66	7	5	2.27	9.07	45	49
1994	KC	42	0	45	48	5	15	50	2	3	4.03	12.69	27	28
1995	KC	54	0	66	60	7	25	49	2	3	3.43	11.65	31	32

Surely the only pitcher in either league who has earned at least $28 in each of the last five years; nevertheless, the interior stats were a little off for the second year in a row.

MIKE MOORE   Age 36   Bid: $0

Year	Team	G	GS	IP	H	HR	BB	SO	W	L	ERA	Ratio	Sv	$
1991	OAK	33	33	210	176	11	105	153	17	8	2.96	12.04	0	22
1992	OAK	36	36	223	229	20	103	117	17	12	4.12	13.40	0	4
1993	DET	36	36	214	227	35	89	89	13	9	5.22	13.31	0	-3
1994	DET	25	25	154	152	27	89	62	11	10	5.42	14.05	0	0
1995	DET	25	25	133	179	24	68	64	5	15	7.53	16.76	0	-30

Went out with a bang, the way we always thought he would.

JAMIE MOYER Age 33

Bid: $1

Year	Team	G	GS	IP	H	HR	BB	SO	W	L	ERA	Ratio	Sv	$
1991	STL	8	7	31	38	5	16	20	0	5	5.74	15.51	0	-7
1993	BAL	25	25	152	154	11	38	90	12	9	3.43	11.37	0	19
1994	BAL	23	23	149	158	23	38	87	5	7	4.77	11.84	0	10
1995	BAL	27	18	116	117	18	30	65	8	6	5.21	11.44	0	9

A top-notch R3 if no one buys him.

MIKE MUSSINA Age 27

Bid: $30

Year	Team	G	GS	IP	H	HR	BB	SO	W	L	ERA	Ratio	Sv	$
1991	BAL	12	12	88	77	7	21	52	4	5	2.87	10.06	0	12
1992	BAL	32	32	241	212	16	48	130	18	5	2.54	9.71	0	40
1993	BAL	25	25	168	163	20	44	117	14	6	4.46	11.11	0	15
1994	BAL	24	24	176	163	19	42	99	16	5	3.06	10.46	0	48
1995	BAL	32	32	222	187	24	50	158	19	9	3.29	9.62	0	50

Mussina shows why the formula has to keep changing. His ERA — not just his ratio — was better last year than in 1992, relative to the league. And he won the equivalent of 21 games last season.

CHARLES NAGY Age 29

Bid: $17

Year	Team	G	GS	IP	H	HR	BB	SO	W	L	ERA	Ratio	Sv	$
1991	CLE	33	33	211	228	15	66	109	10	15	4.13	12.52	0	4
1992	CLE	33	33	252	245	11	57	169	17	10	2.96	10.79	0	29
1993	CLE	9	9	49	66	6	13	30	2	6	6.29	14.61	0	-6
1994	CLE	23	23	169	175	15	48	108	10	8	3.45	11.85	0	29
1995	CLE	29	29	178	194	20	61	139	16	6	4.55	12.89	0	15

He had 14 Quality Starts, and I must have seen the box scores of every one of them; just guessing I would have said that his ERA was closer to 3.00.

JEFF NELSON Age 29

Bid: $5

Year	Team	G	GS	IP	H	HR	BB	SO	W	L	ERA	Ratio	Sv	$
1992	SEA	66	0	81	71	7	44	46	1	7	3.44	12.78	6	4
1993	SEA	71	0	60	57	5	34	61	5	3	4.35	13.65	1	2

Year	Team	G	GS	IP	H	HR	BB	SO	W	L	ERA	Ratio	Sv	$
1994	SEA	28	0	42	35	3	20	44	0	0	2.76	11.69	0	7
1995	SEA	62	0	79	58	4	27	96	7	3	2.17	9.72	2	26

Long relievers are short lived.

CHAD OGEA   Age 25   Bid: $4

Year	Team	G	GS	IP	H	HR	BB	SO	W	L	ERA	Ratio	Sv	$
1994	CLE	4	1	16	21	2	10	11	0	1	6.06	17.08	0	-4
1995	CLE	20	14	106	95	11	29	57	8	3	3.05	10.50	0	23

The bid might not be quite enough to get him if his name comes up early, and in bad leagues it won't be enough to get him late.

DARREN OLIVER   Age 25   Bid: $3

Year	Team	G	GS	IP	H	HR	BB	SO	W	L	ERA	Ratio	Sv	$
1993	TEX	2	0	3	2	1	1	4	0	0	2.70	8.10	0	1
1994	TEX	43	0	50	40	4	35	50	4	0	3.42	13.50	2	9
1995	TEX	17	7	49	47	3	32	39	4	2	4.22	14.51	0	2

Has a good arm if it's sound.

GREGG OLSON   Age 29   Bid: $2

Year	Team	G	GS	IP	H	HR	BB	SO	W	L	ERA	Ratio	Sv	$
1991	BAL	72	0	74	74	1	29	72	4	6	3.18	12.58	31	23
1992	BAL	60	0	61	46	3	24	56	1	5	2.05	10.27	36	30
1993	BAL	50	0	45	37	1	18	44	0	2	1.60	11.00	29	25
1994	ATL	16	0	15	19	1	13	10	0	2	9.20	19.64	1	-9
1995	KC	23	0	33	28	4	19	21	3	3	4.09	12.82	3	6

Had a superb arm when it was sound.

STEVE ONTIVEROS   Age 35   Bid: $7

Year	Team	G	GS	IP	H	HR	BB	SO	W	L	ERA	Ratio	Sv	$
1993	SEA	14	0	18	18	0	6	13	0	2	1.00	12.00	0	3
1994	OAK	27	13	115	93	7	26	56	6	4	2.65	9.29	0	35

Year	Team	G	GS	IP	H	HR	BB	SO	W	L	ERA	Ratio	Sv	$
1995	OAK	22	22	130	144	12	38	77	9	6	4.37	12.63	0	**11**

He was running on empty in the second half (one win, 6.75 ERA). I'm betting he'll start out with half a tank again.

JESSE OROSCO Age 39
Bid: $1

Year	Team	G	GS	IP	H	HR	BB	SO	W	L	ERA	Ratio	Sv	$
1991	CLE	47	0	46	52	5	15	36	2	0	3.74	13.21	0	**1**
1992	MIL	59	0	39	33	2	13	40	3	1	3.23	10.62	1	**5**
1993	MIL	57	0	57	47	2	17	67	3	5	3.18	10.16	8	**14**
1994	MIL	40	0	39	32	4	26	36	3	1	5.08	13.38	0	**2**
1995	BAL	65	0	50	28	4	27	58	2	4	3.26	9.97	3	**12**

Came in to face a batter here, a batter there; held them to .169 batting average whether they batted left or right; seldom stayed long enough to get a win; almost never was given a chance for a save; and helped a Rotisserie team more than Todd Stottlemyre.

ROGER PAVLIK Age 28
Bid: $11

Year	Team	G	GS	IP	H	HR	BB	SO	W	L	ERA	Ratio	Sv	$
1992	TEX	13	12	62	66	3	34	45	4	4	4.21	14.52	0	**-2**
1993	TEX	26	26	166	151	18	80	131	12	6	3.41	12.50	0	**16**
1994	TEX	11	11	50	61	8	30	31	2	5	7.69	16.27	0	**-14**
1995	TEX	31	31	192	174	19	90	149	10	10	4.37	12.40	0	**14**

For once I disagree with the prices; he had a better year than in 1993. Could earn $30.

TROY PERCIVAL Age 26
Bid: $19

Year	Team	G	GS	IP	H	HR	BB	SO	W	L	ERA	Ratio	Sv	$
1991	(A)	28	0	38	23	0	18	63	2	0	1.41	9.63	12	**x**
1992	(A)	11	0	11	6	0	8	16	1	1	5.07	11.82	2	**x**
1992	(AA)	20	0	19	18	1	11	21	3	0	2.37	13.74	5	**x**
1993	(AAA)	18	0	19	24	0	13	19	0	1	6.27	17.85	4	**x**
1994	(AAA)	49	0	61	63	4	29	73	2	6	4.13	13.57	15	**x**
1995	CAL	62	0	74	37	6	26	94	3	2	1.95	7.66	3	**27**

Unbelievable numbers here. The only pitcher who might play better in a Strat-O-Matic game is

AL pitchers

Charlton (AL stats only). Percival was sensational in the last week, pitching like Rod Beck a few years ago, and, unfortunately, as often. The only reason the Angels shouldn't give him the closer's job is that Lee Smith can't do his job. Nobody will be surprised if he out-earns Smith anyway.

MELIDO PEREZ Age 30 Bid: R3

Year	Team	G	GS	IP	H	HR	BB	SO	W	L	ERA	Ratio	Sv	$
1991	CHW	49	8	136	111	15	52	128	8	7	3.12	10.81	1	**16**
1992	NYY	33	33	248	212	16	93	218	13	16	2.87	11.08	0	**25**
1993	NYY	25	25	163	173	22	64	148	6	14	5.19	13.09	0	**-5**
1994	NYY	22	22	151	134	16	58	109	9	4	4.10	11.42	0	**22**
1995	NYY	13	12	69	70	10	31	44	5	5	5.58	13.11	0	**0**

He's the Perez who gets no joy out of life, is not a flake, and might come back.

ANDY PETTITE Age 24 Bid: $10

Year	Team	G	GS	IP	H	HR	BB	SO	W	L	ERA	Ratio	Sv	$
1994	(AA)	11	11	73	60	5	18	50	7	2	2.71	9.62	0	x
1994	(AAA)	16	16	97	101	3	21	61	7	2	2.98	11.32	0	x
1995	(AAA)	2	2	11	7	0	0	8	0	0	.00	5.73	0	x
1995	NYY	31	26	175	183	15	63	114	12	9	4.17	12.65	0	16

He's hittable; he's not *that* different from lefties like Karl and Krivda. Part of his mystique is that he's a Yankee, part that he pitches like Ruth in front of the fans: 8-2, 2.62 ERA at home. The 6.24 ERA on the road? Totally baffling. He gave up 95 hits and 10 home runs in 75 innings, which accounts but doesn't explain.

JIM PITTSLEY Age 22 KC Bid: R1

Year	Team	G	GS	IP	H	HR	BB	SO	W	L	ERA	Ratio	Sv	$
1994	(A)	27	27	162	154	15	42	171	11	5	3.17	10.89	0	x
1995	(AAA)	8	8	48	38	5	16	39	4	1	3.21	10.13	0	x
1995	KC	1	1	3	7	3	1	0	0	0	13.50	21.60	0	-3

When did Pitsley have this unfortunate outing at Kansas City? On August 4, he had surgery on his right elbow. ("The good news" says Baseball America, "was that he had only a slight tear and didn't need Tommy John surgery as initially feared.") What I'm wondering is, did the elbow pop before, during or after such a shellacking?

Also, did it all happen in the fourth inning (he pitched 3.1)? If it was spread out over four, that's Boone's fault.

ERIC PLUNK Age 32

Bid: $5

Year	Team	G	GS	IP	H	HR	BB	SO	W	L	ERA	Ratio	Sv	$
1991	NYY	43	8	112	128	18	62	103	2	5	4.76	15.31	0	-12
1992	CLE	58	0	72	61	5	38	50	9	6	3.64	12.43	4	10
1993	CLE	70	0	71	61	5	30	77	4	5	2.79	11.54	15	19
1994	CLE	41	0	71	61	3	37	73	7	2	2.54	12.42	3	21
1995	CLE	56	0	64	48	5	27	71	6	2	2.67	10.55	2	18

Two-for-five in save opportunities. One thing that no doubt limited them was that he had nine bases stolen against him. Facing as many batters as Kevin Brown, he would have given up 24. He also had a little problem Close & Late: batters hit .246 against him, compared to .211 overall.

Maybe he didn't grab the occasion when fortune presented itself, but for the fourth straight year he earned in double figures. Look for other middle relievers about whom that can be said (hence the bid). For the third straight year, Eric Plunk had a ratio that was far better than the league's.

JIM POOLE Age 30

Bid: $1

Year	Team	G	GS	IP	H	HR	BB	SO	W	L	ERA	Ratio	Sv	$
1991	TEX/BAL	29	0	42	29	3	12	38	3	2	2.36	8.79	1	10
1992	BAL	6	0	3	3	0	1	3	0	0	.00	10.80	0	1
1993	BAL	55	0	50	30	2	21	29	2	1	2.15	9.12	2	13
1994	BAL	38	0	20	32	4	11	18	1	0	6.64	19.03	0	-6
1995	CLE	42	0	50	40	7	17	41	3	3	3.75	10.19	0	9

Close & Late, batters hit .113 against him (.217 overall). With runners in scoring position they hit .156, and indeed Poole was third in the league (behind Christopher and Assenmacher) in that hardly trivial category. The only chink in his 1995 armor, really, is the number of gopher balls; his ERA indicates he had the good grace to give them up with his own men on. He finished only nine games (compared to Plunk's 22) and had zero save opportunities.

ARIEL PRIETO Age 26

Bid: $3

Year	Team	G	GS	IP	H	HR	BB	SO	W	L	ERA	Ratio	Sv	$
1995	OAK	14	9	58	57	4	32	37	2	6	4.97	13.81	0	-1

Prediction: In 1997, Havana will have a team in the United Baseball League.

BRAD RADKE

Age 23   Bid: $5

Year	Team	G	GS	IP	H	HR	BB	SO	W	L	ERA	Ratio	Sv	$
1994	(AAA)	29	28	186	167	9	34	123	12	9	2.66	9.73	0	x
1995	MIN	29	28	181	195	32	47	75	11	14	5.32	12.03	0	8

Flyball pitchers want their G/F's to be radical, and his is (.78). If he can just split the difference between the HR totals in the past two years, he will be a very successful major league pitcher.

ALBERTO REYES

Age 25   Bid: R2

Year	Team	G	GS	IP	H	HR	BB	SO	W	L	ERA	Ratio	Sv	$
1994	(AA)	60	0	69	68	4	13	60	2	2	3.25	10.57	35	x
1995	MIL	27	0	33	19	3	18	29	1	1	2.43	9.99	1	9

The hopeful one.

CARLOS REYES

Age 27   Bid: R3

Year	Team	G	GS	IP	H	HR	BB	SO	W	L	ERA	Ratio	Sv	$
1994	OAK	27	9	78	71	10	44	57	0	3	4.15	13.27	1	2
1995	OAK	40	1	69	71	10	28	48	4	6	5.09	12.91	0	2

The one who was pitching at the end of the year.

ARTHUR RHODES

Age 26   Bid: R1

Year	Team	G	GS	IP	H	HR	BB	SO	W	L	ERA	Ratio	Sv	$
1991	BAL	8	8	36	47	4	23	23	0	3	8.00	17.50	0	-12
1992	BAL	15	15	94	87	6	38	77	7	5	3.63	11.93	0	7
1993	BAL	17	17	86	91	16	49	49	5	6	6.51	14.71	0	-11
1994	BAL	10	10	53	51	8	30	47	3	5	5.81	13.84	0	-2
1995	BAL	19	9	75	68	13	48	77	2	5	6.21	13.86	0	-7

Hard-throwing lefties remain R1's until they quit.

DAVE RIGHETTI

Age 37   Bid: R3

Year	Team	G	GS	IP	H	HR	BB	SO	W	L	ERA	Ratio	Sv	$
1991	SF	61	0	72	64	4	28	51	2	7	3.39	11.55	24	18
1992	SF	54	4	78	79	4	36	47	2	7	5.06	13.21	3	-6

Year	Team	G	GS	IP	H	HR	BB	SO	W	L	ERA	Ratio	Sv	$
1993	SF	51	0	47	58	11	17	31	1	1	5.70	14.26	1	-6
1994	TOR	20	0	20	22	5	19	14	0	1	10.18	18.15	0	-12
1995	CHW	10	9	49	65	6	18	29	3	2	4.20	15.14	0	0

Or become Rags.

BILL RISLEY Age 29   Bid: $3

Year	Team	G	GS	IP	H	HR	BB	SO	W	L	ERA	Ratio	Sv	$
1992	MON	1	1	5	4	0	1	2	1	0	1.80	9.00	0	2
1993	MON	2	0	3	2	1	2	2	0	0	6.00	12.00	0	0
1994	SEA	37	0	52	31	7	19	61	9	6	3.44	8.600	0	23
1995	SEA	45	0	60	55	7	18	65	2	1	3.13	10.89	1	11

Second half burn-out knocks his price down to where it should have been anyway.

MARIANO RIVERA Age 26   Bid: $5

Year	Team	G	GS	IP	H	HR	BB	SO	W	L	ERA	Ratio	Sv	$
1995	(AAA)	7	7	30	25	2	3	30	2	2	2.10	8.40	0	x
1995	NYY	19	10	67	71	11	30	51	5	3	5.51	13.57	0	0

Was Wetteland in the play-offs, now wants to be him in season.

JOE ROA Age 24   Bid: R2

Year	Team	G	GS	IP	H	HR	BB	SO	W	L	ERA	Ratio	Sv	$
1994	(AA)	3	3	20	18	0	1	11	2	1	1.80	8.55	0	x
1994	(AAA)	25	25	168	184	16	34	74	8	8	3.49	11.70	0	x
1995	(AAA)	25	24	165	168	9	28	93	17	3	3.50	10.69	0	x
1995	CLE	1	1	6	9	1	2	0	0	1	6.00	16.50	0	-1

Successful, to say the least, at Buffalo, then faced 28 batters in his major league debut without getting one K.

RICH ROBERTSON Age 27   Bid: $3

Year	Team	G	GS	IP	H	HR	BB	SO	W	L	ERA	Ratio	Sv	$
1993	PIT	9	0	9	15	0	4	5	0	1	6.00	19.00	0	-3

Year	Team	G	GS	IP	H	HR	BB	SO	W	L	ERA	Ratio	Sv	$
1994	PIT	8	0	16	20	2	10	8	0	0	6.89	17.23	0	-6
1995	MIN	25	4	52	48	4	31	38	2	0	3.83	13.76	0	2

The Butch Henry of 1996.

Which reminds me, I forgot Butch Henry. Very likely will miss the full season, but he's on the Red Sox winter roster. An R2 in leagues with carry-over reserve lists.

KEN ROBINSON   Age 26   Bid: $1

Year	Team	G	GS	IP	H	HR	BB	SO	W	L	ERA	Ratio	Sv	$
1995	(AAA)	38	0	50	37	6	12	61	5	3	3.22	8.82	2	x
1995	TOR	21	0	39	25	7	22	31	1	2	3.69	10.85	0	5

Gets short-changed because he's 5'9", 170.

FRANK RODRIGUEZ   Age 23   Bid: $2

Year	Team	G	GS	IP	H	HR	BB	SO	W	L	ERA	Ratio	Sv	$
1992	(A)	25	25	149	125	11	65	129	12	7	3.09	11.48	0	x
1993	(AA)	28	26	171	147	17	78	151	7	11	3.74	11.84	0	x
1994	(AAA)	28	28	186	182	18	60	160	8	13	3.92	11.71	0	x
1995	(AAA)	13	2	27	19	2	8	18	1	1	4.00	9.00	2	x
1995	BO/MIN	25	18	106	114	11	57	59	5	8	6.13	14.56	0	-9

This is his entire professional career and to me it's plain he's not developing. The same fastball that was a terror in Lynchburg in 1992 is going to be deposited all too often into the seats of the Metrodome.   But he'll make the Twins and he's not going to slip through the auction altogether, so I don't have the luxury of hedging my bet with an R1.

KENNY ROGERS   Age 31   Bid: $18

Year	Team	G	GS	IP	H	HR	BB	SO	W	L	ERA	Ratio	Sv	$
1991	TEX	63	9	110	121	14	61	73	10	10	5.42	14.94	5	-4
1992	TEX	81	0	79	80	7	26	70	3	6	3.09	12.13	6	8
1993	TEX	35	33	208	210	18	71	140	16	10	4.10	12.14	0	16
1994	TEX	24	24	167	169	24	52	120	11	8	4.46	11.89	0	20
1995	TEX	31	31	208	192	26	76	140	17	7	3.38	11.60	0	35

The $18 puts him in a class by himself, between Kevin Brown and Chuck Finley, and that's that.

SCOTT RUFFCORN Age 26

Bid: R3

Year	Team	G	GS	IP	H	HR	BB	SO	W	L	ERA	Ratio	Sv	$
1993	CHW	3	2	10	9	2	10	2	0	2	8.10	17.10	0	-3
1994	CHW	2	2	6	15	1	5	3	0	2	12.79	28.42	0	-7
1995	CHW	4	0	8	10	0	13	5	0	0	7.88	25.88	0	-5

A 5.63 ERA in three starts at Birmingham (AA) last year, a 99.99 ERA in two starts at Nashville (AAA). Ootcha kootcha.

JEFF RUSSELL Age 34

Bid: $11

Year	Team	G	GS	IP	H	HR	BB	SO	W	L	ERA	Ratio	Sv	$
1991	TEX	68	0	79	71	11	26	52	6	4	3.29	11.00	30	27
1992	OAK	59	0	66	55	3	25	48	4	3	1.63	10.85	30	30
1993	BOS	51	0	47	39	1	14	45	1	4	2.70	10.22	33	27
1994	BOS/CLE42		0	41	43	5	16	28	1	6	5.09	13.06	17	14
1995	TEX	37	0	33	36	3	9	21	1	0	3.03	12.40	20	20

At the eleventh hour — that is, when he's once again the only saves candidate in the Texas bullpen — price has to go up a dollar or two.

KEN RYAN Age 27

Bid: R2

Year	Team	G	GS	IP	H	HR	BB	SO	W	L	ERA	Ratio	Sv	$
1992	BOS	7	0	7	4	2	5	5	0	0	6.43	11.57	1	0
1993	BOS	47	0	50	43	2	29	49	7	2	3.60	12.96	1	7
1994	BOS	42	0	48	46	1	17	32	2	3	2.44	11.81	13	22
1995	BOS	28	0	33	34	4	24	34	0	4	4.96	15.98	7	1

Don't know what happened to him, but it continued happening at Double-A Trenton (5.82 ERA) and Triple-A Pawtucket (6.30), probably not in that order.

AARON SELE Age 26

Bid: $10

Year	Team	G	GS	IP	H	HR	BB	SO	W	L	ERA	Ratio	Sv	$
1993	BOS	18	18	112	100	5	48	93	7	2	2.74	11.93	0	15
1994	BOS	22	22	143	140	13	60	105	8	7	3.83	12.56	0	18
1995	BOS	6	6	32	32	3	14	21	3	1	3.06	12.80	0	6

It's interesting to speculate who suffered more adversity last year, Bere or Sele.

PAUL SHUEY   Age 25   Bid: R2

Year	Team	G	GS	IP	H	HR	BB	SO	W	L	ERA	Ratio	Sv	$
1994	CLE	14	0	12	14	1	12	16	0	1	8.49	20.06	5	-2
1995	CLE	7	0	6	5	0	5	5	0	2	4.26	14.21	0	0

Only pitched 27 innings at Buffalo (AAA), but the results were impressive: 21 H, 2 HR, 7 BB, 27 SO, 2.63 ERA, 11 saves.

BILL SIMAS   Age 24   Bid: $2

Year	Team	G	GS	IP	H	HR	BB	SO	W	L	ERA	Ratio	Sv	$
1995	(AAA)	30	0	38	44	1	14	44	6	3	3.55	13.74	6	x
1995	(AAA)	7	0	12	12	0	3	12	1	1	3.86	11.25	0	x
1995	CHW	14	0	14	15	1	10	16	1	1	2.57	16.07	0	1

Kept the ball in the park in all three venues (Vancouver and Nashville, besides Comiskey). Two of the walks with the White Sox were intentional.

MIKE SIROTKA   Age 25   Bid: $3

Year	Team	G	GS	IP	H	HR	BB	SO	W	L	ERA	Ratio	Sv	$
1994	(A)	27	27	197	183	11	58	173	12	9	3.07	11.01	0	x
1995	(AA)	16	16	101	95	11	22	79	7	6	3.20	10.43	0	x
1995	(AAA)	8	8	54	51	4	13	34	1	5	2.83	10.67	0	x
1995	CHW	6	6	34	39	2	17	19	1	2	4.19	14.68	0	0

He may have been lucky he only faced 20 left-handed batters in the majors; they batted .368 against him... He might point out that if gave the next four the collar, that would drop a bit. In any event, at a somewhat ripe age, he's had a meteoric rise.

LEE SMITH   Age 38   Bid: $25

Year	Team	G	GS	IP	H	HR	BB	SO	W	L	ERA	Ratio	Sv	$
1991	STL	67	0	73	70	5	13	67	6	3	2.34	10.23	47	42
1992	STL	70	0	75	62	4	26	60	4	9	3.12	10.56	43	38
1993	STL/NY	63	0	58	53	11	14	60	2	4	3.88	10.40	46	32
1994	BAL	41	0	38	34	6	11	42	1	4	3.29	10.57	33	37
1995	CAL	52	0	49	42	3	25	43	0	5	3.47	12.22	37	32

Will he be embarrassed if Percival out earns him?
    Nah.

ZANE SMITH Age 35

Year	Team	G	GS	IP	H	HR	BB	SO	W	L	ERA	Ratio	Sv	$
1991	PIT	35	35	228	234	15	29	120	16	10	3.20	10.38	0	21
1992	PIT	23	22	141	138	8	19	56	8	8	3.06	10.02	0	13
1993	PIT	14	14	83	97	5	22	32	3	7	4.55	12.90	0	-2
1994	PIT	25	24	157	162	18	34	57	10	8	3.27	11.24	0	23
1995	BOS	24	21	111	144	7	23	47	8	8	5.61	13.58	0	-1

He admitted during the winter that he was out of shape last season. Typical lefthander's way of applying for a job. Got me to move him from R3.

CLINT SODOWSKY Age 23

Bid: $2

Year	Team	G	GS	IP	H	HR	BB	SO	W	L	ERA	Ratio	Sv	$
1994	(A)	19	18	110	111	5	34	73	6	3	3.83	11.86	0	x
1995	(AA)	19	19	124	102	4	50	77	5	5	2.55	11.03	0	x
1995	(AAA)	9	9	60	47	5	30	32	5	1	2.85	11.55	0	x
1995	DET	6	6	23	24	4	18	14	2	2	5.01	16.20	0	-1

Sparky loved Sodowsky, said he had nothing more to prove, then pitched him twice in the last week: a 9.00 ERA and 27.00 ratio. He already had 201 IP under his belt for the year, so that couldn't have been the reason.

STEVE SPARKS Age 30

Bid: $1

Year	Team	G	GS	IP	H	HR	BB	SO	W	L	ERA	Ratio	Sv	$
1993	(AAA)	29	28	180	174	17	80	104	9	13	3.84	12.70	0	x
1994	(AAA)	28	27	184	183	23	68	105	10	12	4.46	12.28	0	x
1995	MIL	33	27	202	210	17	86	96	9	11	4.63	13.19	0	6

Just following in the wake.

MIKE STANTON Age 29

Bid: $1

Year	Team	G	GS	IP	H	HR	BB	SO	W	L	ERA	Ratio	Sv	$
1991	ATL	74	0	78	62	6	21	54	5	5	2.88	9.58	7	15
1992	ATL	65	0	64	59	6	20	44	5	4	4.10	11.17	8	8
1993	ATL	63	0	52	51	4	29	43	4	6	4.67	13.85	27	14

Year	Team	G	GS	IP	H	HR	BB	SO	W	L	ERA	Ratio	Sv	$
1994	ATL	49	0	46	41	2	26	35	3	1	3.55	13.20	3	6
1995	ATL	26	0	19	31	3	6	13	1	1	5.59	17.22	1	-3
1995	BOS	22	0	21	17	3	8	10	1	0	3.00	10.71	0	4

Needed to get away from National League hitters.

DAVE STEVENS Age 26

Bid: $6

Year	Team	G	GS	IP	H	HR	BB	SO	W	L	ERA	Ratio	Sv	$
1993	(AA)	11	11	70	69	7	35	49	6	1	4.22	13.37	0	x
1993	(AAA)	24	0	34	24	3	14	29	4	0	4.19	10.06	4	x
1994	MIN	24	0	45	55	6	23	24	5	2	6.80	15.60	0	-5
1994	(AAA)	23	0	43	41	2	16	30	6	2	1.67	11.93	3	x
1995	MIN	56	0	66	74	14	32	47	5	4	5.07	14.53	10	7

An extreme flyball pitcher, which is apparent without knowing that his G/F ratio was .79. Slugging average against him was .512. Will need a large quantity of saves to make up for his qualitatives.

TODD STOTTLEMYRE Age 32

Bid: $15

Year	Team	G	GS	IP	H	HR	BB	SO	W	L	ERA	Ratio	Sv	$
1991	TOR	34	34	219	194	21	75	116	15	8	3.78	11.05	0	19
1992	TOR	28	27	174	175	20	63	98	12	11	4.50	12.31	0	4
1993	TOR	30	28	177	204	11	69	98	11	12	4.84	13.91	0	-2
1994	TOR	26	19	141	149	19	48	105	7	7	4.22	12.60	1	14
1995	OAK	31	31	210	228	26	80	205	14	7	4.55	13.22	0	11

Bid should blow away the opposition in all but strikeout leagues.

JEFF SUPPAN Age 21

Bid: $6

Year	Team	G	GS	IP	H	HR	BB	SO	W	L	ERA	Ratio	Sv	$
1993	(R)	10	9	58	52	0	16	64	4	3	2.18	10.55	0	x
1994	(A)	27	27	174	153	10	50	173	13	7	3.26	10.50	0	x
1995	(AA)	15	15	99	86	5	26	88	6	2	2.36	10.18	0	x
1995	(AAA)	7	7	46	50	9	9	32	2	3	5.32	11.54	0	x

Year	Team	G	GS	IP	H	HR	BB	SO	W	L	ERA	Ratio	Sv	$
1995	BOS	8	3	23	29	4	5	19	1	2	5.96	13.50	0	-1

This is all of Suppan's pro experience.

My feeling is, he was going through a dead-arm period, as luck would have it, just when the Red Sox called him up. After being beaten around the ears, he was sent down to Pawtucket (AAA), and got beat up some more. The Red Sox called him back to hang out in September, he got into some games — and threw gas. I saw him in one of his games: fastballs that hitters could not get around on, sliders that froze them. The guy's an ace. My last $6 goes to him before Dave Stevens, that's a promise.

JULIAN TAVAREZ   Age 23   Bid: $9

Year	Team	G	GS	IP	H	HR	BB	SO	W	L	ERA	Ratio	Sv	$
1993	(A)	18	18	119	102	6	28	107	11	5	2.42	9.83	0	x
1993	(AA)	3	2	19	14	0	1	11	2	1	.95	7.11	0	x
1993	CLE	8	7	37	53	7	13	19	2	2	6.57	16.05	0	-6
1994	(AAA)	26	26	176	167	15	43	102	15	6	3.48	10.74	0	x
1994	CLE	1	1	2	6	1	1	0	0	1	21.60	37.80	0	-4
1995	CLE	57	0	85	76	7	21	68	10	2	2.44	10.27	0	26

No Cora he in any play-off game, he seemed a little overly wrought by his team's defeat; perhaps had more than was legal riding on the outcome?

BOB TEWKSBURY   Age 35   Bid: $4

Year	Team	G	GS	IP	H	HR	BB	SO	W	L	ERA	Ratio	Sv	$
1991	STL	30	30	191	206	13	38	75	11	12	3.25	11.50	0	11
1992	STL	33	32	233	217	15	20	91	16	5	2.16	9.150	0	36
1993	STL	32	32	214	258	15	20	97	17	10	3.83	11.71	0	16
1994	STL	24	24	156	190	19	22	79	12	10	5.32	12.26	0	2
1995	TEX	21	21	130	169	8	20	53	8	7	4.58	13.12	0	6

His year to fool them was probably last year.

LARRY THOMAS   Age 26   Bid: $2

Year	Team	G	GS	IP	H	HR	BB	SO	W	L	ERA	Ratio	Sv	$
1994	(AA)	24	24	144	159	17	53	77	5	10	4.63	13.25	0	x
1995	(AA)	35	0	40	24	0	15	47	4	1	1.34	8.78	2	x

Year	Team	G	GS	IP	H	HR	BB	SO	W	L	ERA	Ratio	Sv	$
1995	CHW	17	0	14	8	1	6	12	0	0	1.32	9.22	0	4

A long-time prospect who looks like he might have found his niche.

MIKE TIMLIN   Age 30   Bid: $7

Year	Team	G	GS	IP	H	HR	BB	SO	W	L	ERA	Ratio	Sv	$
1991	TOR	63	3	108	94	6	50	85	11	6	3.16	11.96	3	15
1992	TOR	26	0	44	45	0	20	35	0	2	4.12	13.40	1	-2
1993	TOR	54	0	56	63	7	27	49	4	2	4.69	14.55	1	-1
1994	TOR	34	0	40	41	5	20	38	0	1	5.18	13.73	2	-1
1995	TOR	31	0	42	38	1	17	36	4	3	2.14	11.79	5	15

Great numbers, for some reason, and Toronto's closer niche is wide open.

SALOMON TORRES   Age 24   Bid: R2

Year	Team	G	GS	IP	H	HR	BB	SO	W	L	ERA	Ratio	Sv	$
1993	SF	8	8	45	37	5	27	23	3	5	4.03	12.90	0	1
1994	SF	16	14	84	95	10	34	42	2	8	5.44	13.77	0	-10
1995	SF	4	1	8	13	4	7	2	0	1	9.00	22.50	0	-5
1995	SEA	16	13	72	87	12	42	45	3	8	6.00	16.13	0	-10

Bad combination: ground ball pitcher (G/F 1.86) who gives up the long ball.

TODD VAN POPPEL   Age 24   Bid: $6

Year	Team	G	GS	IP	H	HR	BB	SO	W	L	ERA	Ratio	Sv	$
1991	OAK	1	1	5	7	1	2	6	0	0	9.66	17.38	0	-2
1993	OAK	16	16	84	76	10	62	47	6	6	5.04	14.79	0	-4
1994	OAK	23	23	117	108	20	89	83	7	10	6.09	15.20	0	-12
1995	OAK	36	14	138	125	16	56	122	4	8	4.88	11.78	0	6

He'll be on everyone's sleeper list, so you might have to go higher if he's on yours.

ED VOSBERG   Age 34   Bid: R3

Year	Team	G	GS	IP	H	HR	BB	SO	W	L	ERA	Ratio	Sv	$
1994	OAK	16	0	14	16	2	5	12	0	2	3.95	13.83	0	0

Year	Team	G	GS	IP	H	HR	BB	SO	W	L	ERA	Ratio	Sv	$
1995	TEX	44	0	36	32	3	16	36	5	5	3.00	12.00	4	12

Nothing wrong with his numbers last year.

TIM WAKEFIELD   Age 29   Bid: $11

Year	Team	G	GS	IP	H	HR	BB	SO	W	L	ERA	Ratio	Sv	$
1992	PIT	13	13	92	76	3	35	51	8	1	2.15	10.86	0	13
1993	PIT	24	20	128	145	14	75	59	6	11	5.61	15.43	0	-17
1995	BOS	27	27	195	163	22	68	119	16	8	2.95	10.64	0	42

One of the hardest things about him: spring training could push his price as high as $20 or as low as $5 without telling us much.

DUANE WARD   Age 32   Bid: R2

Year	Team	G	GS	IP	H	HR	BB	SO	W	L	ERA	Ratio	Sv	$
1991	TOR	81	0	107	80	3	33	132	7	6	2.77	9.48	23	32
1992	TOR	79	0	101	76	5	39	103	7	4	1.95	10.21	12	26
1993	TOR	71	0	72	49	4	25	97	2	3	2.13	9.29	45	42
1995	TOR	4	0	3	11	0	5	3	0	1	27.00	54.00	0	-7

Did his whole arm get caught in a threshing machine?

JOHN WASDIN   Age 23   Bid: R2

Year	Team	G	GS	IP	H	HR	BB	SO	W	L	ERA	Ratio	Sv	$
1994	(A)	6	4	27	17	2	5	30	3	1	1.69	7.33	0	x
1994	(AA)	21	21	142	126	13	29	108	12	3	3.43	9.82	0	x
1995	(AAA)	29	28	174	193	26	38	111	12	8	5.52	11.95	0	x
1995	OAK	5	2	17	14	4	3	6	1	1	4.67	8.83	0	3

Edmonton (AAA) is not a place to build your confidence (team ERA 5.13) but he evidently was willing to challenge hitters in the majors, where he showed perhaps too-good control and not enough velocity.

SCOTT WATKINS

Age 26   Bid: R1

Year	Team	G	GS	IP	H	HR	BB	SO	W	L	ERA	Ratio	Sv	$
1994	(AA)	11	0	14	13	1	4	11	1	0	4.61	10.93	3	x
1994	(AAA)	46	0	57	73	10	28	47	2	6	6.75	15.95	3	x
1995	(AAA)	45	0	55	45	4	13	57	4	2	2.80	9.49	20	x
1995	MIN	27	0	22	22	2	11	11	0	0	5.40	13.71	0	-2

Tremendous numbers at Salt Lake (AAA), where the team ERA was 5.03. Had only two save opportunities with the Twins. Most likely will start the season in Triple-A again, to give Stevens breathing space; then he'll get his shot at being the closer.

BILL WEGMAN

Age 33   Bid: R3

Year	Team	G	GS	IP	H	HR	BB	SO	W	L	ERA	Ratio	Sv	$
1991	MIL	28	28	193	176	16	40	89	15	7	2.84	10.06	0	30
1992	MIL	35	35	262	251	28	55	127	13	14	3.20	10.52	0	26
1993	MIL	20	18	121	135	13	34	50	4	14	4.48	12.61	0	1
1994	MIL	19	19	116	140	14	26	59	8	4	4.51	12.92	0	10
1995	MIL	37	4	71	89	14	21	50	5	7	5.35	14.01	2	1

May have some value in long relief; finished as a starter (9.24 ERA).

JOHN WETTELAND

Age 29   Bid: $40

Year	Team	G	GS	IP	H	HR	BB	SO	W	L	ERA	Ratio	Sv	$
1991	LA	6	0	9	5	0	3	9	1	0	.00	8.00	0	3
1992	MTL	67	0	83	64	6	36	99	4	4	2.92	10.80	37	34
1993	MTL	70	0	85	58	3	28	113	9	3	1.37	9.07	43	50
1994	MTL	52	0	64	46	5	21	68	4	6	2.83	9.47	25	37
1995	NYY	60	0	61	40	6	14	66	1	5	2.93	7.92	31	39

If Jose Mesa had a 1.13 ERA and 9.28 ratio, what would John Wetteland's ERA have been if he were Mesa and still had his own ratio?

No, can't start falling through the looking glass — not with the entire National League ahead of me — but you know what I'm saying. He lost some big ball games with the Yankees; there's no denying it. Relievers will tell you, however, that they look at each game and each year and each team as a brand new day.

MATT WHITESIDE
Age 28
Bid: $1

Year	Team	G	GS	IP	H	HR	BB	SO	W	L	ERA	Ratio	Sv	$
1992	TEX	20	0	28	26	1	11	13	1	1	1.93	11.89	4	6
1993	TEX	60	0	73	78	7	23	39	2	1	4.32	12.45	1	2
1994	TEX	47	0	61	68	6	28	37	2	2	5.02	14.16	1	-1
1995	TEX	40	0	53	48	5	19	46	5	4	4.08	11.38	3	11

It looks like he deserved a better ERA and more than four save opportunities.

BOB WICKMAN
Age 27
Bid: $3

Year	Team	G	GS	IP	H	HR	BB	SO	W	L	ERA	Ratio	Sv	$
1992	NYY	8	8	50	51	2	20	21	6	1	4.11	12.70	0	3
1993	NYY	41	19	140	156	13	69	70	14	4	4.63	14.46	4	4
1994	NYY	53	0	70	54	3	27	56	5	4	3.09	10.41	6	24
1995	NYY	63	1	80	77	6	33	51	2	4	4.05	12.38	1	6

Used to get a lot of cheap wins and now is owed some.

WOODY WILLIAMS
Age 29
Bid: $3

Year	Team	G	GS	IP	H	HR	BB	SO	W	L	ERA	Ratio	Sv	$
1993	TOR	30	0	88	40	2	22	24	3	1	4.38	6.34	0	1
1994	TOR	38	0	59	44	5	33	56	1	3	3.64	11.68	0	8
1995	TOR	23	3	54	44	6	28	41	1	2	3.69	12.07	0	5

Better buy than Wickman if he's healthy.

BOBBY WITT
Age 32
Bid: $2

Year	Team	G	GS	IP	H	HR	BB	SO	W	L	ERA	Ratio	Sv	$
1991	TEX	17	16	89	84	4	74	82	3	7	6.09	16.04	0	-15
1992	TX/OAK	31	31	193	183	16	114	126	10	14	4.29	13.85	0	-4
1993	OAK	35	33	220	226	16	91	131	14	13	4.21	12.97	0	9
1994	OAK	24	24	136	151	22	70	111	8	10	5.04	14.66	0	-2
1995	FLA	19	19	111	104	8	47	95	2	7	3.90	12.28	0	2

Year	Team	G	GS	IP	H	HR	BB	SO	W	L	ERA	Ratio	Sv	$
1995	TEX	10	10	61	81	4	21	46	3	4	4.55	14.97	-1	-1

If you're worried about your innings, you'll be fighting for him in the crapshoot.

BOB WOLCOTT Age 22

Bid: $3

Year	Team	G	GS	IP	H	HR	BB	SO	W	L	ERA	Ratio	Sv	$
1995	(AA)	12	12	86	60	6	13	53	7	3	2.20	7.64	0	x
1995	(AAA)	13	13	79	94	10	16	43	6	3	4.08	12.53	0	x
1995	SEA	7	6	37	43	6	14	19	3	2	4.42	13.99	0	2

If you have the innings and you're allowed to drop pitchers, a much better pick in the crapshoot. Piniella did okay.

KURT ABBOTT   SS   Age 27   Bid: $12

Year	Team	G	AB	R	H	BB	SO	D	T	HR	RBI	SB	CS	BA	$
1993	OAK	20	61	11	15	3	20	1	0	3	9	2	0	.246	2
1994	FLA	101	345	41	86	16	98	17	3	9	33	3	0	.249	7
1995	FLA	120	420	60	107	36	110	18	7	17	60	4	3	.255	**14**

The bids for hitters add up to $2,100. The average hitter that is bought in the auction will earn $13. Abbott could very well be above average this year, but he has no speed to speak of — which is a sure thing — and the chances are he still won't hit at or above the league average. The power, I think, is fully expressed, and he's not a great fielder. Counterbalancing the negatives is the fact that he's a shortstop.

BOB ABREU   OF   Age 22   Bid: R2

Year	Team	G	AB	R	H	BB	SO	D	T	HR	RBI	SB	CS	BA	$
1993	(A)	129	474	62	134	51	90	21	17	5	55	10	14	.283	x
1994	(AA)	116	400	61	121	42	81	25	9	16	73	12	10	.303	x
1995	(AAA)	114	415	72	126	67	120	24	17	10	75	16	14	.304	x

The reserve pick categories are explained briefly in the first AL hitter comment and are described in more detail in the prediction chapter.

Abreu's strikeouts are, in essence, what keeps him from being an R1. Although he played in the PCL, his own home ballpark in Tucson must be huge: 61 homers hit there by both teams, 91 on the road. The batting average was much higher at home (.304/.276) and there were a ton more doubles (298/251) and triples (79/42) hit in the Toros' ballpark.

Nowadays we can even dig up the lefty-righty splits of Triple-A prospects (all of these numbers are taken from Stats Inc.'s terrific green book), and for Abreu it's interesting. In 76 AB he hit .355 against lefties.

The flip is that he hit righties at a .289 clip, which was exactly the Toros' batting average, and on it goes.

EDGARDO ALFONZO   2B,3B   Age 22   Bid: $11

Year	Team	G	AB	R	H	BB	SO	D	T	HR	RBI	SB	CS	BA	$
1994	(AA)	127	498	89	146	64	55	34	2	15	75	14	11	.293	x
1995	NYM	101	335	26	93	12	37	13	5	4	41	1	1	.278	8

His youth and my getting to watch him a lot on the Mets are what explain this bid price.

MOISES ALOU   OF   Age 29   Bid: $27

Year	Team	G	AB	R	H	BB	SO	D	T	HR	RBI	SB	CS	BA	$
1992	MTL	115	341	53	96	25	46	28	2	9	56	16	2	.282	**20**
1993	MTL	136	482	70	138	38	53	29	6	18	85	17	6	.286	**26**
1994	MTL	107	422	81	143	42	63	31	5	22	78	7	6	.339	**39**
1995	MTL	93	344	48	94	29	56	22	0	14	58	4	3	.273	**15**

There are many reasons to bid more than I think a player is going to earn. No pricing system can evaluate position scarcity or injury risk; those factors have to be taken into account by bids. Upside is another. I may not have a great feeling about Alou for this season, but I'll pay a little more than I think he's going to be worth on the basis of how seriously I could be wrong.

SHANE ANDREWS   3B,1B Age 24   Bid: $2

Year	Team	G	AB	R	H	BB	SO	D	T	HR	RBI	SB	CS	BA	$
1993	(AA)	124	442	77	115	64	118	29	1	18	70	10	6	.260	x
1994	(AAA)	137	460	79	117	80	126	25	2	16	85	6	5	.254	x
1995	MTL	84	220	27	47	17	68	10	1	8	31	1	1	.214	2

I don't think Shane Andrews has much chance at all, frankly, of becoming a decent major league hitter, but he's got twice as good a chance as a lot of players that will be available.

ERIC ANTHONY   OF   Age 28   Bid: $3

Year	Team	G	AB	R	H	BB	SO	D	T	HR	RBI	SB	CS	BA	$
1991	HOU	39	118	11	18	12	41	6	0	1	7	1	0	.153	**-3**
1992	HOU	137	440	45	105	38	98	15	1	19	80	5	4	.239	**19**
1993	HOU	145	486	70	121	49	88	19	4	15	66	3	5	.249	**11**
1994	SEA	79	262	31	62	23	66	14	1	10	30	6	2	.237	**7**
1995	CIN	47	134	19	36	13	30	6	0	5	23	2	1	.269	**6**

Has a better chance than Andrews, but I wouldn't say it's 50% better.

ALEX ARIAS   SS,3B   Age 28   Bid: $1

Year	Team	G	AB	R	H	BB	SO	D	T	HR	RBI	SB	CS	BA	$
1992	CHC	32	99	14	29	11	13	6	0	0	7	0	0	.293	2
1993	FLA	96	249	27	67	27	18	5	1	2	20	1	1	.269	3
1994	FLA	59	113	4	27	9	19	5	0	0	15	0	1	.239	0

Year	Team	G	AB	R	H	BB	SO	D	T	HR	RBI	SB	CS	BA	$
1995	FLA	94	216	22	58	22	20	9	2	3	26	1	0	.269	5

Available.

BILLY ASHLEY   OF   Age 25   Bid: R2

Year	Team	G	AB	R	H	BB	SO	D	T	HR	RBI	SB	CS	BA	$
1992	LA	29	95	6	21	5	34	5	0	2	6	0	0	.221	0
1993	LA	14	37	0	9	2	11	0	0	0	0	0	0	.243	0
1994	LA	2	6	0	2	0	2	1	0	0	0	0	0	.333	0
1995	LA	81	215	17	51	25	88	5	0	8	27	0	0	.237	4

Perhaps should be an R1, that's how big his upside still is. But he's got to figure out what he needs to do in the minors. Even if he has a 6'7" ego, the major league pitchers will destroy it.

RICH AUDE   1B   Age 24   Bid: R3

Year	Team	G	AB	R	H	BB	SO	D	T	HR	RBI	SB	CS	BA	$
1993	PIT	13	26	1	3	1	7	1	0	0	4	0	0	.115	-1
1995	PIT	42	109	10	27	6	20	8	0	2	19	1	2	.248	2

I was higher on him last year than Ashley; give up on him now. Oh, I guess he should be an R2 — he did a lot of hitting at Calgary (.564 SA) — but he reminds me of Dave McCarty.

RICH AURELIA   SS   Age 24   Bid: $3

Year	Team	G	AB	R	H	BB	SO	D	T	HR	RBI	SB	CS	BA	$
1994	(AA)	129	458	67	107	53	74	18	6	12	57	10	13	.234	x
1995	(AA)	64	226	29	74	27	26	17	1	4	42	10	3	.327	x
1995	(AAA)	71	258	42	72	35	29	12	0	5	34	2	2	.279	x
1995	SF	9	19	4	9	1	2	3	0	2	4	1	0	.474	3

Not a threat to Clayton. No way. The Giants got him for nothing — from Texas, for Burkett, and the Rangers didn't even get Burkett — so don't worry, Royce. I mean it. The nine games for the Giants, while you were relaxing, were a fluke. So was his binge at Shreveport (AA) earlier in the year. Look at what he did in Double-A the year before; that's more like it. He hit .309 the year before that, in A ball; .337 the year before that, in Rookie ball, but pay no attention. Those are off the screen.

– 129 –   **NL hitters**

BRAD AUSMUS C Age 27

Bid: $12

Year	Team	G	AB	R	H	BB	SO	D	T	HR	RBI	SB	CS	BA	$
1993	SD	49	160	18	41	6	28	8	1	5	12	2	0	.256	3
1994	SD	101	327	45	82	30	63	12	1	7	24	5	1	.251	6
1995	SD	103	328	44	96	31	56	16	4	5	34	16	5	.293	15

Steals will go down but batting average might actually go up.

JEFF BAGWELL 1B Age 28

Bid: $38

Year	Team	G	AB	R	H	BB	SO	D	T	HR	RBI	SB	CS	BA	$
1991	HOU	156	554	79	163	75	116	26	4	15	82	7	4	.294	25
1992	HOU	162	586	87	160	84	97	34	6	18	96	10	6	.273	28
1993	HOU	142	535	76	171	62	73	37	4	20	88	13	4	.320	32
1994	HOU	110	400	104	147	65	65	32	2	39	116	15	4	.368	63
1995	HOU	114	448	88	130	79	102	29	0	21	87	12	5	.290	28

Had an almost $30 off-year. Almost $20 less than I predicted.

JASON BATES SS,2B Age 25

Bid: $3

Year	Team	G	AB	R	H	BB	SO	D	T	HR	RBI	SB	CS	BA	$
1994	(AAA)	125	458	68	131	60	57	19	5	10	76	4	6	.286	x
1995	COL	116	322	42	86	42	70	17	4	8	46	3	6	.267	10

Chance of more of same but no chance of more.

ALLEN BATTLE OF Age 27

Bid: $1

Year	Team	G	AB	R	H	BB	SO	D	T	HR	RBI	SB	CS	BA	$
1993	(AA)	108	390	71	107	45	75	24	12	3	40	20	12	.274	x
1994	(AAA)	132	520	104	163	59	82	44	7	6	69	23	8	.313	x
1995	(AAA)	47	164	28	46	28	32	12	1	3	18	7	1	.280	x
1995	STL	61	118	13	32	15	26	5	0	0	2	3	3	.271	1

They must say he looks like Willie McGee because that's who he looks like. He bats right and doesn't play like him.

TREY BEAMON OF   Age 22

Bid: R1

Year	Team	G	AB	R	H	BB	SO	D	T	HR	RBI	SB	CS	BA	$
1993	(A)	104	373	64	101	48	60	18	6	0	45	19	6	.271	x
1994	(AA)	112	434	69	140	33	53	18	9	5	47	24	9	.323	x
1995	(AAA)	118	452	74	151	39	55	29	5	5	62	18	8	.334	x

"Has shown he is a flat-out good hitter," an opposing manager in the PCL told Baseball America. "Has to work on his intensity."

No problem, intensity can be learned.

However, these stats that he compiled last year at Calgary, a new venue for the Pirates, may not be flat-out good hitters' stats. Calgary is where Rich Aude looked good again. Sam Horn hit .333 and slugged .697. The Cannons' catcher, Keith Osik, hit .336 and slugged .525, after hitting .212 and slugging .331 at Buffalo the year before.

But I still like Beamon, maybe especially if he's not motivated yet.

DAVID BELL 2B   Age 23

Bid: $2

Year	Team	G	AB	R	H	BB	SO	D	T	HR	RBI	SB	CS	BA	$
1993	(AA)	129	483	69	141	43	54	20	2	9	60	3	4	.292	x
1994	(AAA)	134	481	66	141	41	54	17	4	18	88	2	5	.293	x
1995	(AAA)	70	254	34	69	22	37	11	1	8	34	0	3	.272	x
1995	CLE	2	2	0	0	0	0	0	0	0	0	0	0	.000	0
1995	STL	39	144	13	36	4	25	7	2	2	19	1	2	.250	2

I saw him in a few games in September. Does not have the bat.

DEREK BELL OF   Age 27

Bid: $30

Year	Team	G	AB	R	H	BB	SO	D	T	HR	RBI	SB	CS	BA	$
1991	TOR	18	28	5	4	6	5	0	0	0	1	3	2	.143	0
1992	TOR	61	161	23	39	15	34	6	3	2	15	7	2	.242	4
1993	SD	150	542	73	142	23	122	19	1	21	72	26	5	.262	24
1994	SD	108	434	54	135	29	88	20	0	14	54	24	8	.311	35
1995	HOU	112	452	63	151	33	71	21	2	8	86	27	9	.334	35

Needs to cork his bat.

JAY BELL   SS   Age 30   Bid: $13

Year	Team	G	AB	R	H	BB	SO	D	T	HR	RBI	SB	CS	BA	$
1991	PIT	157	608	96	164	52	99	32	8	16	67	10	6	.270	**20**
1992	PIT	159	632	87	167	55	103	36	6	9	55	7	5	.264	**15**
1993	PIT	154	604	102	187	77	122	32	9	9	51	16	10	.310	**23**
1994	PIT	110	424	68	117	49	82	35	4	9	45	2	0	.276	**13**
1995	PIT	138	530	79	139	55	110	28	4	13	55	2	5	.262	**11**

The bids, above all, are preferences, and, in the middle rounds of the draft, if you don't like what you've done so far, you might prefer Abbott.

MARVIN BENARD   OF   Age 26   Bid: $4

Year	Team	G	AB	R	H	BB	SO	D	T	HR	RBI	SB	CS	BA	$
1994	(AA)	125	454	66	143	31	58	32	3	4	48	24	13	.315	x
1995	(AAA)	111	378	70	115	50	66	14	6	6	32	10	13	.304	x
1995	SF	13	34	5	13	1	7	2	0	1	4	1	0	.382	3

Bats left, is 5'9", 180. Has hit .300 at every level except the first (.236 in 64 games at Everett in 1992). Has found the defense against his speed more daunting at every level. Won't be Deion but may be the Giants' centerfielder.

YAMIL BENITEZ   OF   Age 23   Bid: R2

Year	Team	G	AB	R	H	BB	SO	D	T	HR	RBI	SB	CS	BA	$
1993	(A)	111	411	70	112	29	99	21	5	15	61	18	7	.273	x
1994	(AA)	128	475	58	123	36	134	18	4	17	91	18	15	.259	x
1995	(AAA)	127	474	66	123	44	128	24	6	18	69	14	6	.259	x
1995	MTL	14	39	8	15	1	7	2	1	2	7	0	2	.385	4

In addition to his good audition for the Expos, Yamil gets some attention for doing as well or better at Triple-A than he had done at Double-A the previous year, in just about every respect. On the other hand, if he hadn't, the Expos never would have given him a call.

SEAN BERRY   3B   Age 30   Bid: $20

Year	Team	G	AB	R	H	BB	SO	D	T	HR	RBI	SB	CS	BA	$
1991	KC	31	60	5	8	5	23	3	0	0	1	0	0	.133	-3
1992	MTL	24	57	5	19	1	11	1	0	1	4	2	1	.333	3

Year	Team	G	AB	R	H	BB	SO	D	T	HR	RBI	SB	CS	BA	$
1993	MTL	122	299	50	78	41	70	15	2	14	49	12	2	.261	**15**
1994	MTL	103	320	43	89	32	50	19	2	11	41	14	0	.278	**19**
1995	MTL	103	314	38	100	25	53	22	1	14	55	3	8	.318	**20**

Will surpass his old buddy from the AL, Jeff Conine.

DANTE BICHETTE OF Age 32 Bid: $43

Year	Team	G	AB	R	H	BB	SO	D	T	HR	RBI	SB	CS	BA	$
1991	MIL	134	445	53	106	22	107	18	3	15	59	14	8	.238	**15**
1992	MIL	112	387	37	111	16	74	27	2	5	41	18	7	.287	**17**
1993	COL	141	538	93	167	28	99	43	5	21	89	14	8	.310	**31**
1994	COL	116	484	74	147	19	70	33	2	27	95	21	8	.304	**45**
1995	COL	139	579	102	197	22	96	38	2	40	128	13	9	.340	**54**

After hitting well over .360 in his two seasons in Mile High Stadium, Bichette's average had no place to go but down. So said the smart money:

```
1995 Predictions: BICHETTE
                 AB      HR      RBI     SB      BA
Patton          575      29      109     16      .301
James           544      20       77     21      .281
Benson          540      24       98     20      .295
Shandler        550      22       89     18      .293
Mann            619      28       99     22      .288
```

Since Bichette managed to go to the plate as many times as most of us forecast anyway last year, I don't really have to scale down the projections (although I should) to get an idea of how far off we were in the power categories.

Then when the strike finally was settled, we all rushed back to our Ouija boards. The question was, what would the truncated spring do to the already rather thin pitching ranks? I unfortunately never found out how Bill James, John Benson, Ron Shandler and Steve Mann answered this, but I did find two people to cross-check my own revised forecasts against seconds before rolling up my sleeves in front of a speaker phone on April 19 (hooking up with Peter Golenbock again in the Baseball Weekly NL league).

```
Strike-adjusted Predictions: BICHETTE
                 AB      HR      RBI     SB      BA
Patton          525      28      102     16      .312
Hunt            500      26       86     17      .291
Kreutzer        580      23       96     21      .295
```

John Hunt had published his projections that very day in the newspaper that was paying the phone bill. Peter Kreutzer's numbers were posted on the ESPNet SportsZone — so impressing my partner that you will be seeing Kreutzer's predictions in Golenbock's book this year. My new predictions went out on April 17 to the buyers of *Patton $ On Disk*.

The new stat predictions, I should say; the bid limits associated with them were mailed on the same day to anyone who sent in an envelope. My recommended bid for Bichette had gone from $37 in the book to $39 in the update, and he was now the seventh most highly priced hitter overall, so I was moving in the right direction.

```
Top 10 NL hitters
            earned avg            Heath Data    - touts -
Name         1995  sal  +/-        Pts    Rk    AP   JH   $94
BICHETTE,D    54   30   24        61.0    6     39   26   45
SANDERS,R     44   31   13        60.6    8     28   31   26
BONDS,B       43   46   -2        52.5   78     53   43   53
SOSA,S        42   38    5        64.2    1     38   32   40
LARKIN,B      42   26   16        56.1   25     28   31   26
WALKER,L      41   38    3        57.6   15     41   38   39
GWYNN,T       41   29   12        55.2   36     30   29   41
PIAZZA,M      39   31    8        61.4    5     40   30   35
BIGGIO,C      37   29    8        56.1   25     35   29   40
MONDESI,R     35   29    6        60.7    7     27   23   29
    average   42   33    9        58.5   21     36   31   37
```

The information in this chart is explained in the Belle comment. The three veteran, no-keeper leagues in Appendix A are the Baseball Weekly NL league, the Hollywood Stars in California, and It's Only Cricket, a league in Brooklyn that every year insist on a level playing field. The freeze-list league, shown for comparison's sake, is Scrooges NL, bad old boys from Mississippi, they must want us to think, since they go by such names as Tax Avoiders, Wild Turkeys and Big Knockers

Two things stand out. The average of the ten best hitters, $42, is a lot of moolah; it's $2 more than the ten best in the AL, where supposedly the better hitters reside.

And the average salary of $32, $1 more than the average in the AL, means that these hitters were highly predictable. They were 78% predictable, essentially (33/42), since the market tries to push the best hitters to par, while the cheapest one in the entire lot cost $26. There simply isn't a flyer in sight.

This is a success-oriented sort, so it's not surprising that all ten hitters are affiliated with winning Rotisserie teams (break-even is 52 points). It is surprising, however, how much more of an impact they seem to have on races than the AL group had. In 27 Heath leagues, teams that drafted these hitters ended up with 58.5 points, on average. The average rank of the hitters is 21. All told, 180 hitters were drafted by at least 10 teams and are tracked in this fashion. So, in a field of 180 contestants, to rank 21 is the same as ranking 1.4 in a twelve-team competition (21/180 x 12). Teams that bought just one of these hitters finished closer to first than to second.

In a three-way battle between myself, Hunt and the average league, I get Bichette, Bonds, Walker, Gwynn, Piazza and Biggio; Hunt gets Sanders and Larkin; the league gets Mondesi. Since I've already spent $238, we'll give the league Sosa.

CRAIG BIGGIO 2B Age 30   Bid: $33

Year	Team	G	AB	R	H	BB	SO	D	T	HR	RBI	SB	CS	BA	$
1991	HOU	149	546	79	161	53	71	23	4	4	46	19	6	.295	20
1992	HOU	162	613	96	170	94	95	32	3	6	39	38	15	.277	24
1993	HOU	155	610	98	175	77	93	41	5	21	64	15	17	.287	24
1994	HOU	114	437	88	139	62	58	44	5	6	56	39	4	.318	40
1995	HOU	141	553	123	167	80	85	30	2	22	77	33	8	.302	37

Appendix B shows that Biggio's running game contributed $12 to his salary. The pricing system doesn't give full credit to the running game (the league total for $SB is smaller than the league total for either $HR or $RBI), which does not make sense, theoretically. In practice, each steal is less likely to improve a team in the standings, because lots of teams punt the running game. The power categories are always more tightly contested, and so the bids further pinch down on speed in order to pay the power bill.

I'd discuss this further, except there's a good chance Biggio will be in the American League this year, and if the move takes place early enough, he should be moved. Suffice it to say, if he is in the American League and he steals 33 bases, they'll be worth about $3 more.

JEFF BLAUSER SS Age 30   Bid: $7

Year	Team	G	AB	R	H	BB	SO	D	T	HR	RBI	SB	CS	BA	$
1991	ATL	129	352	49	91	54	59	14	3	11	54	5	6	.259	13
1992	ATL	123	343	61	90	46	82	19	3	14	46	5	5	.262	15
1993	ATL	161	597	110	182	85	109	29	2	15	73	16	6	.305	27
1994	ATL	96	380	56	98	38	64	21	4	6	45	1	3	.258	7
1995	ATL	115	431	60	91	57	107	16	2	12	31	8	5	.211	2

A worrisome slump that he simply never kicked. In his best month, May, he hit .234.

BARRY BONDS OF Age 31   Bid: $45

Year	Team	G	AB	R	H	BB	SO	D	T	HR	RBI	SB	CS	BA	$
1991	PIT	153	510	95	149	107	73	28	5	25	116	43	13	.292	46
1992	PIT	140	473	109	147	127	69	36	5	34	103	39	8	.311	53
1993	SF	159	539	129	181	126	79	38	4	46	123	29	12	.336	56
1994	SF	112	391	89	122	74	43	18	1	37	81	29	9	.312	53
1995	SF	144	506	109	149	120	83	30	7	33	104	31	10	.294	43

To me, the 1996 bid price for Bonds is for sissies, just as yours was last year.

```
          Top 10 salaries, NL hitters
                earned avg           Heath Data    - touts -
          Name         1995  sal  +/-   Pts    Rk     AP   JH   |  $94
          BONDS,B        43   46   -2 | 52.5   78  |  53   43   |   53
          BAGWELL,J      28   39  -12 | 47.9  148  |  47   41   |   63
          WALKER,L       41   38    3 | 57.6   15  |  41   38   |   39
          MCGRIFF,F      26   38  -11 | 45.2  170  |  39   32   |   44
          SOSA,S         42   38    5 | 64.2    1  |  38   32   |   40
          GRISSOM,M      18   37  -19 | 44.6  175  |  45   34   |   33
          SHEFFIELD,G    24   36  -12 | 53.5   64  |  37   32   |   32
          WILLIAMS,Ma    26   35   -8 | 51.4   95  |  35   25   |   36
          ALOU,M         15   32  -17 | 56.9   19  |  36   32   |   39
          GALARRAGA,A    33   32    1 | 55.1   39  |  40   36   |   42
             average     30   37   -7 | 52.9   80  |  41   35   |   42
```

He had earned $53 the year before, $56 the year before that, $53 the year before that, and the most that three leagues could come up with was $46? The players as a group — all of them in their primes — earned $42 on average in 1994, and three leagues docked them an average of $5?

We're not talking pitchers here.

The three leagues that make up these averages do have different personalities, as we can see from the following:

NL hitters	BW	HSS	IOC	SCN	f
BONDS,B	43	46	48	57	f
BAGWELL,J	39	39	40	43	f
WALKER,L	37	41	36	34	f
MCGRIFF,F	34	37	42	40	f
SOSA,S	34	46	33	33	
GRISSOM,M	35	39	37	41	
SHEFFIELD,G	34	40	35	27	f
WILLIAMS,Ma	35	35	34	42	
ALOU,M	31	36	28	26	f
GALARRAGA,A	30	30	35	33	f
average	35	39	37	38	

The header above the table reads: **– leagues –**

Baseball Weekly consistently low-balls, the Hollywood Stars go for it. The Crickets chirp in the middle. ("I say, we *are* the average league.")

The Scrooges freeze all but three of these hitters — at such huge prices that the only free agent they have the money left to get down and dirty over, really, is Matt Williams.

In a three-way battle with Hunt and the average league, I get Bonds, Bagwell, Walker, McGriff, Grissom, Sheffield, Alou and Galarraga; the league wins tie-breakers with me, for obvious reasons (eight of them), for Sosa and Williams.

Just pretending I can afford them, do I want these hitters?

They lose an average of $7 each (all ten), so, from that standpoint, no.

However, even losing $7, they are associated with winning teams. The teams that drafted them ended up with 52.9 points on average. They ranked 80 out of 180, which equates to finishing fifth.

May not be where you want to finish, but keep in mind: If the market succeeded in its goal of pushing the best hitters to par — the ones it thinks will be best — the teams that bought them would finish between sixth and seventh.

AARON BOONE   3B   Age 23   Bid: R4

Year	Team	G	AB	R	H	BB	SO	D	T	HR	RBI	SB	CS	BA	$
1994	(R)	67	256	48	70	36	35	15	5	7	55	6	3	.273	x
1995	(AA)	23	66	6	15	5	12	3	0	0	3	2	0	.227	x
1995	(A)	108	395	61	103	43	77	19	1	14	50	11	7	.261	x

Would he be profiled if his name wasn't Aaron?

BRET BOONE   2B   Age 28   Bid: $18

Year	Team	G	AB	R	H	BB	SO	D	T	HR	RBI	SB	CS	BA	$
1992	SEA	33	129	15	25	4	34	4	0	4	15	1	1	.194	1
1993	SEA	76	271	31	68	17	52	12	2	12	38	2	3	.251	8
1994	CIN	108	381	59	122	24	74	25	2	12	68	3	4	.320	26
1995	CIN	138	513	63	137	41	84	34	2	15	68	5	1	.267	16

His career year may not be 1996 but it wasn't 1994.

JEFF BRANSON

SS,3B   Age 29   Bid: $5

Year	Team	G	AB	R	H	BB	SO	D	T	HR	RBI	SB	CS	BA	$
1992	CIN	72	115	12	34	5	16	7	1	0	15	0	1	.296	3
1993	CIN	125	381	40	92	19	73	15	1	3	22	4	1	.241	1
1994	CIN	58	109	18	31	5	16	4	1	6	16	0	0	.284	6
1995	CIN	122	331	43	86	44	69	18	2	12	45	2	1	.260	10

Could do as well or better in the same role.

RICO BROGNA

1B   Age 26   Bid: $23

Year	Team	G	AB	R	H	BB	SO	D	T	HR	RBI	SB	CS	BA	$
1992	DET	9	26	3	5	3	5	1	0	1	3	0	0	.192	0
1994	NYM	39	131	16	46	6	29	11	2	7	20	1	0	.351	12
1995	NYM	134	495	72	143	39	111	27	2	22	76	0	0	.289	22

Possible break-out year coming up, not that he hasn't raised eyebrows already.

JACOB BRUMFIELD

OF   Age 31   Bid: $5

Year	Team	G	AB	R	H	BB	SO	D	T	HR	RBI	SB	CS	BA	$
1992	CIN	24	30	6	4	2	4	0	0	0	2	6	0	.133	1
1993	CIN	103	272	40	73	21	47	17	3	6	23	20	8	.268	12
1994	CIN	68	122	36	38	15	18	10	2	4	11	6	3	.311	9
1995	PIT	116	402	64	109	37	71	23	2	4	26	22	12	.271	12

He's climbed the ladder as far as he can.

DAMON BUFORD

OF   Age 26   Bid: $2

Year	Team	G	AB	R	H	BB	SO	D	T	HR	RBI	SB	CS	BA	$
1993	BAL	53	79	18	18	9	19	5	0	2	9	2	2	.228	1
1994	BAL	4	2	2	1	0	1	0	0	0	0	0	0	.500	0
1995	BAL	24	32	6	2	6	7	0	0	0	2	3	1	.063	-1
1995	NYM	44	136	24	32	19	28	5	0	4	12	7	7	.235	4

This item in the New York Times in November:

    "The Mets' medical report included Rico Brogna (minor surgery to repair cartilage in his right knee), Dave Mlicki (bone chips removed from his elbow), Todd Hundley (cast on left wrist slightly fractured in the final game of the season) and Damon Buford (sprained ankle falling off a skateboard). All should be ready by spring training."

Thought you would want to know.

SCOTT BULLETT   OF   Age 27   Bid: $1

Year	Team	G	AB	R	H	BB	SO	D	T	HR	RBI	SB	CS	BA	$
1993	PIT	23	55	2	11	3	15	0	2	0	4	3	2	.200	0
1995	CHC	104	150	19	41	12	30	5	7	3	22	8	3	.273	7

Fifth-outfielder sleeper.

ELLIS BURKS   OF   Age 31   Bid: $13

Year	Team	G	AB	R	H	BB	SO	D	T	HR	RBI	SB	CS	BA	$
1991	BOS	130	474	56	119	39	81	33	3	14	56	6	11	.251	13
1992	BOS	66	235	35	60	25	48	8	3	8	30	5	2	.255	8
1993	CHW	146	499	75	137	60	97	24	4	17	74	6	9	.275	18
1994	COL	42	149	33	48	16	39	8	3	13	24	3	1	.322	15
1995	COL	103	278	41	74	39	72	10	6	14	49	7	3	.266	14

Was just a tad better than the average hitter — in Colorado!

MIKE BUSCH   3B   Age 27   Bid: R3

Year	Team	G	AB	R	H	BB	SO	D	T	HR	RBI	SB	CS	BA	$
1994	(AAA)	126	460	73	121	50	101	23	3	27	83	2	3	.263	x
1995	(AAA)	121	443	68	119	42	103	32	1	18	62	2	2	.269	x
1995	LA	13	17	3	4	0	7	0	0	3	6	0	0	.235	2

The plight of the scabs who were called up didn't get my sympathy, but to a man they didn't ask for it. They were tough people who had scuffled to a certain level in their profession, were going no further, and knew it. Maybe management had enough sense not to call the ones who weren't *really* tough up to sit next to —

BRETT BUTLER   OF   Age 38   Bid: $17

Year	Team	G	AB	R	H	BB	SO	D	T	HR	RBI	SB	CS	BA	$
1991	LA	161	615	112	182	108	79	13	5	2	38	38	28	.296	25
1992	ATL	157	553	86	171	95	67	14	11	3	39	41	21	.309	28
1993	LA	156	607	80	181	86	69	21	10	1	42	39	19	.298	24

Year	Team	G	AB	R	H	BB	SO	D	T	HR	RBI	SB	CS	BA	$
1994	LA	111	417	79	131	68	52	13	9	8	33	27	8	.314	30
1995	LA	129	513	78	154	67	51	18	9	1	38	32	8	.300	22

— who is really tough.

And was shocked beyond belief that the fans could have turned Mike Busch into a folk hero. I would have been, too.

Brett Butler had nothing to gain whatever by the strike. He was striking for Mike Busch, or would have been if Busch had been the tiniest amount more talented. Butler himself, remember, teetered on the edge of extinction himself for a couple of years. In 1982, his second season with the Braves, he hit .217. Had two extra-base hits in 240 AB. The next season he had 21 doubles, 13 triples and 5 homers. He stole 39 bases and was sent back to the dugout, dusting his uniform, 23 times. He was then and is now 5'10" and about 160 pounds. Mike Busch has been 6'5", 225 all his adult life.

It's interesting that Brett retreated. All the Dodgers did. The laid-back LA fans booed them into submission. It took that long for me to realize — because I do take sides — that baseball has gotten itself into such a world of hurt that a little old labor agreement isn't going to mend it right away.

MIGUEL CAIRO   2B   Age 22   Bid: R4

Year	Team	G	AB	R	H	BB	SO	D	T	HR	RBI	SB	CS	BA	$
1994	(A)	133	533	76	155	34	37	23	4	2	48	44	23	.291	x
1995	(AA)	107	435	53	121	26	31	20	1	1	41	33	16	.278	x

He's 6'0", 160; bats right. Born in Anaco, Venezuela. Signed with the Dodgers in 1990 when he was 17. Hit .315 at Vero Beach (A) in 1993. Led the California League in caught stealing in 1994. Hopes to take DeShields' job.

KEN CAMINITI   3B   Age 33   Bid: $28

Year	Team	G	AB	R	H	BB	SO	D	T	HR	RBI	SB	CS	BA	$
1991	HOU	152	574	65	145	46	85	30	3	13	80	4	5	.253	15
1992	HOU	135	506	68	149	44	68	31	2	13	62	10	4	.294	24
1993	HOU	143	543	75	142	49	88	31	0	13	75	8	5	.262	15
1994	HOU	111	406	63	115	43	71	28	2	18	75	4	3	.283	24
1995	SD	143	526	74	159	69	94	33	0	26	94	12	5	.302	34

A good year turned into a career year in September, but he will continue to enjoy being out of the Astrodome (home slugging average .525, compared to .466 in 1994.)

JOHN CANGELOSI   OF   Age 33   Bid: $3

Year	Team	G	AB	R	H	BB	SO	D	T	HR	RBI	SB	CS	BA	$
1992	PIT	73	85	12	16	18	16	2	0	1	6	6	5	.188	-1
1994	NYM	62	111	14	28	19	20	4	0	0	4	5	1	.252	2
1995	HOU	90	201	46	64	48	42	5	2	2	18	21	5	.318	14

A comeback to rival John Travolta's.

CHUCK CARR   OF   Age 27   Bid: $8

Year	Team	G	AB	R	H	BB	SO	D	T	HR	RBI	SB	CS	BA	$
1991	NYM	12	11	1	2	0	2	0	0	0	1	1	0	.182	-1
1992	STL	22	64	8	14	9	6	3	0	0	3	10	2	.219	3
1993	FLA	142	551	75	147	49	74	19	2	4	41	58	22	.267	26
1994	FLA	106	433	61	114	22	71	19	2	2	30	32	8	.263	19
1995	FLA	105	308	54	70	46	49	20	0	2	20	25	11	.227	6

I bought this lemon two years in a row, so I hate him, don't get me wrong, but now's precisely when you don't want to throw him on someone else's junk heap. Platooning with Tavarez, he could be very effective. Hit .310 against lefties.

MARK CARREON   1B,OF   Age 32   Bid: $16

Year	Team	G	AB	R	H	BB	SO	D	T	HR	RBI	SB	CS	BA	$
1991	NYM	106	254	18	66	12	26	6	0	4	21	2	1	.260	5
1992	DET	101	336	34	78	22	57	11	1	10	41	3	1	.232	7
1993	SF	78	150	22	49	13	16	9	1	7	33	1	0	.327	10
1994	SF	51	100	8	27	7	20	4	0	3	20	0	0	.270	4
1995	SF	117	396	53	119	23	37	24	0	17	65	0	1	.301	20

Fine hitter. Should have completely shed the notion that he's a platoon player (slugged .502 against righthanders) or can't play every day (slugged .505 in September). (Slugged .490 on the season.) The one concern would be if he starts out the season in a slump; often reputations that you think you've shed are still clinging to you.

RAUL CASANOVA   C   Age 23   Bid: R2

Year	Team	G	AB	R	H	BB	SO	D	T	HR	RBI	SB	CS	BA	$
1993	(A)	76	227	32	58	21	46	12	0	6	30	0	1	.256	x

Year	Team	G	AB	R	H	BB	SO	D	T	HR	RBI	SB	CS	BA	$
1994	(A)	123	471	83	160	43	97	27	2	23	120	1	4	.340	x
1995	(AA)	89	306	42	83	25	51	18	0	12	44	4	1	.271	x

Did not follow up his Piazza-like 1994 in the California league with a Piazza-like 1995, but he progressed in the right direction. Injuries slowed him at times at Memphis; he'll get a chance to hone his skills and pad his stats at Las Vegas this year, then be brought up to the Padres late in the season. He's now listed as 6'0", 192 in the green book, so he may also be still growing. He bats both and is said to have a strong arm.

VINNY CASTILLA   3B   Age 28   Bid: $30

Year	Team	G	AB	R	H	BB	SO	D	T	HR	RBI	SB	CS	BA	$
1991	ATL	12	5	1	1	0	2	0	0	0	0	0	0	.200	0
1992	ATL	9	16	1	4	1	4	1	0	0	1	0	0	.250	0
1993	COL	105	337	36	86	13	45	9	7	9	30	2	5	.255	6
1994	COL	52	130	16	43	7	23	11	1	3	18	2	1	.331	9
1995	COL	139	527	82	163	30	87	34	2	32	90	2	8	.309	34

I open the pages of last year's book looking for edification as to why I proposed a $2 bid for Vinny Castilla and find: "It's his bad luck that Walt Weiss has become Cal Ripken all of a sudden." So I obviously didn't think Vinny was Cal Ripken.

In the update, don't ask me why, his stock had dropped to $1.

```
Top 10 profits, NL hitters
              earned avg        Heath Data    - touts -
Name          1995  sal  +/-     Pts   Rk     AP   JH  | $94
CASTILLA,V     34    9   24      55.0   41      1   17 |  9
BICHETTE,D     54   30   24      61.0    6     39   26 | 45
CARREON,M      20    1   19      47.3  153      2      |  4
YOUNG,E        26    9   17      55.6   30      8   16 | 17
LARKIN,B       42   26   16      56.1   25     28   31 | 26
KARROS,E       34   19   15      58.2   12     16   14 | 14
MERCED,O       25   10   15      54.1   56      7   12 | 14
EISENREICH,    21    7   14      52.3   82      6   13 | 15
CAMINITI,K     34   20   14      55.6   31     20   18 | 24
GRACE,M        32   18   14      58.2   12     19   17 | 14
  average      32   15   17      55.3   45     15   16 | 18
```

This is a surprise-oriented sort, and the only who's only half surprised is John Hunt; he had a 50% success rate overall (16/32). The market and I were 47% successful, 53% surprised. By far the best predictor of 1995 was 1994 (56%).

In a three-way battle, Hunt would get Castilla (great call, John), Young (another), Larkin, Merced and Eisenreich; I would get Bichette, Carreon and Grace; the average league would get Karros and take Caminiti from me in a tie-breaker. The John Birch League (1994) would beat us all out for Bichette, Carreon, Young, Merced, Eisenreich and Caminiti.

It's worth noting, though, that $15 is a lot to pay for a surprise. In the American League (Cora comment), the corresponding hitters cost $7; from a certain standpoint those hitters were more than twice as big surprises. The AL group had bigger profits ($21), but the National League hitters had bigger earnings — they gave their teams better stats — and the circumstantial evidence in the Heath Leagues is about the same: the ten biggest bargains in the National League were likewise bought by teams that on average finished third (45/180 x 12).

ANDUJAR CEDENO   SS   Age 26   Bid: $4

Year	Team	G	AB	R	H	BB	SO	D	T	HR	RBI	SB	CS	BA	$
1991	HOU	67	251	27	61	9	74	13	2	9	36	4	3	.243	8
1992	HOU	71	220	15	38	14	71	13	2	2	13	2	0	.173	-4
1993	HOU	149	505	69	143	48	97	24	4	11	56	9	7	.283	16
1994	HOU	98	342	38	90	29	79	26	0	9	49	1	1	.263	11
1995	SD	120	390	42	82	28	92	16	2	6	31	5	3	.210	-1

His average salary was $14, only $6 less than Caminiti's; bettors for some reason were even more bullish, comparatively, over Cedeno's move to San Diego. Baseball Weekly, bearish on Bonds and just about every other expensive hitter, pushed Cedeno to $18. There may be a willingness to put a call or call a put on Andujar this year, but whichever it is, I'm out of it.

ROGER CEDENO   OF   Age 21   Bid: R2

Year	Team	G	AB	R	H	BB	SO	D	T	HR	RBI	SB	CS	BA	$
1993	(AA)	122	465	70	134	45	90	13	8	4	30	28	20	.288	x
1994	(AAA)	104	383	84	123	51	57	18	5	4	49	30	13	.321	x
1995	(AAA)	99	367	67	112	53	56	19	9	2	44	23	18	.305	x
1995	LA	40	42	4	10	3	10	2	0	0	3	1	0	.238	0

Still young enough to be an R5, he's had too much exposure to be an R1.

ARCHI CIANFROCCO   1B   Age 29   Bid: $1

Year	Team	G	AB	R	H	BB	SO	D	T	HR	RBI	SB	CS	BA	$
1992	MTL	86	232	25	56	11	66	5	2	6	30	3	0	.241	6
1993	SD	96	296	30	72	17	69	11	2	12	48	2	0	.243	8
1994	SD	59	146	9	32	3	39	8	0	4	13	2	0	.219	1
1995	SD	51	118	22	31	11	28	7	0	5	31	0	2	.263	6

It's not that I don't understand Mike Bush's position — it's the question, what wouldn't you do to feed your family if it was starving? — it's just that it's impossible to admire it. Archi Cianfrocco, who if anything had less of a future in the majors, said no thank you to being a replacement. He went to Las Vegas, hardly with the Padres' blessing, and hit .311. For once virtue seems to have had an additional reward.

DAVE CLARK　　OF　Age 33　　　　　　　　　　Bid: $1

Year	Team	G	AB	R	H	BB	SO	D	T	HR	RBI	SB	CS	BA	$
1991	KC	11	10	3	2	1	1	0	0	0	1	0	0	.200	0
1992	CHC	23	33	3	7	6	8	0	0	2	7	0	0	.212	1
1993	PIT	110	277	43	75	38	58	11	2	11	46	1	0	.271	10
1994	PIT	86	223	37	66	22	48	11	1	10	46	2	2	.296	15
1995	PIT	77	196	30	55	24	38	6	0	4	24	3	3	.281	6

Hit .310 in 71 at-bats in the cleanup position, which is a sad comment on the Pirates.

PHIL CLARK　OF　Age 28　　　　　　　　　　Bid: R3

Year	Team	G	AB	R	H	BB	SO	D	T	HR	RBI	SB	CS	BA	$
1992	DET	23	54	3	22	6	9	4	0	1	5	1	0	.407	4
1993	SD	102	240	33	75	8	31	17	0	9	33	2	0	.313	12
1994	SD	61	149	14	32	5	17	6	0	5	20	1	2	.215	2
1995	SD	75	97	12	21	8	18	3	0	2	7	0	2	.216	-1

A penny stock that crashed.

ROYCE CLAYTON　SS　Age 26　　　　　　　　　　Bid: $7

Year	Team	G	AB	R	H	BB	SO	D	T	HR	RBI	SB	CS	BA	$
1991	SF	9	26	0	3	1	6	1	0	0	2	0	0	.115	-1
1992	SF	98	321	31	72	26	63	7	4	4	24	8	4	.224	4
1993	SF	153	549	54	155	38	91	21	5	6	70	11	10	.282	16
1994	SF	108	385	38	91	30	74	14	6	3	30	23	3	.236	11
1995	SF	138	509	56	124	38	109	29	3	5	58	24	9	.244	12

Relax, Royce. You will get paid. But I strongly advise your backers to buy Aurilia.

GREG COLBRUNN　1B　Age 26　　　　　　　　　　Bid: $19

Year	Team	G	AB	R	H	BB	SO	D	T	HR	RBI	SB	CS	BA	$
1992	MTL	52	168	12	45	6	34	8	0	2	18	3	2	.268	5
1993	MTL	70	153	15	39	6	33	9	0	4	23	4	2	.255	5
1994	FLA	47	155	17	47	9	27	10	0	6	31	1	1	.303	10

Year	Team	G	AB	R	H	BB	SO	D	T	HR	RBI	SB	CS	BA	$
1995	FLA	138	528	70	146	22	69	22	1	23	89	11	3	.277	**26**

Oddly enough, he didn't hit well against lefties at all (.215). Only hit three homers against them. It's not that lefties are especially good in the National League; in fact, they were significantly easier to hit than righthanders last year (.268 vs. .262).

I'm hemming and hawing while I'm trying to think what the bid limit should be for Colbrunn, but, as we all know, the only real consideration is his health.

JEFF CONINE OF Age 30 Bid: $28

Year	Team	G	AB	R	H	BB	SO	D	T	HR	RBI	SB	CS	BA	$
1992	KC	28	91	10	23	8	23	5	2	0	9	0	0	.253	**1**
1993	FLA	162	595	75	174	52	135	24	3	12	79	2	2	.292	**19**
1994	FLA	115	451	60	144	40	92	27	6	18	82	1	2	.319	**31**
1995	FLA	133	483	72	146	66	94	26	2	25	105	2	0	.302	**31**

A slow fade in the second half (.285), but that's still a three-category player (barely).

SCOTT COOPER 3B Age 28 Bid: $4

Year	Team	G	AB	R	H	BB	SO	D	T	HR	RBI	SB	CS	BA	$
1991	BOS	14	35	6	16	2	2	4	2	0	7	0	0	.457	**3**
1992	BOS	123	337	34	93	37	33	21	0	5	33	1	1	.276	**8**
1993	BOS	156	526	67	147	58	81	29	3	9	63	5	2	.279	**14**
1994	BOS	104	369	49	104	30	65	16	4	13	53	0	3	.282	**14**
1995	STL	118	374	29	86	49	85	18	2	3	40	0	3	.230	**0**

Go to $6 if LaRussa seems to like him.

WIL CORDERO SS,OF Age 24 Bid: $21

Year	Team	G	AB	R	H	BB	SO	D	T	HR	RBI	SB	CS	BA	$
1992	MTL	45	126	17	38	9	31	4	1	2	8	0	0	.302	**4**
1993	MTL	138	475	56	118	34	60	32	2	10	58	12	3	.248	**11**
1994	MTL	110	415	65	122	41	62	30	3	15	63	16	3	.294	**29**
1995	MTL	131	514	64	147	36	88	35	2	10	49	9	5	.286	**16**

Was a flop in the outfield. Made a lot of errors, had a terrible zone rating, and didn't hit.

On the other hand, he was indeed a flop at shortstop. He tied for last in fielding percentage (among regulars), was last in range, last in double plays, and probably was last in zone rating

(.817, compared to .883 for the position).

But he played 105 games at shortstop, 87 to spare, and has an outfielder's bat.

TRIPP CROMER
SS   Age 28   Bid: $1

Year	Team	G	AB	R	H	BB	SO	D	T	HR	RBI	SB	CS	BA	$
1993	STL	10	23	1	2	1	6	0	0	0	0	0	0	.087	-2
1994	STL	2	0	1	0	0	0	0	0	0	0	0	0	.000	0
1995	STL	105	345	36	78	14	66	19	0	5	18	0	0	.226	-2

Tripp shared last place in fielding percentage with Wil. He had an excellent zone rating, though (.924), and hit more homers than anyone expected. His batting average, sadly, was maybe a little high as well.

MIDRE CUMMINGS
OF   Age 24   Bid: $2

Year	Team	G	AB	R	H	BB	SO	D	T	HR	RBI	SB	CS	BA	$
1993	PIT	13	36	5	4	4	9	1	0	0	3	0	0	.111	-2
1994	PIT	24	86	11	21	4	18	4	0	1	12	0	0	.244	1
1995	PIT	59	152	13	37	13	30	7	1	2	15	1	0	.243	1

John Mehno in a September issue of *The Sporting News*: "Veteran players have been put off by casual habits of certain rookies. Inexperienced players far outnumber veterans, one reason for a clubhouse atmosphere that needs to be improved."

We do wish he'd just start naming names at this point, but we don't have to go into that clubhouse.

Elsewhere in the same report he quotes Leyland: "You don't compare yourself to other guys hitting .230, you compare yourself to the best players in the league. That's the only way you're going to get good."

Which pretty much nails it down.

DARREN DAULTON
C   Age 34   Bid: $16

Year	Team	G	AB	R	H	BB	SO	D	T	HR	RBI	SB	CS	BA	$
1991	PHI	89	285	36	56	41	66	12	0	12	42	5	0	.196	6
1992	PHI	145	485	80	131	88	103	32	5	27	109	11	2	.270	34
1993	PHI	147	510	90	131	117	111	35	4	24	105	5	0	.257	21
1994	PHI	69	257	43	77	33	43	17	1	15	56	4	1	.300	21
1995	PHI	98	342	44	85	55	52	19	3	9	55	3	0	.249	9

Position scarcity, meet knees that have had their share of home plate collisions before the season starts.

And when the dust has settled, Daulton's number eight:

Top 10 losses, NL hitters

Name	earned 1995	avg sal	+/-	Heath Data Pts	Rk	- touts - AP	JH	$94
FLOYD,C	-2	19	-20	53.8	60	29	22	14
GRISSOM,M	18	37	-19	44.6	175	45	34	33
DYKSTRA,L	6	24	-18	45.6	164	27	26	13
ALOU,M	15	32	-17	56.9	19	36	32	39
HOLLINS,Dav	3	19	-16	47.4	152	15	10	2
CEDENO,A	-1	14	-15	46.6	160	14	14	11
COOPER,S	0	14	-14	49.3	128	8	13	14
DAULTON,D	9	22	-13	52.5	77	21	20	21
SHEFFIELD,G	24	36	-12	53.5	64	37	32	32
BLAUSER,J	2	14	-12	51.3	97	12	12	7
average	7	23	-16	50.2	110	24	22	19

Interestingly, the market bet more on these hitters last year than they earned in '94; and so did Hunt; and so, especially, did I. This is a list of failed puts, or calls.

In a three-way battle, Floyd, Grissom, Dykstra, Alou and Sheffield go to me; you guys get Hollins, Cooper, Daulton and Blauser; and the only way Hunt gets anyone is if we agree to let go of Cedeno. We do.

The players earn an average of $7 after being expected to earn — by, let's say, you guys — an average of $23. Does that make them 30% predictable?

Well, they return 30 cents on the dollar, that's the simpler way of putting it. The ten biggest AL busts (Delgado comment) returned 25 cents. The teams that were foolish enough to buy the AL duds finished with 49.3 points, in eighth place. The buyers of the ten most disappointing NL hitters scored a little better in points and finished seventh (110/180 x 12).

Even though there are anomalies (what's Alou doing so high?), there seems to be an almost relentless circumstantial logic. Taken as a group, the most unreliable NL hitters were a little more reliable than the most unreliable AL hitters, and their teams, as a result, weren't quite as damaged.

Freeze lists barely seem to matter.

NL hitters	— leagues — BW	HSS	IOC	SCN	f
FLOYD,C	23	17	16	10	f
GRISSOM,M	35	39	37	41	
DYKSTRA,L	22	25	25	25	
ALOU,M	31	36	28	26	f
HOLLINS,Dav	16	20	20	19	
CEDENO,A	18	11	13	13	
COOPER,S	11	12	18	18	
DAULTON,D	24	20	21	22	f
SHEFFIELD,G	34	40	35	27	f
BLAUSER,J	15	13	13	11	
average	23	23	23	21	

The owners in Scrooges thought they had four pretty good freezes, but every one of them lost money (just not as much), while inflation pressure pushed Scrooges to spend more than the non-freeze leagues on Grissom and Cooper. They end up spending almost as much per player.

The other three leagues have some differences of opinion, but not one of them can say it had a better inkling of the ten biggest disasters. Nor can any league be called the bigger fool.

Stage Three from coast to coast.

ANDRE DAWSON   OF   Age 40   Bid: $1

Year	Team	G	AB	R	H	BB	SO	D	T	HR	RBI	SB	CS	BA	$
1991	CHC	149	563	69	153	22	80	21	4	31	104	4	5	.272	30

NL hitters   – 146 –

Year	Team	G	AB	R	H	BB	SO	D	T	HR	RBI	SB	CS	BA	$
1992	CHC	143	542	60	150	30	70	27	2	22	90	6	2	.277	**29**
1993	BOS	121	461	44	126	17	49	29	1	13	67	2	1	.273	**14**
1994	BOS	75	292	34	70	9	53	18	0	16	48	2	2	.240	**10**
1995	FLA	79	226	30	58	9	45	10	3	8	37	0	0	.257	**7**

I don't think he'll make it to one more starting line, but if he does, a most worthy and noble fifth outfielder.

DELINO DESHIELDS   2B   Age 27   Bid: $15

Year	Team	G	AB	R	H	BB	SO	D	T	HR	RBI	SB	CS	BA	$
1991	MTL	151	563	83	134	95	151	15	4	10	51	56	23	.238	**26**
1992	MTL	135	530	82	155	54	108	19	8	7	56	46	15	.292	**31**
1993	MTL	123	481	75	142	72	64	17	7	2	29	43	10	.295	**23**
1994	LA	89	320	51	80	54	53	11	3	2	33	27	7	.250	**16**
1995	LA	127	425	66	109	63	83	18	3	8	37	39	14	.256	**19**

His goofy swing is the problem. If it got results, it would be called a wristy uppercut.

MIKE DEVEREAUX OF   Age 33   Bid: $4

Year	Team	G	AB	R	H	BB	SO	D	T	HR	RBI	SB	CS	BA	$
1991	BAL	149	608	82	158	47	115	27	10	19	59	16	9	.260	**21**
1992	BAL	156	653	76	180	44	94	29	11	24	107	10	8	.276	**30**
1993	BAL	131	527	72	132	43	99	31	3	14	75	3	3	.250	**12**
1994	BAL	85	301	35	61	22	72	8	2	9	33	1	2	.203	**-2**
1995	CHW	92	333	48	102	25	51	21	1	10	55	6	6	.306	**17**
1995	ATL	29	55	7	14	2	11	3	0	1	8	2	0	.255	**2**

Destination — like a few hundred others — unknown; with leverage like that, the Braves ought to be able to get his signature on their own contract. In his prime Devereaux was a superb center fielder and he still can hit lefties (.299 for the years in this scan, .308 last year). He earned his $800,000 last year and will sign for maybe a third as much this year.

MARIANO DUNCAN   SS,2B,1B   Age 32   Bid: $3

Year	Team	G	AB	R	H	BB	SO	D	T	HR	RBI	SB	CS	BA	$
1991	CIN	100	333	46	86	12	57	7	4	12	40	5	4	.258	**12**

Year	Team	G	AB	R	H	BB	SO	D	T	HR	RBI	SB	CS	BA	$
1992	PHI	142	574	71	153	17	108	40	3	8	50	23	3	.267	19
1993	PHI	124	496	68	140	12	88	26	4	11	73	6	5	.282	17
1994	PHI	88	347	49	93	17	72	22	1	8	48	10	2	.268	15
1995	CIN	81	265	36	76	5	62	14	2	6	36	1	3	.287	9

Same as Devereaux: a free agent — sorry about that — who should stay put. Hit .291 against lefties last year, has hit .298 against them in the last five years; dropped down to the $350,000 tax bracket last year, and hasn't stopped.

SHAWON DUNSTON   SS   Age 33   Bid: $14

Year	Team	G	AB	R	H	BB	SO	D	T	HR	RBI	SB	CS	BA	$
1991	CHC	142	492	59	128	23	64	22	7	12	50	21	6	.260	18
1992	CHC	18	73	8	23	3	13	3	1	0	2	2	3	.315	2
1993	CHC	7	10	3	4	0	1	2	0	0	2	0	0	.400	1
1994	CHC	88	331	38	92	16	48	19	0	11	35	3	8	.278	13
1995	CHC	127	477	58	141	10	75	30	6	14	69	10	5	.296	23

Hit .216 in August, .239 the last month. As a free-agent-to-be, it undoubtedly cost him, but not as much as he may think. The four years prior to 1995 had him already in the $3,775,000 tax bracket.

JERMAINE DYE OF   Age 22   Bid: R2

Year	Team	G	AB	R	H	BB	SO	D	T	HR	RBI	SB	CS	BA	$
1994	(A)	135	506	73	151	33	82	41	1	15	98	19	10	.298	x
1995	(AA)	104	403	50	115	27	74	26	4	15	71	4	8	.285	x

Baseball America's No. 3 prospect in the Southern League, he's 6'4", 195; bats right; was a 17th-round draft pick by the Braves in '93. "Power, speed, grace, intelligence, maturity. When managers talk about Dye, any glowing word will do." Devereaux has heard of him.

LENNY DYKSTRA   OF   Age 33   Bid: $23

Year	Team	G	AB	R	H	BB	SO	D	T	HR	RBI	SB	CS	BA	$
1991	PHI	63	246	48	73	37	20	13	5	3	12	24	4	.297	14
1992	PHI	85	345	53	104	40	32	18	0	6	39	30	5	.301	23
1993	PHI	161	637	143	194	129	64	44	6	19	66	37	12	.305	36
1994	PHI	84	315	68	86	68	44	26	5	5	24	15	4	.273	13

Year	Team	G	AB	R	H	BB	SO	D	T	HR	RBI	SB	CS	BA	$
1995	PHI	62	254	37	67	33	28	15	1	2	18	10	5	.264	6

On the cover of my current issue of Baseball Weekly, Ryne Sandberg and his new wife Margaret are smiling broadly. Next to them runs the headline: Why Ryno's Coming Back.

Kind of buried on page 4 of this issue (November 8-14; I'm assuming most of you give the paper a rest for this month) is a much smaller headline: Revived "Game of the Week" Highlights New TV Deal.

I would say even Paul White was taking a rest, because what that means is, there will be baseball this season.

It really wasn't a sure thing until then. Hard to believe, but it wasn't. Now the owners have signed up to what looks like a great deal for everyone.

You'll know all about it by the time this book is in your hands, but to summarize just for reference: more networks, more games, more post-season (yippee — all!), and more money.

Not a lot more, not like the old days, but $11 million per team for the next 5 years, as compared to $7 million per team last year from The Baseball Network. That's $4 million more. It's not enough to pay for Dykstra, in the Phillies' case, but it might pay for the rest of the team.

"With no labor agreement in place, the new TV deal includes a clause whereby the networks don't have to pay in the event of a work stoppage."

Duh.

"We are grateful to our fans, whose interest remains strong," Selig is quoted as saying.

Paul White should have left out the comma.

I don't blame fans for defecting, and I understand their refusal to support either side, but let us be clear: The owners did this.

They couldn't handle the open market, couldn't even figure out the rules, and got so confused about what to do that they stopped the game at the peak of its popularity, in the middle of its best season ever.

The solution they imposed on the players during the strike, it soon became apparent, just made matters worse for the owners. Revenue sharing (without sharing the books) contingent on a salary cap (based on a percent of the revenue).

Steinbrenner was completely candid. Sure, I'll give the Pirates some money. Just can't be mine. Has to be Mattingly's.

The players expressed a willingness to be part of the solution, if the owners let them see the problem. They wouldn't.

The market should be allowed to solve this, said the players. After all, this is America. Without any agreement at all, old or new, that's just what has happened. Won't be long before the players need a union to protect their wages.

No, I believe in free enterprise, I really do; I'm all for the United Baseball League. And I realize a great many players are jerks.

Which brings us to Dykstra. It couldn't be more fitting that on the very day I open my copy of Baseball Weekly to see that baseball's troubles are over, that a TV deal is in place (was this even reported in the regular sports sections?), who should pop up on my screen but Nails.

Give those dudes what they want, he said; I'm not getting mine.

If just a couple of other stars had said that, curtains for the players; they would have been squashed, which was the point all along.

Bonds. Ripken. Molitor. Glavine. Fielder. Stewart. Gwynn.

I would say between them they kissed off $20 million. With virtue as the only conceivable reward.

JIM EISENREICH   OF   Age 37   Bid: $11

Year	Team	G	AB	R	H	BB	SO	D	T	HR	RBI	SB	CS	BA	$
1991	KC	135	375	47	113	20	35	22	3	2	47	5	3	.301	13
1992	KC	113	353	31	95	24	36	13	3	2	28	11	6	.269	9
1993	PHI	153	362	51	115	26	36	17	4	7	54	5	0	.318	17
1994	PHI	104	290	42	87	33	31	15	4	4	43	6	2	.300	15
1995	PHI	129	377	46	119	38	44	22	2	10	55	10	0	.316	21

He's up to .288 lifetime, and this year will be his thirteenth season. Tip of the hat! But keep the applause down.

TONY EUSEBIO   C   Age 29   Bid: $9

Year	Team	G	AB	R	H	BB	SO	D	T	HR	RBI	SB	CS	BA	$
1991	HOU	10	19	4	2	6	8	1	0	0	0	0	0	.105	-1
1994	HOU	55	159	18	47	8	33	9	1	5	30	0	1	.296	9
1995	HOU	113	368	46	110	31	59	21	1	6	58	0	2	.299	14

He wore down in August (.280) and September (.215). Had some trouble batting fifth (.268 in 138 AB); was very comfortable batting seventh (.322 in 115 AB).

CARL EVERETT   OF   Age 26   Bid: $18

Year	Team	G	AB	R	H	BB	SO	D	T	HR	RBI	SB	CS	BA	$
1993	FLA	11	19	0	2	1	9	0	0	0	0	1	0	.105	-1
1994	FLA	16	51	7	11	3	15	1	0	2	6	4	0	.216	2
1995	NYM	79	289	48	75	39	67	13	1	12	54	2	5	.260	11

Turns out that he is definitely a player. Ball jumps off his bat. Good arm. Not base-stealing fast but get out of the way when he slides. It's going to be a while before we'll know whether Mets or Marlins got the better deal.

STEVE FINLEY   OF   Age 31   Bid: $24

Year	Team	G	AB	R	H	BB	SO	D	T	HR	RBI	SB	CS	BA	$
1991	HOU	159	596	84	170	42	65	28	10	8	54	34	18	.285	26
1992	HOU	162	607	84	177	58	63	29	13	5	55	44	9	.292	30
1993	HOU	142	545	69	145	28	65	15	13	8	44	19	6	.266	14
1994	HOU	94	373	64	103	28	52	16	5	11	33	13	7	.276	17

Year	Team	G	AB	R	H	BB	SO	D	T	HR	RBI	SB	CS	BA	$
1995	SD	139	562	104	167	59	62	23	8	10	44	36	12	.297	**28**

The season was a month too long for him to have his first .300 year (.236 in September). With another year studying Tony Gwynn's live videos, he'll do it this time.

DARRIN FLETCHER   C   Age 29   Bid: $7

Year	Team	G	AB	R	H	BB	SO	D	T	HR	RBI	SB	CS	BA	$
1991	PHI	46	136	5	31	5	15	8	0	1	12	0	1	.228	**0**
1992	MTL	83	222	13	54	14	28	10	2	2	26	0	2	.243	**3**
1993	MTL	133	396	33	101	34	40	20	1	9	60	0	0	.255	**8**
1994	MTL	94	285	28	74	25	23	18	1	10	57	0	0	.260	**12**
1995	MTL	110	350	42	100	32	23	21	1	11	45	0	1	.286	**12**

Even though he cost $8 last year, $7 should be enough now, because it's obvious that he's found his level. Fine hitter, though; seldom strikes out.

CLIFF FLOYD   1B   Age 23   Bid: $9

Year	Team	G	AB	R	H	BB	SO	D	T	HR	RBI	SB	CS	BA	$
1993	MTL	10	31	3	7	0	9	0	0	1	2	0	0	.226	**0**
1994	MTL	100	334	43	94	24	63	19	4	4	41	10	3	.281	**14**
1995	MTL	29	69	6	9	7	22	1	0	1	8	3	0	.130	**-2**

Was flailing before his injury. Said he'd just as soon not play first when he came back, which I'm sure sent a chill through baseball circles.

CHAD FONVILLE   SS,2B Age 25   Bid: $9

Year	Team	G	AB	R	H	BB	SO	D	T	HR	RBI	SB	CS	BA	$
1994	(A)	68	283	41	87	41	31	7	3	0	16	22	8	.307	**x**
1995	MTL/LA	102	320	43	89	23	42	6	1	0	16	20	7	.278	**9**

Not much was made of the fact that he jumped all the way from A ball. Why he was still at Single-A in 1994, after hitting .306 there in 1993, is another question. Anyway, he made the jump and gave both Offerman and DeShields more competition than they could handle. He doesn't have the arm or the range to be a full time shortstop.

MICAH FRANKLIN   OF   Age 24   Bid: R2

Year	Team	G	AB	R	H	BB	SO	D	T	HR	RBI	SB	CS	BA	$
1993	(A)	20	69	10	16	10	19	1	1	3	6	0	1	.232	x
1993	(A)	102	343	56	90	47	109	14	4	17	68	6	1	.262	x
1994	(A)	42	150	44	45	27	48	7	0	21	44	7	0	.300	x
1994	(AA)	79	279	46	77	33	79	17	0	10	40	2	2	.276	x
1995	(AAA)	110	358	64	105	47	95	28	0	21	71	3	3	.293	x

He's been a bit like a bush league Albert Belle; he apparently scares people on the field and off.
He's only 60 195, is a switch-hitter, and has been traded from the Mets to the Reds to the Pirates.
Many of the 21 home runs (in 42 games) that he hit in Single-A in 1994 were hit in the bandbox
in Winston Salem.

Last year he played at Calgary with Aude, Horn and the others. His batting average compares
rather poorly to the Cannons' .302 team batting average. But the long ball is the long ball,
anytime, anywhere. And the other Cannons really didn't have that many in their arsenals. Only
two others reached double figures, in fact: Keith Osik, the catcher, who had 10; and Dale Sveum,
the third baseman, who had 12

ANDRES GALARRAGA   1B   Age 35   Bid: $32

Year	Team	G	AB	R	H	BB	SO	D	T	HR	RBI	SB	CS	BA	$
1991	MTL	107	375	34	82	23	86	13	2	9	33	5	6	.219	4
1992	STL	95	325	38	79	11	69	14	2	10	39	5	4	.243	10
1993	COL	120	470	71	174	24	73	35	4	22	98	2	4	.370	37
1994	COL	103	417	77	133	19	93	21	0	31	85	8	3	.319	42
1995	COL	143	554	89	155	32	146	29	3	31	106	12	2	.280	33

Had a .571 slugging average at Coors Field, .452 on the road. Eighteen of his home runs were hit
at home. And he was way behind everyone else.

Altogether, there were 241 homers hit by the Rockies and their opponents at home; in road
games the Rockies and their opponents combined for 119. Right-handed batters hit 172 homers
in Coors Field, 75 on the road.

Left-handed batters found the fences easier to reach, too, and that was not the case in Mile
High Stadium. For both power and batting average, Coors Field was an even better place to hit
in than Mile High Stadium.

RON GANT   OF   Age 31   Bid: $28

Year	Team	G	AB	R	H	BB	SO	D	T	HR	RBI	SB	CS	BA	$
1991	ATL	154	561	101	141	71	104	35	3	32	105	34	15	.251	37
1992	ATL	153	544	74	141	45	101	22	6	17	80	32	10	.259	30

Year	Team	G	AB	R	H	BB	SO	D	T	HR	RBI	SB	CS	BA	$
1993	ATL	157	606	113	166	67	117	27	4	36	117	26	9	.274	**38**
1995	CIN	119	410	79	113	74	108	19	4	29	88	23	8	.276	**33**

In light of how devastating Gant was as the clean-up hitter (15 homers in 127 AB), it's odd that he did most of his hitting in the No. 3 spot (13 homers in 272 AB). He hit .298 with runners in scoring position and, get this, .418 Close & Late. In 55 such knuckle-biting AB, he had an .855 slugging average! He hit 17 of his homers on the road last year, which should make it even harder for the Reds to let him go.

CARLOS GARCIA   2B   Age 28   Bid: $12

Year	Team	G	AB	R	H	BB	SO	D	T	HR	RBI	SB	CS	BA	$
1991	PIT	12	24	4	6	1	8	0	2	0	1	0	0	.250	**0**
1992	PIT	22	39	4	8	0	9	1	0	0	4	0	0	.205	**0**
1993	PIT	141	546	77	147	31	67	25	5	12	47	18	11	.269	**16**
1994	PIT	98	412	49	114	16	67	15	2	6	28	18	9	.277	**17**
1995	PIT	104	367	41	108	25	55	24	2	6	50	8	4	.294	**15**

A nice little safety deposit box in the middle infield.

KARIM GARCIA   OF   Age 20   LA   Bid: R1

Year	Team	G	AB	R	H	BB	SO	D	T	HR	RBI	SB	CS	BA	$
1994	(A)	121	452	72	120	37	112	28	10	21	84	8	3	.265	**x**
1995	(AAA)	124	474	88	151	38	102	26	10	20	90	12	6	.319	**x**
1995	LA	13	20	1	4	0	4	0	0	0	0	0	0	.200	**-1**

The big debate about Karim Garcia is his age. Was he really only 19 last year? Apparently, a lot of managers in the PCL didn't think so.

Even if he did fib a little on his passport (he's from Mexico), there's no denying that he almost won the triple crown in Triple-A after making the jump from Single-A. Everyone agrees his right-fielder's arm is among the best in baseball. A left-handed batter, he will have trouble against lefties in the majors this year (.250 against lefties at Albuquerque), but he'll be facing them.

STEVE GIBRALTER   OF   Age 23   Bid: R2

Year	Team	G	AB	R	H	BB	SO	D	T	HR	RBI	SB	CS	BA	$
1994	(A)	121	452	72	120	37	112	28	10	21	84	8	3	.265	**x**
1995	(AAA)	124	474	88	151	38	102	26	10	20	90	12	6	.319	**x**
1995	LA	13	20	1	4	0	4	0	0	0	0	0	0	.200	**-1**

Gibralter's break-through season ended in mid-July, when he tore ligaments in his thumb. He was leading the American Association in homers and ribbies and had a .616 slugging average. As young as he is, this was his sixth pro season, and he had never before slugged above .500. He's 6'0", 190; bats right. Ron Gant, I doubt, knows who he is.

DERRICK GIBSON OF Age 21 Bid: R5

Year	Team	G	AB	R	H	BB	SO	D	T	HR	RBI	SB	CS	BA	$
1994	(A)	73	284	47	75	29	102	19	5	12	57	14	4	.264	x
1995	(A)	135	506	91	148	29	136	16	10	32	115	31	13	.292	x

Gibson is Baseball America's No. 4 prospect in the South Atlantic League. He bats right and is 6'2", 228 — "a cross between Bo Jackson and Frank Thomas," according to one manager. If so, even remotely so, there are going to be some rockets leaving Coors Field one of these years, because he belongs to the Rockies.

BERNARD GILKEY OF Age 29 Bid: $17

Year	Team	G	AB	R	H	BB	SO	D	T	HR	RBI	SB	CS	BA	$
1991	STL	81	268	28	58	39	33	7	2	5	20	14	8	.216	5
1992	STL	131	384	56	116	39	52	19	4	7	43	18	12	.302	20
1993	STL	137	557	99	170	56	66	40	5	16	70	15	10	.305	26
1994	STL	105	380	52	96	39	65	22	1	6	45	15	8	.253	13
1995	STL	121	480	73	143	42	70	33	4	17	69	12	6	.298	25

Has had just one bad year in the last four, so what is it about him that worries me?

JOE GIRARDI C Age 31 Bid: $6

Year	Team	G	AB	R	H	BB	SO	D	T	HR	RBI	SB	CS	BA	$
1991	CHC	21	47	3	9	6	6	2	0	0	6	0	0	.191	0
1992	CHC	91	270	19	73	19	38	3	1	1	12	0	2	.270	3
1993	COL	86	310	35	90	24	41	14	5	3	31	6	6	.290	9
1994	COL	93	330	47	91	21	48	9	4	4	34	3	3	.276	9
1995	COL	125	462	63	121	29	76	17	2	8	55	3	3	.262	9

Without his Coors fix, he would have hit .228.

LUIS GONZALEZ OF Age 28 Bid: $12

Year	Team	G	AB	R	H	BB	SO	D	T	HR	RBI	SB	CS	BA	$
1991	HOU	137	473	51	120	40	101	28	9	13	69	10	7	.254	16

Year	Team	G	AB	R	H	BB	SO	D	T	HR	RBI	SB	CS	BA	$
1992	HOU	122	387	40	94	24	52	19	3	10	55	7	7	.243	12
1993	HOU	154	540	82	162	47	83	34	3	15	72	20	9	.300	27
1994	HOU	112	392	57	107	49	57	29	4	8	67	15	13	.273	21
1995	CHC	133	471	69	130	57	63	29	8	13	69	6	8	.276	17

While very good hitters do seem to get better as they approach 30, the merely okay hitters seem to go into a decline.

MARK GRACE 1B Age 32 Bid: $27

Year	Team	G	AB	R	H	BB	SO	D	T	HR	RBI	SB	CS	BA	$
1991	CHC	160	619	87	169	70	53	28	5	8	58	3	4	.273	14
1992	CHC	158	603	72	185	72	36	37	5	9	79	6	1	.307	26
1993	CHC	155	594	86	193	71	32	39	4	14	98	8	4	.325	30
1994	CHC	106	403	55	120	48	41	23	3	6	44	0	1	.298	14
1995	CHC	143	552	97	180	65	46	51	3	16	92	6	2	.326	32

A very good hitter.

TONY GRAFFANINO 2B Age 24 Bid: R3

Year	Team	G	AB	R	H	BB	SO	D	T	HR	RBI	SB	CS	BA	$
1993	(A)	123	459	78	126	45	78	30	5	15	69	24	11	.275	x
1994	(AA)	124	440	66	132	50	53	28	3	7	52	29	7	.300	x
1995	(AAA)	50	179	20	34	15	49	6	0	4	17	2	2	.190	x

A sleeper who went into a coma.

WILLIE GREENE 3B Age 24 Bid: R2

Year	Team	G	AB	R	H	BB	SO	D	T	HR	RBI	SB	CS	BA	$
1992	CIN	29	93	10	25	10	23	5	2	2	13	0	2	.269	3
1993	CIN	15	50	7	8	2	19	1	1	2	5	0	0	.160	-1
1994	CIN	16	37	5	8	6	14	2	0	0	3	0	0	.216	-1
1995	(AAA)	91	325	57	79	38	67	12	2	19	45	3	3	.243	x
1995	CIN	8	19	1	2	3	7	0	0	0	0	0	0	.105	-1

Was passed by Pokey Reese, his own teamate at Indianapolis, as a top 10 prospect.

TOMMY GREGG OF   Age 32

Bid: $1

Year	Team	G	AB	R	H	BB	SO	D	T	HR	RBI	SB	CS	BA	$
1995	(AAA)	34	124	30	48	21	13	10	1	9	32	7	0	.387	x
1995	FLA	72	156	20	37	16	33	5	0	6	20	3	1	.237	4

Good year as a pinch-hitter envisioned. Won't press his luck on the bases.

MARQUIS GRISSOM   OF   Age 29

Bid: $29

Year	Team	G	AB	R	H	BB	SO	D	T	HR	RBI	SB	CS	BA	$
1991	MTL	148	558	73	149	34	89	23	9	6	39	76	17	.267	35
1992	MTL	159	653	99	180	42	81	39	6	14	66	78	13	.276	45
1993	MTL	157	630	104	188	52	76	27	2	19	95	53	10	.298	43
1994	MTL	110	475	96	137	41	66	25	4	11	45	36	6	.288	33
1995	ATL	139	551	80	142	47	61	23	3	12	42	29	9	.258	18

When a slump lasts all season, is it a slump? And it began in 1994, really.

MARK GRUDZIELANEK   SS,3B   Age 26

Bid: $3

Year	Team	G	AB	R	H	BB	SO	D	T	HR	RBI	SB	CS	BA	$
1994	(AA)	122	488	92	157	43	66	37	3	11	66	32	10	.322	x
1995	(AAA)	49	181	26	54	10	17	9	1	1	22	12	1	.298	x
1995	MTL	78	269	27	66	14	47	12	2	1	20	8	3	.245	3

He wasn't supposed to *have* minor league stats last year, but since he does, we have an almost textbook example of climbing the ladder three rungs in two years without getting any better. That's not to say he won't.

VLADIMIR GUERRERO   OF   Age 20

Bid: R5

Year	Team	G	AB	R	H	BB	SO	D	T	HR	RBI	SB	CS	BA	$
1994	(A)	37	137	24	43	29	71	13	3	5	25	0	7	.314	x
1995	(A)	110	421	77	140	30	45	21	10	16	63	12	7	.333	x

He's 6'1", 185, and, according to some, better than Andruw Jones. He's also compared to Rondell White, who will be a free agent by the time Vladimir's ready.

WILTON GUERRERO   SS   Age 21   Bid: R2

Year	Team	G	AB	R	H	BB	SO	D	T	HR	RBI	SB	CS	BA	$
1994	(A)	110	402	55	118	29	71	11	4	1	32	23	20	.294	x
1995	(AA)	95	382	53	133	26	63	13	6	0	26	21	22	.348	x
1995	(AAA)	14	49	10	16	1	7	1	1	0	2	2	3	.327	x

The Texas League batting champion, he continued to plunk hits at Albuquerque for 14 games. He could very easily take over at shortstop for the Dodgers sometime this season, but he's not going to be given many steal signs. Wilton bats right and is 5'11", 145; if he teams up with Fonville, we'll need binoculars.

MIKE GULAN   3B   Age 25   Bid: R2

Year	Team	G	AB	R	H	BB	SO	D	T	HR	RBI	SB	CS	BA	$
1994	(A)	120	466	39	113	26	108	30	2	8	56	2	8	.242	x
1995	(AA)	64	242	47	76	11	52	16	3	12	48	4	2	.314	x
1995	(AAA)	58	195	21	46	10	53	10	4	5	27	2	2	.236	x

Is the step up to Double-A the biggest one?

Mike Gulan, a Cardinals hopeful, made it with ease, and then fell on his face at Louisville. "His slick, effortless fielding," in the words of Baseball America, may be enough to keep him climbing. The Cardinals sure hope so.

TONY GWYNN   OF   Age 36   Bid: $37

Year	Team	G	AB	R	H	BB	SO	D	T	HR	RBI	SB	CS	BA	$
1991	SD	134	530	69	168	34	19	27	11	4	62	8	8	.317	22
1992	SD	128	520	77	165	46	16	27	3	6	41	3	6	.317	19
1993	SD	122	489	70	175	36	19	41	3	7	59	14	1	.358	29
1994	SD	110	419	79	165	48	19	35	1	12	64	5	0	.394	41
1995	SD	135	535	82	197	35	15	33	1	9	90	17	5	.368	41

Has finally passed Wade Boggs in lifetime batting average (.336 to .334). Interestingly, he's only eleventh in career OBA, trailing the likes of John Olerud and Dave Magadan. Last year he also led the league in batting with runners in scoring position (.394). Close & Late, he hit .388, and he hit .636 with the bases loaded.

TODD HANEY   2B   Age 30   Bid: $1

Year	Team	G	AB	R	H	BB	SO	D	T	HR	RBI	SB	CS	BA	$
1992	MTL	7	10	0	3	0	0	1	0	0	1	0	0	.300	0

Year	Team	G	AB	R	H	BB	SO	D	T	HR	RBI	SB	CS	BA	$
1994	CHC	17	37	6	6	3	3	0	0	1	2	2	1	.162	0
1995	CHC	25	73	11	30	7	11	8	0	2	6	0	0	.411	6

The most recent of the .400 hitters.

DAVE HANSEN 3B Age 27 Bid: R3

Year	Team	G	AB	R	H	BB	SO	D	T	HR	RBI	SB	CS	BA	$
1991	LA	53	56	3	15	2	12	4	0	1	5	1	0	.268	2
1992	LA	132	341	30	73	34	49	11	0	6	22	0	2	.214	0
1993	LA	84	105	13	38	21	13	3	0	4	30	0	1	.362	9
1994	LA	40	44	3	15	5	5	3	0	0	5	0	0	.341	2
1995	LA	100	181	19	52	28	28	10	0	1	14	0	0	.287	3

If the Dodgers don't bring back Wallach, Hansen's in the picture — almost no one else is. At this point, however, even he may not be too happy about that. He had a .933 fielding percentage in the 58 games that he was asked to take the field.

CHARLIE HAYES 3B Age 30 Bid: $16

Year	Team	G	AB	R	H	BB	SO	D	T	HR	RBI	SB	CS	BA	$
1991	PHI	142	460	34	106	16	75	23	1	12	53	3	3	.230	8
1992	NYY	142	509	52	131	28	100	19	2	18	66	3	5	.257	16
1993	COL	157	573	89	175	43	82	45	2	25	98	11	6	.305	32
1994	COL	113	423	46	122	36	71	23	4	10	50	3	6	.288	17
1995	PHI	141	529	58	146	50	88	30	3	11	85	5	1	.276	18

The kind of player the United Baseball League will be buying next year. They will play at a level that's far above Triple-A.

JOSE HERNANDEZ 2B,SS,3B Age 26 Bid: $2

Year	Team	G	AB	R	H	BB	SO	D	T	HR	RBI	SB	CS	BA	$
1994	CHC	56	132	18	32	8	29	2	3	1	9	2	2	.242	1
1995	CHC	93	245	37	60	13	69	11	4	13	40	1	0	.245	8

Is sure to hit a *few* homers, and you can move him around between three weak positions.

RICHARD HIDALGO   OF   Age 20   Bid: R2

Year	Team	G	AB	R	H	BB	SO	D	T	HR	RBI	SB	CS	BA	$
1993	(A)	111	403	49	109	30	76	23	3	10	55	21	13	.270	x
1994	(A)	124	476	68	139	23	80	47	6	12	76	12	12	.292	x
1995	(AA)	133	489	59	130	32	76	28	6	14	59	8	9	.266	x

Was one of the youngest players in Double-A last year and will be one of the youngest in Triple-A this year. Hidalgo is meant to be a five-tool player, although he won't run in the majors. His arm is said to be exeptional.

GLENALLEN HILL   OF   Age 31   Bid: $25

Year	Team	G	AB	R	H	BB	SO	D	T	HR	RBI	SB	CS	BA	$
1991	TOR/CLE	72	221	29	57	23	54	8	2	8	25	6	4	.258	8
1992	CLE	102	369	38	89	20	73	16	1	18	49	9	6	.241	15
1993	CLE/CHC	97	261	33	69	17	71	14	2	15	47	8	3	.264	15
1994	CHC	89	269	48	80	29	57	12	1	10	38	19	6	.297	23
1995	SF	132	497	71	131	39	98	29	4	24	86	25	5	.264	29

I wouldn't count on 25 steals again, but I'm willing to count on Glenallen, which is amazing enough. Batting behind Williams all year, he could easily drive in 100 runs.

TODD HOLLANDSWORTH   OF Age 23   Bid: R2

Year	Team	G	AB	R	H	BB	SO	D	T	HR	RBI	SB	CS	BA	$
1994	(AAA)	132	505	80	144	46	96	31	5	19	91	15	9	.285	x
1995	(AAA)	10	38	9	9	6	8	2	0	2	4	1	0	.237	x
1995	LA	41	103	16	24	10	29	2	0	5	13	2	1	.233	3

Just didn't quite play enough for the Dodgers to become an R3.

DAMON HOLLINS   OF   Age 22   Bid: R4

Year	Team	G	AB	R	H	BB	SO	D	T	HR	RBI	SB	CS	BA	$
1993	(R)	62	240	37	77	19	30	15	2	7	51	10	2	.321	x
1994	(A)	131	485	76	131	45	115	28	0	23	88	12	7	.270	x
1995	(AA)	129	466	64	115	44	120	26	2	18	77	6	6	.247	x

The 1993 season was a repeat in Rookie ball; maybe that's why he did so well. Highly, highly touted going into the 1994 season, he clearly has made little or no progress. The Braves would love him to get off to a good start in Double-A this year so they can trade him to the Padres.

THOMAS HOWARD   OF   Age 31   Bid: $5

Year	Team	G	AB	R	H	BB	SO	D	T	HR	RBI	SB	CS	BA	$
1991	SD	106	281	30	70	24	57	12	3	4	22	10	7	.249	7
1992	SD/CLE	122	361	37	100	17	60	15	2	2	32	15	8	.277	12
1993	CLE/CIN	112	319	48	81	24	63	15	3	7	36	10	7	.254	9
1994	CIN	83	178	24	47	10	30	11	0	5	24	4	2	.264	7
1995	CIN	113	281	42	85	20	37	15	2	3	26	17	8	.302	14

Shaky performance by Darren Lewis gave him an opportunity that he took good advantage of. If the Reds can't find another taker for Lewis and his guaranteed salary, Howard could be in a platoon.

TRINIDAD HUBBARD   OF   Age 32   Bid: R3

Year	Team	G	AB	R	H	BB	SO	D	T	HR	RBI	SB	CS	BA	$
1994	COL	18	25	3	7	3	4	1	1	1	3	0	0	.280	1
1995	COL	24	58	13	18	8	6	4	0	3	9	2	1	.310	4

Hubbard and McCracken and Pulliam — best outfield in the minors last year. Oh, you'll get a lot of Park Factor nattering from effete snobs, and Magic Year types will tell you 32, 26 and 28 are a little old for the *minors*, but enough: Hubbard (12-66-37-.340), McCracken (3-28-17-.361), and Pulliam (25-91-6-.327) put up the numbers at Colorado Springs. Hubbard kept it up in Denver. He had a .537 slugging average. Against *righthanders* he hit .414 and slugged .759. Righthanders. If that wasn't good enough for the Rockies, and it wasn't — well, it wasn't good enough for Rotisserie Leagues. But you should see the fight over him in Strat-O-Matic.

TODD HUNDLEY   C   Age 27   Bid: $17

Year	Team	G	AB	R	H	BB	SO	D	T	HR	RBI	SB	CS	BA	$
1991	NYM	21	60	5	8	6	14	0	1	1	7	0	0	.133	-1
1992	NYM	123	358	32	75	19	76	17	0	7	32	3	0	.209	3
1993	NYM	130	417	40	95	23	62	17	2	11	53	1	1	.228	4
1994	NYM	91	291	45	69	25	73	10	1	16	42	2	1	.237	10
1995	NYM	90	275	39	77	42	64	11	0	15	51	1	0	.280	14

Position scarcity, meet Magic Year. Let's just hope there isn't a home plate collision.

BRIAN L. HUNTER   OF   Age 25   Bid: $26

Year	Team	G	AB	R	H	BB	SO	D	T	HR	RBI	SB	CS	BA	$
1993	(AA)	133	523	84	154	34	85	22	5	10	52	35	18	.294	x
1994	(AAA)	128	513	113	191	52	52	28	9	10	51	49	14	.372	x
1994	HOU	6	24	2	6	1	6	1	0	0	0	2	1	.250	1
1995	(AAA)	38	155	28	51	17	13	5	1	1	16	11	3	.329	x
1995	HOU	78	321	52	97	21	52	14	5	2	28	24	7	.302	17

A foolishly high bid, but that's what it will take, and I want him.

BRIAN HUNTER   1B   Age 28   Bid: R3

Year	Team	G	AB	R	H	BB	SO	D	T	HR	RBI	SB	CS	BA	$
1991	ATL	97	271	32	68	17	48	16	1	12	50	0	2	.251	10
1992	ATL	102	238	34	57	21	50	13	2	14	41	1	2	.239	12
1993	ATL	37	80	4	11	2	15	3	1	0	8	0	0	.138	-3
1994	CIN	85	256	34	60	17	56	16	1	15	57	0	0	.234	11
1995	CIN	40	79	9	17	11	21	6	0	1	9	2	1	.215	0

Nominate Brian Hunter first. It's up to them to ask, "Do you mean, Brian L?"

BUTCH HUSKEY   3B   Age 24   Bid: $7

Year	Team	G	AB	R	H	BB	SO	D	T	HR	RBI	SB	CS	BA	$
1993	NYM	13	41	2	6	1	13	1	0	0	3	0	0	.146	-2
1995	(AAA)	109	394	66	112	39	88	18	1	28	87	8	6	.284	x
1995	NYM	28	90	8	17	10	16	1	0	3	11	1	0	.189	0

An R1 if he starts at Norfolk.

ALEX OCHOA   OF   Age 24   Bid: $2

Year	Team	G	AB	R	H	BB	SO	D	T	HR	RBI	SB	CS	BA	$
1993	(A)	137	532	84	147	46	67	29	5	13	90	34	13	.276	x
1994	(AA)	134	519	77	156	49	67	25	2	14	82	28	15	.301	x
1995	(AAA)	91	336	41	92	26	50	18	2	8	46	17	7	.274	x
1995	(AAA)	34	123	17	38	14	12	6	2	2	15	7	3	.309	x

Year	Team	G	AB	R	H	BB	SO	D	T	HR	RBI	SB	CS	BA	$
1995	NYM	11	37	7	11	2	10	1	0	0	0	1	0	.297	1

This guy *has* a great arm. Can he hit?
    Swing seems too long to me.

JOSE OFFERMAN SS Age 27   Bid: $2

Year	Team	G	AB	R	H	BB	SO	D	T	HR	RBI	SB	CS	BA	$
1991	LA	52	113	10	22	25	32	2	0	0	3	3	2	.195	-1
1992	LA	149	534	67	139	57	98	20	8	1	30	23	16	.260	11
1993	LA	158	590	77	159	71	75	21	6	1	62	30	13	.269	17
1994	LA	72	243	27	51	38	38	8	4	1	25	2	1	.210	-2
1995	LA	119	429	69	123	69	67	14	6	4	33	2	7	.287	9

The Dodgers' disenfranchise player.

JOSE OLIVA 3B Age 25   Bid: R3

Year	Team	G	AB	R	H	BB	SO	D	T	HR	RBI	SB	CS	BA	$
1994	ATL	19	59	9	17	7	10	5	0	6	11	0	1	.288	5
1995	ATL/STL	70	183	15	26	12	46	5	0	7	20	0	0	.142	-4

Long swings = short careers.

REY ORDONEZ SS Age 24   Bid: R3

Year	Team	G	AB	R	H	BB	SO	D	T	HR	RBI	SB	CS	BA	$
1994	(A)	79	314	47	97	14	28	21	2	2	40	11	6	.309	x
1994	(AA)	48	191	22	50	4	18	10	2	1	20	4	3	.262	x
1995	(AAA)	125	439	49	94	27	50	21	4	2	50	11	13	.214	x

Does Castro root for these guys?

JOE ORSULAK OF Age 34   Bid: $1

Year	Team	G	AB	R	H	BB	SO	D	T	HR	RBI	SB	CS	BA	$
1991	BAL	143	486	57	135	28	45	22	1	5	43	6	2	.278	12
1992	BAL	117	391	45	113	28	34	18	3	4	39	5	4	.289	12
1993	NYM	134	409	59	116	28	25	15	4	8	35	5	4	.284	11

Year	Team	G	AB	R	H	BB	SO	D	T	HR	RBI	SB	CS	BA	$
1994	NYM	96	292	39	76	16	21	3	0	8	42	4	2	.260	10
1995	NYM	108	290	41	82	19	35	19	2	1	37	1	3	.283	7

Still a most professional — and quick — bat.

WILLIS OTANEZ   3B   Age 23   Bid: R2

Year	Team	G	AB	R	H	BB	SO	D	T	HR	RBI	SB	CS	BA	$
1993	(A)	95	325	34	85	29	63	11	2	10	39	1	4	.262	x
1994	(A)	131	476	77	132	53	98	27	1	19	72	4	2	.277	x
1995	(A)	92	354	39	92	28	59	24	0	10	53	1	1	.260	x
1995	(AA)	27	100	8	24	6	25	4	1	1	7	0	1	.240	x

There's nothing to like in his 1995 lines, but he was a hot prospect a year ago, and the Dodgers need a third baseman and a Rookie of the Year.

ERIC OWENS   2B   Age 25   Bid: R2

Year	Team	G	AB	R	H	BB	SO	D	T	HR	RBI	SB	CS	BA	$
1994	(AA)	134	523	73	133	54	86	17	3	3	36	38	14	.254	x
1995	(AAA)	108	427	86	134	52	61	24	8	12	63	33	12	.314	x
1995	CIN	2	2	0	2	0	0	0	0	0	1	0	0	1.000	1

Jumped from nowhere to No. 3 prospect in the American Association. Torn anterior-cruciate ligament stopped his season in mid-August. A fourth-round pick of the Reds in 1992, he's 6'1", 194; bats right. Torn ACL's are no big deal anymore.

CLAUD JAYHAWK OWENS   C   Age 27   Bid: R3

Year	Team	G	AB	R	H	BB	SO	D	T	HR	RBI	SB	CS	BA	$
1993	COL	33	86	12	18	6	30	5	0	3	6	1	0	.209	0
1994	COL	6	12	4	3	3	3	0	1	0	1	0	0	.250	0
1995	COL	18	45	7	11	2	15	2	0	4	12	0	0	.244	3

Matt Nokes has more upside to us, but the Rockies make the call.

CHARLIE O'BRIEN   C   Age 35   Bid: $1

Year	Team	G	AB	R	H	BB	SO	D	T	HR	RBI	SB	CS	BA	$
1991	NYM	69	168	16	31	17	25	6	0	2	14	0	2	.185	-2

Year	Team	G	AB	R	H	BB	SO	D	T	HR	RBI	SB	CS	BA	$
1992	NYM	68	156	15	33	16	18	12	0	2	13	0	1	.212	0
1993	NYM	67	188	15	48	14	14	11	0	4	23	1	1	.255	3
1994	ATL	51	152	24	37	15	24	11	0	8	28	0	0	.243	6
1995	ATL	67	198	18	45	29	40	7	0	9	23	0	1	.227	3

Time for Javy to start catching Maddux; he needs Run Support more than Charlie.

TOM PAGNOZZI   C   Age 33   Bid: $1

Year	Team	G	AB	R	H	BB	SO	D	T	HR	RBI	SB	CS	BA	$
1991	STL	140	459	36	121	36	63	24	5	2	57	9	13	.264	11
1992	STL	139	485	33	121	28	64	26	3	7	44	2	5	.249	8
1993	STL	92	330	31	85	19	30	15	1	7	41	1	0	.258	6
1994	STL	70	243	21	66	21	39	12	1	7	40	0	0	.272	9
1995	STL	62	219	17	47	11	31	14	1	2	15	0	1	.215	-3

LaRussa will find that Steinbach he's not.

MARK PARENT   C   Age 34   Bid: $3

Year	Team	G	AB	R	H	BB	SO	D	T	HR	RBI	SB	CS	BA	$
1991	TEX	3	1	1	0	0	1	0	0	0	0	0	0	.000	0
1992	TEX	17	34	4	8	3	7	1	0	2	4	0	0	.235	1
1993	BAL	22	54	7	14	3	14	2	0	4	12	0	0	.259	3
1994	CHC	44	99	8	26	13	24	4	0	3	16	0	1	.263	3
1995	CHC	81	265	30	62	26	69	11	0	18	38	0	0	.234	9

Had a .742 slugging average against lefties. Cubs were forced to use him against righties, too, though.

JAY PAYTON OF   Age 23   Bid: R1

Year	Team	G	AB	R	H	BB	SO	D	T	HR	RBI	SB	CS	BA	$
1994	(A)	58	219	219	80	23	18	18	2	3	37	10	2	.365	x
1994	(AA)	8	25	25	7	2	3	1	0	0	1	1	1	.280	x
1995	(AA)	85	357	59	123	29	32	20	3	14	54	16	7	.345	x
1995	(AAA)	50	196	33	47	11	22	11	4	4	30	11	3	.240	x

Payton had a shot at the Eastern League triple crown when he got the call to Triple-A. Before suffering an arm injury (that required surgery), he played enough to show that he should have started in Triple-A anyway. If his arm is sound he won't be there long.

GERONIMO PENA   2B   Age 29   Bid: $2

Year	Team	G	AB	R	H	BB	SO	D	T	HR	RBI	SB	CS	BA	$
1991	STL	104	185	38	45	18	45	8	3	5	17	15	5	.243	8
1992	STL	62	203	31	62	24	37	12	1	7	31	13	8	.305	15
1993	STL	74	254	34	65	25	71	19	2	5	30	13	5	.256	9
1994	STL	83	213	33	54	24	54	13	1	11	34	9	1	.254	13
1995	STL	32	101	20	27	16	30	6	1	1	8	3	2	.267	2

Still batting both, he continued to whack lefties (.379) and flail against righties (.222). At Louisville, he hit .381 in six games and then, as far as I can tell, left the game to think about which way he'll bat this year.

TERRY PENDLETON   3B   Age 35   Bid: $16

Year	Team	G	AB	R	H	BB	SO	D	T	HR	RBI	SB	CS	BA	$
1991	ATL	153	586	94	187	43	70	34	8	22	86	10	2	.319	35
1992	ATL	160	640	98	199	37	67	39	1	21	105	5	2	.311	37
1993	ATL	161	633	81	172	36	97	33	1	17	84	5	1	.272	18
1994	ATL	77	309	25	78	12	57	18	3	7	30	2	0	.252	6
1995	FLA	133	513	70	149	38	84	32	1	14	78	1	2	.290	20

He's good for another year.

ROBERTO PETAGINE   1B   Age 25   Bid: R3

Year	Team	G	AB	R	H	BB	SO	D	T	HR	RBI	SB	CS	BA	$
1994	(AAA)	65	247	53	78	35	54	19	0	10	44	3	1	.316	x
1994	HOU	8	7	0	0	1	3	0	0	0	0	0	0	.000	-1
1995	SD	89	124	15	29	26	41	8	0	3	17	0	0	.234	1
1995	(AAA)	19	56	8	12	13	17	2	1	1	5	1	0	.214	x

His early-season success must have been the result of keying on a certain pitch in a certain location, and refusing to offer at anything else. As late as May 14, he had a .700 slugging average and .647 on-base average. Word got around, though, and he never saw that certain pitch in that location again.

J.R. PHILLIPS   1B   Age 26   Bid: R3

Year	Team	G	AB	R	H	BB	SO	D	T	HR	RBI	SB	CS	BA	$
1993	SF	11	16	1	5	0	5	1	1	1	4	0	0	.313	1
1994	SF	15	38	1	5	1	13	0	0	1	3	1	0	.132	-1
1995	SF	92	231	27	45	19	69	9	0	9	28	1	1	.195	1

Once again took frustrations out at Phoenix (.631 SA in 360 AB), but he was Carreon by then.

MIKE PIAZZA   C   Age 27   Bid: $43

Year	Team	G	AB	R	H	BB	SO	D	T	HR	RBI	SB	CS	BA	$
1992	LA	21	69	5	16	4	12	3	0	1	7	0	0	.232	1
1993	LA	149	547	81	174	46	86	24	2	35	112	3	4	.318	37
1994	LA	107	405	64	129	33	65	18	0	24	92	1	3	.319	35
1995	LA	112	434	82	150	39	80	17	0	32	93	1	0	.346	39

He's 116% better than Lopez, the next best catcher, in Appendix B, and will be again. Karros is 3% better than Galarraga in Appendix B, but probably won't be this year. Biggio is 54% better than Veras, and Veras will close that gap. Castilla is decimals better than Caminiti, and neither will be at the top in next year's book. Larkin is 82% better than Dunston, and was a close second to Cordero in last year's book. Bichette is 23% better than Reggie Sanders and 26% better than Bonds in this year's Appendix B. Even Greg Maddux is only 74% better than Nomo, the next best player at his position.

PHIL PLANTIER   OF   Age 27   Bid: $4

Year	Team	G	AB	R	H	BB	SO	D	T	HR	RBI	SB	CS	BA	$
1991	BOS	53	148	27	49	23	38	7	1	11	35	1	0	.331	12
1992	BOS	108	349	46	86	44	83	19	0	7	30	2	3	.246	6
1993	SD	138	462	67	111	61	124	20	1	34	100	4	5	.240	22
1994	SD	96	341	44	75	36	91	21	0	18	41	3	1	.220	8
1995	HOU/SD	76	216	33	55	28	48	6	0	9	34	1	1	.255	7

He failed to hit one home run in the Astrodome, but, back with San Diego, he only hit one at home. His slugging average while with the Astros was .456; with the Padres .385.

LUIS POLONIA   OF   Age 31   Bid: $2

Year	Team	G	AB	R	H	BB	SO	D	T	HR	RBI	SB	CS	BA	$
1991	CAL	150	604	92	179	52	74	28	8	2	50	48	23	.296	34

Year	Team	G	AB	R	H	BB	SO	D	T	HR	RBI	SB	CS	BA	$
1992	CAL	149	577	88	165	45	64	17	4	0	35	51	21	.286	28
1993	CAL	152	576	75	156	48	53	17	6	1	32	55	24	.271	27
1994	NYY	95	350	62	109	37	36	21	6	1	36	20	12	.311	22
1995	NYY	67	238	37	62	25	29	9	3	2	15	10	4	.261	6
1995	ATL	28	53	6	14	3	9	7	0	0	2	3	0	.264	1

If Klesko goes to first and Polonia platoons in left field, push the bid as high as $10.

DANTE POWELL   OF   Age 22   Bid: R4

Year	Team	G	AB	R	H	BB	SO	D	T	HR	RBI	SB	CS	BA	$
1994	(A)	41	165	31	51	19	47	15	1	5	25	27	1	.309	x
1995	(A)	135	505	74	125	46	131	23	8	10	70	43	12	.248	x

To drop 60 points in batting average, just moving from slow A to fast A, and still be a top 10 prospect takes a lot of talent. "He shows flashes of potential that can quickly disappear," according to Baseball America, which rated him No. 5 in the California League. "The same reputation dogged him at Cal Sate Fullerton." It's too early, though, to call him a dog straight out. He's 6'2", 185; bats right. The Giants made him their first pick in the '94 draft. "He can track down just about anything," says the Visalia manager. "And he can throw at least as well as any center fielder his age."

JODY REED   2B   Age 33   Bid: $2

Year	Team	G	AB	R	H	BB	SO	D	T	HR	RBI	SB	CS	BA	$
1991	BOS	153	618	87	175	60	53	42	2	5	60	6	5	.283	15
1992	BOS	143	550	64	136	62	44	27	1	3	40	7	8	.247	6
1993	LA	132	445	48	123	38	40	21	2	2	31	1	3	.276	5
1994	MIL	108	399	48	108	57	34	22	0	2	37	5	4	.271	8
1995	SD	131	445	58	114	59	38	18	1	4	40	6	4	.256	6

Jody is, ahem, once again free to sign with anyone who wants him.

POKEY REESE   SS   Age 23   Bid: R3

Year	Team	G	AB	R	H	BB	SO	D	T	HR	RBI	SB	CS	BA	$
1993	(AA)	102	345	35	73	23	77	17	4	3	37	8	5	.212	x
1994	(AA)	134	484	77	130	43	75	23	4	12	49	21	4	.269	x
1995	(AAA)	89	343	51	82	36	81	21	1	10	46	8	8	.239	x

What a team they had at Indianapolis! Pokey's the No. 4 prospect in the American Association and the hitters ahead of him are teammates Gibraltar and Owens. Willie Greene also makes it onto the list. The team had a .611 winning percentage, won the pennant by 6 games, then got swept by Louisville in the playoffs. That's baseball, as we say each year.

Pokey was the Reds' first-round pick back in '91, so he's taking his sweet time. He's 6'0"; bats right. Fielding — I know I should have told you earlier, but I thought you knew — is his game. "This is an exciting player defensively," says one manager. "He's very acrobatic," says another. "His arm is probably the best infielder's arm in the league."

EDGAR RENTERIA SS Age 20   Bid: R2

Year	Team	G	AB	R	H	BB	SO	D	T	HR	RBI	SB	CS	BA	$
1994	(A)	128	439	46	111	35	56	15	1	0	36	6	11	.253	x
1995	(AA)	135	508	70	147	32	85	15	7	7	68	30	11	.289	x

Drafted as a free agent by the Marlins in '92, he could pose a threat to Abbott this year. Again, it's the glove that will bring him to the majors, but his offensive game improved dramatically in Double-A, where he was one of the Eastern League's youngest players. A switch-hitter, 6'1", 172, he's "clay ready to be molded," in the words of Baseball America. "He's fluid," says a rival manager. "The kid knows how to play the game."

ADAM RIGGS 2B Age 23   Bid: R5

Year	Team	G	AB	R	H	BB	SO	D	T	HR	RBI	SB	CS	BA	$
1994	(R)	62	234	55	73	31	38	20	3	5	44	19	8	.312	x
1995	(A)	134	542	111	196	59	93	39	5	24	106	31	10	.362	x

Adam Riggs hit more than 100 points higher than Dante Powell in the California League, hit more than twice as many homers, stole some bases himself, played second, and finished five rungs further down as a prospect, the last one on the list.

The two knocks against him were his fielding and his age. I admit he's a bit old to be an R5, but he looks like too good a hitter to be an R4, and I don't hold his fielding against him. He's 5'11", 180, and was drafted in the 22nd round in 1994 by the Dodgers, who aren't hung up on defense either.

BIP ROBERTS 2B,OF Age 32   Bid: $20

Year	Team	G	AB	R	H	BB	SO	D	T	HR	RBI	SB	CS	BA	$
1991	SD	117	424	66	119	37	71	13	3	3	32	26	11	.281	17
1992	CIN	147	532	92	172	62	54	34	6	4	45	44	16	.323	33
1993	CIN	83	292	46	70	38	46	13	0	1	18	26	6	.240	8
1994	SD	105	403	52	129	39	57	15	5	2	31	21	7	.320	25
1995	SD	73	296	40	90	17	36	14	0	2	25	20	2	.304	15

Says he will be in mint condition.

HENRY RODRIGUEZ OF,1B Age 28 Bid: $3

Year	Team	G	AB	R	H	BB	SO	D	T	HR	RBI	SB	CS	BA	$
1992	LA	53	146	11	32	8	30	7	0	3	14	0	0	.219	1
1993	LA	76	176	20	39	11	39	10	0	8	23	1	0	.222	3
1994	LA	104	306	33	82	17	58	14	2	8	49	0	1	.268	11
1995	LA/MTL	45	138	13	33	11	28	4	1	2	15	0	1	.239	1

Hit more home runs in one spring training game than he did for both teams he played on combined. Probably more important to Floyd buyers than Segui buyers.

SCOTT ROLEN 3B Age 21 Bid: R2

Year	Team	G	AB	R	H	BB	SO	D	T	HR	RBI	SB	CS	BA	$
1994	(A)	138	513	83	151	55	90	34	5	14	72	4	0	.294	x
1995	(A)	66	238	45	69	37	46	13	2	10	39	1	0	.290	x
1995	(AA)	20	76	16	22	7	14	3	0	3	15	1	0	.289	x

The Phillies' Minor League Player of the Year — before you say anything: Gene Schall really wasn't half bad.

REY SANCHEZ 2B,SS,3B Age 28 Bid: $1

Year	Team	G	AB	R	H	BB	SO	D	T	HR	RBI	SB	CS	BA	$
1991	CHC	13	23	1	6	4	3	0	0	0	2	0	0	.261	0
1992	CHC	74	255	24	64	10	17	14	3	1	19	2	1	.251	3
1993	CHC	105	344	35	97	15	22	11	2	0	28	1	1	.282	4
1994	CHC	96	291	26	83	20	29	13	1	0	24	2	5	.285	6
1995	CHC	114	428	57	119	14	48	22	2	3	27	6	4	.278	8

Becomes Ryno's spear-carrier; would like to throw it at him.

RYNE SANDBERG 2B Age 36 Bid: $10

Year	Team	G	AB	R	H	BB	SO	D	T	HR	RBI	SB	CS	BA	$
1990	CHC	155	615	116	188	50	84	30	3	40	100	25	7	.306	44
1991	CHC	158	585	104	170	87	89	32	2	26	100	22	8	.291	37
1992	CHC	158	612	100	186	68	73	32	8	26	87	17	6	.304	40
1993	CHC	117	456	67	141	37	62	20	0	9	45	9	2	.309	18

Year	Team	G	AB	R	H	BB	SO	D	T	HR	RBI	SB	CS	BA	$
1994	CHC	57	223	36	53	23	40	9	5	5	24	2	3	.238	3

What do you think?

Anyway, $10 is a starting point. I wouldn't go past $15.

DEION SANDERS   OF   Age 28   Bid: $10

Year	Team	G	AB	R	H	BB	SO	D	T	HR	RBI	SB	CS	BA	$
1991	ATL	54	110	16	21	12	23	1	2	4	13	11	3	.191	4
1992	ATL	97	303	54	92	18	52	6	14	8	28	26	9	.304	21
1993	ATL	95	272	42	75	16	42	18	6	6	28	19	7	.276	13
1994	CIN	92	375	58	106	32	63	17	4	4	28	38	16	.283	27
1995	SF	85	343	48	92	27	60	11	8	6	28	24	9	.268	14

Another $10 that's just sort of set aside for him. I doubt he's going to play baseball again. Too difficult.

REGGIE SANDERS   OF   Age 28   Bid: $42

Year	Team	G	AB	R	H	BB	SO	D	T	HR	RBI	SB	CS	BA	$
1991	CIN	9	40	89	8	0	9	0	0	1	3	1	1	.200	0
1992	ATL	116	385	50	104	48	98	26	6	12	36	16	7	.270	18
1993	CIN	138	496	90	136	51	118	16	4	20	83	27	10	.274	28
1994	CIN	107	400	66	105	41	114	20	8	17	62	21	9	.263	26
1995	CIN	133	484	91	148	69	122	36	6	28	99	36	12	.306	44

Some touts, when they're wrong about a player, never say die; they keep running him down until, ultimately, they're right. I tend to overreact the other way. Reggie Sanders is great! The hell with his little skid in September, his abysmal playoffs — in fact, they are just going to drive him to an even better year.

BENITO SANTIAGO   C   Age 31   Bid: $10

Year	Team	G	AB	R	H	BB	SO	D	T	HR	RBI	SB	CS	BA	$
1991	SD	152	580	60	155	23	114	22	3	17	87	8	10	.267	22
1992	SD	106	386	37	97	21	52	21	0	10	42	2	5	.251	10
1993	FLA	139	469	49	108	37	88	19	6	13	50	10	7	.230	8
1994	FLA	101	337	35	92	25	57	14	2	11	41	1	2	.273	12

Year	Team	G	AB	R	H	BB	SO	D	T	HR	RBI	SB	CS	BA	$
1995	CIN	81	266	40	76	24	48	20	0	11	44	2	2	.286	**13**

Lured out of Homestead at the eleventh hour for $550,000, Benito must have snuck his eyes sideways on the bench more than once — like Johnny in the Budweiser commercial — at Hal Morris, who was being paid $3.3 million. As fellow free agents this year, they aren't going to change places; knowing Benito, he'll probably look to Japan.

STEVE SCARSONE 3B   Age 30   Bid: $1

Year	Team	G	AB	R	H	BB	SO	D	T	HR	RBI	SB	CS	BA	$
1992	BAL/PHI	18	30	3	5	2	12	0	0	0	0	0	0	.167	**-2**
1993	SF	44	103	16	26	4	32	9	0	2	15	0	1	.252	**2**
1994	SF	52	103	21	28	10	20	8	0	2	13	0	2	.272	**3**
1995	SF	80	233	33	62	18	82	10	3	11	29	3	2	.266	**9**

Hit .457 on the first pitch, .156 with two strikes.

What that means is, he's not going to hit 11 homers in 233 AB again, even if he gets 233 AB. Still, he's become a master of sneak attacks.

GENE SCHALL   1B   Age 26   Bid: R2

Year	Team	G	AB	R	H	BB	SO	D	T	HR	RBI	SB	CS	BA	$
1994	(AAA)	127	463	54	132	50	86	35	4	16	89	9	1	.285	**x**
1995	(AAA)	92	320	52	100	49	54	25	4	12	63	3	3	.313	**x**
1995	PHI	24	65	2	15	6	16	2	0	0	5	0	0	.231	**-1**

With Jefferies sitting out the final week, Schall went 1-for-16. But he's not trying to be Lou Gehrig. After two-and-a-half years in Triple-A, he'll settle for Wally Pipp.

DAVID SEGUI   1B,OF   Age 29   Bid: $17

Year	Team	G	AB	R	H	BB	SO	D	T	HR	RBI	SB	CS	BA	$
1991	BAL	86	212	15	59	12	19	7	0	2	22	1	1	.278	**5**
1992	BAL	113	189	22	44	20	23	9	0	1	17	1	0	.233	**1**
1993	BAL	146	450	54	123	58	53	27	0	10	60	2	1	.273	**12**
1994	NYM	92	336	46	81	33	43	17	1	10	43	0	0	.241	**6**
1995	NY/MTL	130	456	68	141	40	47	25	4	12	68	2	7	.309	**21**

Luckily there's no need for Floyd to play first anymore. It would be very interesting to learn if any real-life GM's would still take Floyd ahead of Segui. Would you?

SCOTT SERVAIS

C   Age 29   Bid: $5

Year	Team	G	AB	R	H	BB	SO	D	T	HR	RBI	SB	CS	BA	$
1991	HOU	16	37	0	6	4	8	3	0	0	6	0	0	.162	-1
1992	HOU	77	205	12	49	11	25	9	0	0	15	0	0	.239	0
1993	HOU	85	258	24	63	22	45	11	0	11	32	0	0	.244	6
1994	HOU	78	251	27	49	10	44	15	1	9	41	0	0	.195	1
1995	CHC	80	264	38	70	32	52	22	0	13	47	2	2	.265	12

In the second half, he batted .310, hit 10 home runs, and drove Wilkins out of town.

GARY SHEFFIELD

OF   Age 28   Bid: $33

Year	Team	G	AB	R	H	BB	SO	D	T	HR	RBI	SB	CS	BA	$
1991	MIL	50	175	25	34	19	15	12	2	2	22	5	5	.194	1
1992	SD	146	557	87	184	48	40	34	3	33	100	5	6	.330	46
1993	FLA	140	494	67	145	47	64	20	5	20	73	17	5	.294	26
1994	FLA	87	322	61	89	51	50	16	1	27	78	12	6	.276	32
1995	FLA	63	213	46	69	55	45	8	0	16	46	19	4	.324	24

The Baseball Weekly leagues are still kind of patching together their rules. In the NL league, Al Chaby had to cut Sheffield, because we are only allowed five players at a time on reserve, and Sheffield was out for the season. Wasn't he?

No, not quite, as it turned out. This player with the reputation of being unable to play through pain picked up a bat in the beginning of September, wrapped his thumb around it, and was in the lineup the next day.

Dottie Enrico happened to have the most money left at that point and picked him up. In the four weeks that she had him on her team, Sheffield hit .377-7-20 with 4 stolen bases.

Okay, Dottie, *okay*. You planned it. You were smart to hold your money until September, when all sorts of weird things happen. Still doesn't make Chaby feel any better.

CRAIG SHIPLEY

3B   Age 33   Bid: $1

Year	Team	G	AB	R	H	BB	SO	D	T	HR	RBI	SB	CS	BA	$
1991	SD	37	91	6	25	2	14	3	0	1	6	0	1	.275	2
1992	SD	52	105	7	26	2	21	6	0	0	7	1	1	.248	1
1993	SD	105	230	25	54	10	31	9	0	4	22	12	3	.235	5
1994	SD	81	240	32	80	9	28	14	4	4	30	6	6	.333	16
1995	HOU	92	232	23	61	8	28	8	1	3	24	6	1	.263	5

Drayton McLane really expects to draw 2.5 million this year?

DAVE SILVESTRI   SS,2B Age 28   Bid: R3

Year	Team	G	AB	R	H	BB	SO	D	T	HR	RBI	SB	CS	BA	$
1992	NYY	7	13	3	4	0	3	0	2	0	1	0	0	.308	0
1993	NYY	7	21	4	6	5	3	1	0	1	4	0	0	.286	1
1994	NYY	12	18	3	2	4	9	0	1	1	2	0	1	.111	-1
1995	NYY	17	21	4	2	4	9	0	0	1	4	0	0	.095	-1
1995	MTL	39	72	12	19	9	27	6	0	2	7	2	0	.264	2

If he makes the Expos, he played 7 games at second for the Yankee and thus qualifies at both middle infield positions.

You never know — it could make a difference!

MIKE SIMMS   1B   Age 29   Bid: R3

Year	Team	G	AB	R	H	BB	SO	D	T	HR	RBI	SB	CS	BA	$
1995	(AAA)	85	319	56	94	35	65	26	8	13	66	10	2	.295	x
1995	HOU	50	121	14	31	13	28	4	0	9	24	1	2	.256	7

With his career audition (No. 5) last year, he deserves a sixth.

DON SLAUGHT   C   Age 37   Bid: $1

Year	Team	G	AB	R	H	BB	SO	D	T	HR	RBI	SB	CS	BA	$
1991	PIT	77	220	19	65	21	32	17	1	1	29	1	0	.295	7
1992	PIT	87	255	26	88	17	23	17	3	4	37	2	2	.345	15
1993	PIT	116	377	34	113	29	56	19	2	10	55	2	1	.300	15
1994	PIT	76	240	21	69	34	31	7	0	2	21	0	0	.288	6
1995	PIT	35	112	13	34	9	8	6	0	0	13	0	0	.304	3

Which of two possible categories did he help more in? Take a guess, then check out Appendix B.

DWIGHT SMITH   OF   Age 32   Bid: $1

Year	Team	G	AB	R	H	BB	SO	D	T	HR	RBI	SB	CS	BA	$
1991	CHC	90	167	16	38	11	32	7	2	3	21	2	3	.228	3
1992	CHW	109	217	28	60	13	40	10	3	3	24	9	8	.276	9
1993	CHC	111	310	51	93	25	51	17	5	11	35	8	6	.300	15
1994	BAL	73	196	31	55	12	37	7	2	8	30	2	4	.281	9

Year	Team	G	AB	R	H	BB	SO	D	T	HR	RBI	SB	CS	BA	$
1995	ATL	103	131	16	33	13	35	8	2	3	21	0	3	.252	3

A bigger part of the Braves than the stats suggest.

OZZIE SMITH   SS   Age 41   Bid: $1

Year	Team	G	AB	R	H	BB	SO	D	T	HR	RBI	SB	CS	BA	$
1991	STL	150	550	96	157	83	36	30	3	3	50	35	9	.285	24
1992	STL	132	518	73	153	59	34	20	2	0	31	43	9	.295	23
1993	STL	141	545	75	157	43	18	22	6	1	53	21	8	.288	17
1994	STL	98	381	51	100	38	26	18	3	3	30	6	3	.262	7
1995	STL	44	156	16	31	17	12	5	1	0	11	4	3	.199	-2

Don't play this year, Ozzie. Don't make us bid more for Tripp Cromer.

ROBERT SMITH   3B   Age 22   Bid: R2

Year	Team	G	AB	R	H	BB	SO	D	T	HR	RBI	SB	CS	BA	$
1994	(A)	127	478	49	127	41	112	27	2	12	71	18	7	.266	x
1995	(AA)	127	444	75	116	40	109	27	3	14	58	12	6	.261	x

He's the No. 2 prospect in the Southern League and coming faster than the stats suggest. Drafted in the eleventh round in 1992 out of high school by the Braves, he's 6'3", 183; bats right. He has — need I say? — "a strong and accurate arm." He also has "quick hands and quick feet." So, if he just holds his own against Triple-A pitching, and Klesko's at first, and Chipper's at third, and Luis Polonia is in left field...

SAMMY SOSA   OF   Age 27   Bid: $41

Year	Team	G	AB	R	H	BB	SO	D	T	HR	RBI	SB	CS	BA	$
1991	CHW	116	316	39	64	14	98	10	1	10	33	13	6	.203	7
1992	CHC	67	262	41	68	19	63	7	2	8	25	15	7	.260	12
1993	CHC	159	598	92	156	38	135	25	5	33	93	36	11	.261	35
1994	CHC	105	426	59	128	25	92	17	6	25	70	22	13	.300	40
1995	CHC	144	564	89	151	58	134	17	3	36	119	34	7	.268	42

Slammin' Sammy even played the field last year. Highest range factor in the league for right fielders and tied Mondesi and Walker for the most assists. Undoubtedly Sosa was challenged more often, and perhaps he just had a lot of balls hit his way, but his zone rating also was excellent (.887, compared to .815 for the MLB average in right field). He played in every game, showed more discipline at the plate, hit 21 homers in the second half, and is a strong candidate to be this year's MVP.

KELLY STINNETT   C   Age 26   Bid: $1

Year	Team	G	AB	R	H	BB	SO	D	T	HR	RBI	SB	CS	BA	$
1994	NYM	47	150	20	38	11	28	6	2	2	14	2	0	.253	3
1995	NYM	77	196	23	43	29	65	8	1	4	18	2	0	.219	0

Can get back to his 1994 form.

KEVIN STOCKER   SS   Age 26   Bid: $2

Year	Team	G	AB	R	H	BB	SO	D	T	HR	RBI	SB	CS	BA	$
1993	PHI	70	259	46	84	30	43	12	3	2	31	5	0	.324	11
1994	PHI	82	271	38	74	44	41	11	2	2	28	2	2	.273	6
1995	PHI	125	412	42	90	43	75	14	3	1	32	6	1	.218	-2

Overrated last year (average salary $4), he'll earn $6 this year.

MARK SWEENEY   1B   Age 26   Bid: R3

Year	Team	G	AB	R	H	BB	SO	D	T	HR	RBI	SB	CS	BA	$
1995	(AAA)	69	226	48	78	43	33	14	2	7	59	3	1	.345	x
1995	(AAA)	22	76	15	28	14	8	8	0	2	22	2	0	.368	x
1995	STL	37	77	5	21	10	15	2	0	2	13	1	1	.273	3

Who *is* Mark Sweeney? Hitting .345 at Vancouver may be no biggie — the Angels didn't think so — but hitting .368 at Louisville would have led the American Association by 43 points, with enough AB. Plus he draws walks. Plus he doesn't strike out.

He'd be a George Plimpton character if he hit home runs.

TONY TARASCO   OF   Age 26   Bid: $8

Year	Team	G	AB	R	H	BB	SO	D	T	HR	RBI	SB	CS	BA	$
1993	ATL	24	35	6	8	0	5	2	0	0	2	0	1	.229	0
1994	ATL	87	132	16	36	9	17	6	0	5	19	5	0	.273	8
1995	MTL	126	438	64	109	51	78	18	4	14	40	24	3	.249	16

He was too good to be true at the beginning — it was starting to look like the Expos just know baseball better than anyone else does — then worse then bad in the second half. Quick bat, quick feet keep us interested.

ED TAUBENSEE
C   Age 27   Bid: $6

Year	Team	G	AB	R	H	BB	SO	D	T	HR	RBI	SB	CS	BA	$
1991	CLE	26	66	5	16	5	16	2	1	0	8	0	0	.242	0
1992	HOU	104	297	23	66	31	78	15	0	5	28	2	1	.222	3
1993	HOU	94	288	26	72	21	44	11	1	9	42	1	0	.250	7
1994	CIN	66	187	29	53	15	31	8	2	8	21	2	0	.283	9
1995	CIN	80	218	32	62	22	52	14	2	9	44	2	2	.284	11

Good hitter for the second straight year, still a catcher.

JESUS TAVAREZ
OF   Age 25   Bid: $7

Year	Team	G	AB	R	H	BB	SO	D	T	HR	RBI	SB	CS	BA	$
1994	FLA	17	39	4	7	1	5	0	0	0	4	1	1	.179	-1
1995	FLA	63	190	31	55	16	27	6	2	2	13	7	5	.289	6

Won't be worth more than Carr if they platoon.

JASON THOMPSON
1B   Age 25   Bid: R3

Year	Team	G	AB	R	H	BB	SO	D	T	HR	RBI	SB	CS	BA	$
1993	(A)	66	240	36	72	37	47	25	1	7	38	3	2	.300	x
1994	(A)	68	253	57	91	37	58	19	2	13	63	1	1	.360	x
1994	(AA)	63	215	35	56	28	77	17	2	8	46	0	1	.260	x
1995	(AA)	137	475	62	129	62	131	20	1	20	64	7	3	.272	x

His slugging average the second time in Double-A was 26 points lower.

ROBBIE THOMPSON
2B   Age 34   Bid: $4

Year	Team	G	AB	R	H	BB	SO	D	T	HR	RBI	SB	CS	BA	$
1991	SF	144	492	74	129	63	95	24	5	19	48	14	7	.262	19
1992	SF	128	443	54	115	43	75	25	1	14	49	5	9	.260	15
1993	SF	128	494	85	154	45	97	30	2	19	65	10	4	.312	26
1994	SF	35	129	13	27	15	32	8	2	2	7	3	1	.209	-1
1995	SF	95	336	51	75	42	76	15	0	8	23	1	2	.223	0

One more Robbie Thompson burst before the candle goes out?

RYAN THOMPSON
OF   Age 28   Bid: $6

Year	Team	G	AB	R	H	BB	SO	D	T	HR	RBI	SB	CS	BA	$
1992	NYM	30	108	15	24	8	24	7	1	3	10	2	2	.222	2
1993	NYM	80	288	34	72	19	81	19	2	11	26	2	7	.250	6
1994	NYM	98	334	39	75	28	94	14	1	18	59	1	1	.225	11
1995	NYM	75	267	39	67	19	77	13	0	7	31	3	1	.251	6

Can put a charge in the ball when he guesses right.

OZZIE TIMMONS
OF   Age 25   Bid: $4

Year	Team	G	AB	R	H	BB	SO	D	T	HR	RBI	SB	CS	BA	$
1994	(AAA)	126	440	63	116	36	93	30	2	22	66	0	3	.264	x
1995	CHC	77	171	30	45	13	32	10	1	8	28	3	0	.263	7

His MLE of 1994, whatever it was, was not 1995.

ANDY VAN SLYKE
OF   Age 35   Bid: $2

Year	Team	G	AB	R	H	BB	SO	D	T	HR	RBI	SB	CS	BA	$
1991	PIT	138	491	87	130	71	85	24	7	17	83	10	3	.265	22
1992	PIT	154	614	103	199	58	99	45	12	14	89	12	3	.324	35
1993	PIT	83	323	42	100	24	40	13	4	8	50	11	2	.310	17
1994	PIT	105	374	41	92	52	72	18	3	6	30	7	0	.246	6
1995	BAL	17	63	6	10	5	15	1	0	3	8	0	0	.159	-1
1995	PHI	63	214	26	52	28	41	10	2	3	16	7	0	.243	3

Has his wit still intact, which is not bad after the way he's played.

JOHN VANDER WAL
OF,1B   Age 30   Bid: $1

Year	Team	G	AB	R	H	BB	SO	D	T	HR	RBI	SB	CS	BA	$
1991	MTL	21	61	4	13	1	18	4	1	1	8	0	0	.213	0
1992	MTL	105	213	21	51	24	36	8	2	4	20	3	0	.239	4
1993	MTL	106	215	34	50	27	30	7	4	5	30	6	3	.233	4
1994	COL	91	110	12	27	16	31	3	1	5	15	2	1	.245	4
1995	COL	105	101	15	35	16	23	8	1	5	21	1	1	.347	8

The best National League DH and a cheap way to get your Coors.

EDGARD VELASQUEZ OF   Age 20

Bid: R5

Year	Team	G	AB	R	H	BB	SO	D	T	HR	RBI	SB	CS	BA	$
1994	(A)	119	447	50	106	23	120	22	3	11	39	9	9	.237	x
1995	(A)	131	497	74	149	40	102	25	6	13	69	7	10	.300	x

An R5 because he's a Rockies' prospect, but he'd be an R4 anyway. Showed plenty of power for his size: 5'11", 171 (so far). In the entire Carolina League, there were only two other .300 hitters. "Has a short, compact stroke that will supply good power for a center fielder," according to Baseball America's sources. "Managers named him the best defensive outfielder in the league and" — it goes without saying — "said he had the strongest arm in the league." Although he hasn't stolen many bases yet, "that will come with experience."

QUILVIO VERAS   2B   Age 24

Bid: $27

Year	Team	G	AB	R	H	BB	SO	D	T	HR	RBI	SB	CS	BA	$
1993	(AA)	128	444	87	136	91	62	19	7	2	51	52	23	.306	x
1994	(AAA)	123	457	71	114	59	56	22	4	0	43	40	18	.249	x
1995	FLA	124	440	86	115	80	68	20	7	5	32	56	21	.261	24

The other legitimate Rookie of the Year contender on the Marlins, he was great a lead-off hitter, not just a base-stealer, and had one of the best zone ratings of any second basemen. Hit equally well from either side, best month was his last. He and Johnson have better chances than Nomo or Chipper to win the MVP award before they're through.

JOSE VIZCAINO   SS   Age 28

Bid: $4

Year	Team	G	AB	R	H	BB	SO	D	T	HR	RBI	SB	CS	BA	$
1991	CHC	93	145	7	38	5	18	5	0	0	10	2	1	.262	2
1992	CHC	86	285	25	64	14	35	10	4	1	17	3	0	.225	0
1993	CHC	151	551	74	158	46	71	19	4	4	54	12	9	.287	15
1994	NYM	103	410	47	105	33	62	13	3	3	33	1	11	.256	3
1995	NYM	135	509	66	146	35	76	21	5	3	56	8	3	.287	14

Had a great year with the Mets — one of his greatest achievements was hitting .315 in the No. 8 position — but no power and no speed, with an average batting average, has a $4 salary cap.

LARRY WALKER   OF   Age 29

Bid: $39

Year	Team	G	AB	R	H	BB	SO	D	T	HR	RBI	SB	CS	BA	$
1991	MTL	137	487	59	141	42	102	30	2	16	64	14	9	.290	24
1992	MTL	143	528	85	159	41	97	31	4	23	93	18	6	.301	38

Year	Team	G	AB	R	H	BB	SO	D	T	HR	RBI	SB	CS	BA	$
1993	MTL	138	490	85	130	80	76	24	5	22	86	29	7	.265	28
1994	MTL	103	395	76	127	47	74	44	2	19	86	15	5	.322	39
1995	COL	131	494	96	151	49	72	31	5	36	101	16	3	.306	41

According to Bill James, Larry Walker "looks for all the world as if he should have played for the 1956 Yankees. He's got the whole package — the swagger, the talent, the left-handed power. The 1950s body."

So James is still on his game.

TIM WALLACH 3B Age 38 Bid: $5

Year	Team	G	AB	R	H	BB	SO	D	T	HR	RBI	SB	CS	BA	$
1991	MTL	151	577	60	130	50	100	22	1	13	73	2	4	.225	8
1992	MTL	150	537	53	120	50	90	29	1	9	59	2	2	.223	6
1993	LA	133	477	42	106	32	70	19	1	12	62	0	2	.222	4
1994	LA	113	414	68	116	46	80	21	1	23	78	0	2	.280	25
1995	LA	97	327	24	87	27	69	22	2	9	38	0	0	.266	8

The Dodgers released him, but that's free agency: they'll buy him back.

JEROME WALTON OF Age 30 Bid: $2

Year	Team	G	AB	R	H	BB	SO	D	T	HR	RBI	SB	CS	BA	$
1994	CIN	46	68	10	21	4	12	4	0	1	9	1	3	.309	4
1995	CIN	102	162	32	47	17	25	12	1	8	22	10	7	.290	11

Has scuffled back to being a good bench player. There was a time when an .893 OBS (on-base+ slugging) and a sabermetrician for an agent would have made him rich.

PAT WATKINS OF Age 23 Bid: R3

Year	Team	G	AB	R	H	BB	SO	D	T	HR	RBI	SB	CS	BA	$
1993	(R)	66	235	46	63	22	44	10	3	6	30	15	4	.268	x
1994	(A)	132	524	107	152	62	84	24	5	27	83	31	13	.290	x
1995	(A)	27	107	14	22	10	24	3	1	4	13	1	0	.206	x
1995	(AA)	105	358	57	104	33	53	26	2	12	57	5	5	.291	x

He pounded out his 1994 numbers at Winston-Salem; same place Micah Franklin pounded out his. Last year he played 27 games there again, before being promoted, despite himself, to Double-A Chattanooga. Did he hit well there or not?

The team batting average was .280. He was only marginally better than that. His .475 slugging average was only 50 points higher than the team slugging average, and three teammates hit more homers: Jamie Dismuke, 20; Don Rohrmeier, 17; and Adam Hyzdu, 13. Conclusion? If he's a prospect, I'm an airplane.

JOHN WEHNER 3B,OF   Age 29   Bid: R3

Year	Team	G	AB	R	H	BB	SO	D	T	HR	RBI	SB	CS	BA	$
1991	PIT	37	106	15	36	7	17	7	0	0	7	3	0	.340	5
1992	PIT	55	123	11	22	12	22	6	0	0	4	3	0	.179	-2
1993	PIT	29	35	3	5	6	10	0	0	0	0	0	0	.143	-2
1994	PIT	2	4	1	1	0	1	1	0	0	3	0	0	.250	0
1995	PIT	52	107	13	33	10	17	0	3	0	5	3	1	.308	3

Has always had desire — turns doubles into triples — just can't reach the seats.

WALT WEISS SS   Age 33   Bid: $3

Year	Team	G	AB	R	H	BB	SO	D	T	HR	RBI	SB	CS	BA	$
1991	OAK	40	133	15	30	12	14	6	1	0	13	6	0	.226	2
1992	OAK	103	316	36	67	43	39	5	2	0	21	6	3	.212	-1
1993	FLA	158	500	50	133	79	73	14	2	1	39	7	3	.266	6
1994	COL	110	423	58	106	56	58	11	4	1	32	12	7	.251	6
1995	COL	137	427	65	111	98	57	17	3	1	25	15	3	.260	7

Great year. His on-base average went up 67 points (he led the league in % Pitches Taken); he showed a little more pop, picked the right time to steal a base. What makes the 98 walks even more remarkable is that he spent most of the year batting in the eighth position. There's a theory that you should go up hacking in that spot. But by taking the walk, you get the pitcher out of the way for the next inning, which drives the opposing manager up the wall. Also, with John Vander Wal on the bench, the No. 9 spot was a threat.

RONDELL WHITE   OF   Age 24   Bid: $25

Year	Team	G	AB	R	H	BB	SO	D	T	HR	RBI	SB	CS	BA	$
1993	MTL	23	73	9	19	7	16	3	1	2	15	1	2	.260	3
1994	MTL	40	97	16	27	9	18	10	1	2	13	1	1	.278	4
1995	MTL	130	474	87	140	41	87	33	4	13	57	25	5	.295	26

Conservative bid; for some reason, I don't see him running a lot.

MARK WHITEN
OF   Age 29   Bid: $6

Year	Team	G	AB	R	H	BB	SO	D	T	HR	RBI	SB	CS	BA	$
1991	TOR/CLE	116	407	46	99	30	85	18	7	9	45	4	3	.243	8
1992	CLE	148	508	73	129	72	102	19	4	9	43	16	12	.254	14
1993	STL	152	562	81	142	58	110	13	4	25	99	15	8	.253	23
1994	STL	92	334	57	98	37	75	18	2	14	53	10	5	.293	23
1995	BOS	32	108	13	20	8	23	3	0	1	10	1	0	.185	-2
1995	PHI	60	212	38	57	31	63	10	1	11	37	7	0	.269	12

The trade of Scott Cooper for Mark Whiten gets the You're Both Ugly award of the decade. Of the century, had not Whiten returned to the NL and started hittin'.

DARRELL WHITMORE
OF   Age 27   Bid: R3

Year	Team	G	AB	R	H	BB	SO	D	T	HR	RBI	SB	CS	BA	$
1993	FLA	76	250	24	51	10	72	8	2	4	19	4	2	.204	-1
1994	FLA	9	22	1	5	3	5	1	0	0	0	0	1	.227	-1
1995	FLA	27	58	6	11	5	15	2	0	1	2	0	0	.190	-1

Injured? Released? Didn't play in the minors.

RICK WILKINS
C   Age 28   Bid: $4

Year	Team	G	AB	R	H	BB	SO	D	T	HR	RBI	SB	CS	BA	$
1991	CHC	86	203	21	45	19	56	9	0	6	22	3	3	.222	4
1992	CHC	83	244	20	66	28	53	9	1	8	22	0	2	.270	8
1993	CHC	136	446	78	135	50	99	23	1	30	73	2	1	.303	27
1994	CHC	100	313	44	71	40	86	25	2	7	39	4	3	.227	4
1995	CHC/HOU	65	202	30	41	46	61	3	0	7	19	0	0	.203	0

Hit .250 with the Astros; they were hoping for more than one home run.

EDDIE WILLIAMS
1B   Age 30   Bid: $9

Year	Team	G	AB	R	H	BB	SO	D	T	HR	RBI	SB	CS	BA	$
1994	SD	49	175	32	58	15	26	11	1	11	42	0	1	.331	17
1995	SD	97	296	35	77	23	47	11	1	12	47	0	0	.260	10

NL hitters

Plagued by small injuries but that couldn't have been all. Future again in doubt.

MATT WILLIAMS   3B   Age 30   Bid: $38

Year	Team	G	AB	R	H	BB	SO	D	T	HR	RBI	SB	CS	BA	$
1991	SF	157	589	72	158	33	128	24	5	34	98	5	5	.268	30
1992	SF	146	529	58	120	39	109	13	5	20	66	7	7	.227	16
1993	SF	145	579	105	170	27	80	33	4	38	110	1	3	.294	33
1994	SF	112	445	74	119	33	87	16	3	43	96	1	0	.267	36
1995	SF	76	283	53	95	30	58	17	1	23	65	2	0	.336	26

He's the National League threat to Maris. Of course.

Name	G	AB	HR	RBI	SB	BA	$
WILLIAMS,Ma	162	603	49	139	4	.336	56

That's last season expanded out to 162 games. Maybe he wasn't going to hit 60 homers (leaving aside the small detail that it's hard to hit homers on the DL) but he was on a pace to damn near earn $60. Without running.

In 1994, he *was* going to beat Maris.

Name	G	AB	HR	RBI	SB	BA
WILLIAMS,Ma	162	644	62	139	1	.267

Even Stats Inc. thinks so. The computer they played the season out on (in?) produced 62-144-1-.264 final 1994 stats for Matt Williams — in 159 games. He just looks brittle in the five-year scan because (1) he was hurt last year and (2) the game has *been* brittle for the last two years.

1995 proj.	G	AB	HR	RBI	SB	BA
BICHETTE,D	156	651	45	144	15	.340
WALKER,L	147	556	41	114	18	.306
SOSA,S	162	635	41	134	38	.268
BONDS,B	162	569	37	117	35	.294
KARROS,E	161	620	36	118	5	.298

These are the top five home-run hitters in the league last year, with the season expanded to 162 games. We see that no one in the NL was going to threaten Maris, in fact, last season. Sosa might have joined the 40-40 club, though. Bichette would have had the most RBI's since, I don't know, Hack Wilson. We also see that Sosa, Bonds and Karros between them missed one game.

1994 proj.	G	AB	HR	RBI	SB	BA
WILLIAMS,MA	157	624	60	135	1	.267
BAGWELL,J	154	561	55	163	21	.368
BONDS,B	157	548	52	114	41	.312
MCGRIFF,F	158	594	48	132	10	.318
GALARRAGA,A	144	585	43	119	11	.319

Just a reminder that two years ago, with only slightly more hitting overall, there were likely going to be three hitters — and there could have been four — who hit 50 homers in the National League.

The longer a season runs, the more things level out; there's no question about that. For all we know, the 1994 home run champion would have been Galarraga with 47.

Perhaps we should come at it from the other direction, though. What are the odds that 47 will be enough this year?

NIGEL WILSON OF   Age 26   Bid: R3

Year	Team	G	AB	R	H	BB	SO	D	T	HR	RBI	SB	CS	BA	$
1992	(AA)	137	521	85	143	33	137	34	7	26	69	13	8	.274	x
1993	(AAA)	96	370	66	108	25	108	26	7	17	68	8	3	.292	x
1993	FLA	7	16	0	0	0	11	0	0	0	0	0	0	.000	-2
1994	(AAA)	87	314	50	97	22	79	24	1	12	62	2	3	.309	x
1995	(AAA)	82	304	53	95	13	95	27	3	17	51	5	3	.313	x
1995	CIN	5	7	0	0	0	4	0	0	0	0	0	0	.000	-1

Contributed handsomely to the Reds' team at Indianapolis (his slugging average was almost as high as Steve Gibralter's); he even showed enough for the Reds to call him up for a few games. The first hitter selected in the expansion draft now has gone hitless in 23 at-bats in the majors with no walks and 15 strikeouts.

RON WRIGHT   1B   Age 20   Bid: R5

Year	Team	G	AB	R	H	BB	SO	D	T	HR	RBI	SB	CS	BA	$
1994	(R)	45	169	10	29	10	21	9	0	1	16	1	0	.172	x
1995	(A)	135	527	93	143	62	118	23	1	32	104	2	0	.271	x

The No. 6 prospect in the South Atlantic League, he's 6'0", 210; bats right; is said to be a Jeff Bagwell clone; and — it's sickening — belongs to the Braves.

ERIC YOUNG   2B,OF   Age 29   Bid: $18

Year	Team	G	AB	R	H	BB	SO	D	T	HR	RBI	SB	CS	BA	$
1992	LA	49	132	9	34	8	9	1	0	1	11	6	1	.258	4
1993	COL	144	490	82	132	63	41	16	8	3	42	42	19	.269	20
1994	COL	90	228	37	62	38	17	13	1	7	30	18	7	.272	17
1995	COL	120	366	68	116	49	29	21	9	6	36	35	12	.317	26

Hit .406 in July, .404 in September, .331 at home, .269 with two strikes (third in the league), .366 ahead in the count, .404 Close & Late, .316 batting lead-off... A timid bid, I admit it. Defense does count a little.

KEVIN YOUNG   3B   Age 27   Bid: R3

Year	Team	G	AB	R	H	BB	SO	D	T	HR	RBI	SB	CS	BA	$
1992	PIT	10	7	2	4	2	0	0	0	0	4	1	0	.571	2
1993	PIT	141	449	38	106	36	82	24	3	6	47	2	2	.236	3

Year	Team	G	AB	R	H	BB	SO	D	T	HR	RBI	SB	CS	BA	$
1994	PIT	59	122	15	25	8	34	7	2	1	11	0	2	.205	-2
1995	PIT	56	181	13	42	8	53	9	0	6	22	1	3	.232	3

Hit well at Calgary (.356), where Rich Aude...

TODD ZEILE 3B,1B   Age 30   Bid: $16

Year	Team	G	AB	R	H	BB	SO	D	T	HR	RBI	SB	CS	BA	$
1991	STL	155	565	76	158	62	94	36	3	11	81	17	11	.280	24
1992	STL	126	439	51	113	68	70	18	4	7	48	7	10	.257	12
1993	STL	157	571	82	158	70	76	36	1	17	103	5	4	.277	21
1994	STL	113	415	62	111	52	56	25	1	19	75	1	3	.267	20
1995	STL/CHC	113	426	50	105	34	76	22	0	14	52	1	0	.246	9

Even more listless with the Cubs: .227-9-30 in 299 AB, 3 homers in Wrigley.

JOHN ZUBER   1B   Age 26   Bid: R3

Year	Team	G	AB	R	H	BB	SO	D	T	HR	RBI	SB	CS	BA	$
1993	(A)	129	494	70	152	49	47	37	5	5	49	6	6	.308	x
1994	(AA)	138	498	81	146	71	71	29	5	9	71	2	4	.293	x
1995	(AAA)	119	418	53	120	49	68	19	5	3	50	1	2	.287	x

Is 6'1", 175; bats left; plays for the Phillies; and hopes he has better luck than Eddie Zambrano as Hitter Z.

National League Pitchers

JUAN ACEVEDO   Age 25   Bid: R2

Year	Team	G	GS	IP	H	HR	BB	SO	W	L	ERA	Ratio	Sv	$
1993	(A)	27	20	118	119	8	58	107	9	8	4.40	13.50	0	x
1994	(AA)	26	26	174	142	15	38	161	17	6	2.37	9.31	0	x
1995	COL	17	11	66	82	15	20	40	4	6	6.44	13.98	0	-9
1995	(AAA)	3	3	15	18	0	7	7	1	1	6.14	15.00	0	x
1995	(AAA)	2	2	3	0	0	1	2	0	0	.00	3.00	0	x

His great Double-A numbers in 1994 were compiled at New Haven in the Eastern League, perhaps the best place in the Rockies' organization for pitchers to gain self-esteem; then the curious decision was made for Acevedo to bypass Colorado Springs and start right off in the city of Denver. By the time he was sent down to confidence school, his arm may have been hurting.

By now, it was the Mets who were fire-selling, the Rockies who were going for broke — don't you love it? — and he was bartered for Bret Saberhagen. The inevitable comparison would be to Doyle Alexander for John Smoltz, except that Doyle did pitch well for the Tigers and Smoltz's arm wasn't hurting.

TAVO ALVAREZ   Age 24   Bid: $1

Year	Team	G	GS	IP	H	HR	BB	SO	W	L	ERA	Ratio	Sv	$
1994	(AAA)	25	25	141	163	10	55	77	7	10	4.22	13.91	0	x
1995	(AA)	3	3	16	17	0	5	14	2	1	2.25	12.38	0	x
1995	(AAA)	3	3	22	17	1	5	11	2	1	2.49	9.00	0	x
1995	MTL	8	8	37	46	2	14	17	1	5	6.75	14.46	0	-8

Tavo Alvarez was mediocre at best at Ottawa in 1994. The only way to account for his limited minor league play last year is that he also must have had arm trouble. But he pitched well, particularly back at Ottawa. Then pitched badly enough at Montreal to drag a Rotisserie team down about four points in the standings. I'd take a $1 chance on him this year, if he makes the Expos, because he's an extreme groundball pitcher (G/F 2.66).

LUIS AQUINO   Age 31   Bid: R3

Year	Team	G	GS	IP	H	HR	BB	SO	W	L	ERA	Ratio	Sv	$
1991	KC	38	1	157	152	10	47	80	8	4	3.44	11.41	3	14
1992	KC	15	0	68	81	5	20	11	3	6	4.52	13.43	0	-2
1993	FLA	38	13	111	115	6	40	67	6	8	3.42	12.61	0	6
1994	FLA	29	1	51	39	3	22	22	2	1	3.73	10.84	0	6

Year	Team	G	GS	IP	H	HR	BB	SO	W	L	ERA	Ratio	Sv	$
1995	SF	34	0	42	57	6	13	26	0	3	5.10	14.88	2	**-5**

Aquino could be history, at last, and he could earn $6 this year. If the latter, it would mean that he boosted a team that had him the whole time about three points in the standings; as innocuous as he was in 1994, he contributed enough wins to gain a point right there, and his qualitative contributions easily were enough for another two points.

But no team will have him the whole time this year. There are a zillion R3's in the next chapter, and Luis Aquino is standing in for most of them.

RENE AROCHA   Age 30   Bid: $1

Year	Team	G	GS	IP	H	HR	BB	SO	W	L	ERA	Ratio	Sv	$
1993	STL	32	29	188	197	20	31	96	11	8	3.78	10.91	0	**15**
1994	STL	45	7	83	94	9	21	62	4	4	4.01	12.47	11	**13**
1995	STL	41	0	50	55	6	18	25	3	5	3.99	13.23	0	**1**

The R3's could be $1 pitchers and the $1 pitchers could be R3's. All told, there are 108 pitchers with bid values, adding up to exactly $1,020. That's what the average Stage Three league spends on pitching. If yours spends more, add to the bid values for pitchers and subtract from hitters, always keeping the total bid limit at $3,120.

MATT ARRANDALE   Age 25   Bid: R4

Year	Team	G	GS	IP	H	HR	BB	SO	W	L	ERA	Ratio	Sv	$
1993	(A)	12	12	69	77	6	14	53	3	4	4.59	11.93	0	x
1994	(A)	9	9	59	65	0	11	29	3	4	3.36	11.59	0	x
1994	(A)	19	19	133	112	2	21	121	15	3	1.76	9.00	0	x
1995	(AA)	47	3	69	72	1	22	24	3	5	3.28	12.26	2	x

Very curious that a pitcher who won 18 games in A-ball in 1994 would be switched to relief, long relief at that. If he was having arm trouble (as the BB/SO rate suggests), long relief would seem to be the worse place for Arrandale to be.

He remains an R4 — long-range possibility — because he was a hot prospect just a short time ago.

ANDY ASHBY   Age 28   Bid: $17

Year	Team	G	GS	IP	H	HR	BB	SO	W	L	ERA	Ratio	Sv	$
1991	PHI	8	8	42	41	5	19	26	1	5	6.00	12.86	0	**-6**
1992	PHI	10	8	37	42	6	21	24	1	3	7.54	15.32	0	**-10**
1993	SD	32	21	123	168	19	56	77	3	10	6.80	16.39	1	**-28**

Year	Team	G	GS	IP	H	HR	BB	SO	W	L	ERA	Ratio	Sv	$
1994	SD	24	24	164	145	16	43	121	6	11	3.40	10.30	0	**23**
1995	SD	31	31	193	180	17	62	150	12	10	2.94	11.30	0	**25**

The best combination in the world — a strikeout groundball pitcher (G/F 2.10) — whose best years, if he doesn't have arm trouble, are right in front of him.

PEDRO ASTACIO   Age 26   Bid: $3

Year	Team	G	GS	IP	H	HR	BB	SO	W	L	ERA	Ratio	Sv	$
1992	LA	11	11	82	80	1	20	43	5	5	1.98	10.98	0	**10**
1993	LA	31	31	186	165	14	68	122	14	9	3.57	11.25	0	**18**
1994	LA	23	23	149	142	18	47	108	6	8	4.29	11.42	0	**8**
1995	LA	48	11	104	103	12	29	80	7	8	4.24	11.42	0	**7**

Still worth a $3 flyer. The bid limit may not seem like much, but there will be two Pedro Astacios at the end of the auction for every spot that is left to fill.

STEVE AVERY   Age 26   Bid: $16

Year	Team	G	GS	IP	H	HR	BB	SO	W	L	ERA	Ratio	Sv	$
1991	ATL	35	35	210	189	21	65	137	18	8	3.38	10.87	0	**19**
1992	ATL	35	35	234	216	14	71	129	11	11	3.20	11.05	0	**12**
1993	ATL	35	35	223	216	14	43	125	18	6	2.94	10.44	0	**32**
1994	ATL	24	24	152	127	15	55	122	8	3	4.04	10.80	0	**16**
1995	ATL	29	29	173	165	22	52	141	7	13	4.67	11.27	0	**5**

Now, good *starting* pitchers — they are scarce. Even if you think Avery's a bum (there's an ever-growing host of scarcely disinterested former fans who think so), the bid limit is what you better make sure someone else pays for him.

My own opinion?

I want him. But I've been burned by Avery.

WILLIE BANKS   Age 27   Bid: R3

Year	Team	G	GS	IP	H	HR	BB	SO	W	L	ERA	Ratio	Sv	$
1991	MIN	5	3	17	21	1	12	16	1	1	5.71	17.14	0	**-3**
1992	MIN	16	12	71	80	6	37	37	4	4	5.70	14.83	0	**-8**
1993	MIN	31	0	171	186	17	78	138	11	12	4.04	13.87	0	**4**
1994	CHC	23	23	138	139	16	56	91	8	12	5.40	12.69	0	**-4**

Year	Team	G	GS	IP	H	HR	BB	SO	W	L	ERA	Ratio	Sv	$
1995	C/LA/FL	25	15	91	106	14	58	62	2	6	5.66	16.28	0	-17

Was only a shade worse than the average starting pitcher, believe it or not, in his 15 starts (4.22 ERA vs. 4.20 for the league). Started nine games for the Marlins.

BRIAN BARBER   Age 23   Bid: $2

Year	Team	G	GS	IP	H	HR	BB	SO	W	L	ERA	Ratio	Sv	$
1994	(AA)	6	6	36	31	4	16	54	1	3	3.25	11.75	0	x
1994	(AAA)	19	18	85	79	7	46	95	4	7	5.38	13.24	1	x
1995	(AAA)	20	19	107	105	14	40	94	6	5	4.70	12.20	0	x
1995	STL	9	4	29	31	4	16	27	2	1	5.22	14.42	0	-2

So far, it's been all talk and not much show for Brian Barber. That's still better than no show, which happens so often. Fair number of strikeouts with the Cardinals.

JOSE BAUTISTA   Age 31   Bid: R3

Year	Team	G	GS	IP	H	HR	BB	SO	W	L	ERA	Ratio	Sv	$
1993	CHC	58	7	112	105	11	27	63	10	3	2.82	10.64	2	19
1994	CHC	58	0	69	75	10	17	45	4	5	3.89	11.94	1	7
1995	SF	52	6	101	120	24	26	45	3	8	6.44	13.05	0	-13

A hundred innings of Jose Bautista kills teams like the Giants, who have to have the innings.

ROD BECK   Age 27   Bid: $27

Year	Team	G	GS	IP	H	HR	BB	SO	W	L	ERA	Ratio	Sv	$
1991	SF	31	0	52	53	4	13	38	1	1	3.78	11.35	1	1
1992	SF	65	0	92	62	4	15	87	3	3	1.76	7.53	17	31
1993	SF	76	0	79	57	11	13	86	3	1	2.16	7.94	48	46
1994	SF	48	0	49	49	10	13	39	2	4	2.77	11.47	28	31
1995	SF	60	0	59	60	7	21	42	5	6	4.45	12.43	33	27

He just eked out Trevor Hoffman for the highest salary among relievers last year (by 33 cents):

```
Top 10 salaries, NL pitchers
                  earned avg         Heath Data    - touts -
NL pitchers       1995   sal  +/-    Pts    Rk     AP   JH  | $94
MADDUX,G          68     36   32     68.1   1      40   40  |  72
BECK,R            27     33   -6     57.9   16     36   31  |  31
HOFFMAN,T         33     33    0     59.6   5      33   32  |  32
MYERS,R           29     32   -3     51.8   64     27   28  |  19
ROJAS,M           21     30  -10     57.1   21     28   30  |  28
RIJO,J             3     26  -23     54.6   39     24   29  |  21
DRABEK,D           0     24  -24     49.3   84     23   28  |  38
FRANCO,J          32     24    8     55.7   33     28   29  |  31
HILL,K            -6     24  -30     51.9   60     17   27  |  31
SABERHAGEN,B       7     23  -16     54.8   37     20   28  |  46
   average        21     29   -7     56.1   36     28   30  |  35
```

Just as in the AL, relievers have lost a lot of cachet in recent years. And just as in the AL, it's nothing personal. In Beck's case, his heroic 1993 effort late in the season seems to have taken something out of his arm permanently.

It's quite shocking, really, that only five of the ten most expensive pitchers last year were closers. It would seem that nine teams either don't have closers or don't have closers who are deemed any good, and yet there was no scarcity of saves in the league — either last year or the year before. In both years, slightly more than half of the wins were accompanied by saves.

Perhaps the significance here is that half of the ten most expensive pitchers *are* starters. Maybe it's the scarcity of starting pitching that's causing this.

In any event, the value of looking at the list is to see how the group as a whole performed. Did the ten most coveted pitchers last year do their job? Or, as conventional wisdom would have it, did they break our hearts as usual?

Four of them ranged from horrible to lousy. And altogether they lost $7 each.

On the other hand, they earned $21 each. The average pitcher is worth $8.67; they were far better than twice above average.

Teams that bought these pitchers finished with an average of 56.1 points — much better than the teams that bought the ten most expensive hitters (52.9 points — Bonds comment). A total of 120 pitchers were bought in at least ten Heath leagues; the teams that bought the 10 highest-paid finished 36th out of 120. In other words, in a 12-team race, they finished between third and fourth (36/120 x 12 = 3.6).

We are getting to be very ambitious indeed when finishing in the money breaks our hearts.

Another way to look at it is that the most expensive pitchers returned 72 cents on the dollar (21/29); they were 72% reliable.

They would have returned 75 cents on my dollar and 70 cents on John Hunt's.

They only returned 60 cents on their 1994 dollars (21/35); that must be what Hunt, myself and you were thinking when we decided they were getting pay cuts, not raises, from us.

ALAN BENES   Age 24   Bid: $6

Year	Team	G	GS	IP	H	HR	BB	SO	W	L	ERA	Ratio	Sv	$
1995	(AAA)	11	11	56	37	5	14	54	4	2	2.41	8.20	0	x
1995	STL	3	3	16.0	24	2	4	20	1	2	8.44	15.75	0	-5

Look at the BB/SO! This guy rears back and fires! No one touched him in his last game. A guy with that kind of stuff doesn't even have to think about pitching. Could have gotten here on talent alone. May not have learned a damn thing yet.

MIKE BIRKBECK
Age 35   Bid: R3

Year	Team	G	GS	IP	H	HR	BB	SO	W	L	ERA	Ratio	Sv	$
1995	(AAA)	9	9	53	52	2	13	39	5	3	2.36	11.04	0	x
1995	NYM	4	4	28	22	2	2	14	0	1	1.63	7.81	0	7

Mike Birkbeck takes it one year at a time, and last year is the only year that counts. Don't waste a reserve pick on him this year, but before it's over, he'll earn something for somebody.

WILLIE BLAIR
Age 31   Bid: R3

Year	Team	G	GS	IP	H	HR	BB	SO	W	L	ERA	Ratio	Sv	$
1992	HOU	29	8	79	74	5	25	48	5	7	4.00	11.33	0	2
1993	COL	46	18	146	184	20	42	84	6	10	4.75	13.93	0	-8
1994	COL	47	1	78	98	9	39	68	0	5	5.79	15.88	3	-16
1995	SD	40	12	114	112	11	45	83	7	5	4.34	12.39	0	4

Willie Blair may be worth a reserve pick. I'm as shocked as you are.

DOUG BOCHTLER
Age 25   Bid: $2

Year	Team	G	GS	IP	H	HR	BB	SO	W	L	ERA	Ratio	Sv	$
1994	(AAA)	22	20	100	116	11	48	86	3	7	5.20	14.76	0	x
1995	(AAA)	18	2	36	31	5	26	32	2	3	4.25	14.25	1	x
1995	SD	34	0	45	38	5	19	45	4	4	3.57	11.32	1	7

Seriously good numbers. The difference between what he did at San Diego and what he did in Triple-A is intriguing.

PEDRO BORBON
Age 28   Bid: $1

Year	Team	G	GS	IP	H	HR	BB	SO	W	L	ERA	Ratio	Sv	$
1994	(AAA)	59	0	81	66	3	41	85	3	4	2.79	11.89	4	x
1995	ATL	41	0	32	29	2	17	33	2	2	3.09	12.94	2	4

Pitched for the honor of the family.

TOBY BORLAND
Age 27   Bid: $1

Year	Team	G	GS	IP	H	HR	BB	SO	W	L	ERA	Ratio	Sv	$
1994	PHI	24	0	34	31	1	14	26	1	0	2.36	11.80	1	6

Year	Team	G	GS	IP	H	HR	BB	SO	W	L	ERA	Ratio	Sv	$
1995	PHI	50	0	74	81	3	37	59	1	3	3.77	14.35	6	**1**

Kept the ball in the park. Didn't disgrace himself. But sure wasn't the Phillies closer.

RICKY BOTTALICO   Age 26   Bid: $21

Year	Team	G	GS	IP	H	HR	BB	SO	W	L	ERA	Ratio	Sv	$
1993	(A)	13	0	20	19	0	5	19	1	0	2.75	10.80	4	**x**
1993	(AA)	49	0	72	63	4	26	65	3	3	2.25	11.13	20	**x**
1994	(AAA)	19	0	22	32	4	22	22	3	1	8.87	11.13	3	**x**
1994	PHI	3	0	3	3	0	1	3	0	0	.00	12.00	0	**1**
1994	(AA)	38	0	43	29	6	10	51	2	2	2.53	11.13	22	**x**
1995	PHI	62	0	88	50	7	42	87	5	3	2.46	9.44	1	**19**

You read it here first: Bottalico will be their closer this year.
   If this is the first book you bought.

RYAN BOWEN   Age 28   Bid: R3

Year	Team	G	GS	IP	H	HR	BB	SO	W	L	ERA	Ratio	Sv	$
1991	HOU	14	13	72	73	4	36	49	6	4	5.15	13.69	0	**-5**
1992	HOU	11	9	34	48	8	30	22	0	7	10.96	20.85	0	**-21**
1993	FLA	27	27	157	156	11	87	98	8	12	4.42	13.96	0	**-5**
1994	FLA	8	8	47	50	9	19	32	1	5	4.94	13.12	0	**-3**
1995	FLA	4	3	17	23	3	12	15	2	0	3.78	18.90	0	**-2**

There's a certain distinction in having compiled minus numbers in all five years of the scan.

JEFF BRANTLEY   Age 32   Bid: $28

Year	Team	G	GS	IP	H	HR	BB	SO	W	L	ERA	Ratio	Sv	$
1991	SF	67	0	95	78	8	52	81	5	2	2.45	12.27	15	**16**
1992	SF	56	4	92	67	8	45	86	7	7	2.95	11.00	7	**14**
1993	SF	53	12	114	112	19	46	76	5	6	4.28	12.51	0	**0**
1994	CIN	50	0	65	46	6	28	63	6	6	2.48	10.19	15	**31**
1995	CIN	56	0	70	53	11	20	62	3	2	2.82	9.34	28	**34**

Brantley earned $1 more than Trevor Hoffman, cost $9 less, and ranked 26 places lower in the

Heath league trackings.

Top 10 NL pitchers

NL pitchers	earned 1995	avg sal	+/-	Heath Data Pts	Rk	- touts - AP	JH	$94
MADDUX,G	68	36	32	68.1	1	40	40	72
NOMO,H	39	6	33	56.0	29	R2		
WORRELL,To	38	12	26	50.7	73	22	17	18
HENKE,T	38	22	16	49.6	82	24	23	22
SCHOUREK,P	37	4	33	58.5	12	3	10	5
WOHLERS,M	35	5	30	53.5	48	5	16	2
BRANTLEY,J	34	19	15	55.7	31	20	17	31
VALDES,I	33	8	25	54.2	46	7		8
HOFFMAN,T	33	33	0	59.6	5	33	32	32
FRANCO,Jo	32	24	8	55.7	33	28	29	31
average	39	17	22	56.2	36	18	18	22

What does that mean? Is it an anomaly, or did silly owners buy Brantley and wise owners buy Hoffman? Just asking, since Peter Golenbock and I bought both in the Baseball Weekly league.

Here's what you paid, in more detail.

NL pitchers	— leagues — BW	HSS	IOC	SCN	f
MADDUX,G	36	37	35	35	f
NOMO,H	5		13	9	
WORRELL,To	18	13	6	15	f
HENKE,T	19	23	23	30	
SCHOUREK,P	9	3	1	2	
WOHLERS,M	8	5	2	2	
BRANTLEY,J	21	20	15	21	
VALDES,I	13	8	3		
HOFFMAN,T	35	33	30	13	f
FRANCO,Jo	26	25	21	21	f
average	19	17	15	15	

These are the ten best pitchers, in fact, so you have to say Baseball Weekly whips the Hollywood Stars and It's Only Crickets, the other two non-freeze leagues.

Between Baseball Weekly, Hunt and myself, Baseball Weekly gets Nomo, Brantley, Valdes and Hoffman; Hunt gets Schourek, Wohlers and Franco; I get Worrell and Henke; and Hunt and I tie for Maddux.

That's according to what Hunt and I advised to pay and what Baseball Weekly actually paid. Since both Hunt and I were in the Baseball Weekly league, and he got Wohlers but didn't get Schourek or Franco, and I didn't get Worell or Henke but did get Hoffman, Brantley and Maddux, it gets confusing.

How is it that the ten best NL pitchers, earning profits of $22 each — each one of them nearly a $40 pitcher — were bought by teams that finished with an average of 56.2 points, one measly tenth of a point better than the ten most expensive pitchers, who lost $7 each?

A head-scratcher. An anomaly for sure. But worth thinking about.

JAMIE BREWINGTON   Age 24   Bid: $2

Year	Team	G	GS	IP	H	HR	BB	SO	W	L	ERA	Ratio	Sv	$
1995	(AA)	16	16	88	72	8	55	74	8	3	3.06	12.99	0	x
1995	SF	13	13	75	68	8	45	45	6	4	4.54	13.50	0	0

Probably should be an R1 — snap him up right away on reserve — but he's not going got make it to the reserve draft. There can't be any leagues left that don't allow the dropping of pitchers, because all those owners have expired, but if you can't both deactivate and reserve Brewington (in the BW league, we can cut healthy, all-too active pitchers, but we can only reserve injured pitchers), then he may not be worth the risk. He's too young, too inexperienced, too wild, and is an extreme flyball pitcher (G/F 0.68).

DOUG BROCAIL   Age 29   Bid: R3

Year	Team	G	GS	IP	H	HR	BB	SO	W	L	ERA	Ratio	Sv	$
1992	SD	3	3	14	17	2	5	15	0	0	6.43	14.14	0	-3
1993	SD	24	24	128	143	16	42	70	4	13	4.56	12.97	0	-4
1994	SD	12	0	17	21	1	5	11	0	0	5.82	13.76	0	-3
1995	HOU	36	7	77	87	10	22	39	6	4	4.19	12.69	1	4

The innings were divided equally between starting and relieving, and he was fine as a reliever (3.03 ERA).

Curiously, relievers in the National League had only slightly better ERAs than starters last year (4.14 ERA for relievers, 4.20 for starters). It's certainly not the case that relievers are better than starters, and although they don't have to pitch as long, that's not it either; it's that no starter has ever ruined a reliever's stats.

JIM BULLINGER   Age 30   Bid: $5

Year	Team	G	GS	IP	H	HR	BB	SO	W	L	ERA	Ratio	Sv	$
1992	CHC	39	9	85	72	9	54	36	2	8	4.66	13.34	7	-2
1993	CHC	15	0	17	18	1	9	10	1	0	4.32	14.58	1	0
1994	CHC	33	10	100	87	6	34	72	6	2	3.60	10.89	2	16
1995	CHC	24	24	150	152	14	65	93	12	8	4.14	13.02	0	6

Bid price may be a little high (7.56 ERA the last month), but the Cubs are going to be hot this year.

DAVE BURBA   Age 29   Bid: $4

Year	Team	G	GS	IP	H	HR	BB	SO	W	L	ERA	Ratio	Sv	$
1991	SEA	22	2	37	34	6	14	16	2	2	3.68	11.78	1	3
1992	SF	23	11	71	80	4	31	47	2	7	4.97	14.14	0	-9
1993	SF	54	5	95	95	14	37	88	10	3	4.25	12.46	0	5
1994	SF	57	0	74	59	5	45	84	3	6	4.38	12.65	0	1
1995	SF/CIN	52	9	107	90	9	51	96	10	4	3.97	11.90	0	10

Had a G/F ratio of 1.23, which is worth noting only because he used to be an extreme flyball pitcher. Had a 3.27 ERA with Cincinnati and a 3.88 ERA as a starter. Inasmuch as he made all nine starts with the Reds, he must have been sensational in his six relief appearances in a Reds' uniform.

JOHN BURKETT
Age 31   Bid: $4

Year	Team	G	GS	IP	H	HR	BB	SO	W	L	ERA	Ratio	Sv	$
1991	SF	36	34	207	223	19	60	131	12	11	4.18	12.32	0	0
1992	SF	32	32	190	194	13	45	107	13	9	3.84	11.34	0	7
1993	SF	34	34	232	224	18	40	145	22	7	3.65	10.26	0	30
1994	SF	25	25	159	176	14	36	85	6	8	3.62	11.97	0	12
1995	FLA	30	30	188	208	22	57	126	14	14	4.30	12.66	0	8

In Appendix B we can see the sad truth that, as good as Burkett was, he only helped in one category.

PAUL BYRD
Age 25   Bid: $1

Year	Team	G	GS	IP	H	HR	BB	SO	W	L	ERA	Ratio	Sv	$
1995	(AAA)	22	10	87	71	6	21	61	3	5	2.79	9.52	6	x
1995	NYM	17	0	22	18	1	7	26	2	0	2.05	10.23	0	6

Excellent numbers, especially with the Mets. Could easily earn double-figures this year, and you can probably get him in the reserve draft.

TOM CANDIOTTI
Age 38   Bid: $7

Year	Team	G	GS	IP	H	HR	BB	SO	W	L	ERA	Ratio	Sv	$
1991	TOR	34	34	238	202	12	73	167	13	13	2.65	10.40	0	32
1992	LA	32	32	204	177	13	63	152	11	15	3.00	10.61	0	15
1993	LA	33	32	214	192	12	71	155	8	10	3.12	11.08	0	18
1994	LA	23	22	153	149	9	54	102	7	7	4.12	11.94	0	8
1995	LA	30	30	190	187	18	58	141	7	14	3.50	11.58	0	14

There's no reason to be afraid of Candiotti because of his age, and so maybe I'm just afraid of him.

HECTOR CARRASCO
Age 26   Bid: $2

Year	Team	G	GS	IP	H	HR	BB	SO	W	L	ERA	Ratio	Sv	$
1994	CIN	45	0	56	42	3	30	41	5	6	2.24	11.50	6	19
1995	CIN	64	0	87	86	1	46	64	2	7	4.12	13.60	5	1

He clearly lost something. The one home run is his best stat.

LARRY CASIAN   Age 30   Bid: 0

Year	Team	G	GS	IP	H	HR	BB	SO	W	L	ERA	Ratio	Sv	$
1991	MIN	15	0	18	28	4	7	6	0	0	7.36	17.18	0	-6
1992	MIN	6	0	7	7	0	1	2	1	0	2.70	10.80	0	1
1993	MIN	54	0	57	59	1	14	31	5	3	3.02	11.59	1	9
1994	MN/CLE	40	0	49	73	12	16	20	1	5	7.35	16.35	1	-13
1995	CHC	42	0	23	23	1	15	11	1	0	1.93	14.66	0	2

Such an interesting effort, presumably his last, that it's worth a look at. Casian was brought in strictly to face lefties, and they hit .308 against him. He did not get even two outs per appearance. The 47 right-handed batters he was forced to face (mostly pinch-hitters, no doubt) hit only .189 against him, but, really, all they needed to do was stand there: he walked ten of them. Inning per inning, Casian surely has the biggest differential in Appendix B between $ERA and ($Rto), meaning he was one lucky pitcher.

FRANK CASTILLO   Age 27   Bid: $14

Year	Team	G	GS	IP	H	HR	BB	SO	W	L	ERA	Ratio	Sv	$
1991	CHC	18	4	112	107	5	33	73	6	7	4.35	11.28	0	1
1992	CHC	33	33	205	179	19	63	135	10	11	3.46	10.61	0	11
1993	CHC	29	25	141	162	20	39	84	5	8	4.84	12.80	0	-5
1994	CHC	4	4	23	25	3	5	19	2	1	4.30	11.74	0	2
1995	CHC	29	29	188	179	22	52	135	11	10	3.21	11.06	0	23

A typical pitcher, right?

Maybe yes, maybe no. Is $9 a lot or a little to pay for a pitcher?

```
Top 10 profits, NL pitchers
              earned avg          Heath Data    - touts -
NL pitchers   1995  sal   +/-     Pts    Rk     AP   JH    | $94
NOMO,H         39    6    33      56.0   29     R2         |
SCHOUREK,P     37    4    33      58.5   12     3    10    | 5
MADDUX,G       68    36   32      68.1   1      40   40    | 72
WOHLERS,M      35    5    30      53.5   48     5    16    | 2
WORRELL,To     38    12   26      50.7   73     22   17    | 18
VALDES,I       33    8    25      54.2   46     7          | 8
REED,Steve     23    1    22      61.1   4      R2         | 0
NAVARRO,J      25    2    22      51.8   63     3    8     | -13
CASTILLO,F     23    2    21      56.8   25     R3         | 2
SLOCUMB,H      29    10   19      59.1   7      5    15    | 9
   average     35    9    26      57.0   31     9    11    | 10
```

Frank Castillo was vintage crapshoot. There's no question that the crapshoot extends to $2 and in some leagues it extends to $3. Meaning it takes $3 to have your pick of the litter at the end. It does *not* extend to $4. Pete Schourek was not in the crapshoot. No pitcher that is listed with a $4 bid limit in this book is deemed to be what you're hoping you don't hit. Only three of the ten pitchers who returned the biggest profits in the league last year had their humble beginnings in the truly huge underclass that comprises the crapshoot. Not only is the $9 average salary a lot to pay, it's more than the average pitcher is going to earn ($8.67).

The group earned $10 in 1994; the $1 discount by the market is the smallest we've seen for any group. Comparatively speaking, a turn for the better is being predicted.

My overall take is the same as the market's, while Hunt seems to have a special intuition about many of these pitchers. He gets a lot of credit for Wohlers, Navarro and especially Slocumb. In the three-way battle, he also takes Schourek easily and once again has to toss a coin with me for Maddux.

I'm almost shut out completely (I do get Worrell again); you guys are way ahead of Hunt and I on Hideo Nomo; then you out blink me for Valdes and pick up Reed and Castillo in the crapshoot.

Total luck.

No, no; you guys are tough. A closer look confirms this.

NL pitchers	— leagues —				
	BW	HSS	IOC	SCN	f
NOMO,H	5		13	9	
SCHOUREK,P	9	3	1	2	
MADDU│,G	36	37	35	35	f
WOHLERS,M	8	5	2	2	
WORRELL,To	18	13	6	15	f
VALDES,I	13	8	3		
REED,Steve	1		2	1	
NAVARRO,J		3	4	11	
CASTILLO,F	3	1	2		
SLOCUMB,H	4	9	18	3	f
average	10	8	9	10	

Even Castillo involved a bit of scuffling; Reed was the only one who was virtually uncontested. The march of time (BW drafted 4/19, HSS 4/30, IOC 5/4, SCN 5/9) was plainly a big factor. Someone in Scrooge's, who may even have been thinking of not freezing Slocumb at some point in the winter, came into their draft smiling.

It would be fun to see how that team did, but Scrooge's is not in the packet of league information that Jerry Heath sent me. I do have the Hollywood Stars...

The Bel Air Bobs bought Slocumb and finished sixth.

The Buffalo Soldiers bought Wohlers and finished third.

The Hojay Greys bought Schourek and finished fourth.

The Screwballs bought Valdes and finished eighth.

The Winos — here you go — they bought Navarro and finished first.

Still, not all that much of a success-oriented search. And it is in fact pretty much in accord with the more global circumstantial evidence that is found under "Heath Data" in the chart above. With average profits of $26, wouldn't you expect the teams that bought these pitchers to make out like bandits? The data suggests otherwise.

The teams finished with an average of 57 points. The average rank of these pitchers works out to a third-place finish in a 12-team league (31/120 x 12). Nothing wrong with that.

But, compared to the other groups that we've looked at, the profits don't seem to mean much. Teams that bought the top ten pitchers period (forgetting profits) finished with 56.2 points. Teams that bought the ten most expensive pitchers (and incurred losses) finished with 56.1 points. How far back is that?

What's going on here? When you look at groups of ten, can it all be dismissed as an anomaly?

JASON CHRISTIANSEN

Age 26   Bid: $2

Year	Team	G	GS	IP	H	HR	BB	SO	W	L	ERA	Ratio	Sv	$
1994	(AA)	28	0	39	30	2	14	43	2	1	2.09	10.15	2	x
1994	(AAA)	33	0	34	19	3	16	39	3	1	2.41	9.26	0	x
1995	PIT	63	0	56	49	5	34	53	1	3	4.15	13.26	0	-2

A sleeper (average salary $3) who at least didn't fleece anyone.

BRAD CLONTZ

Age 25   Bid: $3

Year	Team	G	GS	IP	H	HR	BB	SO	W	L	ERA	Ratio	Sv	$
1993	(A)	51	0	75	69	5	26	79	1	7	2.75	11.40	10	x
1994	(AA)	39	0	45	32	5	10	49	1	2	1.20	8.40	27	x
1994	(AAA)	24	0	25	19	1	9	21	0	0	2.10	10.08	11	x
1995	ATL	59	0	69	71	5	22	55	8	1	3.65	12.13	4	12

I tried to get Hunt interested in one of our relievers in the Baseball Weekly league. We had Hoffman, Brantley and Bruce Ruffin; he had Wohlers. Clontz was getting the saves. "Hey, John, want one of our relievers? ... Not yet? You mean you still think Wohlers is going to do anything? ... You do? How come?"

"I went to college with Brad Clontz," said John. "And he can't pitch."

Now *that's* networking.

STEVE COOKE

Age 26   Bid: R2

Year	Team	G	GS	IP	H	HR	BB	SO	W	L	ERA	Ratio	Sv	$
1992	PIT	11	0	23	22	2	4	10	2	0	3.52	10.17	1	3
1993	PIT	32	32	211	207	22	59	132	10	10	3.89	11.36	0	11
1994	PIT	25	23	134	157	21	46	74	4	11	5.02	13.60	0	-10

Made one start at Augusta (A): 5 IP, 2 hits, 1 walk, 5 K's, no runs. One start at Carolina (AA): 5 IP, 5 hits, 5 walks, 4 K's, 4 runs. An R1, or even as much as $5, or an R3, depending on spring training.

JOHN CUMMINGS

Age 27   Bid: R3

Year	Team	G	GS	IP	H	HR	BB	SO	W	L	ERA	Ratio	Sv	$
1993	SEA	10	8	46	59	6	16	19	0	6	6.02	14.57	0	-7
1994	SEA	17	8	64	66	7	37	33	2	4	5.63	14.48	0	-5
1995	LA	35	0	39	38	3	10	21	3	1	3.00	11.08	0	6

Avoid.

RICH DELUCIA Age 31 Bid: $2

Year	Team	G	GS	IP	H	HR	BB	SO	W	L	ERA	Ratio	Sv	$
1991	SEA	32	31	182	176	31	78	98	12	13	5.09	12.56	0	-1
1992	SEA	30	11	84	100	13	35	66	3	3	5.49	14.46	1	-9
1993	SEA	30	1	43	46	5	23	48	3	3	4.64	14.44	0	-2
1994	CIN	8	0	11	9	4	5	15	0	0	4.22	11.81	0	0
1995	STL	56	1	82	63	9	36	76	8	7	3.39	10.82	0	13

While Hunt and I were dickering, Mike Vogel, who produces *Outside Pitch*, a magazine for Orioles fans, was on cruise control. He won the Baseball Weekly NL league wire-to-wire. His pitching staff included Rich DeLucia, who was picked up after the first week to replace David Nied. Even though Vogel was in first place, I wasn't paying that much attention to him — it was early — and I had absolutely no premonition when I opened my stat packet from Heath Data for Period # 4. My eyes popped out. Vogel had 11 wins that week!

Eleven!

Has anyone ever seen anything close to that? I've seen six wins before. I think I've seen seven. I'm sure I've never seen eight. I'd remember.

I called Mike after the season was over to congratulate him — to shake my head along with him over the fact that he ended up with a grand total of 62 wins — sixty-two! — and I asked him if he could reconstruct that particular week, in which *he had eleven wins!* He was happy to. This is what came in the mail.

"The week of May 16-22:

"Tues, 5/16   Slocumb, Smoltz

"Wed, 5/17   Swindell

"Thu, 5/18   Christiansen"

Time out. Can you imagine how you would feel, reading the box scores on Friday morning, if you saw a W after Christiansen, win number 4 that week?

"Friday, 5/19 Beck"

Win number 5. Beck blew the save. But wins are worth more than saves.

"Sat, 5/20   Beck, Tyler Green, Hudek."

You're hallucinating.

"Sun, 5/21   DeLucia, Smoltz, Swindell"

You've fainted. It's okay; you don't miss anything.

"Mon, 5/22   On the seventh day, they rested."

JERRY DIPOTO Age 28 Bid: $1

Year	Team	G	GS	IP	H	HR	BB	SO	W	L	ERA	Ratio	Sv	$
1993	CLE	46	0	56	57	0	30	41	4	4	2.40	13.90	11	13
1994	CLE	7	0	16	26	1	10	9	0	0	8.04	20.68	0	-8
1995	NYM	58	0	79	77	2	29	49	4	6	3.78	12.13	2	6

Solid plugger. Keeps the ball in the park and on the ground (G/F 2.78).

GLENN DISHMAN   Age 25   Bid: R2

Year	Team	G	GS	IP	H	HR	BB	SO	W	L	ERA	Ratio	Sv	$
1995	(AAA)	14	14	106	91	12	20	64	6	3	2.55	9.42	0	x
1995	SD	19	16	97	104	11	34	43	4	8	5.01	12.80	0	-3

Will get hammered. But I could be wrong.

JIM DOUGHERTY   Age 28   Bid: R3

Year	Team	G	GS	IP	H	HR	BB	SO	W	L	ERA	Ratio	Sv	$
1993	(AA)	52	0	53	39	3	21	55	2	2	1.87	10.19	36	x
1994	(AAA)	55	0	59	70	9	30	49	5	4	4.12	15.25	21	x
1995	(AAA)	8	0	11	11	1	5	12	1	0	3.27	13.09	1	x
1995	HOU	56	0	68	76	7	25	49	8	4	4.92	13.43	0	2

Good example of a minor-league saves artist in the majors.

DOUG DRABEK Age 33   Bid: $14

Year	Team	G	GS	IP	H	HR	BB	SO	W	L	ERA	Ratio	Sv	$
1991	PIT	35	35	235	245	16	62	142	15	14	3.07	11.77	0	14
1992	PIT	34	34	257	218	17	54	177	15	11	2.77	9.54	0	29
1993	HOU	34	34	238	242	18	60	157	9	18	3.79	11.44	0	11
1994	HOU	23	23	165	132	14	45	121	12	6	2.84	9.67	0	38
1995	HOU	31	31	185	205	18	54	143	10	9	4.77	12.60	0	0

Was last year an anomaly? That is the question.

```
Top 10 losses, NL pitchers
                  earned avg          Heath Data    - touts -
NL pitchers       1995  sal  +/-      Pts    Rk     AP   JH  | $94
HILL,K              -6   24  -30      51.9   60     17   27    31
JACKSON,D          -17   11  -28      44.5  113      9   16    28
FREEMAN,M          -16   10  -26      42.4  119      6    6    25
DRABEK,D             0   24  -24      49.3   84     23   28    38
RIJO,J               3   26  -23      54.6   39     24   29    21
TRACHSEL,S         -11   12  -23      47.6   95     15   15    21
MULHOLLAND,T       -16    7  -22      37.2  122      1   10   -11
BENES,Andy           1   19  -18      48.5   90     17   18    16
JACOME,J           -13    5  -18      44.6  112      2         10
BANKS,W            -17    0  -18      43.0  118      1         -4
        average     -9   14  -23      46.4   95     12   15    17
```

Because it's such a hard question to answer, let's talk about the group.

They cost $14 each so a lot was expected of them. The only one picked up in the crapshoot — gingerly, at that (just BW) — was Willie Banks. On the other hand, the market pays $3 less for these pitchers than they earned last year; greater caution is being exercised than for the top ten profits.

In the three-way battle, I bounce up off the canvas and come back ducking. I don't get Hill or Jackson or Freeman or Drabek or Rijo or Mulholland or Benes or Jacome. I do get my share of Trachsel, a strange throat disease, and I wasn't quite careful enough about where I stepped to avoid Banks. Hunt gets Hill, Jackson, Drabek, Rijo, Mulholland and his half of Trachsel (but, having bought so many bargains, he has plenty of immunities). You get Freeman, Benes and Jacome.

There are many other remedies to these pitchers, of course, besides crippling injury or banishment to the American League. Owners probably stuck with Rijo until he went on the DL and stayed with Benes as well as Hill to the end, but surely they didn't absorb ($9) worth of stats per pitcher. It was probably around ($6). Teams that bought even one of these pitchers finished with an average of 46.4 points. About halfway between ninth and tenth (95/120 x 12).

DARREN DREIFORT   Age 25   Bid: R2

Year	Team	G	GS	IP	H	HR	BB	SO	W	L	ERA	Ratio	Sv	$
1994	LA	27	0	29	45	0	15	22	0	5	6.21	18.62	6	-6
1994	(AA)	8	8	35	36	0	13	32	3	1	2.80	12.60	0	x
1994	(AAA)	1	1	6	8	1	3	3	1	0	5.68	15.63	0	x

Did not pitch at all last year.

Peter Golenbock and I made him one of our reserve picks in the Baseball Weekly league. Since the reserve draft only went four deep, it was an incredible blunder.

We might go back to the pitchers in the previous comment for a second.

```
                      — leagues —
   NL pitchers      BW   HSS  IOC  SCN f
   HILL,K           24    21   26   26 f
   JACKSON,D        15    12    7   10
   FREEMAN,M        10    11    9    8
   DRABEK,D         23    24   26   20 f
   RIJO,J           26    25   27   28
   TRACHSEL,S       12    11   13   10 f
   MULHOLLAND,T     11     5    4    9
   BENES,Andy       19    19   20   20
   JACOME,J          6     4    6    3
   BANKS,W           1
        average     15    15   15   15
```

These are the bombs. The only two in the whole group that you could tolerate on your team were Rijo and Benes. Even Drabek dragged you down. (Less than a penny's worth of damage, but every fraction of a penny counts.) Let's catalog the horrors, at least in Baseball Weekly.

Michael Laub, who publishes the National League Rotisserie Analyst, a biweekly newsletter, bought Ken Hill, and he finished — wait a minute: might as well get this all over with. He also bought Drabek and Mulholland, and he finished last by 17 points. (He finished second in 1994.)

Only one other person came out of the auction carrying two bombs. Al Chaby, co-author of the Fantasy Baseball Scouting Report, bought Danny Jackson and Trachsel, and he finished 17 points ahead of Laub. (First division in 1994.)

Steve Mann, author of The Mann Fantasy Baseball Guide, bought the third biggest single bomb, Marvin Freeman, and he finished with 50 points, good for sixth. (This space is blank. The one vow I made for this year was to be a lot nicer.)

So that takes care of six bombs.

The next biggest of the remaining bombs is Jose Rijo. Ron Shandler, the Baseball Forecaster, bought Rijo and came within a heartbeat of trading him to me for Saberhagen, before Rijo went down. Ron finished half a point behind Mann. (Third in 1994.)

The next biggest unaccounted-for bomb, Andy Benes, went to Dottie Enrico and Susan Asmore, co-founders the first all-female Rotisserie league in the country; this new entry in the league finished ninth, two points behind Shandler.

The second smallest bomb, Jacome, exploded briefly in John Snider's luggage. John, who works in the investing field, walked away from it (Jacome, I mean) to finish fourth with 57 points.

And the smallest bomb, Banks, I'm sorry to say, was not bought in the Baseball Weekly league after all.

I goofed. Lots of leagues *did* buy Willie Banks. (Loo $1, WGN $3, BIN $3, NEWP $1, MSR $1...) but lots of leagues took a pass, and it seems my league was one of them. Sorry about that. One does get groggy late at night. One looks back constantly, but one moves constantly forward.

JOEY EISCHEN   Age 26   Bid: R2

Year	Team	G	GS	IP	H	HR	BB	SO	W	L	ERA	Ratio	Sv	$
1994	MTL	1	0	1	4	0	0	1	0	0	54.01	54.01	0	-3
1995	LA	17	0	20	19	1	11	15	0	0	3.10	13.28	0	0

Eischen was pitching well at Ottawa when the Expos traded him to the Dodgers, and he proceeded to pitch impeccably at Albuquerque (16 IP, 8 hits, 3 BB, 14 SO, no runs), which is hard to do. So he's still a prospect.

Nope. Can't let it go.

Appendix A really is set in stone right now, and space is always a concern, but if Willie Banks really doesn't belong in the top 10 losses chart, it can't go unfixed.

```
The true top 10 losses, NL pitchers
                earned  avg            Heath Data    - touts -
NL pitchers      1995   sal   +/-       Pts    Rk     AP    JH
HILL,K             -6    24   -30       51.9   60     17    27
JACKSON,D         -17    11   -28       44.5  113      9    16
FREEMAN,M         -16    10   -26       42.4  119      6     6
DRABEK,D            0    24   -24       49.3   84     23    28
RIJO,J              3    26   -23       54.6   39     24    29
TRACHSEL,S        -11    12   -23       47.6   95     15
MULHOLLAND,T      -16     7   -22       37.2  122      1    10
BENES,Andy          1    19   -18       48.5   90     17    18
JACOME,J          -13     5   -18       44.6  112      2
SWIFT,B            -3    15   -18       43.6  116     10    10
      average      -8    15   -23       46.4   95     12    14
```

Well, I got lucky.

Scott Newman didn't. The publisher of the Sandlot Shrink bought Billy Swift in the Baseball Weekly league, and he finished fifth with 55 points. (Not bad at all; he obviously spent the rest of his money well.)

But where I got lucky was in Swift's apparent impact in 120 Heath leagues. He's not at all like Willie Banks, but it happens that Swift's teams finished with almost the same number of points and, out of 120 pitchers, Swift only ranks two places higher. So nothing has changed for the group.

It's how the groups finish that's important.

JOHN ERICKS   Age 28   Bid: $1

Year	Team	G	GS	IP	H	HR	BB	SO	W	L	ERA	Ratio	Sv	$
1995	(AAA)	5	5	29	20	2	13	25	2	1	2.48	10.24	0	x
1995	PIT	19	18	106	108	7	50	80	3	9	4.58	13.42	0	-5

John Ericks spread his losses among three different teams in BW last year, including Patton/Golenbock's.

JEFF FASSERO   Age 33   Bid: $4

Year	Team	G	GS	IP	H	HR	BB	SO	W	L	ERA	Ratio	Sv	$
1991	MTL	51	0	55	39	1	17	42	2	5	2.44	9.11	8	13
1992	MTL	70	0	86	81	1	34	63	8	7	2.84	12.08	1	8
1993	MTL	56	15	150	119	7	54	140	12	5	2.29	10.40	1	27
1994	MTL	21	21	139	119	13	40	119	8	6	2.99	10.32	0	26
1995	MTL	30	30	189	207	15	74	164	13	14	4.33	13.38	0	3

Maybe will bounce back. Maybe will get worse.

One thing that was deceptive about how the bidding went for the ten biggest bombs was the $15 average for everyone. Did you notice that? All four leagues, even the freeze list league, ended up taking the same beating.

```
       The true top 10 losses, NL pitchers
                    — leagues —
       NL pitchers    BW   HSS  IOC  SCN f
       HILL,K         24   21   26   26  f
       JACKSON,D      15   12    7   10
       FREEMAN,M      10   11    9    8
       DRABEK,D       23   24   26   20  f
       RIJO,J         26   25   27   28
       TRACHSEL,S     12   11   13   10  f
       MULHOLLAND,T   11    5    4    9
       BENES,Andy     19   19   20   20
       JACOME,J        6    4    6    3
       SWIFT,B        14   14   17   10
           average    16   15   16   14
```

With Swift in and Banks out, there isn't the same conformity.

In the crapshoot, the differences of opinion may be huge, but they aren't expressed in the salaries (by definition). But perhaps what should be emphasized is not that leagues have different opinions about the more expensive pitchers; despite the differences, isn't there an amazing amount of agreement?

Look at Marvin Freeman. How did four leagues make four such similar predictions?

Was there a $20 salary cap on Andy Benes?

The answers are (1) leagues aren't making predictions and (2) yes.

SID FERNANDEZ   Age 33   Bid: $8

Year	Team	G	GS	IP	H	HR	BB	SO	W	L	ERA	Ratio	Sv	$
1991	NYM	8	8	44	36	4	9	31	1	3	2.86	9.20	0	**5**
1992	NYM	32	32	215	162	12	67	193	14	11	2.73	9.60	0	**26**
1993	NYM	18	18	120	82	17	36	81	5	6	2.93	8.87	0	**19**
1994	BAL	19	19	115	109	27	46	95	6	6	5.15	12.10	0	**7**
1995	BAL	8	7	28	36	9	17	31	0	4	7.39	17.04	0	**-8**
1995	PHI	11	11	65	48	11	21	79	6	1	3.34	9.60	0	**13**

One reason there was even a salary cap on Jose Rio is that Sid Fernandez was coming along. Why pay for it if you can get it free?

rk	NL pitchers	earned 1995	avg sal	rk	NL pitchers	earned 1995	avg sal
1	LESKANIC,C	20		11	WELLS,Davi	9	
2	ISRINGHAUSEN	16		12	PETKOVSEK	9	
3	DELUCIA,R	13		13	WILLIAMS,Mik	9	
4	HAMMOND,C	13		14	MATHEWS,TJ	9	
5	FERNANDZ,S	13		15	HENNEMAN,M	8	
6	MATHEWS,T	12		16	PENA,Aleja	8	
7	MORGAN,M	12		17	HABYAN,J	7	
8	FOSSAS,T	11		18	BIRKBECK	7	
9	BURBA,D	10		19	MINOR,B	7	
10	RITZ,K	9		20	MLICKI,Da	7	

These are the top 20 freebies last year. All told, 65 pitchers in the National League cost not one cent (at the auction) and earned $1 or more during the season. That's a lot of free loot.

For comparison, the hitter freebies:

rk	NL hitters	earned 1995	avg sal	rk	NL hitters	earned 1995	avg sal
1	CANGELOSI,J	14		11	TAVAREZ,JE	6	
2	MAY,D	13		12	REED,Jo	6	
3	LIVINGSTONE,	12		13	HANEY,T	6	
4	WHITEN,M	12		14	CIANFROCCO,	6	
5	WALTON,J	11		15	GALLAGHER,D	5	
6	FONVILLE,C	10		16	BOGAR,T	4	
7	SCARSONE,S	9		17	MARSH,T	4	
8	JONES,Chr	9		18	HUBBARD,T	4	
9	LONGMIRE,T	8		19	GREGG,T	4	
10	SIMMS,M	7		20	BENITEZ,Y	4	

Darnell Coles is hitter number 54, the last one to earn more than half a dollar. Nice loot, but nothing like the pitchers.

John Hunt is well aware of this. That's why you didn't see him owning any of the bombs. While he's telling *you* to spend your money, he's sitting on the sidelines, laughing. The most expensive pitcher he bought in the BW auction cost $9 (P.A. Martinez — ha-ha!) He spent a grand total of $49 on pitchers. Only one of them was minimum wage, and he was his best starter (Pat Rapp). He also made two great $8 buys (Wohlers and Hampton).

The junk was discarded quickly — replaced, alas, by more junk. There were 31 different pitchers supplying his stats by the end of the year, only one continuously (Wohlers) and five discontinuously (that is, came back either from the DL or the scrap heap for encores: Hampton, Parris, Rapp, Rueter and White.) Three of the top 20 freebies listed above graced Hunt's roster briefly (Fossas, Habyan and Petkovsek), but he didn't have the patience for the drip from Fossas (who would?) and happened to get Petkovsek in one of his off-weeks. John missed all the biggies. I'd love to know what he bid on Leskanic, Isringhausen, Wells and Henneman — to pass on El Sid would have been more than understandable — but John keeps us in the dark about the blind bids, the losing ones, even after he's unsealed them.

So, while Hunt did avoid each of the 10 biggest bombs, he got blasted. And finished tenth. (First in 1994, when he had the looter's touch.)

The other teams who escaped the bombs spent some money. Stu Baron of Baron's On Deck paid $90 for his pitchers and finished third. Jim Dressel and Rick Wilson of the Fantasy Baseball Journal spent $92 and finished in a tie for seventh. Mike Vogel, the winner, spent $88 for his pitchers.

Patton/Golenbock spent $157. We finished second. We finished exactly with the point total that we expected (74), but to spend an average of $17 per pitcher and not get one of the bombs was a matter of pure luck.

BRYCE FLORIE Age 26   Bid: $2

Year	Team	G	GS	IP	H	HR	BB	SO	W	L	ERA	Ratio	Sv	$
1994	SD	9	0	9	8	0	3	8	0	0	.96	10.61	0	3
1995	SD	47	0	69	49	8	38	68	2	2	3.01	11.40	1	8

He's one of the gems in Appendix A with an average salary of 33 cents, but lest we get completely carried away, here's the entire list:

```
                        earned avg
       rk  NL pitchers   1995  sal   +/-  |   AP    JH
        1  HENRY,Do        14    0    14  |
        2  PLESAC,Dan       8    0     7  |   R3     8
        3  FLORIE,B         8    0     7  |   R3
        4  DIPOTO,J         6    0     6  |    5    10
        5  BORLAND,T        1    0     1  |    7     4
        6  SHAW,J           1    0     1  |    2     5
        7  WILLIAMS,To      1    0     0  |
        8  BAILEY,C         0    0    -1  |    1
        9  DYER,M          -1    0    -1  |   R3
       10  WOODALL,B       -2    0    -3  |   R2
       11  MADDU|,M        -3    0    -3  |   R2
       12  WENDELL,T       -4    0    -4  |   R3
       13  NIED,D          -7    0    -7  |    2
       14  ACEVEDO,J       -9    0    -9  |   R1
       15  GREEN,Ty       -10    0   -11  |          9
       16  WILLIAMS,Br    -10    0   -11  |   R3
       17  OLIVARES,O     -12    0   -12  |   R1
          average       -1.19 0.33 -1.52  | 1.00  2.12
```

Decimals are definitely in order.

Hunt was a big DiPoto fan, and I give him credit for the Tyler Green call. At his zenith I'm sure Tyler had earned $9. Plesac, on the other hand, I don't understand.

I was also a DiPoto fan, and I went ape over Toby Borland. I really thought he had a chance of being Slocumb.

The reason you don't see the Heath trackings is that Heath only tracks pitchers who appear on the draft rosters of at least ten of his leagues.

Anyway, Bryce Flories was tough. The thing I like best about him? You guessed it. Despite the gophers, an extreme, I mean extreme, groundball pitcher: G/F 3.29, 3.39 for both seasons.

TONY FOSSAS   Age 38   Bid: R3

Year	Team	G	GS	IP	H	HR	BB	SO	W	L	ERA	Ratio	Sv	$
1991	BOS	64	0	57	49	3	28	29	3	2	3.47	12.16	1	4
1992	BOS	60	0	30	31	1	14	19	1	2	2.43	13.65	2	3
1993	BOS	71	0	40	38	4	15	39	1	1	5.18	11.93	0	-1
1994	BOS	44	0	34	35	6	15	31	2	0	4.76	13.24	1	2
1995	STL	58	0	37	28	1	10	40	3	0	1.47	9.33	0	11

If you did have the patience last year, he helped your team in the qualitative categories more than Mike Morgan did. It's hard to believe, but that's why Appendix B is still hogging space in this book.

   That said, who wants him? Game's supposed to be fun.

KEVIN FOSTER   Age 27   Bid: $7

Year	Team	G	GS	IP	H	HR	BB	SO	W	L	ERA	Ratio	Sv	$
1993	PHI	2	1	7	13	3	7	6	0	1	14.85	27.00	0	-7
1994	CHC	13	13	81	70	7	35	75	3	4	2.89	11.67	0	11
1995	CHC	30	28	168	149	32	65	146	12	11	4.51	11.49	0	10

Outstanding athlete. Runs like the wind. Can hit a bit (.250, one home run). Throws smoke. But he must learn fear. A 2/1 BB/HR rate gets good hitters very excited.

JOHN FRANCO   Age 34   Bid: $25

Year	Team	G	GS	IP	H	HR	BB	SO	W	L	ERA	Ratio	Sv	$
1991	NYM	52	0	55	61	2	18	45	5	9	2.93	12.85	30	23
1992	NYM	31	0	33	24	1	11	20	6	2	1.64	9.55	15	21
1993	NYM	35	0	36	46	6	19	29	4	3	5.20	16.10	10	3
1994	NYM	47	0	50	47	2	19	42	1	4	2.70	11.88	30	31
1995	NYM	48	0	52	48	4	17	41	5	3	2.44	11.32	29	32

Fine year. Bet carefully on another.

MARVIN FREEMAN   Age 33   Bid: R3

Year	Team	G	GS	IP	H	HR	BB	SO	W	L	ERA	Ratio	Sv	$
1991	ATL	34	0	48	37	2	13	34	1	0	3.00	9.38	1	5
1992	ATL	58	0	64	61	7	29	41	7	5	3.22	12.59	3	6

Year	Team	G	GS	IP	H	HR	BB	SO	W	L	ERA	Ratio	Sv	$
1993	ATL	21	0	24	24	1	10	25	2	0	6.08	12.93	0	-2
1994	COL	19	18	113	113	10	23	67	10	2	2.80	10.86	0	25
1995	COL	22	18	95	122	15	41	61	3	7	5.89	15.50	0	-16

The R3 population is so huge that it really needs a secondary sort within it. For the purposes of the book, maybe Freeman should be an R2. But I just see negative number for him from now on, even if he's healthy, and even if he's not in Colorado.

SCOTT GENTILE   Age 25   Bid: R2

Year	Team	G	GS	IP	H	HR	BB	SO	W	L	ERA	Ratio	Sv	$
1993	(A)	25	25	138	132	8	54	108	8	9	4.03	12.13	0	x
1994	(AA)	6	2	10	16	1	25	14	0	1	17.42	36.90	0	x
1994	(A)	53	1	65	44	0	19	90	5	2	1.93	8.72	26	x
1995	(AA)	37	0	50	36	3	15	48	2	2	3.44	9.18	11	x

He's the Expos' prospect who finished 1994 with a 40-game scoreless streak. Looks like he did more than well enough at Harrisburg last year to start out this year at Ottawa.

TOM GLAVINE   Age 30   Bid: $24

Year	Team	G	GS	IP	H	HR	BB	SO	W	L	ERA	Ratio	Sv	$
1991	ATL	34	34	247	201	17	69	192	20	11	2.55	9.85	0	34
1992	ATL	33	33	225	197	6	70	129	20	8	2.76	10.68	0	25
1993	ATL	36	36	239	236	16	90	120	22	6	3.20	12.26	0	24
1994	ATL	25	25	165	173	10	70	140	13	9	3.97	13.23	0	10
1995	ATL	29	29	199	182	9	66	127	16	7	3.08	11.23	0	28

The pricing system every now and then really does what it's supposed to. With the hitting explosion in 1993, we see that Glavine pretty much repeated 1992. Then in 1994, despite winning 13 games in two-thirds of a season, he struggled. Last year was one of his very best.

Some details from the Stats Inc. records bureau: Glavine had the third lowest SLG Allowed (behind Maddux and Nomo) and the second lowest HR per IP (behind Maddux). He tied Burkett for most GDP per 9 IP. With runners on, he allowed batters to hit .234, fifth lowest in the league (minimum 200 BFP). Close & Late, batters hit .235. After 106+ pitches, he was able to fan only 7 of 49, walked 6, and allowed 8 hits (a .186 batting average). In September he got a little tired (4.11 ERA) and then found his second wind when Stats Inc. stopped counting.

DWIGHT GOODEN

Age 31

Bid: R3

Year	Team	G	GS	IP	H	HR	BB	SO	W	L	ERA	Ratio	Sv	$
1991	NYM	27	27	190	185	12	56	150	13	7	3.60	11.42	0	10
1992	NYM	31	31	206	197	11	70	145	10	13	3.67	11.67	0	4
1993	NYM	29	29	209	188	16	61	149	12	15	3.45	10.74	0	20
1994	NYM	7	7	41	46	9	15	40	3	4	6.31	13.28	0	-5

Too late to get baseball well.

MIKE GRACE

Age 26

Bid: $2

Year	Team	G	GS	IP	H	HR	BB	SO	W	L	ERA	Ratio	Sv	$
1994	(A)	15	15	80	84	6	20	45	5	5	4.82	11.70	0	x
1995	(AA)	24	24	147	137	13	35	118	13	6	3.54	10.53	0	x
1995	(AAA)	2	2	17	17	0	2	13	2	0	1.59	10.06	0	x
1995	PHI	2	2	11	10	0	4	7	1	1	3.18	11.12	0	2

His numbers look terrific. Haven't seen him pitch.

TYLER GREEN

Age 26

Bid: R3

Year	Team	G	GS	IP	H	HR	BB	SO	W	L	ERA	Ratio	Sv	$
1993	PHI	3	2	7	16	1	5	7	0	0	7.36	25.77	0	-4
1995	PHI	26	25	141	157	15	66	85	8	9	5.31	14.27	0	-10

If he's in the rotation, he's an R1 among R3's in the reserve draft.
By the way, there *is* a secondary sort in the software program (details in the PS).

TOMMY GREENE

Age 29

Bid: R3

Year	Team	G	GS	IP	H	HR	BB	SO	W	L	ERA	Ratio	Sv	$
1991	PHI	36	27	208	177	19	66	154	13	7	3.38	10.53	0	16
1992	PHI	13	12	64	75	5	34	39	3	3	5.32	15.25	0	-10
1993	PHI	31	30	200	175	12	62	167	16	4	3.42	10.67	0	24

Year	Team	G	GS	IP	H	HR	BB	SO	W	L	ERA	Ratio	Sv	$
1994	PHI	7	7	36	37	5	22	28	2	0	4.54	14.89	0	-3
1995	PHI	11	6	34	45	6	20	24	0	5	8.29	17.38	0	-14

An R2 among R3's?

Nope. I don't think so. R3 all the way at this point.

JOEY HAMILTON Age 25 Bid: $18

Year	Team	G	GS	IP	H	HR	BB	SO	W	L	ERA	Ratio	Sv	$
1994	SD	16	16	109	98	7	29	61	9	6	2.98	10.52	0	24
1995	SD	31	30	204	189	17	56	123	6	9	3.08	10.79	0	21

Quite astonishingly, he's not listed among the leaders in Tough Losses. With a 3.61 Run Support and 19 Quality Starts, he sure got his share of tough No Decisions. There is definitely something called Pay Back.

CHRIS HAMMOND Age 30 Bid: $7

Year	Team	G	GS	IP	H	HR	BB	SO	W	L	ERA	Ratio	Sv	$
1991	CIN	20	19	100	92	4	48	50	7	7	4.06	12.64	0	0
1992	CIN	28	26	147	149	13	55	79	7	10	4.22	12.46	0	-4
1993	FLA	32	32	191	207	18	66	108	11	12	4.66	12.86	0	-2
1994	FLA	13	13	73	79	5	23	40	4	4	3.07	12.52	0	8
1995	FLA	25	24	161	157	17	47	126	9	6	3.80	11.40	0	13

Included in the software program is something called, simply enough, Rtg. It's a weighted ratio. The formula is (hits+.5*BB+1.5*HR)/IP. The idea is that walks aren't as bad as hits and home runs are the worst kinds of hits.

The rating seldom tells you anything surprising about pitchers that you know are good. Joey Hamilton gets an excellent rating (1.18) and he had a great ERA.

But what about Hammond, whose ERA went up last year while his ratio went down?

Without the rating, we can see that he did have a little problem with the long ball, but the rating says he really was pitching better, much better than the year before. He had 1.27 rating in 1995, 1.34 in 1994. If he had the "correct" ERA in 1994, it should have gotten better in 1995.

The average pitcher last year had 4.18 ERA and 1.35 rating. A little work on the calculator — 1.27/1.35 x 4.18 = 3.93 — shows what Hammond's "correct" ERA would have been, so, if anything, his actual ERA was a little bit lower than he might have deserved.

In which case, he was either very lucky in 1994 or very tough in the clutch.

And maybe he was left in too long last year. Here's something interesting: .226 BA against him on the first 75 pitches, .247 on pitches 76-90, .375 on pitches 91-105, and .436 on pitches 106+, when he faced an inexplicable 41 batters.

Good Lord! He gave up 6 home runs to those batters! Batters had a .949 slugging average after 106 pitches!

That will ruin your rating.

He had decent Run Support (5.70) and made 12 Quality Starts. With runners in scoring position, batters only hit .184 against him; *that* will help your ERA. Close & Late they hit .386. Which I guess we already knew. Not one base was stolen against him. Only 7 CS, so they knew better than to try.

This stuff is from the Stats Inc. blue book. In the back of the red book, under Special Pitching Leaders, sure enough, Hammond leads in SB% Allowed (I thought 7 attempts might not be enough to qualify.) And in BA Allowed ScPos, Hammond's .184 is second in the league. He's between Maddux and Nomo — pretty good company.

What *else* can I find? Anything?

His ERA by months is sort of the same as by pitch-count. April 1.74, June 2.51, July 2.92, August 7.77, September/October 5.19. Only 15 strikeouts in 33 innings in August; 31 in 35 innings the last month.

He made one start on three-days' rest (now why would they do that with the number of arm problems he's had?) and pitched superbly: 8 innings, one run, 2 hits, 3 BB, 6 SO, and one tough No Decision.

Look, I'm worried about Chris Hammond, too. I'm not saying I'm not. Give me Joey Hamilton any day.

But the trouble is, you're not going to.

MIKE HAMPTON Age 23   Bid: $12

Year	Team	G	GS	IP	H	HR	BB	SO	W	L	ERA	Ratio	Sv	$
1993	SEA	13	3	17	28	3	17	8	1	3	9.53	23.82	1	-9
1994	HOU	44	0	41	46	4	16	24	2	1	3.70	13.50	0	1
1995	HOU	24	24	151	141	13	49	115	9	8	3.35	11.35	0	16

Hampton's rating was 1.23 last year and going down (2.75 ERA in September/October). Might have to find more money for him in the update.

PETE HARNISCH Age 29   Bid: $5

Year	Team	G	GS	IP	H	HR	BB	SO	W	L	ERA	Ratio	Sv	$
1991	HOU	33	33	217	169	14	83	172	12	9	2.70	10.47	0	22
1992	HOU	34	34	207	182	18	64	164	9	10	3.70	10.71	0	7
1993	HOU	33	33	218	171	20	79	185	16	9	2.98	10.34	0	30
1994	HOU	17	17	95	100	13	39	62	8	5	5.40	13.17	0	-2
1995	NYM	18	18	110	111	13	24	82	2	8	3.68	11.05	0	7

This bid assumes good health. No matter how well he pitches in the spring, it's not going higher in the update.

TOM HENKE Age 38   Bid: $26

Year	Team	G	GS	IP	H	HR	BB	SO	W	L	ERA	Ratio	Sv	$
1991	TOR	49	0	50	33	4	11	53	0	2	2.32	7.87	32	29

Year	Team	G	GS	IP	H	HR	BB	SO	W	L	ERA	Ratio	Sv	$
1992	TOR	57	0	56	40	5	22	46	3	2	2.26	10.02	34	30
1993	TEX	66	0	74	55	7	27	79	5	5	2.91	9.93	40	38
1994	TEX	37	0	38	33	6	12	39	3	6	3.79	10.66	15	22
1995	STL	52	0	54	42	2	18	48	1	1	1.82	9.94	36	38

The Tom Henke of old.

Brian Harvey's scan was not something you wanted to see. He planned to start throwing again in November and is an R2.

MIKE HENNEMAN Age 34   Bid: $19

Year	Team	G	GS	IP	H	HR	BB	SO	W	L	ERA	Ratio	Sv	$
1991	DET	60	0	84	81	2	34	61	10	2	2.88	12.27	21	24
1992	DET	60	0	77	75	6	20	58	2	6	3.96	11.06	24	18
1993	DET	63	0	72	69	4	32	58	5	3	2.64	12.68	24	24
1994	DET	30	0	35	43	5	17	27	1	3	5.19	15.58	8	3
1995	DET	29	0	29	24	0	9	24	0	1	1.53	10.13	18	21
1995	HOU	21	0	21	21	1	4	19	0	1	3.00	10.71	8	8

Pitched himself closer to home and, you would think, out of retirement.

DOUG HENRY Age 32   Bid: $2

Year	Team	G	GS	IP	H	HR	BB	SO	W	L	ERA	Ratio	Sv	$
1991	MIL	32	0	36	16	1	14	28	2	1	1.00	7.50	15	20
1992	MIL	68	0	65	64	6	24	52	1	4	4.02	12.18	29	17
1993	MIL	54	0	54	67	7	25	38	4	4	5.56	15.33	17	-8
1994	MIL	25	0	31	32	7	23	20	2	3	4.60	15.80	0	-1
1995	NYM	51	0	67	48	7	25	62	3	6	2.96	9.81	4	14

In the update, he'll probably have half his salary given to Mike Hampton.

GIL HEREDIA Age 30   Bid: $1

Year	Team	G	GS	IP	H	HR	BB	SO	W	L	ERA	Ratio	Sv	$
1991	SF	7	4	33	27	4	7	13	0	2	3.82	9.27	0	1
1992	MTL	20	5	45	44	4	20	22	2	3	4.23	12.89	0	-2

Year	Team	G	GS	IP	H	HR	BB	SO	W	L	ERA	Ratio	Sv	$
1993	MTL	20	9	57	66	4	14	40	4	2	3.92	12.56	2	3
1994	MTL	39	3	75	85	7	13	62	6	3	3.46	11.71	0	11
1995	MTL	40	18	119	137	7	21	74	5	6	4.31	11.95	1	4

Indistinguishable from an R3.

DUSTIN HERMANSON   Age 23

Bid: R1

Year	Team	G	GS	IP	H	HR	BB	SO	W	L	ERA	Ratio	Sv	$
1994	(AA)	16	0	21	13	0	6	30	1	0	.43	8.14	8	x
1994	(AAA)	7	0	7	6	1	5	6	0	0	6.14	14.14	3	x
1995	(AAA)	31	0	36	35	5	29	42	0	1	3.50	16.00	11	x
1995	SD	26	0	32	35	8	22	19	3	1	6.82	16.20	0	-6

A big mistake if the Padres don't give him at least a month of Triple-A.

XAVIER HERNANDEZ   Age 30

Bid: R3

Year	Team	G	GS	IP	H	HR	BB	SO	W	L	ERA	Ratio	Sv	$
1991	HOU	32	6	63	66	6	32	55	2	7	4.71	14.00	3	-4
1992	HOU	77	0	111	81	5	42	96	9	1	2.11	9.97	7	23
1993	HOU	72	0	97	75	6	28	101	4	5	2.61	9.59	9	21
1994	NYY	31	0	40	48	7	21	37	4	4	5.85	15.53	6	3
1995	CIN	59	0	90	95	8	31	84	7	2	4.60	12.60	3	5

Indistinguishable from a $1 pitcher.

TREVOR HOFFMAN   Age 28

Bid: $27

Year	Team	G	GS	IP	H	HR	BB	SO	W	L	ERA	Ratio	Sv	$
1993	SD	67	0	90	80	10	39	79	4	6	3.90	11.90	5	6
1994	SD	47	0	56	39	4	20	68	4	4	2.57	9.48	20	32
1995	SD	55	0	53	48	10	14	52	7	4	3.88	10.46	31	33

Home runs up, strikeouts down; arm may have been hurting, although, like any good closer, he would never admit it.

DARREN HOLMES   Age 30   Bid: $7

Year	Team	G	GS	IP	H	HR	BB	SO	W	L	ERA	Ratio	Sv	$
1991	MIL	40	0	76	90	6	27	59	1	4	4.72	13.80	3	-4
1992	MIL	41	0	42	35	1	11	31	4	4	2.55	9.78	6	12
1993	COL	62	0	67	56	6	20	60	3	3	4.05	10.26	25	20
1994	COL	29	0	28	35	5	24	33	0	3	6.35	18.74	3	-9
1995	COL	68	0	67	59	3	28	61	6	1	3.24	11.75	14	20

Home ERA of 2.95! Although he seems much happier when he's not the closer, Leskanic could pull
a Darren Holmes.

JOHN HUDEK   Age 29   Bid: R1

Year	Team	G	GS	IP	H	HR	BB	SO	W	L	ERA	Ratio	Sv	$
1994	HOU	42	0	39	24	5	18	39	0	2	2.97	9.61	16	20
1995	HOU	19	0	20	19	3	5	29	2	2	5.40	10.80	7	6

It's not enough to break down, he had to get an ERA like that in the process?

You glance at the ratio, glance at the home runs, and you don't need the rating (1.30) to know
that fortune treated him most unkindly.

JASON ISRINGHAUSEN   Age 23   Bid: $15

Year	Team	G	GS	IP	H	HR	BB	SO	W	L	ERA	Ratio	Sv	$
1994	(A)	14	14	101	76	2	27	59	6	4	2.23	9.18	0	x
1994	(AA)	14	14	92	78	6	23	69	5	4	3.02	9.88	0	x
1995	(AAA)	12	12	87	64	2	24	75	9	1	1.55	9.10	0	x
1995	(AA)	6	6	41	26	1	12	59	2	1	2.85	8.34	0	x
1995	NYM	14	14	93	88	6	31	55	9	2	2.81	11.52	0	16

The one caution is as simple as baseball isn't: it's been too simple so far. The curve is
mind-blowing. The fastball ain't for sissies.

DANNY JACKSON   Age 34   Bid: $2

Year	Team	G	GS	IP	H	HR	BB	SO	W	L	ERA	Ratio	Sv	$
1991	CHC	17	14	71	89	8	48	31	1	5	6.75	17.45	0	-21
1992	PIT	34	34	201	211	6	77	97	8	13	3.84	12.87	0	-5
1993	PHI	32	32	210	214	12	80	120	12	11	3.77	12.58	0	8

Year	Team	G	GS	IP	H	HR	BB	SO	W	L	ERA	Ratio	Sv	$
1994	PHI	25	25	179	183	13	46	129	14	6	3.26	11.49	0	**28**
1995	STL	19	19	101	120	10	48	52	2	12	5.90	15.02	0	**-17**

Slightly stronger post All-Star (4.54 ERA). Pitched less, too (38 IP). You can be forgiven if you wait until the reserve round.

MIKE JACKSON   Age 31   Bid: $2

Year	Team	G	GS	IP	H	HR	BB	SO	W	L	ERA	Ratio	Sv	$
1991	SEA	72	0	89	64	5	34	74	7	7	3.25	9.95	14	**22**
1992	SF	67	0	82	76	7	33	80	6	6	3.73	11.96	2	**4**
1993	SF	81	0	77	58	7	24	70	6	6	3.03	9.54	1	**14**
1994	SF	36	0	42	23	4	11	51	3	2	1.49	7.23	4	**22**
1995	CIN	40	0	49	38	5	19	41	6	1	2.39	10.47	2	**14**

Life-expectancy of his arm is perhaps one more year, but that's nothing new for Mike.

BOBBY JONES   Age 26   Bid: $10

Year	Team	G	GS	IP	H	HR	BB	SO	W	L	ERA	Ratio	Sv	$
1993	NYM	9	9	62	61	6	22	35	2	4	3.65	12.11	0	**2**
1994	NYM	24	24	160	157	10	56	80	12	7	3.15	11.98	0	**23**
1995	NYM	30	30	196	209	20	53	127	10	10	4.19	12.05	0	**8**

He's *not* going to be mediocre, the way he was in the second half (5.48 ERA). He either fixes whatever it was and wins 20 games or goes completely south.

TODD JONES   Age 28   Bid: $9

Year	Team	G	GS	IP	H	HR	BB	SO	W	L	ERA	Ratio	Sv	$
1993	HOU	27	0	37	28	4	15	25	1	2	3.13	10.37	2	**5**
1994	HOU	48	0	73	52	3	26	63	5	2	2.72	9.66	5	**23**
1995	HOU	68	0	100	89	8	52	96	6	5	3.07	12.73	15	**20**

Misused in the first half, when he had a 1.83 ERA and only 6 saves, he was overused in the second, when he had 4.53 ERA in 35 games. Had 8 BB and 27 SO in July, 12 BB and 14 SO in August. He also might be a place to steal some money from to bid more for Hampton.

DARRYL KILE Age 27

Bid: $2

Year	Team	G	GS	IP	H	HR	BB	SO	W	L	ERA	Ratio	Sv	$
1991	HOU	37	22	154	144	16	84	100	7	11	3.69	13.35	0	-3
1992	HOU	22	22	125	124	8	63	90	5	10	3.95	13.43	0	-6
1993	HOU	32	26	172	152	12	69	141	15	8	3.51	11.59	0	17
1994	HOU	24	24	148	153	13	82	105	9	6	4.57	14.32	0	-5
1995	HOU	25	21	127	114	5	73	113	4	12	4.96	13.25	0	-7

I picture negative innings for the rest of his career, which he'll keep extending with his moments of brilliance.

MARC KROON Age 23

Bid: R2

Year	Team	G	GS	IP	H	HR	BB	SO	W	L	ERA	Ratio	Sv	$
1994	(A)	26	26	143	143	14	81	153	11	6	4.83	14.10	0	x
1995	(AA)	22	19	115	90	12	61	123	7	5	3.51	11.82	0	x
1995	SD	2	0	2	1	0	2	2	0	1	10.80	16.20	0	-1

Nice stats for the most part; now needs Triple-A in his resume.

MARK LEITER Age 33

Bid: $6

Year	Team	G	GS	IP	H	HR	BB	SO	W	L	ERA	Ratio	Sv	$
1991	DET	38	15	135	125	16	50	103	9	7	4.21	11.67	0	5
1992	DET	35	14	112	116	9	43	75	8	5	4.18	12.78	0	4
1993	DET	27	13	107	111	17	44	70	6	6	4.73	13.08	0	1
1994	CAL	40	7	95	99	13	35	71	4	7	4.72	12.65	2	7
1995	SF	30	29	196	185	19	55	129	10	12	3.82	11.04	0	17

What little trick did Mark Leiter learn? He was a solid plugger, really, in the American league, but it's not as if he had never been given a chance in a rotation before. He had 7 complete games last year, after 3 in his career, and one of his most amazing stats is that from the seventh inning on, batters hit only .142 against him.

Pitching in the Stick was not his secret; he had a slightly higher home ERA.

Batters hit .325 against him with runners in scoring position, but .185 Close & Late.

Sometimes it does no good to look too closely. You shut your eyes and bid, then go to the movies on the nights he pitches.

CURT LESKANIC   Age 28   Bid: $14

Year	Team	G	GS	IP	H	HR	BB	SO	W	L	ERA	Ratio	Sv	$
1993	COL	18	8	57	59	7	27	30	1	5	5.37	13.58	0	**-6**
1994	COL	8	3	22	27	2	10	17	1	1	5.64	14.91	0	**-4**
1995	COL	76	0	98	83	7	33	107	6	3	3.40	10.65	10	**20**

What would it cost to buy him, Holmes and Ruffin?

Would you want to do that for any team, much less the Rockies?

Probably not. Buy one of them — you know one of them is going to be a great price — and you'll think you have the right one for the rest of the draft.

JON LIEBER   Age 26   Bid: R2

Year	Team	G	GS	IP	H	HR	BB	SO	W	L	ERA	Ratio	Sv	$
1994	PIT	17	17	109	116	12	25	71	6	7	3.73	11.68	0	**11**
1995	PIT	21	12	73	103	7	14	45	4	7	6.32	14.49	0	**-10**

Arm problem? Continued to get tattooed at Calgary (122 hits, 7.01 ERA in 77 IP).

ESTEBAN LOAIZA   Age 24   Bid: $1

Year	Team	G	GS	IP	H	HR	BB	SO	W	L	ERA	Ratio	Sv	$
1994	(AA)	24	24	154	169	15	30	115	10	5	3.79	11.63	0	**x**
1995	PIT	32	31	173	205	21	55	85	8	9	5.16	13.55	0	**-9**

Guess what Esteban did last year? Threw fewer pitches per batter than Greg Maddux. Maddux is between Loaiza (3.28) and Mulholland (3.36).

It may not be a totally bizarre stat, though. It means they throw strikes and the batters get a piece of the ball. Loaiza's young and probably very brash; last year might have been a learning experience.

GREG MADDUX Age 30   Bid: $42

Year	Team	G	GS	IP	H	HR	BB	SO	W	L	ERA	Ratio	Sv	$
1991	CHC	37	37	263	232	18	66	198	15	11	3.35	10.20	0	**21**
1992	CHC	35	35	268	201	7	70	199	20	11	2.18	9.10	0	**42**
1993	ATL	36	36	267	228	14	52	197	20	10	2.36	9.44	0	**49**
1994	ATL	25	25	202	150	4	31	156	16	6	1.56	8.06	0	**72**
1995	ATL	28	28	210	147	8	23	181	19	2	1.63	7.30	0	**68**

Has now passed Koufax on the all-time greatest pitchers list, and people are even beginning to think he's kind of sexy.

There are other similarities. Maddux, we tend to forget, had a shaky first few years in the majors. In his September call-up in 1986, he gave up 44 hits in 31 innings, lost four out of six decisions, and had a 5.52 ERA. The following year, he gave up 181 hits and 74 walks in 156 inning, lost 14 out of 20 decisions, and had 5.61 ERA. Then he got good, and that's why, even though he's still played two fewer seasons than Koufax did, he's only 15 wins behind Koufax right now.

Well, it's true; you can't count on anything in baseball. It's possible he won't win 15 games in the next two years, and even if he does, he hasn't yet.

The reason he's better than Koufax, already, is that Koufax reigned supreme when pitchers reigned supreme. Greg Maddux has been getting better and better and better while pitching in general has been going to hell. Or the batters have been getting better and better and better.

It doesn't matter which. And it's that simple.

PEDRO A. MARTINEZ   Age 27   Bid: R3

Year	Team	G	GS	IP	H	HR	BB	SO	W	L	ERA	Ratio	Sv	$
1993	SD	32	0	37	23	4	13	32	3	1	2.43	8.76	0	9
1994	SD	48	1	68	52	4	49	52	3	2	2.90	13.30	3	8
1995	HOU	25	0	21	29	3	16	17	0	0	7.40	19.60	0	-9

This is John Hunt's Pedro Martinez.

PEDRO J. MARTINEZ   Age 24   Bid: $23

Year	Team	G	GS	IP	H	HR	BB	SO	W	L	ERA	Ratio	Sv	$
1992	LA	2	1	8	6	0	1	8	0	1	2.25	7.88	0	1
1993	LA	65	2	107	76	5	57	119	10	5	2.61	11.19	2	18
1994	MTL	24	23	145	115	11	45	142	11	5	3.42	9.95	1	29
1995	MTL	30	30	195	158	21	66	174	14	10	3.51	10.36	0	27

And this is the Pedro Martinez who, according to one of John's columns over the winter, is the only starting pitcher besides Maddux to earn $20 in each of the last two years.

Is that true?

Best 1994 starting pitchers

NL pitchers	$94	$95	avg sal	+/-	Heath Data Pts	Heath Data Rk	- touts - AP	- touts - JH
MADDUX,G	72	68	36	32	68.1	1	40	40
SABERHAGEN,B	46	7	23	-16	54.8	37	20	28
DRABEK,D	38	0	24	-24	49.3	84	23	28
HILL,K	31	-6	24	-30	51.9	60	17	27
MARTINEZ,PJ	29	27	19	8	58.9	9	21	26
JACKSON,D	28	-17	11	-28	44.5	113	9	16
FASSERO,J	26	3	20	-17	47.5	97	10	25
HAMILTON,J	24	21	15	7	59.5	6	8	25
ASHBY,A	23	25	11	14	56.0	30	15	17
JONES,B	23	8	12	-4	55.7	31	12	17
REYNOLDS,S	22	19	13	7	57.3	19	9	20
RIJO,J	21	3	26	-23	54.6	39	24	29
TRACHSEL,S	21	-11	12	-23	47.6	95	15	15
MERCKER,K	20	3	13	-10	51.8	65	11	20
average (14)	30	11	18	-7	54.1	49	17	24

Not in my book.

But it's almost true. The only pitchers I would add to the list are Hamilton and Ashby. (Reynolds misses by about 20 cents.)

John is not being careless, he's just not right.

According to my formulas. Jerry Heath's prices, which Hunt uses for retrospective values, have Ashby and Hamilton earning less than $20 in one year or the other, if not in both.

I think there's a fatal error in Jerry's seemingly foolproof method (he plugs players into a mid-place team in each of his leagues and sees how it affects the standings), but that's stuff for masochists. It's worth taking a look at this whole group of starting pitchers, each of whom was a $20 winner in 1994 (according to me) for another reason: they are still winners in 1995.

Yes, they dropped off badly, from $30 on average to $11. Yes, as cautious as the market is, it still pays $18 per pitcher and gets hosed $7 on each one. But the teams that bought these pitchers finished with 54.1 points. On average, they finished fifth (49/120 x 12).

How can that be? Don't profits mean anything?

Maybe what needs to be emphasized is that they were, in fact, in real life, pretty good pitchers. These are the average 1995 stats of all of the pitchers in the chart above:

IP	W	Sv	ERA	Ratio	$W	$S	$ERA	$Rto	$TOT
164	9	0	4.00	11.99	9	0	1	1	11.09

They would have been 10-game winners in a full season and they had, on the whole, good innings. The average pitcher is only worth $8.67, and the average starting pitcher, who can only contribute in three categories, has slightly negative innings. (The ERA of starters was 6 points higher than the ERA of relievers in the NL last year.) The average starting pitcher probably earns less than $8.

Or the fact that they are associated with winning teams could be a 14-pitcher anomaly. I'm not saying I ever seek or enjoy a $7 beating. You only grudgingly accept *any* kind of loss, even with inflation.

Look at Saberhagen, Drabek, Hill, Fassero, Jones, Rijo, Merker... 1995 compared to 1994... I mean, if those aren't typical pitchers...

John, one question: You expected us to pay $24 for these bums?

RAMON MARTINEZ   Age 28   Bid: $16

Year	Team	G	GS	IP	H	HR	BB	SO	W	L	ERA	Ratio	Sv	$
1991	LA	33	33	220	190	18	69	150	17	13	3.27	10.58	0	20

Year	Team	G	GS	IP	H	HR	BB	SO	W	L	ERA	Ratio	Sv	$
1992	LA	25	25	151	141	11	69	101	8	11	4.00	12.54	0	-2
1993	LA	32	32	212	202	15	104	127	10	12	3.44	13.01	0	7
1994	LA	24	24	170	160	18	56	119	12	7	3.97	11.44	0	18
1995	LA	30	30	206	176	19	81	138	17	7	3.66	11.21	0	24

Don't worry about John. He has 52 chances to get back at me. Let's look at real-life salaries for, I promise, the very last time.

What's happened is that USA Today has finally published its annual major league salary survey. Up until now, all I've seen is salaries in snippets. Now I can self-score myself for my Murray Chass predictions in last year's book. (He's a New York Times reporter who is obsessed with salaries; to tell you the truth, I could care less what professional athletes make, but I would like to see baseball survive.)

```
AP's predicted 1995 real life salaries vs. actual salaries
                              — 1995 —
  1995 free agents   1994 salary      predicted         actual      dif.
  Terry Mulholland    $3,350,000       $500,000      $1,250,000      60%
  Mark Grace          $4,400,000     $3,500,000      $4,375,000      20%
  Kevin Brown         $4,225,000     $4,000,000      $4,225,000       5%
  Tim Wallach         $3,412,000     $2,000,000      $2,002,200       0%
  Jack McDowell       $5,300,000     $5,400,000      $5,400,000       0%
  Jeff Blauser        $3,750,000     $3,500,000      $3,420,000      -2%
  Larry Walker        $4,025,000     $5,500,000      $5,019,382     -10%
  Paul Assenmacher    $2,583,334       $950,000        $787,000     -21%
  Steve Ontiversos      $120,000     $1,200,000        $965,000     -24%
  Tom Henke           $3,752,625     $3,000,000      $2,325,000     -29%
  Terry Pendleton     $3,200,000     $2,200,000      $1,600,000     -38%
  Brett Butler        $3,500,000     $3,500,000      $2,000,000     -75%
  Gregg Jefferies     $4,600,000     $5,400,000      $3,000,000     -80%
  Benito Santiago     $3,800,000     $2,100,000        $650,000    -223%
  Mike Gallego        $1,575,000     $1,000,000        $300,000    -233%
  Andy Van Slyke      $3,550,000     $2,200,000        $600,000    -267%
  Frank Viola         $4,333,334     $1,500,000        $190,000    -689%
         average      $3,498,605     $2,791,176      $2,241,681     -25%
           total     $59,476,293    $47,450,000     $38,108,582     -25%
```

There were more but I know how unpopular Murray Chass is.

The idea is not to show how smart I was, just how distressingly *dim* the owners have been all along. On the right is the difference between what I predicted and what in fact happened in the signing up of free agents last year. I was trying to show in broad strokes how much money the owners were going to save under the *existing system*, the very thing the players said they'd be thrilled to see continue, and the owners outfoxed me; they saved, just in this group here, half a million dollars more per player than I thought they would!

For these 17 players — free agents of every ilk and description — they saved $1.2 million per player, $21.4 million overall.

The players are ranked in the order of how much the owners outfoxed me: don't we see a light bulb going on? I don't know the dates that these contracts were signed, but I'm pretty sure the longer the players waited to sign, the more they were sorry they hadn't taken an earlier offer.

Now that the owners have figured out all sorts of ingenious ways to grant players their freedom, the official free-agent-to-be figure of a little over 150 is just the starting point. More than 300 major league players will be given a taste of Adam Smith's cruel broth, with more than 500 minor league free agents waiting thirstily at the door. Russ McGinnis, Mike Oquist, Greg Blosser,

Pork Chop Pough, Tuffy Rhodes, Jack Voigt, Eric Wedge, Henry Cotto, Pete Rose Jr., Keith Kessinger, Brad Pennington, Jim Tatum, Dave Staton, Patrick Lennon, Curtis Pride, Ben Rivera, Dale Sveum, Nelson Simmons, Jeff McNeeley, Nate Minchey, Gary Thurman, Brian Turang, Sam Horn, John Marzano, Mike Huff, Wally Whitehurst... You know every one of them.

Ramon Martinez, one of the very best of the 150, received $3,925,000 last year. He earned it. Had his second great year in a row (has averaged $20 of play money in that time). Won three more games than his little brother, had about the same ERA and doesn't pay all that much attention to ratio. He's won 91 games lifetime, Pedro only 35. He knows his little brother only earned $270,000 last year; there are no secrets in this family. And he knows his brother gets to go to arbitration this year. These two guys are hip, and he gets a lot of sass from Pedro about that.

TERRY MATHEWS   Age 31   Bid: $4

Year	Team	G	GS	IP	H	HR	BB	SO	W	L	ERA	Ratio	Sv	$
1994	FLA	24	2	43	45	4	9	21	2	1	3.35	11.30	0	6
1995	FLA	57	0	83	70	9	27	72	4	4	3.38	10.56	3	12

Who are these Mathews?

T.J. MATHEWS   Age 26   Bid: $3

Year	Team	G	GS	IP	H	HR	BB	SO	W	L	ERA	Ratio	Sv	$
1995	(AAA)	32	7	67	60	2	27	50	9	4	2.70	11.69	0	x
1995	STL	23	0	30	21	1	11	28	1	1	1.52	9.71	2	9

Are they brotthers?

CHUCK MCELROY   Age 28   Bid: R3

Year	Team	G	GS	IP	H	HR	BB	SO	W	L	ERA	Ratio	Sv	$
1991	CHC	71	0	101	73	7	57	92	6	2	1.95	11.55	3	14
1992	CHC	72	0	84	73	5	51	83	4	7	3.55	13.34	6	3
1993	CHC	49	0	47	51	4	25	31	2	2	4.56	14.45	0	-3
1994	CIN	52	0	58	52	3	15	38	1	2	2.34	10.46	5	15
1995	CIN	44	0	40	46	5	15	27	3	4	6.02	13.61	0	-4

Forget him. As I've said before.

GREG MCMICHAEL   Age 29   Bid: $6

Year	Team	G	GS	IP	H	HR	BB	SO	W	L	ERA	Ratio	Sv	$
1993	ATL	74	0	92	68	3	29	89	2	3	2.06	9.52	19	27
1994	ATL	51	0	59	66	1	19	47	4	6	3.84	13.04	21	21

Year	Team	G	GS	IP	H	HR	BB	SO	W	L	ERA	Ratio	Sv	$
1995	ATL	67	0	81	64	8	32	74	7	2	2.79	10.71	2	**17**

Good way to get with a juggernaut that's still rolling.

KENT MERCKER   Age 28   Bid: $6

Year	Team	G	GS	IP	H	HR	BB	SO	W	L	ERA	Ratio	Sv	$
1991	ATL	50	4	73	56	5	35	62	5	3	2.58	11.17	6	**12**
1992	ATL	53	0	68	51	4	35	49	3	2	3.42	11.33	6	**7**
1993	ATL	43	8	66	52	2	36	59	3	1	2.86	12.00	0	**6**
1994	ATL	20	17	112	90	16	45	111	9	4	3.45	10.82	0	**20**
1995	ATL	29	26	143	140	16	61	102	7	8	4.15	12.65	0	**3**

If he does become some other team's second or third starter, maybe that's how he'll pitch.

DAN MICELI   Age 25   Bid: $18

Year	Team	G	GS	IP	H	HR	BB	SO	W	L	ERA	Ratio	Sv	$
1993	PIT	9	0	5	6	0	3	4	0	0	5.06	15.19	0	**-1**
1994	PIT	28	0	27	28	5	11	27	2	1	5.93	12.84	2	**0**
1995	PIT	58	0	58	61	7	28	56	4	4	4.66	13.81	21	**14**

Fell apart in the last month. Probably just tired.

DOUG MILLION   Age 20   Bid: R4

Year	Team	G	GS	IP	H	HR	BB	SO	W	L	ERA	Ratio	Sv	$
1994	(R)	3	3	12	8	0	3	19	1	0	1.50	8.25	0	**x**
1994	(A)	10	10	58	50	4	21	75	5	3	2.34	11.02	0	**x**
1995	(A)	24	23	111	111	6	79	85	5	7	4.62	15.41	0	**x**

Eddie Epstein in *The Minor League Scouting Report Notebook*, a new book from Stats Inc.: "Million (great name for a baseball player) is very refined for a high school pitcher, which can be good or bad. Sometimes a high school pitcher has skills beyond his years because he has pitched a lot of innings, too many for his own good."

He's a Rockies' prospect, furthermore, so I was getting a little carried away anyway, making him an R5 in last year's book.

MIKE MIMBS   Age 27   Bid: $1

Year	Team	G	GS	IP	H	HR	BB	SO	W	L	ERA	Ratio	Sv	$
1994	(AA)	32	21	154	130	11	61	145	11	4	3.46	11.16	0	x
1995	PHI	35	19	137	127	10	75	93	9	7	4.15	13.30	1	3

Only Nomo and Maddux were tougher with runners on (minimum 200 BFP). The difference is that they were a lot tougher (.181 and .185 vs. .216 for Mimbs) and Mimbs had more BFP with runners on, in far fewer innings.

DAVE MLICKI   Age 28   Bid: $3

Year	Team	G	GS	IP	H	HR	BB	SO	W	L	ERA	Ratio	Sv	$
1992	CLE	4	4	22	23	3	16	16	0	2	4.98	16.20	0	-4
1993	CLE	3	3	13	11	2	6	7	0	0	3.38	11.48	0	1
1995	NYM	29	25	161	160	23	54	123	9	7	4.26	11.99	0	7

Has surprisingly good stuff. May have finally left arm problems behind.

RAMON MOREL   Age 21   Bid: R2

Year	Team	G	GS	IP	H	HR	BB	SO	W	L	ERA	Ratio	Sv	$
1994	(A)	28	27	169	157	8	24	152	10	7	2.83	9.64	0	x
1995	(A)	12	12	73	80	2	13	44	3	7	3.47	11.47	0	x
1995	(AA)	10	10	69	71	4	10	34	3	7	3.52	10.57	0	x
1995	PIT	5	0	6	6	0	2	3	0	1	2.84	11.37	0	1

I would not put this slender package in my own luggage — not activated — if perchance he flies north with the Pirates from Florida.

MIKE MORGAN   Age 36   Bid: $6

Year	Team	G	GS	IP	H	HR	BB	SO	W	L	ERA	Ratio	Sv	$
1991	LA	34	34	236	197	12	61	140	14	10	2.78	9.83	1	28
1992	CHC	34	34	240	203	14	79	123	16	8	2.55	10.58	0	25
1993	CHC	32	32	208	206	15	74	111	10	15	4.03	12.13	0	6
1994	CHC	15	15	81	111	12	35	57	2	10	6.69	16.29	0	-23
1995	STL	21	21	131	133	12	34	61	7	7	3.56	11.44	0	12

Nomo is number two in Behind in Count, with no sight of Maddux. (There's minimum BFP of 125, so that explains it.) It's clearly a bad idea to be behind in the count, because the batting averages run from Nomo (.262) to Bullinger (.285), who's tenth best in the league. Mike Morgan's .178 batting average against when Behind in the Count becomes rather impressive.

Don't be too surprised if you see Terry Mulholland profiled next in next year's book.

RANDY MYERS Age 30

Bid: $31

Year	Team	G	GS	IP	H	HR	BB	SO	W	L	ERA	Ratio	Sv	$
1991	CIN	58	12	132	116	8	80	108	6	13	3.55	13.36	6	2
1992	SD	66	0	80	84	7	34	66	3	6	4.29	13.33	38	24
1993	CHC	73	0	75	65	7	26	86	2	4	3.11	10.87	53	38
1994	CHC	38	0	40	40	3	16	32	1	5	3.79	12.50	21	19
1995	CHC	57	0	56	49	7	28	59	1	2	3.88	12.45	38	29

I'm thinking of actually projecting pitcher stats in *Patton $ On Disk* (details in the PS), and if I do, the other Still Nasty Boy will be the saves leader by a wide margin. Cubs are going to give Cincy all they can handle.

JAIME NAVARRO Age 29

Bid: $12

Year	Team	G	GS	IP	H	HR	BB	SO	W	L	ERA	Ratio	Sv	$
1991	MIL	34	34	234	237	18	73	114	15	12	3.92	11.92	0	13
1992	MIL	34	34	246	224	14	64	100	17	11	3.33	10.54	0	27
1993	MIL	35	34	214	254	21	73	114	11	12	5.33	13.73	0	-8
1994	MIL	29	10	90	115	10	35	65	4	9	6.62	15.06	0	-13
1995	CHC	29	29	200	194	19	56	128	14	6	3.28	11.23	0	25

Assuming Jaimie Navarro stays in shape.

DANNY NEAGLE Age 27

Bid: $11

Year	Team	G	GS	IP	H	HR	BB	SO	W	L	ERA	Ratio	Sv	$
1991	MIN	7	3	20	28	3	7	14	0	1	4.05	15.75	0	x
1992	PIT	55	6	86	81	9	43	77	4	6	4.48	12.93	2	-3
1993	PIT	50	7	81	82	10	37	73	3	5	5.31	13.17	1	-5
1994	PIT	24	24	137	135	18	49	122	9	10	5.12	12.09	0	2
1995	PIT	31	31	210	221	20	45	150	13	8	3.43	11.42	0	22

Price enforce to at least $10. Otherwise Hunt will get him.

ROBB NEN Age 26 Bid: $24

Year	Team	G	GS	IP	H	HR	BB	SO	W	L	ERA	Ratio	Sv	$
1993	TEX	9	3	23	28	1	26	12	1	1	6.35	21.44	0	-8
1993	FLA	15	1	33	35	5	20	27	1	0	7.02	14.85	0	-7
1994	FLA	44	0	58	46	6	17	60	5	5	2.95	9.78	15	27
1995	FLA	62	0	66	62	6	23	68	0	7	3.29	11.65	23	20

Don't know what Nen's problem was last year, but I'm pretty sure it's over.

DAVID NIED Age 27 Bid: R2

Year	Team	G	GS	IP	H	HR	BB	SO	W	L	ERA	Ratio	Sv	$
1992	ATL	6	2	23	10	0	5	19	3	0	1.17	5.87	0	8
1993	COL	16	16	87	99	8	42	46	5	9	5.17	14.59	0	-7
1994	COL	22	22	122	137	15	47	74	9	7	4.80	13.57	0	-1
1995	COL	2	0	4	11	2	3	3	0	0	20.77	29.08	0	-7

Looks like both he and Nigel Wilson have gone up in flames.

JAMES NIX Age 25 Bid: R2

Year	Team	G	GS	IP	H	HR	BB	SO	W	L	ERA	Ratio	Sv	$
1994	(A)	29	28	169	168	23	87	139	11	10	4.58	13.58	0	x
1995	(AA)	40	5	84	84	8	30	71	3	5	3.20	12.21	2	x

If this guy pans out, it's John Benson's tip. I had never heard of Nix until I made a point of getting my hands on Benson's October monthly to see if pricing was an issue anymore. Nix is mentioned as one of the players to watch in the AZL. "A product of Texas A&M," Benson writes, "Nix has been working out of the pen for Mesa. After 13 innings he was unscored upon and surrendered just six hits while striking out 14." By the time I checked him out, Nix was up to 18 IP, still no runs, 9 hits, 0 walks and 18 K. Hmmm... The two-year scan indicates the switch (back) to the pen was the right move for him.

HIDEO NOMO Age 27 Bid: $25

Year	Team	G	GS	IP	H	HR	BB	SO	W	L	ERA	Ratio	Sv	$
1995	(A)	1	1	5	6	0	1	6	0	1	3.38	12.60	0	x
1995	LA	28	28	191	124	14	78	236	13	6	2.54	9.50	0	39

He's the one-man reason that Maddux isn't *quite* as dominant — in crude Patton $ and in all the esoteric stuff in the back of the Stats Inc. books — as he was in 1994. If you take Nomo out of the league, without even replacing him with a replacement player like Craig McMurtry, the league

ERA goes up two points, the ratio three points and you have the same context as the year before.

Many of the esoteric categories have been mentioned already, but it's such a wonderful battle that it should be recapped. In overall batting average against, Nomo is first, Maddux second. With runners on, Nomo is first, Maddux is second. With none on, Nomo is first, Maddux is third (Schilling comes between them; in all cases the minimum BFP is 200). With two strikes, Nomo is first, Maddux is second. Ahead in the count, Nomo is first, Maddux is second. Behind in the count, Nomo is first, Maddux doesn't qualify. With runners in scoring position, Maddux is first and Nomo is third (behind Hammond). Close & Late, Nomo is first and Maddux is fourth (behind Neagle and Bottalico; the minimum BFP for this category is 40, and Bottalico, with 204 AB, faced twice as many batters Close & Late as anyone else in baseball last year — that's an *amazing* stat).

In HR per 9 IP, Maddux is first, Nomo is fifth (Glavine, Rapp and Smiley in between). Versus RHB, Nomo is first, Maddux is second (tied with Burba). Versus LHB, Maddux is first, Nomo is second. In OBP Allowed (darn close to ratio), Maddux is first, Nomo is second. In SLG Allowed (more relevant to ERA), Maddux is first, Nomo is second.

Nomo had significantly better run support (4.75 vs. 4.34) and undoubtedly equally worse defensive support (which does sneak into the ERA and ratio, for sure). Both pitchers were easy to run on (29 SB in 34 tries against Nomo, 26 in 32 against Maddux — something for you to work on, Greg.) Nomo led the league in strikeouts by a wide margin, but Maddux was third, and he nearly lapped the next best pitcher (Reynolds) in SO/BB. Nomo was a little more effective than Maddux after the sixth inning, but Maddux pitched many more innings in the same number of starts.

Nomo had the best ERA at home of anybody in baseball. Maddux had the best ERA on the road of anybody in baseball. Maddux had the best ERA in either league on grass, Nomo was second. Maddux had the best ERA in either league on turf — and finally, finally, Nomo can't take it anymore. He had a 4.55 ERA in five starts on turf.

Kind of surprising, since Nomo (G/F 0.85) is an extreme flyball pitcher, while Maddux (G/F 3.03) is as extreme the other way.

DONOVAN OSBORNE   Age 27   Bid: $3

Year	Team	G	GS	IP	H	HR	BB	SO	W	L	ERA	Ratio	Sv	$
1992	STL	34	29	179	193	14	38	104	11	9	3.77	11.61	0	5
1993	STL	26	26	156	153	18	47	83	10	7	3.76	11.56	0	11
1995	STL	19	19	113	112	17	34	82	4	6	3.81	11.59	0	6

Got better as the season went along.

ANTONIO OSUNA   Age 23   Bid: $4

Year	Team	G	GS	IP	H	HR	BB	SO	W	L	ERA	Ratio	Sv	$
1993	(A)	14	0	18	19	2	5	20	0	2	4.91	12.00	2	x
1994	(AA)	35	0	46	19	0	18	53	1	2	.98	7.24	19	x
1994	(AAA)	6	0	6	5	0	1	8	0	0	.00	9.00	4	x
1995	LA	39	0	45	39	5	20	46	2	4	4.43	11.89	0	1

One of those pitchers who will take a fair amount of money off the table if he's nominated early. I'd do it. Obviously throws hard, but his control could get worse.

LANCE PAINTER Age 28 Bid: R3

Year	Team	G	GS	IP	H	HR	BB	SO	W	L	ERA	Ratio	Sv	$
1993	COL	10	6	39	52	5	9	16	2	2	6.00	14.08	0	-5
1994	COL	15	14	74	91	9	26	41	4	6	6.11	14.29	0	-11
1995	COL	33	1	45	55	9	10	36	3	0	4.37	12.90	1	2

The pen could save him.

CHAN HO PARK Age 23 Bid: R1

Year	Team	G	GS	IP	H	HR	BB	SO	W	L	ERA	Ratio	Sv	$
1994	LA	2	0	4	5	1	5	6	0	0	11.25	22.50	0	-4
1994	(AA)	20	20	101	91	4	57	100	5	7	3.55	13.19	0	x
1995	(AAA)	23	22	110	93	10	76	101	6	7	4.91	13.83	0	x
1995	LA	2	1	4	2	1	2	7	0	0	4.50	9.00	0	0

Decent stats at Albuquerque, two strong games in September, plus the lure of the East.

STEVE PARRIS Age 28 Bid: R2

Year	Team	G	GS	IP	H	HR	BB	SO	W	L	ERA	Ratio	Sv	$
1994	(A)	17	17	57	58	7	21	48	3	3	3.63	12.47	0	x
1995	(AA)	14	14	90	61	2	16	86	9	1	2.51	7.70	0	x
1995	PIT	15	15	82	89	12	33	61	6	6	5.38	13.39	0	-3

Old enough to be an R3, and he has had some seasoning in Triple-A (in '92 and '93), but the stats at Double-A last year are simply too good to ignore.

ALEJANDRO PENA Age 37 Bid: $1

Year	Team	G	GS	IP	H	HR	BB	SO	W	L	ERA	Ratio	Sv	$
1991	ATL	59	0	82	74	6	22	62	8	1	2.40	10.49	15	23
1992	ATL	41	0	42	40	7	13	34	1	6	4.07	11.36	15	11
1994	PIT	22	0	29	22	4	10	27	3	2	5.02	10.05	7	10
1995	BOS	17	0	24	33	5	12	25	1	1	7.40	16.64	0	-6
1995	FL/ATL	27	0	31	22	3	7	39	2	0	2.61	8.42	0	8

Threw like there was no tomorrow.

CARLOS PEREZ　Age 25　Bid: $10

Year	Team	G	GS	IP	H	HR	BB	SO	W	L	ERA	Ratio	Sv	$
1994	(AA)	12	11	79	55	5	18	69	7	2	1.94	8.32	0	x
1994	(AAA)	17	17	119	130	8	41	82	7	5	3.33	12.93	0	x
1995	MTL	28	23	141	142	18	28	106	10	8	3.69	10.83	0	17

The Triple-A numbers in '94 sure don't suggest the kind of stuff he possessed. Kept on whiffing 'em in the second half, to their chagrin, even though his other numbers started to slide.

MIKE PEREZ　Age 31　Bid: R3

Year	Team	G	GS	IP	H	HR	BB	SO	W	L	ERA	Ratio	Sv	$
1991	STL	14	0	17	19	1	7	7	0	2	5.82	13.76	0	-3
1992	STL	77	0	93	70	4	32	46	9	3	1.84	9.87	0	17
1993	STL	65	0	73	65	4	20	58	7	2	2.48	10.53	7	18
1994	STL	36	0	31	52	5	10	20	2	3	8.71	18.00	12	-4
1995	CHC	68	0	71	72	8	27	49	2	6	3.66	12.49	2	4

Could be a typical middle reliever.

ROBERT PERSON　Age 26　Bid: $4

Year	Team	G	GS	IP	H	HR	BB	SO	W	L	ERA	Ratio	Sv	$
1994	(AA)	31	23	159	124	18	68	130	9	6	3.45	10.87	0	x
1995	(AA)	26	7	67	46	4	25	65	5	4	3.11	9.54	7	x
1995	(AAA)	5	4	32	30	2	13	33	2	1	4.50	12.09	0	x
1995	NYM	3	1	12	5	1	2	10	1	0	.75	5.25	0	6

Continued to overpower batters in the AZL; throws harder than any Met.

MARK PETKOVSEK　Age 30　Bid: $1

Year	Team	G	GS	IP	H	HR	BB	SO	W	L	ERA	Ratio	Sv	$
1993	PIT	26	0	32	43	7	9	14	3	0	6.96	14.47	0	-5
1995	STL	26	21	137	136	11	35	71	6	6	4.00	11.21	0	9

In 8 starts at Louisville last year: 54 IP, 38 H, 3 HR, 8 BB, 30 SO, 2.32 ERA, 4 wins. Rest of career is a blank.

RICKY PICKETT   Age 26   Bid: R2

Year	Team	G	GS	IP	H	HR	BB	SO	W	L	ERA	Ratio	Sv	$
1995	(AA)	40	0	47	22	3	44	69	4	5	3.28	12.64	9	x
1995	(AA)	14	0	21	9	1	9	23	2	0	1.71	7.71	3	x

He's been pulled from the back pages of the Stats Inc. green book, where his 12.24 K per 9 IP is easily the best rate in the high minors.

First he pitched at Chattanooga (Reds), then at Shreveport (Giants) last year, so he may have been par t of the Burba trade. In that control can be learned, could becomea big part. A smallish lefty (6'0", 185).

DAN PLESAC   Age 34   Bid: R3

Year	Team	G	GS	IP	H	HR	BB	SO	W	L	ERA	Ratio	Sv	$
1991	MIL	45	10	92	92	12	39	61	2	7	4.29	12.77	8	3
1992	MIL	44	4	79	64	5	35	54	5	4	2.96	11.28	1	9
1993	CHC	57	0	63	74	10	21	47	2	1	4.74	13.64	0	-4
1994	CHC	54	0	55	61	9	13	53	2	3	4.61	12.18	1	1
1995	PIT	58	0	60	53	3	27	57	4	4	3.58	11.93	3	8

Much safer end-game fill-in than Petkovsek; easier to say, too.

MARK PORTUGAL   Age 33   Bid: $6

Year	Team	G	GS	IP	H	HR	BB	SO	W	L	ERA	Ratio	Sv	$
1991	HOU	32	27	168	163	19	59	120	10	12	4.49	11.87	1	0
1992	HOU	18	16	101	76	7	41	62	6	3	2.66	10.39	0	10
1993	HOU	33	33	208	194	10	77	131	18	4	2.77	11.73	0	26
1994	SF	21	21	137	135	17	45	87	10	8	3.93	11.80	0	14
1995	SF/CIN	31	31	182	185	17	56	96	11	10	4.01	11.94	0	11

Was Mark Portugal for the Giants and Mark Portugal for Cincinnati.

JAY POWELL   Age 24   Bid: R1

Year	Team	G	GS	IP	H	HR	BB	SO	W	L	ERA	Ratio	Sv	$
1994	(A)	26	20	123	132	13	54	87	7	7	4.96	13.61	0	x
1995	(AA)	50	0	53	42	2	15	53	5	4	1.87	9.68	0	x
1995	FLA	9	0	8	7	0	6	4	0	0	1.08	14.04	0	1

The closer's job at Portland (AA) obviously agreed with him. This is not just another wily old minor leaguer racking up saves, although I'm not sure what he is.

BILL PULSIPHER
Age 22   Bid: $8

Year	Team	G	GS	IP	H	HR	BB	SO	W	L	ERA	Ratio	Sv	$
1993	(A)	6	6	43	34	1	12	29	2	3	2.08	9.55	0	x
1993	(A)	13	13	96	63	2	39	102	7	3	2.24	9.53	0	x
1994	(AA)	28	28	201	179	18	89	171	14	9	3.22	12.00	0	x
1995	(AAA)	13	13	92	84	3	33	63	6	4	3.14	11.45	0	x
1995	NYM	17	17	127	122	11	45	81	5	7	3.98	11.87	0	6

In his first pro season in 1992: 6-3, 2.84. So he's cocky for good reason. Adversity *will* make his acquaintance sometime soon.

PAT RAPP
Age 28   Bid: $8

Year	Team	G	GS	IP	H	HR	BB	SO	W	L	ERA	Ratio	Sv	$
1992	SF	3	2	10	8	0	6	3	0	2	7.20	12.60	0	-2
1993	FLA	16	16	94	101	7	39	57	4	6	4.02	13.40	0	-1
1994	FLA	24	23	133	132	13	69	75	7	8	3.85	13.57	0	3
1995	FLA	28	28	167	158	10	76	102	14	7	3.44	12.59	0	16

The only knock is the walks.

STEVE REED
Age 30   Bid: $4

Year	Team	G	GS	IP	H	HR	BB	SO	W	L	ERA	Ratio	Sv	$
1992	SF	18	0	16	13	2	3	11	1	0	2.30	9.19	0	3
1993	COL	64	0	84	80	13	30	51	9	5	4.48	11.74	3	7
1994	COL	61	0	64	79	9	26	51	3	2	3.94	14.77	3	0
1995	COL	71	0	84	61	8	21	79	5	2	2.14	8.79	3	23

Key was conquering the altitude: 3.07 ERA at home (5.02 lifetime).

BRYAN REKAR
Age 24   Bid: $5

Year	Team	G	GS	IP	H	HR	BB	SO	W	L	ERA	Ratio	Sv	$
1994	(A)	22	19	111	120	3	31	91	6	6	3.48	12.24	0	x
1995	(AA)	12	12	80	65	4	16	80	6	3	2.13	9.11	0	x

Year	Team	G	GS	IP	H	HR	BB	SO	W	L	ERA	Ratio	Sv	$
1995	(AAA)	7	7	48	29	0	13	39	4	2	1.49	7.88	0	x
1995	COL	15	14	85	95	11	24	60	4	6	4.98	12.60	0	-2

What's an oxymoron?

Bryan Rekar. The first great Rockies' pitcher.

SHANE REYNOLDS Age 28   Bid: $12

Year	Team	G	GS	IP	H	HR	BB	SO	W	L	ERA	Ratio	Sv	$
1994	HOU	33	14	124	128	10	21	110	8	5	3.05	10.81	0	22
1995	HOU	30	30	189	196	15	37	175	10	11	3.47	11.08	0	19

2.82 ERA at home. Slight concern about the way he tired in the last month.

ARMANDO REYNOSO Age 26

Year	Team	G	GS	IP	H	HR	BB	SO	W	L	ERA	Ratio	Sv	$
1991	ATL	6	5	23	26	4	10	10	2	1	6.17	13.89	0	-3
1992	ATL	3	1	8	11	2	2	2	1	0	4.69	15.25	1	0
1993	COL	30	30	189	206	22	63	117	12	11	4.00	12.81	0	5
1994	COL	9	9	52	54	5	22	25	3	4	4.82	13.07	0	-1
1995	COL	20	18	93	116	12	36	40	7	7	5.32	14.71	0	-7

The average Rockies' pitcher.

CHUCK RICCI   Age 27   Bid: R2

Year	Team	G	GS	IP	H	HR	BB	SO	W	L	ERA	Ratio	Sv	$
1995	(AAA)	68	0	65	48	6	24	66	4	3	2.49	9.97	25	x
1995	PHI	7	0	10	9	0	3	9	1	0	1.80	10.80	0	3

Not a threat to Bottalico but he is to Borland.

JOSE RIJO   Age 31   Bid: $15

Year	Team	G	GS	IP	H	HR	BB	SO	W	L	ERA	Ratio	Sv	$
1991	CIN	30	30	204	165	8	55	172	15	6	2.51	9.69	0	29
1992	CIN	33	33	211	185	15	44	171	15	10	2.56	9.77	0	27
1993	CIN	36	36	257	218	19	62	227	14	9	2.48	9.79	0	40

Year	Team	G	GS	IP	H	HR	BB	SO	W	L	ERA	Ratio	Sv	$
1994	CIN	26	26	172	177	16	52	171	9	6	3.08	11.96	0	21
1995	CIN	14	14	69	76	6	22	62	5	4	4.17	12.78	0	3

The bid is just reserving some money for him. Don't spend it all on Rekar if he's out.

KEVIN RITZ Age 31 Bid: R1

Year	Team	G	GS	IP	H	HR	BB	SO	W	L	ERA	Ratio	Sv	$
1991	DET	11	5	15	17	1	22	9	0	3	11.74	23.40	0	-5
1992	DET	23	11	80	88	4	44	57	2	5	5.60	14.85	0	-7
1994	COL	15	15	74	88	5	35	53	5	6	5.62	15.03	0	-9
1995	COL	31	28	173	171	16	65	120	11	11	4.21	12.25	2	9

Incredible resurrection, but until the reserve round I'm staying at the Plaza.

KEVIN ROGERS Age 27 Bid: R3

Year	Team	G	GS	IP	H	HR	BB	SO	W	L	ERA	Ratio	Sv	$
1992	SF	6	6	34	37	4	13	26	0	2	4.24	13.24	0	-3
1993	SF	64	0	81	71	3	28	62	2	2	2.68	11.05	0	8
1994	SF	9	0	10	10	1	6	7	0	0	3.48	13.94	0	0

Ten good innings at San Jose, four bad ones at Phoenix.

MEL ROJAS Age 29 Bid: $25

Year	Team	G	GS	IP	H	HR	BB	SO	W	L	ERA	Ratio	Sv	$
1991	MTL	37	0	48	42	4	13	37	3	3	3.75	10.31	6	7
1992	MTL	68	0	101	71	2	34	70	7	1	1.43	9.39	10	27
1993	MTL	66	0	88	80	6	30	48	5	8	2.95	11.21	10	16
1994	MTL	58	0	84	71	11	21	84	3	2	3.32	9.86	16	28
1995	MTL	59	0	68	69	2	29	61	1	4	4.12	13.03	30	21

Had great stuff in the games I saw him pitch.

KIRK RUETER Age 25 Bid: $3

Year	Team	G	GS	IP	H	HR	BB	SO	W	L	ERA	Ratio	Sv	$
1993	MTL	14	14	86	85	5	18	31	8	0	2.73	10.82	0	14

Year	Team	G	GS	IP	H	HR	BB	SO	W	L	ERA	Ratio	Sv	$
1994	MTL	20	20	92	106	11	23	50	7	3	5.17	12.57	0	0
1995	MTL	9	9	47	38	3	9	28	5	3	3.23	8.94	0	11

Great numbers, except for the SO, which show he's on that razor's edge.

BRUCE RUFFIN   Age 32   Bid: $10

Year	Team	G	GS	IP	H	HR	BB	SO	W	L	ERA	Ratio	Sv	$
1991	PHI	31	15	119	125	6	38	85	4	7	3.78	12.33	0	-1
1992	MIL	25	6	58	66	7	41	45	1	6	6.67	16.60	0	-14
1993	COL	59	12	140	145	10	69	126	6	5	3.87	13.79	2	0
1994	COL	56	0	56	55	6	30	65	4	5	4.04	13.74	16	15
1995	COL	37	0	34	26	1	19	23	0	1	2.12	11.91	11	12

3.57 home ERA: 0.55 on the road. It would be interesting to know what his G/F was at Coors Field; overall it was 2.29. Leskanic won't get all the saves.

JOHNNY RUFFIN   Age 24   Bid: R2

Year	Team	G	GS	IP	H	HR	BB	SO	W	L	ERA	Ratio	Sv	$
1993	CIN	21	0	38	36	4	11	30	2	1	3.58	11.23	2	4
1994	CIN	51	0	70	57	7	27	44	7	2	3.09	10.80	1	17
1995	CIN	10	0	13	4	0	11	11	0	0	1.35	10.13	0	3

His numbers at Indianapolis were a continuation of his numbers at Cincinnati: 50 IP, 27 H, 3 HR, 37 BB, 58 SO, 2.90 ERA. Three wins. No saves.

BRET SABERHAGEN   Age 32   Bid: $10

Year	Team	G	GS	IP	H	HR	BB	SO	W	L	ERA	Ratio	Sv	$
1991	KC	28	28	196	165	12	45	136	13	8	3.07	9.63	0	29
1992	NYM	17	15	98	84	6	27	81	3	5	3.50	10.23	0	5
1993	NYM	19	19	139	131	11	17	93	7	7	3.29	9.56	0	18
1994	NYM	24	24	177	169	13	13	143	14	4	2.74	9.24	0	46
1995	COL	25	25	153	165	21	33	100	7	6	4.18	11.65	0	7

Wants to get out of Dodge. Double price if he does.

ROGER SALKELD   Age 25   Bid: R3

Year	Team	G	GS	IP	H	HR	BB	SO	W	L	ERA	Ratio	Sv	$
1993	SEA	3	2	14	13	0	4	13	0	0	2.51	10.67	0	2
1994	SEA	13	13	59	76	7	45	46	2	5	7.17	18.46	0	-19

Now in the Reds' organization, he had some success at Indianapolis (12-2 in 20 starts: 119 IP, 96 H, 86 SO, 4.22 ERA). He was once considered better than Van Poppel.

I can tell I'm not impressing you National League-onlies.

SCOTT SANDERS   Age 27   Bid: R1

Year	Team	G	GS	IP	H	HR	BB	SO	W	L	ERA	Ratio	Sv	$
1993	SD	9	9	52	54	4	23	37	3	3	4.13	13.24	0	0
1994	SD	23	20	111	103	10	48	109	4	8	4.78	12.24	1	0
1995	SD	17	15	90	79	14	31	88	5	5	4.30	11.00	0	6

Should I reserve $10 for him —

CURT SCHILLING   Age 29   Bid: $10

Year	Team	G	GS	IP	H	HR	BB	SO	W	L	ERA	Ratio	Sv	$
1991	HOU	56	0	76	79	2	39	71	3	5	3.81	14.04	8	2
1992	PHI	42	26	226	165	11	59	147	14	11	2.35	8.91	2	35
1993	PHI	34	34	235	234	23	57	186	16	7	4.02	11.13	0	17
1994	PHI	13	13	82	87	10	28	58	2	8	4.48	12.57	0	-1
1995	PHI	17	17	116	96	12	26	114	7	5	3.57	9.47	0	18

— or for him?

If I set money aside for all of them, there's nothing left for Bryan Rekar.

JASON SCHMIDT   Age 23   Bid: R1

Year	Team	G	GS	IP	H	HR	BB	SO	W	L	ERA	Ratio	Sv	$
1994	(AA)	24	24	141	135	9	54	131	8	7	3.65	12.06	0	x
1995	(AAA)	19	19	116	97	2	48	95	8	6	2.25	11.25	0	x
1995	ATL	9	2	25	27	2	18	19	2	2	5.76	16.20	0	-4

A legitimate R1. Should start out at Richmond, and is bound to get the call soon. Just not necessarily from the Braves.

Has any pitching coach made it to the Hall of Fame? My votes go to Ray Miller, who says throw strikes, change speeds, pitch fast; and to Leo Mazzone, who seconds that, but the amazing thing about Mazzone is that his pitchers never, ever break down. John Smoltz has tried, but Mazzone won't let him.

Last year, the Braves started Matt Murray in one game, probably to show-case him, and gave Jason Schmidt two starts — that's how good they think he is. Five pitchers started all the other games.

In 1994, Mike Bielecki and Brad Woodall each got one start. The same five started all the others. In 1993, Merker took over from Pete Smith toward the end. In other words, the same five basically started all those games. In 1992, pre-Maddux, Mazzone used two fifth starters (Bielecki and Smith), and that was enough to bring on David Nied and Armando Reynoso for three starts in September.

Elias would be able to tell us if any pitching staff going back to the dead-ball era has ever had such stability.

Changing speeds is a hard thing to quantify, but the Braves allowed the fewest walks and had the quickest games in the majors.

Damn. No they didn't. The Reds, the Expos, and, amazingly, the Mets all had fewer walks. But I'll stick with the quickest-games assertion, even though I can't find that information.

The Braves starters had a 3.25 ERA, more than half a run better than the relievers.

Schmidt's stats were ruined in one bad game for the Braves. Relieving.

PETE SCHOUREK   Age 27   Bid: $24

Year	Team	G	GS	IP	H	HR	BB	SO	W	L	ERA	Ratio	Sv	$
1991	NYM	35	8	86	82	7	43	67	5	4	4.27	13.03	2	-1
1992	NYM	22	21	136	137	9	44	60	6	8	3.64	11.98	0	1
1993	NYM	41	18	128	168	13	45	72	5	12	5.96	14.94	0	-18
1994	CIN	22	10	81	90	11	29	69	7	2	4.09	13.17	0	5
1995	CIN	29	29	190	158	17	45	160	18	7	3.22	9.60	0	37

Dallas Green is a front-runner. If the young Mets do well, he'll be the right manager for them; he'll have them thinking they're better than they are. If they stumble, he'll have them thinking they're gutless wonders who will never harness their talent. May Pete Schourek rub it in forever.

TIM SCOTT   Age 29   Bid: $1

Year	Team	G	GS	IP	H	HR	BB	SO	W	L	ERA	Ratio	Sv	$
1991	SD	2	0	1	2	0	0	1	0	0	9.00	18.00	0	0
1992	SD	34	0	38	39	4	21	30	4	1	5.26	14.34	0	-3
1993	MTL	56	0	72	69	4	34	65	7	2	3.01	12.94	1	8
1994	MTL	40	0	53	51	0	18	37	5	2	2.70	11.64	1	12
1995	MTL	62	0	63	52	6	23	57	2	0	3.98	10.66	2	6

Still poppin' them up: G/F 0.84.

RUDY SEANEZ   Age 27

Bid: $1

Year	Team	G	GS	IP	H	HR	BB	SO	W	L	ERA	Ratio	Sv	$
1991	CLE	5	0	5	10	2	7	7	0	0	16.20	30.60	0	-6
1993	SD	3	0	3	8	1	2	1	0	0	13.50	27.00	0	-3
1994	LA	17	0	24	24	2	9	18	1	1	2.66	12.55	0	3
1995	LA	37	0	35	39	5	18	29	1	3	6.75	14.80	3	-5

Rotisserie owners are like Dallas Green, as we see in Appendix A.

HEATHCLIFF SLOCUMB   Age 30

Bid: $7

Year	Team	G	GS	IP	H	HR	BB	SO	W	L	ERA	Ratio	Sv	$
1991	CHC	52	0	63	53	3	30	34	2	1	3.45	11.92	1	2
1992	CHC	30	0	36	52	3	21	27	0	3	6.50	18.25	1	-11
1993	CHC	10	0	11	7	0	4	4	1	0	3.38	9.28	0	2
1993	CLE	20	0	27	28	3	16	18	3	1	4.28	14.49	0	1
1994	PHI	52	0	72	75	0	28	58	5	1	2.86	12.82	0	9
1995	PHI	61	0	65	64	2	35	63	5	6	2.89	13.64	32	29

Assuming the roles are reversed, should still be an effective combination with Bottalico.

JOHN SMILEY   Age 31

Bid: $18

Year	Team	G	GS	IP	H	HR	BB	SO	W	L	ERA	Ratio	Sv	$
1991	PIT	33	33	208	194	17	44	129	20	8	3.08	10.31	0	25
1992	MIN	34	34	241	205	17	65	163	16	9	3.21	10.08	0	29
1993	CIN	18	18	106	117	15	31	60	3	9	5.62	12.61	0	-8
1994	CIN	24	24	159	169	18	37	112	11	10	3.86	11.68	0	17
1995	CIN	28	27	177	173	11	39	124	12	5	3.46	10.80	0	22

Strong temptation to bid into the 20's; salary scan says don't.

JOHN SMOLTZ   Age 29

Bid: $18

Year	Team	G	GS	IP	H	HR	BB	SO	W	L	ERA	Ratio	Sv	$
1991	ATL	36	36	230	206	16	77	148	14	13	3.80	11.09	0	10
1992	ATL	35	35	247	206	17	80	215	15	12	2.85	10.43	0	22

Year	Team	G	GS	IP	H	HR	BB	SO	W	L	ERA	Ratio	Sv	$
1993	ATL	35	35	244	208	23	100	208	15	11	3.62	11.38	0	19
1994	ATL	21	21	135	120	15	48	113	6	10	4.14	11.23	0	10
1995	ATL	29	29	193	166	15	72	193	12	7	3.18	11.12	0	24

Ditto.

EVERETT STULL   Age 23   Bid: R2

Year	Team	G	GS	IP	H	HR	BB	SO	W	L	ERA	Ratio	Sv	$
1993	(A)	15	15	82	68	8	59	85	4	9	3.83	13.94	0	x
1994	(A)	27	26	147	116	3	78	165	10	10	3.31	11.88	0	x
1995	(AA)	24	24	127	114	12	79	132	3	12	5.54	13.68	0	x

Got stalled at Harrisburg (AA), then shifted into gear in the AZL (2.75 ERA, 35 K in 36 IP). Just
needs an off speed pitch to go with his hard stuff, which is plainly superior.

BILLY SWIFT   Age 34   Bid: $5

Year	Team	G	GS	IP	H	HR	BB	SO	W	L	ERA	Ratio	Sv	$
1991	SEA	71	0	90	74	3	26	48	1	2	1.99	9.96	17	24
1992	SF	30	22	165	144	6	43	77	10	4	2.08	10.22	1	22
1993	SF	34	34	233	195	18	55	157	21	8	2.82	9.67	0	41
1994	SF	17	17	109	109	10	31	62	8	7	3.38	11.52	0	16
1995	COL	19	19	106	122	12	43	68	9	3	4.94	14.05	0	-3

Price enforce to $3.

GREG SWINDELL   Age 31   Bid: $1

Year	Team	G	GS	IP	H	HR	BB	SO	W	L	ERA	Ratio	Sv	$
1991	CLE	33	33	238	241	21	31	169	9	16	3.48	10.29	0	21
1992	CIN	31	31	214	210	14	41	138	12	8	2.70	10.57	0	19
1993	HOU	31	30	190	215	24	40	124	12	13	4.16	12.06	0	7
1994	HOU	24	24	148	175	20	26	74	8	9	4.37	12.20	0	6
1995	HOU	33	26	153	180	21	39	96	10	9	4.47	12.88	0	2

Salary scan says minus dollars.

JEFF TABAKA   Age 32   Bid: R3

Year	Team	G	GS	IP	H	HR	BB	SO	W	L	ERA	Ratio	Sv	$
1994	PIT/SD	39	0	41	32	1	27	32	3	1	5.27	12.95	1	0
1995	SD/HOU	34	0	31	27	2	17	25	1	0	3.23	12.91	0	1

The fourth time in Triple-A was a charm: 1.99 ERA in 19 games at Las Vegas. More to the point, 2.22 ERA in 24 games with the Astros.

KEVIN TAPANI   Age 32   Bid: $3

Year	Team	G	GS	IP	H	HR	BB	SO	W	L	ERA	Ratio	Sv	$
1991	MIN	34	34	244	225	23	40	135	16	9	2.99	9.77	0	35
1992	MIN	34	34	220	226	17	48	138	16	11	3.97	11.21	0	16
1993	MIN	36	35	226	243	21	57	150	12	15	4.43	11.96	0	10
1994	MIN	24	24	156	181	13	39	91	11	7	4.62	12.69	0	14
1995	MIN	20	20	134	155	21	34	88	6	11	4.92	12.73	0	4
1995	LA	13	11	57	72	8	14	43	4	2	5.05	13.58	0	-2

National League was no tonic. Also went from a hitters' park to a pitchers' park. On the other hand, he did go from a solid defensive team to a — ?

Well, according to Mike Gimbel, a consultant for player evaluation for the Red Sox and Baseball Weekly AL participant, the *Dodgers* had a good defensive team.

In one of John Hunt's columns in November, the Gimbel ratings were shown and to some extent explained. "Gimbel eschews errors and fielding percentage; rather, he looks at balls hit into a player's defensive area for a better read on the player's abilities." That's a lot of looking! "Analyzing more than 3,000 balls put in play, per team, he measured each player against the composite of all his opponents at his position at his home park and at the combined away parks when the player is on the road."

Some things you just have to take on faith.

And yet Gimbel's ratings are extremely interesting precisely because they don't accord with what we think we have observed and/or with what we have read: the whole Dodger team has become a Jose Offerman joke.

It would not seem that Gimbel has access to the observations of the Stats Inc. scorers. They give Offerman a bad zone rating (compared to the average shortstop) and Fonville — he's awful, man (as well as below average at second). DeShields has a positive zone rating, Wallach's is slightly positive, Mondesi's is average, Butler's is below average, Kelly's is average in left (terrible in center)... So maybe these are the observations of Gimbel's own network, and what that would mean is, people are seeing different things.

Which is, of course, the case. Scout after scout put his reputation on the line, based on what he thought he saw in Jose Offerman. What did he lack?

He obviously lacked something, and now we see things differently.

And we read in Mike Gimbel's data pretty much what we want to read.

The Twins had the best defense in the American League? Okay. As Hunt aptly observed in his column, that doesn't raise your estimation of Twins pitchers one bit.

The Dodgers had a better defense than the Braves? We ignore that.

The Cardinals had the worst defense in the league? We pay attention to that. We think about it.

And then we know Ozzie was great.

TOM THOBE Age 26

Year	Team	G	GS	IP	H	HR	BB	SO	W	L	ERA	Ratio	Sv	$
1994	(AAA)	48	2	88	65	2	26	57	7	0	1.84	9.31	5	x
1995	ATL	3	0	3	7	0	0	2	0	0	10.80	18.90	0	-2

This is the good Thobe. He's 6'6", 195; throws left. The not-so good Thobe, J.J., is 6'6", 220, throws right, plays for the Expos, and doesn't strike anybody out.

MARK THOMPSON Age 25

Bid: $1

Year	Team	G	GS	IP	H	HR	BB	SO	W	L	ERA	Ratio	Sv	$
1994	COL	2	2	9	16	2	8	5	1	1	9.00	24.00	0	-6
1995	COL	21	5	51	73	7	22	30	2	3	6.53	16.76	0	-13

At least take him in the reserve draft. Bad stats hide the fact that he really stepped forward for the Rockies in the crucial last week: 3 games, 5.2 IP, no runs, 5 K's.

STEVE TRACHSEL Age 25

Bid: $5

Year	Team	G	GS	IP	H	HR	BB	SO	W	L	ERA	Ratio	Sv	$
1993	CHC	3	3	20	16	4	3	14	0	2	4.58	8.70	0	1
1994	CHC	22	22	146	133	19	54	108	9	7	3.21	11.53	0	21
1995	CHC	30	29	161	174	25	76	117	7	13	5.15	14.00	0	-11

His worst month was his last. May, by contrast, was precisely what people bet $12 on: 33 IP, 21 H, 11 BB, 22 SO, 2.48 ERA. There must have been arm trouble.

UGUETH URBINA Age 22

Bid: R1

Year	Team	G	GS	IP	H	HR	BB	SO	W	L	ERA	Ratio	Sv	$
1994	(AA)	21	21	121	96	11	43	86	9	3	3.28	10.34	0	x
1995	(A)	2	2	9	4	0	1	11	1	0	.00	5.00	0	x
1995	(AAA)	13	11	68	46	1	26	55	6	2	3.04	9.53	0	x
1995	MTL	7	4	23	26	6	14	15	2	2	6.17	15.43	0	-3

Starts in Ottawa, comes up for good in May.

ISMAEL VALDES
Age 22   Bid: $19

Year	Team	G	GS	IP	H	HR	BB	SO	W	L	ERA	Ratio	Sv	$
1993	(AA)	3	2	13	12	0	0	11	1	0	1.38	8.31	0	x
1994	(AA)	8	8	53	54	4	9	55	2	3	3.38	10.70	0	x
1994	(AAA)	8	8	45	44	1	13	39	4	1	3.40	11.40	0	x
1994	LA	21	1	28	21	2	10	28	3	1	3.18	9.85	0	8
1995	LA	33	27	198	168	17	51	150	13	11	3.05	9.97	1	33

Glen Waggoner (presumably) in last year's RLBA book: "Call him Ismael if you want, but with his gas you ought to call him Exxon Valdes. The Dodgers love his Hershiser-like mechanics and poise. We love the 1.118 ratio in three minor league seasons coming into last year. We love the fact that his *highest* minor league ERA was 2.42... And we especially love the idea of getting him cheap, at least this once."

Great comment, Glenn. With more gas, less hype, you might have gotten him at your $5 bid price ($8 average salary in Appendix A), and I doubt mine will do it this year.

SERGIO VALDEZ
Age 30   Bid: R3

Year	Team	G	GS	IP	H	HR	BB	SO	W	L	ERA	Ratio	Sv	$
1991	CLE	6	0	16	15	3	5	11	1	0	5.51	11.25	0	-3
1992	MTL	27	0	37	25	2	12	32	0	2	2.41	8.92	0	4
1993	MTL	4	0	3	4	1	1	2	0	0	9.00	15.00	0	-1
1994	BOS	12	1	14	25	4	8	4	0	1	8.16	20.72	0	-8
1995	SF	13	11	66	78	12	17	29	4	5	4.75	12.89	0	-1

An oil spill waiting to happen.

FERNANDO VALENZUELA
Age 35   Bid: R3

Year	Team	G	GS	IP	H	HR	BB	SO	W	L	ERA	Ratio	Sv	$
1991	CAL	2	2	7	14	1	3	5	0	2	12.15	21.86	0	-7
1993	BAL	32	31	179	179	18	79	78	8	10	4.94	13.00	0	-2
1994	PHI	8	7	45	42	8	7	19	1	2	3.00	9.80	0	8
1995	SD	29	15	90	101	16	34	57	8	3	4.98	13.45	0	-1

Only one of his 8 wins was picked up in the Baseball Weekly league (by Stu Baron back in May, counterbalanced by 6.35 ERA, 17.47 ratio). In September, P/G chose to go to Valdez.

BILL VANLANDINGHAM
Age 25   Bid: $5

Year	Team	G	GS	IP	H	HR	BB	SO	W	L	ERA	Ratio	Sv	$
1994	SF	16	14	84	70	4	43	56	8	2	3.54	12.11	0	12
1995	SF	18	18	123	124	14	40	95	6	3	3.67	12.03	0	8

Seems to be a pitcher who knows how to win.

DAVE VERES
Age 29   Bid: $4

Year	Team	G	GS	IP	H	HR	BB	SO	W	L	ERA	Ratio	Sv	$
1994	HOU	32	0	41	39	4	7	28	3	3	2.41	10.10	1	12
1995	HOU	72	0	103	89	5	30	94	5	1	2.26	10.36	1	20

His rating (weighted ratio) was 1.08 — tremendous. He's right behind Worrell among relievers; and ahead of all starters, of course, except for one that he can just wave at (Nomo, 0.96) and another that he can't even see (0.81).

RON VILLONE
Age 26   Bid: $4

Year	Team	G	GS	IP	H	HR	BB	SO	W	L	ERA	Ratio	Sv	$
1994	(AA)	41	5	79	56	7	68	94	6	7	3.86	14.13	8	x
1995	SEA	19	0	19	20	6	23	26	0	2	7.91	20.02	0	-8
1995	(AAA)	22	0	30	9	1	19	43	1	0	.61	8.40	13	x
1995	SD	19	0	26	24	5	11	37	2	1	4.21	12.27	1	2

When the Padres picked up Villone for Benes, they didn't see much point in leaving him in Tacoma (AAA). The rating for that stat line you see?
   0.67.

FRANK VIOLA
Age 36   Bid: R3

Year	Team	G	GS	IP	H	HR	BB	SO	W	L	ERA	Ratio	Sv	$
1991	NYM	35	35	231	259	25	54	132	13	15	3.97	12.18	0	2
1992	BOS	35	35	238	214	13	89	121	13	12	3.44	11.46	0	17
1993	BOS	29	29	184	180	12	72	91	11	8	3.14	12.35	0	18
1994	BOS	6	6	31	34	2	17	9	1	1	4.65	14.81	0	-1
1995	CIN	3	3	14	20	3	3	4	0	1	6.28	14.44	0	-3

Whatever he does this year, you know that right now he's got his best career stats, so here they are: 175-147, 3.69 ERA. Started all but one of his 415 games, completed 74. Pitched the one game in relief in 1983, but since he started 34 games that year, it can fairly be said he didn't miss a turn in the rotation from his call-up from Toledo early in 1982 until his sixth start with the Red Sox in 1994, when he broke down. Who's Gehrig's pitching equivalent — anyone know? Ripken's streak started in 1982.

TERRELL WADE Age 23 Bid: R2

Year	Team	G	GS	IP	H	HR	BB	SO	W	L	ERA	Ratio	Sv	$
1994	(AA)	21	21	107	87	7	58	105	9	3	3.83	12.20	0	x
1994	(AAA)	4	4	24	23	1	15	26	2	2	2.63	14.25	0	x
1995	(AAA)	24	23	142	137	10	63	124	10	9	4.56	12.68	0	x
1995	ATL	3	0	4	3	1	4	3	0	1	4.50	15.75	0	-1

May not be ready, but it's time to find out.

BILLY WAGNER Age 25 Bid: R1

Year	Team	G	GS	IP	H	HR	BB	SO	W	L	ERA	Ratio	Sv	$
1993	(A)	7	7	29	25	3	25	31	1	3	4.08	15.52	0	x
1994	(A)	26	26	153	99	9	91	204	8	9	3.29	11.18	0	x
1995	(AA)	12	12	70	49	7	36	77	2	2	2.57	10.93	0	x
1995	(AAA)	13	13	76	70	3	32	80	5	3	3.18	12.08	0	x
1995	HOU	1	0	0	0	0	0	0	0	0	.00	.00	0	0

So much easier to say R1 than $10.

PAUL WAGNER Age 28 Bid: $1

Year	Team	G	GS	IP	H	HR	BB	SO	W	L	ERA	Ratio	Sv	$
1992	(AAA)	8	8	39	51	1	14	19	3	3	5.49	15.00	0	x
1992	(AA)	19	19	122	104	3	47	101	6	6	3.03	11.14	0	x
1993	PIT	44	17	141	143	15	42	114	8	8	4.27	11.78	2	6
1994	PIT	29	17	120	136	7	50	86	7	8	4.59	13.99	0	-3
1995	PIT	33	25	165	174	18	72	120	5	16	4.80	13.42	1	-7

Another good call by Waggoner in the RLBA book: "Will he end up being a starter or reliever? We don't know, and we're beginning to suspect that it doesn't matter."

Hey, as Glen would say, it's a long course; we hitch a ride with anyone we can.

DONNIE WALL Age 28

Bid: R3

Year	Team	G	GS	IP	H	HR	BB	SO	W	L	ERA	Ratio	Sv	$
1994	(AAA)	26	24	148	171	9	35	84	11	8	4.43	12.53	0	x
1995	(AAA)	28	28	177	190	5	32	119	17	6	3.30	11.29	0	x
1995	HOU	6	5	24	33	5	5	16	3	1	5.55	14.05	0	-1

Kept winning in the majors, just not for Rotisserie teams.

ALLEN WATSON Age 25

Bid: $1

Year	Team	G	GS	IP	H	HR	BB	SO	W	L	ERA	Ratio	Sv	$
1993	STL	16	15	86	90	11	28	49	6	7	4.60	12.35	0	1
1994	STL	22	22	116	130	15	53	74	6	5	5.52	14.24	0	-12
1995	STL	21	19	114	126	17	41	49	7	9	4.96	13.15	0	-3

Lefties have more lives. Otherwise David Weathers would follow.

DAVID WELLS Age 36

Bid: $17

Year	Team	G	GS	IP	H	HR	BB	SO	W	L	ERA	Ratio	Sv	$
1991	TOR	40	28	198	188	24	49	106	15	10	3.72	10.75	1	20
1992	TOR	41	14	120	138	16	36	62	7	9	5.40	13.05	2	-4
1993	DET	32	30	187	183	26	42	139	11	9	4.19	10.83	0	17
1994	DET	16	16	111	113	13	24	71	5	7	3.96	11.07	0	17
1995	DET	18	18	130	120	17	37	83	10	3	3.04	10.84	0	27
1995	CIN	11	11	73	74	6	16	50	6	5	3.59	11.15	0	9

Bill James in his book last year: "A weighty left-hander with a legitimate fastball, good control, and strong pitching instincts. He had his elbow scoped last April, and at season's end was pitching extremely well. He's kind of a fat John Smiley — a fine pitcher, really, but stuck working for the Tigers because people don't feel they can count on him. Capable of winning 16-18 games."

DAVID WEST Age 31

Bid: R3

Year	Team	G	GS	IP	H	HR	BB	SO	W	L	ERA	Ratio	Sv	$
1991	MIN	15	12	71	66	13	28	52	4	4	4.54	11.86	0	2
1992	MIN	9	3	28	32	3	20	19	1	3	6.99	16.52	0	-7
1993	PHI	76	0	86	60	6	51	87	6	4	2.92	11.57	3	12

Year	Team	G	GS	IP	H	HR	BB	SO	W	L	ERA	Ratio	Sv	$
1994	PHI	31	14	99	74	7	61	83	4	10	3.55	12.27	0	**7**
1995	PHI	8	8	38	34	5	19	25	3	2	3.79	12.55	0	**3**

He may *think* he's rehabbing, but he won't show up in Florida looking like Orel Hershiser. Turk Wendell was trimmed to save space above, even though he could pick up some wins in middle relief for the Cubs, who are going to be hot this year.

GABE WHITE   Age 24   Bid: R3

Year	Team	G	GS	IP	H	HR	BB	SO	W	L	ERA	Ratio	Sv	$
1994	MTL	7	5	24	24	4	11	17	1	1	6.08	13.31	1	**-2**
1995	MTL	19	1	26	26	7	9	25	1	2	7.01	12.27	0	**-4**

Popped them up (G/F 0.42) when they didn't hit it out.

BRIAN WILLIAMS   Age 27   Bid: R3

Year	Team	G	GS	IP	H	HR	BB	SO	W	L	ERA	Ratio	Sv	$
1991	HOU	2	2	12	11	2	4	4	0	1	3.75	11.25	0	**0**
1992	HOU	16	16	96	92	10	42	54	7	6	3.92	12.52	0	**0**
1993	HOU	42	5	82	76	7	38	56	4	4	4.83	12.51	3	**0**
1994	HOU	20	13	78	112	9	41	49	6	5	5.74	17.58	0	**-17**
1995	SD	44	6	72	79	3	38	75	3	10	6.00	14.63	0	**-10**

Lots of K's, good G/F (1.57); normally, that's a tough combination.

PAUL WILSON   Age 23   Bid: R1

Year	Team	G	GS	IP	H	HR	BB	SO	W	L	ERA	Ratio	Sv	$
1994	(R)	3	3	12	8	0	4	13	0	2	3.00	9.00	0	**x**
1994	(A)	8	8	37	32	3	17	37	0	5	5.06	11.92	0	**x**
1995	(AA)	16	16	120	89	5	24	127	6	3	2.17	8.48	0	**x**
1995	(AAA)	10	10	66	59	3	20	67	5	3	2.85	10.77	0	**x**

He even got scuffed up a bit at St. Lucie (A) in '94, so I don't know what else he needs. Probably a few more innings in Triple-A. If he doesn't get them, put him between Isringhausen and Pulsipher on your wish list. He's far the largest of the three (6'5", 235).

MARK WOHLERS

Age 26   Bid: $40

Year	Team	G	GS	IP	H	HR	BB	SO	W	L	ERA	Ratio	Sv	$
1991	ATL	17	0	20	17	1	13	13	3	1	3.20	13.73	2	3
1992	ATL	32	0	35	28	0	14	17	1	2	2.55	10.70	4	6
1993	ATL	46	0	48	37	2	22	45	6	2	4.50	11.06	0	5
1994	ATL	51	0	51	51	1	33	58	7	2	4.59	14.82	1	2
1995	ATL	65	0	65	51	2	24	90	7	3	2.09	10.44	25	35

Why the teams that bought Wohlers only finished with an average of 53.5 points (top 10 pitchers, Brantley comment) is not at all clear. As a freeze for next year at $5, he'll be in the top five in the Heath trackings.

TODD WORRELL

Age 36   Bid: $29

Year	Team	G	GS	IP	H	HR	BB	SO	W	L	ERA	Ratio	Sv	$
1992	STL	67	0	64	45	4	25	64	5	3	2.11	9.84	3	13
1993	LA	35	0	101	46	6	11	31	1	1	6.05	5.10	5	-6
1994	LA	38	0	42	37	4	12	44	6	5	4.29	10.50	11	18
1995	LA	59	0	62	50	4	19	61	4	1	2.02	9.96	32	38

His teams finished with only 50.7 points — below .500 — and he actually earned more than Wohlers, turning almost as big a profit (Castillo comment), and yet it still doesn't seem quite as strange. Must be something about Todd Worrell.

ANTHONY YOUNG

Age 30   Bid: R3

Year	Team	G	GS	IP	H	HR	BB	SO	W	L	ERA	Ratio	Sv	$
1991	NYM	10	8	49	48	4	12	20	2	5	3.10	10.95	0	3
1992	NYM	52	13	121	134	8	31	64	2	14	4.17	12.27	15	6
1993	NYM	39	10	100	103	8	42	62	1	16	3.77	13.01	3	0
1994	CHC	20	19	115	103	12	46	65	4	6	3.92	11.69	0	7
1995	CHC	32	1	41	47	5	14	15	3	4	3.70	13.28	2	3

Maybe even Anthony Young will be hot this year.

Chapter 2
Predictions

If the strike did one thing it was get forecasters agreeing on how much hitting there would be for the first time in years. A lot. There wasn't anybody who didn't think April would be a disaster for pitchers; many predicted pitchers would need at least until the end of May to get in shape; and some, like myself, thought the rush to start the season might mess them up for the entire year.

ERA by month

	AL	NL	MLB
April	5.20	4.22	4.69
May	4.79	4.33	4.56
June	4.63	4.01	4.32
July	4.69	4.09	4.39
August	4.98	4.17	4.57
Sept/Oct	4.38	4.30	4.34
1995	4.71	4.18	4.45

As it turns out, it seems there was indeed some disruption in the American League but none to speak of in the National League. For both leagues combined, April shows the highest ERA, but how unusual is that?

ERA by month

	AL	NL	MLB
April	5.01	4.38	4.70
May	4.88	4.04	4.44
June	4.78	4.24	4.51
July	4.63	4.34	4.49
August	4.65	3.86	4.26
Sept/Oct			
1994	4.80	4.21	4.50

It's not unusual, and in fact there was more hitting in April of 1994 than there was in last year's partial April that followed an unusually long lay-off and a sharply reduced preparation period.

To that, all you can say is go figure.

And I really don't see anything else in either chart that sheds much light on either of these dark seasons. In 1994, there was a slight downward trend in overall ERA, followed by a fairly noticeable drop in August, causing me to speculate that September would have continued to see a reduction in hitting — but face it, who knows?

Last year, August had the second most hitting after April, and September had the second best pitching after June. Don't ask me what that tells us.

I worry about this more than most people, because my theory is, if I can get the big picture right, I'm bound to get the little pictures right more often than other people who are in the prediction business.

This was the big-picture forecast in last year's book:

Book predictions

	AB	HR	RBI	SB	BA
AL	78400	2283	10472	1381	.267
NL	73500	2036	9525	1505	.269

And this was the update picture:

Update predictions

	AB	HR	RBI	SB	BA
AL	71400	2210	9720	1272	.269
NL	65800	1921	8607	1465	.271

And this was the actual picture (NL pitchers do not sit for this portrait):

1995 league totals

	AB	HR	RBI	SB	BA
AL	69522	2164	9691	1331	.270
NL	64926	1897	8478	1595	.271

Then we quickly better reduce the book picture by 144/162 to bring it more in line with the actual AB, even though that isn't a category:

Book predictions scaled to actual season

	AB	HR	RBI	SB	BA
AL	69689	2029	9308	1228	.267
NL	65333	1810	8467	1338	.269

Thus we can see that, while in neither case do I have a firm grip on reality — there are those who say I never do — between the book and the update, I have it pretty well surrounded.

A concession that I had to make last year I have to make again: no team-by-team predictions. Hardly any point, back in November where I am, and even when you're reading this book, chances are, hundreds of players will still be floating free.

I've stuck with my at-bat cap for each league, optimistically counting, yet again, on 162 games; but a good case can be made that I shouldn't. Not that I should under-predict AB — although a case can be made for that, too — but that I should over-predict. That's what Bill James does, and he presents his usual compelling reasons for his way of doing things in this year's *Major League Handbook*:

"We have long arguments every year about how much playing time to project for who. What I always argue, and I win as many as I lose, is that if a young player can play, we should project him to play. My thinking is this: if a young player comes along, and you turn to us to see what kind of hitter he is, and we don't tell you, then we've failed you. We haven't told you what we know.

"On the other hand, if we project him to bat 537 times and he doesn't, so what? You didn't really think we knew who was going to play how much, did you?"

He discusses in detail the problem of trying to guess if Matt Lawton, Rich Becker or someone else will get the 550 AB that the center field position in Minnesota offers.

"We could project 275 at bats for each of them, rub our hands contentedly and say we've got the position covered. But have we really minimized the error?"

It's not a rhetorical question. He explains in detail why the mathematical answer to that is no. (Unless, of course, nobody wins the job and they in fact do split the AB.)

"So making the projected at bats match the available playing time doesn't really do anything to minimize the error. It's a compromise; it guarantees that you'll be half wrong. I'd rather be right half the time and wrong half the time than half wrong all the time."

I've met Bill James, and there is something about him that definitely reminds me of Will Rogers.

For starters, they are/were both very funny, and I got a good laugh when I read that line. Humor, though, is itself an odd duck: it exposes what's false without necessarily telling what's true.

You won't be half-wrong, Bill, if Becker and Lawton *do* split the job; and, at least while their battling for it, don't they have to? So that's one point which you could have made, and which I'm sure was discussed in your various arguments with your colleagues, but you didn't, because it would have torn your joke to shreds.

My next question is, who's failing who here? The way you put it — "You didn't really think we knew who was going to play how much, did you? — kind of puts me on the defensive, but once I've recovered: yes, damn it, that's *exactly* what I thought you might tell me. We *know* Becker and Lawton are going to be in a battle; who's going to win it?

I flip to the relevant pages and see Becker (9-52-16-.282 in 444 AB) and see Lawton (17-78-27-.270 in 564 AB) and I see that Lawton does beat Becker out, but not this year, and I'm not sure why.

Nope — cancel that. Cheap joke, nothing more.

The projection for Lawton is bold, it's what we're looking for; James quite obviously does think Lawton's ready. Not me. I'll be shocked if he puts up numbers that approach these this year (and I'll change my mind if he doesn't cool down in the AZL), and, furthermore, there's no *way* Becker posts these numbers. I was a big Becker fan myself, until I actually saw him play.

Cheap joke No. 2. James, I'm sure, watches at least as many games as I do, and he may have even talked to Rich Becker at some point. I do not talk to baseball players. They scare me.

Cheap joke No. 3. I don't talk to baseball players because I just don't get the chance (but it's also true that I'm not the sort of person to go up to someone — Rich Becker or anyone else — and ask him why he's not very good at what he does).

But I would ask James dozens of questions if I got the chance. (I did get a chance two years ago, when were riding in the same car from New York to Hackensack to shoot the ESPN pre-season special; amid chit-chat, the only serious question I got around to asking him was, Why did he ever join the Baseball Weekly tout league? His answer: "Because I'm not very good at saying no to people." He did last year.) The question I would ask with regard to the hitter projections is, Why not one more line, showing the totals?

How far over is he on at-bats?

He devotes 400 lines to 400 players (which is interesting in itself: he's over-projecting at-bats but under-projecting the number of people who will get them), and it would be such a simple matter to have line 401 show what it all adds up to. Each line is so fantastically detailed: not simply HR, but D, T, BB and SO; not just SB but CS. I'd like to see how many CS there are overall, compared to SB. It's not that I expect to see anything outlandish, but I am curious.

Following the projections for 400 hitters in 1996 is a page called "These Guys Can Play Too and Might Get a Shot." There are 24 such hitters on this list, which, James writes, "includes players that we wouldn't expect to play next year, but who we feel have the ability to play if they get the chance." Almost all 24 of them are hitters worthy of our consideration (such as Bob Abreu, Trey Beamon, Brian Giles, Todd Greene, Robin Jennings, Brooks Kieschnick, Jose Malave, Ruben Rivera and Todd Walker) and the MLE's that are shown for them definitely have useful information. But how exactly does projecting 409 AB for Brian Giles differ from projecting 444 for Rich Becker? Is one a lesser so-what if it doesn't happen? Is that the difference?

James has as much as admitted there isn't room for Rich Becker even. I guess he's saying that Rich Becker has a better chance of making him wrong somewhere else than Brian Giles has.

I'm not trying to be cute, nor am I nit-picking. The question of what to do with every one of the 24 players he names is *the* question of forecasting. A good number of them will make brief appearances in the majors this year, while a few will play a lot of the season and have significant impacts. How does showing what they all will do if they all play a lot help us identify who the few will be?

This is not to say that I don't listen to Bill James. I always do. "What we know is, Matt Lawton can play. So what I say is, let's make a strong statement that Matt Lawton can play. If Tom Kelly doesn't give him a chance to show it, that's on him." I listen to that. I like it. Makes sense, and makes me smile.

Then I naturally look for an answer to this, since I do it differently. You can make the same statement — not as dramatically but just as accurately — about a player's potential in 100 AB as in 500 AB. The player isn't generating the stats, we are; and any amount of AB can be representative of how well we think the player will play, if he plays.

Ultimately, it comes down to the fact that there's some cussed element in me that resists projecting 1,008 AB for Matt Lawton and Rich Becker. I just can't do it, not wittingly. Maybe the best resolution of this issue is to say, some forecasters should project both of them fully out, and some shouldn't.

My method is to start with line 401. I ask myself, how much hitting is there going to be in each league this year? The fourth year after expansion; pitchers may finally have their act together again. Ball seemed a little less juiced last year than two years ago. No new stadiums to throw things askew. (The only new stadium that hasn't been a hitters's stadium is the one the Hurt plays in.) Farmer's almanac says it's going to be cold in April and blowing in at Wrigley (that's not a tip; only have my Stats Inc. books so far)...

The ERA's that I pin on the wall for 1996 are 4.40 for the AL, 4.00 for the NL — still a lot of hitting, ample for me to have fun with, but less than last year (4.71 in the AL and 4.18 in the NL). With a calculator I work out the number of HR, RBI, SB and BA needed to produce ERA's like these (allowing for league differences) and pin these numbers up on the wall. Then I crank up The Projector in *Patton $ On Disk* and start building toward them player by player, and this part really is fun.

Haven't done it yet for this year — it's the last thing I do — but it will be fun.

I've already done the hard part, which is the bids. The bids are serious business. The bids are bets, the predictions are guesses.

Clearly, each player is grounded in the year before. For example, suppose Piazza doesn't get hurt and the season is completed and he gets 547 AB, as he did in 1993. Rounding that off to the nearest 25, I enter 550 for Piazza in his data box; the program asks "ProRate? Y/N", I hit the Y key with a vengeance. Into the data box pops a new Piazza (with all secondary stats, the ones we pay close attention to but aren't worth anything, expanded as well):

```
Piazza — first try
  AB    H    HR   RBI   SB    BA      $
 550   190   40   117    1   .345    46
```

The one thing that's not simply multiplied by 550/434 here is the salary; if it were it would be $49. That is, if the formula used in this year's book, which judged Piazza's 1995 stats to be worth $39, were simply thrown into The Projector, the pro-rated stats would be worth $49.

The Projector has a prediction formula that's tailored to the predicted overall stats. No matter much how much hitting there is in the National League this season — whether there's more, or as I'm predicting, whether there's less — it will be worth around $2,500. That figure varies somewhat, depending on how much "free loot" comes along, but the stats of the hitters we buy in the draft will be worth $2,184 (according to the pricing theory that this book is based on). The prediction formula for 1996 judges the pro-rated stats that you see above to be worth $46.

In essence, the formula puts Piazza's expanded stats in the context of a full season, which pushes his price down, but it expects less hitting by the average player, and that pushed Piazza back up a bit.

The question is, is it a good prediction either way — price or stats?

Seems a bit much, doesn't it? I recommended a bid limit of $43 for Piazza and that *had* to include position scarcity, I'm sure it did; so, without even fussing with the stats themselves, let's enter $40 in Piazza's data box and see what happens.

```
Piazza — second try
  AB    H    HR   RBI   SB    BA      $
 550   181   35   111    1   .329    40
```

Two tries does it, I think. This seems reasonable. Very much within Piazza's reach. Just can't get hurt.

If I was 100% confident that Piazza *won't* get hurt, for these stats, from a catcher? I'd bid $45.

If you don't see this precise prediction for Piazza in the tables that follow, it means, in the end, I couldn't leave well enough alone. There was a third try, a fourth try.

And so it goes, for over 600 hitters.

Matt Williams will be fun.

The batting average is going to be much harder to figure than the home runs. Do you split the difference between .336 and .267?

Since Bill James has by far the harshest deadline for getting his projections to the printer, I can already show you his 1996 Matt Williams (which most of you, I imagine, have already seen; the projections are in the *Stats Major League Handbook*, which, incredibly, you can buy at the beginning of November):

Predictions

Bill James: Matt Williams this year

AB	H	HR	RBI	SB	BA	$
539	146	36	100	2	.271	28

The price, I'm sure you realize, is my prediction formula applied to his predicted stats. There is a Bill James pricing system, but it must be for Bill James fantasy baseball; it's not for Rotisserie.

So forget the price — do you like the stats?

His method couldn't be more opposed to mine. Yet by no means are we looking at a simple weighted average. Age is a big factor. And such matters as BB/SO ratio, undoubtedly, are taken into account. The formula has never been divulged.

Which is fine. James has given us a lifetime of formulas to play with. Probably the formula that generates the projections simply isn't readable; the point is, it is a formula. James is hands-off and proud of it.

Right off the bat, in his essay in this year's *Handbook*, he lists Our Projection of players who would hit 30 home runs in 1995 next to a list of Actual Factual.

"As you can see, we projected only 14 players to hit 30 or more home runs. In fact, 21 players hit 30 or more home runs. This is normal. Since we always project players to have typical seasons, rather than good seasons, we will always under-project the players who have career years."

Let's take a look:

Our Projection	HR	Actual Factual	HR	AP Projection	HR
Ken Griffey Jr.	41	Albert Belle	50	Frank Thomas	51
Albert Belle	40	Dante Bichette	40	Albert Belle	47
Frank Thomas	40	Jay Buhner	40	Jeff Bagwell	46
Barry Bonds	38	Frank Thomas	40	Barry Bonds	45
Juan Gonzalez	38	Mark McGwire	39	Ken Griffey Jr.	43
Matt Williams	38	Rafael Palmeiro	39	Matt Williams	43
Fred McGriff	36	Mo Vaughn	39	Fred McGriff	40
Manny Ramirez	36	Sammy Sosa	36	Gary Sheffield	40
Cecil Fielder	34	Larry Walker	36	Andres Galarraga	37
Tim Salmon	34	Gary Gaetti	35	Cecil Fielder	37
Jeff Bagwell	30	Tim Salmon	34	Juan Gonzalez	37
Jose Canseco	30	Barry Bonds	33	Mo Vaughn	37
Mike Piazza	30	Jim Edmonds	33	Bob Hamelin	35
Sammy Sosa	30	Vinny Castilla	32	Mike Piazza	35
		Eric Karros	32	Sammy Sosa	34
		Mike Piazza	32	Tim Salmon	34
		Mickey Tettleton	32	Joe Carter	33
		Cecil Fielder	31	Dave Justice	32
		Andres Galarraga	31	Jay Buhner	32
		Tino Martinez	31	Jose Canseco	32
		Manny Ramirez	31	Chili Davis	31
				Kevin Mitchell	31
				Ryan Klesko	31
				Manny Ramirez	30
				Rafael Plameiro	30
				Ruben Sierra	30

Look who else has horned in. Couldn't help it.

The corollary seems to be, if you allow yourself to meddle, human nature being what it is, you're going to over-project the players who have career years. Not just in terms of numbers of players but numbers of homers, Actual Factual seems to sit right between us. The computer and the sentimentalist have reality surrounded.

James points out that eight of the players he projected to hit 30 homers did, and five of the other six missed "simply because they were hurt... As a group, they hit more home runs per at bat (.064) than we projected for them (.061), but just missed too much playing time, between injuries and the strike, to reach 30." That leaves one unaccounted for; wouldn't you know it would be the one player for whom failing to hit 30 homers truly is atypical. "The sixth player... was the Crime Dog, who had his string of 30-homer seasons snapped by the shortened schedule. He hit 27 homers; there is very little doubt that, with another 18 games, he would have cleared the barrier."

Well, if you're going to be like *that*, Bill, I'm going to claim the Crime Dog, too, so Actual Factual, which was closer to me anyway — it really wasn't in the middle (BJ 14, AF 21, AP 26 30-homer hitters) — comes closer in my direction, and away from yours.

Also, all five players that you cry-babied over (Griffey, Canseco, Bagwell, Williams and Gonzalez) I can cry-baby over.

Can I tell you something about Gary Sheffield, while I wipe my eyes? He had an HR-per-AB rate of .075. Just because your formula only projected 25 HR for him doesn't mean I don't deserve a hankie.

Speaking of HR rates, what about that Juan Gonzalez? Wasn't he awesome? HR/AB rate of .077. Crime Dog's was only .051. So if we're going to give ourselves McGriff, why not give ourselves Gonzalez (hit .417 the last week) — what do you say?

The score now is BJ 14, AF 23, AP 26.

Had either Canseco (24 HR) or Williams (23) been hot in the final 18 games, one more of our picks would have gone over the 30-homer mark.

And why limit ourselves to our picks? The better way to ask the question is, how many hitters did we predict would hit 30 homers in a full season and how many reasonably would have in a full season? Five other hitters, besides McGriff and Gonzalez, were nestled in the 29-27 HR bracket at the end: Reggie Sanders, Edgar Martinez, Ron Gant, Tony Phillips and John Valentin. The truth is, Actual Factual would probably have passed me.

And I'm going to be just as much of a pest about similarity scores, head to head. On just homers, clearly James and I tie on, say, Salmon: can't be any argument about that. But do we get a similarity score of 1,000?

No, because we projected 162 games, and in 162 games Salmon projects to 38 HR. I'm not as close to Albert as I look (he projects to 56 HR). James is not as close to Thomas as he looks (Thomas projects to 45 HR).

Putting all that aside, a method that unabashedly seeks a player's "typical year," even if it hasn't happened yet (Manny Ramirez), successfully projects 8 players to hit 30 or more home runs. My method of simply guessing is successful on 13.

Which means, of course, that I make 13 bad guesses; 13 that at the very least are overly optimistic about home runs (and indeed are optimistic across the board). Not only are they bad guesses, but they miss reality by a much wider margin than James does: he said Bagwell would hit 30-113-14-.310, I said Bagwell would hit 46-130-6-.329.

So that's the warning. Sometimes I beat the hell out of Bill James, and sometimes he beats the hell out of me.

Overall? Well, it's like this. Since 1992, James and all the other mechanical forecasters have been at a disadvantage. Their formulas did not foresee the effects of expansion. I anticipated these effects, and then when a juiced up baseball was added to the mix, I went with that, too. So I was able to make some wild predictions and get away with quite a few of them. Stat-generating prediction formulas (my prediction formulas do generate stats in the prediction formulas, if you enter the dollar amounts in the data boxes, but it's still more accurate to say that they measure the values of the stats that are predicted)... where was I? Oh: stat-generating formulas — hell, mechanical forecasts — need stability to be successful. The more chaotic baseball is, the better my guesses will look — if I guess right about the big picture.

This will be an interesting year, a good contest between my method and the mechanical forecasts. I'm looking for a slight tilt back in the direction of the pitcher — for reasons already discussed — and there's been so much hitting in the last few years that data upon which mechanical projections depend will finally have brought the projected hitters up to speed. Bill James and I might have pretty much the same line 401 this year.

As a customer service, I'm going to try very hard to be different.

I'll be very disappointed if my Matt Williams looks like his Matt Williams.

He won't — we already know that — but it's shorthand for saying I hope to be very different in the particulars. When I reach Jeff Bagwell, I'm going to look at my bid value for him, and of course look at his five-year scan, and then I'm going to start knocking the numbers around in his data box until they look like good guesses.

If I discover something in the process that inclines me to change the bid for Bagwell, then, unfortunately, here's how it has to be done: I change the bid here, *in the prediction chapter*, and leave the first chapter as it is.

The bid in the previous chapter is the beta bid. It's the one that was on the screen when I wrote the comment. Often the comments and the bids are linked. Not only that, but if I change the bid as much as $1 for Bagwell, I have to award that $1 to someone else. It's easy to do in the software program, hard to do in the numerous files for chapter one that are already being transformed into the printed word.

As I make predictions, I'll work team by team, even though I well realize the teams I'm looking at in November won't be the teams you'll be looking at in March. I don't have to be totally strict, but it helps me stay within my overall at-bat cap. Roberto Alomar will not be a Blue Jay, and I'm not bothering to list the Blue Jays on one page in this book, but I'll be predicting what Alomar's going to do this year as if he's a Blue Jay. Unless his status has officially changed before my cut-off (December 1), you'll find "Tor" after his name; you'll be able to tell that the context is non-specific at the time of the prediction. If he signs with the Dodgers before December 1, you'll find him in NL charts with "LA" after his name, and the predictions will have been adjusted to a known destination. For perhaps the first week of December, I may yet be able to sneak big signings into the charts.

Alomar will be one of the harder players to predict, even if I do know where he's playing. He's precisely the sort of player that I want to make slightly more dashing guesses about this year. Before the bids — which have only evolved in the last few years — I felt the pull of the typical, just like James, because that's what betting is all about. The bids, hopefully, have liberated me; I should be able to depend more on hunch and intuition for people like Roberto Alomar, and whether that's good or bad is what we're going to discover.

If baseball does have a return to normalcy this season (and remember, with expansion looming again in 1998, it won't last long), maybe we'll learn if Bill James is right. Do players normally do what they normally do? Or do they normally zig and zag?

Obviously, they zig and zag to some extent; we'd sure hate this game if they didn't. But if I let the predictions themselves zig and zag a little bit more than they have in the past, just a bit, will I be more in step or out of step with Actual Factual than if I played it like James does, whose predictions are my bids?

Explanation of the Charts

The **hitters** are predicted in full, including runs scored. Under $ is what the predicted stats will be worth this year if the overall assumptions about how much hitting there's going to be are more or less correct. Under Bid is the recommended bid price beyond which you shouldn't go.

There are numerous reasons why the bid price might differ from what the hitter is predicted to earn. Reasons that the bid might be higher include —

> Position scarcity: the hitter is a giant at a weak position.
> Investment safety: the hitter is durable, reliable and good.
> Upside: the hitter could easily go way past the stats that are predicted.
> Hedging: the prediction is grim but I could be wrong.
> Good stats: players who cost $40 and earn $40 help more than players who cost $10 and earn $10, in this or any pricing system.

Reasons that the bid might be lower include —

- ➤ Performance risk: the player has fallen short of expectations before.
- ➤ Physical risk: the player gets hurt a lot.
- ➤ Downside: the prediction is so optimistic that it's the upper limit of what the player can do.
- ➤ Hedging: the prediction is optimistic but I could be wrong.
- ➤ Possible punting: much of the player's value is in SB, the easiest category to bail out of.
- ➤ No upside: there's about a $10 ceiling on what the hitter can do.
- ➤ Life's not fair (or linear): hitters with a $5 ceiling get the minimum wage.

The full season is predicted and thus the predicted stats for hitters add up to around $2,500. The hitters that are bought in the auction will earn $2,184, exactly, in the average league. (The predictions for these hitters will somewhat exceed $2,184, simply because predictions never adequately anticipate injuries.)

Bid prices go to the expected top 168 hitters who will be available this April, and the bids add up to $2,100, exactly. The reason the bid prices for hitters add up to less than what the hitters will earn is that the bid prices for pitchers add up to more than what the pitchers will earn.

The **pitchers** who are bought in the auction will earn $936, but that includes many, many negative earning. The minimum bid is $1. Most leagues spend a little more than $1,000 on pitching. The bid prices for pitchers — the expected top 108 pitchers available in April — add up to $1,020, an arbitrary figure.

Thus the bids for the expected top 276 players add up to $3,120, and you can make adjustments from there. You are encouraged to. The more time you are able to put into customizing your bid prices, the better off you will be at the auction. Separating yourself from the crowd, without departing from common sense, is the whole key to the game. (There is plenty of scribble space in the margins for changing bids, entering freezes or even tracking the auction.)

The stats for pitchers in the charts are the actual 1995 stats, *not predictions*. Under $ is what the pitchers earned in 1995, not what they are expected to earn this year. The stats are real, and the $ are really what the pitchers earned in 1995. According to my formulas.

The bids for pitchers are the predictions. They predict an order of earnings much more than earnings themselves. And they don't really predict an order of earnings so much as a simple preference, all things considered. The predicted earnings of a pitcher with a $5 bid price might be more than the predicted earnings of a pitcher with a $10 price, if I were predicting earnings, but I'm still not doing that. Maybe next year and maybe even this year in the software program (details in the PS).

That leaves us with the battle that often wins the war, the reserve draft.

When the auction is over and 276 players have been bought, less than half the players who will play in each major league have been accounted for. The idea of reserving players is to have them play for you, at the appropriate time, for nothing. Even Ultra leagues, soaking up an additional 204 players, don't get them all (they get about two-thirds), but they certainly get most of the important ones. The reserve list designations are my attempt to predict who the best unbought players will be.

There are five classifications, and some of them don't have the same meanings for pitchers as they do for hitters.

Reserve List 1 (R1):

Top prospects who should appear in the majors well before September and contribute significant stats. Pitcher R1's may contribute significantly bad stats, of course, but history shows that the best pitcher call-ups are better each year than the best hitter call-ups. These pitchers often are very hard to identify beforehand, however, whereas most of the good hitters can be seen coming from miles away.

For self-scoring purposes in next year's book, we'll say that all R1's will earn $5 next year, a figure that's much lower than the best R1's will be worth and much higher than the average R1 will be worth.

(Quick review of last year's R1's: the vast majority started out on major league teams and so were bid on. People like Clontz, Cordova and Brian L. Hunter. The best unbought R1 was Jimmy Haynes, who earned $8. The worst was Glenn Dishman, who earned ($3). In between them were seven other players who obviously didn't do much.)

Reserve List 2 (R2):

Most hitter R2's have at least gotten as far as Double-A already. They'll probably start in Triple-A and have a good chance of being called up in September. They won't contribute much this year, but they could very easily be worth the $10 or even $15 (leagues vary on this matter) that they will cost as freezes next year. The R2 hitter payoff normally is in the following season.

R2 pitchers are much more likely to have an influence this year, for better or for worse, while they are more unlikely to be players that you'll want to freeze for even $10 next year. A few veteran pitchers that I don't want to be lost in the next group are given R2 designations.

For self-scoring purposes, we'll say that the average hitter R2 will earn $2, the average pitcher R2 will lose $1. We will also predict that the five best pitcher R2's will be worth much more than the five best hitter R2's.

(Even here, the majority ended up being available in auctions last year. Players like Garret Anderson and Carlos Perez, while several who weren't available, like Dwayne Hosey, were bought anyway. The best unbought R2 was Chad Ogea $23. The two next R2's that no league in Appendix A bought were veterans Chris Hammond and Mike Morgan, worth $13 and $12. The best unbought hitting R2 was Herbert Perry $7. The worst unbought R2 was Scott Klingenbeck ($17). A total of 34 other unbought R2's earned more than Klingenbeck and less than Morgan. Quite obviously, the best pitchers were far better than the best hitters.)

Reserve List 3 (R3):

The R3 hitters are boring. They are veterans who didn't make the top 168 hitters or Triple-A players who don't even do much for Triple-A Rotisserie Leagues. John Cangelosi was the quintessential, though hardly typical, R3 in last year's book.

R3 pitchers are incendiary. They are the veterans on major league staffs who you don't dare put on your opening day rosters. Mike Moore is a good example of a pitcher who should have been and R3 but instead had a $1 bid price in last year's book. Danny Darwin was an R3 who should have been an R3. Frank Castillo is an example of an R3 who should have had a $1 bid price.

Many veteran minor league pitchers are also R3's. It means I think they have more hope than the countless more who aren't listed.

For scoring purposes, make hitters worth $1 each, pitchers ($3) each. The average pitcher on this list will undoubtedly lose more than $3.

(Best unbought R3: Honeycutt $15. Best hitter: Cangelosi $14. Worst R3: Bryan Hickerson ($17). (Darwin ($18) was bought by one league.) The average unbought R3 pitcher, of whom there were 54, earned ($1.07). The average unbought R3 hitter, numbering 45, earned $2.84.)

Reserve List 4 (R4):

Hitters and pitchers alike are so far from the major league scene that they should be thought of strictly as futures. In other words, they are promising enough to take up space on your farm team.

Leagues with extensive farm systems should examine every single R4 under a magnifying glass; most of them aren't profiled, so to get a picture of them you'll have to buy books that have many more pictures, such as John Benson's *A to Z*, or that concentrate exclusively on prospects, such as Eddie Epstein's *Scouting Notebook*, a great new offering from Stats Inc.

The rest of you should leave room on the brain pan for the next group, unless you really think you could have picked Jason Isringhausen out of the 27 NLP R4's in last year's book.

(Best R4 hitter: Yami Benitez $4. Besides Isringhuasen, the only other R4 prospect to earn anything was Mike Mordecai $3. Several R4 prospects got ahead of themselves and lost something, such as Jeff Suppan ($1) and Ugueth Urbina ($3).)

Reserve List 5 (R5)

Here, in the heart of *Baseball America*, everyone can dream. The future is not now, not this year — never, no way — but maybe... maybe if you stare *real hard*, you'll spot this year's Johnny Damon among them. Could happen.

R5's are seriously serious picks for leagues with even limited farm systems. In leagues that award low fixed salaries to farm-system players when they finally do arrive, R5's are snapped up in the first round. It's a much surer bet that Ruben Rivera will eventually produce than that Frank Castillo will have a good season.

Last year, I wrote, "The R4's as a group may get to the majors a step ahead of the R5's, but when both groups have taken the last step, the R5's will run away from the R4's. That's the theory, anyway." Now it looks like the R5's as a group are going to sprint out ahead as soon as this year.

(Damon already has; Rivera also reached the majors, as did Jose Herrera and Karim Garcia; Paul Wilson and Todd Greene — if they're not available themselves — are prime R1's; Andruw Jones moved up to the R1 of R5's; and it was a small group to begin with.)

The idea is that you work from the top and the bottom towards the center. Predicted values for reserve list hitters can be a help selecting within each group, but, of course, playing time is the key. A hitter who's predicted to earn $3 in 75 AB has received more of an endorsement as a prospect than a hitter who's predicted to earn $4 in 150 AB.

The R1's should contain the most concentrated value. R3's should have the most total value (as long as negatives are counted as zero for pitchers — precisely why they are on reserve); however, this territory is so vast it's hard to figure out where to stake your claim.

Just as the predicted stats and bids can keep changing right up to the second that Adam Summers, who turns all of this into the printed word, finally puts his foot down, I can keep adding reserve list picks as I find them. Any R1's and R5's that you see listed who don't have profiles are late additions, ones that have passed a very strict standard, indeed — because who likes to confess his ignorance? — so I suggest you track them down.

Or just name them. Last name and team they play for. Position next, if someone asks. Then the age; then even bats or throws left or right, before you say the first initial, because at that moment everyone will know that you, too, are whistling in the dark.

1996 AL hitters — alphabetical

Name	B	Tm	Age	C123SO	AB	R	HR	RBI	SB	BA	$	Bid
M Aldrete	L	Cal	35	-F---O	75	9	1	12	0	.267	2	1
M Alexander	R	Bal	25	--Dts-	250	38	2	23	12	.232	5	2
L Alicea	B	Bos	30	--D---	425	63	4	46	9	.261	9	5
R Alomar	B	Tor	28	--D---	550	74	15	69	25	.296	28	32
S Alomar	R	Cle	30	C-----	350	51	12	51	0	.286	12	10
R Amaral	R	Sea	34	------O	175	31	0	12	14	.274	7	2
R Amaro	B	Cle	31	------O	50	4	1	5	0	.220	0	R3
B Anderson	L	Bal	32	------O	600	116	17	69	28	.258	23	22
G Anderson	L	Cal	24	------O	525	77	17	90	3	.299	23	25
G Arias	R	Cal	24	---T--	0	0	0	0	0	.000	0	R2
C Baerga	B	Cle	27	--D---	600	104	15	94	8	.305	27	29
H Baines	L	Bal	37	------	425	65	21	72	0	.294	20	17
B Barberie	B	Bal	28	--Dt--	225	35	1	23	2	.258	3	1
K Bartee	B	Min	24	------O	0	0	0	0	0	.000	0	R4

Name	B	Tm	Age	C123SO	AB	R	HR	RBI	SB	BA	$	Bid
K Bass	B	Bal	37	-----O	150	16	2	16	5	.260	4	R3
H Battle	R	Tor	24	---T--	100	14	1	6	1	.230	0	R3
D Bautista	R	Det	24	-----O	225	23	6	18	3	.204	0	2
R Becker	B	Min	24	-----O	275	31	3	23	7	.258	5	2
A Belle	R	Cle	29	-----O	575	125	51	131	3	.304	43	45
G Berroa	R	Oak	31	-----O	550	82	19	87	3	.273	19	18
M Blowers	R	Sea	31	-f-T-o	425	55	19	84	0	.252	14	12
W Boggs	L	NY	38	-f-T--	500	82	5	68	1	.330	20	15
B Bonilla	B	Bal	33	---T-O	550	111	31	111	1	.305	32	35
M Bordick	R	Oak	30	-----S-	500	50	5	42	7	.258	7	4
D Boston	L	Tor	24	-F----	100	12	3	11	2	.250	3	R2
D Brady	B	Chi	26	--D---	125	21	1	18	6	.248	4	R2
D Bragg	L	Sea	26	-----O	0	0	0	0	0	.000	0	R3
S Brosius	R	Oak	29	-FdTsO	450	76	14	43	2	.251	8	5
J Brown	R	Bal	29	-----O	25	4	0	2	3	.200	1	R3
J Buhner	R	Sea	31	-----O	550	95	35	122	1	.251	25	27
J Burnitz	L	Cle	27	-----O	50	28	2	7	1	.260	2	R2
M Cameron	R	Chi	23	-----O	125	11	1	16	5	.208	1	R3
J Canseco	R	Bos	31	-----o	450	67	25	84	1	.278	21	23
P Carey	L	Bal	28	-F----	0	0	0	0	0	.000	0	R3
J Carter	R	Tor	36	-f---O	575	72	25	88	9	.257	21	24
D Cedeno	B	Tor	27	--DtS-	175	19	2	15	0	.234	0	R3
W Chamberla	R	Oth	30	-----O	0	0	0	0	0	.000	0	R3
J Cirillo	R	Mil	26	-fDTs-	500	80	7	51	3	.266	9	5
J Clark	R	Min	32	-f---O	175	26	4	19	1	.274	4	2
T Clark	B	Det	24	-F----	275	26	11	45	1	.247	8	R1
W Clark	L	Tex	32	-F----	500	88	13	95	1	.282	18	18
A Cole	L	Min	30	-----O	0	0	0	0	0	.000	0	R3
M Coleman	R	Bos	20	-----O	0	0	0	0	0	.000	0	R4
V Coleman	B	Sea	34	-----O	375	50	0	15	31	.259	13	14
B Cookson	R	Bos	26	-----O	75	6	1	9	0	.267	1	R3
R Coomer	R	Min	29	-F-t-o	150	22	5	28	0	.273	5	R2
J Cora	B	Sea	31	--D-s-	400	52	0	36	13	.268	9	6
M Cordova	R	Min	26	-----O	550	83	25	89	14	.269	25	26
S Cox	L	Oak	21	-F----	0	0	0	0	0	.000	0	R5
F Cruz	R	Oak	24	----S-	50	0	0	10	2	.200	1	0
I Cruz	L	Det	28	-F----	50	4	2	5	0	.220	1	R3
C Curtis	R	Det	27	-----O	625	105	19	65	31	.258	25	24
M Cuyler	B	Det	27	-----O	75	12	0	4	1	.213	0	0
J Damon	L	KC	22	-----O	575	101	11	75	25	.294	27	25
C Davis	B	Cal	36	------	550	101	24	104	0	.291	25	23
R Davis	R	NY	26	-f-T--	450	64	18	68	0	.242	11	8
C Delgado	L	Tor	24	-f---O	450	57	19	64	0	.253	12	15
A Diaz	B	Sea	27	-----O	350	56	2	35	22	.254	12	4
E Diaz	R	Tex	21	--D---	0	0	0	0	0	.000	0	R4
E Diaz	R	Cle	23	C-----	0	0	0	0	0	.000	0	R4
G Disarcina	R	Cal	28	----S-	450	74	5	51	6	.284	12	9
R Durham	B	Chi	24	--D---	550	81	9	67	24	.267	20	16
D Easley	R	Cal	26	--D-S-	125	12	2	12	3	.224	1	R3
J Edmonds	L	Cal	26	-----O	575	110	30	108	4	.278	27	28
D Erstad	L	Cal	22	-----O	150	4	4	15	1	.293	5	R1
A Espinoza	R	Cle	34	-fDTS-	125	13	2	14	0	.256	2	1
J Fabregas	L	Cal	26	C-----	250	26	2	24	0	.256	2	1
R Faneyte	R	Oak	27	-----O	0	0	0	0	0	.000	0	R3
S Fasano	R	KC	24	Cf----	150	12	3	12	0	.240	1	R3
K Felder	R	Mil	25	-----O	50	5	1	5	0	.240	1	R2

Name	B	Tm	Age	C123SO	AB	R	HR	RBI	SB	BA	$	Bid
F Fermin	R	Oth	32	--D-S-	0	0	0	0	0	.000	0	R3
T Fernandez	B	NY	34	--d-S-	400	59	3	46	5	.245	5	2
C Fielder	R	Det	32	-F----	550	76	30	91	0	.253	19	20
J Flaherty	R	Det	28	C-----	400	44	7	43	0	.245	4	1
A Fox	L	NY	25	---TS-	100	11	2	9	3	.250	2	R2
M Franklin	B	Det	24	------O	100	6	4	9	0	.250	2	R2
L Frazier	B	Tex	31	--d--O	150	28	0	12	16	.213	5	1
J Frye	R	Tex	29	--D---	425	51	3	39	4	.278	8	2
T Fryman	R	Det	27	---T--	575	85	22	88	3	.264	19	21
G Gaetti	R	KC	37	-f-T--	550	78	29	100	2	.255	21	18
G Gagne	R	KC	34	----S-	500	67	6	56	5	.252	8	5
N Garcpprra	R	Bos	22	----S-	0	0	0	0	0	.000	0	R2
B Gates	B	Oak	26	-fD---	575	65	7	66	6	.273	13	12
J Giambi	L	Oak	25	-F-T--	250	37	5	31	1	.264	5	2
B Gil	R	Tex	23	----S-	475	41	12	55	3	.223	5	3
B Giles	L	Cle	25	------O	50	5	2	6	0	.280	2	R2
J Girardi	R	NY	31	C-----	425	54	4	47	0	.252	4	3
C Gomez	R	Det	25	--D-S-	525	59	9	59	4	.248	8	6
L Gomez	R	Bal	29	-f-T--	100	11	3	9	0	.230	1	R3
A Gonzalez	R	Tor	23	---tS-	475	66	12	54	5	.242	8	9
J Gonzalez	R	Tex	26	------o	525	79	40	111	1	.282	31	28
C Goodwin	L	Bal	23	------O	475	65	2	37	41	.255	19	13
T Goodwin	L	KC	27	------O	475	70	2	27	51	.274	25	19
C Grebeck	R	Chi	31	--dTS-	150	16	1	19	0	.253	2	1
S Green	L	Tor	23	------O	525	74	26	84	6	.307	29	26
T Greene	R	Cal	25	C-----	100	5	6	19	0	.260	4	R1
M Greenwell	L	Bos	32	------O	500	71	13	75	5	.290	19	18
R Greer	L	Tex	27	-f---O	425	57	10	59	1	.264	10	7
B Grieve	L	Oak	20	------O	0	0	0	0	0	.000	0	R4
K Griffey	L	Sea	26	------O	575	115	39	120	7	.329	43	46
J Grotewald	L	KC	30	-f-----	0	0	0	0	0	.000	0	R3
G Guevara	B	Sea	23	--d-S-	0	0	0	0	0	.000	0	R4
O Guillen	L	Chi	32	----S-	525	63	1	51	7	.251	6	5
C Hale	L	Min	31	-fdt--	75	6	0	12	0	.267	1	R3
B Hamelin	L	KC	28	-f----	350	31	17	52	0	.226	7	2
D Hamilton	L	Mil	31	------O	450	61	5	49	12	.271	12	5
J Hammonds	R	Bal	25	------O	425	39	7	51	4	.278	11	8
T Hansen	R	Sea	29	------O	0	0	0	0	0	.000	0	R3
S Hare	L	Oth	29	-f---O	0	0	0	0	0	.000	0	R3
B Haselman	R	Bos	30	Cf-t--	175	25	3	24	0	.257	3	1
S Hatteberg	L	Bos	26	C-----	25	2	0	3	0	.240	0	R3
R Henderson	R	Oak	37	------O	375	57	6	44	25	.288	20	19
J Herrera	L	Oak	23	------O	175	17	2	8	3	.251	2	R2
B Higginson	L	Det	25	------O	450	65	16	56	5	.233	9	8
D Hocking	L	Min	26	----S-	75	12	1	9	2	.227	1	R3
C Hoiles	R	Bal	31	C-----	400	60	22	66	2	.253	15	14
D Hollins	B	Bos	30	-F----	50	11	2	8	0	.240	1	R2
D Hosey	B	Bos	29	------O	550	75	11	52	17	.289	20	12
D Howard	B	KC	29	-fD-SO	200	18	0	14	4	.240	1	R3
R Hudler	R	Cal	32	-fD--O	125	14	1	14	5	.240	3	1
D Hulse	L	Mil	28	------O	300	40	1	35	14	.253	8	3
T Hunter	R	Min	20	------O	0	0	0	0	0	.000	0	R4
J Hurst	R	Chi	24	------O	0	0	0	0	0	.000	0	R4
J Huson	L	Bal	31	--DTs-	175	26	1	20	6	.257	4	1
R Ibanez	R	Sea	24	C-----	0	0	0	0	0	.000	0	R4
D Jackson	R	Cle	22	----S-	0	0	0	0	0	.000	0	R4

Name	B	Tm	Age	C123SO	AB	R	HR	RBI	SB	BA	$	Bid
J Jaha	R	Mil	30	-F----	500	85	24	88	0	.294	23	19
C James	R	Bos	33	------o	125	12	4	13	1	.264	3	R3
D James	L	NY	33	-f---O	150	15	1	18	2	.287	4	1
S Javier	B	Oak	32	---t-O	525	89	5	60	36	.269	23	18
R Jefferson	B	Bos	27	-f---O	150	24	5	30	0	.273	6	1
D Jeter	R	NY	22	-----S-	150	25	1	16	7	.280	6	R1
L Johnson	L	Chi	32	------O	625	97	5	54	38	.291	28	25
W Joyner	L	KC	34	-F----	525	73	13	84	1	.295	19	18
R Karkovice	R	Chi	32	C-----	425	57	17	67	2	.216	7	2
P Kelly	R	NY	28	--D---	475	55	5	50	7	.251	7	3
W Kirby	L	Cle	32	------O	150	22	1	11	7	.240	3	1
D Klassen	R	Mil	21	----S-	0	0	0	0	0	.000	0	R4
C Knoblauch	R	Min	27	--D-s-	575	110	8	64	45	.325	39	35
R Knorr	R	Tor	27	C-----	375	51	7	46	1	.216	1	1
J Ladd	R	Tor	25	C-----	0	0	0	0	0	.000	0	R2
C Latham	R	Min	23	------O	100	8	2	7	3	.240	2	R2
M Lavallier	L	Chi	35	C-----	175	12	1	33	0	.257	3	R3
M Lawton	L	Min	24	------O	425	72	8	45	15	.266	14	11
S Leius	R	Min	30	---Ts-	300	40	5	36	0	.247	4	1
J Levis	L	Cle	28	C-----	25	1	0	4	0	.280	1	R3
J Leyritz	R	NY	32	CF----	275	38	7	38	1	.284	9	5
P Listach	B	Mil	28	--DtSo	225	22	1	16	14	.236	5	2
K Lockhart	L	KC	31	--Dt--	350	51	4	42	9	.280	11	4
K Lofton	L	Cle	29	------O	600	125	12	60	71	.342	54	47
M Lopez	R	KC	21	---tS-	0	0	0	0	0	.000	0	R4
M Loretta	R	Mil	24	--d-S-	125	32	1	7	2	.264	2	R2
T Lowery	R	Tex	25	------O	0	0	0	0	0	.000	0	R3
S Lydy	R	Oak	27	------O	0	0	0	0	0	.000	0	R3
B Lyons	R	Chi	36	Cf----	50	5	1	9	0	.240	1	0
M Macfarlan	R	Bos	32	C-----	400	46	15	55	0	.230	7	5
S Mack	R	Oth	34	------O	0	0	0	0	0	.000	0	R4
R Mahay	L	Bos	25	------O	0	0	0	0	0	.000	0	0
J Malave	R	Bos	25	------O	125	14	5	18	1	.264	4	R1
J Manto	R	Bal	31	-f-T--	50	5	2	8	0	.240	1	R3
N Martin	B	Chi	29	--Dtso	150	15	1	15	4	.233	2	R3
A Martinez	L	Tor	23	C-----	225	14	2	29	0	.240	2	R3
D Martinez	L	Chi	31	-F---O	325	49	4	36	5	.265	7	2
E Martinez	R	Sea	33	-f-t--	525	118	24	110	0	.333	33	29
T Martinez	L	Sea	28	-F----	550	94	27	96	0	.304	28	29
J Marzano	R	Tex	33	C-----	50	8	1	10	0	.260	1	R3
D Masteller	L	Min	28	-F---O	0	0	0	0	0	.000	0	R3
M Matheny	B	Mil	25	C-----	175	13	3	22	0	.234	2	R3
D Mattingly	L	Oth	35	-F----	0	0	0	0	0	.000	0	0
B Mayne	L	KC	28	C-----	375	28	2	32	0	.264	4	1
W McGee	B	Oth	37	------O	0	0	0	0	0	.000	0	R3
R McGuire	L	Bos	24	-F----	0	0	0	0	0	.000	0	R2
M McGwire	R	Oak	32	-F----	525	118	53	133	0	.265	35	28
M McLemore	B	Tex	31	--D--O	425	65	2	35	17	.256	10	6
P Meares	R	Min	27	----So	475	67	11	59	9	.261	13	10
H Mercedes	R	KC	26	C-----	50	8	1	10	0	.220	1	0
M Merullo	L	Min	30	Cf----	175	17	1	24	0	.257	2	1
M Mieske	R	Mil	28	------O	275	42	14	55	1	.244	10	3
P Molitor	R	Min	39	-------	550	67	18	69	16	.293	25	21
J Mosquera	R	Tor	24	C-----	0	0	0	0	0	.000	0	R4
L Mouton	R	Chi	28	------O	450	56	13	68	3	.284	16	11
P Munoz	R	Min	27	-f---O	450	45	16	54	5	.262	13	14

Name	B	Tm	Age	C123SO	AB	R	HR	RBI	SB	BA	$	Bid
E Murray	B	Cle	40	-F----	500	74	21	92	1	.284	21	21
G Myers	L	Cal	30	C-----	275	34	7	38	0	.269	7	2
R Myers	L	KC	23	-----O	75	8	0	6	6	.253	3	R2
T Naehring	R	Bos	29	---T--	475	62	7	55	0	.295	13	9
P Nevin	R	Det	25	---t-O	200	18	3	24	0	.215	0	2
W Newson	L	Sea	31	-----O	0	0	0	0	0	.000	0	R3
D Nilsson	L	Mil	26	cf---O	500	74	21	85	1	.272	19	18
O Nixon	B	Tex	37	-----O	625	92	0	47	52	.288	30	24
T Nixon	L	Bos	22	-----O	0	0	0	0	0	.000	0	R4
L Norman	R	KC	27	-----O	50	7	0	5	0	.220	0	0
S Nunez	R	KC	21	--D---	0	0	0	0	0	.000	0	R4
J Nunnally	L	KC	24	-----O	375	61	13	49	8	.237	10	7
T O'Leary	L	Bos	26	-----O	425	63	14	59	4	.287	16	13
P O'Neill	L	NY	33	-----O	550	95	24	95	1	.304	27	29
S Obando	R	Bal	26	-----O	50	4	2	5	0	.260	1	R3
J Olerud	L	Tor	27	-F----	525	76	9	59	1	.293	15	16
J Oliver	R	Mil	30	Cf----	350	44	6	49	1	.271	8	3
L Ortiz	R	Tex	26	---T--	50	4	2	8	0	.220	1	R3
S Owen	B	Cal	35	--dTS-	0	0	0	0	0	.000	0	R3
M Pagliarul	L	Tex	36	-f-T--	75	8	0	8	0	.240	0	0
O Palmeiro	L	Cal	27	-----O	50	7	0	2	1	.260	1	R3
R Palmeiro	L	Bal	31	-F----	600	93	39	112	2	.300	35	38
D Palmer	R	Tex	27	---T--	500	118	31	89	0	.280	24	24
C Paquette	R	Oak	27	-f-TsO	225	33	9	38	3	.213	5	1
R Pemberton	R	Det	26	-----O	300	30	3	41	2	.303	10	R2
T Pena	R	Cle	39	C-----	225	21	3	23	0	.244	2	1
S Penn	B	Det	26	--D---	200	21	0	8	9	.225	1	R3
E Perez	R	Cal	26	---T--	75	10	2	12	1	.267	3	R2
R Perez	R	Tor	27	-----O	125	11	2	11	0	.272	2	1
T Perez	B	Tor	22	--dtS-	100	12	1	8	0	.230	0	R3
H Perry	R	Cle	26	-F-t--	225	31	4	31	1	.293	7	6
T Phillips	B	Cal	37	---T-O	575	120	18	57	14	.268	19	19
G Pirkl	R	Sea	25	-F----	75	4	2	5	0	.253	1	R3
A Pozo	R	Sea	22	--D---	100	14	2	12	3	.260	3	R2
K Puckett	R	Min	35	--dtsO	575	86	23	105	1	.310	29	33
T Raines	B	Chi	36	-----O	525	80	9	61	14	.276	17	16
M Ramirez	R	Cle	24	-----O	550	101	37	123	5	.311	38	36
J Randa	R	KC	26	--dT--	75	6	2	8	0	.227	1	R3
L Raven	R	Cal	27	-----O	0	0	0	0	0	.000	0	R2
J Reboulet	R	Min	32	cfdTS-	200	36	3	21	0	.265	3	1
D Relaford	B	Sea	22	----S-	0	0	0	0	0	.000	0	R4
T Rhodes	L	Oth	27	-----O	0	0	0	0	0	.000	0	0
B Ripken	R	Cle	31	--Dt--	50	11	2	8	0	.280	2	R3
C Ripken	R	Bal	35	----S-	600	86	18	91	0	.268	17	20
R Rivera	R	NY	22	-----O	200	20	8	21	5	.240	6	R1
L Roberts	B	Tor	25	-----O	0	0	0	0	0	.000	0	R4
A Rodriguez	R	Sea	20	----S-	525	71	20	69	10	.257	17	18
C Rodriguez	B	Bos	28	--Dts-	50	8	0	6	0	.240	0	R3
I Rodriguez	R	Tex	24	C-----	500	56	12	68	0	.282	14	16
S Rodriguez	R	Det	25	--D-s-	125	16	0	7	5	.208	0	0
T Salmon	R	Cal	27	-----O	550	111	37	112	5	.289	33	36
J Samuel	R	KC	35	-Fd--o	200	27	9	33	2	.245	6	1
K Seitzer	R	Mil	34	-F-T--	525	58	8	77	2	.295	17	11
R Sexson	R	Cle	21	-F----	0	0	0	0	0	.000	0	R5
T Shumpert	R	Oth	29	--Dts-	0	0	0	0	0	.000	0	R3
R Sierra	B	NY	30	-----O	550	80	18	94	1	.256	16	15

Predictions—AL alpha

Name	B	Tm	Age	C123SO	AB	R	HR	RBI	SB	BA	$	Bid
D Singleton	L	Mil	23	-----O	50	3	0	2	3	.200	0	R3
M Smith	R	Bal	26	-----O	250	25	6	35	1	.236	4	1
M Smith	L	KC	20	-F----	0	0	0	0	0	.000	0	R4
C Snopek	R	Chi	25	---Ts-	225	31	4	26	1	.276	5	2
J Snow	R	Cal	28	-F----	575	86	23	90	1	.277	21	19
L Sojo	R	Sea	30	--D-So	225	30	1	24	0	.271	3	2
P Sorrento	L	Cle	30	-F----	375	60	28	96	1	.267	22	17
S Spiezio	R	Oak	23	---T--	125	11	4	11	1	.248	2	R2
E Sprague	R	Tor	28	-f-T--	525	77	17	69	0	.242	9	7
S Stahoviak	L	Min	26	-F-T--	250	26	2	21	3	.252	3	R3
M Stairs	L	Oak	27	-----O	175	15	4	25	0	.274	5	2
M Stanley	R	NY	33	C-----	425	64	17	79	0	.264	15	17
T Steinbach	R	Oak	34	Cf----	425	42	12	63	0	.273	12	12
T Steverson	R	Det	24	-----O	100	26	2	14	4	.240	3	R3
S Stewart	R	Tor	22	-----O	200	12	0	12	9	.265	5	R1
D Strange	B	Sea	32	--dT-o	125	15	1	16	0	.264	2	1
D Strawberr	L	NY	34	-----o	250	40	10	39	0	.244	6	7
F Stubbs	L	Det	36	-F---O	100	11	1	16	0	.250	2	R3
C Stynes	R	KC	23	--D---	100	19	1	11	3	.250	2	R2
B Surhoff	L	Mil	31	CF---O	525	86	9	82	5	.307	21	18
L Sutton	L	KC	25	-F----	100	8	3	10	0	.250	2	R2
M Sweeney	R	KC	22	C-----	100	8	2	9	0	.260	2	R2
D Tartabull	R	Oak	33	-----O	350	43	11	45	1	.243	7	8
J Tatum	R	Bos	28	c----O	25	2	1	3	0	.240	1	R3
M Tettleton	B	Tex	35	cf---O	500	88	31	85	0	.242	17	14
F Thomas	R	Chi	28	-F----	550	134	48	127	3	.325	45	47
J Thome	L	Cle	25	---T--	525	106	29	101	5	.278	26	29
R Tingley	B	Det	36	Cf----	100	11	2	14	0	.220	1	0
L Tinsley	B	Bos	27	-----O	325	53	1	32	11	.268	8	4
A Tomberlin	L	Oak	29	------	0	0	0	0	0	.000	0	R3
A Trammell	R	Det	38	-----S-	200	25	2	20	1	.255	2	1
C Tremie	R	Chi	26	C-----	25	1	0	2	0	.120	0	0
M Tucker	L	KC	25	-----O	225	28	8	23	2	.236	4	5
B Turang	R	Sea	29	--d--O	0	0	0	0	0	.000	0	R3
C Turner	R	Cal	27	C-----	25	0	0	2	0	.160	0	R3
T Unroe	R	Mil	25	-F----	0	0	0	0	0	.000	0	R3
J Valentin	R	Bos	26	-----S-	550	107	24	86	10	.289	27	28
J Valentin	R	Min	20	C-----	0	0	0	0	0	.000	0	R5
J Valentin	B	Mil	26	---tS-	500	91	17	69	19	.248	18	11
D Valle	R	Tex	35	Cf----	100	9	1	6	0	.240	0	0
G Vaughn	R	Mil	30	-------	300	49	11	43	4	.220	6	1
M Vaughn	L	Bos	28	-F----	575	96	37	118	5	.287	33	36
R Velarde	R	Cal	33	--DTSO	500	81	11	62	4	.276	14	7
R Ventura	L	Chi	28	-F-T--	550	84	27	100	0	.287	25	26
F Vina	L	Mil	26	--Dts-	150	23	0	14	3	.240	1	R3
J Vitiello	R	KC	26	-f----	150	15	7	33	1	.273	7	2
O Vizquel	B	Cle	29	-----S-	525	77	2	47	21	.259	13	11
J Voigt	R	Tex	30	-f---O	75	10	2	9	0	.240	1	R3
M Walbeck	B	Min	26	C-----	400	40	3	45	1	.263	6	2
T Walker	L	Min	23	--D---	175	25	8	25	4	.263	7	R1
T Ward	B	Mil	31	-----O	150	21	3	21	5	.240	4	R3
C Weinke	L	Tor	23	-F----	0	0	0	0	0	.000	0	R4
L Whitaker	L	Det	39	--D---	325	42	13	52	0	.274	11	6
D White	R	Det	26	-F---o	50	3	1	3	0	.200	0	0
C Widger	R	Sea	25	C----o	150	11	2	17	1	.233	1	1
B Williams	B	NY	27	-----O	575	94	22	93	10	.299	29	30

Name	B	Tm	Age	C123SO	AB	R	HR	RBI	SB	BA	$	Bid
G Williams	B	Oak	26	C-----	225	36	6	39	0	.271	7	3
G Williams	R	NY	29	-----O	175	31	5	26	7	.234	6	2
H Williams	L	Chi	25	-F----	0	0	0	0	0	.000	0	R4
D Wilson	R	Sea	27	C-----	425	40	5	49	0	.261	6	4
E Wilson	B	Cle	21	----S-	0	0	0	0	0	.000	0	R4
D Winfield	R	Cle	44	------	0	0	0	0	0	.000	0	0
C Worthingt	R	Tex	31	---T--	75	4	2	6	0	.213	0	R3
E Young	R	Oak	27	-----O	125	22	3	13	0	.216	0	R3
G Zaun	B	Bal	25	C-----	125	15	3	16	1	.256	3	1
Totals					77700	2269		1255		.269	2584	
					11277	10696						2100

1996 AL pitchers — alphabetical

The only predictions are the recommended bid limits for this year; the stats are the 1995 major league stats for each pitcher and the $ values are what the stats were worth in 1995.

Name	T	Tm	Age	IP	SO	W	Sv	ERA	Ratio	$	Bid
J Abbott	L	Cal	28	197	86	11	0	3.70	12.47	20	10
M Acre	R	Oak	27	52	47	1	0	5.71	13.85	-4	2
R Aguilera	R	Bos	34	55	52	3	32	2.60	9.60	39	35
P Ahearne	R	Det	22	10	4	0	0	11.70	22.50	-7	0
J Alberro	R	Tex	26	20	10	0	0	7.40	16.55	-6	0
W Alvarez	L	Chi	26	175	118	8	0	4.32	13.58	6	14
B Anderson	R	Cal	25	99	45	6	0	5.87	12.64	-1	R2
L Andujar	R	Chi	23	30	9	2	0	3.26	11.87	5	3
K Appier	R	KC	28	201	185	15	0	3.89	10.86	31	25
P Assenmach	L	Cle	35	38	40	6	0	2.82	10.33	12	1
B Ayala	R	Sea	26	71	77	6	19	4.44	13.05	21	5
S Baker	L	Oak	25	3	3	0	0	9.83	24.54	-2	0
J Baldwin	R	Chi	25	14	10	0	0	12.89	25.16	-13	R2
S Bankhead	R	NY	32	39	20	1	0	6.00	13.85	-3	0
B Bark	L	Bos	27	2	0	0	0	0.00	11.57	1	R2
T Belcher	R	Sea	34	179	96	10	0	4.52	13.85	5	3
S Belinda	R	Bos	29	69	57	8	10	3.10	10.20	26	4
A Benes	R	Sea	28	63	45	7	0	5.86	15.00	-2	14
A Benitez	R	Bal	23	47	56	1	2	5.66	13.97	-2	R1
J Bere	R	Chi	25	137	110	8	0	7.19	16.80	-26	10
S Bergman	R	Det	26	135	86	7	0	5.12	15.69	-8	R3
M Bertotti	L	Chi	26	14	15	1	0	12.56	21.35	-9	0
M Bielecki	R	Cal	36	75	45	4	0	5.97	13.26	-3	R3
B Black	L	Cle	39	47	34	4	0	6.85	15.02	-5	R3
B Blomdahl	R	Det	25	24	15	0	1	7.77	18.12	-8	0
B Boehringe	R	NY	27	17	10	0	0	13.76	23.43	-15	R3
J Boever	R	Det	35	98	71	5	3	6.39	15.69	-11	R3
R Bolton	R	Chi	27	22	10	0	0	8.18	19.23	-9	R3
R Bones	R	Mil	27	200	77	10	0	4.63	13.52	5	2
J Borowski	R	Bal	24	7	3	0	0	1.23	11.04	2	R9
C Bosio	R	Sea	33	170	85	10	0	4.92	14.82	-3	2
S Boskie	R	Cal	29	111	51	7	0	5.64	12.25	2	1
M Brandenbu	R	Tex	25	27	21	0	0	5.93	14.16	-3	0
B Brewer	L	KC	28	45	31	2	0	5.56	14.69	-3	R2
J Briscoe	R	Oak	28	18	19	0	0	8.35	22.58	-10	0
K Brown	R	Bal	31	172	117	10	0	3.60	10.60	28	19
T Browning	R	KC	36	10	3	0	0	8.10	16.20	-3	R3
M Bunch	R	KC	24	40	19	1	0	5.63	12.60	-1	R9

Name	T	Tm	Age	IP	SO	W	Sv	ERA	Ratio	$	Bid
T Burrows	L	Tex	27	44	22	2	1	6.45	15.92	-6	0
M Butcher	R	Cal	31	51	29	6	0	4.73	14.02	4	R3
R Carmona	R	Sea	23	47	28	2	1	5.66	16.80	-6	R2
T Castillo	L	Tor	33	72	38	1	13	3.22	10.90	20	3
N Charlton	L	Sea	33	47	58	2	14	1.51	7.36	29	33
M Christoph	R	Det	32	61	34	4	1	3.82	12.47	8	R2
M Clark	R	Cle	28	124	68	9	0	5.27	13.35	3	7
T Clark	R	Bal	35	39	18	2	1	3.46	12.69	5	R3
R Clemens	R	Bos	33	140	132	10	0	4.18	12.92	12	23
B Colon	R	Cle	20	0	0	0	0	0.00	0.00	0	R5
D Cone	R	NY	33	229	191	18	0	3.57	11.11	38	27
J Converse	R	KC	24	23	14	1	1	6.56	16.97	-4	0
D Cook	L	Tex	33	57	53	0	2	4.53	13.89	0	0
R Cormier	L	Bos	29	115	69	7	0	4.07	12.68	10	1
B Cornett	R	Tor	27	5	4	0	0	9.01	21.60	-3	0
J Corsi	R	Oak	34	45	26	2	2	2.20	11.40	11	R3
D Cox	R	Tor	36	45	38	1	0	7.40	18.00	-13	R3
T Crabtree	L	Tor	26	32	21	0	0	3.09	12.09	3	R2
J Cummings	L	Sea	27	5	4	0	0	11.82	25.31	-4	0
J D'Amico	R	Mil	20	0	0	0	0	0.00	0.00	0	R4
R Darling	R	Oak	35	104	69	4	0	6.23	14.71	-11	0
D Darwin	R	Tex	40	99	58	3	0	7.45	14.73	-17	0
T Davis	L	Sea	25	24	19	2	0	6.38	18.00	-4	R2
S Davison	R	Sea	25	4	3	0	0	6.24	16.61	-1	0
J Dedrick	R	Bal	27	7	3	0	0	2.35	16.43	0	R3
J DeSilva	R	Bal	28	8	1	1	0	7.28	15.58	-1	R3
J Dettmer	R	Tex	26	0	0	0	0	27.03	54.00	-1	0
R Dibble	R	Mil	32	26	26	1	1	7.18	21.19	-9	R3
J Doherty	R	Det	29	113	46	5	6	5.10	13.30	5	2
M Drews	R	NY	21	0	0	0	0	0.00	0.00	0	R5
D Eckersley	R	Oak	41	50	40	4	29	4.83	11.44	28	22
C Eldred	R	Mil	28	23	18	1	0	3.42	12.93	3	6
A Embree	L	Cle	26	24	23	3	1	5.11	14.23	2	5
S Erickson	R	Bal	28	196	106	13	0	4.81	12.83	10	8
V Eshelman	L	Bos	27	81	41	6	0	4.85	13.44	3	R1
H Fajardo	R	Tex	25	15	9	0	0	7.80	14.40	-4	R3
J Farrell	R	Cle	34	4	4	0	0	3.86	13.50	0	R3
A Fernandez	R	Chi	26	203	159	12	0	3.80	11.71	25	24
S Fernandez	L	Bal	33	28	31	0	0	7.39	17.03	-8	0
M Fetters	R	Mil	31	34	33	0	22	3.38	15.58	16	12
C Finley	L	Cal	33	203	195	15	0	4.21	12.63	19	17
D Fleming	L	KC	26	80	40	1	0	5.96	15.41	-11	R3
T Fortugno	L	Chi	33	38	24	1	0	5.59	11.40	0	R3
B Givens	L	Mil	30	107	73	5	0	4.95	14.25	-2	R1
G Gohr	R	Det	28	10	12	1	0	0.87	10.45	4	2
T Gordon	R	KC	27	189	119	12	0	4.43	13.95	7	6
J Granger	L	KC	24	0	0	0	0	0.00	0.00	0	R2
J Grimsley	R	Cle	28	34	25	0	1	6.09	18.26	-8	0
K Gross	R	Tex	35	183	106	9	0	5.54	14.16	-7	4
E Guardado	L	Min	25	91	71	4	2	5.12	14.19	-1	R3
M Gubicza	R	KC	33	213	81	12	0	3.75	11.98	24	5
E Gunderson	L	Bos	30	12	9	2	0	5.11	16.05	0	R3
J Guzman	R	Tor	29	135	94	4	0	6.32	14.90	-16	4
J Habyan	R	Cal	32	32	25	1	0	4.13	13.22	1	R3
D Hall	R	Tor	31	16	11	0	3	4.41	16.53	1	R1
C Haney	L	KC	27	81	31	3	0	3.65	12.28	8	R3

Name	T	Tm	Age	IP	SO	W	Sv	ERA	Ratio	$	Bid
E Hanson	R	Bos	31	186	139	15	0	4.24	11.86	22	14
M Harkey	R	Cal	29	127	56	8	0	5.44	14.27	-3	R3
L Hawkins	R	Min	23	27	9	2	0	8.67	17.00	-8	1
J Haynes	R	Bal	23	24	22	2	0	2.25	8.62	8	7
R Helling	R	Tex	25	12	5	0	0	6.57	18.24	-4	R3
D Henry	R	Det	34	8	9	1	5	6.24	21.81	2	R3
P Hentgen	R	Tor	27	200	135	10	0	5.11	14.62	-5	13
W Heredia	R	Tex	24	12	6	0	0	3.75	18.00	-2	R2
R Hernandez	R	Chi	31	59	84	3	32	3.92	13.72	28	28
O Hershiser	R	Cle	37	167	111	16	0	3.87	10.86	30	20
G Hibbard	L	Sea	31	0	0	0	0	0.00	0.00	0	R3
K Hill	R	Cle	30	74	48	4	0	3.98	13.14	5	12
S Hitchcock	L	NY	25	168	121	11	0	4.71	11.92	14	5
R Honeycutt	L	NY	42	45	21	5	2	2.96	9.66	15	R3
C Howard	L	Tex	30	4	2	0	0	0.00	9.00	1	R3
S Howe	L	NY	38	49	28	6	2	4.96	15.24	3	R3
J Hudson	R	Bos	25	46	29	0	1	4.11	14.87	-1	R2
R Huisman	R	KC	27	9	12	0	0	7.45	13.96	-2	R3
E Hurtado	R	Tor	25	77	33	5	0	5.45	14.02	-2	R2
M Ignasiak	R	Mil	30	39	26	4	0	5.90	16.79	-4	0
J Jacome	L	KC	25	84	39	4	0	5.36	13.07	-1	R2
M James	R	Cal	28	55	36	3	1	3.88	12.13	7	R3
D Johns	L	Oak	28	54	25	5	0	4.61	11.52	7	R2
R Johnson	L	Sea	32	214	294	18	0	2.48	9.40	58	37
D Jones	R	Bal	38	46	42	0	22	5.01	13.69	15	11
R Jordan	L	Tor	26	15	10	1	1	6.60	18.60	-3	0
S Kamieniec	R	NY	32	89	43	7	0	4.02	13.25	8	3
M Karchner	R	Chi	29	32	24	4	0	1.69	12.65	9	2
S Karl	L	Mil	24	124	59	6	0	4.14	13.86	5	2
S Karsay	R	Oak	24	0	0	0	0	0.00	0.00	0	R2
J Key	L	NY	35	30	14	1	0	5.64	13.65	-2	14
B Keyser	R	Chi	29	92	48	5	0	4.97	13.74	0	R3
M Kiefer	R	Mil	27	49	41	4	0	3.44	11.60	9	1
K King	L	Sea	27	3	3	0	0	12.29	19.63	-2	0
S Klingenbe	R	Min	25	79	42	2	0	7.12	16.15	-17	0
R Krivda	L	Bal	26	75	53	2	0	4.54	12.07	4	2
M Langston	L	Cal	35	200	142	15	0	4.63	12.40	16	17
M Lee	L	Bal	31	33	27	2	1	4.86	13.23	2	R3
D Leiper	R	Oak	34	22	10	1	0	3.57	14.29	1	R3
A Leiter	L	Tor	30	183	153	11	0	3.64	13.28	16	6
J Lima	R	Det	23	73	37	3	0	6.11	12.58	-3	5
F Lira	R	Det	24	146	89	9	1	4.31	12.73	12	2
G Lloyd	L	Mil	29	32	13	0	4	4.50	10.13	6	R3
B Looney	L	Bos	26	4	2	0	0	17.37	30.86	-6	0
B Looper	R	Oth	21	0	0	0	0	0.00	0.00	0	R5
A Lopez	R	Cle	24	23	22	0	0	3.13	9.39	4	R2
A Lorraine	L	Chi	23	8	5	0	0	3.38	5.62	2	R2
M Maddux	R	Bos	34	89	65	4	1	3.61	10.14	16	3
M Magnante	L	KC	33	44	28	1	0	4.23	12.29	2	R3
P Mahomes	R	Min	25	94	67	4	3	6.37	13.98	-6	R3
J Manzanill	R	NY	28	17	11	0	0	2.08	14.54	2	R3
D Martinez	R	Cle	41	187	99	12	0	3.08	10.59	36	17
B Maxcy	R	Det	25	52	20	4	0	6.88	15.82	-8	0
K McCaskill	R	Chi	35	81	50	6	2	4.89	14.44	2	R3
B McDonald	R	Bal	28	80	62	3	0	4.16	11.81	7	13
J McDowell	R	NY	30	217	157	15	0	3.93	11.95	26	21

Name	T	Tm	Age	IP	SO	W	Sv	ERA	Ratio	$	Bid
R McDowell	R	Tex	35	85	49	7	4	4.02	12.70	13	3
R Meacham	R	KC	28	59	30	4	2	4.98	13.72	3	R3
J Mecir	R	Sea	26	4	3	0	0	0.00	13.50	1	R9
P Menhart	R	Mil	27	7	6	0	0	9.83	24.54	-5	0
J Mesa	R	Cle	30	64	58	3	46	1.13	9.28	57	41
J Middlebrk	R	Oth	21	0	0	0	0	0.00	0.00	0	R5
A Mills	R	Bal	29	23	16	3	0	7.44	18.78	-5	R3
A Miranda	L	Mil	26	74	45	4	1	5.23	16.05	-5	1
M Mohler	L	Oak	27	23	15	1	1	3.04	12.93	4	R3
R Monteleon	R	Cal	33	9	5	1	0	2.00	11.00	3	R3
J Montgomer	R	KC	34	65	49	2	31	3.43	11.65	32	29
J Moyer	L	Bal	33	115	65	8	0	5.21	11.44	9	1
O Munoz	R	Min	30	35	25	2	0	5.61	14.52	-2	0
M Murray	R	Bos	25	3	1	0	0	18.92	37.80	-5	R2
M Mussina	R	Bal	27	221	158	19	0	3.29	9.62	50	30
M Myers	L	Det	27	6	4	1	0	9.96	19.89	-2	0
C Nagy	R	Cle	29	178	139	16	0	4.55	12.89	15	17
J Nelson	R	Sea	29	78	96	7	2	2.17	9.72	25	5
C Nitkowski	L	Det	23	39	13	1	0	7.09	16.70	-9	R2
C Ogea	R	Cle	25	106	57	8	0	3.05	10.49	23	4
D Oliver	L	Tex	25	49	39	4	0	4.22	14.51	2	3
G Olson	R	KC	35	33	21	3	3	4.09	12.82	6	2
S Ontiveros	R	Oak	35	129	77	9	0	4.37	12.63	11	7
M Oquist	R	Bal	28	54	27	2	0	4.17	15.33	-1	0
R Orellano	L	Bos	23	0	0	0	0	0.00	0.00	0	R2
J Orosco	L	Bal	39	49	58	2	3	3.26	9.97	12	1
J Parra	R	Min	23	61	29	1	0	7.59	15.32	-14	R2
B Patterson	L	Cal	37	53	41	5	0	3.04	10.29	13	R3
J Patterson	R	NY	27	3	3	0	0	2.70	16.20	0	R3
D Pavlas	R	NY	33	5	3	0	0	3.18	12.70	0	R3
R Pavlik	R	Tex	28	191	149	10	0	4.37	12.40	14	11
B Penningto	L	Bal	27	6	10	0	0	8.11	18.90	-3	R3
T Percival	R	Cal	26	74	94	3	3	1.95	7.66	27	19
M Perez	R	NY	30	69	44	5	0	5.58	13.11	1	R3
A Pettite	L	NY	24	175	114	12	0	4.17	12.65	16	10
H Pichardo	R	KC	26	64	43	8	1	4.36	13.50	8	R3
J Pierce	R	Bos	26	15	12	0	0	6.60	18.00	-4	R3
J Pittsley	R	KC	22	3	0	0	0	13.51	21.60	-3	R1
E Plunk	R	Cle	32	64	71	6	2	2.67	10.55	18	5
J Poole	L	Cle	30	50	41	3	0	3.76	10.19	9	1
A Prieto	R	Oak	26	58	37	2	0	4.97	13.81	-1	3
S Radinsky	L	Chi	28	38	14	2	1	5.45	14.92	-2	R3
B Radke	R	Min	23	181	75	11	0	5.32	12.03	8	5
A Reyes	R	Mil	25	33	29	1	1	2.43	9.99	8	R2
C Reyes	R	Oak	32	69	48	4	0	5.09	12.91	2	R3
A Rhodes	L	Bal	27	75	77	2	0	6.21	13.86	-7	R1
B Rigby	R	Oak	22	0	0	0	0	0.00	0.00	0	R4
D Righetti	L	Chi	37	49	29	3	0	4.20	15.14	0	R3
R Rightnowa	R	Mil	31	36	22	2	1	5.40	13.01	1	R3
B Risley	R	Sea	29	60	65	2	1	3.13	10.89	11	3
M Rivera	R	NY	26	67	51	5	0	5.51	13.56	0	5
J Roa	R	Cle	24	6	0	0	0	6.01	16.50	-1	R2
S Roberson	L	Mil	24	84	40	6	0	5.76	14.83	-5	R3
R Robertson	L	Min	27	51	38	2	0	3.83	13.76	2	3
K Robinson	R	Tor	26	39	31	1	0	3.69	10.85	5	1
F Rodriguez	R	Min	23	105	59	5	0	6.13	14.56	-9	2

Name	T	Tm	Age	IP	SO	W	Sv	ERA	Ratio	$	Bid
J Rogers	R	Tor	29	23	13	2	0	5.71	14.83	-1	R3
K Rogers	L	Tex	31	208	140	17	0	3.38	11.59	35	18
S Ruffcorn	R	Chi	26	8	5	0	0	7.88	25.87	-5	R3
J Russell	R	Tex	34	32	21	1	20	3.03	12.40	19	10
K Ryan	R	Bos	27	32	34	0	7	4.96	15.98	1	R2
S Sanderson	R	Cal	39	39	23	1	0	4.12	11.90	3	R3
M Sanford	R	Min	29	18	17	0	0	5.30	15.43	-2	R3
B Scanlan	R	Mil	29	83	29	4	0	6.59	15.66	-12	0
A Sele	R	Bos	26	32	21	3	0	3.06	12.80	6	10
J Shaw	R	Chi	29	9	6	0	0	6.52	12.10	-1	R9
P Shuey	R	Cle	25	6	5	0	0	4.27	14.21	0	R2
B Simas	R	Chi	24	14	16	1	0	2.57	16.07	1	2
M Sirotka	R	Chi	25	34	19	1	0	4.20	14.68	0	3
L Smith	R	Cal	38	49	43	0	37	3.47	12.22	32	25
Z Smith	L	Bos	35	110	47	8	0	5.61	13.58	-1	R2
C Sodowsky	R	Det	23	23	14	2	0	5.02	16.20	-1	2
S Sparks	R	Mil	30	202	96	9	0	4.63	13.19	6	1
M Stanton	L	Bos	29	21	10	1	0	3.00	10.71	4	1
D Stevens	R	Min	26	65	47	5	10	5.07	14.53	7	6
T Stottlemy	R	Oak	31	209	205	14	0	4.55	13.22	11	16
J Suppan	R	Bos	21	22	19	1	0	5.96	13.50	-1	6
J Tavarez	R	Cle	23	85	68	10	0	2.44	10.27	26	9
S Taylor	L	Tex	28	15	10	1	0	9.40	17.61	-6	0
D Telgheder	R	Oak	29	25	16	1	0	5.61	14.37	-2	R2
B Tewksbury	R	Tex	35	129	53	8	0	4.58	13.12	7	4
L Thomas	L	Chi	26	13	12	0	0	1.32	9.22	4	2
M Thomas	L	Mil	26	1	0	0	0	0.00	20.25	0	R3
M Timlin	R	Tor	30	42	36	4	5	2.14	11.79	15	7
D Torres	R	KC	26	44	28	1	0	6.09	14.82	-5	R2
S Torres	R	Sea	24	72	45	3	0	6.00	16.12	-10	R2
M Trombley	R	Min	29	97	68	4	0	5.62	13.73	-4	R3
T Vanegmond	R	Bos	27	6	5	0	0	9.46	20.25	-3	R3
T VanPoppel	R	Oak	24	138	122	4	0	4.88	11.77	5	6
E Vosberg	L	Tex	34	36	36	5	4	3.00	12.00	12	R3
T Wakefield	R	Bos	29	195	119	16	0	2.95	10.64	42	11
D Ward	R	Tor	32	2	3	0	0	27.03	54.00	-7	R2
J Ware	R	Tor	25	26	18	2	0	5.47	16.75	-3	R2
J Wasdin	R	Oak	23	17	6	1	0	4.68	8.83	3	R2
S Watkins	L	Min	26	21	11	0	0	5.40	13.71	-2	R1
B Wegman	R	Mil	33	70	50	5	2	5.35	14.01	1	R3
D Wengert	R	Oak	26	29	16	1	0	3.34	12.74	3	R3
J Wetteland	R	NY	29	61	66	1	31	2.94	7.92	39	40
M Whiteside	R	Tex	28	53	46	5	3	4.08	11.38	11	1
S Whiteside	L	Det	25	3	2	0	0	14.74	27.00	-4	R3
K Wickander	L	Mil	31	23	11	0	1	1.93	11.96	5	R3
B Wickman	R	NY	27	80	51	2	1	4.05	12.37	6	3
W Williams	R	Tor	29	53	41	1	0	3.69	12.07	5	3
B Witt	R	Tex	32	61	46	3	0	4.55	14.97	-1	2
S Wojci'wsk	L	Oak	25	48	13	2	0	5.18	14.61	-2	R3
B Wolcott	R	Sea	22	36	19	3	0	4.42	13.99	2	3
J Wright	R	Cle	20	0	0	0	0	0.00	0.00	0	R5
Total											1020

1996 NL hitters — alphabetical

Name	B	Tm	Age	C123SO	AB	R	HR	RBI	SB	BA	$	Bid
K Abbott	R	Fla	27	-----S-	475	58	18	61	2	.251	12	13
B Abreu	L	Hou	22	------O	0	0	0	0	0	.000	0	R2
I Alcantrat	R	Mon	23	---T--	0	0	0	0	0	.000	0	R4
E Alfonzo	R	NY	22	--DTs-	525	38	7	64	1	.282	13	11
J Allenswor	R	Pit	24	------O	0	0	0	0	0	.000	0	R3
M Alou	R	Mon	29	------O	525	95	23	92	8	.288	26	27
S Andrews	R	Mon	24	-F-T--	150	18	5	21	0	.213	2	2
E Anthony	L	Cin	28	-f---O	150	21	6	25	3	.233	5	2
A Arias	R	Fla	28	--dTS-	150	15	1	18	0	.253	2	1
B Ashley	R	LA	25	------O	150	14	7	23	0	.233	4	R2
R Aude	R	Pit	25	-F----	75	6	2	13	0	.240	2	R3
R Aurilia	R	SF	24	-----S-	225	35	5	31	3	.262	6	3
B Ausmus	R	SD	27	Cf----	400	50	3	38	10	.303	13	12
J Bagwell	R	Hou	28	-F----	550	112	34	116	11	.311	40	37
J Barry	B	NY	27	------O	0	0	0	0	0	.000	0	R3
J Bates	B	Col	25	--DtS-	275	34	5	38	1	.273	7	3
A Battle	R	StL	27	------O	125	13	0	7	3	.256	1	R3
T Beamon	L	Pit	22	------O	250	41	5	34	9	.284	10	R1
T Belk	R	Cin	25	-F----	0	0	0	0	0	.000	0	R3
D Bell	R	StL	23	--Dt--	250	22	3	32	1	.248	3	2
D Bell	R	Hou	27	------O	550	84	14	86	24	.311	32	30
J Bell	R	Pit	30	---tS-	575	85	11	59	2	.273	13	13
R Belliard	R	Atl	34	--D-S-	125	7	0	4	0	.208	-1	0
M Benard	L	SF	26	------O	250	36	2	29	7	.264	6	4
Y Benitez	R	Mon	24	------O	100	15	4	17	0	.240	3	R3
M Benjamin	R	SF	30	--dTs-	225	21	2	14	12	.213	2	R3
S Berry	R	Mon	30	-f-T--	525	75	23	91	5	.270	22	20
D Berryhill	B	Oth	32	Cf----	0	0	0	0	0	.000	0	0
D Bichette	R	Col	32	------O	550	101	45	127	8	.318	46	42
C Biggio	R	Hou	30	--D---	600	112	17	71	29	.288	29	33
J Blauser	R	Atl	30	-----S-	500	70	11	42	7	.228	5	6
G Blum	R	Mon	23	--D-s-	0	0	0	0	0	.000	0	R4
T Bogar	R	NY	29	-fdTSo	125	14	0	17	0	.272	2	R3
B Bonds	L	SF	31	------O	525	126	34	107	32	.307	44	45
A Boone	R	Cin	23	---T--	0	0	0	0	0	.000	0	R4
B Boone	R	Cin	27	--D---	550	75	21	85	4	.282	22	18
J Booty	R	Fla	20	----S-	0	0	0	0	0	.000	0	R4
P Borders	R	Oth	32	C-----	0	0	0	0	0	.000	0	R3
T Bradshaw	L	StL	27	------O	50	6	1	5	0	.240	1	R3
J Branson	L	Cin	29	-fdTS-	350	45	12	55	2	.251	10	5
J Brito	R	Col	30	C-----	75	7	0	10	1	.213	0	0
R Brogna	L	NY	26	-F----	525	79	24	82	1	.295	25	23
J Browne	B	Fla	30	--Dt-O	125	14	1	9	0	.256	1	R3
J Brumfield	R	Pit	31	------O	450	69	3	28	23	.262	11	5
D Buford	R	NY	25	------O	200	34	5	17	9	.245	5	2
S Bullett	L	Chi	27	------O	125	15	2	18	6	.272	5	1
E Burks	R	Col	31	------O	350	51	17	60	8	.266	17	13
M Busch	R	LA	27	-f-T--	0	0	0	0	0	.000	0	R3
B Butler	L	LA	39	------O	550	83	1	40	34	.295	20	17
R Butler	L	Phi	26	------O	0	0	0	0	0	.000	0	R3
M Cairo	R	LA	22	--D---	0	0	0	0	0	.000	0	R4
K Caminiti	B	SD	33	---T--	575	73	25	96	5	.290	28	28
J Cangelosi	B	Hou	33	------O	175	40	1	15	18	.257	7	4

Name	B	Tm	Age	C123SO	AB	R	HR	RBI	SB	BA	$	Bid
R Carabello	B	StL	27	--D---	0	0	0	0	0	.000	0	R3
C Carr	L	Fla	27	-----O	100	17	0	6	12	.270	5	3
M Carreon	R	SF	32	-F---O	525	66	19	81	1	.291	22	17
R Casanova	R	SD	23	C-----	0	0	0	0	0	.000	0	R4
P Castellan	R	Col	26	---T--	0	0	0	0	0	.000	0	R3
V Castilla	R	Col	28	---Ts-	550	82	31	95	1	.285	28	28
A Castillo	R	NY	20	C-----	0	0	0	0	0	.000	0	R4
J Castro	R	LA	24	---Ts-	0	0	0	0	0	.000	0	R3
A Cedeno	R	SD	26	---tS-	450	50	11	42	7	.227	5	3
R Cedeno	B	LA	21	------O	125	11	0	6	5	.248	1	R2
A Cianfrocc	R	SD	29	-Fdtso	175	29	4	43	0	.246	5	1
D Clark	L	Pit	33	------O	200	30	4	24	3	.280	6	1
P Clark	R	SD	28	-f---O	75	9	2	8	0	.213	0	R3
R Clayton	R	SF	26	-----S-	500	55	4	51	19	.252	11	7
D Clyburn	R	Cin	22	------O	0	0	0	0	0	.000	0	R4
G Colbrunn	R	Fla	26	-F----	475	62	20	79	7	.284	22	21
D Coles	R	StL	33	-F-T-o	0	0	0	0	0	.000	0	R3
L Collier	R	Pit	23	-----S-	0	0	0	0	0	.000	0	R4
J Conine	R	Fla	30	-f---O	550	83	24	112	1	.289	27	28
S Cooper	L	StL	28	---T--	425	32	7	50	2	.238	5	4
W Cordero	R	Mon	24	-----SO	500	65	19	67	6	.274	19	21
C Counsell	L	Col	25	-----S-	100	11	1	8	2	.230	1	R3
T Cromer	R	StL	28	--d-S-	325	33	7	18	0	.234	1	1
M Cummings	L	Pit	24	------O	225	18	3	21	1	.240	2	2
D Daulton	L	Phi	34	C-----	375	50	13	66	6	.259	14	16
A Dawson	R	Fla	41	------O	175	22	6	28	0	.251	5	1
S Decker	R	Fla	30	Cf----	50	4	1	4	0	.220	0	R3
D Deshields	L	LA	27	--D---	475	73	8	41	36	.265	19	15
M Devereaux	R	Atl	33	------O	225	32	6	36	3	.267	8	4
M Duncan	R	Cin	33	-FDtSo	250	33	6	33	2	.272	7	3
S Dunston	R	Chi	33	-----S-	500	64	14	72	8	.266	16	14
J Dye	R	Atl	22	------O	75	6	3	8	1	.240	2	R2
L Dykstra	L	Phi	33	------O	500	74	12	50	27	.276	21	21
J Eisenreic	L	Phi	37	------O	400	46	8	57	4	.300	15	11
A Encarnaci	R	Pit	22	C-----	275	30	3	16	1	.222	-1	R3
T Eusebio	R	Hou	29	C-----	300	37	4	47	0	.307	11	9
C Everett	B	NY	26	------O	550	91	25	102	4	.258	22	18
S Finley	L	SD	31	------O	575	107	7	48	38	.304	27	24
D Fletcher	L	Mon	29	C-----	375	45	9	57	0	.283	12	7
K Flora	R	Phi	26	------O	50	8	1	4	2	.200	0	R3
C Floyd	L	Mon	23	-F---o	450	65	6	53	13	.262	12	9
C Fonville	B	LA	25	--D-So	475	63	0	23	29	.259	10	9
B Fordyce	R	NY	25	C-----	0	0	0	0	0	.000	0	R3
M Franco	L	Chi	26	-fDt--	0	0	0	0	0	.000	0	R3
A Galarraga	R	Col	35	-F----	550	87	35	102	7	.275	30	32
D Gallagher	R	Phi	35	------O	75	5	1	7	0	.280	1	R3
R Gant	R	Cin	31	------O	475	85	27	91	19	.259	27	28
C Garcia	R	Pit	28	--D-s-	525	55	5	57	6	.288	14	12
F Garcia	R	Pit	23	---t-O	0	0	0	0	0	.000	0	R4
K Garcia	L	LA	20	------O	125	25	5	30	2	.256	6	R1
P Geisler	L	Phi	26	------O	0	0	0	0	0	.000	0	R3
S Gibralter	R	Cin	23	------O	50	4	1	5	0	.260	1	R2
D Gibson	R	Col	21	------O	0	0	0	0	0	.000	0	R5
B Gilkey	R	StL	29	------O	500	70	13	57	10	.286	18	17
E Giovanola	L	Atl	27	--Dts-	0	0	0	0	0	.000	0	R3
L Gonzalez	L	Chi	28	------O	400	58	10	58	7	.278	14	12

Predictions—NL alpha

Name	B	Tm	Age	C123SO	AB	R	HR	RBI	SB	BA	$	Bid
M Grace	L	Chi	32	-F----	575	109	12	90	1	.317	25	27
T Graffanin	R	Atl	24	--D---	0	0	0	0	0	.000	0	R3
W Greene	L	Cin	24	---T--	50	2	2	5	0	.220	1	R2
T Gregg	L	Fla	32	-f---O	150	19	5	19	2	.273	5	1
M Grissom	R	Atl	29	------O	600	83	17	58	38	.277	27	28
M Grudziela	R	Mon	26	--dTS-	200	32	1	15	4	.255	2	3
V Guerrero	R	Mon	20	------O	0	0	0	0	0	.000	0	R5
W Guerrero	R	LA	21	-----S-	75	8	0	3	3	.253	1	R2
M Gulan	R	StL	25	---T--	50	4	1	5	0	.240	1	R2
R Gutierrez	R	Hou	26	---tS-	175	21	1	13	4	.263	3	1
C Gwynn	L	LA	31	-f---O	0	0	0	0	0	.000	0	R3
T Gwynn	L	SD	36	------O	550	82	8	105	12	.364	37	37
D Hajek	R	Hou	28	--D---	100	14	1	11	2	.280	3	R3
T Haney	R	Chi	30	--Dt--	125	18	3	10	1	.288	4	R3
D Hansen	L	LA	27	---T--	125	12	0	9	0	.280	1	R3
L Harris	B	Cin	31	-FdT-o	125	20	1	10	6	.248	2	R3
C Hayes	R	Phi	31	---T--	550	60	11	88	5	.271	17	16
S Hemond	R	StL	30	C-d---	100	9	2	7	0	.190	0	R3
C Hernandez	R	LA	29	C-----	75	2	1	6	0	.187	0	0
J Hernandez	R	Chi	26	--DTS-	175	26	9	28	0	.240	5	2
R Hidalgo	R	Hou	20	------O	75	9	3	10	1	.240	2	R2
G Hill	R	SF	31	------O	550	81	27	102	18	.258	27	25
T Hilton	L	Col	22	-F----	0	0	0	0	0	.000	0	R5
R Holbert	R	SD	25	--d-So	75	11	2	5	4	.200	1	R3
N Holdren	R	Col	24	-F----	0	0	0	0	0	.000	0	R4
R Holifield	L	Phi	25	------O	0	0	0	0	0	.000	0	R4
T Hollandsw	L	LA	23	------O	125	19	5	19	1	.240	3	R2
D Hollins	L	Atl	22	------O	0	0	0	0	0	.000	0	R4
T Houston	R	Atl	25	C-----	0	0	0	0	0	.000	0	R3
T Howard	B	Cin	31	------O	325	48	3	30	19	.277	11	5
M Hubbard	R	Chi	25	C-----	75	6	2	6	0	.200	0	R3
T Hubbard	R	Col	32	------O	75	16	3	11	2	.280	3	R3
T Hundley	B	NY	27	C-----	425	59	22	78	1	.280	20	18
B Hunter	R	Hou	25	------O	575	93	4	51	41	.311	29	26
B Hunter	R	Cin	28	-F---o	75	8	3	8	1	.213	1	R3
B Huskey	R	NY	24	---T-o	250	22	8	30	2	.244	5	R1
T Hyers	L	SD	24	-F----	0	0	0	0	0	.000	0	R3
P Incavigil	R	Oth	32	------O	0	0	0	0	0	.000	0	R3
G Jefferies	B	Phi	28	-F---O	575	105	12	79	16	.334	32	27
R Jennings	L	Chi	24	------O	50	4	1	4	0	.260	1	R2
B Johnson	R	SD	28	Cf----	200	19	2	26	0	.250	2	1
C Johnson	R	Fla	24	C-----	475	60	19	64	2	.255	14	15
H Johnson	B	Chi	35	-fdTso	0	0	0	0	0	.000	0	R3
M Johnson	L	Pit	28	-F----	250	35	17	41	1	.220	8	3
A Jones	R	Atl	19	------O	0	0	0	0	0	.000	0	R5
C Jones	R	NY	30	-f---O	175	31	7	29	1	.280	7	1
C Jones	B	Atl	24	---T-O	575	93	25	94	6	.270	24	26
B Jordan	R	StL	29	------O	550	87	25	84	17	.267	26	27
K Jordan	R	Phi	26	--Dt--	175	25	3	17	1	.234	1	R3
D Justice	L	Atl	30	------O	475	83	27	89	3	.272	24	26
E Karros	R	LA	28	-F----	575	84	26	98	2	.283	26	26
M Kelly	R	Atl	26	------O	0	0	0	0	0	.000	0	R3
R Kelly	R	LA	31	------O	475	54	9	53	21	.276	18	17
J Kendall	R	Pit	22	C-----	175	18	2	24	1	.286	5	R1
J Kent	R	NY	28	--D---	525	75	22	81	3	.276	21	21
B Kieschnck	L	Chi	24	-f---O	75	14	3	15	0	.253	3	R1

Name	B	Tm	Age	C123SO	AB	R	HR	RBI	SB	BA	$	Bid
J King	R	Pit	31	-FdTs-	500	65	16	91	3	.256	16	16
M Kingery	L	Col	35	-f---O	275	51	5	25	10	.280	9	3
R Klesko	L	Atl	25	-f---O	475	69	33	101	7	.278	30	27
P Konerko	R	LA	20	C-----	0	0	0	0	0	.000	0	R4
B Kosko	R	Col	29	---T--	0	0	0	0	0	.000	0	R3
B Kowitz	L	Atl	26	------	0	0	0	0	0	.000	0	R3
T Laker	R	Mon	26	C-----	50	6	1	7	0	.240	1	R3
T Lampkin	R	SF	32	C-----o	100	10	1	11	0	.260	1	R3
R Lankford	L	StL	29	------O	550	101	20	88	27	.265	27	28
M Lansing	R	Mon	28	--D-s-	525	60	6	62	23	.269	17	14
B Larkin	R	Cin	32	----S-	525	103	16	86	32	.328	38	36
D Lee	R	SD	20	---T--	0	0	0	0	0	.000	0	R5
M Lemke	B	Atl	30	--D---	425	44	5	40	2	.254	5	2
M Leonard	L	SF	31	------O	0	0	0	0	0	.000	0	R3
D Lewis	R	Cin	28	------O	300	41	1	15	20	.253	7	9
M Lewis	R	Cin	26	--dTs-	200	29	5	35	0	.275	7	7
M Liebertha	R	Phi	24	C-----	175	21	2	23	1	.263	3	1
N Liriano	B	Pit	32	--Dts-	225	24	3	25	0	.267	4	R3
S Livingsto	L	SD	30	-Fdt--	175	23	4	28	1	.274	6	2
J Lofton	B	Cin	22	--D---	0	0	0	0	0	.000	0	R4
T Long	L	NY	20	-F----	0	0	0	0	0	.000	0	R5
T Longmire	L	Phi	27	------O	125	25	4	22	1	.288	5	1
J Lopez	R	Atl	25	C-----	450	61	18	75	2	.287	20	21
J Mabry	L	StL	25	-F---O	500	45	8	52	0	.290	13	13
D Magadan	L	Hou	33	-f-T--	350	43	4	47	1	.286	9	6
K Manwaring	R	SF	30	C-----	400	21	3	37	0	.248	2	1
T Marsh	R	Phi	30	------O	100	11	2	13	0	.270	3	R3
A Martin	L	Pit	28	------O	475	74	15	59	14	.274	18	15
D May	L	Hou	27	-f---O	375	47	8	65	1	.283	13	8
C McBride	R	Atl	22	---T--	0	0	0	0	0	.000	0	R4
D McCarty	R	SF	26	-f---O	75	3	1	7	0	.240	3	R3
Q McCracken	R	Col	26	------O	100	15	0	8	5	.270	3	R2
R McDavid	R	SD	24	------O	0	0	0	0	0	.000	0	R3
F McGriff	L	Atl	32	-F----	550	90	29	105	7	.289	31	35
B McMillion	L	Fla	24	------O	50	7	2	7	1	.280	2	R2
B McRae	B	Chi	28	------O	625	116	13	53	30	.285	24	20
R Mejia	R	Col	24	--D---	75	7	1	5	1	.240	1	R3
O Merced	B	Pit	29	-F---O	525	75	11	80	1	.286	17	16
O Miller	R	Hou	27	----S-	400	43	7	44	2	.258	7	4
K Mitchell	R	Oth	34	-f---O	0	0	0	0	0	.000	0	R1
R Mondesi	R	LA	25	------O	575	99	37	109	18	.277	36	34
M Morandini	L	Phi	30	--D---	475	62	5	41	7	.276	10	5
M Mordecai	R	Atl	28	-fDtso	175	22	6	21	2	.280	6	2
R Morman	R	Fla	34	-f---O	0	0	0	0	0	.000	0	R3
B Morris	L	Chi	23	--D---	0	0	0	0	0	.000	0	R4
H Morris	L	Cin	23	-F----	475	70	19	72	5	.288	21	21
J Mouton	R	Hou	27	------O	275	38	3	24	23	.258	10	6
N Munoz	R	LA	25	C-----	0	0	0	0	0	.000	0	R3
C Murray	R	SF	24	------O	0	0	0	0	0	.000	0	R3
B Natal	R	Fla	30	C-----	75	3	3	10	0	.213	1	R3
B Nelson	R	Phi	22	----S-	0	0	0	0	0	.000	0	R4
M Newfield	R	SD	23	------O	325	35	7	41	0	.271	8	9
M Nieves	B	SD	24	-f---O	225	30	13	36	1	.204	5	2
M Nokes	L	Col	32	C-----	75	7	4	12	0	.227	2	1
C O'Brien	R	Atl	35	C-----	150	12	4	17	0	.253	3	1
A Ochoa	R	NY	24	------O	450	82	6	41	5	.264	8	5

Predictions—NL alpha

Name	B	Tm	Age	C123SO	AB	R	HR	RBI	SB	BA	$	Bid
J Offerman	B	LA	27	----S-	275	31	0	21	2	.255	1	2
J Oliva	R	StL	25	-f-T--	75	6	2	8	0	.227	1	R3
J Oquendo	B	StL	32	--DtSo	150	21	1	13	0	.213	0	0
R Ordonez	R	NY	24	-----S-	0	0	0	0	0	.000	0	R3
J Orsulak	L	NY	34	-f---O	175	24	2	24	1	.291	5	1
W Otanez	R	LA	23	---T--	75	6	3	7	0	.240	1	R2
R Otero	B	NY	23	------O	75	11	1	5	5	.227	1	R3
E Owens	R	Cin	25	---T--	50	11	1	9	2	.280	2	R2
J Owens	R	Col	27	C-----	375	57	7	58	0	.243	6	2
T Pagnozzi	R	StL	33	C-----	425	32	4	35	0	.261	4	1
M Parent	R	Chi	34	C-----	150	16	10	21	0	.240	5	3
J Patterson	B	SF	29	--D---	175	21	1	11	7	.223	1	R3
J Payton	R	NY	24	------O	100	20	3	17	1	.280	4	R1
S Pegues	R	Pit	28	------O	75	6	1	6	0	.253	1	R3
G Pena	R	StL	29	--D---	425	84	4	33	9	.266	8	4
T Pendleton	R	Fla	35	---T--	500	67	15	75	0	.270	15	16
E Perez	R	Atl	28	Cf----	0	0	0	0	0	.000	0	R3
G Perry	L	StL	35	-F-----	75	3	1	8	0	.240	1	R3
R Petagine	L	SD	25	-F---o	0	0	0	0	0	.000	0	R3
C Peterson	R	Pit	22	------O	0	0	0	0	0	.000	0	R4
J Phillips	L	SF	26	-F---o	200	23	9	24	0	.210	2	R3
M Piazza	R	LA	27	C-----	550	96	35	111	2	.329	40	43
P Plantier	L	SD	27	------O	225	33	8	35	0	.249	6	4
L Polonia	L	Atl	31	------O	175	17	0	10	9	.303	6	2
D Powell	R	SF	23	------O	0	0	0	0	0	.000	0	R2
C Pride	L	Mon	27	------O	0	0	0	0	0	.000	0	R3
H Pulliam	R	Col	28	------O	75	11	6	16	0	.267	5	R2
E Pye	R	LA	29	---T--	0	0	0	0	0	.000	0	R3
J Reed	L	SF	33	C-----	75	7	1	5	0	.253	1	R3
J Reed	R	SD	33	--D-s-	375	47	2	32	3	.256	4	2
P Reese	R	Cin	23	----S-	0	0	0	0	0	.000	0	R3
E Renteria	B	Fla	20	----S-	75	10	1	8	2	.253	2	R2
K Rhodes	L	Oth	27	------O	0	0	0	0	0	.000	0	R3
A Riggs	R	LA	23	--D---	0	0	0	0	0	.000	0	R5
K Roberson	B	NY	28	------O	0	0	0	0	0	.000	0	R3
B Roberts	B	SD	32	--D-sO	475	100	3	40	31	.309	22	20
H Rodriguez	L	Mon	28	-f---O	175	16	3	18	0	.251	2	2
S Rolen	R	Phi	21	---T--	125	12	4	17	1	.256	3	R2
R Sanchez	R	Chi	28	--D-s-	100	12	0	6	1	.280	1	1
R Sandberg	R	Chi	36	--D---	525	55	10	48	8	.251	9	10
D Sanders	L	SF	28	------O	300	41	5	24	20	.277	12	10
R Sanders	R	Cin	28	------O	550	100	30	107	34	.282	39	42
F Santangel	R	Mon	31	--d--O	0	0	0	0	0	.000	0	R3
B Santiago	R	Cin	31	Cf----	350	48	9	50	1	.269	10	10
S Scarsone	R	SF	30	-fdT--	125	17	5	15	1	.248	3	1
G Schall	R	Phi	26	-F---o	75	4	1	5	0	.253	1	R2
K Sefcik	R	Phi	25	---T--	0	0	0	0	0	.000	0	R3
D Segui	B	Mon	29	-F---O	550	82	14	75	2	.302	21	17
S Servais	R	Chi	29	C-----	400	53	14	55	0	.248	9	5
D Sheaffer	R	StL	34	Cf-t--	200	23	4	28	0	.230	2	1
G Sheffield	R	Fla	27	------O	500	95	37	99	23	.296	40	32
C Shipley	R	Hou	33	-fdTs-	225	22	4	27	3	.271	6	1
J Siddall	L	Mon	28	C-----	0	0	0	0	0	.000	0	R3
D Silvestri	R	Mon	28	-fdtSo	75	12	2	7	1	.240	1	R3
M Simms	R	Hou	29	-F---o	100	11	7	19	0	.250	5	R3
B Simonton	R	SF	24	-F----	0	0	0	0	0	.000	0	R4

Name	B	Tm	Age	C123SO	AB	R	HR	RBI	SB	BA	$	Bid
D Slaught	R	Pit	37	C-----	200	21	2	28	0	.295	6	1
D Smith	L	Atl	32	------O	150	18	3	24	0	.267	4	R3
O Smith	B	StL	41	-----S-	300	32	1	26	10	.233	3	2
R Smith	R	Atl	22	---T--	75	6	3	9	0	.253	2	R2
S Sosa	R	Chi	27	------O	600	119	42	126	40	.267	45	41
T Spehr	R	Mon	29	C-----	175	12	4	14	0	.257	3	1
B Spiers	R	NY	30	--dT--	0	0	0	0	0	.000	0	R3
K Stinnett	R	NY	26	C-----	175	20	5	17	0	.234	2	1
K Stocker	R	Phi	26	-----S-	450	46	4	39	7	.227	2	2
D Stovall	B	StL	23	------O	0	0	0	0	0	.000	0	R4
M Sweeney	L	StL	26	-F---o	125	15	3	21	1	.312	6	R3
T Tarasco	L	Mon	25	------O	250	34	5	20	11	.272	8	7
E Taubensee	L	Cin	27	Cf----	225	30	6	42	0	.267	7	6
J Tavarez	B	Fla	25	------O	150	17	1	10	5	.253	2	1
J Thompson	L	SD	25	-F----	0	0	0	0	0	.000	0	R3
M Thompson	L	Hou	37	------O	100	10	2	14	3	.240	3	R3
R Thompson	R	SF	34	--D---	375	58	10	38	2	.245	6	4
R Thompson	R	NY	28	------O	400	58	11	45	3	.248	8	6
O Timmons	R	Chi	25	------O	175	29	9	27	2	.251	7	4
A Van Slyke	L	Phi	35	------O	300	36	4	26	7	.243	4	2
J VanderWal	L	Col	30	-F---o	150	19	6	29	0	.313	8	1
G Varsho	R	Phi	34	------O	75	5	1	8	1	.253	1	R3
E Velasquez	R	Col	20	------O	0	0	0	0	0	.000	0	R4
Q Veras	B	Fla	25	--D--o	575	125	8	44	75	.264	32	27
J Vizcaino	B	NY	28	--d-S-	525	64	2	50	3	.272	8	4
L Walker	L	Col	29	------O	525	102	38	107	12	.324	43	39
T Wallach	R	LA	38	-f-T--	375	26	8	43	0	.261	7	5
J Walton	B	Cin	30	-f---O	125	24	4	16	7	.304	7	2
P Watkins	R	Cin	23	------O	0	0	0	0	0	.000	0	R4
L Webster	L	Phi	31	C-----	75	9	1	6	0	.253	1	R3
M Webster	B	LA	37	------O	0	0	0	0	0	.000	0	R3
J Wehner	R	Pit	29	c--TsO	125	15	1	14	7	.280	5	R3
W Weiss	B	Col	32	----S-	475	80	0	26	15	.255	5	3
D White	B	Fla	33	------O	550	85	12	68	22	.282	22	18
R White	R	Mon	24	------O	575	81	14	79	21	.285	25	25
M Whiten	B	Phi	29	------O	525	86	19	78	9	.250	17	11
D Whitmore	L	Fla	27	------O	0	0	0	0	0	.000	0	R3
R Wilkins	L	Hou	29	Cf----	275	42	11	36	0	.211	3	3
E Williams	R	SD	31	-F----	325	38	13	51	0	.262	11	8
M Williams	R	SF	30	---T--	575	107	60	132	4	.283	46	38
N Wilson	L	Cin	25	------O	0	0	0	0	0	.000	0	R3
P Wilson	R	NY	21	------O	0	0	0	0	0	.000	0	R4
R Wright	R	Atl	20	-F----	0	0	0	0	0	.000	0	R5
D Young	R	StL	22	------O	0	0	0	0	0	.000	0	R4
E Young	R	Col	29	--D--O	550	101	8	53	51	.273	26	18
K Young	R	Pit	27	-f-T--	75	5	2	9	0	.227	1	R3
T Zeile	R	Chi	30	-F-T-o	525	62	18	75	4	.257	16	17
E Zosky	R	Fla	28	--d-S-	0	0	0	0	0	.000	0	R3
J Zuber	L	Phi	24	-F----	0	0	0	0	0	.000	0	R3
Totals					72800	2104		1567	.271	2579		
						10271		9712			2100	

1996 NL pitchers — alphabetical

The only predictions are the recommended bid limits for this year; the stats are the 1995 major league stats for each pitcher and the $ values are what the stats were worth in 1995.

Name	T	Tm	Age	IP	SO	W	Sv	ERA	Ratio	$	Bid
K Abbott	L	Phi	28	28	21	2	0	3.81	13.98	1	R3
J Acevedo	R	NY	26	65	40	4	0	6.44	13.98	-9	R2
T Alvarez	R	Mon	24	37	17	1	0	6.75	14.46	-7	1
L Aquino	R	SF	31	42	26	0	2	5.10	14.88	-5	0
R Arocha	R	StL	30	49	25	3	0	3.99	13.23	1	1
M Arrandale	R	StL	25	0	0	0	0	0.00	0.00	0	R4
A Ashby	R	SD	28	192	150	12	0	2.94	11.30	25	17
P Astacio	R	LA	26	104	80	7	0	4.24	11.42	7	3
S Avery	L	Atl	26	173	141	7	0	4.67	11.27	5	16
C Bailey	R	StL	25	3	5	0	0	7.37	9.82	-1	R3
R Bailey	R	Col	25	81	33	7	0	4.98	14.05	-2	R3
W Banks	R	Phi	27	90	62	2	0	5.66	16.28	-17	R3
B Barber	R	StL	23	29	27	2	0	5.22	14.42	-2	2
S Barton	L	SF	32	44	22	4	1	4.26	11.37	5	R3
J Bautista	R	SF	31	100	45	3	0	6.44	13.05	-13	R3
R Beck	R	SF	27	58	42	5	33	4.45	12.43	28	27
A Benes	R	StL	24	16	20	1	0	8.44	15.75	-5	6
A Berumen	R	SD	25	44	42	2	1	5.69	14.82	-5	R2
M Birkbeck	R	NY	35	27	14	0	0	1.63	7.81	7	R3
W Blair	R	SD	30	114	83	7	0	4.34	12.39	4	R3
D Bochtler	R	SD	25	45	45	4	1	3.57	11.32	7	2
P Borbon	L	Atl	28	32	33	2	2	3.09	12.94	4	1
T Borland	R	Phi	27	74	59	1	6	3.77	14.35	1	1
R Bottalico	R	Phi	26	87	87	5	1	2.46	9.44	19	21
R Bowen	R	Fla	28	16	15	2	0	3.78	18.90	-2	R3
J Brantley	R	Cin	32	70	62	3	28	2.82	9.34	34	28
J Brewingto	R	SF	24	75	45	6	0	4.54	13.50	0	2
D Brocail	R	Hou	29	77	39	6	1	4.19	12.68	4	R3
J Bullinger	R	Chi	30	150	93	12	0	4.14	13.02	7	5
D Burba	R	Cin	29	106	96	10	0	3.97	11.90	10	4
E Burgos	L	SF	30	8	12	0	0	8.65	21.60	-5	0
J Burkett	R	Fla	31	188	126	14	0	4.30	12.66	8	4
P Byrd	R	NY	25	22	26	2	0	2.05	10.22	6	1
T Candiotti	R	LA	38	190	141	7	0	3.50	11.58	13	7
H Carrasco	R	Cin	26	87	64	2	5	4.12	13.60	1	2
A Carter	L	Phi	27	7	6	0	0	6.14	7.36	0	R3
L Casian	L	Chi	30	23	11	1	0	1.93	14.66	2	0
F Castillo	R	Chi	27	188	135	11	0	3.21	11.06	23	14
J Castillo	R	NY	26	0	0	0	0	0.00	0.00	0	R3
J Christian	L	Pit	26	56	53	1	0	4.15	13.26	-2	2
B Clontz	R	Atl	25	69	55	8	4	3.65	12.13	12	3
S Cooke	L	Pit	26	0	0	0	0	0.00	0.00	0	R2
J Cummings	L	LA	26	39	21	3	0	3.00	11.08	6	R3
O Daal	L	LA	24	20	11	4	0	7.20	19.80	-5	0
M DeJean	R	Col	25	0	0	0	0	0.00	0.00	0	R2
J DeLeon	R	Mon	35	8	12	0	0	7.57	15.12	-2	R3
R DeLucia	R	StL	31	82	76	8	0	3.39	10.82	13	2
J Deshaies	L	Phi	35	5	6	0	0	20.27	27.00	-8	0
M Dewey	R	SF	31	31	32	1	0	3.13	13.36	1	R3
J DiPoto	R	NY	28	78	49	4	2	3.78	12.13	6	1
G Dishman	L	SD	25	97	43	4	0	5.01	12.80	-3	R2

Name	T	Tm	Age	IP	SO	W	Sv	ERA	Ratio	$	Bid
J Dougherty	R	Hou	28	67	49	8	0	4.92	13.43	2	R3
D Drabek	R	Hou	33	185	143	10	0	4.77	12.60	0	14
D Dreifort	R	LA	25	0	0	0	0	0.00	0.00	0	R2
R Drese	R	Oth	21	0	0	0	0	0.00	0.00	0	R4
E DuBose	L	Oth	19	0	0	0	0	0.00	0.00	0	R5
M Dunbar	L	Fla	27	7	5	0	0	11.58	29.57	-7	0
M Dyer	R	Pit	29	74	53	4	0	4.34	13.38	0	R3
T Edens	R	Chi	35	3	2	1	0	6.01	27.00	-1	0
J Eischen	L	LA	26	20	15	0	0	3.10	13.28	0	R2
D Elliott	R	SD	27	2	3	0	0	0.00	13.50	0	R3
J Ericks	R	Pit	28	106	80	3	0	4.59	13.41	-5	1
S Estes	L	SF	23	17	14	0	0	6.75	10.90	-2	R6
B Eversgerd	L	Mon	27	21	8	0	0	5.14	13.28	-2	R3
J Fassero	L	Mon	33	189	164	13	0	4.33	13.38	3	4
S Fernandez	L	Phi	33	64	79	6	0	3.34	9.60	13	8
P Fletcher	R	Phi	29	13	10	1	0	5.40	16.20	-2	0
D Florence	L	NY	29	12	5	3	0	1.50	17.25	3	R3
B Florie	R	SD	26	68	68	2	1	3.01	11.40	7	2
T Fossas	L	StL	38	36	40	3	0	1.47	9.33	11	R3
K Foster	R	Chi	27	167	146	12	0	4.51	11.49	10	7
J Franco	L	NY	35	51	41	5	29	2.44	11.32	32	25
J Frascator	R	StL	26	32	21	1	0	4.41	15.15	-3	0
W Fraser	R	Mon	32	25	12	2	2	5.61	11.92	1	R3
M Freeman	R	Col	33	94	61	3	0	5.89	15.50	-16	R3
S Frey	L	Phi	32	17	7	0	1	2.12	7.41	5	R3
R Garces	R	Fla	24	24	22	0	0	4.44	13.31	-2	R3
M Gardner	R	Fla	34	102	87	5	1	4.49	13.37	-1	R3
S Gentile	R	Mon	25	0	0	0	0	0.00	0.00	0	R2
T Glavine	R	Atl	30	198	127	16	0	3.08	11.23	28	24
P Gomez	R	SF	28	14	15	0	0	5.14	18.00	-4	0
D Gooden	R	NY	31	0	0	0	0	0.00	0.00	0	R3
J Gott	R	Pit	36	31	19	2	3	6.03	14.36	-2	R3
M Grace	R	Phi	26	11	7	1	0	3.18	11.12	2	2
J Grahe	R	Col	28	56	27	4	0	5.08	15.25	-5	R3
T Green	R	Phi	26	140	85	8	0	5.31	14.27	-10	R2
T Greene	R	Phi	29	33	24	0	0	8.29	17.37	-14	R3
E Gunderson	R	NY	30	24	19	1	0	3.70	12.20	1	R3
M Guthrie	R	LA	30	19	19	0	0	3.66	12.81	0	R3
J Guzman	R	Chi	32	0	0	0	0	0.00	0.00	0	R3
J Habyan	R	StL	32	40	35	3	0	2.88	10.40	8	R3
J Hamilton	R	SD	25	204	123	6	0	3.08	10.79	21	18
C Hammond	L	Fla	30	161	126	9	0	3.80	11.40	13	7
M Hampton	L	Hou	23	150	115	9	0	3.35	11.35	16	12
L Hancock	L	Pit	28	14	6	0	0	1.93	7.71	3	R3
G Hansell	R	LA	25	19	13	0	0	7.45	16.29	-6	R3
P Harnisch	R	NY	29	110	82	2	0	3.68	11.04	7	5
G Harris	R	Mon	40	48	47	2	0	2.61	11.36	7	R3
G Harris	R	Phi	31	19	9	2	0	4.26	12.79	1	R3
D Hartgrave	L	Hou	29	36	24	2	0	3.22	11.39	4	R3
B Harvey	R	Fla	27	0	0	0	0	0.00	0.00	-3	R2
T Henke	R	StL	38	54	48	1	36	1.82	9.94	38	26
M Henneman	R	Hou	34	21	19	0	8	3.00	10.71	8	19
B Henry	L	Mon	27	126	60	7	0	2.84	11.44	16	R2
D Henry	R	NY	34	67	62	3	4	2.96	9.80	14	2
G Heredia	R	Mon	30	119	74	5	1	4.31	11.95	4	1
D Hermanson	R	SD	23	31	19	3	0	6.82	16.20	-6	R1

Name	T	Tm	Age	IP	SO	W	Sv	ERA	Ratio	$	Bid
J Hernandez	R	Fla	29	7	5	0	0	11.58	19.28	-5	R3
X Hernandez	R	Cin	30	90	84	7	3	4.60	12.60	5	R3
B Hickerson	L	Col	32	48	40	3	1	8.57	18.06	-17	R3
T Hoffman	R	SD	28	53	52	7	31	3.88	10.46	33	27
D Holmes	R	Col	30	66	61	6	14	3.24	11.75	20	7
C Hook	R	SF	27	52	40	5	0	5.50	14.45	-3	0
J Hope	R	Pit	25	2	2	0	0	30.89	46.28	-6	R3
J Hudek	R	Hou	29	20	29	2	7	5.40	10.80	6	R1
J Isringhau	R	NY	23	93	55	9	0	2.81	11.52	16	15
D Jackson	L	StL	32	100	52	2	0	5.90	15.02	-17	2
M Jackson	R	Cin	31	49	41	6	2	2.39	10.47	14	2
K Jarvis	R	Cin	26	79	33	3	0	5.70	14.01	-9	R3
J Johnstone	R	Fla	27	4	3	0	0	3.86	17.36	-1	0
B Jones	R	NY	28	195	127	10	0	4.19	12.05	8	10
T Jones	R	Hou	28	99	96	6	15	3.07	12.73	20	9
J Juden	R	Phi	25	62	47	2	0	4.02	12.06	2	R2
R Karp	L	Phi	26	2	2	0	0	4.50	18.00	0	R2
D Kile	R	Hou	27	127	113	4	0	4.96	13.25	-7	2
M Kroon	R	SD	23	1	2	0	0	10.81	16.20	-1	R2
B Krueger	L	SD	38	7	6	0	0	7.05	19.96	-3	0
D Leiper	L	Mon	33	22	12	0	2	2.86	9.00	5	R3
M Leiter	R	SF	32	195	129	10	0	3.82	11.04	17	6
C Leskanic	R	Col	28	98	107	6	10	3.40	10.65	20	14
R Lewis	R	Fla	30	36	32	0	0	3.75	11.25	1	R3
J Lieber	R	Pit	26	72	45	4	0	6.32	14.49	-10	R2
E Loaiza	R	Pit	24	172	85	8	0	5.16	13.55	-9	1
G Maddux	R	Atl	30	209	181	19	0	1.63	7.30	68	42
R Manzanill	R	Pit	32	3	1	0	0	4.91	12.27	0	R3
P Martinez	L	Hou	27	20	17	0	0	7.40	19.60	-9	R3
P Martinez	R	Mon	24	194	174	14	0	3.51	10.35	27	23
R Martinez	R	LA	28	206	138	17	0	3.66	11.21	24	16
T Mathews	R	StL	26	29	28	1	2	1.52	9.71	9	3
T Mathews	R	Fla	31	82	72	4	3	3.38	10.56	12	4
T Mauser	R	SD	29	5	9	0	0	9.54	20.65	-3	0
D May	L	Atl	24	4	1	0	0	11.26	22.50	-3	R2
J McCurry	R	Pit	26	61	27	1	1	5.02	16.52	-10	0
C McElroy	L	Cin	28	40	27	3	0	6.03	13.61	-4	R3
G McMichael	R	Atl	29	80	74	7	2	2.79	10.71	17	6
K Mercker	R	Atl	28	143	102	7	0	4.15	12.65	3	6
D Miceli	R	Pit	25	58	56	4	21	4.66	13.81	15	18
D Million	L	Col	20	0	0	0	0	0.00	0.00	0	R4
M Mimbs	L	Phi	27	136	93	9	1	4.15	13.30	4	1
B Minor	R	NY	30	46	43	4	1	3.66	10.99	7	R3
D Mintz	R	SF	27	19	7	1	0	7.45	17.69	-6	0
D Mlicki	R	NY	28	160	123	9	0	4.26	11.99	7	3
R Morel	R	Pit	21	6	3	0	0	2.84	11.37	0	R2
M Morgan	R	StL	36	131	61	7	0	3.56	11.44	12	6
T Mulhollan	R	SF	33	149	65	5	0	5.80	13.77	-16	R3
B Munoz	R	Phi	28	15	6	0	0	5.75	13.79	-2	R2
M Munoz	R	Col	30	43	37	2	2	7.42	16.69	-11	0
M Myers	L	Fla	27	2	0	0	0	0.00	18.00	0	0
R Myers	L	Chi	33	55	59	1	38	3.88	12.45	29	31
C Nabholz	L	Chi	29	23	21	0	0	5.40	13.88	-3	0
J Navarro	R	Chi	29	200	128	14	0	3.28	11.23	25	12
D Neagle	L	Pit	27	209	150	13	0	3.43	11.42	21	11
R Nen	R	Fla	26	65	68	0	23	3.29	11.65	20	24

Name	T	Tm	Age	IP	SO	W	Sv	ERA	Ratio	$	Bid
R Nichols	R	Atl	31	6	3	0	0	5.41	25.65	-3	0
D Nied	R	Col	27	4	3	0	0	20.79	29.08	-7	R2
H Nomo	R	LA	27	191	236	13	0	2.54	9.50	39	25
O Olivares	R	Phi	28	41	22	1	0	6.91	16.85	-12	R3
D Osborne	L	StL	27	113	82	4	0	3.81	11.59	6	3
A Osuna	R	LA	30	44	46	2	0	4.43	11.89	1	4
L Painter	L	Col	28	45	36	3	1	4.37	12.90	2	R3
V Palacios	R	StL	32	40	34	2	0	5.80	14.95	-6	R3
C Park	R	LA	23	4	7	0	0	4.50	9.00	0	R1
J Parrett	R	StL	34	76	71	4	0	3.64	11.62	6	R3
S Parris	R	Pit	28	82	61	6	0	5.38	13.39	-3	R2
A Pena	R	Atl	37	31	39	2	0	2.61	8.42	8	1
B Penningto	L	Cin	27	9	7	0	0	5.59	18.62	-3	R3
C Perez	L	Mon	25	141	106	10	0	3.69	10.82	17	10
M Perez	R	Chi	31	71	49	2	2	3.66	12.49	4	R3
Y Perez	L	Fla	28	46	47	2	1	5.21	12.15	-1	R3
R Person	R	NY	26	12	10	1	0	0.75	5.25	6	4
M Petkovsek	R	StL	30	137	71	6	0	4.00	11.21	9	1
D Plesac	L	Pit	34	60	57	4	3	3.58	11.93	7	R3
M Portugal	R	Cin	33	181	96	11	0	4.01	11.94	11	6
J Powell	R	Fla	24	8	4	0	0	1.08	14.04	1	R1
R Powell	L	Pit	28	29	20	0	0	6.98	17.29	-10	0
T Pugh	R	Cin	29	98	38	6	0	3.84	12.08	7	R3
B Pulsipher	L	NY	22	126	81	5	0	3.98	11.86	5	8
P Quantrill	R	Phi	27	179	103	11	0	4.67	12.85	1	1
P Rapp	R	Fla	28	167	102	14	0	3.44	12.58	16	8
S Reed	R	Col	30	84	79	5	3	2.14	8.78	23	4
B Rekar	R	Col	24	85	60	4	0	4.98	12.60	-2	4
S Reynolds	R	Hou	28	189	175	10	0	3.47	11.08	19	12
A Reynoso	R	Col	30	93	40	7	0	5.32	14.71	-7	R3
C Ricci	R	Phi	27	10	9	1	0	1.80	10.80	2	R2
J Rijo	R	Cin	31	69	62	5	0	4.17	12.78	3	15
K Ritz	R	Col	31	173	120	11	2	4.21	12.25	10	R1
B Rivera	R	Chi	27	5	2	0	0	5.41	18.00	-1	R3
F Rodriguez	R	LA	23	10	5	1	0	2.53	13.50	2	R2
R Rodriguez	L	StL	33	1	0	0	0	0.00	0.00	1	0
K Rogers	L	SF	27	0	0	0	0	0.00	0.00	0	R3
M Rojas	R	Mon	29	67	61	1	30	4.12	13.03	21	25
J Roper	R	SF	24	8	6	0	0	12.39	23.63	-7	R3
J Rosselli	L	SF	24	30	7	2	0	8.70	17.70	-11	R3
K Rueter	L	Mon	25	47	28	5	0	3.23	8.93	11	3
B Ruffin	L	Col	32	34	23	0	11	2.12	11.91	12	10
J Ruffin	R	Cin	24	13	11	0	0	1.35	10.13	3	R1
B Saberhage	R	Col	32	153	100	7	0	4.18	11.65	7	10
S Sanders	R	SD	27	90	88	5	0	4.30	11.00	6	R1
C Schilling	R	Phi	29	116	114	7	0	3.57	9.46	18	10
J Schmidt	R	Atl	23	25	19	2	0	5.76	16.20	-4	R1
P Schourek	L	Cin	27	190	160	18	0	3.22	9.60	37	24
T Scott	R	Mon	29	63	57	2	2	3.98	10.66	6	1
R Seanez	R	LA	27	34	29	1	3	6.75	14.80	-5	R2
S Service	R	SF	28	31	30	3	0	3.19	11.03	5	R3
J Shaw	R	Mon	29	62	45	1	3	4.62	12.13	1	R3
H Slocumb	R	Phi	30	65	63	5	32	2.89	13.64	29	7
A Small	R	Fla	24	6	5	1	0	1.42	18.47	1	R2
J Smiley	L	Cin	31	176	124	12	0	3.46	10.80	22	18
P Smith	R	Cin	30	24	14	1	0	6.66	13.68	-4	0

Name	T	Tm	Age	IP	SO	W	Sv	ERA	Ratio	$	Bid
J Smoltz	R	Atl	29	192	193	12	0	3.18	11.12	24	18
D Springer	R	Phi	31	22	15	0	0	4.84	12.09	-1	0
R Springer	R	Phi	27	26	32	0	0	3.71	10.80	1	R3
E Stull	R	Mon	24	0	0	0	0	0.00	0.00	0	R2
T Sturtze	R	Chi	25	2	0	0	0	9.01	13.50	-1	0
S Sullivan	R	Cin	25	3	2	0	0	4.91	14.73	0	R6
D Swartzbau	R	Chi	28	7	5	0	0	0.00	9.82	2	R3
B Swift	R	Col	34	105	68	9	0	4.94	14.05	-3	5
G Swindell	L	Hou	31	153	96	10	0	4.47	12.88	3	1
J Tabaka	L	Hou	32	30	25	1	0	3.23	12.91	1	R3
K Tapani	R	LA	32	57	43	4	0	5.05	13.58	-2	3
J Thobe	R	Mon	25	4	0	0	0	9.01	20.25	-2	R3
T Thobe	L	Atl	26	3	2	0	0	10.81	18.90	-2	R3
M Thompson	R	Col	25	51	30	2	0	6.53	16.76	-12	1
S Torres	R	SF	24	8	2	0	0	9.01	22.50	-5	R3
S Trachsel	R	Chi	25	160	117	7	0	5.15	14.00	-11	5
T Urbani	L	StL	28	82	52	3	0	3.70	13.06	2	0
U Urbina	R	Mon	22	23	15	2	0	6.17	15.43	-3	R1
I Valdes	R	LA	22	197	150	13	1	3.05	9.97	33	19
C Valdez	R	SF	24	14	7	0	0	6.14	16.57	-4	R6
S Valdez	R	SF	31	66	29	4	0	4.75	12.89	-1	R3
F Valenzuel	L	SD	36	90	57	8	0	4.98	13.45	-1	R3
B Vanlandin	R	SF	25	122	95	6	0	3.67	12.03	8	5
D Veres	R	Hou	29	103	94	5	1	2.26	10.36	20	4
R Veres	R	Fla	30	48	31	4	1	3.88	12.57	4	R3
R Villone	L	SD	26	25	37	2	1	4.21	12.27	2	4
F Viola	L	Cin	36	14	4	0	0	6.28	14.44	-3	R3
T Wade	L	Atl	23	4	3	0	0	4.50	15.75	-1	R2
B Wagner	L	Hou	25	0	0	0	0	0.00	0.00	0	R1
P Wagner	R	Pit	28	165	120	5	1	4.80	13.42	-7	1
M Walker	R	Chi	31	44	20	1	1	3.22	13.90	1	R3
P Walker	R	NY	27	17	5	1	0	4.59	14.77	-1	0
D Wall	R	Hou	28	24	16	3	0	5.55	14.05	-1	R3
A Watson	L	StL	25	114	49	7	0	4.96	13.14	-2	1
D Weathers	R	Fla	26	90	60	4	0	5.98	15.54	-15	R3
D Wells	L	Cin	33	72	50	6	0	3.59	11.15	9	17
T Wendell	R	Chi	29	60	50	3	0	4.92	14.17	-4	R3
D West	R	Phi	31	38	25	3	0	3.79	12.55	3	R3
G White	L	Mon	24	25	25	1	0	7.02	12.27	-4	R2
R White	R	Pit	27	55	29	2	0	4.75	13.74	-3	R3
B Williams	R	SD	27	72	75	3	0	6.00	14.62	-10	R3
M Williams	R	Phi	31	87	57	3	0	3.29	10.98	9	2
P Wilson	R	NY	23	0	0	0	0	0.00	0.00	0	R1
T Wilson	L	SF	30	82	38	3	0	3.92	13.06	1	R3
M Wohlers	R	Atl	26	64	90	7	25	2.09	10.44	35	40
B Woodall	L	Atl	27	10	5	1	0	6.10	18.29	-2	R3
T Worrell	R	SD	28	13	13	1	0	4.73	14.85	-1	R2
T Worrell	R	LA	36	62	61	4	32	2.02	9.96	38	29
A Young	R	Chi	30	41	15	3	2	3.70	13.28	4	R3
Total											1020

1996 AL hitters — by bid limits

Upper case means at least 18 games (or the majority) played at a position; lower case means at least one game played. Many R3's and zero bids have been cut, without changing the #'s.

Catchers

#	Name	B	Tm	Age	C123SO	AB	R	HR	RBI	SB	BA	$	Bid
1-	B Surhoff	L	Mil	31	CF---O	525	86	9	82	5	.307	21	18
2-	M Stanley	R	NY	33	C-----	425	64	17	79	0	.264	15	17
3-	I Rodriguez	R	Tex	24	C-----	500	56	12	68	0	.282	14	16
4-	C Hoiles	R	Bal	31	C-----	400	60	22	66	2	.253	15	14
5-	T Steinbach	R	Oak	34	Cf----	425	42	12	63	0	.273	12	12
6-	S Alomar	R	Cle	30	C-----	350	51	12	51	0	.286	12	10
7-	M Macfarlan	R	Bos	32	C-----	400	46	15	55	0	.230	7	5
8-	J Leyritz	R	NY	32	CF----	275	38	7	38	1	.284	9	5
9-	D Wilson	R	Sea	27	C-----	425	40	5	49	0	.261	6	4
10-	J Oliver	R	Mil	30	Cf----	350	44	6	49	1	.271	8	3
11-	G Williams	B	Oak	26	C-----	225	36	6	39	0	.271	7	3
12-	J Girardi	R	NY	31	C-----	425	54	4	47	0	.252	4	3
13-	G Myers	L	Cal	30	C-----	275	34	7	38	0	.269	7	2
14-	R Karkovice	R	Chi	32	C-----	425	57	17	67	2	.216	7	2
15-	M Walbeck	B	Min	26	C-----	400	40	3	45	1	.263	6	2
16-	B Mayne	L	KC	28	C-----	375	28	2	32	0	.264	4	1
17-	T Pena	R	Cle	39	C-----	225	21	3	23	0	.244	2	1
18-	J Flaherty	R	Det	28	C-----	400	44	7	43	0	.245	4	1
19-	J Fabregas	L	Cal	26	C-----	250	26	2	24	0	.256	2	1
20-	M Merullo	L	Min	30	Cf----	175	17	1	24	0	.257	2	1
21-	G Zaun	B	Bal	25	C-----	125	15	3	16	1	.256	3	1
22-	B Haselman	R	Bos	30	Cf-t--	175	25	3	24	0	.257	3	1
23-	R Knorr	R	Tor	27	C-----	375	51	7	46	1	.216	1	1
24-	C Widger	R	Sea	25	C----o	150	11	2	17	1	.233	1	1
31-	J Valentin	B	Min	20	C-----	0	0	0	0	0	.000	0	R5

First Basemen

#	Name	B	Tm	Age	C123SO	AB	R	HR	RBI	SB	BA	$	Bid
1-	F Thomas	R	Chi	28	-F----	550	134	48	127	3	.325	45	47
2-	R Palmeiro	L	Bal	31	-F----	600	93	39	112	2	.300	35	38
3-	M Vaughn	L	Bos	28	-F----	575	96	37	118	5	.287	33	36
4-	T Martinez	L	Sea	28	-F----	550	94	27	96	0	.304	28	29
5-	M McGwire	R	Oak	32	-F----	525	118	53	133	0	.265	35	28
6-	E Murray	B	Cle	40	-F----	500	74	21	92	1	.284	21	21
7-	C Fielder	R	Det	32	-F----	550	76	30	91	0	.253	19	20
8-	J Snow	R	Cal	28	-F----	575	86	23	90	1	.277	21	19
9-	J Jaha	R	Mil	30	-F----	500	85	24	88	0	.294	23	19
10-	W Joyner	L	KC	34	-F----	525	73	13	84	1	.295	19	18
11-	W Clark	L	Tex	32	-F----	500	88	13	95	1	.282	18	18
12-	P Sorrento	L	Cle	30	-F----	375	60	28	96	1	.267	22	17
13-	J Olerud	L	Tor	27	-F----	525	76	9	59	1	.293	15	16
14-	H Perry	R	Cle	26	-F-t--	225	31	4	31	1	.293	7	6
15-	J Giambi	L	Oak	25	-F-T--	250	37	5	31	1	.264	5	2
16-	D Martinez	L	Chi	31	-F---O	325	49	4	36	5	.265	7	2
17-	J Samuel	R	KC	35	-Fd--o	200	27	9	33	2	.245	6	1
18-	M Aldrete	L	Cal	35	-F---O	75	9	1	12	0	.267	2	1
19-	R McGinnis	R	KC	33	-F-t-o	0	0	0	0	0	.000	0	0
21-	D White	R	Det	26	-F---o	50	3	1	3	0	.200	0	0
22-	T Clark	B	Det	24	-F----	275	26	11	45	1	.247	8	R1
23-	D Boston	L	Tor	24	-F----	100	12	3	11	2	.250	3	R2

#	Name	B	Tm	Age	C123SO	AB	R	HR	RBI	SB	BA	$	Bid
24-	D Hollins	B	Bos	30	-F----	50	11	2	8	0	.240	1	R2
25-	R McGuire	L	Bos	24	-F----	0	0	0	0	0	.000	0	R2
26-	L Sutton	L	KC	25	-F----	100	8	3	10	0	.250	2	R2
27-	R Coomer	R	Min	29	-F-t-o	150	22	5	28	0	.273	5	R2
28-	I Cruz	L	Det	28	-F----	50	4	2	5	0	.220	1	R3
29-	G Pirkl	R	Sea	25	-F----	75	4	2	5	0	.253	1	R3
30-	S Dunn	R	Min	26	-F----	0	0	0	0	0	.000	0	R3
31-	P Carey	L	Bal	28	-F----	0	0	0	0	0	.000	0	R3
32-	T Unroe	R	Mil	25	-F----	0	0	0	0	0	.000	0	R3
33-	S Stahoviak	L	Min	26	-F-T--	250	26	2	21	3	.252	3	R3
34-	D Masteller	L	Min	28	-F---O	0	0	0	0	0	.000	0	R3
35-	F Stubbs	L	Det	36	-F---O	100	11	1	16	0	.250	2	R3
36-	D Mattingly	L	Oth	35	-F----	0	0	0	0	0	.000	0	R3
37-	M Smith	L	KC	20	-F----	0	0	0	0	0	.000	0	R4
38-	H Williams	R	Chi	25	-F----	0	0	0	0	0	.000	0	R4
39-	C Weinke	L	Tor	23	-F----	0	0	0	0	0	.000	0	R4
40-	S Cox	L	Oak	21	-F----	0	0	0	0	0	.000	0	R5
41-	R Sexson	R	Cle	21	-F----	0	0	0	0	0	.000	0	R5

Second Basemen

#	Name	B	Tm	Age	C123SO	AB	R	HR	RBI	SB	BA	$	Bid
1-	C Knoblauch	R	Min	27	--D-s-	575	110	8	64	45	.325	39	35
2-	R Alomar	B	Tor	28	--D---	550	74	15	69	25	.296	28	32
3-	C Baerga	B	Cle	27	--D---	600	104	15	94	8	.305	27	29
4-	R Durham	B	Chi	24	--D---	550	81	9	67	24	.267	20	16
5-	B Gates	B	Oak	26	-fD---	575	65	7	66	6	.273	13	12
6-	R Velarde	R	Cal	33	--DTSO	500	81	11	62	4	.276	14	7
7-	J Cora	B	Sea	31	--D-s-	400	52	0	36	13	.268	9	6
8-	L Whitaker	L	Det	39	--D---	325	42	13	52	0	.274	11	6
9-	J Cirillo	R	Mil	26	-fDTs-	500	80	7	51	3	.266	9	5
10-	L Alicea	B	Bos	30	--D---	425	63	4	46	9	.261	9	5
11-	K Lockhart	L	KC	31	--Dt--	350	51	4	42	9	.280	11	4
12-	P Kelly	R	NY	28	--D---	475	55	5	50	7	.251	7	3
13-	J Frye	R	Tex	29	--D---	425	51	3	39	4	.278	8	2
14-	P Listach	B	Mil	28	--DtSo	225	22	1	16	14	.236	5	2
15-	M Alexander	R	Bal	25	--Dts-	250	38	2	23	12	.232	5	2
16-	R Hudler	R	Cal	32	-fD--O	125	14	1	14	5	.240	3	1
17-	B Barberie	B	Bal	28	--Dt--	225	35	1	23	2	.258	3	1
18-	J Huson	L	Bal	31	--DTs-	175	26	1	20	6	.257	4	1
19-	S Rodriguez	R	Det	25	--D-s-	125	16	0	7	5	.208	0	0
27-	T Walker	L	Min	23	--D---	175	25	8	25	4	.263	7	R1
28-	C Stynes	R	KC	23	--D---	100	19	1	11	3	.250	2	R2
29-	A Pozo	R	Sea	22	--D---	100	14	2	12	3	.260	3	R2
30-	D Brady	B	Chi	26	--D---	125	21	1	18	6	.248	4	R2
31-	N Martin	B	Chi	29	--Dtso	150	15	1	15	4	.233	2	R3
32-	D Easley	R	Cal	26	--D-S-	125	12	2	12	3	.224	1	R3
33-	S Penn	B	Det	26	--D---	200	21	0	8	9	.225	1	R3
34-	B Ripken	R	Cle	31	--Dt--	50	11	2	8	0	.280	2	R3
35-	T Shumpert	R	Oth	29	--Dts-	0	0	0	0	0	.000	0	R3
36-	D Howard	B	KC	29	-fD-SO	200	18	0	14	4	.240	1	R3
37-	C Rodriguez	B	Bos	28	--Dts-	50	8	0	6	0	.240	0	R3
38-	F Vina	L	Mil	26	--Dts-	150	23	0	14	3	.240	1	R3
39-	E Diaz	R	Tex	21	--D---	0	0	0	0	0	.000	0	R4
40-	S Nunez	R	KC	21	--D---	0	0	0	0	0	.000	0	R4

Shortstops

#	Name	B	Tm	Age	C123SO	AB	R	HR	RBI	SB	BA	$	Bid
1-	J Valentin	R	Bos	26	-----S-	550	107	24	86	10	.289	27	28
2-	C Ripken	R	Bal	35	-----S-	600	86	18	91	0	.268	17	20
3-	A Rodriguez	R	Sea	20	-----S-	525	71	20	69	10	.257	17	18
4-	J Valentin	B	Mil	26	---tS-	500	91	17	69	19	.248	18	11
5-	O Vizquel	B	Cle	29	-----S-	525	77	2	47	21	.259	13	11
6-	P Meares	R	Min	27	-----So	475	67	11	59	9	.261	13	10
7-	A Gonzalez	R	Tor	23	---tS-	475	66	12	54	5	.242	8	9
8-	G Disarcina	R	Cal	28	-----S-	450	74	5	51	6	.284	12	9
9-	C Gomez	R	Det	25	--D-S-	525	59	9	59	4	.248	8	6
10-	O Guillen	L	Chi	32	-----S-	525	63	1	51	7	.251	6	5
11-	G Gagne	R	KC	34	-----S-	500	67	6	56	5	.252	8	5
12-	M Bordick	R	Oak	30	-----S-	500	50	5	42	7	.258	7	4
13-	B Gil	R	Tex	23	-----S-	475	41	12	55	3	.223	5	3
14-	T Fernandez	B	NY	34	--d-S-	400	59	3	46	5	.245	5	2
15-	L Sojo	R	Sea	30	--D-So	225	30	1	24	0	.271	3	2
16-	A Trammell	R	Det	38	-----S-	200	25	2	20	1	.255	2	1
17-	J Reboulet	R	Min	32	cfdTS-	200	36	3	21	0	.265	3	1
18-	C Grebeck	R	Chi	31	--dTS-	150	16	1	19	0	.253	2	1
25-	D Jeter	R	NY	22	-----S-	150	25	1	16	7	.280	6	R1
26-	M Loretta	R	Mil	24	--d-S-	125	32	1	7	2	.264	2	R2
27-	N Garcpprra	R	Bos	22	-----S-	0	0	0	0	0	.000	0	R2
28-	F Fermin	R	Oth	32	--D-S-	0	0	0	0	0	.000	0	R3
29-	D Hocking	L	Min	26	-----S-	75	12	1	9	2	.227	1	R3
30-	T Perez	B	Tor	22	--dtS-	100	12	1	8	0	.230	0	R3
31-	D Cedeno	B	Tor	27	--DtS-	175	19	2	15	0	.234	0	R3
32-	D Relaford	B	Sea	22	-----S-	0	0	0	0	0	.000	0	R4
33-	M Lopez	R	KC	21	---tS-	0	0	0	0	0	.000	0	R4
34-	D Jackson	R	Cle	22	-----S-	0	0	0	0	0	.000	0	R4
35-	D Klassen	R	Mil	21	-----S-	0	0	0	0	0	.000	0	R4
36-	E Wilson	B	Cle	21	-----S-	0	0	0	0	0	.000	0	R4
37-	G Guevara	B	Sea	23	--d-S-	0	0	0	0	0	.000	0	R4

Third Basemen

#	Name	B	Tm	Age	C123SO	AB	R	HR	RBI	SB	BA	$	Bid
1-	B Bonilla	B	Bal	33	---T-O	550	111	31	111	1	.305	32	35
2-	J Thome	L	Cle	25	---T--	525	106	29	101	5	.278	26	29
3-	R Ventura	L	Chi	28	-F-T--	550	84	27	100	0	.287	25	26
4-	D Palmer	R	Tex	27	---T--	500	118	31	89	0	.280	24	24
5-	T Fryman	R	Det	27	---T--	575	85	22	88	3	.264	19	21
6-	T Phillips	B	Cal	37	---T-O	575	120	18	57	14	.268	19	19
7-	G Gaetti	R	KC	37	-f-T--	550	78	29	100	2	.255	21	18
8-	W Boggs	L	NY	38	-f-T--	500	82	5	68	1	.330	20	15
9-	M Blowers	R	Sea	31	-f-T-o	425	55	19	84	0	.252	14	12
10-	K Seitzer	R	Mil	34	-F-T--	525	58	8	77	2	.295	17	11
11-	T Naehring	R	Bos	29	---T--	475	62	7	55	0	.295	13	9
12-	R Davis	R	NY	26	-f-T--	450	64	18	68	0	.242	11	8
13-	E Sprague	R	Tor	28	-f-T--	525	77	17	69	0	.242	9	7
14-	S Brosius	R	Oak	29	-FdTsO	450	76	14	43	2	.251	8	5
15-	C Snopek	R	Chi	25	---Ts-	225	31	4	26	1	.276	5	2
16-	D Strange	B	Sea	32	--dT-o	125	15	1	16	0	.264	2	1
17-	A Espinoza	R	Cle	34	-fDTS-	125	13	2	14	0	.256	2	1
18-	C Paquette	R	Oak	27	-f-TsO	225	33	9	38	3	.213	5	1
19-	S Leius	R	Min	30	---Ts-	300	40	5	36	0	.247	4	1
29-	C Worthingt	R	Tex	31	---T--	75	4	2	6	0	.213	0	R3
30-	H Battle	R	Tor	24	---T--	100	14	1	6	1	.230	0	R3

Predictions—AL bid limits

#	Name	B	Tm	Age	C123SO	AB	R	HR	RBI	SB	BA	$	Bid
31-	L Gomez	R	Bal	29	-f-T--	100	11	3	9	0	.230	1	R3
32-	L Ortiz	R	Tex	26	---T--	50	4	2	8	0	.220	1	R3
33-	J Randa	R	KC	26	--dT--	75	6	2	8	0	.227	1	R3
34-	S Owen	B	Cal	35	--dTS-	0	0	0	0	0	.000	0	R3

Outfielders

#	Name	B	Tm	Age	C123SO	AB	R	HR	RBI	SB	BA	$	Bid
1-	K Lofton	L	Cle	29	------O	600	125	12	60	71	.342	54	47
2-	K Griffey	L	Sea	26	------O	575	115	39	120	7	.329	43	46
3-	A Belle	R	Cle	29	------O	575	125	51	131	3	.304	43	45
4-	T Salmon	R	Cal	27	------O	550	111	37	112	5	.289	33	36
5-	M Ramirez	R	Cle	24	------O	550	101	37	123	5	.311	38	36
6-	K Puckett	R	Min	35	--dtsO	575	86	23	105	1	.310	29	33
7-	B Williams	B	NY	27	------O	575	94	22	93	10	.299	29	30
8-	P O'Neill	L	NY	33	------O	550	95	24	95	1	.304	27	29
9-	J Edmonds	L	Cal	26	------O	575	110	30	108	4	.278	27	28
10-	J Buhner	R	Sea	31	------O	550	95	35	122	1	.251	25	27
11-	S Green	L	Tor	23	------O	525	74	26	84	6	.307	29	26
12-	M Cordova	R	Min	26	------O	550	83	25	89	14	.269	25	26
13-	L Johnson	L	Chi	32	------O	625	97	5	54	38	.291	28	25
14-	G Anderson	L	Cal	24	------O	525	77	17	90	3	.299	23	25
15-	J Damon	L	KC	22	------O	575	101	11	75	25	.294	27	25
16-	O Nixon	B	Tex	37	------O	625	92	0	47	52	.288	30	24
17-	C Curtis	R	Det	27	------O	625	105	19	65	31	.258	25	24
18-	J Carter	R	Tor	36	-f---O	575	72	25	88	9	.257	21	24
19-	B Anderson	L	Bal	32	------O	600	116	17	69	28	.258	23	22
20-	R Henderson	R	Oak	37	------O	375	57	6	44	25	.288	20	19
21-	T Goodwin	L	KC	27	------O	475	70	2	27	51	.274	25	19
22-	M Greenwell	L	Bos	32	------O	500	71	13	75	5	.290	19	18
23-	G Berroa	R	Oak	31	------O	550	82	19	87	3	.273	19	18
24-	D Nilsson	L	Mil	26	cf---O	500	74	21	85	1	.272	19	18
25-	S Javier	B	Oak	32	----t-O	525	89	5	60	36	.269	23	18
26-	T Raines	B	Chi	36	------O	525	80	9	61	14	.276	17	16
27-	C Delgado	L	Tor	24	-f---O	450	57	19	64	0	.253	12	15
28-	R Sierra	B	NY	30	------O	550	80	18	94	1	.256	16	15
29-	M Tettleton	B	Tex	35	cf---O	500	88	31	85	0	.242	17	14
30-	V Coleman	B	Sea	34	------O	375	50	0	15	31	.259	13	14
31-	P Munoz	R	Min	27	-f---O	450	45	16	54	5	.262	13	14
32-	C Goodwin	L	Bal	23	------O	475	65	2	37	41	.255	19	13
33-	T O'Leary	L	Bos	26	------O	425	63	14	59	4	.287	16	13
34-	D Hosey	B	Bos	29	------O	550	75	11	52	17	.289	20	12
35-	L Mouton	R	Chi	28	------O	450	56	13	68	3	.284	16	11
36-	M Lawton	L	Min	24	-f---O	425	72	8	45	15	.266	14	11
37-	B Higginson	L	Det	25	------O	450	65	16	56	5	.233	9	8
38-	J Hammonds	R	Bal	25	------O	425	39	7	51	4	.278	11	8
39-	D Tartabull	R	Oak	33	------O	350	43	11	45	1	.243	7	8
40-	R Greer	L	Tex	27	-f---O	425	57	10	59	1	.264	10	7
41-	J Nunnally	L	KC	24	------O	375	61	13	49	8	.237	10	7
42-	M McLemore	B	Tex	31	--D--O	425	65	2	35	17	.256	10	6
43-	D Hamilton	L	Mil	31	------O	450	61	5	49	12	.271	12	5
44-	M Tucker	L	KC	25	------O	225	28	8	23	2	.236	4	5
45-	A Diaz	B	Sea	27	------O	350	56	2	35	22	.254	12	4
46-	L Tinsley	B	Bos	27	------O	325	53	1	32	11	.268	8	4
47-	D Hulse	L	Mil	28	------O	300	40	1	35	14	.253	8	3
48-	M Mieske	R	Mil	28	------O	275	42	14	55	1	.244	10	3
49-	M Stairs	L	Oak	27	------O	175	15	4	25	0	.274	5	2

Predictions—AL bid limits

# Name	B	Tm	Age	C123SO	AB	R	HR	RBI	SB	BA	$	Bid
50- G Williams	R	NY	29	------O	175	31	5	26	7	.234	6	2
51- J Clark	R	Min	32	-f----O	175	26	4	19	1	.274	4	2
52- R Becker	B	Min	24	------O	275	31	3	23	7	.258	5	2
53- P Nevin	R	Det	25	---t-O	200	18	3	24	0	.215	0	2
54- D Bautista	R	Det	24	------O	225	23	6	18	3	.204	0	2
55- R Amaral	R	Sea	34	------O	175	31	0	12	14	.274	7	2
56- W Kirby	L	Cle	32	------O	150	22	1	11	7	.240	3	1
57- M Smith	R	Bal	26	------O	250	25	6	35	1	.236	4	1
58- L Frazier	B	Tex	31	--d--O	150	28	0	12	16	.213	5	1
59- D James	L	NY	33	-f---O	150	15	1	18	2	.287	4	1
60- R Perez	R	Tor	27	------O	125	11	2	11	0	.272	2	1
69- J Malave	R	Bos	25	------O	125	14	5	18	1	.264	4	R1
70- R Rivera	R	NY	22	------O	200	20	8	21	5	.240	6	R1
71- D Erstad	L	Cal	22	------O	150	4	4	15	1	.293	5	R1
72- S Stewart	R	Tor	22	------O	200	12	0	12	9	.265	5	R1
73- L Raven	R	Cal	27	------O	0	0	0	0	0	.000	0	R2
74- C Latham	R	Min	23	------O	100	8	2	7	3	.240	2	R2
75- R Pemberton	R	Det	26	------O	300	30	3	41	2	.303	10	R2
76- M Franklin	B	Det	24	------O	100	6	4	9	0	.250	2	R2
77- J Burnitz	L	Cle	27	------O	50	28	2	7	1	.260	2	R2
78- K Felder	R	Mil	25	------O	50	5	1	5	0	.240	1	R2
79- J Herrera	L	Oak	23	------O	175	17	2	8	3	.251	2	R2
80- R Myers	L	KC	23	------O	75	8	0	6	6	.253	3	R2
81- B Giles	L	Cle	25	------O	50	5	2	6	0	.280	2	R2
83- K Bass	B	Bal	37	------O	150	16	2	16	5	.260	4	R3
84- D Singleton	L	Mil	23	------O	50	3	0	2	3	.200	0	R3
85- T Steverson	R	Det	24	------O	100	26	2	14	4	.240	3	R3
86- J Tatum	R	Bos	28	c-----O	25	2	1	3	0	.240	1	R3
87- O Palmeiro	L	Cal	27	------O	50	7	0	2	1	.260	1	R3
88- A Cole	L	Min	30	------O	0	0	0	0	0	.000	0	R3
89- W McGee	B	Oth	37	------O	0	0	0	0	0	.000	0	R3
91- D Bragg	L	Sea	26	------O	0	0	0	0	0	.000	0	R3
94- M Cameron	R	Chi	23	------O	125	11	1	16	5	.208	1	R3
95- R Faneyte	R	Oak	27	------O	0	0	0	0	0	.000	0	R3
97- R Amaro	B	Cle	31	------O	50	4	1	5	0	.220	0	R3
98- T Hansen	R	Sea	29	------O	0	0	0	0	0	.000	0	R3
99- B Cookson	R	Bos	26	------O	75	6	1	9	0	.267	1	R3
101- W Newson	L	Sea	31	------O	0	0	0	0	0	.000	0	R3
102- W Chamberla	R	Oth	30	------O	0	0	0	0	0	.000	0	R3
104- G Thurman	R	Oth	31	------O	0	0	0	0	0	.000	0	R3
105- C Maldonado	R	Oth	35	------O	0	0	0	0	0	.000	0	R3
106- E Davis	R	Oth	34	------O	0	0	0	0	0	.000	0	R3
107- J Brown	R	Bal	29	------O	25	4	0	2	3	.200	1	R3
108- J Voigt	R	Tex	30	-f---O	75	10	2	9	0	.240	1	R3
109- D Gallagher	R	Oth	35	------O	0	0	0	0	0	.000	0	R3
110- T Ward	B	Mil	31	------O	150	21	3	21	5	.240	4	R3
111- T Lowery	R	Tex	25	------O	0	0	0	0	0	.000	0	R3
112- E Young	R	Oak	27	------O	125	22	3	13	0	.216	0	R3
113- S Obando	R	Bal	26	------O	50	4	2	5	0	.260	1	R3
114- M Coleman	R	Bos	20	------O	0	0	0	0	0	.000	0	R4
115- L Roberts	B	Tor	25	------O	0	0	0	0	0	.000	0	R4
116- T Nixon	L	Bos	22	------O	0	0	0	0	0	.000	0	R4
117- M Christens	R	Cal	19	------O	0	0	0	0	0	.000	0	R4
118- B Grieve	L	Oak	20	------O	0	0	0	0	0	.000	0	R4
119- S Mack	R	Oth	34	------O	0	0	0	0	0	.000	0	R4
120- J Hurst	R	Chi	24	------O	0	0	0	0	0	.000	0	R4

Predictions—AL bid limits

#	Name	B	Tm	Age	C123SO	AB	R	HR	RBI	SB	BA	$	Bid
121-	K Bartee	B	Min	24	-----O	0	0	0	0	0	.000	0	R4
122-	T Hunter	R	Min	20	-----O	0	0	0	0	0	.000	0	R4

Designated Hitters

#		Name	B	Tm	Age	C123SO	AB	R	HR	RBI	SB	BA	$	Bid
1	-	E Martinez	R	Sea	33	-f-t--	525	118	24	110	0	.333	33	29
2	-	J Gonzalez	R	Tex	26	-----o	525	79	40	111	1	.282	31	28
3	-	C Davis	B	Cal	36	------	550	101	24	104	0	.291	25	23
4	-	J Canseco	R	Bos	31	-----o	450	67	25	84	1	.278	21	23
5	-	P Molitor	R	Min	39	------	550	67	18	69	16	.293	25	21
6	-	H Baines	L	Bal	37	------	425	65	21	72	0	.294	20	17
7	-	D Strawberr	L	Oth	34	-----o	250	40	10	39	0	.244	6	7
8	-	B Hamelin	L	KC	28	-f-----	350	31	17	52	0	.226	7	2
9	-	J Vitiello	R	KC	26	-f-----	150	15	7	33	1	.273	7	2
10	-	G Vaughn	R	Mil	30	------	300	49	11	43	4	.220	6	1
11	-	R Jefferson	B	Bos	27	-f---o	150	24	5	30	6	.273	6	1
15	-	C Hale	L	Min	31	-fdt--	75	6	0	12	0	.267	1	R3
17	-	C James	R	Bos	33	-----o	125	12	4	13	1	.264	3	R3
19	-	K Maas	R	Oth	31	-f-----	0	0	0	0	0	.000	0	R3
20	-	S Horn	L	Tex	32	------	0	0	0	0	0	.000	0	R3
21	-	J Grotewald	L	KC	30	-f-----	0	0	0	0	0	.000	0	R3

1996 AL pitchers — by bid limits

The only predictions are the recommended bid limits for this year; the stats are the 1995 major league stats for each pitcher and the $ values are what the stats were worth in 1995.

#	Name	T	Tm	Age	IP	SO	W	Sv	ERA	Ratio	$	Bid
1-	J Mesa	R	Cle	30	64	58	3	46	1.13	9.28	57	41
2-	J Wetteland	R	NY	29	61	66	1	31	2.94	7.92	39	40
3-	R Johnson	L	Sea	32	214	294	18	0	2.48	9.40	58	37
4-	R Aguilera	R	Bos	34	55	52	3	32	2.60	9.60	39	35
5-	N Charlton	L	Sea	33	47	58	2	14	1.51	7.36	29	33
6-	M Mussina	R	Bal	27	221	158	19	0	3.29	9.62	50	30
7-	J Montgomer	R	KC	34	65	49	2	31	3.43	11.65	32	29
8-	R Hernandez	R	Chi	31	59	84	3	32	3.92	13.72	28	28
9-	D Cone	R	NY	33	229	191	18	0	3.57	11.11	38	27
10-	K Appier	R	KC	28	201	185	15	0	3.89	10.86	31	25
11-	L Smith	R	Cal	38	49	43	0	37	3.47	12.22	32	25
12-	A Fernandez	R	Chi	26	203	159	12	0	3.80	11.71	25	24
13-	R Clemens	R	Bos	33	140	132	10	0	4.18	12.92	12	23
14-	D Eckersley	R	Oak	41	50	40	4	29	4.83	11.44	28	22
15-	J McDowell	R	NY	30	217	157	15	0	3.93	11.95	26	21
16-	O Hershiser	R	Cle	37	167	111	16	0	3.87	10.86	30	20
17-	K Brown	R	Bal	31	172	117	10	0	3.60	10.60	28	19
18-	T Percival	R	Cal	26	74	94	3	3	1.95	7.66	27	19
19-	K Rogers	L	Tex	31	208	140	17	0	3.38	11.59	35	18
20-	C Nagy	R	Cle	29	178	139	16	0	4.55	12.89	15	17
21-	D Martinez	R	Cle	41	187	99	12	0	3.08	10.59	36	17
22-	C Finley	L	Cal	33	203	195	15	0	4.21	12.63	19	17
23-	M Langston	L	Cal	35	200	142	15	0	4.63	12.40	16	17
24-	T Stottlemy	R	Oak	31	209	205	14	0	4.55	13.22	11	16
25-	E Hanson	R	Bos	31	186	139	15	0	4.24	11.86	22	14
26-	A Benes	R	Sea	28	63	45	7	0	5.86	15.00	-2	14
27-	J Key	L	NY	35	30	14	1	0	5.64	13.65	-2	14
28-	W Alvarez	L	Chi	26	175	118	8	0	4.32	13.58	6	14

#	Name	T	Tm	Age	IP	SO	W	Sv	ERA	Ratio	$	Bid
29-	B McDonald	R	Bal	28	80	62	3	0	4.16	11.81	7	13
30-	P Hentgen	R	Tor	27	200	135	10	0	5.11	14.62	-5	13
31-	K Hill	R	Cle	30	74	48	4	0	3.98	13.14	5	12
32-	M Fetters	R	Mil	31	34	33	0	22	3.38	15.58	16	12
33-	D Jones	R	Bal	38	46	42	0	22	5.01	13.69	15	11
34-	T Wakefield	R	Bos	29	195	119	16	0	2.95	10.64	42	11
35-	R Pavlik	R	Tex	28	191	149	10	0	4.37	12.40	14	11
36-	A Pettite	L	NY	24	175	114	12	0	4.17	12.65	16	10
37-	J Russell	R	Tex	34	32	21	1	20	3.03	12.40	19	10
38-	J Bere	R	Chi	25	137	110	8	0	7.19	16.80	26	10
39-	A Sele	R	Bos	26	32	21	3	0	3.06	12.80	6	10
40-	J Abbott	L	Cal	28	197	86	11	0	3.70	12.47	20	10
41-	J Tavarez	R	Cle	23	85	68	10	0	2.44	10.27	26	9
42-	S Erickson	R	Bal	28	196	106	13	0	4.81	12.83	10	8
43-	S Ontiveros	R	Oak	35	129	77	9	0	4.37	12.63	11	7
44-	M Clark	R	Cle	28	124	68	9	0	5.27	13.35	3	7
45-	J Haynes	R	Bal	23	24	22	2	0	2.25	8.62	8	7
46-	M Timlin	R	Tor	30	42	36	4	5	2.14	11.79	15	7
47-	J Suppan	R	Bos	21	22	19	1	0	5.96	13.50	-1	6
48-	A Leiter	L	Tor	30	183	153	11	0	3.64	13.28	16	6
49-	C Eldred	R	Mil	28	23	18	1	0	3.42	12.93	3	6
50-	T VanPoppel	R	Oak	24	138	122	4	0	4.88	11.77	5	6
51-	D Stevens	R	Min	26	65	47	5	10	5.07	14.53	7	6
52-	T Gordon	R	KC	27	189	119	12	0	4.43	13.95	7	6
53-	S Hitchcock	L	NY	25	168	121	11	0	4.71	11.92	14	5
54-	B Radke	R	Min	23	181	75	11	0	5.32	12.03	8	5
55-	E Plunk	R	Cle	32	64	71	6	2	2.67	10.55	18	5
56-	M Gubicza	R	KC	33	213	81	12	0	3.75	11.98	24	5
57-	M Rivera	R	NY	26	67	51	5	0	5.51	13.56	0	5
58-	J Nelson	R	Sea	29	78	96	7	2	2.17	9.72	25	5
59-	J Lima	R	Det	23	73	37	3	0	6.11	12.58	-3	5
60-	A Embree	L	Cle	26	24	23	3	1	5.11	14.23	2	5
61-	B Ayala	R	Sea	26	71	77	6	19	4.44	13.05	21	5
62-	K Gross	R	Tex	35	183	106	9	0	5.54	14.16	-7	4
63-	S Belinda	R	Bos	29	69	57	8	10	3.10	10.20	26	4
64-	B Tewksbury	R	Tex	35	129	53	8	0	4.58	13.12	7	4
65-	C Ogea	R	Cle	25	106	57	8	0	3.05	10.49	23	4
66-	J Guzman	R	Tor	29	135	94	4	0	6.32	14.90	16	4
67-	B Wickman	R	NY	27	80	51	2	1	4.05	12.37	6	3
68-	R Robertson	L	Min	27	51	38	2	0	3.83	13.76	2	3
69-	A Prieto	R	Oak	26	58	37	2	0	4.97	13.81	-1	3
70-	W Williams	R	Tor	29	53	41	1	0	3.69	12.07	5	3
71-	T Belcher	R	Sea	34	179	96	10	0	4.52	13.85	5	3
72-	T Castillo	L	Tor	33	72	38	1	13	3.22	10.90	20	3
73-	D Oliver	L	Tex	25	49	39	4	0	4.22	14.51	2	3
74-	L Andujar	R	Chi	23	30	9	2	0	3.26	11.87	5	3
75-	S Kamieniec	R	NY	32	89	43	7	0	4.02	13.25	8	3
76-	R McDowell	R	Tex	35	85	49	7	4	4.02	12.70	13	3
77-	M Sirotka	R	Chi	25	34	19	1	0	4.20	14.68	0	3
78-	B Risley	R	Sea	29	60	65	2	1	3.13	10.89	11	3
79-	B Wolcott	R	Sea	22	36	19	3	0	4.42	13.99	2	3
80-	M Maddux	R	Bos	34	89	65	4	1	3.61	10.14	16	3
81-	F Rodriguez	R	Min	23	105	59	5	0	6.13	14.56	-9	2
82-	C Bosio	R	Sea	33	170	85	10	0	4.92	14.82	-3	2
83-	G Gohr	R	Det	28	10	12	1	0	0.87	10.45	4	2
84-	M Acre	R	Oak	27	52	47	1	0	5.71	13.85	-4	2

Predictions—AL bid limits

#	Name	T	Tm	Age	IP	SO	W	Sv	ERA	Ratio	$	Bid
85-	R Bones	R	Mil	27	200	77	10	0	4.63	13.52	5	2
86-	J Doherty	R	Det	29	113	46	5	6	5.10	13.30	5	2
87-	M Karchner	R	Chi	29	32	24	4	0	1.69	12.65	9	2
88-	G Olson	R	KC	35	33	21	3	3	4.09	12.82	6	2
89-	B Witt	R	Tex	32	61	46	3	0	4.55	14.97	-1	2
90-	S Karl	L	Mil	24	124	59	6	0	4.14	13.86	5	2
91-	C Sodowsky	R	Det	23	23	14	2	0	5.02	16.20	-1	2
92-	R Krivda	L	Bal	26	75	53	2	0	4.54	12.07	4	2
93-	B Simas	R	Chi	24	14	16	1	0	2.57	16.07	1	2
94-	L Thomas	L	Chi	26	13	12	0	0	1.32	9.22	4	2
95-	F Lira	R	Det	24	146	89	9	1	4.31	12.73	12	2
96-	P Assenmach	L	Cle	35	38	40	6	0	2.82	10.33	12	1
97-	R Cormier	L	Bos	29	115	69	7	0	4.07	12.68	10	1
98-	J Moyer	L	Bal	33	115	65	8	0	5.21	11.44	9	1
99-	M Whiteside	R	Tex	28	53	46	5	3	4.08	11.38	11	1
100-	M Stanton	L	Bos	29	21	10	1	0	3.00	10.71	4	1
101-	M Kiefer	R	Mil	27	49	41	4	0	3.44	11.60	9	1
102-	J Orosco	L	Bal	39	49	58	2	3	3.26	9.97	12	1
103-	K Robinson	R	Tor	26	39	31	1	0	3.69	10.85	5	1
104-	A Miranda	L	Mil	26	74	45	4	1	5.23	16.05	-5	1
105-	S Sparks	R	Mil	30	202	96	9	0	4.63	13.19	6	1
106-	J Poole	L	Cle	30	50	41	3	0	3.76	10.19	9	1
107-	L Hawkins	R	Min	23	27	9	2	0	8.67	17.00	-8	1
108-	S Boskie	R	Cal	29	111	51	7	0	5.64	12.25	2	1
185-	S Watkins	L	Min	26	21	11	0	0	5.40	13.71	-2	R1
186-	V Eshelman	L	Bos	27	81	41	6	0	4.85	13.44	3	R1
187-	A Rhodes	L	Bal	27	75	77	2	0	6.21	13.86	-7	R1
188-	A Benitez	R	Bal	23	47	56	1	2	5.66	13.97	-2	R1
189-	J Pittsley	R	KC	22	3	0	0	0	13.51	21.60	-3	R1
190-	D Hall	R	Tor	31	16	11	0	3	4.41	16.53	1	R1
191-	B Givens	L	Mil	30	107	73	5	0	4.95	14.25	-2	R1
192-	D Johns	L	Oak	28	54	25	5	0	4.61	11.52	7	R2
193-	M Christoph	R	Det	32	61	34	4	1	3.82	12.47	8	R2
194-	D Torres	R	KC	26	44	28	1	0	6.09	14.82	-5	R2
195-	M Murray	R	Bos	25	3	1	0	0	18.92	37.80	-5	R2
196-	D Telgheder	R	Oak	29	25	16	1	0	5.61	14.37	-2	R2
197-	J Wasdin	R	Oak	23	17	6	1	0	4.68	8.83	3	R2
198-	B Anderson	R	Cal	25	99	45	6	0	5.87	12.64	-1	R2
199-	A Lorraine	L	Chi	23	8	5	0	0	3.38	5.62	2	R2
200-	T Crabtree	L	Tor	26	32	21	0	0	3.09	12.09	3	R2
201-	J Jacome	L	KC	25	84	39	4	0	5.36	13.07	-1	R2
202-	K Ryan	R	Bos	27	32	34	0	7	4.96	15.98	1	R2
203-	J Parra	R	Min	23	61	29	1	0	7.59	15.32	14	R2
204-	A Reyes	R	Mil	25	33	29	1	1	2.43	9.99	8	R2
205-	C Nitkowski	L	Det	23	39	13	1	0	7.09	16.70	-9	R2
206-	Z Smith	L	Bos	35	110	47	8	0	5.61	13.58	-1	R2
207-	M Bunch	R	KC	24	40	19	1	0	5.63	12.60	-1	R2
208-	B Bark	L	Bos	27	2	0	0	0	0.00	11.57	1	R2
209-	R Carmona	R	Sea	23	47	28	2	1	5.66	16.80	-6	R2
210-	S Torres	R	Sea	24	72	45	3	0	6.00	16.12	10	R2
211-	D Ward	R	Tor	32	2	3	0	0	27.03	54.00	-7	R2
212-	J Hudson	R	Bos	25	46	29	0	1	4.11	14.87	-1	R2
213-	J Ware	R	Tor	25	26	18	2	0	5.47	16.75	-3	R2
214-	J Roa	R	Cle	24	6	0	0	0	6.01	16.50	-1	R2
215-	E Hurtado	R	Tor	25	77	33	5	0	5.45	14.02	-2	R2
216-	P Shuey	R	Cle	25	6	5	0	0	4.27	14.21	0	R2

Predictions—bid limits

#	Name	T	Tm	Age	IP	SO	W	Sv	ERA	Ratio	$	Bid
217-	R Orellano	L	Bos	23	0	0	0	0	0.00	0.00	0	R2
218-	S Karsay	R	Oak	24	0	0	0	0	0.00	0.00	0	R2
219-	J Granger	L	KC	24	0	0	0	0	0.00	0.00	0	R2
220-	J Baldwin	R	Chi	25	14	10	0	0	12.89	25.16	13	R2
221-	B Brewer	L	KC	28	45	31	2	0	5.56	14.69	-3	R2
222-	T Davis	L	Sea	25	24	19	2	0	6.38	18.00	-4	R2
223-	A Lopez	R	Cle	24	23	22	0	0	3.13	9.39	4	R2
224-	W Heredia	R	Tex	24	12	6	0	0	3.75	18.00	-2	R2
225-	H Fajardo	R	Tex	25	15	9	0	0	7.80	14.40	-4	R3
226-	B Black	L	Cle	39	47	34	4	0	6.85	15.02	-5	R3
227-	D Cox	R	Tor	36	45	38	1	0	7.40	18.00	13	R3
230-	M Butcher	R	Cal	31	51	29	6	0	4.73	14.02	4	R3
231-	J Deleon	R	Oth	35	67	53	5	0	5.19	11.70	5	R3
232-	J Dedrick	R	Bal	27	7	3	0	0	2.35	16.43	0	R3
233-	J Corsi	R	Oak	34	45	26	2	2	2.20	11.40	11	R3
234-	T Clark	R	Bal	35	39	18	2	1	3.46	12.69	5	R3
236-	M James	R	Cal	28	55	36	3	1	3.88	12.13	7	R3
237-	D Righetti	L	Chi	37	49	29	3	0	4.20	15.14	0	R3
238-	S Wojci'wsk	L	Oak	25	48	13	2	0	5.18	14.61	-2	R3
239-	J Boever	R	Det	35	98	71	5	3	6.39	15.69	11	R3
242-	G Lloyd	L	Mil	29	32	13	0	4	4.50	10.13	6	R3
243-	J Mecir	R	Sea	26	4	3	0	0	0.00	13.50	1	R3
244-	M Trombley	R	Min	29	97	68	4	0	5.62	13.73	-4	R3
245-	R Helling	R	Tex	25	12	5	0	0	6.57	18.24	-4	R3
246-	J Rogers	R	Tor	29	23	13	2	0	5.71	14.83	-1	R3
247-	R Rightnowa	R	Mil	31	36	22	2	1	5.40	13.01	1	R3
248-	S Ruffcorn	R	Chi	26	8	5	0	0	7.88	25.87	-5	R3
249-	R Fermin	R	Oak	23	1	0	0	0	13.51	33.75	-2	R3
250-	P Mahomes	R	Min	25	94	67	4	3	6.37	13.98	-6	R3
251-	J Manzanill	R	NY	28	17	11	0	0	2.08	14.54	2	R3
252-	M Sanford	R	Min	29	18	17	0	0	5.30	15.43	-2	R3
253-	S Bergman	R	Det	26	135	86	7	0	5.12	15.69	-8	R3
255-	E Guardado	L	Min	25	91	71	4	2	5.12	14.19	-1	R3
256-	J Shaw	R	Chi	29	9	6	0	0	6.52	12.10	-1	R3
257-	K McCaskill	R	Chi	35	81	50	6	2	4.89	14.44	2	R3
258-	M Magnante	L	KC	33	44	28	1	0	4.23	12.29	2	R3
259-	E Gunderson	L	Bos	30	12	9	2	0	5.11	16.05	0	R3
260-	R Bolton	R	Chi	27	22	10	0	0	8.18	19.23	-9	R3
261-	R Meacham	R	KC	28	59	30	4	2	4.98	13.72	3	R3
262-	J Habyan	R	Cal	32	32	25	1	0	4.13	13.22	1	R3
263-	J Borowski	R	Bal	24	7	3	0	0	1.23	11.04	2	R3
264-	T Fortugno	L	Chi	33	38	24	1	0	5.59	11.40	0	R3
265-	C Haney	L	KC	27	81	31	3	0	3.65	12.28	8	R3
266-	B Keyser	R	Chi	29	92	48	5	0	4.97	13.74	0	R3
267-	A Mills	R	Bal	29	23	16	3	0	7.44	18.78	-5	R3
268-	M Harkey	R	Cal	29	127	56	8	0	5.44	14.27	-3	R3
269-	M Mohler	L	Oak	27	23	15	1	1	3.04	12.93	4	R3
272-	C Reyes	R	Oak	32	69	48	4	0	5.09	12.91	2	R3
273-	M Lee	L	Bal	31	33	27	2	1	4.86	13.23	2	R3
274-	M Bielecki	R	Cal	36	75	45	4	0	5.97	13.26	-3	R3
276-	D Henry	R	Det	34	8	9	1	5	6.24	21.81	2	R3
279-	J Ausanio	R	NY	30	37	36	2	1	5.73	15.53	-3	R3
280-	S Roberson	L	Mil	24	84	40	6	0	5.76	14.83	-5	R3
281-	G Hibbard	L	Sea	31	0	0	0	0	0.00	0.00	0	R3
282-	J Pierce	R	Bos	26	15	12	0	0	6.60	18.00	-4	R3
283-	D Fleming	L	KC	26	80	40	1	0	5.96	15.41	11	R3

Predictions—AL bid limits

#	Name	T	Tm	Age	IP	SO	W	Sv	ERA	Ratio	$	Bid
284-	R Dibble	R	Mil	32	26	26	1	1	7.18	21.19	-9	R3
285-	R Honeycutt	L	NY	42	45	21	5	2	2.96	9.66	15	R3
286-	E Vosberg	L	Tex	34	36	36	5	4	3.00	12.00	12	R3
288-	S Howe	L	NY	38	49	28	6	2	4.96	15.24	3	R3
289-	S Sanderson	R	Cal	39	39	23	1	0	4.12	11.90	3	R3
290-	R Huisman	R	KC	27	9	12	0	0	7.45	13.96	-2	R3
291-	J Patterson	R	NY	27	3	3	0	0	2.70	16.20	0	R3
292-	B Wegman	R	Mil	33	70	50	5	2	5.35	14.01	1	R3
293-	T Vanegmond	R	Bos	27	6	5	0	0	9.46	20.25	-3	R3
294-	S Whiteside	L	Det	25	3	2	0	0	14.74	27.00	-4	R3
295-	D Wengert	R	Oak	26	29	16	1	0	3.34	12.74	3	R3
296-	B Boehringe	R	NY	27	17	10	0	0	13.76	23.43	15	R3
297-	M Perez	R	NY	30	69	44	5	0	5.58	13.11	1	R3
298-	S Radinsky	L	Chi	28	38	14	2	1	5.45	14.92	-2	R3
299-	K Wickander	L	Mil	31	23	11	0	1	1.93	11.96	5	R3
300-	H Pichardo	R	KC	26	64	43	8	1	4.36	13.50	8	R3
301-	J D'Amico	R	Mil	20	0	0	0	0	0.00	0.00	0	R4
302-	B Rigby	R	Oak	22	0	0	0	0	0.00	0.00	0	R4
303-	B Looper	R	Oth	21	0	0	0	0	0.00	0.00	0	R5
304-	B Colon	R	Cle	20	0	0	0	0	0.00	0.00	0	R5
305-	M Drews	R	NY	21	0	0	0	0	0.00	0.00	0	R5
306-	J Middlebrk	R	Oth	21	0	0	0	0	0.00	0.00	0	R5
307-	J Wright	R	Cle	20	0	0	0	0	0.00	0.00	0	R5

1996 NL hitters — by bid limits

Upper case means at least 18 games (or the majority) played at a position; lower case means at least one game played. Many R3's and zero bids have been cut, without changing the #'s.

Catchers

#	Name	B	Tm	Age	C123SO	AB	R	HR	RBI	SB	BA	$	Bid
1-	M Piazza	R	LA	27	C-----	550	96	35	111	2	.329	40	43
2-	J Lopez	R	Atl	25	C-----	450	61	18	75	2	.287	20	21
3-	T Hundley	B	NY	27	C-----	425	59	22	78	1	.280	20	18
4-	D Daulton	L	Phi	34	C-----	375	50	13	66	6	.259	14	16
5-	C Johnson	R	Fla	24	C-----	475	60	19	64	2	.255	14	15
6-	B Ausmus	R	SD	27	Cf----	400	50	3	38	10	.303	13	12
7-	B Santiago	R	Cin	31	Cf----	350	48	9	50	1	.269	10	10
8-	T Eusebio	R	Hou	29	C-----	300	37	4	47	0	.307	11	9
9-	D Fletcher	L	Mon	29	C-----	375	45	9	57	0	.283	12	7
10-	E Taubensee	L	Cin	27	Cf----	225	30	6	42	0	.267	7	6
11-	S Servais	R	Chi	29	C-----	400	53	14	55	0	.248	9	5
12-	M Parent	R	Chi	34	C-----	150	16	10	21	0	.240	5	3
13-	R Wilkins	L	Hou	29	Cf----	275	42	11	36	0	.211	3	3
14-	J Owens	R	Col	27	C-----	375	57	7	58	0	.243	6	2
15-	D Slaught	R	Pit	37	C-----	200	21	2	28	0	.295	6	1
16-	D Sheaffer	R	StL	34	Cf-t--	200	23	4	28	0	.230	2	1
17-	M Nokes	L	Col	32	C-----	75	7	4	12	0	.227	2	1
18-	C O'Brien	R	Atl	35	C-----	150	12	4	17	0	.253	3	1
19-	T Pagnozzi	R	StL	33	C-----	425	32	4	35	0	.261	4	1
20-	K Manwaring	R	SF	30	C-----	400	21	3	37	0	.248	2	1
21-	K Stinnett	R	NY	26	C-----	175	20	5	17	0	.234	2	1
22-	B Johnson	R	SD	28	Cf----	200	19	2	26	0	.250	2	1
23-	T Spehr	R	Mon	29	C-----	175	12	4	14	0	.257	3	1
24-	M Liebertha	R	Phi	24	C-----	175	21	2	23	1	.263	3	1
31-	J Kendall	R	Pit	22	C-----	175	18	2	24	1	.286	5	R1

#	Name	B	Tm	Age	C123SO	AB	R	HR	RBI	SB	BA	$	Bid
34-	E Perez	R	Atl	28	Cf----	0	0	0	0	0	.000	0	R3
35-	A Encarnaci	R	Pit	22	C-----	275	30	3	16	1	.222	-1	R3
36-	T Laker	R	Mon	26	C-----	50	6	1	7	0	.240	1	R3
37-	B Natal	R	Fla	30	C-----	75	3	3	10	0	.213	1	R3
38-	J Reed	L	SF	33	C-----	75	7	1	5	0	.253	1	R3
39-	T Houston	R	Atl	25	C-----	0	0	0	0	0	.000	0	R3
41-	T Lampkin	R	SF	32	C----o	100	10	1	11	0	.260	1	R3
42-	S Hemond	R	StL	30	C-d---	100	9	2	7	0	.190	0	R3
43-	S Decker	R	Fla	30	Cf----	50	4	1	4	0	.220	0	R3
45-	L Webster	L	Phi	31	C-----	75	9	1	6	0	.253	1	R3
47-	P Konerko	R	LA	20	C-----	0	0	0	0	0	.000	0	R4
48-	A Castillo	R	NY	20	C-----	0	0	0	0	0	.000	0	R4
49-	R Casanova	R	SD	23	C-----	0	0	0	0	0	.000	0	R4

First Basemen

#	Name	B	Tm	Age	C123SO	AB	R	HR	RBI	SB	BA	$	Bid
1-	J Bagwell	R	Hou	28	-F----	550	112	34	116	11	.311	40	37
2-	F McGriff	L	Atl	32	-F----	550	90	29	105	7	.289	31	35
3-	A Galarraga	R	Col	35	-F----	550	87	35	102	7	.275	30	32
4-	G Jefferies	B	Phi	28	-F---O	575	105	12	79	16	.334	32	27
5-	M Grace	L	Chi	32	-F----	575	109	12	90	1	.317	25	27
6-	E Karros	R	LA	28	-F----	575	84	26	98	2	.283	26	26
7-	R Brogna	L	NY	26	-F----	525	79	24	82	1	.295	25	23
8-	H Morris	L	Cin	23	-F----	475	70	19	72	5	.288	21	21
9-	G Colbrunn	R	Fla	26	-F----	475	62	20	79	7	.284	22	21
10-	M Carreon	R	SF	32	-F---O	525	66	19	81	1	.291	22	17
11-	D Segui	B	Mon	29	-F---O	550	82	14	75	2	.302	21	17
12-	O Merced	B	Pit	29	-F---O	525	75	11	80	1	.286	17	16
13-	J Mabry	L	StL	25	-F---O	500	45	8	52	0	.290	13	13
14-	C Floyd	L	Mon	23	-F---o	450	65	6	53	13	.262	12	9
15-	E Williams	R	SD	31	-F----	325	38	13	51	0	.262	11	8
16-	M Johnson	L	Pit	28	-F----	250	35	17	41	1	.220	8	3
17-	S Livingsto	L	SD	30	-Fdt--	175	23	4	28	1	.274	6	2
18-	J VanderWal	L	Col	30	-F---o	150	19	6	29	0	.313	8	1
19-	A Cianfrocc	R	SD	29	-Fdtso	175	29	4	43	0	.246	5	1
20-	G Schall	R	Phi	26	-F---o	75	4	1	5	0	.253	1	R2
21-	M Sweeney	L	StL	26	-F----	125	15	3	21	1	.312	6	R3
22-	M Simms	R	Hou	29	-F---o	100	11	7	19	0	.250	5	R3
23-	J Zuber	L	Phi	24	-F----	0	0	0	0	0	.000	0	R3
24-	R Aude	R	Pit	25	-F----	75	6	2	13	0	.240	2	R3
25-	R Petagine	L	SD	25	-F---o	0	0	0	0	0	.000	0	R3
26-	T Belk	R	Cin	25	-F----	0	0	0	0	0	.000	0	R3
27-	G Perry	L	StL	35	-F----	75	3	1	8	0	.240	1	R3
28-	B Hunter	R	Cin	28	-F---o	75	8	3	8	1	.213	1	R3
29-	J Thompson	L	SD	25	-F----	0	0	0	0	0	.000	0	R3
30-	J Phillips	L	SF	26	-F---o	200	23	9	24	0	.210	2	R3
32-	B Simonton	R	SF	24	-F----	0	0	0	0	0	.000	0	R4
33-	N Holdren	R	Col	24	-F----	0	0	0	0	0	.000	0	R4
34-	R Wright	R	Atl	20	-F----	0	0	0	0	0	.000	0	R5
35-	T Hilton	L	Col	22	-F----	0	0	0	0	0	.000	0	R5
36-	T Long	L	NY	20	-F----	0	0	0	0	0	.000	0	R5

Second Basemen

#	Name	B	Tm	Age	C123SO	AB	R	HR	RBI	SB	BA	$	Bid
1-	C Biggio	R	Hou	30	--D---	600	112	17	71	29	.288	29	33
2-	Q Veras	B	Fla	25	--D--o	575	125	8	44	75	.264	32	27

Predictions—NL bid limits

#	Name	B	Tm	Age	C123SO	AB	R	HR	RBI	SB	BA	$	Bid
3-	J Kent	R	NY	28	--D---	525	75	22	81	3	.276	21	21
4-	B Roberts	B	SD	32	--D-sO	475	100	3	40	31	.309	22	20
5-	B Boone	R	Cin	27	--D---	550	75	21	85	4	.282	22	18
6-	E Young	R	Col	29	--D--O	550	101	8	53	51	.273	26	18
7-	D Deshields	L	LA	27	--D---	475	73	8	41	36	.265	19	15
8-	M Lansing	R	Mon	28	--D-s-	525	60	6	62	23	.269	17	14
9-	C Garcia	R	Pit	28	--D-s-	525	55	5	57	6	.288	14	12
10-	R Sandberg	R	Chi	36	--D---	525	55	10	48	8	.251	9	10
11-	C Fonville	B	LA	25	--D-So	475	63	0	23	29	.259	10	9
12-	M Morandini	L	Phi	30	--D---	475	62	5	41	7	.276	10	5
13-	R Thompson	R	SF	34	--D---	375	58	10	38	2	.245	6	4
14-	G Pena	R	StL	29	--D---	425	84	4	33	9	.266	8	4
15-	J Bates	B	Col	25	--DtS-	275	34	5	38	1	.273	7	3
16-	M Duncan	R	Cin	33	-FDtSo	250	33	6	33	2	.272	7	3
17-	D Bell	R	StL	23	--Dt--	250	22	3	32	1	.248	3	2
18-	M Mordecai	R	Atl	28	-fDtso	175	22	6	21	2	.280	6	2
19-	M Lemke	B	Atl	30	--D---	425	44	5	40	2	.254	5	2
20-	J Reed	R	SD	33	--D-s-	375	47	2	32	3	.256	4	2
24-	E Giovanola	L	Atl	27	--Dts-	0	0	0	0	0	.000	0	R3
25-	N Liriano	B	Pit	32	--Dts-	225	24	3	25	0	.267	4	R3
26-	T Haney	R	Chi	30	--Dt--	125	18	3	10	1	.288	4	R3
27-	J Browne	B	Fla	30	--Dt-O	125	14	1	9	0	.256	1	R3
28-	J Patterson	B	SF	29	--D---	175	21	1	11	7	.223	1	R3
31-	M Franco	L	Chi	26	-fDt--	0	0	0	0	0	.000	0	R3
32-	K Jordan	R	Phi	26	--Dt--	175	25	3	17	1	.234	1	R3
33-	R Mejia	R	Col	24	--D---	75	7	1	5	1	.240	1	R3
34-	D Hajek	R	Hou	28	--D---	100	14	1	11	2	.280	3	R3
35-	G Blum	R	Mon	23	--D-s-	0	0	0	0	0	.000	0	R4
36-	J Lofton	B	Cin	22	--D---	0	0	0	0	0	.000	0	R4
37-	B Morris	L	Chi	23	--D---	0	0	0	0	0	.000	0	R4
38-	M Cairo	R	LA	22	--D---	0	0	0	0	0	.000	0	R4
39-	A Riggs	R	LA	23	--D---	0	0	0	0	0	.000	0	R5

Shortstops

#	Name	B	Tm	Age	C123SO	AB	R	HR	RBI	SB	BA	$	Bid
1-	B Larkin	R	Cin	32	-----S-	525	103	16	86	32	.328	38	36
2-	W Cordero	R	Mon	24	-----SO	500	65	19	67	6	.274	19	21
3-	S Dunston	R	Chi	33	-----S-	500	64	14	72	8	.266	16	14
4-	K Abbott	R	Fla	27	-----S-	475	58	18	61	2	.251	12	13
5-	J Bell	R	Pit	30	---tS-	575	85	11	59	2	.273	13	13
6-	R Clayton	R	SF	26	-----S-	500	55	4	51	19	.252	11	7
7-	J Blauser	R	Atl	30	-----S-	500	70	11	42	7	.228	5	6
8-	J Vizcaino	B	NY	28	--d-S-	525	64	2	50	3	.272	8	4
9-	O Miller	R	Hou	27	-----S-	400	43	7	44	2	.258	7	4
10-	R Aurilia	R	SF	24	-----S-	225	35	5	31	3	.262	6	3
11-	A Cedeno	R	SD	26	---tS-	450	50	11	42	7	.227	5	3
12-	W Weiss	B	Col	32	-----S-	475	80	0	26	15	.255	5	3
13-	M Grudziela	R	Mon	26	--dTS-	200	32	1	15	4	.255	2	3
14-	J Offerman	B	LA	27	-----S-	275	31	0	21	2	.255	1	2
15-	O Smith	B	StL	41	-----S-	300	32	1	26	10	.233	3	2
16-	J Hernandez	R	Chi	26	--DTS-	175	26	9	28	0	.240	5	2
17-	K Stocker	R	Phi	26	-----S-	450	46	4	39	7	.227	2	2
18-	R Gutierrez	R	Hou	26	---tS-	175	21	1	13	4	.263	3	1
19-	T Cromer	R	StL	28	--d-S-	325	33	7	18	0	.234	1	1
20-	A Arias	R	Fla	28	--dTS-	150	15	1	18	0	.253	2	1
23-	E Renteria	B	Fla	20	-----S-	75	10	1	8	2	.253	2	R2

#	Name	B	Tm	Age	C123SO	AB	R	HR	RBI	SB	BA	$	Bid
24-	W Guerrero	R	LA	21	-----S-	75	8	0	3	3	.253	1	R2
25-	P Reese	R	Cin	23	-----S-	0	0	0	0	0	.000	0	R3
26-	C Counsell	L	Col	25	-----S-	100	11	1	8	2	.230	1	R3
27-	R Ordonez	R	NY	24	-----S-	0	0	0	0	0	.000	0	R3
28-	D Silvestri	R	Mon	28	-fdtSo	75	12	2	7	1	.240	1	R3
29-	R Holbert	R	SD	25	--d-So	75	11	2	5	4	.200	1	R3
30-	T Bogar	R	NY	29	-fdTSo	125	14	0	17	0	.272	2	R3
32-	B Nelson	R	Phi	22	-----S-	0	0	0	0	0	.000	0	R4
33-	J Booty	R	Fla	20	-----S-	0	0	0	0	0	.000	0	R4
34-	L Collier	R	Pit	23	-----S-	0	0	0	0	0	.000	0	R4

Outfielders

#	Name	B	Tm	Age	C123SO	AB	R	HR	RBI	SB	BA	$	Bid
1-	B Bonds	L	SF	31	------O	525	126	34	107	32	.307	44	45
2-	R Sanders	R	Cin	28	------O	550	100	30	107	34	.282	39	42
3-	D Bichette	R	Col	32	------O	550	101	45	127	8	.318	46	42
4-	S Sosa	R	Chi	27	------O	600	119	42	126	40	.267	45	41
5-	L Walker	L	Col	29	------O	525	102	38	107	12	.324	43	39
6-	T Gwynn	L	SD	36	------O	550	82	8	105	12	.364	37	37
7-	R Mondesi	R	LA	25	------O	575	99	37	109	18	.277	36	34
8-	G Sheffield	R	Fla	27	------O	500	95	37	99	23	.296	40	32
9-	D Bell	R	Hou	27	------O	550	84	14	86	24	.311	32	30
10-	J Conine	R	Fla	30	-f---O	550	83	24	112	1	.289	27	28
11-	R Gant	R	Cin	31	------O	475	85	27	91	19	.259	27	28
12-	R Lankford	L	StL	29	------O	550	101	20	88	27	.265	27	28
13-	M Grissom	R	Atl	29	------O	600	83	17	58	38	.277	27	28
14-	R Klesko	L	Atl	25	-f---O	475	69	33	101	7	.278	30	27
15-	B Jordan	R	StL	29	------O	550	87	25	84	17	.267	26	27
16-	M Alou	R	Mon	29	------O	525	95	23	92	8	.288	26	27
17-	B Hunter	R	Hou	25	------O	575	93	4	51	41	.311	29	26
18-	D Justice	L	Atl	30	------O	475	83	27	89	3	.272	24	26
19-	G Hill	R	SF	31	------O	550	81	27	102	18	.258	27	25
20-	R White	R	Mon	24	------O	575	81	14	79	21	.285	25	25
21-	S Finley	L	SD	31	------O	575	107	7	48	38	.304	27	24
22-	L Dykstra	L	Phi	33	------O	500	74	12	50	27	.276	21	21
23-	B McRae	B	Chi	28	------O	625	116	13	53	30	.285	24	20
24-	D White	B	Fla	33	------O	550	85	12	68	22	.282	22	18
25-	C Everett	B	NY	26	------O	550	91	25	102	4	.258	22	18
26-	R Kelly	R	LA	31	------O	475	54	9	53	21	.276	18	17
27-	B Gilkey	R	StL	29	------O	500	70	13	57	10	.286	18	17
28-	B Butler	L	LA	39	------O	550	83	1	40	34	.295	20	17
29-	A Martin	L	Pit	28	------O	475	74	15	59	14	.274	18	15
30-	E Burks	R	Col	31	------O	350	51	17	60	8	.266	17	13
31-	L Gonzalez	L	Chi	28	------O	400	58	10	58	7	.278	14	12
32-	J Eisenreic	L	Phi	37	------O	400	46	8	57	4	.300	15	11
33-	M Whiten	B	Phi	29	------O	525	86	19	78	9	.250	17	11
34-	D Sanders	L	SF	28	------O	300	41	5	24	20	.277	12	10
35-	D Lewis	R	Cin	28	------O	300	41	1	15	20	.253	7	9
36-	M Newfield	R	SD	23	------O	325	35	7	41	0	.271	8	9
37-	D May	L	Hou	27	-f---O	375	47	8	65	1	.283	13	8
38-	T Tarasco	L	Mon	25	------O	250	34	5	20	11	.272	8	7
39-	R Thompson	R	NY	28	------O	400	58	11	45	3	.248	8	6
40-	J Mouton	R	Hou	27	------O	275	38	3	24	23	.258	10	6
41-	T Howard	B	Cin	31	------O	325	48	3	30	19	.277	11	5
42-	J Brumfield	R	Pit	31	------O	450	69	3	28	23	.262	11	5
43-	A Ochoa	R	NY	24	------O	450	82	6	41	5	.264	8	5

#	Name	B	Tm	Age	C123SO	AB	R	HR	RBI	SB	BA	$	Bid
44-	P Plantier	L	SD	27	-----O	225	33	8	35	0	.249	6	4
45-	J Cangelosi	B	Hou	33	-----O	175	40	1	15	18	.257	7	4
46-	M Benard	L	SF	26	-----O	250	36	2	29	7	.264	6	4
47-	M Devereaux	R	Atl	33	-----O	225	32	6	36	3	.267	8	4
48-	O Timmons	R	Chi	25	-----O	175	29	9	27	2	.251	7	4
49-	M Kingery	L	Col	35	-f---O	275	51	5	25	10	.280	9	3
50-	C Carr	L	Fla	27	-----O	100	17	0	6	12	.270	5	3
51-	L Polonia	L	Atl	31	-----O	175	17	0	10	9	.303	6	2
52-	D Buford	R	NY	25	-----O	200	34	5	17	9	.245	5	2
53-	J Walton	B	Cin	30	-f---O	125	24	4	16	7	.304	7	2
54-	M Nieves	B	SD	24	-f---O	225	30	13	36	1	.204	5	2
55-	H Rodriguez	L	Mon	28	-f---O	175	16	3	18	0	.251	2	2
56-	E Anthony	L	Cin	28	-f---O	150	21	6	25	3	.233	5	2
57-	A Van Slyke	L	Phi	35	-----O	300	36	4	26	7	.243	4	2
58-	M Cummings	L	Pit	24	-----O	225	18	3	21	1	.240	2	2
59-	T Longmire	L	Phi	27	-----O	125	25	4	22	1	.288	5	1
60-	A Dawson	R	Fla	41	-----O	175	22	6	28	0	.251	5	1
61-	S Bullett	L	Chi	27	-----O	125	15	2	18	6	.272	5	1
62-	T Gregg	L	Fla	32	-f---O	150	19	5	19	2	.273	5	1
63-	J Orsulak	L	NY	34	-f---O	175	24	2	24	1	.291	5	1
64-	J Tavarez	B	Fla	25	-----O	150	17	1	10	5	.253	2	1
65-	C Jones	R	NY	30	-f---O	175	31	7	29	1	.280	7	1
66-	D Clark	L	Pit	33	-----O	200	30	4	24	3	.280	6	1
68-	K Mitchell	R	Oth	34	-f---O	0	0	0	0	0	.000	0	R1
69-	T Beamon	L	Pit	22	-----O	250	41	5	34	9	.284	10	R1
70-	K Garcia	L	LA	20	-----O	125	25	5	30	2	.256	6	R1
71-	J Payton	R	NY	24	-----O	100	20	3	17	1	.280	4	R1
72-	B Kieschnck	L	Chi	24	-f---O	75	14	3	15	0	.253	3	R1
73-	B Abreu	L	Hou	22	-----O	0	0	0	0	0	.000	0	R2
74-	S Gibralter	R	Cin	23	-----O	50	4	1	5	0	.260	1	R2
75-	B Ashley	R	LA	25	-----O	150	14	7	23	0	.233	4	R2
76-	R Hidalgo	R	Hou	20	-----O	75	9	3	10	1	.240	2	R2
77-	H Pulliam	R	Col	28	-----O	75	11	6	16	0	.267	5	R2
78-	T Hollandsw	L	LA	23	-----O	125	19	5	19	1	.240	3	R2
79-	R Cedeno	B	LA	21	-----O	125	11	0	6	5	.248	1	R2
80-	B McMillion	L	Fla	24	-----O	50	7	2	7	1	.280	2	R2
81-	D Powell	R	SF	23	-----O	0	0	0	0	0	.000	0	R2
82-	Q McCracken	R	Col	26	-----O	100	15	0	8	5	.270	3	R2
83-	J Dye	R	Atl	22	-----O	75	6	3	8	1	.240	2	R2
84-	R Jennings	L	Chi	24	-----O	50	4	1	4	0	.260	1	R2
85-	C Pride	L	Mon	27	-----O	0	0	0	0	0	.000	0	R3
86-	B Kowitz	L	Atl	26	-----O	0	0	0	0	0	.000	0	R3
88-	J Allenswor	R	Pit	24	-----O	0	0	0	0	0	.000	0	R3
89-	C Murray	R	SF	24	-----O	0	0	0	0	0	.000	0	R3
90-	K Flora	R	Phi	26	-----O	50	8	1	4	2	.200	0	R3
91-	G Varsho	R	Phi	34	-----O	75	5	1	8	1	.253	1	R3
92-	T Hubbard	R	Col	32	-----O	75	16	3	11	2	.280	3	R3
96-	M Thompson	L	Hou	37	-----O	100	10	2	14	3	.240	3	R3
97-	D Smith	L	Atl	32	-----O	150	18	3	24	0	.267	4	R3
98-	R McDavid	R	SD	24	-----O	0	0	0	0	0	.000	0	R3
99-	R Holifield	L	Phi	25	-----O	0	0	0	0	0	.000	0	R3
100-	R Otero	B	NY	23	-----O	75	11	1	5	5	.227	1	R3
102-	D McCarty	R	SF	26	-f---O	75	3	1	7	0	.240	0	R3
103-	S Pegues	R	Pit	28	-----O	75	6	1	6	0	.253	1	R3
106-	N Wilson	L	Cin	25	-----O	0	0	0	0	0	.000	0	R3
107-	A Battle	R	StL	27	-----O	125	13	0	7	3	.256	1	R3

#	Name	B	Tm	Age	C123SO	AB	R	HR	RBI	SB	BA	$	Bid
108-	T Marsh	R	Phi	30	-----O	100	11	2	13	0	.270	3	R3
109-	M Leonard	L	SF	31	-----O	0	0	0	0	0	.000	0	R3
110-	J Barry	B	NY	27	-----O	0	0	0	0	0	.000	0	R3
111-	Y Benitez	R	Mon	24	-----O	100	15	4	17	0	.240	3	R3
114-	P Clark	R	SD	28	-f---O	75	9	2	8	0	.213	0	R3
115-	K Roberson	B	NY	28	-----O	0	0	0	0	0	.000	0	R3
116-	T Bradshaw	L	StL	27	-----O	50	6	1	5	0	.240	1	R3
117-	M Kelly	R	Atl	26	-----O	0	0	0	0	0	.000	0	R3
118-	D Whitmore	L	Fla	27	-----O	0	0	0	0	0	.000	0	R3
119-	F Santangel	R	Mon	31	--d--O	0	0	0	0	0	.000	0	R3
120-	F Garcia	R	Pit	23	---t-O	0	0	0	0	0	.000	0	R4
121-	D Hollins	L	Atl	22	-----O	0	0	0	0	0	.000	0	R4
122-	E Velasquez	R	Col	20	-----O	0	0	0	0	0	.000	0	R4
123-	P Wilson	R	NY	21	-----O	0	0	0	0	0	.000	0	R4
124-	P Watkins	R	Cin	23	-----O	0	0	0	0	0	.000	0	R4
125-	D Young	R	StL	22	-----O	0	0	0	0	0	.000	0	R4
126-	D Stovall	B	StL	23	-----O	0	0	0	0	0	.000	0	R4
127-	C Peterson	R	Pit	22	-----O	0	0	0	0	0	.000	0	R4
128-	D Clyburn	R	Cin	22	-----O	0	0	0	0	0	.000	0	R4
129-	V Guerrero	R	Mon	20	-----O	0	0	0	0	0	.000	0	R5
130-	A Jones	R	Atl	19	-----O	0	0	0	0	0	.000	0	R5
131-	D Gibson	R	Col	21	-----O	0	0	0	0	0	.000	0	R5

1996 NL pitchers — by bid limits

The only predictions are the recommended bid limits for this year; the stats are the 1995 major league stats for each pitcher and the $ values are what the stats were worth in 1995.

#	Name	T	Tm	Age	IP	SO	W	Sv	ERA	Ratio	$	Bid
1-	G Maddux	R	Atl	30	209	181	19	0	1.63	7.30	68	42
2-	M Wohlers	R	Atl	26	64	90	7	25	2.09	10.44	35	40
3-	R Myers	L	Chi	33	55	59	1	38	3.88	12.45	29	31
4-	T Worrell	R	LA	36	62	61	4	32	2.02	9.96	38	29
5-	J Brantley	R	Cin	32	70	62	3	28	2.82	9.34	34	28
6-	R Beck	R	SF	27	58	42	5	33	4.45	12.43	28	27
7-	T Hoffman	R	SD	28	53	52	7	31	3.88	10.46	33	27
8-	T Henke	R	StL	38	54	48	1	36	1.82	9.94	38	26
9-	J Franco	L	NY	35	51	41	5	29	2.44	11.32	32	25
10-	H Nomo	R	LA	27	191	236	13	0	2.54	9.50	39	25
11-	M Rojas	R	Mon	29	67	61	1	30	4.12	13.03	21	25
12-	T Glavine	R	Atl	30	198	127	16	0	3.08	11.23	28	24
13-	R Nen	R	Fla	26	65	68	0	23	3.29	11.65	20	24
14-	P Schourek	L	Cin	27	190	160	18	0	3.22	9.60	37	24
15-	P Martinez	R	Mon	24	194	174	14	0	3.51	10.35	27	23
16-	R Bottalico	R	Phi	26	87	87	5	1	2.46	9.44	19	21
17-	M Henneman	R	Hou	34	21	19	0	8	3.00	10.71	8	19
18-	I Valdes	R	LA	22	197	150	13	1	3.05	9.97	33	19
19-	J Hamilton	R	SD	25	204	123	6	0	3.08	10.79	21	18
20-	D Miceli	R	Pit	25	58	56	4	21	4.66	13.81	15	18
21-	J Smiley	L	Cin	31	176	124	12	0	3.46	10.80	22	18
22-	J Smoltz	R	Atl	29	192	193	12	0	3.18	11.12	24	18
23-	A Ashby	R	SD	28	192	150	12	0	2.94	11.30	25	17
24-	D Wells	L	Cin	33	72	50	6	0	3.59	11.15	9	17
25-	S Avery	L	Atl	26	173	141	7	0	4.67	11.27	5	16
26-	R Martinez	R	LA	28	206	138	17	0	3.66	11.21	24	16
27-	J Isringhau	R	NY	23	93	55	9	0	2.81	11.52	16	15

#	Name	T	Tm	Age	IP	SO	W	Sv	ERA	Ratio	$	Bid
28-	J Rijo	R	Cin	31	69	62	5	0	4.17	12.78	3	15
29-	F Castillo	R	Chi	27	188	135	11	0	3.21	11.06	23	14
30-	D Drabek	R	Hou	33	185	143	10	0	4.77	12.60	0	14
31-	C Leskanic	R	Col	28	98	107	6	10	3.40	10.65	20	14
32-	M Hampton	L	Hou	23	150	115	9	0	3.35	11.35	16	12
33-	J Navarro	R	Chi	29	200	128	14	0	3.28	11.23	25	12
34-	S Reynolds	R	Hou	28	189	175	10	0	3.47	11.08	19	12
35-	D Neagle	L	Pit	27	209	150	13	0	3.43	11.42	21	11
36-	B Jones	R	NY	28	195	127	10	0	4.19	12.05	8	10
37-	C Perez	L	Mon	25	141	106	10	0	3.69	10.82	17	10
38-	B Ruffin	L	Col	32	34	23	0	11	2.12	11.91	12	10
39-	B Saberhage	R	Col	32	153	100	7	0	4.18	11.65	7	10
40-	C Schilling	R	Phi	29	116	114	7	0	3.57	9.46	18	10
41-	T Jones	R	Hou	28	99	96	6	15	3.07	12.73	20	9
42-	S Fernandez	L	Phi	33	64	79	6	0	3.34	9.60	13	8
43-	B Pulsipher	L	NY	22	126	81	5	0	3.98	11.86	5	8
44-	P Rapp	R	Fla	28	167	102	14	0	3.44	12.58	16	8
45-	T Candiotti	R	LA	38	190	141	7	0	3.50	11.58	13	7
46-	K Foster	R	Chi	27	167	146	12	0	4.51	11.49	10	7
47-	C Hammond	L	Fla	30	161	126	9	0	3.80	11.40	13	7
48-	D Holmes	R	Col	30	66	61	6	14	3.24	11.75	20	7
49-	H Slocumb	R	Phi	30	65	63	5	32	2.89	13.64	29	7
50-	A Benes	R	StL	24	16	20	1	0	8.44	15.75	-5	6
51-	M Leiter	R	SF	32	195	129	10	0	3.82	11.04	17	6
52-	G McMichael	R	Atl	29	80	74	7	2	2.79	10.71	17	6
53-	K Mercker	R	Atl	28	143	102	7	0	4.15	12.65	3	6
54-	M Morgan	R	StL	36	131	61	7	0	3.56	11.44	12	6
55-	M Portugal	R	Cin	33	181	96	11	0	4.01	11.94	11	6
56-	J Bullinger	R	Chi	30	150	93	12	0	4.14	13.02	7	5
57-	P Harnisch	R	NY	29	110	82	2	0	3.68	11.04	7	5
58-	B Swift	R	Col	34	105	68	9	0	4.94	14.05	-3	5
59-	S Trachsel	R	Chi	25	160	117	7	0	5.15	14.00	-11	5
60-	B Vanlandin	R	SF	25	122	95	6	0	3.67	12.03	8	5
61-	D Burba	R	Cin	29	106	96	10	0	3.97	11.90	10	4
62-	J Burkett	R	Fla	31	188	126	14	0	4.30	12.66	8	4
63-	J Fassero	L	Mon	33	189	164	13	0	4.33	13.38	3	4
64-	T Mathews	R	Fla	31	82	72	4	3	3.38	10.56	12	4
65-	A Osuna	R	LA	30	44	46	2	0	4.43	11.89	1	4
66-	R Person	R	NY	26	12	10	1	0	0.75	5.25	6	4
67-	S Reed	R	Col	30	84	79	5	3	2.14	8.78	23	4
68-	B Rekar	R	Col	24	85	60	4	0	4.98	12.60	-2	4
69-	D Veres	R	Hou	29	103	94	5	1	2.26	10.36	20	4
70-	R Villone	L	SD	26	25	37	2	1	4.21	12.27	2	4
71-	P Astacio	R	LA	26	104	80	7	0	4.24	11.42	7	3
72-	B Clontz	R	Atl	25	69	55	8	4	3.65	12.13	12	3
73-	T Mathews	R	StL	26	29	28	1	2	1.52	9.71	9	3
74-	D Mlicki	R	NY	28	160	123	9	0	4.26	11.99	7	3
75-	D Osborne	L	StL	27	113	82	4	0	3.81	11.59	6	3
76-	K Rueter	L	Mon	25	47	28	5	0	3.23	8.93	11	3
77-	K Tapani	R	LA	32	57	43	4	0	5.05	13.58	-2	3
78-	B Barber	R	StL	23	29	27	2	0	5.22	14.42	-2	2
79-	D Bochtler	R	SD	25	45	45	4	1	3.57	11.32	7	2
80-	J Brewingto	R	SF	24	75	45	6	0	4.54	13.50	0	2
81-	H Carrasco	R	Cin	26	87	64	2	5	4.12	13.60	1	2
82-	J Christian	L	Pit	26	56	53	1	0	4.15	13.26	-2	2
83-	R DeLucia	R	StL	31	82	76	8	0	3.39	10.82	13	2

Predictions—NL bid limits

#	Name	T	Tm	Age	IP	SO	W	Sv	ERA	Ratio	$	Bid
84-	B Florie	R	SD	26	68	68	2	1	3.01	11.40	7	2
85-	M Grace	R	Phi	26	11	7	1	0	3.18	11.12	2	2
86-	D Henry	R	NY	34	67	62	3	4	2.96	9.80	14	2
87-	D Jackson	L	StL	32	100	52	2	0	5.90	15.02	-17	2
88-	M Jackson	R	Cin	31	49	41	6	2	2.39	10.47	14	2
89-	D Kile	R	Hou	27	127	113	4	0	4.96	13.25	-7	2
90-	M Williams	R	Phi	31	87	57	3	0	3.29	10.98	9	2
91-	T Alvarez	R	Mon	24	37	17	1	0	6.75	14.46	-7	1
92-	R Arocha	R	StL	30	49	25	3	0	3.99	13.23	1	1
93-	P Borbon	L	Atl	28	32	33	2	2	3.09	12.94	4	1
94-	T Borland	R	Phi	27	74	59	1	6	3.77	14.35	1	1
95-	P Byrd	R	NY	25	22	26	2	0	2.05	10.22	6	1
96-	J DiPoto	R	NY	28	78	49	4	2	3.78	12.13	6	1
97-	J Ericks	R	Pit	28	106	80	3	0	4.59	13.41	-5	1
98-	G Heredia	R	Mon	30	119	74	5	1	4.31	11.95	4	1
99-	E Loaiza	R	Pit	24	172	85	8	0	5.16	13.55	-9	1
100-	M Mimbs	L	Phi	27	136	93	9	1	4.15	13.30	4	1
101-	A Pena	R	Atl	37	31	39	2	0	2.61	8.42	8	1
102-	M Petkovsek	R	StL	30	137	71	6	0	4.00	11.21	9	1
103-	P Quantrill	R	Phi	27	179	103	11	0	4.67	12.85	1	1
104-	T Scott	R	Mon	29	63	57	2	2	3.98	10.66	6	1
105-	G Swindell	L	Hou	31	153	96	10	0	4.47	12.88	3	1
106-	M Thompson	R	Col	25	51	30	2	0	6.53	16.76	-12	1
107-	P Wagner	R	Pit	28	165	120	5	1	4.80	13.42	-7	1
108-	A Watson	L	StL	25	114	49	7	0	4.96	13.14	-2	1
109-	L Aquino	R	SF	31	42	26	0	2	5.10	14.88	-5	0
153-	D Hermanson	R	SD	23	31	19	3	0	6.82	16.20	-6	R1
154-	J Hudek	R	Hou	29	20	29	2	7	5.40	10.80	6	R1
155-	C Park	R	LA	23	4	7	0	0	4.50	9.00	0	R1
156-	J Powell	R	Fla	24	8	4	0	0	1.08	14.04	1	R1
157-	K Ritz	R	Col	31	173	120	11	2	4.21	12.25	10	R1
158-	J Ruffin	R	Cin	24	13	11	0	0	1.35	10.13	3	R1
159-	S Sanders	R	SD	27	90	88	5	0	4.30	11.00	6	R1
160-	J Schmidt	R	Atl	23	25	19	2	0	5.76	16.20	-4	R1
161-	U Urbina	R	Mon	22	23	15	2	0	6.17	15.43	-3	R1
162-	B Wagner	L	Hou	25	0	0	0	0	0.00	0.00	0	R1
163-	P Wilson	R	NY	23	0	0	0	0	0.00	0.00	0	R1
164-	J Acevedo	R	NY	26	65	40	4	0	6.44	13.98	-9	R2
165-	A Berumen	R	SD	25	44	42	2	1	5.69	14.82	-5	R2
166-	S Cooke	L	Pit	26	0	0	0	0	0.00	0.00	0	R2
167-	M DeJean	R	Col	25	0	0	0	0	0.00	0.00	0	R2
168-	G Dishman	L	SD	25	97	43	4	0	5.01	12.80	-3	R2
169-	D Dreifort	R	LA	25	0	0	0	0	0.00	0.00	0	R2
170-	J Eischen	L	LA	26	20	15	0	0	3.10	13.28	0	R2
171-	S Gentile	R	Mon	25	0	0	0	0	0.00	0.00	0	R2
172-	T Green	R	Phi	26	140	85	8	0	5.31	14.27	-10	R2
173-	B Harvey	R	Fla	27	0	0	0	0	0.00	0.00	-3	R2
175-	J Juden	R	Phi	25	62	47	2	0	4.02	12.06	2	R2
176-	R Karp	L	Phi	26	2	2	0	0	4.50	18.00	0	R2
177-	M Kroon	R	SD	23	1	2	0	0	10.81	16.20	-1	R2
178-	J Lieber	R	Pit	26	72	45	4	0	6.32	14.49	-10	R2
179-	D May	L	Atl	24	4	1	0	0	11.26	22.50	-3	R2
180-	R Morel	R	Pit	21	6	3	0	0	2.84	11.37	0	R2
181-	B Munoz	R	Phi	28	15	6	0	0	5.75	13.79	-2	R2
182-	D Nied	R	Col	27	4	3	0	0	20.79	29.08	-7	R2
183-	S Parris	R	Pit	28	82	61	6	0	5.38	13.39	-3	R2

#	Name	T	Tm	Age	IP	SO	W	Sv	ERA	Ratio	$	Bid
184-	C Ricci	R	Phi	27	10	9	1	0	1.80	10.80	2	R2
185-	F Rodriguez	R	LA	23	10	5	1	0	2.53	13.50	2	R2
186-	R Seanez	R	LA	27	34	29	1	3	6.75	14.80	-5	R2
187-	A Small	R	Fla	24	6	5	1	0	1.42	18.47	1	R2
188-	E Stull	R	Mon	24	0	0	0	0	0.00	0.00	0	R2
189-	T Wade	L	Atl	23	4	3	0	0	4.50	15.75	-1	R2
190-	G White	L	Mon	24	25	25	1	0	7.02	12.27	-4	R2
191-	T Worrell	R	SD	28	13	13	1	0	4.73	14.85	-1	R2
192-	K Abbott	L	Phi	28	28	21	2	0	3.81	13.98	1	R3
193-	T Adams	R	Chi	23	18	15	1	1	6.50	16.00	-3	R3
194-	C Bailey	R	StL	25	3	5	0	0	7.37	9.82	-1	R3
195-	R Bailey	R	Col	25	81	33	7	0	4.98	14.05	-2	R3
196-	W Banks	R	Phi	27	90	62	2	0	5.66	16.28	-17	R3
197-	S Barton	L	SF	32	44	22	4	1	4.26	11.37	5	R3
198-	J Bautista	R	SF	31	100	45	3	0	6.44	13.05	-13	R3
199-	M Birkbeck	R	NY	35	27	14	0	0	1.63	7.81	7	R3
200-	W Blair	R	SD	30	114	83	7	0	4.34	12.39	4	R3
201-	R Bowen	R	Fla	28	16	15	2	0	3.78	18.90	-2	R3
202-	D Brocail	R	Hou	29	77	39	6	1	4.19	12.68	4	R3
204-	J Castillo	R	NY	26	0	0	0	0	0.00	0.00	0	R3
205-	D Creek	R	StL	27	6	10	0	0	0.00	6.75	3	R3
206-	J Cummings	L	LA	26	39	21	3	0	3.00	11.08	6	R3
207-	J DeLeon	R	Mon	35	8	12	0	0	7.57	15.12	-2	R3
208-	M Dewey	R	SF	31	31	32	1	0	3.13	13.36	1	R3
209-	J Dougherty	R	Hou	28	67	49	8	0	4.92	13.43	2	R3
215-	T Fossas	L	StL	38	36	40	3	0	1.47	9.33	11	R3
217-	M Freeman	R	Col	33	94	61	3	0	5.89	15.50	-16	R3
218-	S Frey	L	Phi	32	17	7	0	1	2.12	7.41	5	R3
219-	R Garces	R	Fla	24	24	22	0	0	4.44	13.31	-2	R3
220-	M Gardner	R	Fla	34	102	87	5	1	4.49	13.37	-1	R3
221-	D Gooden	R	NY	31	0	0	0	0	0.00	0.00	0	R3
223-	J Grahe	R	Col	28	56	27	4	0	5.08	15.25	-5	R3
224-	T Greene	R	Phi	29	33	24	0	0	8.29	17.37	-14	R3
225-	E Gunderson	R	NY	30	24	19	1	0	3.70	12.20	1	R3
226-	M Guthrie	R	LA	30	19	19	0	0	3.66	12.81	0	R3
227-	J Guzman	R	Chi	32	0	0	0	0	0.00	0.00	0	R3
234-	J Hernandez	R	Fla	29	7	5	0	0	11.58	19.28	-5	R3
235-	X Hernandez	R	Cin	30	90	84	7	3	4.60	12.60	5	R3
261-	K Rogers	L	SF	27	0	0	0	0	0.00	0.00	0	R3
262-	J Roper	R	SF	24	8	6	0	0	12.39	23.63	-7	R3
263-	J Rosselli	L	SF	24	30	7	2	0	8.70	17.70	-11	R3
264-	S Service	R	SF	28	31	30	3	0	3.19	11.03	5	R3
265-	J Shaw	R	Mon	29	62	45	1	3	4.62	12.13	1	R3
266-	R Springer	R	Phi	27	26	32	0	0	3.71	10.80	1	R3
269-	J Tabaka	L	Hou	32	30	25	1	0	3.23	12.91	1	R3
289-	D Coggin	R	Phi	20	0	0	0	0	0.00	0.00	0	R4
290-	R Drese	R	Oth	21	0	0	0	0	0.00	0.00	0	R4
291-	R Hunter	R	Phi	21	0	0	0	0	0.00	0.00	0	R4
292-	S Johnston	L	Phi	20	0	0	0	0	0.00	0.00	0	R4
293-	D Million	L	Col	20	0	0	0	0	0.00	0.00	0	R4
294-	T Mounce	R	Hou	20	0	0	0	0	0.00	0.00	0	R4
295-	J Paniagua	R	Mon	22	0	0	0	0	0.00	0.00	0	R4
296-	J Wright	R	Col	21	0	0	0	0	0.00	0.00	0	R4
297-	E DuBose	L	Oth	19	0	0	0	0	0.00	0.00	0	R5
298-	J Jones	R	Fla	20	0	0	0	0	0.00	0.00	0	R5

Predictions—NL bid limits

Chapter 3
Notes for Masochists

Oscar Wilde said, "Never write a love letter, never throw one away." He could have been talking about numbers nerds. Here's an e-mail trail from September to November for you to follow in the order that I received and sent messages. The real-time chronology is sometimes out of order (the modern day equivalent of going to the post office one day and mailing a Dear John letter; going the next day and finding a letter that unmistakably hints at getting married). Peter Kreutzer is the principal Other, with Les Leopold ever lurking in the background; they are each contributing numbers to Peter Golenbock's book this year. Much irrelevant material has been deleted and in a few cases the censor's knife has been wielded. [Clarifications have been added where absolutely necessary, which is not to say they clear much up.]

16-Sep-95 23:43 EDT   **Sb: Re: last week**   **Fm: Ron Shandler**
You wrote:
> Thanks for the transactions. I didn't even realize there wasn't a trading deadline at some point. Any interest in Hoffman for Reynolds?
    With just as much of a meager shot at making a move in wins as in saves, I'll pass. A few weeks earlier and this would've been more intriguing. Thanks anyway.

17-Sep-95 00:55 EDT   **Sb: Re:contact**   **Fm: Eric A. Lindow**
What with traveling and moving, I haven't accomplished much of anything on our endeavors so far. Sunday night should be fine to call- try the home number as the Patton/Lindow line may not have a phone attached to it.

18-Sep-95 10:23:00   **Sb: moves 9/18**   **To: Peter Kreutzer [SWAT]**
The Moose... activate Ben McDonald, drop Hurtado; activate Burnitz, drop Frazier Please pass on the phone number up here in chilly woods. Also, for hot stove purposes, maybe those two proposals I sent you?

18-Sep-95 18:19:00   **Sb: late call**   **To: Peter Kreutzer**
Moose forgot to say in earlier message, activate Leius, drop Worthington. Minny game is just beginning now, hope it's OK.

19-Sep-95 13:47 EDT   **Sb: Re: late call**   **Fm: Peter Kreutzer**
Your six o'clock call in is the sort of transaction I've had to turn down a number of times this year. The most painful involved Goodman, twice, when he was languishing with about 11 points. My test has to do with a rather imprecise determination as to whether anyone could possibly object and/or claim that precedent has been set. For this reason I've been most strict this year: I don't want to have to make these decisions—ever.

19-Sep-95 19:41 EDT   **Sb: hi!**   **Fm: Brett Summers**
Dave is downstairs sawing a board so he has a place to put the brains tomorrow.
He's coming to my class to give a talk on neuroanatomy, and real dead human
brains kind of come with the territory. I only wish we hadn't had chicken soup
for dinner. Reminds me of mom's longstanding chicken abstinence after she
visited the anatomy lab for art purposes. Yuck.

21-Sep-95 16:21 EDT   **Sb: labr**   **Fm: INTERNET:JHunt [BW SWAT]**
hey, alex, here are last week's deals:

baron reserves alfonzo, activates wallach; cuts webster, activates c.johnson; cuts j.ruffin, claims byrd-1; cuts orsulak, claims simms-1 shandler cuts battle, claims newfield-1; cuts leiper, claims m.williams-1 hunt activates aude, cuts busch; cuts blair, claims ericks-1; cuts leonard, claims ochoa-1 enrico reserves alou, claims buford-8 p/g reserves bip, claims haney-

looks like you guys need a bad couple of weeks from vogel's pitchers, and that wacky strategy will work!

21-Sep-95 19:07:00   **Sb: Re: Skyline**   **To: Colin Summers**

Another problem is that Stone is missing. Slipped out the door this morning when we were loading the car for Tiny. We couldn't catch him, then went inside and left the door open, and he hasn't been seen since.

21-Sep-95 19:15:00   **Sb: Stone is missing!**   **To: Brett Summers**

He got out while we were helping Tiny load up her car in the middle of the morning, eluded capture, refused the open door invitation, and hasn't been seen since. Now it's dark. We'll leave the sliding door open all night and hopefully in the morning he'll be scratching at the bedroom door, especially up for breakfast.

21-Sep-95 21:44 EDT   **Sb: Re: Skyline**   **Fm: Colin Summers**

Very sad about Stone. I hope he has the sense to stay away from the road. And I hope he is getting his fill out there. I would open the van, if I were you. He probably knows that as well as he knows the house.
—Colin

21-Sep-95 16:41 EDT   **Sb: Message from Internet**   **Fm: lcarlson**
Dear Alex,

I appreciate the time you took yesterday to discuss the process you follow to get your book to us each year. I now have a better understanding of how much writing you do in the short time after the season ends. In view of that, I thank you very much for agreeing to move your due date up from December 12th to December 7th. That will help us immensely.

Our Sales Department appreciates that you are making the text as up-to-date as possible, but they have been anxious about getting the printed books sooner. As I explained yesterday, putting the book on an earlier schedule is urgent for our Sales and Production Departments. I am now alerting them that the final, finished manuscript will arrive on camera-ready disk on Thursday, December 7th. Kate is also pleased with this news.

22-Sep-95 18:56:00   **Sb: Re: The Client**   **To: Colin Summers**

Stone's back, which Pog is kicking me off the computer to tell you [and Brett] about.

22-Sep-95 18:51:00   **Sb: next yr's book**   **To: >Internet:jhunt**
I have the April 19 issue of Baseball Weekly and can type all your bid values into a spreadsheet, but it would be a lot quicker if I had a master list that was sorted alphabetically. I was wondering if you have such a thing in a spreadsheet of your own that you could send to me on email? Four simple lists would be the ticket — hitters and pitchers in each league alphabetically, with '95 projected dollar values — although if you also make stat projections, I'd of course be interested in those, too . . . Is it safe to say LABR's going to abort next year? You gave it so little play this time around because people found it to be less than entertaining? I definitely keep hearing that

about my appendixes — don't look back, no one cares — trouble is, looking ahead can be done in about 10 pages!

23-Sep-95 19:34 EDT   Sb: Re: next yr's book   Fm: INTERNET:JHunt

shoot, I spiked all those files with the predictions. but please feel free to use what you like- I haven't looked to see how accurate they were, but I don't think I happened to nail too many. (also feel free to give me the proper dissing for the billy ashley prognostication). as for labr, I think there will always be a labr in some form - it's just too valuable as a draft tool to see the results of our auctions. but yeah, most correspondence dealing with labr has been positive about the reduced coverage. (i've gotten a handful of complaints from people who wanted to see more, but it wouldn't take a great leap of imagination to assume they originated from some league members). good luck with the book - I hope things go a little more smoothly next spring. I gotta think they'll have an agreement by then. shhhyeahhhright

24-Sep-95 13:47:00   Sb: Re: next yr's book   To: INTERNET:JHunt

Well, I've been typing in your $V's for AL hitters, and here's a question: Are your values generated strictly by the projected stats? For example, you have nine $17 hitters of various descriptions; is there some sort of formula that says Sandy Alomar and Rich Becker figure to be worth the same? Or do intangibles such as risk and position scarcity play a part? What's interesting is that I sent out the Spring Training Update to the book at exactly the same time you were preparing this for BW. On a flyer like Higginson we are remarkably close. I predict basically the same stat line and my mechanical formula says those stats are also worth $17. But the bid price in the Update is $11. The $6 I don't want to risk on Higginson gets sent toward safer bets — like, you know, Olerud. Anyway, what I'm trying to figure out is, should I be comparing your prices to my supposedly objective stat values or to my admittedly subjective bid values?

24-Sep-95 19:39:00   Sb: another query   To: Walter Shapiro

When you buy players with no salary, like Bonilla, I realize they become toppers the following season, if you freeze them. But what about dropped players like Mattingly? Is he now a topper for next year, which is hardly why we bought him back but is still better than $13? And I need to know by tomorrow at noon what the call is on Jeter. [Must be activated off reserve roster this year to have option of freezing him next year at $15?]

24-Sep-95 7:37 EDT   Sb: Re: query   Fm: Walter Shapiro

alex: all in good time, all in good time. Nabobs so depressed by performance of pitching staff — roughly 30 ER in last 30 IP with just one win — that I have not thought about anything — including the rules regarding Derek Jeter. Promise you an answer sometime today. All the best, the Nabobs

24-Sep-95 20-Sep-95   Sb:Re:another query   Fm:Walter Shapiro

Alex: I was about to look up the answer to your last query, when this one came in...Mattingly is a topper for next year, no if ands or buts... As for what, I am doing tomorrow, I am almost too depressed to care. No hitting and no pitching is a dynamite combination with a week to go in the season... I would love Bobby Witt or Steve Sparks, but I assume they will either go to the Veecks and the Bags respectively, or else I'd guess wrong and be out bid...

I will answer your Derek Jeter question in the near future.

The Nabobs, who have lost their Natter.

24-Sep-95 20:51 EDT   Sb: Re:another query   Fm: Walter Shapiro

Alex--Have now checked the constitution. Here goes the rules as they apply to Derek Jeter and any of his ilk . . .

25-Sep-95 11:57:00   **Sb: last call**   **To: Peter Kreutzer**

1) The Moose will bid $1 for shunned (and shuddery, of course) B.Witt; drop even more terrifying Jacome. If we don't get him, we'll activate Suppan, drop Jacome.

2) Claim Mieske, drop Masteller. If we don't get him we'll activate Brian Giles, drop Masteller.

3) Activate Snopek, drop Worthington.

4) Activate Jeter [DH], drop Donnie from the ballgame.

25-Sep-95 16:00 EDT   **Sb: labr, etc.**   **Fm: INTERNET:JHunt**

pretty quiet final week: baron cuts byrd, claims wall-9; p/g cuts hemond, claims perez-1; cuts decker, claims siddall-1; cuts haney, claims wehner-1; cuts vanderwal, claims tavarez-5 vogel cuts pulsipher, claims bochtler-9; cuts guthrie, claims cummings-9; cuts swindell, claims minor-9

    I can't believe bochtler went so long without being claimed - I certainly could've used him.

    as for the projections, I can't believe we were so close on higgy - I thought i'd be alone in my lofty expectation. but I also can't believe he's hit for such a low average, but that's another story. but yes, my dollar formula was based solely on the predicted stats and an approximate pool of talent in a standard roto league. of course, my predicted stats took into account injury risk (mcgwire, etc.)

25-Sep-95 12:16:00   **Sb: unclaims**   **To: Peter Kreutzer**

Key stat in the Minnesota boxscore: T - 2:19. Twins and White Sox hitters running up to the plate and flailing at anything. Bere probably would have walked 10, if that's any comfort, in normal times. Tonight we'll have to watch Karl and Nitkowski — Karl's by no means a meaningless game — to test the hypothesis that what you want in the last week is control-artist lefties in games that don't count.

25-Sep-95 12:30:00   **Sb: I get it now**   **To: Walter Shapiro**

Thanks for the rules clarifications. Do you have any thoughts about making them a little easier to memorize in the future?

25-Sep-95 16:26 EDT   **Sb: tilting at windmills**   **Fm: Stoneburn**

Peter Kreutzer. unavailable, so don't know who went where, etc. assume you've seen stats. bags

26-Sep-95 12:11 EDT   **Sb: Last swat**   **Fm: Peter Kreutzer**

    $ CLAIMS

    BURN BAGS claim D Singleton (OF) for $3. Drop C Pacquette. Remaining: None

    NATTERING NABOBS claim Robertson (P) for $2. Drop K Wickander. Remaining: None

    VEECKS claim S Sparks for $4. Drop E Plunk. Remaining: None.

    MOOSE FACTORY claim B Witt (P) for $1. Drop J Jacome. Remaining: None.

No More Swats until next year, unless there is a playoff game, in which case: Ups and downs—October 2.

26-Sep-95 8:04:00   **Sb: Re: tilting at windmills**   **To: Stoneburn**

Will you still be using Benson's book? Even though it's not a popular exercise, if only for change of pace I like to check out the forecasts now and then, and Benson's are the only ones I don't have. Fact that he costs twice as much as anyone else can't have anything to do with it.

26-Sep-95 19:28 EDT   **Sb: Re: I get it now**   **Fm: Walter Shapiro**

. . . I can't see whether it matters if I finish 6th with 49.0 points or finish sixth with 55.0. (Hell, it matters, otherwise I wouldn't have called sports phone six times for the updates on today's Angels vs Seattle [Benes] game).

The truth about this season that seems to leap out at me is that someone could have done very well just trading at fair prices for underachieving ballplayers in early July. (Albert Belle and Paul Molitor leap to mind, as well as the Alex Fernandez's and Jack McDowell's of this world who are keeping Starr in first place). It seems to me that we all underestimated exactly how long it would take many players to recover from the long layoff. We all instinctively knew that May would not be typical, but for many players the quasi-spring-training lasted through the July 4th holiday. My guess, and it's only guess, is that there will be much wider discrepancies for players on 1st half vs. second half stats than is usual. (One way to measure it would be to count the number of hitters whose combined BA and SLG average rises or falls by more than .200 between the 1st half and second half) and compare that number with, say, 1993.

The collapse of the Angels was also statistically explicable, since they clearly had a disproportionate number of hitters who were thriving in the early going. Had we played a 162 game season, I would bet that Jim Edmonds would end up hitting .260 and having a Slugging Average around .440. (He'll be frozen in the ADL, of course, but I do wonder what the range of prices for him in startup leagues will be next year. I've always been a skeptic and I wouldn't go over $16, since I take his second-half swoon very seriously).

Obviously, we must should take a look at our rules, since we really haven't gotten our act together on that score in about three years.

Totally favor doing away with the Derek Jeter inequity, but not retroactively.

26-Sep-95 21:17 EDT   **Sb: Re: Stone is missing!**   **Fm: Brett Summers**

Is stone back yet? No other e-mails so I don't know if he has come home or not...

26-Sep-95 8:16:00   **Sb: delay**   **To: Brett Summers**

Something's wrong with your email. I didn't get your query about Stone until this morning, and you obviously haven't gotten message Peg sent days ago . He showed up the next morning, very nonchalant. Where he spent the night is anyone's guess. The day before though, Lorraine Harrington was cleaning her living room when she heard a noise upstairs. She went up to check and found a cat in Joe's closet.

27-Sep-95 10:43 EDT   **Sb: Last swat**   **Fm: Peter Kreutzer**

Interesting idea but I would guess that somewhat wild power pitchers would benefit most from flailing. Doesn't Ted Williams chart show it harder to hit pitches at the edges and outside the strike zone? And isn't the benefit of wildness to the hitter with the patience to wait for a meatball?

These days, mostly, I can't bring myself to recalculate to see what would've happened if I hadn't dropped Witt and Sparks. Going into yesterday I'm pretty sure I was ahead, but if I have them I don't activate Bere (2 decent starts notwithstanding) and have 2 more wins. Maybe I even drop Witt yesterday. it's a hard game.

27-Sep-95 10:43 EDT   **Sb: Re:unclaims**   **Fm: Peter Kreutzer**

I tend to agree with Stoneburn, the prediction comparisons in the player comments don't often throw much light. What I'll be doing if Peter G's publisher can be convinced there won't be a strike next year is comparing the prices/predictions of the various touts in one place. I'd like your spring training price list because I'm curious, but also because I'd like to do a study of the variations.

I'm not sure about your lefty control pitcher theory, but game times have plummeted.

This is not turning into a week for improbable come-from-behind victories (unless you're a Cubs fan). Nova's pitchers are not cooperating. It will take a crumble of Scanlan-like proportions for the powerless but speedy ones not to walk away with 50% of our UBL money.

29-Sep-95 08:18 EDT   Sb: various   **Fm: Stoneburn**

pls give me mailing address and i'll send benson plus b. america. has bruce called you re. ubl news? he has much to say . . . kirby gets jaw broken, fan angry with yet one more late homer charges randy m, cochran compares fuhrman to hitler . .. what is world coming to!!?

01-Oct-95 16:57 EDT   Sb: Re: endgame   **Fm: Peter Kreutzer**

The only game info I've seen today is Mussina's brill job, which reminds me why I dumped Sparks and Witt (more than Sparks' rather ineffective outing). The problem for me is that Nova's pitching needed to suffer big time (and didn't) for me to have any shot at the big prize, so as far as I know I'm rooting for Hitchcock not to get the win in today's Yankee game—with the thought of sneaking into second. In fact I'm rooting for him to get hammered beyond recognition, because that's what it will take.

I'd love to take tomorrow off to watch the playoff. Will it be on free tv?

01-Oct-95 9:19:00   Sb: one more!   **To: Walter Shapiro**

What fun for the Nabobs, getting to watch Langston and Junior go at each other. But I am also psyched for this game. Angels have dodged infamy already, but to beat Randy Jonson in Seattle — the odds in favor of the Mariners (9:5) must be a record for a play-off, and are still modest! If Colin weren't so busy out in Vegas I'd call him up and ask him to put $100 on the Angels.

02-Oct-95 01:03 EDT   Sb: Re: endgame   **Fm: Peter Kreutzer**

It turns out that as I wrote you this afternoon the Yanks and Hitchcock had already won, and that I was much more in danger of falling into fourth place than challenging for second. I expect there will be surprises in tomorrow's stats, and mostly hope that the pennant hangs in the balance throughout the playoff. I mean our pennant. So I activate Eduardo Perez and root for Rich Monteleone to win.

2-Oct-95 11:52:00   Sb: Re: endgame   **To: Peter Kreutzer**

The Langston thing curdled my soul. Ugliest TV shot I've ever seen. Obviously, earlier, when we could lip-read Langston and he was saying[ ]-something-or other, he was saying [ ] you, Hudler. Then he has to sit next to him and glare. And Hudler keeps looking out to the field and clapping his hands. I don't know what the hell was happening with Miller and Morgan. This was better than any footage in 10,000 hours of Simpson coverage and they are damn near totally oblivious. Langston had been pitching like a lion, true, but so had Hudler been playing like one. Hulder was a dope, of course, turning his back on the play, but no one ever notices if Langston makes the play that he was supposed to. Finally, Langston's HOLDING the ball was incredible — one of the great reflex feats I've ever seen — which M & M barely mention. The other thing that they completely missed was the play a moment later by Salmon. They're all over Blowers for not tagging up, but he would have been out easily, inning over, still 1-0, instead of on the next pitch Sojo hitting a squib that Snow should have at least stopped from going through. If it's 1-0, does Phillips hit that HR? To me, Snow's failure was bigger — more important and less excusable — than Hudler's.

03-Oct-95 18:08 EDT   Sb: Re: one more!   **Fm: Walter Shapiro**

Alex: It was actually a great game. I will probably remember Sojo's base-clearing inside-the-park-error-filled whatchamacallit long after I will remember who won the individual rounds of the playoffs. The one thing that I can say in defense of the wildcard system is that it seems to increase the likelihood of sudden-death one-game playoffs. And games like yesterday when everything was on the line is what baseball is all about.

Langston [a Nabob] may not be the best pitcher in baseball, but he certainly is the most expressive figure in defeat. I felt worse about his defeat than the OJ verdict.

Have heard about the standings from Starr, but have not seen them. My condolences to the misbegotten Moose and the star-crossed Bags. Nabobs moderately happy with their final surge to fifth place.

Only four and a half months until pitchers and catchers.

04-Oct-95 01:19 EDT   Sb: Lang(ston)s his head in shame   Fm: Peter Kreutzer

The Langston-Hudler moment made me wonder about those cut-up scrappy personalities managers love so much. I don't think I saw Hudler this year without it being mentioned how often his hustle runs him into many, if not as many, stupid mistakes as it runs him out of. This may have been the ESPN guys each time, how many other chances did I get to see the Halos, but if true it may explain in part Langston's ire. I can't quite figure out what he was thinking on that play, or how he could miss Langston's botch.

Sojo's hit is snow of a different color. Since the bat sheared off and flew in the same direction as the spinning ball, it's hard to see JT's miscue as a mental error. Yeah, it's great if he can knock it down, but hard to say he should've. I think.

04-Oct-95 09:26 EDT   Sb: UPDATES   Fm: Stoneburn

where is jack ruby now that we really need him??

post-season has little reality, yet. see stats? anyway, i'm back in ny and trying to come to grips with idea of oj becoming even richer and more famous.

5-Oct-95 14:13:00   Sb: mail   To: Steve Stoneburn

I went to our little post office today and got the Benson books. Thanks very much.   Did you read the two op-ed pieces in yesterday's Times? Scott Turow and Frank Rich? To understand the jurors is, perhaps, to forgive them.

5-Oct-95 15:09:00   Sb: yoohoo   To: Mark Starr

Nice going, Nova! Haven't seen the standings yet but I gather Hackers gave you a scare. But it just makes that artificial chocolate whatever all the sweeter, doesn't it?

5-Oct-95 15:13:00   Sb: nice try, hackers   To: Steven Levy

You at least put a good scare into Nova.   What's your scouting report on Radke? Did you ever watch him pitch? Anything that might help when his name pops up on the screen would be welcome.

6-Oct-95 9:31:00   Sb: etc   To: >Internet:shandler

Well, Ron, you did it, you saved the game from the Sweeney Plan (no power). Ismael Valdes was the difference. Did Vogel come to you with that or did you go to him? Hunt says there will be a league next year, but I don't know...

06-Oct-95 10:15 EDT   Sb: Re: nice try, hackers   Fm: Steven Levy

It's frustrating to know that any combination of little things could have taken me over — one point in BA, or two wins, or two HRs and a stolen base...

The key trade of the season for me was Goodman trading Salmon for Jeff Russel when he know I was shopping Smith and Fetters. Either one of those guys would have been better for him, and I would have probably thrown in another worthwhile player. But he never called me. So I traded Smith to Starr.

Radke will be a good pitcher. I put him on our reserve list because Chris had just come from Minneapolis with the local paper saying that Radke shined in spring training and would be in the rotation after the first few weeks. He is gutsy, and seems to be one of those guys who will stick it out for the win. Of course chances for that don't come too often on his team, but what was impressive was something like a five game winning streak in August-early September — the league didn't figure him out, he was doing the figuring. This from a rookie suddenly in the pressure position of being the ace of the staff.

06-Oct-95 16:48 EDT   Sb: Re: yoohoo   Fm: Mark Starr

At my age, more than a scare. Who asked the Bags [also punting power] to hit three home runs that last week while they were sinking out of sight with a .183 BA. Anyway, all's well that ends well, though I didn't need the added agony of the playoff game. I had it won on Sunday, then had a chance to lose it Monday if his guys went something like 5-8. Tall order with Randy Johnson pitching, but that didn't mean I didn't sweat. In the end, they went 1-5, the BA point was safe and I have my second championship—once a decade whether I need it or not.

07-Oct-95 20:33 EDT   Sb: stats   Fm: Eric A. Lindow

I got the games by position and am integrating it into the database before I send the info on. The only shortcoming I see in this list is that most players lack first initials.

08-Oct-95 10:56 EDT   Sb: Re: numbers   Fm: Peter Kreutzer

Was out to dinner and didn't see last night's game, unfortunately. I think Buck's great accomplishment (I refuse to credit Stick) is to have wrested the image of the Yankees, at least on the field, away from the Big Man. It actually makes them an easy team to like and root for.

9-Oct-95 10:33:00   Sb: Re: numbers   To: Peter Kreutzer

Well, I doubt you were out to dinner last night. Luckily, I switched allegiances just in time. Shots of the owner up in his booth and Sierra at the plate were the last Straws. But what a great scamper by Griffey! All those Double Martinez signs were portents! No one — not Bob Gibson, not Steve Blass, not Orel Hershiser, not Rod Beck (in the regular season) — has ever been a mightier warrior than Randy Johnson. And now, and now... does the wiped out Northeast Nation get the Braves or Indians on Tuedsay? Better match-up in the NL; much more fun to watch AL.

09-Oct-95 10:18 EDT   Sb: Re: etc   Fm: Ron Shandler

He came to me, looking for Valdes. I was in the market to move one of my frontline starting pitchers for some speed and at the time, was more reluctant to move Shane Reynolds than the unproven-over-a-full-season-of-play rookie Valdes. Shows how smart I was . . . Still, congratulations on 2nd place and the perfect implementation of the Sweeney Plan. You just can't account for a wire-to-wire season like Vogel put in.

10-Oct-95 01:48 EDT   Sb: O Buck!   Fm: Peter Kreutzer

I sat glued to the TV, eating leftovers cold. Even the insipid posturings of Brent Mussberger couldn't wreck the game. From my seat I could see Cone falter, see him running out of gas. Even if it took an extra batter for Buck, how could he not go to the pen? I suppose he would've looked bad if Rivera or Pettite or Black Jack had given up the tying run, but doesn't he look bad now?

And then it looked like Piniella had made the same mistake, sticking with Johnson an inning too long. It is the brilliance of the game that the two situations were so congruent, so comparable, so immediate. Talent and guts only take you so far, and then you need strength and flexibility. That's what managing a pitching staff is all about. Piniella made the same mistake, only he had Edgar Martinez to fix it. I suppose if you're going to go down it may as well be with your best.

I would've yanked Cone after the walk to Tino (at least I think it was a walk, but then Mussberger kept calling it a hit, and because I wasn't keeping score at home I grew unsure...).

My warrior vote goes to Jack Morris, game 7 for the Twins. But then, Mike Scott never had a chance to go the extra yard.

11-Oct-95 11:31 EDT   Sb: photo   Fm: Adam P. Summers

Ask Lindy if he is interested in trying to sell the computer program via the world wide web.

Every year I ask you to get a visa account. This would be an added incentive. A potential 40 million people have access to the web sites.

13-Oct-95 07:57 EDT   Sb: trip west   Fm: Adam P. Summers
The next day Colin and I drove around LA. We saw Marc Sedaka and his new hovel. It has a great view which will be less great after a mudslide or earthquake moves him (or his upslope neighbors) downslope. Dinner was at a neat place where you pick all the materials for a stir fry and they do it in front of you. It was a contest to see who could get the most stuff in the all you can eat bowl. I won, but I could not eat half of what I picked since I ended up with a stirfry the size of my head.

Next morning Colin, Ilya and I went blading. Nell was excluded on the grounds that it is not fair to go if you can't risk falling down. In her current state she would weeble rather than fall so it was judged not risky enough. We did the strand from Hermosa to the factories just south of the airport. Ilya mentioned choking fumes further along so we did not proceed to El Segundo. After a nice breakfast Ilya and I drove around in pink death fetching a motorcycle...got to go. maybe more monday or tuesday.

17-Oct-95 16:01 EDT   Sb: Question regarding formulas   Fm: M ROTHSCHILD
Mr. Patton,
Let me start off by saying that I am a great admirer of your work. I wish I could tell you that I won my league thanks to you, but in this great age of information, our commissioner chose the USA Today on- line service as our stat service, and it crashed four times. The fourth time, came right after the all-star break, when I was in first place, but that was when the money was returned and the league ended.

I am currently trying to adapt the principles you have developed for my own personal use for a basketball league. I spoke to Eric Lindow and he informed me of your e-mail address. My question takes you back to probably your first publication on the pricing system which is a chapter in Peter Golenbock's book published in 1987. In this explanation of the system, you say there are 1392 total points generated by the players in the draft in a twelve team league. This comes out to 116 points per team. (by the way there is a misprint in the formula on page 99 which continues to torment me by making me think there's 113 points per team) I'd like to know how you came about the total of 1392. Was it just by figuring out the marginal value of the "average hitter", for instance, and then multiplying the points and average player earned by the total hitters in the league? I believe this to be the case considering my experience so far with basketball, but considering the time you put into devising the formulas (I know, because I've put in a ridiculous amount trying to translate them) I find it hard to believe that any numbers you use are arbitrary, which is what 1392 becomes. I'd greatly appreciate any insight you could provide on this matter.
Sincerely,
Matt Rothschild

17-Oct-95 23:44 EDT   Sb: All Praises   Fm: Peter Kreutzer
Kenny Lofton is great. So is baseball, although I wish I could've seen a NLCS game. It's weird to have not.

18-Oct-95 9:11:00   Sb: Re: All Praises   To: Peter Kreutzer
Another incredible game. It was as if the intense concentration all nine players needed to hold down the Indians finally got to the Mariners. If Wilson had paid attention to the way Lofton caught the 27th out the night before, he would have know he was coming... Great camera work.

The two best shots, which surprisingly they chose not to repeat, were the one up the third base line, the foreshortening effect being only partly what put Lofton right on Espinoza ass, and the one down the third base line, where you see Wilson's disgust at missing the ball shuddering though his body, and you see Lofton, yep, right on Espinoza's ass.   Baseball is great, and the two teams in the Series deserve to be called great. There's even a certain symmetry in their getting there, the Braves also demolishing by far the better of their two opponents and having trouble with the one that was really quite weak, that was running on fumes. They didn't have to show all four games in the first round, but it seems to me that for both rounds there was always an EST and PST game the same night. It would have been so easy to show all regional games without competition, in prime time, and still show a second game. The owners have sniffed too many fumes. I really think they are brain-damaged. The combination of success in business, constant failure with THEIR fantasy teams, is lethal. Is it possible that baseball is not going to heal itself over the winter, despite the wonderful medicine that the players are administering nightly?

18-Oct-95 09:28 EDT   **Sb: CATCH UP**   **Fm: Stoneburn**
SPENT ALL LAST WK IN ATLANTA AND NOW BACK THERE FIGHTING THROUGH MANAGEMENT BUY-OUT VS KILL; MUCH MUCH TENSION. WHO NEEDS IT ... CAN'T SAY WRONG GUYS GETTING TO PLAY BRAVES. MY COMPANY HAS BOX SEATS TO ALL ATLANTA HOME GAMES, BUT OF COURSE I WON'T BE THERE NEXT WK WHEN I COULD TAKE ADVANTAGE.CHEERS. BAGS

18-Oct-95 22:38:00   **Sb: pod**   **To: Eric Lindow**
Well, I've got the hitter stats in a new directory, POD96, but it's pretty messy. I don't know how you keep all this stuff straight. I copied mail2.bin to both nlp94.pww and nlp95.pww, and the working files in EVA and PRO show the new data for NL hitters, but now what? Do I rename nlp94.pww nlp95.pww, since that's what it is, and nlp95.pww nlp96.pww? I don't dare. The directory will make more sense to me, but it might not make a bit of sense to the exes...

19-Oct-95 11:46:00   **Sb: just missed**   **To: Mike Walsh**
Hi Mike, Alex here (I hope you've got your email ID-ing your correspondents by now). Been meaning to tell you that a couple of days ago I was down in Salisbury meeting with Nancy Cahan and Pat Sermon and someone from Random House about flogging this year's book. I had no idea I was in your area, but just as we were breaking up, Nancy said, "I know someone else who plays this game, Michael Walsh." So I said, show me where he lives, I'd like to meet him (just kidding), and we dropped by. Banged on the door, tracked down some distant banging in the attic, found a carpenter who said you had just gone to New York. Too bad. Great spot you have. Nancy said you've got a novel out? Way to go. (We don't get much news up here in Vermont.) The great thing is, I was trying to explain to Nancy who played this game — which seemed more hopeful than trying to explain what the game was — and I said it was in fact played by people who were all too busy: far from the get-a-lifers that Mike Lupica is constantly trashing; people who had too many lives. So later when she remembered that you were in a league, it was like, bingo. Anyway, Peg and I are here in Manchester at least until December... Good luck flogging your book. Trust all goes well in your lives, or most of them, we mustn't be greedy.

19-Oct-95 11:52 EDT   **Sb: X.400 Delivery Report**   **Fm: X.400 Gateway**
Delivery report for message 951019154204 71461.2046 FHJ89-2
    Subject: just missed
    To: X400:(c=us;a=mci;s=0003783638)
    Status: Delivery failed
    Time: 15:42:02 GMT 19-Oct-95
    Reason: 1 - Transfer Failure

Diagnostic: 0 - Unrecognized ORName
Explanation: Recipient name is not valid on the receiving mail system.

20-Oct-95 19:21:00   **Sb: query**   **To: Walter Shapiro**

Hey there, Walter — you get the feeling like I do Indians are going to mash Braves? But that's not the query. I tried to send a message to Mike Walsh a couple days ago and it was sent back. Used to work, so Mike probably has scampered on to a new address. Do you happen to have it?

22-Oct-95 0:23:00   **Sb: notes 10/21**   **To: Eric Lindow**

I'm wondering if Team 29 should become Free Agent instead of Other. That's what 99% of Others are. If there's room, we could still have Team 30 as Other, which could include Japan, colleges, high school, Cuba, retired.   Gallego in AL hitters should be D Gallagher, 35 — all other stats the same.   Garciaper should be M Gallego, 35 — all other stats the same.   I've changed the HR, RBI and SB denominators and am getting basically the right values. I tried to change the BA, but when I switched 4700 AB to 4300 AB, it came out 43000 AB... Made Albert Belle worth ($1100). Did no one ever call this in? If so, shows even cyberspace punks are afraid to mess with Patton $.

24-Oct-95 11:05:00   **Sb: Question regarding formula**   **Fm: M ROTHSCHILD**

Dear Matt —   I wish I could remember how I arrived at the 1392 point total but I can't. I do remember saying that Henderson or Righetti earned more than 12 points in the SB or saves category because all teams start from zero, then the bottom teams get x number of steals or saves. The same thinking applies to total team points: you start counting from zero even though the last-place team will have more than zero.   The more important concept is that the point totals should convert to dollars that add up to league budgets. In my formulas I do this by multiplying 13/6 times whatever the point totals are in each category. In other words, every 6 points that a hitter or pitcher gains for a team are worth $13. (The average hitter gains 6 points and is worth $13; the average pitcher gains 4 points and is worth $8.67.)   Hope this helps with your basketball calculations.   — Alex

24-Oct-95 15:04   **Sb: Question regarding formulas**   **Fm: M ROTHSCHILD**

Alex,

   I figured it out and thought you might be interested to know the answer. I appreciate you responding, anyway.

   In the Golenbock book, you use 5.71 points for the average hitter, rather than 6. I know that you currently use 6 because it's based on the ratio of hitters to an average player (14 vs. 23) The 6 points is a misnomer, however, and it is based on the multipliers (4.1 for HRs, 14.27 for RBIs, 4.3 for SBs) which are based on the league averages and the spread each category to gain an additional place. Once the multipliers are adjusted, for any given year, the average player always earns 6 points.   The misnomer comes from this:

   A team made up of 14 average hitters, in a twelve owner league does not earn 14 * 6 points as is suggested. Rather, the team earns 6 points in each quantitative category * 3 quantitative categories = 18 points in the standings. So actually an average player earns 18/14 (1.29) points in the quantitative categories, not 6.

   Hence, the 1392 is a somewhat arbitrary number and was broken down in that book to 959 for hitters, 433 for pitchers.

   5.71 points/hitter * 14 hitters/team * 12 teams/league = 959 points/league (hitters only)

   3.99 points/pitcher * 9 pitchers/team * 12 teams/league = 431 points/league

   But this is incorrect, because the 5.71 is incorrect.

   Actually, with your new numbers, hitters generate 1008 points per league (6 * 14 * 12)

   With the corrected/normalized numbers, hitters generate

      (18 points for average team/14 hitters) * 14 * 12 = 216 points, and 1008/216 = 6/1.29

I'm not sure if your averaged category multipliers are arbitrary (I think they are), but if you understand what I've written (I'm not sure I do) there should not be a need for them to be arbitrary once you know the league averages for BA, AB, and H you can solve for the multipliers. I'm not sure exactly how, yet, but once I figure out the formula, I'll let you know.

I hope this was clear and more than a waste of your time. Also, I'd like to suggest you explain the idea that the 6 points generated, while accurate, has really no meaning whatsoever, in your new book. I'd like to hear from you again on your thoughts regarding this. Matt

24-Oct-95 11:29:00   Sb: eva/pro   To: Eric Lindow

In POD96 I've now got eva95.exe and pro96.exe, both copied from the eva95.exe that you sent me. So they both have the same hitter formulas, which is fine for now; however, they also seem to be drawing on the same data files. When I change the working file in PRO96, the working file in EVA95 also changes. That shouldn't happen, should it? I would think PRO96 would draw from alh95.pww and EVA95 would draw from alh94.pww. So you see that things are more than a little confused.

24-Oct-95 20:26:00   Sb: Re: forecasts   To: Peter Kreutzer

I will be barely tracking the forecasters this year, but I will occasionally compare you, me and Hunt in the revised forecasts. So, please refresh me as to where these were seen last year? Somewhere in cyberspace, I know, but where exactly? And I am correct that you will be publishing '96 projections in Peter's book? Also, when did you make these projections? I'm assuming, based on the at-bats, that they are strike adjusted. The first guy I am doing is your man Albert. He hit more home runs JUST AS A BONEMAN than you predicted! Just kidding. But I trust you've scratched your head over Jerry Heath's price for him. $31? Good grief. I've always said the best pricing test would be a retrospective draft. Buying players after the season ends. I'm pretty sure the 1995 Albert Belle would go for more than $31. Don't you think? And, of course, what's screwy is that Jerry has Manny at $27, only $4 less than Albert.

25-Oct-95 11:08 EDT   Sb: Re: forecasts   Fm: Peter Kreutzer

The forecasts I sent you were strike adjusted and put together about a week before the season, although as I peruse them I'm struck by how grounded in the mechanical predictions we concocted last November they are. They appeared on the ESPNet SportsZone on the World Wide Web.

One of the things I started messing with, in an attempt to find a way to generalize enough from year to year so that I could get context-sensitive prices without sorting and resorting players for each year (oh, if I were a programmer), has lead to a second, retrospective, evaluative pricing system. That is, if you were to draft players after the season was over and their stats were complete, what would you pay for them? Which is what you're talking about.

Maybe we should do this. If we got 12 teams to submit price lists, and then sorted them out as if we were drafting, we'd end up with 12 teams putting prices on known quantities. Are you game? It could be interesting.

25-Oct-95 19:45:00   Sb: Re: forecasts   To: Peter Kreutzer

Definitely game! That's what my prices ARE. Who took how much of the pie. I'm telling you, you'll be whupped! Sign me up.

27-Oct-95 11:25 EDT   Sb: Re: forecasts   Fm: Peter Kreutzer

I'll get us a game: I'm thinking each team submits a list of 168 players and 108 pitchers w/ prices, ranked from most to least expensive. Someone (me), will conduct a "draft", starting with the top name on list 1, checking all the other lists, and giving the player to the team that's made the high bid. I think you should always top the next high bid by 1, rather than committing to the bid you make (That is if you make the high bid on Belle at $50, and Jerry Heath has the next highest bid at $34, you get Belle for $35, not $50). Once the draft is complete, player stats are totaled and voila! A winner.

I think $100 per team would make it interesting. And that we should use our usual minimums for ABs and IP. The only problem I can foresee is one team ending up with a ludicrous # of saves or steals. If that happens because of their valuation system, so be it. But if it's just bad luck, well, it doesn't seem like much fun.

When Albert hit the homer on Wednesday I thought: Hmm, nice adjustment. As the Maddux pitch approached the plate on Thursday I could see it was in the same spot, and when he hit it the same way I almost certainly decided to freeze him. I mean, wow! Whatta game.

27-Oct-95 23:21:00   Sb: forecasts   To: Peter Kreutzer

Put me in the game, but we need more than just you, me and Jerry. I'd quickly go broke, topping all of his prices. You can only afford so many even $32 Albert Belles. (The way to handle Jerry would be to push the scrubs out. Did it feel to you like Alex Rodriguez earned $7 last year?) Now, I detected a tiny hint of agreement between you and Jerry. Something about a valuation system producing a "ludicrous number of saves." No way! There's nothing ludicrous about excess. Too much is never enough, not even if you're Levy. It's obvious that the whole reason Albert is worth only $4 more than Ramirez in Jerry's calculations is that Albert goes right off the charts. He hits 20 more homers than Manny and gets credit for maybe five of them. That's no good. If we believed Jerry, you'd be dropping Albert and I'd be keeping Olerud! I'll mail you POD95 on Monday. Will the Indians be world champs by then? I suspect they will.

28-Oct-95 16:27 EDT   Sb: Re: forecasts   Fm: Peter Kreutzer

I think the game only works if we get 12 takers. Any fewer and we have to make adjustments and then the scientific part of it is gone. I'm not sure how much I agree with Jerry. What I do know is that retrospective valuing is way different than prospective valuing. And it's what lies in the difference that we should be interested in.

Peter's book is on, I guess. Which means less time to suss the difference (Viva!) and more time churning the numbers. Sacre bleu.

Much as I'm rooting for the Cleves, their fatal flaw is lefties. My buddy Jon, is also feeling a Cleveland run. And hell, my prediction was a 3-3 deadlock after six. But I'll bet the Injuns fold tomorrow night. And lose 7 to 2. I hope I'm wrong, there's a special thrill to game 7.

28-Oct-95 23:55 EDT   Sb: New PRO96 and pitcher data files   Fm: Eric A. Lindow

Copy the big file to your POD96 directory as PRO96.EXE. Copy the two small files to the same directory as: ALP95.PWO and NLP95.PWO - this will make the proper filenames for EVA. (Copy as .PWW if you want working files also). Then copy them again, using ALP96.PWO and NLP96.PWO so that you will have prediction files for PRO.

Probably a good idea to back up anything you have done so far before doing the above. although if you get the filenames right you can only affect pitcher data, which I assume you haven't done anything to anyway.

29-Oct-95 9:57:00   Sb: Re: forecasts   To: Peter Kreutzer

Well, Jon and I were wrong. It was a good World Series. Real good, not great. Not enough close plays at home. Glavine was definitely great; Martinez wasn't just hurting, he was throwing meatballs. The Braves were pressing, the seventh game would have been painful indeed (unless you wanted those Cleves, but I'm a National Leaguer deep down). The great thing about Justice is he was telling the truth. The Atlanta fans were a bunch of hide-behind-your-popcorn pantywaists. Gutless glory seekers. Baseball DOES include the fans. You can't have it both ways. Only Ted Turner gets through life on Prozac, and does anything. Justice said he never had felt so much pressure, the whole day had been the worst of his life. He wasn't as great as Glavine by any stretch, but what he did was more amazing because he was unable to block the pressure out. . . . I like the National League but I sure don't like those Lemke/Belliard/Glavine innings. (Didn't you have the feeling Glavine might do some damage if Belliard would just get on?) If someone's on, though, the sacrifice situation — with the third baseman playing a foot from the plate, the shortstop dashing maybe to second, maybe to third, and so forth — is fun. So what I propose as the final solution to baseball's only real problem is a DH/PH blend: in both leagues, you get one free pinch-hit for the pitcher. Once a game, the pitcher can be replaced by some thug on the bench without having to come out. There's always the threat that way, and there's all sorts of cat and mouse as to when to use it. One thing that would go and be good riddance is the double-switch. It's one of those things that someone like Whitey Herzog thought up and everyone else thinks they have to use, even though they're not bridge players. Last night Hargrove made a fool of himself by sending in Amaro for Ramirez when he brought in Poole. Even Joe Morgan (who I think has really slipped) let that go. The announcers aren't bridge players; they scratch their heads and say this is the National League at it's best, pal. Had the game gone on, they would have woken up to what really happened. Amaro did come up the next inning in what would have been the pitcher's spot — but Poole was taken out anyway! The weeping one, Tavarez (what's that all about?) was brought in to start the next inning. So Amaro (or better, Perry) could have pinch-hit. Meantime, guess who's not in right field anymore? If the Indians score ONE run, one, and the game goes on and on and on, guess who's batting behind Eddie Murray from now on? Tavarez. Eric Plunk. Chad Ogea. Eddie wouldn't see another pitch worth bitching about. One thing about batting orders is that the people at the top come up more often than the people at the bottom; it never fails. Well, I guess I'm getting my work done. If I can figure out how to dump Tapcis into Inword.

02-Nov-95 09:07 EST   **Sb: Re: forecasts**   **Fm: Peter Kreutzer**

Thanks for the disks. I was away a couple days and they were in my box when I got back.

I don't think the designated pinch hitter idea is a bad one, but its still gimmicky. One of Atlanta's problems this year was that Blauser was hurt and not hitting. Lemke managed to pick up some of the slack, but with those three virtual holes (including the pitcher), that lineup was less than fearsome—even with all that meat. That should mean something, and it did. As good as the Braves were they had to come from behind to win over and over again. This year they got lucky. You can bet they won't be next year.

But with Devereaux or Smith AND Klesko in the line up they're a much more powerful offense, and much better defensively. Not that it made any difference in the Series. I say let the pitcher hit and let teams choose between weak hitting middle infielders and good hitters. It will be interesting to see what Davey Johnson, a notorious "defense is no substitute for offense" manager, does in the DH league.

03-Nov-95 19:03 EST   **Sb: Re: forecasts**   **Fm: Peter Kreutzer**

I just ran correlations on the predictions I have entered thus far in my spreadsheet: LABR, Hunt, Your $s, Your Bids, ADL and Me.

Correlation turns each set of predictions into a line, then compares the attitude of the lines. A correlation of 1 means the lines are parallel, a 0 means they create a right angle, a -1 means they're parallel but the correlation is between the first number in one set and the last number in the other, etc.

One challenge in these comparisons is to decide what sets of data to compare. I think sorting by the actual earnings of the players is probably best, since that gives you the group that did it. Then see how well we figured they would do.

Anyway, the best correlation to the Top 100 AL hitters was, drum roll please, Patton dollars. Patton bids, ADL and Me were virtually tied, in that order. Surprisingly, Hunt was a little better than LABR, but well back (.59 to .54).

Part of your success is attributable to your allocation of more money for the hitters. It will be interesting to see what that does to the pitchers.

4-Nov-95 10:16:00   **Sb: Re: forecasts**   **To: Peter Kreutzer**

You're way ahead of me. I don't know a right angle from an angle iron. But what are you comparing all of us to? You're prices? Les's? I'm pretty sure it's not Jerry's.   I use the term similarity score awfully loosely. For years they were something James trotted out to score himself with, and all I could tell about them was that they were ridiculous.

6-Nov-95 8:18:00   **Sb: hey**   **To: Steve Stoneburn**

Thanks for sending the Benson figures. They look sort of like Heath's.

6-Nov-95 8:45:00   **Sb: universal baseball**   **To: Adam Summers**

Guess what the latest UBL hot spot is? Worcester. When I'm visiting you in Amherst, it will be a half hour drive to go watch Don Mattingly play.

Actually, the UBL is in big trouble; they were standing at the altar with Liberty TV, when MLB crooked its finger and Liberty skipped out the side exit. They need two more franchises and don't think they can get them without a TV package already in place.

Stoneburn and Bruce went to a meeting in New York last week, and what they were told is it's a tough sell because everybody thinks baseball is on its last legs. Nothing could be further from the truth. Everyone makes such a big deal of the attendance decline in the majors; far more amazing, I think, is that 25,000 peope still showed up for each and every ballgame. It wasn't that long ago that 10,000 was a good crowd. When teams went over the 1 million mark, they jumped for joy. Then 2 million became the benchmark. Now
it's 3 million. Eight teams teams still drew over 2 million last season and the Rockies and Orioles went over 3 million.

The Houston owner called a press conference to tell Houstonians that if 2.5 milllion of them don't turn out this year, he's going to move! With baseball in the sorry shape it is, and with the sorry Astrodome to go to, 1.3 million turned out last year, and I'd love it if every one of them told Drayton McLane to shove off and take his sorry team with him.

The reason franchises are still worth in the kazillions is that the owners HAVE done one thing right: they've kept their club exclusive. They lost control of the players but they've still got their monopoly. The new team in Arizona doesn't have a stadium, doesn't know if it is in the AL or NL, and won't play until 1998; already it has sold *41,000* season tickets. You could say supply is being kept below demand.

Which is where the UBL should come in. With Worcester as one hot spot and Puerto Rico as another and Brooklyn as another and Mexico City as another and San Jose as another, all it needs really to do is put players on the field, and TV will come. Getting the players is the easiest part. There are right now upwards of 300 major league free agents and 500 minor league free agents, everyone of them desperate to keep playing. (Who in their right mind would prefer to work?) And good players, really good players, are sprouting up everywhere. The team that's my dark horse in the Olympics (to beat the Cubans, not the U.S.) is Japan. Baseball's flourishing in the oddest places, like the Netherlands and Australia. Baseball, much more than football (sorry, Ad), is taking over the world; there just seems to be something about it that is the perfect antidote for the world's frazzled nerves.

The minor leagues have never been more popular. Bill has a season ticket to the Hudson Valley Rengades in Fishkill. It's the only way he can get in.

06-Nov-95 01:19 EST   **Sb: Angle irons**   **Fm: Peter Kreutzer**

Once I did the correlations on the NL things got more interesting. Maybe because my predictions came out on top. Actually, in the AL if you sort on the top 168 players I nearly caught you, too. Hunt did better in the NL too. In any case, the difference between the various predictors and the league bidding, isn't all that great. Which we already knew.

I haven't put together the "Post Season Draft" yet. Les suggested that in addition to submitting prices, that each team also submit a list of players at their prices that would comprise a whole team. Obviously, this can't be a money bet (or has to be a small side wager). It would help even out what could be some very bad luck on the draft. I'm on jury duty this week and have some family obligations, but hopefully I'll get a chance to make some calls.

I didn't enter Hunts stats, just the $ values. Last year I did all the stats for you and James, and that took care of October.

James's similarity scores were an attempt, originally, to sort through the history of baseball and find people with similar profiles. By assigning values to each of the categories and comparing them against the whole database, he'd be able to find players whose careers were somewhat congruent at different junctures in their careers. My recollection is he used these groupings to forecast the future careers of big fat slow catchers and low average high SB centerfielders or whatever. Mostly arbitrary, one suspects, but interesting.

6-Nov-95 8:50:00   **Sb: Re: Angle irons**   **To: Peter Kreutzer**

You're right about James. That's what he was doing... But for scoring himself he withheld a key piece of information: not how many people had 900 similarity scores but what did 900 mean? It wasn't linear — you couldn't say that 900 was 5.8% better than 850, or 928 .1% better than 927, so you were lost. My great advantage (like I've been telling Les for years) is that I'm not a math whiz like you guys. I'm the only one in the industry who can actually publish his formulas. (And, amazingly, that is a popular item in the book.) But I do, of course, pretend to be more ignorant than I am. And you, of course, continue to withhold the critical piece of information! WHAT are you comparing the predictions to? What measurement of the reality? Les's prices? Les (& More — what was that other guy's name) Dollars are damn good (they are the closest to mine); but until I know what you're really doing, I don't have any idea what you're doing.

06-Nov-95 15:21 EST   **Sb: Re: Angle irons**   **Fm: Peter Kreutzer**

Whoops. Yeah, I meant to also say:

Once I started scoring better in the correlations, I had to start examining the role that the pricing system for actual 1995 played. I was using Les's formula from 2 weeks ago to compare, which certainly gives an edge in the evaluation to my projections. Which is why this "Draft at auction a team from the already completed season" is so interesting.

If you drop me your formula for 1995 I'll plug it in and recorrelate. It should be interesting.

8-Nov-95 9:46:00   **Sb: Re: Angle irons**   **To: Peter Kreutzer**

We really are onto something. To me the one remaining mystery of the game (the Rotisserie game) is why a $40 player who earns $40 is more powerful than a $20 player who earns $20. That shouldn't be the case in my pricing system, since mine doesn't have any bends or warps at all. It says 40 is 15% of 260 (.1538461, actually) and 20 is 8% (.076923). But all sorts of circumstantial evidence indicates you'll be mighty happy if Albert brings you $40 for $48 — happier than if Mattingly returned $13 for $13, which is why he's a free agent. In Jerry's world, as I said, Alex Rodriguez earned $7 last year. In mine he earned $4. In mine Albert earned $46 (just about what I expected), not $31. These are huge differences at each end. Clearly, there are warps in Jerry's world if Belle and Ramirez are a mere $4 apart; if Belle is only 15% better (31/27) than Manny Ramirez. What he's doing is, he's underpaying Albert by 48% (46/31) to overpay Alex by 75% (7/4). Anyway, that's what I'm here to say, and I'm more than happy to put any amount of money up against Jerry's prices. He's going to have Alex R's stats and be nicked $5. I'm going to be down $32 and have Albert's stats. I can't wait. So what I'll do is, I'll send you the formulas in Lotus files that I sent Eric. This is fun. If you can figure out how to run this contest we'll get fascinating data. If you can get stuff back to me in time, it's definitely going into the Q&A. But please don't release my industrial secrets (Les is fine, although I don't think he's interested) before the book does.

09-Nov-95 00:16 EST   **Sb: I've got files**   **Fm: Peter Kreutzer**

Thanks for the files. I probably won't open them until the weekend. I have jury duty tomorrow and have to get my predictions to Les ASAP, so there isn't really time 'til then. And I want to review my list and settle it before I look at your prices. I mean, this is science, isn't it? There's also the competitive advantage, but my theory is so radical that it is either going to be a fabulous success or will crash and burn, so I doubt it would do any good to see your prices.

I talked to Steve today and he's in. Hopefully we'll get this together for next week. If you talk to anyone who might want in have them call me. I think we need 12 (we have you, me, Steve and Les so far). Maybe I'll send out some email and fax inquiries.

9-Nov-95 9:19:00   **Sb: Re: I've got files**   **To: Peter Kreutzer**

Steve who? Levy? Stoneburn? Someone else? If you're talking about a real auction, there's no way. No time. I'm not sure what I pictured, but I thought it would be on auto-pilot. Albert's name comes up, and the highest price gets him, at $1 more than the next price, and so on down. The trick was always finding 12 prices. I can think of you, me, Les, Jerry, Benson and — ? Hey, we could call Glen Waggoner and do the NL East.

09-Nov-95 10:57 EST   **Sb: Schedule Crunch**   **Fm: Colin Summers**

The schedule has already started to impinge on the design of the building. Through some miscommunication with the cabinet maker, the cabinets for the master bath and poolbath were not ordered. If they were ordered now from the custom cabinet place we had selected we wouldn't have them until the very end of December. So we have switched to a module cabinet for those spaces. A little more ordinary, a bunch of lines that are not from my hand and exist in many average homes across this desert basin floor. They are checking to see if they can get the formica I selected.

No solution there. It can't be late. They are shooting for a December 1 completition date now. The client hasn't taken a vacation for the past three years. On December 10 he will settle into his new home for a four week break from touring and the live show. Obviously, that sort of vacation can't be moved to January just because we won't have the cabinets ready. So we fall back to the ordinary in a few places.

There are other places that I won't compromise. I don't know where they are yet, but I know that on December 10 there will be some holes in the complete fabric of the house and the reason will be that they need to be custom patched, little odds and ends like a false mirror over a secret cubbyhole. If I took a day out from getting things done I could figure out which things I might not get done in time.

11-Nov-95 00:12 EST   **Sb: Re: I've got files**   **Fm: Peter Kreutzer**

Stoneburn wants to do it.

I pictured it the same way: everyone submits a list of 276 names. The highest priced player is named first and goes to the highest bidder for $1 more than the second highest. And so on. Ties are determined by random selection: for the tied price (not $1 more).

We've got: You, me, Les, Stoneburn. I'll contact the rest of our league: I figured Walter and maybe Levy would be into it, and who knows? And Starr. It's action, after all.

But if you can get some of those other touts in, great. I would think a call to Hunt would do it. He could write about it, and lord knows he needs material now that he's gone weekly. (Four weeks of printing Jerry's prices? Yeesh). And sure, Jerry, too. He wouldn't even have to do anything if we used his list of $s.

In re: action. I thought if it were a friendly group we could make a wager, say a hundred or so, just to make it interesting. I'm game if everyone wants to. If that's a problem I'd forgo the bet: it will be plenty interesting anyway.

If you want to email Hunt and introduce me, I'll take it from there. I don't know how much time I'm going to have (I got on a jury) but I'll find it one way or the other.

11-Nov-95 10:04:00   Sb: idea   To: >Internet:jhunt

Hey, there, John — how's it going? I'm still working away on the book, and you've been doing fine, especially on avoiding the bombs.

    A friend of mine named Peter Kreutzer wants to do a retrospective auction. That is, get 12 people together and buy last year's stats and see who wins THAT league. No forecasting skills, just a rock 'em sock 'em clash of pricing theories. Good idea? It's hot stove time and you might be able to get at least a couple of meals out of this for your own column. (I'm hoping he pulls it together in time for me to get it into the Q&A of my book.) Peter is doing the predictions for Golenbock this year. He's going to get Jerry Heath involved and has a few other people lined up. We need 12, obviously. Maybe you can pull in people like Ron Shandler and John Benson? You can tell them all they have to do is submit a list of 276 players (all of whom were on last year's Opening Day Rosters — not people like Wakefield or league crossovers like Bonilla) with prices for each. From then on it's nothing but auto-pilot. A player's name is nominated and the highest price gets him (at $1 more than the next highest price). Then we give all the stats to Jerry.
Anyway, in case you have time to help out, I gave Kreutzer your email address and you'll be hearing from him. He's already seen MY prices, but what the hell, he's already seen the stats.

11-Nov-95 10:07:00   Sb: price war   To: >Internet:shandler

Hi Ron — I'm sure you are totally snowed under at the moment (me too) but I thought you should see a message I just sent to John Hunt. Hope it explains itself, hope you can join. — Alex

11-Nov-95 10:46:00   Sb: Re: I've got files   To: Peter Kreutzer

What a weird world. While you were sending this message last night, I was wandering outside looking for our cat with a flashlight. I finished off Darren Daulton, went outside to stretch, and the cat flashed out the door. He doesn't know from cold, but the problem was, believe it or not, there's a coyote that comes down to the town. I've seen him twice now. Once when I was writing about Lofton, once when I was writing about Cone, somewhere in there. A movement catches my eye out the window, and there's this big silvery yellow coyote trotting across the lawn. When I say, "Hey you — what should I say about Lofton?" he takes off. Something keeps bringing him to the town and I have the feeling Manchester's cat population is already less than it was.

    So you've seen the message I sent to Hunt. I trust you agree with the key stipulation: no Wakefield, no Bonillas. As for the order, why shouldn't it be random? Why not have Alex Rodriguez come up early? I can tell you from experience in the BW auctions that you can't keeping grabbing the high-priced bargains, no matter how juicy they are. (We almost blew our Sweeney Plan — again — when Bonds stopped at $43!) There can be a strong tilt towards the big tickets in the early rounds, because that's the way we play, but occasionally a Wes Chamberlain should be nominated. We'll have your co-author pick them. I'll be interested to see how Hunt et al respond to this. Am I right that you and Les are separate?

11-Nov-95 19:26 EST   Sb: Re: I've got files   Fm: Peter Kreutzer

Actually, I don't agree with the Wakefield stipulation. The idea is to summarize, say, AL value at the end of the season. Wakefield, Bonilla and, yes, even Mark Whiten, were part of the AL value pool. So if they rank above #168 they should be draftable. You get their AL stats only of course. Makes sense, don't it?

    About Les and me, I was thinking we'd be separate teams. Why not? My pricing system is different than his, though I have to admit I've adjusted it to incorporate what I've learned from him. Just as I've adjusted it to incorporate what I've learned from you. And whoever else helps me understand stuff. But an interesting thing has happened: Both he and I have developed, independently, alternative pricing schemes. We were working on different problems and used different methods, but somehow ended up with prices that are nearly congruent. So the question: If we both use the same scheme do we screw each other up? That wouldn't be any fun at all. So he wants to team up. We may be wrong but at least these new ideas will get a clear shot. I want to think about it some more.

I haven't looked at your prices, and won't until I settle on mine. I mean, I know pretty much what yours are. They're like Les's standard method and my standard method. With differences. But I'd hate to know just what your price is on Albert, or perhaps more importantly on Randy Johnson.

Give the coyote time. If I know my Indian legends he will not only tell you about Lofton, but also Will Pennyfeather. And will keep mum about Chief Knock-a-Homa.

12-Nov-95 10:42:00   **Sb: Re: I've got files**   **To: Peter Kreutzer**

No, it doesn't make sense. Sorry. This available-at-draft thing is something I've tried to get across many times to Les, but he doesn't listen.   Briefly, here it is. We have $260 that we want to spend as best we can in April. We need to know, if Albert does such and such, how much of my $260 does he get? Because everyone's trying to figure the same thing out, the question for all of us is, how much of $3,120 does each player that we buy in the draft get? Another way to put it is, the average player is worth $11.3 (3120/276), and there's not anybody who would argue about THAT.

Players that come along later are what I call "free loot." They get measured by the same pricing system — for reference purposes after the season — so if Bonilla got the same stats as, say, Ripken, and Ripken was worth $25 (I wish), Bonilla was worth $25. For accounting purposes only. For reference. To make books more interesting, or at least fatter. Obviously, you can't buy Bonilla for $25, because he's on the Mets.

That's why the prices for the entire AL at the end of the season go over budget, especially the hitter prices. (So many pitchers that are called "free loot" rip you off so bad that the pitching budget barely rises.) When you do open up my files, you'll see "draft populations" at the top. The AL hitters drafted are massaged by my formulas to earn exactly $2,184. And this is where legitimate debate begins. Why is that?   I say, the average hitter is worth 50% more than the average pitcher, because he contributes in three categories rather than two — and Les says this is baloney. I'm sure he's right. But I've never been able to turn the qualitative categories into quantities, so what I do is, I turn them into zero. I multiply 168 hitters by $13 and that's the hitter budget. The 108 pitchers bought earn an average of $8.67, so the pitcher budget is $936.

I guess this isn't so brief, but I'm basically writing the masochist chapter.

Where I got lucky, Les says, is that I came up with allocations of money by this cockamamie theory that do rather resemble the way leagues allocate money. I counter that hard experience brings leagues ever into closer accord with my theory. Stage One leagues spend well over $936 on pitchers. Stage Two spend less for pitchers than Stage One. Stage Three spend less than Stage Two. Stage Three is the final stage, and, I have to admit, they spend more than $936. Does this mean I'm wrong about what the average pitcher is worth?

It means, simply, that I'm wrong about what the average pitcher is paid. I finally figured out WHY we pay too much when I grew up and stopped giving letter grades for pitchers and started giving them bid prices in the book. What I learned is, you have to bid at least $1! There may not be 108 pitchers that you WANT to do that for, but those are the rules. (In last year's book I speculated that it would be fun to allow the bidding to begin at negative $5; you get a $5 credit if you start with Mike Moore on your team.) The list of acceptable pitchers must run to 108 and to keep the prices for 108 pitchers down to $936, when there aren't any negative pitchers, is just about impossible. So my bids for pitchers add up to $1,020. It's arbitrary as an exact figure but it closely reflects reality. Look at the Heath salary sheet (that I'm sure you've got). Pitcher payrolls last year: ADL $1,080; BW $1,018; RRL $975... So the bid prices for hitters can't add up to $2,184; they have to add up to $2,100, and I'm telling you, making this concession to the real world hurt.   But I've become a big fan of Bid $; in this year's book they get more play than Patton $. Bid $ allow you to pay more for Ripken than he's worth, because he's Ripken, and more for

Piazza because he's a catcher.

Position scarcity, I suspect, is what you've been wrestling with. Your prices are radical because you think you've licked it. If you have, mathematically — wow — I am in awe. And you will definitely win this contest.

As for competing with Les, I do see the problem. From my standpoint it's a problem, too. I'll be getting Albert AND Randy Johnson, there's no suspense there — but how much the rest of you make me pay for them is critical. The prices are what the players earned last year; if you pay them what they deserve, you're in big trouble. You have a $260 team. You finish 6.5. If we can get 12 people lined up with solid pricing systems, it's hard to imagine anybody buying more than $270 worth of stats or less than $250 worth of stats — as measured by each person's system afterward. As measured by Jerry Heath, 12 teams should be packed together not many points on either side of 52 points. It will be the wickedest average point gap in history! So, although I do see your problem, I still think you're wimps.

12-Nov-95 12:15 EST   Sb: Not a wimp   Fm: Peter Kreutzer

Hey, Les is the wimp. I'm ready to go. I added a wrinkle that changes my numbers a little off Les's. And since we started in different places our evals were a little different. I concur that there isn't going to be much spread, but those little differences will count for something. I want to know what.

And of course you're right about the "available at draft" thing. My point is that we're drafting NOW. We know what the AL and the NL did last year, and we know all the players who contributed. I can see that you don't want to figure them in because you're working toward next year's draft, when the same situation will obtain. 168 hitters and 108 pitchers will be taken, no more, no less.

I'm saying once the season is over and we KNOW what everyone's done, the Bonillas and Wakefield become very, very relevant. They wouldn't be, of course, in a league that doesn't allow moves (which would have to be the case in your league that allows negative bidding), but we have all found some way to slipstream them. And you can't argue that the homers and ribbies and good innings and wins they add to the mix don't effect the final price of everyone else in the league. Can you?

(It occurs to me that your league that allows negative bids helps me make my point. If we allowed negative bids in ADL, under our current rules, it's hard to imagine a scenario in which any team could get away with a negative bid. I bid -$20 for Mike Moore—about his 1995 value—and you bid -$19, and we both know that the bidding isn't going to stop until it gets, at least, to $0. Because three weeks into the season we know that whoever gets him can drop him for a middle reliever, who also may be worth less than a $1. But prospectively could be worth more [no pun intended]. And Moore himself, over just three weeks, COULD actually earn positive. So our flexibility, our ability to add a Bonilla or a Wakefield, or for that matter a Hippolito Pichardo, who started the season on a reserve list, affects the prices of the 276 players we draft. What I hoped to learn from this new pricing scheme and our winter game was more about how. And how much.)

As best I can tell, apart from the philosophical/analytical differences, our schism here is a practical one. You have prices without Bonilla and Wakefield. I have prices with them. One prediction I'm certain of: There may be gracious concession but there will be no compromise.

13-Nov-95 12:04 EST   Sb: Re: price war   Fm: Ron Shandler

Alex,

Thanks for the invite, but I'm not sure I'm all that interested in participating. I may be interpreting your idea all wrong, but it seems to me that the concept is a bit flawed. As I understand it, your goal is to determine whose valuation methodology is the most accurate. However, I'm not sure a mock draft is the way to go about it. Some points...

Doesn't this type of "competition" assume that hypothetically, if all 12 team owners used the same valuation method and went into the draft with 12 identical lists, that all 12 SHOULD finish tied? Wouldn't this result HAVE TO be the case in order for an accurate analysis of 12 varying methodologies?

It would seem to me that draft order would be incredibly important. Since there is a small core of players who dominate certain categories, if a team picked 12th, that would put them at a disadvantage. This is unlike a normal draft where an owner who misses out on the superstars can double up on his efforts to land a greater number of mid-level players.

Although all teams would end up with $260 worth of value, what would be there to prevent one team from drafting too deep in any one category? If Player X is the next name on my draft list, hit 25 HRs last year, and my team already has HRs locked up, wouldn't I draft a lower value speedster if I'm short on SBs?

Maybe I'm reading your idea all wrong, but I'm not sure exactly what this type of competition would prove. As of now, I'll pass on this, but let me know if anything changes.
Ron S.

13-Nov-95 12:45:00   **Sb: Re: Not a wimp**   **To: Peter Kreutzer**

I agree with you completely about the way the negative bidding would go. (There are riffs in both previous books about this — one, I believe, even proposing an opening bid of minus $10 for Wakefield! — but I can't for the life of me find them.) And there is an obvious solution to our problem that involves a compromise from me, a concession from you. Change the budgets.

You know those lovely color graphs that Jerry sends us each month? His best case/worse case projections don't do much for me, but the draft rosters vs current rosters is his way of demonstrating empirically what I'm talking about. Get it out (I know you have it, Peter!) and let's look at the Bonemen.

They paid $261 at the draft (so first of all — you should be disqualified!) and the draft roster earned, by Jerry's calculations, $290: that means you bought a good team. You finished second in the hypotheticals, which means, for sure, you did. But for you to earn more than $260 with your draft roster, somebody else had to earn less than $260. Just glancing, five teams come out ahead and seven come out behind, so it looks like the draft rosters do earn about $260 per team in Jerry's system — as they MUST. You can't buy more than $260 worth of value per team if that's what each team is spending. This is the same as to say the average player bought in the draft costs $11.3 and earns $11.3. I mean, if we can't agree on that, then we are at loggerheads, but we can. Can't we? I don't know, Peter. I see you shaking your head. I see you and Les looking at each other. The Moose just doesn't get it. If he only knew a little bit about multiple regressions, maybe we could talk.

To be honest, I'm not dead clear on what Jerry means by "Current A.R. $ earned." I think he means what Albert earned WHILE he was on your active roster, but it's possible he means what Albert earned on the year. But it doesn't matter. What matters is the Bonemen, in this reckoning, again earn more than $260 — and so does EVERY OTHER TEAM... except, alas, me and Stoneburn. How is it that the pretty colors at the bottom go shooting off to the right in all but two cases? Answer: Wakefield and Bonilla. Teams earn more than $260 per team at the end of the season.

This is inarguable, this is not theory. If you don't like Jerry's graphs, look at the stats that we're really paying him for. At the draft we bought 1834 home runs (see hypotheticals); at the end of the year we have 2011 homers (see final standings). These are numbers that can be added up on a calculator, if we have doubts about Jerry. So we have two choices. We either agree that players drafted earn $260 per team, and use that as our starting point. Or we agree that the final stats are worth more than $260 and use that as our starting point. To do the latter, all we have to do is accept your prices or mine.

13-Nov-95 19:10 EST   **Sb: Ohhhhhhhh, I seeeeeeeeee.**   **Fm: Peter Kreutzer**

Wow. A new thought. I didn't really think it was possible. At least not as regards this, but you're right: If we buy $260 worth of stats at the start of the season and we end up with more stats at the end of the season than we bought, they MUST be worth more than $260.

To be honest, using Jerry's chart to prove this is not all that helpful. His "Draft Roster" consists of the up-to-date stats for the guys each team bought at the draft. His "Current Roster" is the up-to-date stats for the guys on each team now.

But more important to our debate, I don't think this new thought changes my argument very much. Here's why, and please feel free to call me stubborn and pig-headed and even dense:

The reason we know, at the start of the season, that the average player is worth $11.30, is because we know there are 276 players and they cost a total of $3120. From there the math is easy. But as you so interestingly point out, when the season is over, the player we paid (for arguments sake) $11.30 for, will not be worth $11.30 even if he generates exactly his projected stats. This is because of all the stats that accumulate that haven't been paid for.

For instance: We paid for 1834 homers. So the average drafted home run hitter whacked 10.92 taters. But the average player, on the year, hit 11.97 homers (2011 divided by 168). Extend this idea across all four (or 3) categories and you have to assume that the hitter you paid $11.30 for at the draft because he was average, will end up being worth (when measured against the final league totals) somewhat less.

Anyway, I think this is a digression that doesn't come to bear on our discussion. About which my argument goes like this: Since our retrospective draft will only claim 168 players and 108 pitchers, we will have no inflation of stats as occurs during the usual year. We know that the 276 players we pay $3120 for will, when the accounting is done, be worth $3120. It doesn't matter whether Bonilla or Wakefield are in their number, because the guys who added surplus to the regular roto season (at the bottom of the pile), will not be drafted in our draft because they rank #277 to #310, let's say.

Which is why I think we should keep the $260 budget and allow any player's 1995 AL stats be bought.

But your point does raise serious questions about how to value the stats of players at the end of the season. I've always indexed everything based on the idea that the 168th hitter and the 108th pitcher were each worth $1 (you have to pay $1 for them). But while this is the proper way to set prices for the draft, for a retrospective pricing system it doesn't seem like it is. And while the ramifications are apparent, what to do about them, alas, is not.

Ps. My total paid for the Bonemen is wrong on Jerry's sheet because he mistakenly gave me John Valentin at the start of the season rather than Jose Valentin. It was a mistake I'd have preferred go uncorrected.

14-Nov-95 08:00 EST   Sb: Re:white elephant   Fm: Adam P. Summers
A horse is a little like a boat. A continuing expense. It is mainly Pam's horse. She has wanted a horse since her last one was put down. This opportunity just came along. I have no real idea of whether it is a bargain or not. I know one thing about horse prices: $.85/lb on the hoof. At around 1000 pounds I could get $850 for the critter tommorow. That is the reaon why horses seldom sell for less than $1000, no one wants to send Silver off to the dog food plant just because they sold him to someone who wanted to turn a quick profit.

14-Nov-95 9:27:00   Sb: Re:white elephant   To: Adam
I love the idea of you and Pam being grifters! But you're right. Silver's dead meat otherwise. It's the kind of can't-fail scheme that I spend two months every year hoping I'll stumble on while I'm writing the book!

14-Nov-95 11:56:00   Sb: Re:Ohhhhhhhh, I seeeeeeeeee.   To: Peter Kreutzer
Hmmm. Now where are we? I've read your message, and you've seen the reply from Shandler that I sent you before that (I try to limit the trips I make into cyberspace to the morning, when

I've got a fresh spacesuit on, and things often go flying both ways), so now we have a whole new set of issues that we haven't even talked about. Plus one less contestant. (What I really was hoping for this morning was a message from Hunt.)   Well, I'll wait for your thoughts re Shandler's non-list. I sort of get what you're saying about the average player changing his stats and, unfortunately, I even more sort of don't. What I know is, Bonilla was not available in our auction last April so we can't buy him now. The very definition of a retrospective draft is to go back to the auction and bid on the players that we bid on then — KNOWING WHAT THEIR STATS ARE.

What we are trying to do is check out measuring systems. We aren't trying to learn who has the better handle on making predictions, or even whose pricing system is more useful for people who will proceed from them to make their own predictions, to set their own bids. The question is one of simple math: whose prices cut the pie up more accurately.   We can agree on the size of the pie in April It's $260 per team. After that — we now agree, so we have made progress — it's more than $260 per team. As soon as one non-drafted player contributes stats to any team in the league the size of the pie changes. (With many pitchers, as we know, it shrinks.) But we can't agree on precisely how much it changes unless we can agree on a way of measuring, and as Shandler points out, if we could do that, we'd all end up with the same team! The reason we are talking, and talking, is that we don't think we quite agree.

You know who we won't hear from either? John Benson. Even though he cites being a CPA/MBA as a reason to buy his books, he has no patience for pricing theory. His retrospective prices are solid, very solid, but he could care less if they are VERY solid. He doesn't like to niggle. He calls me a bean-counter. Used to, when he thought that I'd be hurt. When he saw me crowing about it in my books, he stopped.   Benson's contention is that pricing is maybe 20% of the game and predicting is 80%. The splits may be 10/90, I'm not sure, and that's fine too. He's absolutely right: It's a waste of time to split hairs over by far the less important side of the yin and the yang of Rotisserie baseball. I just enjoy wasting time. (But don't, alas, have time to straighten out that metaphor.) After discovering that I had tweaked the stolen-base denominator this year just far enough to cheat Lofton, in my judgement, out of $1, I tweaked the denominator back, and thus had to change the prices in every spreadsheet for every player — pitchers as well as hitters — in both leagues. Took a day.

But I'm not a total lunatic. In the end I'm trying to do something useful with my prices, and that is leave a reliable record for readers to refer to in the stat scans of how players performed, in Rotisserie terms, over the last several seasons. When Les totally revamped his system a few years ago, even if it was an improvement (I thought so, since it moved in my direction), he snipped himself off from the past. There's no point in showing multi-year scans if you use multi systems.

When Lofton's five-year scan showed him earning $39 last year, something just didn't feel right. He earned $61 in 1994 and now he earned $39? I had nudged the saves denominator up to pay more for power — because leagues are bunching ever closer together in the power categories and letting speed slip, that's the reality — but I had nudged it too far. I nudged it back. Lofton earned $40, and I felt much better.

Pricing systems have four missions.   1) They try to distribute money in a sensible way between hitters and pitchers.   2) They try to figure out how much the various categories are worth. They recognize that all categories are not created equal. (In a pure scarcity model, Lofton's 1995 stats are worth $51).   3) They attempt to recognize league differences. (Lofton last year in the National League would only have been worth $36).   4) They try to cope — especially nowadays — with the fluctuations from year to year. (Albert's season last year would have been worth $49 in 1992. His full season, had it been played, would have been worth $55.)

What you said in one of your earlier messages about trying to learn something that will help you be a better player? Sounds good, but get real. That's Bensonville. Players don't do exactly what they're supposed to — ever — so don't worry about it. In your formulas. If you have the sense that the possibility of Bonilla coming into the league somehow affects what you're willing to pay for Jeffrey Hammonds, that's good; it should. Lower your bid price. But I'm telling you this, and it's really my last word on the subject: last year Hammonds earned $4. $3.78, to be exact. I

Notes for Masochists

mean, it could go up a few cents if I decide that I cheated him when I tweaked the SB denominator to help out Lofton, but we're talking round numbers here.

14-Nov-95 20:27 EST　　　　　**Sb: Ohhhhhhhh-kay**　　　　　**Fm: Peter Kreutzer**

I don't remember saying that thing about "trying to learn something that will help (me) be a better player." And I like to waste time, too, but a quick trip to the filing cabinet didn't unearth it, so let me say this:

I got off on this tangent because I now have in my computer ALL the stats for ALL the players and pitchers who ever played. What I wanted to find was a reliable pricing system (didn't have to mimic draft prices) that measured roto value for all the seasons—all time. I wanted to do this because I thought it would help me make better mechanical predictions. Out of our discussions, and similar one's I've had with Les, I've also come to believe that there is a significant difference between what a player's stat value and what his draft value is (this, obviously, isn't new at all) and that lying somewhere in that difference is something interesting about the game.

For instance: Yes, all categories are not worth the same. But just because the way the game is played now gives certain weights to certain categories doesn't mean that particular (lack-of) balance is inevitable. One would assume that the smart player is always trying to cut against the grain. Isn't this, at least in part, what the Sweeny players taught us this year? We're not valuing SBs and Pitching enough in the draft and so the money one saves by dropping Power is sufficient to win all the other categories. What we saw in the ADL is that in a league with no freezes (thus, no concentrated cheap power) dumping two categories can be enough to win the whole thing. And you almost pulled the same thing off in LABR.

So, yeah, while pricing is far from the be-all and end-all of the game, it is the only way to get at what's happening in the game. From there we can take off in a number of directions, some interesting, some dead ends, and probably some valuable.

As far as checking out measuring systems goes, I better see your point than I did before. What I'll respond with is, okay, we can do it your way. The important thing is that either way we're measuring 276 players. If those are the players available when we drafted in the spring, or they are the players available when the season is over, the math will be the same (if the 168th player and 108th pitcher must cost a dollar). Only the values for the players will be different.

If we use those players only available in the spring we're STILL getting surplus value. Jeff Manto was drafted by 10 of Jerry's 30 teams, for an average price of $1. Which averaged out over the thirty teams is .33. In our retrospective draft, some team is going to pays $10 (Jerry) for him. That's $10 that last April was spent elsewhere. But when all is said and done the stats for the retrospective league will be worth just $3120, and not a penny more.

Although I think we've made progress, what I agreed to is that we spend $260 for each team in the spring. And we end up with more stats than we paid for when all is said and done. Since, if we were to draft a team when the season was over, it would also be worth $260, I don't agree that the value of the stats increases. In fact, I would argue that the value of the stats decreases. Consider this:

When you draft your team at the start of the season you have to spend $260. For argument sake, you've spent 1/8th your budget ($32.50) on homers. And you've paid the average price for homers (getting 10.8 per player in the bargain). But you know that 10% more homers are going to be available free during the course of the year in waivers and from the reserve list. You have also spent 1/8th your budget on Wins. But you know that 50% more wins are going to be available for free from waivers and the reserve list. Haven't you made a mistake?

Of course you have. You should've spent less money on the Wins and more on the Homers. Which is what teams do. They pay for what is scarce and reliable, and scramble later for abundance (which is abundant because it is less reliable).

But, to get back to our argument, when the season is over, when all the stats are reliable, isn't the true value of those wins the same as the value of those homers? They certainly gain you just as many points in the standings. And if you're only counting the top 168 players and 108 pitchers at the end of the year (as we would be doing in our retrospective draft played by my rules), aren't they worth $260 per team—same as at the start of the year?

The most significant bit of theory that I pull out of this argument is confirmation of your Pay More for Good Players idea. When we add 10% of homers to the league, it doesn't diminish the value of Albert's 50 homers and Buhner's 40. These chunks of homers are scarce and irreplaceable (unless we luck into Edmonds). But it does diminish the value of all those guys who I have on my list projected for 3 or 4 or 5 homers. Sure, if you have those few homers from Ozzie Guillen they add just as much to your team total as Albert's 48th, 49th and 50th. But if you didn't have Ozzie's you'd more than likely have someone else who would hit the same three, someone who didn't cost anything and in that sense they're valueless. So instead of spending $2.60 for those homers (as Les's breakdowns suggest they're worth) you're better off spending $2.60 more for Albert.

Yipes, I do go on. But I spent all day on a jury, with a brutal deliberation. So perhaps I'm especially wound up and contentious. I should say that I'm really enjoying this debate. It's hard from moment to moment to tell what makes sense and what doesn't, but I'm developing a much more rounded picture of all the different ideas aswirl in our game. BTW, I have Hammonds earning $1 ($1.30 to be exact). But then I include Bonilla and Coleman and Johnny Damon, too. Because they all played. And that's why I want to play.

14-Nov-95 20:27 EST   **Sb: shandler's non-list**   **Fm: Peter Kreutzer**

Shandler's points are dead-on.

The fact is that if all teams put in lists with the same values there wouldn't be a deadlock because coinflips would determine ties. And coin flips, while fair, aren't going to end up being distributed evenly.

The second point was of far greater concern to me. I rationalized it thusly: This game is an exercise, one for which we have no precedent. If it doesn't work out, if value in each of the categories isn't distributed in a way consistent with the submitted price list, then we won't have learned all that much from it. But it's also possible that the distortions (if you ended up with way too many homers and not enough steals) would be an accurate reflection of inadequacies in each pricing system. I don't think there's any way to tell until the exercise is over.

It would definitely be better to have an actual draft, so that adjustments could be made, but that seems impractical..

But then Les came up with a better idea: He suggested that each team submit a list of players who add up to $260. If you're the only team to bid on a particular player, you get him. But if two or more teams bid, the high team gets the player. In the next round each team fills the open spots on their roster (created because they weren't the high bidder for a player) with available players and so on, until all 12 rosters are filled.

There is some debate about whether all the teams should know what the other teams's rosters look like. I think, since we want this to be a valuation challenge, that no team should know about the other teams partial rosters. At the start of each round you only know that you have these players, these holes, this much money left and these players available.

But one could argue the other way, too, which would enable each team to change strategies in mid course..

Personally, I think this is a great game for the winter. Will take multiple weeks, and MAY help us understand the valuation issues.

It would also be possible to do both at once.

15-Nov-95 14:40:00   **Sb: Re:Ohhhhhhhh-kay**   **To: Peter Kreutzer**

Uh-oh... Uh-oh... Doubling up on your punches? I may be about to go down for the count.

Trying to respond as briefly as possible to the points in both messages in the order that they're raised...

1) I guess you didn't say anything about being a better player. You keep referring to "learning something interesting" about the game, and because of my own cultural bias I just assume it

means it's going to help you win it.

2) The Sweeney Plan definitely changes values, and that is the whole point. Back when Dollar and Bill and I kept the topper for Frank Thomas every year, we also were punting speed. That way, no matter what the rest of you suckers thought, he was more valuable to us than he was to you, and we topped.

3) When all is said and done, not only will the stats of the retrospective league be worth $3120, and not a penny more, they will be the stats of the restrospective league.

They will BE those stats. Does that help?

(Pardon my manners, Peter, but I'm also having a hard day -- drawing a blank on what to say about Dwight Smith, with the whole rest of the book to go! -- and so I thought a visit to the gym during lunch hour might help. I do, obviously, enjoy it myself.)

Anyway, the stats of the retrospective league will be the retrospective stats. Like I said. And you did, too.

4) Les's idea -- next message (thank God I saw it coming, or it would have caught me as I was walking to the corner after this one) -- is excellent. It would be fun to pick out several different teams worth exactly $260 and then decide which one to submit. There's only one problem. Each team that I submit, if my prices are even halfway decent, will finish at .500. The prices are par. My $260 team is worth $260. What you're trying to do in the auction is buy about $300 worth of stats with your $260 -- in competitve leagues, that's normally enough profits to be in the running -- and the only way you get a $40 profit is if someone else takes a $40 loss. I have to underpay for the players I get, and you have to overpay for the players you get. That's what the contest would be all about.

5) It can't be done. I guess. Not at the rate we're going.

6) Maybe... Here's an idea. Like you say, it's a long off-season. Why don't we get 12 people together in New York (unfortunately, after both our deadlines have passed) and simply start bidding? We could plan it around the winter meeting. It wouldn't take long -- everyone puts 100 bucks on the table, that seems about right -- and away we go. In a weird sort of way, it could be exciting. No haggling over Bobby Bo, no fussing over Wakefield: anyone is fair game. You can buy Barry Bonds, if it makes you happy. Hell, you can buy Bobby Bonds or junk bonds or, by then, probably the whole UBL, and then we send all the AL stats that we bought down to Jerry to sort out for us.

But, um, this isn't quite where we started, is it? Very far from auto-pilot. So I guess, ahem, you better not look at my prices, after all. Don't peek, Peter. Leave those Lotus files alone! And let's get it on.

16-Nov-95 11:53:00   **Sb: trying**   **To: Peter Kreutzer**

Good heavens. No word from you this morning. You must be holed up in a hotel somewhere. Whatever your verdict is, at least you're taking longer than four hours.

(Let's discuss the trial.)

(Just kidding.)

Anyway, the reflective life goes on, and I have thought up a compromise.

The problem I have with what you want is contained in the very top of the Lotus files. When you do open them, you will see "AL drafts" and "NL drafts" at the top of the hitters' stats, and the same thing at the top of the pitchers' stats. These are the average leagues. They are derived from the hypotheticals that Jerry sends me (and I believe Les gets them, too, if you don't). The hypothetical final standings are the very retrospective stats that I'm talking about. No changes after draft day. What we bought in the auction.

The amazing (actually, not so amazing) thing is how similar all the leagues are. Just two examples from NL leagues; WGN -- AB 53627, HR 1654, RBI 7238, SB 1399, BA .275; ERB -- AB 54275, HR 1665, RBI 7329, SB 1368, BA .274. From the AB it's clear they aren't the same hitters, but they're doing virtually the same thing. So, for the hitters, it's very easy to tell almost exactly how big the pie is. And then you just have to carve it up.

As you know, I give each hitter a 50% large slice than each pitcher. Each hitter is decreed to be worth (decreed, not proven, this is the argument) $13. I am my own arbiter and once I've given the average hitter $13, the hitters all told get $2,184 (13 x 168). The reason I don't get a lot of flak for this is that experience by and large bears me out; most leagues spend more than $2,000 on hitting.

And what they are getting from the hitters is almost identical from league to league.

Therefore, when I tailor hitting denominators to match the draft stats of the average league, the total prices for almost any league add up to $2,184. Lots of people do this when they get my book. They don't mess with the formulas, they just go to Appendix A, look up what Patton says so-and-so earned last year, write it down next to the hitters they bought, and add it up. They normally do this once. But if they do it TWELVE times, they get just about $2,184. (In the ADL, we don't. Because of our vapor lock on Gaetti, we were worse than the average league.)

There's $936 left (3120 - 2184). (Or: $8.67 x 108.) Yes, pitching is only 30% of the game; that's the shocking truth. Even though it accounts for 50% of the points. And there are fewer pitchers. That's the profound paradox.

But my job isn't philosophy, it's counting beans, and I'd love to be able to report that when you add up the prices for pitchers in the same way, you get $936. You don't. Here's why.

WGN -- IP 10584, Wins 612, Saves 444, ERA 4.06, Ratio 12.13; ERB -- IP 11203, Wins 649, Saves 448, ERA 3.96, Ratio 11.97.

Those are the pitching stats that the Washington Ghosts bought in DC in April and the Elizabeth River Bushes bought somewhere in Virginia at the same time -- nothing hypothetical here -- and they screw my life up badly because they buy very different stats. They don't buy the same pitchers and the pitchers they do buy don't do the same things.

If ERB bought as many more homers as they bought wins, they'd have 1753 RBI.

It's hard to say about the averages, since achieving a lower ERA is good, achieving a lower batting average is bad, but let's say that's not the case. We'll pretend, in this shadowy world of ours, that more is better in both cases. We figure WGN's ERA is 4.06/3.96 "better" than ERB's ERA, multiply that times ERB's .274 batting average, and get a .281 batting average.

Imagine one league buying 168 hitters who had a .281 batting average and another league buying 168 hitters who had a .274 batting average. You'd have to think one league was using the DH.

The formulas in the book this year award the WGN hitters $2,184. They WERE the average league. The astute Virginians get $2,188; they nip the Washingtonians by .2%.

The WGN pitchers get awarded $928 in the formula. The ERB pitchers get $977. ERB is

5% better. Five percent, not point five. It would be as if they bought $2,299 worth of hitting stats.

You can't buy more than you pay for. That's the one thing I'm sure we've agreed on so far. ERB did not buy $3,165 worth of stats in its auction. It bought, at most, $3,120 worth of stats. (If one team had $5 left at the end, the league bought $3,115 worth of stats.) ERB, using my prices, will find that there's a tiny bit of inflation. Because they were more prescient than the average league, they are going to earn $264 per team (3165/3120 x 260).

That's why this is worth all the fuss. That $4 per team, in a retrospective draft, would be a killer.

You can't spend what you don't have. For my prices to work exactly in THEIR retrospective draft, they'd have to multiply every single price in the book by 3120/3165. That would drop Albert's price from $46 to $45. It might be more relevant to them that it would drop Bichette's from $54 to $53.

Remember Shandler's wise observation. If I end up with even a $259 team, I'm in last.

I've pondered, literally for years, over what I can do to make the pitchers behave themselves. There are solutions. Leagues may not much resemble the average league, but there is an average league. You'll see it at the top of the pitching spreadsheet: WGN, ERB and two other leagues averaged together. The formula makes those stats -- the NL average stats bought in auctions last year -- out to be worth $950. Not $936. The formula makes the average stats bought in the AL out to be worth $912. Not $936. When you have a formula that produces prices that are this different for the two types of Rotisserie leagues -- both using the same rules and having the same budgets -- you know something's flawed.

One solution would be to fiddle with the NL saves denominator until NL pitchers were worth exactly $936 and the AL saves denominator until AL pitchers were worth exactly $936.

Another would be to fiddle with NL wins denominator until the pitchers earned what they were supposed to, and do the same for the AL pitchers.

Or you could fiddle with both denominators until you had it right.

But what would "it" be? How can you change the wins denominator each year, when that's the one category in all of baseball that never changes?

Well, for two years now, I've had to change it. But that's not my fault. I blame that on the owners. Nevertheless, even in the worst of times, there remains one win per game. The saves category fluctuates a little bit and there is a slight league difference (more saves in the NL) but basically half the wins are saved and half aren't. I'll mess around with the first decimal in the saves denominator, and there I draw the line.

Because, to me, the most valuable thing about the prices is seeing everything in relation to everything else. The foundation of the theory is that each two wins that a Rotisserie team gets mean a point in the standings. This year, last year, next year. (Even this is open to debate, of course. No question but that wins get more hotly contested with each year, and the saves category slides.) What I want is a constant off of which I can spin all the other categories, and for me it's wins. Without any constant, it's very hard to see the league differences and yearly fluctuations that really are important. So my pitching prices for any given league are not accurate, and now I've spilled the beans. Here's the compromise. (It's HARD for me to compromise, Peter; takes me a while to warm up.) You tell me who the 276 players we buy in the draft are. Throw in Bonilla, Wakefield, Bonds -- you name it -- just name them first. Remember, there aren't supposed to be any surprises in this draft; this is not a test of predicting. If Bonds is available, and we're counting just AL stats, I assure you I will take him over Hamelin. The one thing I insist can't happen is for me to be sitting there at the end, having spent all my money and filled my entire roster, and then have some wise ass across the table say, "Hey guys, we forgot Gary Gaetti." Personally, I believe since we forgot him we should forget him, but if you like being reminded that's okay. Select your 276 players, send me their names, give me half an hour to fiddle with the decimals -- I might only need ten minutes -- and I'm ready for the gong.

17-Nov-95 12:19 EST   Sb: a stand-up guy   Fm: Peter Kreutzer
I missed yesterday's round cause I was, sans computer, en route to NYC to see Walter's comedy act in the village. What he did is really a remarkable achievement: Got up on a stage in front of about 25 people in a small night club and told jokes. Funny jokes, for the most part. He was nervous, didn't know how to disengage the microphone from the stand so stood there with hands at his side and talked, but he got laughs and warmth back for his trouble. It was good fun, and reminded me most of what I miss about life in NYC. (Less driving).

I'd love to sit down and hold a draft to test these issues, but I think it would take a long time. Perhaps even as long as our regular draft (minus the reserve round). Which is why Les's compromise feels right. Actually, it's hardly a compromise but rather a full-fledged different game.

But what it will measure will be the same, even if we allow everyone to know the results of each round (which will allow for more "drafting" strategy and is probably inevitable, because someone has to decide who gets who each round and that's probably me and clearly if I know then everyone has to know).

Shandler's right that if everyone has a good pricing system then all teams will end up being worth $260, but clearly everyone's pricing system is different. If you'd pay $4 for Hammonds and I'd pay $1, then you're going to get him, unless someone else writes down $5. And just as clearly, Hammonds is worth only one amount. So someone is either going to overpay for him, or the person who doesn't get him is going to spend that $4 on Chuck Knoblauch and get him, but then end up with Milt Cuyler, too. You know what I mean.

From those differences will come value, and winners. And losers.

Which gets to your denominator problems. There was a guy in the alt.baseball.fantasy newsgroup on the internet a few weeks ago who made the observation that no pricing scheme is valid unless it is compiled within the context of a league. Which I think is dead accurrate. What we're doing, trying to make universal values, is impossible because the "average league" is just that: representative, not actual. As soon as people start bidding all the values change. When someone overbids early it means there is less money available for later. When someone chucks steals or power or average, the scale tilts.

Which doesn't mean that universal values aren't important. Everyone who goes into the draft with a comprehensive list of prices for players has assumed universal values. But you know all this. You taught me much about it. My point is that when the draft is done everyone has an opinion about who did better or worse, depending on how their universal values compare to the specific values the league placed on the drafted players. And sometimes those opinions are right. Often, for reasons that can be out of our control, like injuries and trades, they're wrong.

One of the reasons they're wrong is that everything doesn't stop at the draft. The hypotheticals are important, but they don't measure the reserve lists and the waiver claims and trades. I would guess that the two leagues you cite use different reserve systems, or claims systems, which makes their efficiency at plucking value from the pool different. But even if they play with exactly the same rules they'll end up with different results because within the context of each of their leagues different guys have different values. If one team ends up with Fetters, Mesa and Smith, it skews the value of saves up and down the standings.

So when your values show individual leagues (and particularly pitchers) with values that deviate from 3120 you're measuring the various efficiencies and exigencies in each league. It isn't a flaw in your system.

What gets interesting, it just occurred to me, is that your request we designate the 276 players who are draftable before we draft, goes part of the way toward addressing those issues. I had been thinking that part of what makes each of our value systems different is our differing takes on what makes a player draftable. Is #168 Cuyler or Hamelin? From such questions will winners and losers, in my view of the game, be determined. And clearly the decision made in pitching would have more of an impact: How much ERA do you swap for additional WINS? If you know exactly how much total ERA there is, and how many WINS, those decisions become more manageable. And perhaps, all our values move closer together. I'd think so, though I don't know for sure.

I do know that we'll still end up with differences, because once rosters start being firmed up all the values change. For the team that has Lofton, Tom Goodwin is less valuable than for all the other teams (excepting those who are chucking steals). What I also know is that, even if we make the draft open to all players who accumulated AL stats in 1995 (or hell, even if we let teams draft guys who didn't play in the AL, like Bonds--Barry or Bobby) Gaetti isn't going to sneak through because we now know what he was did.

Jorge Fabregas might, but then again he could also end up, again, on a first place team.

In conclusion, at last!, I see your point and am willing to go that way if everyone else will go along (my guess is it creates more problems, but maybe not). We play Les's game, with everyone being apprised of everyone elses rosters after each round. I'm for the $100 side bet but that shouldn't be a barrier to entry. And if I compile the stats I'll submit my list to a disinterested 3rd party before we start and stick to those values. Should I write it up?

18-Nov-95 10:31:00   **Sb: answewered prayers**   **To: Peter Kreutzer**

No, I'm not referring to you're agreeing to whatever it is we're agreeing to, but to the complete list of major league salaries that was published yesterday in USA Today. Did you see it? (Here I am worried about you being sequestered somewhere, your eloquence being put to the test by eleven other increasingly lathered souls, and you're partying with the boys! Stoneburn's review of Walter's act was just as favorable, except Stoneburn didn't find him to be the least nervous.) Remember page 339 that I was so proud of in last year's book. Well, these are the greatest predictions I've ever made. I get incredible similarity scores, and then the real owners go right by me, once they've learned the score. I'll total it up in a player comment. Truman Capote should be writing about this, not Murray Chass. (Capote spells better than I do, but no amount of praying can get me back to the Sb: in Tapcis.)

Anyway, you, me, Les, Walter — we're all stand-up guys. And we can reduce or eliminate the bet, no problem. I just want to be clear, though: we have agreed to identify the 276 players first. Haven't we? And then I do have one other teensy weensy request — but it's not a demand! Can we please have negative bids? I can easily fudge the denominators to give positive values to the top 108 pitchers (whoever we identify as the 108 pitchers ahead of time can — and, of course, in a real auction must — have positive values). But that wouldn't be my pricing system, and it's my pricing system, not my bids that I want to test. The prices are retrospective; this is meant to be a retrospective draft.

I repeat, though, there's no way I'm sitting down now, not after all this sparring. So if you and Les want it to be $1 minimum (frankly, if you're still confused which way we're pointing) give me the list of players and the time-out to fine tune the denominators, as Les might say. Also I hope you're doing something about getting enough people in the ring, because I still haven't heard even boo from Hunt.

18-Nov-95 15:19 EST   Sb: huncarved coffins   Fm: Peter Kreutzer

I didn't see the USA Today list, but I'm going to scoot onto their site on the Web and hope it's there. But it doesn't surprise me, I mean your salary prediction success. You nailed the issue last year, spun my head around. And the players should've paid attention. They'd be making a lot more money if they'd taken the owner's first proposal.

Of course, I'm enough of an idealist that I'm hoping the players are happy how this has gone so far. After all, they still have no cap and have thus far retained their freedom of movement, both of which they were being asked to sacrifice. But it's hard to see this being settled with the memory of the Owners offer of $30M minimum salaries clanking around in the players's collective brain. Surely the owners, having found the Patton religion, aren't going to be making that offer again.

I like the negative bid idea, as I've said, but it won't work in this sort of game. Without a draft's interaction there's no way to keep money from being minted. The market just isn't responsive enough. So while I'd trust that no one would bid -$25 for, say, Mark Holzemer, I think a -$2 for Holzemer would be just as unfair even if it is a "fair value" bid. (After I wrote this I realized that if we designate 108 pitchers all will be bid on, and thought that maybe negs would be okay. But on further reflection, since not all 108 will be bid on in the same round, necessarily, the same problem obtains.)

I can't believe you haven't heard from Hunt. Maybe he talked to Shandler and figured the thing wasn't coming off. What I'll do is write it up and send rules to Shandler, who was interested if his concerns were addressed, which in this format they are, and Hunt and ADLers and anyone else I can think of. We need 7 more bodies/intellects, which doesn't seem that hard.

Are you saying I should put together the list of available players and that will be okay for you? If so, I don't see why we can't designate the pool as players who accumulated stats in the AL in 1995. Then each of us can have our own top 276. But if we have to, well, I can live with that just fine. After all we're testing a pricing scenario. Give me the players's names in advance and I don't have to first figure out who player number 168 is.

18-Nov-95 20:32 EST   Sb: Re: idea   Fm: INTERNET:JHunt

that sounds like a great idea. another good idea would be to get a bunch of us together (maybe in a chat room on the INTERNET or something) and have an auction for a league based solely on '95 stats - the league would be over as soon as the computer compiles the teams. it would be just a simple exercise in drafting, but it could certainly open some eyes. do you like that idea?

19-Nov-95 10:14:00   Sb: Re: huncarved coffins   To: Peter Kreutzer

Now, I have to tell you, this is getting serious. I will admit that I only saw belatedly what an awful malaprop my "ansewered prayers" was; I'd rather think of myself as a subliminal genius than a pisspoor typist. But you missed it. Or did you? That's what's killing me. Is "huncarved coffins" your answer? It's going to ruin my day. Please respond immediately.

Meantime, I've forwarded Hunt's message — which is great! Somehow I don't think it would be a good idea to forward him all our messages; to, you know, like catch him up. And if he comes out of it thinking it was his idea, that's good too. In fact, I can see where I could be trouble if I get involved any bit further. Where I made my mistake was in thinking my BOOK prices are being tested. I can submit any prices I want — you and Hunt just tell me what the rules are — because it's ME who's being tested. That's all anybody cares about. And I'm going to win.

19-Nov-95 11:14 EST   Sb: Re: hunt's in   Fm: Peter Kreutzer

I think forwarding our correspondence on this would overwhelm the clearly overworked young man. I'll send him a note with the basic parameters of what we've been discussing and we'll move on from there.

The idea of conducting the draft on the INTERNET is fine, but won't be any faster than a real draft and means we need to find players who can access IRC. It's possible but I'm a fairly dedicated cybersurfer and have yet to foray into that. My guess is you don't even want to think about it.

In re "winning:" I of course like your bluster, but until we play the game it isn't much but warming air. Personally, I'm pretty sure you will be playing for third unless Les and I cancel each other out.

Fin.

Peter should have the last word, don't you think? Time to put up our dukes.

Draft Populations — hitters

AL 95	AB	H	HR	RBI	SB	BA	$HR	$RBI	$SB	$BA	$TOT
BWAL	55142	15147	1881	7982	1094	.275	755	938	494	1	2188
BZB	54937	15038	1856	7935	1082	.274	745	933	488	0	2165
DDA	55674	15278	1875	8070	1087	.274	752	949	491	1	2192
LSL	55605	15225	1879	8011	1093	.274	754	942	493	0	2189
league	55340	15163	1873	8000	1089	.274	751	940	492	0	2183
team	4612	1264	156	667	91	.274	63	78	41	0	182
player	329	90.3	11.1	47.6	6.5	.274	4	6	3	0	13.00
NL 95	AB	H	HR	RBI	SB	BA	$HR	$RBI	$SB	$BA	$TOT
BWNL	53660	14768	1638	7267	1410	.275	739	945	501	0	2185
BLK	53419	14645	1650	7190	1395	.274	745	935	495	-1	2173
WGN	53627	14741	1654	7238	1399	.275	747	941	497	0	2184
ERB	54275	14870	1665	7329	1368	.274	752	953	486	-2	2188
league	53745	14780	1652	7256	1393	.275	746	943	495	0	2183
team	4479	1232	138	605	116	.275	62	79	41	0	182
player	320	88.0	9.8	43.2	8.3	.275	4	6	3	0	13.00

Draft populations — pitchers

AL 95	IP	W	Sv	ERA	Rto	$W	$S	$ERA	$Rto	$TOT
BWAL	9769	594	403	4.54	12.85	585	312	0	-1	896
BZB	10554	536	418	4.48	12.74	528	324	2	2	856
DDA	10694	635	426	4.52	12.83	626	330	0	0	955
LSL	10689	641	401	4.56	12.87	632	310	-1	-1	939
league	10426	602	412	4.53	12.82	593	319	0	0	912
team	869	50	34	4.53	12.82	49	27	0	0	76
player	97	6	4	4.53	12.82	5	3	0	0	8.46
NL 95	IP	W	Sv	ERA	Rto	$W	$S	$ERA	$Rto	$TOT
BWNL	10528	607	444	3.94	11.87	598	332	3	3	937
BLK	11066	638	444	4.03	12.00	629	332	-1	0	959
ERB	11203	649	448	3.96	11.97	639	335	2	0	977
WGN	10584	612	444	4.06	12.13	603	332	-3	-4	928
league	10845	627	445	4.00	11.99	617	333	0	0	950

| team | 904 | 52 | 45 | 4.00 | 11.99 | 51 | 33 | 0 | 0 | 85 |
| pitcher | 100 | 5.8 | 4.9 | 4.00 | 11.99 | 6 | 4 | 0 | 0 | 9.42 |

American League 1995 formulas

$HR = 13/6*HR/5.4
$RBI = 13/6*RBI/18.43
$SB = 13/6*SB/4.8
$BA = 13/6*((1178.2+H)/(4300+AB)0.274)/0.0012
$W = 13/6*Wins/2.2
$Sv = 13/6*Saves/2.8
$ERA = 13/6*(4.53-(478.16+ER)/((950+IP)/9))/0.04
$Rto = 13/6*(12.82-((1353.22+H+BB)/((950+IP)/9)))/0.07

National League 1995 formulas

$HR = 13/6*HR/4.8
$RBI = 13/6*RBI/16.67
$SB = 13/6*SB/6.1
$BA = 13/6*((1155+H)/(4200+AB)0.275)/0.0012
$W = 13/6*Wins/2.2
$Sv = 13/6*Saves/2.9
$ERA = 13/6*(4-(422.22+ER)/((950+IP)/9))/0.04
$Rto = 13/6*(11.99-((1265.61+H+BB)/((950+IP)/9)))/0.07

American League 1996 prediction formulas
$HR = 13/6*HR/5.4
$RBI = 13/6*HR/19.3
$SB = 13/6*SB/5.4
$BA = 13/6*((1300.8+H)/(4800+AB)0.271)/0.0012
$W = 13/6*Wins/2.5
$Sv = 13/6*Saves/3.7
$ERA = 13/6*(4.25-(495.8+ER)/((1050+IP)/9))/0.04
$Rto = 13/6*(12.5-((1458.3+H+BB)/((1050+IP)/9)))/0.07

National League 1996 prediction formulas
$HR = 13/6*HR/4.9
$RBI = 13/6*HR/18.1
$SB = 13/6*HR/6.7
$BA = 13/6*((1283.1+H)/(4700+AB)0.273)/0.0012
$W = 13/6*Wins/2.5
$Sv = 13/6*Saves/3.8
$ERA = 13/6*(3.9-(454.9+ER)/((1050+IP)/9))/0.04
$Rto = 13/6*(11.85-((1382.5+H+BB)/((1050+IP)/9)))/0.07

Next year's notes will have — in addition to the 1996 actual formulas and 1997 predicted formulas — the 1995 Fight Formulas. To some extent there will be different denominators. All depends on what the game is. And I really expect to learn a lot from this. If Kreutzer and Leopold actually have figured out position scarcity (don't you think that's their secret that they can barely contain?), I may indeed get my nose bloodied. I can admit it to my fellow masochists.

Rest assured you will find the round-by-round in these pages. Should be fascinating viewing to retrospective fight fans.

Not a bad definition of what a masochist is.

Chapter 4
The Death of Rotisserie

So, is this how come the comments were so short? You've been saving space for me?

Already — I don't believe it — you've broken your vow. Just ask the questions.

How come the comments were so short?

I know. Have to hustle. Do you really expect me to spend $68 for Greg Maddux?

No!

You expect me to spend $42, is that it?

You can spend whatever you jolly well feel like, but $42 is the recommended limit of what I think you should spend. The bid prices are rigged in such a way that, however much under them the players come to you, you feel like your getting a good deal; however much over them someone else goes, you feel they're getting a bad deal and you'll get a better deal somewhere else.

So you're saying Maddux is going to earn $42 this year.

Um — okay, you can look at it like that.
    Was that on the card I gave you?

I'm just trying to look at it the way you do. You say Maddux was worth $68 last year but will only be worth $42 this year, so he's only going to be 42/68 as good. Seems to me you're predicting a big fall-off.

The bid is much more a prediction of rank than earnings. If he's the best pitcher in baseball again, as the bid predicts, that's not much of a fall-off (although Maddux could fall a long way and still be the best). As far as earnings go, I'll be surprised if he earns less than $50. But I won't be surprised if I'm terribly wrong. If you know what I mean.

Sure. Plain English: a bid is a bet and a price is a prediction. Right?

A bid is always a bet and a price is almost always an exact measurement. All the prices in chapter one are simply ways of expressing existing stats in a number that we can understand. In chapter two, the prices for hitters are the measurements of predicted stats, and so, yes, those prices are predictions. They are exact measurements now and will turn out to be very inexact predictions.

I was with you, and then you lost me on the last turn.

The prices for hitters in the prediction chapter are measurements of the stats I predict. The bids take into account many factors besides predicted stats. For example —
    What?

I get it. I was just trying to give you your lines, even if they're not on this card. Sometimes you should just answer the questions.

Sorry.

Like you said yourself, you better hope there are some people reading your book for the first time or you're in trouble. But my partner says I have to ask you this one question. Off the record. He must have seen it coming, because he said, no matter what the price is, I have to ask it. Between you and me.

Go ahead.

You really think Maddux was worth $68 last year?

Uh... Yes, I really do. In fact, I know it. I'm willing to bet on it.
   I guess it's too much to hope that you might have read the masochist chapter for once?

Flipped through it. What was that all about? Maybe seeing the m word right at the beginning messed me up or something, but I never could get with it. Nice try though.

The m word?

Marriage. Look, here's the thing: this is me talking, not my partner, because I make the bids. Even if you could guarantee me another year for Maddux like last year — which is what you were talking about, I read that part — I'd rather pay my alimonies than shell out 68 bucks for any player.

Alimonies?

Let's say I spend $68 for him and my budget is exactly what you say it should be, $78: how do I buy 8 more pitchers for $10 and not buy them all in the crapshoot?

First of all, the pitchers are going to end up earning $78 per team, counting all the negatives. The bids for pitchers work out to $85 per team, and that's about what leagues spend, on average. But not only do leagues vary considerably on what they'll spend for pitchers, teams have very different ideas of what to spend. The most important thing is for you to figure out what you're willing to spend — what your own ideal budget is — and adjust the bid limits accordingly. Just make sure every dollar you add to someone is subtracted from someone else. If you take the money from a hitter, it doesn't necessarily mean the stats are going to be worse than what I predict; just that you're not willing to pay as much for them.
   So once again, bids aren't the same as prices.

Now answer the question. How do I buy the rest of my pitchers, no matter what my budget is, after I've forked out $68 for Maddux, even if I do get his stats?

It can be done, I promise you, but you'll have neutralized him. It will be a .500 pitching staff.

Sort of like he's back on the Cubs?

Hey, Cubs are going to be hot. But that's the right idea.

Show me how I get a .500 pitching staff for $85 after I've spent $68 on one pitcher.

I'll show you how you can do it for $78.

Unexpected end

$	Draft roster	IP	W	Sv	ERA	Ratio
68	MADDUX,G	210	19	0	1.63	7.30
2	SWINDELL,G	153	10	0	4.47	12.88
2	WITT,B	111	2	0	3.90	12.28
1	QUANTRILL,P	179	11	0	4.67	12.85
1	BENES,Andy	119	4	0	4.17	12.59
1	WILSON,T	83	3	0	3.92	13.06
1	AROCHA,R	50	3	0	3.99	13.23
1	WALKER,M	45	1	1	3.22	13.90
1	DEWEY,M	32	1	0	3.13	13.36
78	totals	980	54	1	3.63	11.67

In this retrospective draft, the team pays exactly what Maddux is going to be worth and gets it, then fills in with pitchers who do exactly what they are paid to do. In the Baseball Weekly league that I was in, this staff would have finished second in ERA and ratio, second to last in wins and last in saves.

And in my leagues, would have finished first in the qualitatives. Amazing. I guess he would have finished first in BW, except, as Hunt kept telling us, he was already carrying you and Golenbock along with your Sweeney Plan, and you swept the pitching.

Precisely. That's the power of Greg Maddux. He basically wins two categories all by himself. Nobody else in the game does that. Without him, this hypothetical pitching staff has a 4.17 ERA and 12.86 ratio. In the BW league — sorry, but we don't have time to hear about all of yours — that would have been good for eighth in ERA and, get this, *eleventh* in ratio. Hardly worth dropping this team to last in the qualitatives for failing to get the innings, since it's practically there anyway.

I thought we were ignoring that, because this staff doesn't have 1,000 innings even with Maddux.

Recall that back then, when this draft was held, it only needed 888. These pitchers have 100 to spare in a full season.

Is that why he earned so much? Because it was a short season?

There's something to that. The more you pitch, the more chances you have of getting blasted. But if he stayed the same, and the league stayed the same, he would have still been worth $68. It's very easy, even with 144-game stats to produce retrospective pitching staffs that meet the innings requirement.

And they don't screw up?

They *can't* screw up. The retrospective prices produce .500 pitching staffs for $78, no matter how you shake and bake.

$	Draft roster	IP	W	Sv	ERA	Ratio
68	MADDUX,G	210	19	0	1.63	7.30
3	FASSERO,J	189	13	0	4.33	13.38
1	QUANTRILL,P	179	11	0	4.67	12.85
1	BENES,Andy	119	4	0	4.17	12.59
1	CARRASCO,H	87	2	5	4.12	13.60
1	WILSON,T	83	3	0	3.92	13.06
1	BORLAND,T	74	1	6	3.77	14.35
1	SHAW,J	62	1	3	4.62	12.13
1	WALKER,M	45	1	1	3.22	13.90
78	totals	1048	55	15	3.71	11.99

This team substitutes Fassero for Swindell, then fills in with the most IP that $7 can buy. It sacrifices ERA and ratio, although it's still strong in both, and creeps into contention in wins and saves. Another .500 staff, wouldn't you say? With Fassero the only pitcher besides Maddux who's worth more than $1.

It helps to have stats to look at. (You should have done this in the comments.) Let's try the same thing with someone else, somebody that maybe some other people think was worth more than Maddux, like Wohlers.

Okay, we shake Wohlers out onto the plate with --

We'll buy two blue chip starters (Rijo $26, Saberhagen $23: the average salaries in Appendix A); the cheapest of the Atlanta Five (Merker $13); then the maybe-great Bobby Jones for $12 (good price); need one more starter, are thrilled to get Bullinger at $6. That's $80 on starting pitching, so the pen has to be a crapshoot.

Xavier for $3? Not bad; might get a lot of the action if his arm is right. Wohlers $5? That hurt. But could be a stopper yet if he can find the plate. Finally, the last two roster spots, take your pick of remaining pitchers: Blas Minor — you never know — and Mike Perez — how'd he slip through?

A $10 bullpen, a $90 pitching staff loaded with upside (if the saves aren't there, fall back to three categories)... Here's how the cookies crumbled.

$	Draft roster	IP	W	Sv	ERA	Ratio
3	RIJO,J	69	5	0	4.17	12.78
7	SABERHAGEN,B	153	7	0	4.18	11.65
3	MERCKER,K	143	7	0	4.15	12.65
8	JONES,B	196	10	0	4.19	12.05
6	BULLINGER,J	150	12	0	4.14	13.02
7	MINOR,B	47	4	1	3.66	10.99
5	HERNANDEZ,X	90	7	3	4.60	12.60
4	PEREZ,Mike	71	2	2	3.66	12.49
35	WOHLERS,M	65	7	25	2.09	10.44
78	totals	983	61	31	4.01	12.20

What do you think. Where does this team finish in your leagues?

Let's see. I've got the standings right —

That's okay — just roughly.

In the middle in all four categories.

By paying $90 for this staff, you'll have a better-than-average staff if they just break even (earn $90). By getting $78 back — no matter what you paid — you are getting an average staff (9 x $8.67, the worth of the average pitcher).

That was the point I was trying to make to Peter Kreutzer in the previous —
What?

You made it.

I don't think so, or else you wouldn't be still fighting me over Maddux.

Les Leopold was saying, let's submit teams that add up to $260 and I was saying, what does that prove? My $260 teams finish right in the middle. They are par. They are what the stats were worth, and if you get what you pay for, you finish exactly in the middle.

In the retrospective draft, if we ever have it, I even want to include minuses. Because even Terry Mulholland is at par. Here, I'll show you —

What?

I said: at least <u>*switch leagues.*</u>

Oh, that's a good idea... We'll make Cone the big-ticket starter, $27 (average salary in last year's drafts). Then Gordon $9, Bosio $7, Stottlemyre $3, Brian Anderson $3, and — a nomination that backfired — Mike Moore $1. Total for five starting pitchers $50. Try to get lightning in a bottle with Armando Benitez $17, double-up with Darren Hall $15, who some tout is very high on, and fill out with Jose Mesa $3, because you want to get some of the Cleveland action. Total spent on pitching $85.

These are what they earned, together with the stats that earned them:

$	AL pitchers	IP	W	Sv	ERA	Ratio
38	CONE,D	229	18	0	3.57	11.11
7	GORDON,T	189	12	0	4.43	13.95
-3	BOSIO,C	170	10	0	4.92	14.82
11	STOTTLEMYRE,T	210	14	0	4.55	13.22
0	ANDERSON,Bri	100	6	0	5.87	12.64
-30	MOORE,M	133	5	0	7.53	16.76
57	MESA,J	64	3	46	1.13	9.28
0	HALL,D	16	0	3	4.41	16.53
-2	BENITEZ,A	48	1	2	5.66	13.97
78	totals	1158	69	51	4.70	13.37

This pitching staff, if it keeps Mike Moore for all 133 innings, is a little below .500.

Weren't you high on Benitez too?

Hey. Be nice. Besides, I bought Hall myself.

The hitters are exactly the same. If the hitters a team buys get $182 worth of stats, it has an average offense. If it only paid, say, $150 for these hitters, it got a profit on its hitting, but the offense itself is still average. As an example:

sal	Pos	$	Draft roster	AB	HR	RBI	SB	BA
18	C	16	TETTLETON,M	429	32	78	0	.238
4	C	1	BORDERS,P	143	4	13	0	.231
7	2B	1	SHUMPERT,T	47	0	3	3	.234
6	SS	7	GAGNE,G	430	6	49	3	.256
4	SS	1	GIL,B	415	9	46	2	.219
4	1B	25	SNOW,JT	544	24	102	2	.289
17	3B	42	MARTINEZ,E	511	29	113	4	.356
12	3B	2	SABO,C	71	1	8	2	.254
25	OF	33	NIXON,O	589	0	45	50	.295
24	OF	27	WILLIAMS,B	563	18	82	8	.307
20	OF	11	VAUGHN,G	392	17	59	10	.224
18	OF	-2	DELGADO,C	91	3	11	0	.165
8	OF	0	MAY,D	113	1	9	0	.248
1	OF	17	O'LEARY,T	399	10	49	5	.308
168		182	totals	4737	154	667	89	.275

A draft roster of hitters whose prices add up to exactly $182 in retrospect.

The salaries (again from Appendix A) add up to $168, so there were good buys overall. The hypothetical owner that bought this team was conducting a clinic in Stage Four caution: spread the money evenly, buy regulars, never go overboard. And he was being Stage Four crafty: several players at key positions will be out of harm's way as DH's. Meantime he keeps the DH position open, allowing him to take a flyer at the end on Troy O'Leary.

But what kind of offense does he get?

Want me to check my leagues?

No — roughly.

Roughly? I don't think it looks so hot. Maybe that's why you don't want me to check.

Well, there is a little problem. You're not going to like this, but at least hear me out.

In the final standings of *my* league, this offense is indeed below average. It finishes tenth in homers, tenth in ribbies, seventh in steals and fifth in batting average. But in the hypothetical final standings — that is, no changes in rosters all year long — it finishes eighth, seventh, seventh and sixth. It doesn't do better because two teams punted power, but that's another —

You saying you did the Sweeney Plan in both leagues?

I didn't, two other teams did, but let's finish with this first. Clearly, this offense does better in the hypothetical finals — it's close to average — and then slides back in the actual final standings. Why is that?

Because the final standings have stats of players we pick up during the year for nothing.

Exactly. Teams have more HR, RBI amd SB at the end of the year than they bought in the auction.

Why wasn't that a problem with the pitchers?

Because they give you suckey innings along with the wins and saves. Your draft roster is worse off in the final standings in the quantitatives, better off in the qualitatives.

Hmph... Just what I was trying to tell Kreutzer. Don't know why it was so difficult. And it's the only thing that non-masochists need to know. The first test of any pricing formula is, do the prices for the players we buy in the auction add up to $3,120, more or less? If the formula produces prices for all players at the end of the season (there will be more than 600 in each league) adding up to $3,120, it means the prices for the 276 that we bought in the draft are too low.

Don't know why people like Kreutzer and Les Leopold have so much trouble with that, but evidently you don't. Anyway, we can move on.

You look pained.

You done?

I am. Fire away.

Let me say that I'm in kind of in a tough position here. I have your questions on this card and my partner's on this one, and most of the time I don't even get to ask my own questions.

Relax. We'll get to them all. What's the next one?

This one's my partner's, it's not mine... It says, "When he's through explaining Maddux is worth whatever, ask him again."

Ask me again what?

Do you really believe it?

You tell that partner of yours to —
What's this guy's problem anyway? Last year Maddux was worth $72. How come that didn't freak him out?

It did! He's been waiting two years to find out what happened to your pricing system? It used to be good.

Nothing's happened! It's still good!

All right. Say Maddux was worth $72. Here's a question.
I feel sorry for you, but here it goes.
If Maddux was worth $72, how do I buy eight more pitchers with $6?

Simple.
Maddux could earn more than $78. It's not a problem.

Maddux can earn more than the whole pitching staff is worth?

Absolutely.

How do I buy the rest of my pitchers?

With negative bids.

Oh, man, you can't do that!

Why not, in a retrospective draft? Minus $17 for Danny Jackson. If somebody else says minus $16, he's got him. He gets a $16 credit, plus his stats. What's wrong with that?

You add up all these stats and, once again, a $78 pitching staff is a .500 pitching staff. If we skip the innings rule for this one — Greg Maddux and the eight nebbishes — it's sure to earn 26 points.

You know what the next note says?

No idea.

"If you still haven't called his bluff, don't argue. Just show him the other prices."

That's what this is all about? Other people's prices? Am I supposed to change mine because theirs are different?

My partner says, when people catch on to you, you're dead.

Who are we talking about?

Hunt. Benson. Shandler. They're the ones that are out so far.

Can I see them?

Well, first of all, these aren't Hunt's prices; they're Jerry Heath's. Hunt publishes them in Baseball Weekly for the sake of discussion.
    Second, I have no idea how Benson and Shandler come up with their prices, so it would not be fair to comment on them, but, uh...

That's not going to stop you?

Here's what we'll do. First, let's change JH to HD, for Heath Data. Then we'll add my list of prices. Then we'll put the actual stats in front of them. Then we'll look at them. Then we'll let common sense decide this.
    The first group will be my top five pitchers last season, with everything averaged to help us see what's going on.

Top NLP	IP	W	Sv	ERA	Ratio	$HD	$JB	$RS	$AP
MADDUX,G	210	19	0	1.63	7.30	42	41	51	68
NOMO,H	191	13	0	2.54	9.50	30	24	31	39
WORRELL,To	62	4	32	2.02	9.96	29	34	47	38
HENKE,T	54	1	36	1.82	9.94	27	35	49	38
SCHOUREK,P	190	18	0	3.22	9.60	31	22	27	37
average	142	11	14	2.35	8.95	32	31	41	44

What does your common sense tell you?

That Shandler's are the best prices.

Why?

The others are too low. Yours are too high.

According to who?

Me, the bidder. I mean, I'm not going to bid $51 for Maddux or $47 for Worrell, even after the fact, because, just like you were saying, that's par. But common sense tells me these are better prices.

You may be right.

What?

Even though Shandler doesn't spend as much on these pitchers as I do, at least he spends more on the relief pitchers. It could be just a different allocation of money, which is something that reasonable people can argue about. Not spending your money is something that reasonable people would want to avoid.

Now we either go down the pitchers' pay scale or over to the hitters' pay scale. Since Heath and Benson might be allocating much more money to hitters than Shandler or I — which is reasonable — let's go over to the top NL hitters.

NL hitters	AB	HR	RBI	SB	BA	$HD	$JB	$RS	$AP
BICHETTE,D	579	40	128	13	0.340	42	42	38	54
SANDERS,R	484	28	99	36	0.306	38	38	37	44
BONDS,B	506	33	104	31	0.294	38	37	36	43
SOSA,S	564	36	119	34	0.268	37	37	37	42
LARKIN,B	496	15	66	51	0.319	36	39	37	42
average	526	30	103	33	0.305	38	39	37	45

Whose prices are the best now?

Benson's.

Thanks. Why?

They make sense to me. They're what I would pay.

Seriously? You think Bonds only earned $37 last year? A 30-30 season in 144 games? Pretty fair batting average and over 100 RBI's — he's not even three times better than the average hitter?

That's what you say, because you put the average hitter at $13. How do you know Benson's average hitter isn't $11.3?

Good point. Let's look at some average hitters' stats.

NL hitters	AB	HR	RBI	SB	BA	$HD	$JB	$RS	$AP
ABBOTT,Ku	420	17	60	4	0.255	15	12	12	14
MAGADAN,D	348	2	51	2	0.313	13	10	9	14
MAY,D	206	8	41	5	0.301	14	11	10	13
MOUTON,J	298	4	27	25	0.262	14	13	14	13
MORRIS,H	359	11	51	1	0.279	15	10	9	12
average	326	8	46	7	0.280	14	11	11	13

Now who do you like?

Benson or Shandler. These are bums.

Easy to say, but you have to buy somebody, don't you? Can't just stand on the sidelines, waving your money. I've been getting the players up to now, and now Jerry's getting them.

This is starting to be interesting. I really haven't paid attention to other prices for several years. I thought this battle was basically over and we were all sitting together in one big room. But look how far apart Shandler and I are on Magadan.

The main thing is, the average of these five is very close to the average hitter's stats (the average of all 168 hitters bought in auctions last year), and Jerry is making the statement — with his prices, not his mixed with mine — that Bonds is only 2.7 times better than the average hitter (38/14). Do you believe that?

How come he's Jerry and everybody else is their last name?

Because I've talked to Jerry a hundred times about this. If the average hitter is too abstract, compare Bonds and Hal Morris category by category: how can Bonds be only 2.5 times better

(38/15)? He's three times better in homers, two times better in ribbies, 31 times better in steals, and has a better batting average.

So forget Heath.

No, don't forget Heath. Because at least he's spending his money. Remember, I've gotten every player so far, except the two relievers, and now Jerry's starting to buy them.

But there's no way you can afford them all.

As a pricer, there sure is. My budget is $3,120, not $260; as long as I don't go over it — and I don't — I can buy every one of these players at my price, unless someone else has a higher price. So far, Shandler's bought Worrell and Henke; Heath has bought Abbott, May and Morris, with a tie with Shandler for Mouton; and I have taken everyone else.

And Benson's been shut out.

So we have to find out where he makes his move. Here are five average pitchers.

NL pitchers	IP	W	Sv	ERA	Ratio	$HD	$JB	$RS	$AP
RITZ,K	173	11	2	4.21	12.25	13	7	9	9
WILLIAMS,Mik	88	3	0	3.29	10.98	8	5	8	9
VANLANDINGHAM	123	6	0	3.67	12.03	10	5	8	8
JONES,B	196	10	0	4.19	12.05	11	6	7	8
PLESAC,Dan	60	4	3	3.58	11.93	10	5	8	8
average	128	7	1	3.91	11.95	10	6	8	8

Common sense, please?

Benson's still not getting anyone. And Heath has gone crazy

Why? These are the average pitchers, and if the average hitter is worth $11 or so, isn't the pitcher also?

I'm getting a little worried here. I'm not going to be able to go home and face my partner if I let you talk me back into your prices.

I still don't see why you deserted me. Or what you're doing here since you did.

I didn't say you didn't have good ideas.

Everything spins off the prices. But my main idea right now is, you should be happy: you've got quite a range of choices. Was Kevin Ritz worth $13 or $7 or $9? Those aren't small differences.

My gut says $8. I'd pay $8 for these stats.

You want to join our retrospective draft? We need 12 players.
    That's exactly what I would pay.

How much money was it?

Uh, actually, we have 12 players. Now let's quickly look at five hitters and pitchers that I consider to have been of minimal value, and we'll know all we need to know.

NL hitters	AB	HR	RBI	SB	BA	$HD	$JB	$RS	$AP
BENJAMIN,M	186	3	12	11	.220	4	4	5	3
BLAUSER,J	431	12	31	8	.211	4	4	6	2
JOHNSON,H	169	7	22	1	.195	3	1	2	1
RODRIGUEZ,H	138	2	15	0	.239	1	0	1	1
PHILLIPS,JR	231	9	28	1	.195	2	1	3	1
average	231	7	22	4	.210	3	2	3	2

Rounding my prices off to whole numbers (since the others are), I find these stats to be worth an average of $1.60. Shandler says their worth $3.40. Benson's prices average out to $2.00 exactly. Heath figures they're worth $2.80.

Do you think those are small differences?

They're not so small even without the decimals. Shandler's buying all the players now, except HoJo and maybe Rodriguez.

In the retrospective draft that Kreutzer wants to hold, I'm going to argue to break all ties with decimals. Why not?

You would. Anyway, if you're not going to let me in this retrospective draft, would you stop talking about it? Let's see the pitchers.

Here are five of them that I say are worth a dollar, but they are ranked by what they are worth to the cent (from $1.09 for Arocha to $0.64 for Wilson):

NL pitchers	IP	W	Sv	ERA	Ratio	$HD	$JB	$RS	$AP
AROCHA,R	50	3	0	3.99	13.23	3	0	2	1
BORLAND,T	74	1	6	3.77	14.35	2	3	7	1
CARRASCO,H	87	2	5	4.12	13.60	3	3	6	1
QUANTRILL,P	179	11	0	4.67	12.85	6	1	2	1
WILSON,T	83	3	0	3.92	13.06	3	1	2	1
average	95	4	2	4.22	13.30	3	2	4	1

To me, they are truly worth 93 cents each (a difference that would count in a retrospective auction) but here, again, we'll round off my prices —

Because we're trying to learn something useful here.

Right. I pay $1.00 per pitcher, obviously; Shandler pays $3.80, Benson pays $1.60 and Heath pays $3.40.

Look at the differences of opinion on Toby Borland. On Hector Carrasco. On Paul Quantril. How can that be? We're all looking at the same simple immutable facts.

Someone's going to clean up in your retrospective auction. I'm not sure it's you, though.

Who is?

I'm not sure. I mean, I like your prices here, but I still don't like your high ones.

My formulas are dead-simple equations. They very well could be too simple, but I can't bend and warp the prices, even if I want to. One win from Toby Borland is worth the same as one win from Greg Maddux. A stolen base from JR Phillips is worth as much as a stolen base from Quilvio Veras.

In Jerry's prices, Veras, not Philips, gets cheated. He plugs players into the mid-place team in his dozens of leagues and recalculates the standings. Clearly, for many mid-place teams, Quilvio's speed soon becomes surplus; the first ten bases he steals are much more important, in his Heath salary drive, than the last 20 or even 30.

And how do the other two screw up?

It looks to me like Shandler's spending too much for the little guys, not enough for the big guy's, but at least he's spending his money. Just at a rough guess, he'll buy three players to my one, going head to head with the full $3,120 to spend — and I'll get 80%, or more, of the stats.

Benson's not going to get any stats, and I bet the reason is just what we were talking about earlier: he's putting his $3,120 salary cap on the year-end stats, not the stats that we buy in April.

But Jerry's prices, even though they have a problem, are far the most interesting to me. I learn a lot from them.

Remember that they are empirical. Jerry's got the resources and the programming skills to find out what's actually happening in real Rotisserie life. When he says Veras stops being worth that much to the team he's on after a while, you better believe it (and, of course, you trade Veras).

What about smaller players, though. Surely, Borland, Carrasco and Wilson don't take mid-place teams over the top in either wins or saves? Nevertheless, in league after league, Heath finds Carrasco to be worth more than Borland — which is not what Shandler says. He finds Wilson, who has no saves at all, to be worth more than Borland — decidedly not what Shandler says. It's hard to tell what, if any, differences there are in the qualitatives... Is there something we should infer?

Hell, yes. Wins are more important than saves. Each win counts more than a save. You've been saying that for years. My partner right away said that was one of your good ideas.

Be sure to thank him for me.

I've been saying it, but Jerry's been showing it.

The fact that Greg Maddux was far and away the "winningest" pitcher in all the Heath leagues, despite his $36 average salary — doesn't that tell you something?

How come Randy Johnson only ranks tenth in the American League?

Because smart owners weren't so sure about him.

What do you mean?

I'm not sure. I'm just thinking out loud. But that could be it.

We onto something?

Maybe. It's hard to say... The second pitcher behind Maddux in the NL was Mike Hampton. Good pitcher, a lot of touts were high on him (although not me). John Hunt, for instance, had a $6 price for him in Baseball Weekly, then backed that up a week later with $8 in the Baseball Weekly auction. But why Hampton, who only earned $16, would be on more winning teams than Wohlers or Valdes or Schourek, I don't know.

Andy Pettite was the "winningest" pitcher in the AL; teams that bought him finished with an average of 62.7 points. But in 45 leagues, only 12 teams bought him. So that could be an anomaly.

Mesa was second. He turned the largest profit by far of any player in either league — at $54, it may be the highest ever — but the second biggest profit-maker was Johnson, and, as you say, he ranked tenth. Teams that bought David Wells ended up with more points.

Wells was sixth. And Ron Villone was fifth.

Mike Mussina was only No. 19. What's Chris Haney doing at No. 16?

You tell me. Why are you even listing this stuff?

Because I do believe that, in groups of ten, we're being told something. Did you notice, when I switched Banks for Swift in the list of busts in the Drabek comment, not all that much changed? I said I got lucky when the Heath trackings didn't change even a little bit, but what about the average salary? Swift cost $15, Banks almost nothing, and yet the switch only raised the average for all ten pitchers by one dollar.

The most important grouping of ten is, unquestionably, the ten highest salaries. When ten of them get paid such and such and earn such and such and their teams do such and such, there's something to be learned from this.

You kept hinting what it is. One of my questions when I was reading the player comments was, why don't you just say it?.

I did. Didn't I? I thought I said many times: the market is being too cautious. It's not quite pushing the expected ten best players to par. They're not being neutralized. It's almost like a little glitch in Stage Three, looking for profits where there aren't supposed to be any. Very much with the encouragement of these other touts, we're seeing a sort of Stage Two Revisited that's definitely being exploited by certain owners.

Mind telling us what these stages are? That's a question from you new readers.

Sure. Back in Stage One, everybody bolted from the starting gate. They wildly overspent on the star hitters with no speed and spent way too much on pitching, especially starting pitching. They had never even heard of *Baseball America*. The winner was always somebody who kept his money, knew the rookies and cleaned up from the middle rounds on.

In Stage Two, everybody tried to be that somebody. There was too much money at the end and Jackie Robinson wouldn't have earned what was expected of the rookies.

In Stage Three, the final stage, everyone knows everything. Skill is so rampant that it's a game of luck.

Things like the $18 for Delgado — that's not Stage Two?

Oh, there will always be yearnings. If you check Appendix A, you'll see all three stages represented in the bidding for that one player. My league, the American Dreams, had a shoot-out for old time's sake, but Cowtown must have been out of pocket when Delgado's name came up. (Or had he plunged that far in one week? The ADL draft took place the day before the season started; Cowtown's six days later.) Baseball Weekly was being Stage Three cute; pushing Delgado's price a notch higher than it would have otherwise, not because he qualified at catcher, but because, in the BW rules, he would qualify after catching one game, and he was supposed to platoon with Knorr.

Maybe you can show us some of the rounds in your BW league? Let us see what stage people like Hunt belonged to.

No can do this year.

What do you mean? Don't go getting born-again on me with this be-nice stuff.

Here's what happened.

Peter Golenbock and I are pretty busy on the speaker phone — he does the pitchers, I do the hitters — so I asked Dollar Bill, who was down in Florida scouting with me, if he would mind keeping track of the bidding? There was a game in Sarasota that night, so Dollar certainly had something better to do, but he said sure.

Dollar and I were in Winter Haven that afternoon and only got to Peter's house in St. Pete's with half an hour to spare. Peter and I talked over strategy, quickly realized we didn't have one, and once again fell back on the Sweeney plan. I gave a notepad to Dollar, and he wrote down numbers one through 276, and we thought we were all set.

In the first round, Eric Karros was nominated.

Dollar, who knows what Jeff Reboulet batted in 1993, said, "*Who?*"

"Karros," I said, and spelled it.

"Is he a hitter or a pitcher?"

By the second round, Dollar was fired.

You know what? In Stage Three, round-by-rounds are overrated anyway.

They are when you don't have any. Want to do one of my leagues? I've got everything, even the last bids.

No, I'm serious — thanks, anyway — it doesn't matter *when* players come up in Stage Three; it matters *what* is expected. What we really should be doing is looking at subsequent groups of ten highest salaries.

Recall that all four groups of ten most coveted players were associated with winning teams. All four! *That* is amazing. I don't think it has ever happened.

In descending order of points for the teams that bought them:
1) Top 10 salaries, NL pitchers (Beck comment) — 56.1 points.
2) Top 10 salaries, AL pitchers (Cone comment) — 54.8 points.
3) Top 10 salaries, AL hitters (Canseco comment) — 52.9 points.
3) Top 10 salaries, NL hitters (Bonds comment) — 52.9 points.

As we saw in the comments, these may not look like much better than .500 teams (52 points is break-even), but even the hitters average out to a fifth-place finish in a 12-team league.

The hitters lose money.

The NL pitchers lose money.

The AL pitchers actually make money — which means, incontestably, that the group for which the market had its highest expectations *exceeded* them. The biggest anomaly may be *only* 54.8 points. It's all Gene Autry's fault.

I'm surprised you didn't say Herzog's. But back it up a bit. When you say incontestably — isn't that according to your prices? Suppose I buy Benson's —

Go ahead.

I do. Now, for argument's sake, let's say his prices for these ten AL pitchers average out to $28 each. For instance, he has Randy Johnson at $34 last year, right there is $24 difference —

The average player is worth $11 and you're saying Randy Johnson was only three times better?

I'm not, Benson is. And here's the thing. Supposing a lot of people don't believe Randy Johnson was worth $58, no matter what you say; how can you say they are getting more than they expect if they don't agree with what you say they got? They paid $30 and you say they got $34, but Benson says they got $28, and — don't pass out — they agree with Benson.

Very good point. Really.

So let's look at subsequent groups of 10.

Next 10 highest salaries, AL pitchers

		earned	avg		Heath Data		- touts -		
rk	AL pitchers	1995	sal	+/-	Pts	Rk	AP	JH	$94
11	KEY,J	-2	25	-27	49.1	96	22	23	36
12	MCDOWELL,J	26	25	1	55.5	23	22	23	30
13	JONES,Doug	15	24	-10	50.9	80	26	21	35
14	FERNANDEZ,A	25	23	2	54.8	29	18	27	29
15	APPIER,K	31	22	9	55.6	22	25	28	22
16	ECKERSLEY,D	28	22	6	55.6	21	22	22	24
17	ALVAREZ,W	6	21	-15	52.2	61	21	19	31
18	FETTERS,M	16	21	-5	56.9	14	21	21	22
19	MCDONALD,B	7	20	-13	44.1	127	19	21	27
20	MARTINEZ,De	36	20	16	52.8	54	18	19	36
	average	19	22	-3	52.8	53	21	22	29

These are the second ten most coveted pitchers in the AL; the first are shown in the Cone comment. It doesn't matter if you don't like what you see under "earned 1995;" the same measurements are being used for this ten as the other ten, and they measure up as considerably — I mean, considerably — less.

My prices show how big a bite out of the pie a player takes. Apparently, we can't agree how big the pie is, and so forth. But we have to agree, I would think, that I have no bias against this second group of pitchers. If the first group earns an average of $34 and this group earns an average of $19, this group's bite is only 56% as big as the first group's (19/34).

And the market had a big preference for the first group, paying 36% more for it (30/22).

In my prices, the market's a little disappointed, losing $3 per pitcher. In the Heath trackings, the teams that bought them still do pretty well, averaging 52.4 points. But that's a big drop from 54.8 points. Instead of finishing third, on average, they finish fifth (53/129 x 12).

You sure about this stuff?

I'm sure that in 45 Heath leagues, there was this much difference. Jerry Heath doesn't lie.

Who are the next ten?

Next 10 highest salaries, AL pitchers

		earned	avg		Heath Data		- touts -		
rk	AL pitchers	1995	sal	+/-	Pts	Rk	AP	JH	$94
21	HENTGEN,P	-5	19	-25	50.6	87	24	20	37
22	BERE,J	-26	19	-45	51.9	68	17	19	22
23	SELE,A	6	17	-12	54.9	28	12	17	18
24	BENITEZ,A	-2	17	-19	47.4	108	12	9	3
25	NAGY,C	15	16	-1	51.6	72	14	18	29
26	BROWN,K	28	15	13	57.9	8	11	22	-1
27	HALL,D	0	15	-15	51.7	71	15	14	21
28	ELDRED,C	2	14	-12	51.5	74	9	19	16
29	ONTIVEROS,S	11	14	-3	54.3	34	13	18	35
30	CLEMENS,R	12	14	-2	49.8	95	27	20	42
	average	4	16	-12	52.2	65	15	18	22

The average salary is dropping only gradually (72% of what the previous ten pitchers cost); earnings are plunging (21% of what the previous ten earned).

But they're still on winning teams?

That's right. Running quite counter to the conventional wisdom, the 30 most expensive pitchers in the league last year were bought by winning teams.

Where do the losers start kicking in?

In the very next batch:

Next 10 highest salaries, AL pitchers

		earned	avg		Heath Data		- touts -		
rk	AL pitchers	1995	sal	+/-	Pts	Rk	AP	JH	$94
31	LANGSTON,M	16	13	3	53.5	49	15	18	7
32	RUSSELL,JE	20	13	6	53.0	53	19	10	14
33	WARD,D	-7	13	-20	49.8	94	12	18	
34	FINLEY,C	19	12	7	55.1	25	12	20	19
35	ROGERS,K	35	12	23	57.8	9	9	16	20
36	PEREZ,M	0	11	-11	53.8	44	8	16	22
37	TEWKSBURY	6	10	-4	50.2	91	9	13	2
38	SHUEY,P	0	10	-10	45.7	120	R1	8	-2
39	GUZMAN,Ju	-16	10	-26	43.1	128	5	24	-4
40	HOWE,S	3	9	-7	52.6	58	9	17	32
	average	8	11	-3	51.5	67	10	16	11

Even with Kevin Rogers in it, this group averages below 52 points. And that's despite a pretty good return. Getting $8 back per pitcher isn't bad at all; it's 72 cents on the dollar.

In the group above this one, they get 25 cents back. Why would they be on winning teams and not these pitchers?

That's the question, isn't it?

Now we're both asking the questions.

I don't *know* why. But there's been an absolutely steady decline in — let's call it winning percentage as we drop down from the pitchers that people want the most to the ones they're not so sure about: 54.8, 52.8, 52.2, 51.5.

So you're saying we should be surer about the ones we're sure about and pay more for them?

Maybe. Maybe...

Next 10 highest salaries, AL pitchers

		earned	avg		Heath Data		- touts -		
rk	AL pitchers	1995	sal	+/-	Pts	Rk	AP	JH	$94
41	OLIVER,D	2	9	-7	48.0	103	6	8	9
42	BONES,R	5	9	-4	52.1	66	8	15	33
43	CLARK,M	2	9	-7	50.5	88	8	11	22
44	GORDON,T	7	9	-2	50.7	84	8	15	15
45	HENNEMAN,M	21	9	12	54.5	31	11	11	3
46	PLUNK,E	18	8	10	54.1	39	20	19	21
47	ABBOTT,J	20	8	12	54.2	35	4	15	11
48	HERSHISER,O	30	8	22	53.6	46	7	12	7
49	TAPANI,K	4	8	-4	54.2	37	7	12	14
50	ACRE,M	-4	7	-11	52.8	55	5	15	9
	average	11	8	3	52.5	58	8	13	14

But, of course, it can't be that simple. The last group in the top 50 turns this trend around. The pitchers for whom the market pays an average of $8 are clearly better buys than the pitchers for whom it pays an average of $11.

Is this the sweet spot? Is $8 the magic number?

It's my lucky number, so I'm buying nothing but $8 starters from now on. And if you spend $1 more or $1 less, you've got yourself a dud.

What's Hunt doing?

John? He's making predictions. And not one of them is unreasonable. In fact, he's closer to what the pitchers earn overall than either the market or I. But he's in a hurry; he's got both leagues to project for the April 19 issue of Baseball America, and I doubt he's got a salary cap. The market and I have no idea what Mark Acre's going to do, but considering that we do have a salary cap, and we're not even positive Acre won't end up losing $4, our bets are at least as optimistic as Hunt's prediction.

So now we're past the sweet spot? They start losing again?

The $6 group is not pretty:

```
Next 10 highest salaries, AL pitchers
              earned avg          Heath Data    - touts -
   rk AL pitchers 1995  sal  +/-    Pts   Rk    AP   JH  | $94
   51 BOSIO,C      -3    7  -10    52.7   57     3    7  |  8
   52 RHODES,A     -7    7  -14    51.4   79     4   10  | -2
   53 SMITH,Z      -1    7   -8    51.9   67    R1       | 23
   54 FERNANDEZ,S  -8    7  -15    50.0   92     9   13  |  7
   55 BREWER,B     -3    5   -8    52.2   64     5    9  | 16
   56 WICKMAN,B     6    5    1    47.6  107     7   13  | 24
   57 GROSS,K      -7    5  -11    42.4  130     8    6  | 17
   58 KAMIENIECKI   8    5    3    47.9  104     7    8  | 14
   59 RUFFCORN,S   -5    4   -9    47.6  106    R1    2  | -7
   60 PERCIVAL,T   27    4   23    56.5   15    R1       |
      average       1    6   -5    50.0   82     4    7  | 10
```

Whoa! If Percival doesn't slip into it, it is ugly. And I was thinking seven was my lucky number.

Now, now — it's a game of skill. The next group:

```
Next 10 highest salaries, AL pitchers
              earned avg          Heath Data    - touts -
   rk AL pitchers 1995  sal  +/-    Pts   Rk    AP   JH  | $94
   61 RODRIGUEZ,F  -9    4  -13    53.6   47    R1       |
   62 WELLS,D      27    4   23    59.1    6     9   14  | 17
   63 RISLEY,B     11    4    7    51.6   73     7    9  | 23
   64 BALDWIN,J   -13    3  -16    51.5   76    R1       |
   65 BLACK,B      -5    3   -9    51.8   69     1   16  |
   66 HANSON,E     22    3   19    55.1   26     7   13  |  7
   67 LLOYD,G       6    3    3    51.5   75     1    9  |  4
   68 MIRANDA,A    -5    3   -9    53.6   45     5    9  |  0
   69 WEGMAN,B      1    3   -2    46.0  113     3    8  | 10
   70 FLEMING,D   -11    3  -14    48.4  102    R2       | -20
      average       2    3   -1    52.2   63     3    8  |  4
```

What's significant here is that $3 gets you $2. Quite an improvement over $6 getting you $1.

You mean, stay just above the crapshoot? Good place to get bargains?

It is if you get Wells. Not if you get Fleming.

No, things have got to start getting out of line somewhere; the auction would kind of grind to a halt otherwise. We'd refuse to fill out our pitching staffs.

The question on the table is, is pitching as a whole as much of a crapshoot as we think? Down here, of course it is.

Next 10 highest salaries, AL pitchers

		earned	avg		Heath Data		- touts -		
rk	AL pitchers	1995	sal	+/-	Pts	Rk	AP	JH	$94
71	HAWKINS,L	-8	3	-11	52.2	65	R2		
72	PAVLIK,R	14	3	11	56.9	13	R1	10	-14
73	STEVENS,D	7	3	4	56.0	20	R1		-5
74	STOTTLEMYRE	11	3	8	54.2	38	4	7	14
75	ANDERSON,Bri	0	3	-3	49.9	93	2	8	4
76	HITCHCOCK,S	14	3	11	59.6	4	3	7	6
77	MESA,J	57	3	54	62.2	2	4	8	16
78	CORMIER,R	10	2	8	51.8	70	R2	15	2
79	NELSON,J	26	2	24	52.7	56	3	6	7
80	BOEVER,J	-11	2	-12	51.4	77	9	14	16
	average	12	3	9	54.7	44	3	9	5

Suddenly the pickings are a lot better.

How are you deciding which $3 pitchers go where?

The first sort is by the average salaries in Appendix A, so there are decimals. Then the second sort is alphabetical. I do not intervene.

I don't know why you're pointing that out, since this doesn't support what you're saying. This ratty bunch of pitchers has the most profits and the second best winning percentage that we've seen so far.

Correct. And who still has the first? The ten most expensive pitchers.

One tenth of a point. That means something?

It means a lot to me when the one group is somebody we all can agree on. For that very reason, since we're all trying to win, they're not supposed to be winners. They're supposed to be neutralized.

So profits don't mean anything?

Sure they do. This group here earns three times more than their salaries, and that's why they are in fact the second most powerful group.

Isn't it all Mesa?

A lot of it is. Wherever he appeared, this was bound to happen. But take him out of the group and the average of the remaining nine is $7 earnings, $4 profits, and their teams ended up with 53.9 points, which would still be the second winningest group.

Jeff Nelson was awesome.

From that I conclude you had him.

Just once.

And I notice that these prices don't bother you as much.

All of them look fine to me. Except Mesa.

I think either Jerry Heath or Peter Kreutzer sicked you on me. I'd like to know which.

Moving right along:

Next 10 highest salaries, AL pitchers

		earned	avg		Heath Data		- touts -		
rk	AL pitchers	1995	sal	+/-	Pts	Rk	AP	JH	$94
81	CASTILLO,T	20	2	19	52.4	59	2	7	17
82	MOYER,J	9	2	7	45.2	123	3	3	10
83	DELEON,J	5	1	4	50.8	82	2		16
84	BUTCHER,M	3	1	2	48.6	101	R3		-5
85	COX,D	-13	1	-14	51.4	78	4		12
86	DARLING,R	-11	1	-12	45.9	115	1		15
87	ERICKSON,S	10	1	9	50.4	89	4	7	-5
88	MCCASKILL,K	2	1	1	53.4	50	1	3	9
89	MEACHAM,R	2	1	1	48.9	98	4	9	13
90	MILLS,A	-5	1	-6	53.8	43	3	7	3
	average	2	1	1	50.1	84	2	4	9

A most interesting group. That don't do any harm, and yet they're associated with losers.

How do you explain that?

I don't. I mean, no matter how little is paid from now on, there have to be losers, because most of the groups have been winners so far. For each group to get more than 52 points, some other group has to get less. But that does not, I realize, explain why this group does.

It seems especially unfair, since the market did such a good job of being unimpressed by what these pitchers did in 1994. Although I seem more unimpressed than Hunt — and I happen to hit what the group earned on the nose — his tips are more impressive: he says avoid Cox and Darling (before the reserve draft), take a flyer on Tony Castillo.

Why do you suppose Jamie Moyer ranks so far down?

Why does Alan Mills rank so high? But I'm telling you, the big picture is fascinating. Here's the next one:

Next 10 highest salaries, AL pitchers

		earned	avg		Heath Data		- touts -		
rk	AL pitchers	1995	sal	+/-	Pts	Rk	AP	JH	$94
91	REYES,C	2	1	1	44.7	126	1	6	2
92	SCANLAN,B	-12	1	-13	53.1	52	1		8
93	VILLONE	-8	1	-9	59.3	5		2	
94	ASSENMACHER	13	1	12	53.9	41	2	7	7
95	GUTHRIE,M	4	1	4	45.7	119	R3		-3
96	HANEY,C	8	1	7	56.5	16	R3		-5
97	MAHOMES,P	-6	1	-7	47.1	109	1	7	6
98	PENA,A	-6	1	-7	42.5	129	R2		
99	PETTITE,A	16	1	15	62.7	1	R2	2	
100	PICHARDO,H	8	1	7	47.8	105	R3		4
	average	2	1	1	51.3	70	1	2	2

How unstable are *these* pitchers? As a group. Individually, some of them look like they're on Pogo sticks, but as a group they exactly repeat the year before. Somehow, at this level of ineptitude, that seems more surprising than at other levels.

Just to prove this is not rigged, explain again why Villone is a ahead of Assenmacher?

Sure. Villone's average salary in the appendix is $1, Assenmacher's is 67 cents. Anyway, what's to rig? We're going to look at every last pitcher until there's nothing left to look at.

```
12 lowest salaries, AL pitchers
                  earned avg         Heath Data      - touts -
        AL pitchers 1995  sal  +/-    Pts    Rk       AP   JH   $94
101 TAVAREZ,J        26    1   25    54.2    36       R1         -4
102 VAN POPPEL,T      6    1    5    48.9    99       R2        -12
103 WHITESIDE,M      11    1   10    52.2    63       R3         -1
104 BELINDA,S        26    0   26    58.7     7        1    6     1
105 BERGMAN,S        -8    0   -9    50.6    86       R2          0
106 DARWIN,D        -18    0  -18    45.4   121       R3    3    -5
107 GROOM,B         -11    0  -12    53.3    51       R3          3
108 GUBICZA,M        24    0   24    53.8    42        1    4    10
109 LEITER,A         16    0   16    52.3    60        1         -5
110 LILLIQUIST,D     -1    0   -2    50.8    81       R3          2
111 RADINSKY,S       -2    0   -2    45.8   118       R1
112 TIMLIN,M         15    0   14    56.5    17        2         -1
        average       7    0    7    51.9    65        0    1    -1
```

There's still more riff-raff after this in the appendix: players, like Timlin, who were bought by one team, but these are the ones who were on the opening rosters of at least 10 Heath leagues — and thus are tracked — and who were bought by at least one team in Appendix A, and thus have average salaries.

It's a wonderful group, moving from the red in '94 to a solid $7 last year, all for an average salary of 42 cents. And the teams that bought them don't quite finish at .500.

You saying that losers wait until the very end to pick a pitcher?

Could be. Could be. What do you think?

You could look at it like that. You could also say there's still good stuff here at the end. Better stuff than in the two previous groups. Hell, better than in the $6 group, if I remember right.

Oh, you do. Let's just throw it all together and step back and look.

```
              avg earned          Heath Data
NL pitchers   sal  1995  +/-      Pts    Rk   "lg"
Nos.   1-10    30    34    4      54.8    36    3
Nos.  11-20    22    19   -3      52.8    53    5
Nos.  21-30    16     4  -12      52.2    65    6
Nos.  31-40    11     8   -3      51.5    67    6
Nos.  41-50     8    11    3      52.5    58    5
Nos.  51-60     6     1   -5      50.0    82    8
Nos.  61-70     3     2   -1      52.2    63    6
Nos.  71-80     3    12    9      54.7    37    3
Nos.  81-90     1     2    1      50.1    84    8
Nos.  91-100    1     2    1      51.3    70    7
Nos. 101-112    0     7    7      51.9    65    6
       sum    101   102    1       574   680   63
       avg      9     9    0        52    62    6
```

What do you think?

It's kind of blurry. I think I've had enough of this.

Hang in there. One more inning.

First of all, I've switched it so that the average salary is first. We clearly see a gradual descent from paying good money for the first ten pitchers to paying zilch for the last twelve. It's nice and orderly because that's the way we've ordered it.

Then we have what the pitchers earned. This isn't orderly. It bumps its way down to $1, rallies, falls, then rallies at the very end.

You there?

I hear you.

For the Heath trackings, just to give you something you can relate to, I've added how each group would finish in a 12-team league. There are 129 pitchers who are tracked altogether, so if the average rank for one group is 36, the conversion is 36/129 x 12 = a third place finish in a 12-team league.
  That doesn't grab you, huh?

It did when you first explained it. After the fiftieth time, it gets kind of tired.

Well, excuse me.
  Okay, maybe I should have just shown you this chart — skip all the supporting detail — even though I'm the type who likes to see it. Then maybe it would pop out at you.
  For the first 50 most expensive pitchers, are there big losses or big profits?

Big losses.

For the first 50 most expensive pitchers, what's the worst that any group finishes?

Sixth. I can't get as excited about that as you do.

My, we are getting cranky. I suppose you'd like to finish eighth, eighth and seventh, like three of the other groups? Two of them despite the fact that they turn profits.

We went over that. That's what you say; it may not be what Benson says.

After I've balanced the books for you? Why don't you just kick dirt on me and be done with it. I can't impress you.

Balanced what books?

How much did these pitchers cost? In real life. How much did they earn? In my formulas. That's called balancing the books.

Hey, that's pretty neat. No kidding? You get within one dollar overall? That's amazing. Wait until I tell my partner.
  There's no tricks? Because he's going to spot them if there are.

None whatever, the only thing you might tell him is that I've rounded off the numbers putting together the summary. For both average salary and earned 1995 the totals are probably a little high, but high equally.

I hand it to you.
  Does that mean — Benson's books can't balance?

'Fraid so.

Don't hand me that — you love it.

Not really. John's very good at gathering information; that's his passion. He's not into pricing.

Frankly, I bug him about it just because it would be so easy to correct. I ragged him until he finally dropped his optimal bids (almost), and I'll keep ragging him until he nudges his prices up. Everyone has a mission.

Wake up, please. I have one last thing to show you.

What time is it? Where am I?

It's almost time to go home. But we haven't quite come to the real reason I did all this. In the summary — see the average points that all the groups combined get?

Yeah, it's 52, just like you said it would be.

It's not, though. When we open the decimals up, we actually get 52.2 points. That is not possible. Jerry Heath, as I've said, does not make mistakes. So what's going on?

All right, I'll tell you. We stopped counting after 112 pitchers, but there are those 17 more that add up to 129. The three leagues in Appendix A took a pass, but a minimum of ten Heath leagues opened the season with them, and they are tracked, and this is how those pitchers, and their teams, fared:

AL pitchers	earned 1995	avg sal	+/-	Heath Data Pts	Rk	- touts - AP	JH	$94
AUSANIO,J	-3			47.0	110	R2	5	-11
DOHERTY,J	5			47.0	111	1		2
EICHHORN,M				54.3	33	R2		26
ESHELMAN,V	3			53.6	48			
GRIMSLEY,J	-8			49.0	97	R3	3	4
GUTHRIE,M	4			45.7	119	R3		-3
HELLING,R	-4			46.7	112	R2		-3
KARSAY,S				54.6	30	4	11	7
KIEFER,M	9			50.8	82	R2		-4
LILLIQUIST,D	-1			50.8	81	R3		2
MCDOWELL,R	13			44.9	125	1	5	-9
MOORE,M	-30			45.3	122	1	2	0
PENNINGTON,B	-3			45.8	116	R3	4	
SANDERSON,S	3			46.0	114	1		10
STEWART,D	-14			45.0	124	3		-8
WELLS,B	-6			50.3	90	R2		2
WILLIAMS,Mit	-6			45.8	117	3	2	-6
average	-2			48.4	96	1	2	0

It's as if the very first group has been flipped on its head: the market's 17 *least* coveted pitchers (that a few teams still are forced to buy) are as predictably awful.

Well, they're not even that awful, most of them. They are predictably what they are, and yet the damage is considerable! Even though they virtually cost nothing (an average salary in 45 Heath leagues of less than $1) and only lose $2, they have a far, far worse winning percentage than any other group of pitchers. (And this, believe me, is the last group.) Only Mike Moore and Dave Stewart aren't innocuous, and yet teams that open the season with even one pitcher from this list of rejects finish ninth.

How do we explain that?

Is there a certain personality type that is attracted to pitchers that nobody else will have anything to do with?

Hello?

Huh? Attracted to who? Don't go poking into my personal life. Do I ask you why your phone's been disconnected?

I think we're done. Don't you?

Done? No way! I was taking a rest while you did your thing. I've got a bunch of questions I still have to ask you!

Sorry. While you were napping I used up the rest of the pages.

Oh, come on!

In fact, I have to use one more up.

Maybe if I had gotten onto this train in the player comments, I could have followed it through to a conclusion for all the other top-10 salaries lists — that's how important I think it is — but it's too late now. However, I should at least show the next ten players in each group.

Second 10 highest salaries, NL pitchers

		earned	avg		Heath Data		- touts -		
rk	NL pitchers	1995	sal	+/-	Pts	Rk	AP	JH	$94
11	AVERY,S	5	22	-18	49.0	87	21	26	16
12	GLAVINE,T	28	22	6	46.4	108	15	21	10
13	HENKE,T	38	22	16	49.6	82	24	23	22
14	NEN,R	20	21	-1	57.9	18	14	18	27
15	FASSERO,J	3	20	-17	47.5	97	10	25	26
16	BENES,Andy	1	19	-18	48.5	90	17	18	16
17	MARTINEZ,PJ	27	19	8	58.9	9	21	26	29
18	BRANTLEY,J	34	19	15	55.7	31	20	17	31
19	HUDEK,J	6	17	-11	53.8	47	25	15	20
20	SMOLTZ,J	24	17	7	52.0	58	17	15	10
	average	19	20	-1	51.9	63	18	20	21

The top 10 are in the Beck comment. Those pitchers earned $21, so were only marginally better (while both were very good); since they cost $8 more, they incur bigger losses. But those teams do significantly better (56.1 points).

Draw your own conclusions.

Well, in the first place —

Next. (You had your chance.)

Second 10 highest salaries, NL hitters

		earned	avg		Heath Data		- touts -		
	Name	1995	sal	+/-	Pts	Rk	AP	JH	$94
11	SANDERS,R	44	31	13	60.6	8	28	31	26
12	JEFFERIES,G	21	31	-9	47.7	150	35	32	30
13	PIAZZA,M	39	31	8	61.4	5	40	30	35
14	JUSTICE,D	19	30	-11	44.8	174	32	28	26
15	BICHETTE,D	54	30	24	61.0	6	39	26	45
16	BIGGIO,C	37	29	8	56.1	25	35	29	40
17	GWYNN,T	41	29	12	55.2	36	30	29	41
18	MONDESI,R	35	29	6	60.7	7	27	23	29
19	BELL,De	35	27	7	59.7	9	31	27	35
20	CORDERO,W	16	26	-10	50.4	111	24	26	29
	average	34	29	5	55.8	53	32	28	34

This group has a much better winning percentage than the ten most expensive hitters (Bonds comment); not surprising, since it earns $4 more than that group. A $5 profit on a $29 hitter is phenomenal. Teams that buy them finish easily in the money, between third and fourth (53/180 x 12).

So maybe you should —

Next.

Second 10 highest salaries, AL hitters

rk	Name	earned 1995	avg sal	+/-	Heath Data Pts	Rk	- touts - AP	JH	$94
11	MOLITOR,P	18	31	-14	53.6	60	37	29	41
12	PUCKETT,K	30	31	-1	52.6	79	32	29	35
13	KNOBLAUCH,C	44	31	13	56.9	13	32	32	35
14	SALMON,T	39	30	9	57.5	9	32	22	22
15	O'NEILL,P	25	28	-3	52.8	75	32	22	37
16	CURTIS,C	27	28	0	60.6	3	20	23	21
17	SIERRA,R	18	28	-10	51.5	109	30	24	25
18	RAMIREZ,M	34	27	7	54.5	38	29	21	17
19	ANDERSON,B	23	27	-4	54.8	35	28	21	26
20	FRYMAN,T	18	27	-9	46.2	188	27	21	18
	average	28	29	-1	54.1	61	30	24	28

This group brings 96 cents on the dollar, and that's obviously — at least, circumstantially — good enough, because we have another great winning percentage. There are more AL Heath leagues (as well as more hitters in the AL), so the average rank of 61 is almost as good (61/195 x 12 = 3.7).

As in the NL, this second most expensive group of hitters outperforms the highest paid group (Canseco comment). In both leagues, the 10 most expensive pitchers were better — in the AL, decisively better — than the next 10 most expensive pitchers.

Can I?

Feel free.

It's a big drop down to these second hitter groups. Instead of almost $40, you get them at under $30. So maybe that's the play: let the big tickets go by and jump in here.

Well, there's no doubt that's what people were trying to do in Baseball Weekly. The one thing Peter and I swore we wouldn't do this time was price-enforce anyone, and sure enough, when Bonds was the first or second player nominated, the bidding limped to a halt at $43. Can you imagine? But we bit our tongues, because last year, in our first attempt at the Sweeney Plan, we found ourselves suddenly in possession of Bonds for $46. We looked at each other. We were just humble pilgrims from the AL, but was this room for real? We rationalized that Bonds would fit half of the Sweeney Plan, and then would turn into the best pitcher in the league when we found out who that was.

That's when Olbermann wouldn't trade with you?

Right. I know one person who didn't send you here is Keith. He wouldn't argue with the Maddux price, either year. He's the first person who realized that Barry Bonds was no longer the man in the NL.

But look at the first five tiers of hitter salaries, broken down by leagues, to see that, even if leagues start out different, they quickly end up the same.

Most expensive NL hitters

Name	earned 1995	avg sal	+/-	- leagues - BW	HSS	IOC
Nos. 1-10	30	37	-7	35	39	37
Nos. 11-20	34	29	5	28	31	29
Nos. 21-30	22	24	-2	24	24	25
Nos. 31-40	21	20	1	20	20	21
Nos. 41-50	17	17	-1	18	17	17

If you're in that Baseball Weekly auction, would you rather spend $18 for a $17 player or $35 for a $30 player?

Me, I'd pick $28 for $34. I keep seeing that sweet spot.

I keep seeing Stage Three hell. But the answer to that, for some mysterious reason, is $35 for a $30 player.

What's so mysterious about it? You get better stats?

No, $20 worth of stats should be exactly half of $40 worth of stats, the way I price things. But they may not be. In the retrospective draft that we're going to hold, I'll be getting the $40 players — until I can't afford them — so it will be very interesting.

One thing I noticed: you pay $42 for Albert Belle in this retrospective draft, there's no risk involved. You get your $4 profit and wait for the next player. You get Randy Johnson for — my guess is, $49 — and you walk off with $9. Again no risk.

That's what I figure. When push comes to shove, these other guys are going to push their prices for Johnson from the low 40's to the high 40's, and it still won't be enough. I'm going to get bigger profits on a few players than they do with all their scrubs combined, and even though it will be close — it has to be — that should be my edge.

Relax. Don't worry about it. It's going to be a cakewalk.

It is?

But you're still not answering the question. We shelled out $47 for Griffey last year — no problem — so when he crashed, so did we. In that league.

I see. Very clever.
    What you're saying is absolutely right. The more money you put in one player, the more you're at risk. That's why there's this strong resistance to spending full value for the best players. It's not that people are looking for profits, necessarily; it's that, after a certain point, they simply get scared.
    Chatting with Hunt after the auction, I said, "Could you believe that price for Bonds?" I could hear him shaking his head. "It's an awful lot of money to spend on one player," said John.

You saying Hunt's a chicken?

Not at all! He's the one guy in the league who won't hesitate to trade. Hunt's as wily as they come. He sits, and he waits, and he waits, and he lets good bargains go by until he gets a *great* bargain. The most he spent on any player was $30.

For who?

Galarraga. Now don't go getting retrospective on me, that's a great price. Notice in Appendix A Scrooge's froze him for $33. And that's exactly what he earned in a bad year. In the Bonds comment you saw him ranked 39th out of 180 hitters in the Heath trackings.

The deal I noticed was Piazza being number 13 on the salary scale.

Isn't that unbelievable? In Baseball Weekly, Stu Baron paid $32 for him, and that's higher than his average salary! Nuts. The way Peter and I had it divided, I had $100 to buy the hitters, and for a second I almost convinced myself Piazza's batting average would be worth $33 to us.

If anyone still isn't sure what position scarcity is all about, check out how Piazza's teams did; you could say that by ranking fifth out of 180 hitters, he played on teams that finished beyond first (5/180 x 12 = .33).

So why couldn't you and Golenbock just play it straight? Why do the Sweeney Plan and have to skip all these bargains?

Maybe we should have. But if we had, the trick would have been picking the best one. When Bonds went for $43, I would have sworn all the straight players in the room — in this case, on the speaker phone — would have jumped all over Piazza, because of scarcity, but they didn't. The truth is that many of these experts, who definitely do know baseball, were playing straight Rotisserie for only the second time. So in a way it was a Stage Two auction. You can see it throughout the Appendix: $18 for Cedeno, $23 for Floyd, $17 for Rondell White, $18 for Todd Jones — it's a combination of too much money still left to spend and wanting to have something to boast about in touting circles.

Don't I see $29 next to Floyd under AP?

Yep. That's what's so much fun about the Sweeney Plan. You let everyone else take the chances. You're in your own little room, completely bullet proof.

I wonder if you'd be saying that if something happened to Maddux.

At the auction — of course you can be torpedoed by events. During the bidding, you have your own set of values, and they are so far apart from anyone else's that whatever they do doesn't affect you, and you have this soothing sense that they are destroying each other.

Better explain exactly how it works. For your new readers. Your old ones I bet are getting pretty sick of it.

I'm sure they are. But understand that this is the first time I've actually tried the plan myself; the rest has been all talk. It's named for Hugh Sweeney, who himself stole the idea from Bruce Buschel. This was back in the late 80's; all the tricks that I had played on the American Dreams League — buying nothing but hitting, buying nothing but relief pitchers, punting stolen bases — had run their course, many of them no longer options because of changes in the rules.

Who'd you steal these ideas from?

No one. Others were undoubtedly thinking them up at the same time, but back in those frontier days, with a little imagination and daring, you could work an angle that definitely stacked the deck in your favor. Unlike real baseball there is no difference between finishing last and good and last in any category. Anyway, Sweeney got the idea from Buschel that you could punt *two* categories and still end up with 74 points. That's enough to finish in the money, guaranteed, and if you're lucky you might even finish first. Sweeney picked the nine pitchers he wanted, bought his batting average and speed, and fortunately for us jogged off into the sunset for the entire season; without making one roster move, he finished fifth.

That told us something and we put in a minimum-AB rule. For the inaugural draft two years ago, the first thing Peter called into the speaker phone was, "Hey, John, is there a there a minimum IP rule?" Yes, there was. "Is there a minimum AB rule?" No there wasn't. And we were off.

So last year wasn't the first time.

We were foiled by the strike. We had unfinished business.

How'd you do that year? I noticed you didn't tell us when you were saying how everyone else finished.

Sixth. I was pretty sure I could save it for when you got up here. How'd you find me, anyway?

Up where? Where are we?

Very close to the end.

In the auction we spent $157 for our pitchers: Maddux $36, Hoffman $35, Saberhagen $24, Brantley $21, Astacio $14, Ruffin $14, Ashby $10, Cooke $2, Josias Manzanillo $1.

Our hitters were: Stinnett $2, Decker $1, Treadway $1, Vizcaino $2, Branson $1, Phil Clark $1, Magadan $1, Aude $1, Gwynn $26, Butler $22, Carr $19, Darren Lewis $18, Lous Frazier $3, and Dwight Smith $1.

You had $3 left over.

I know; we screwed up. (How'd you figure that out so quick?) And if we had taken a hike like Sweeney, we would have finished with nowhere near 74 points. In the hypothetical final standings — the standings calculated strictly from the draft rosters, no changes — we finished fourth with 60.5 points.

Most of all, you were short of SB.

That's right . . . Yes, that is exactly right. Peter did his job. He nailed down ERA and ratio —

Maddux did.

Peter and Maddux nailed down the qualitatives, and the only reason we were second in saves is that Mike Vogel bought two closers plus Heathcliffe Slocumb. We were tied for fourth in wins in the hypotheticals, but were only seven wins out of first.

We had a .278 batting average, which would have put us in fifth. But that could be corrected easily. People like Stinnett and Aude were bought on spec; if they failed to gain trade value, we simply ditched them.

Steals were a problem. In June we finally had to trade Saberhagen to Hunt for Bip Roberts, and that didn't work out for either side. Then we picked up Fonville on waivers in June. Peter fixed up the rest of it in late July when he traded Phil Clark to Shandler for Cangelosi.

For wins, we just kept buying starting pitchers with our $100 until one of them was Isringhausen.

Vogel finally unloaded one of his relievers to shore up his own starting pitching. In the last week we passed him in both batting average and SB to at least make him feel the heat. He won by a point and a half.

But since you got your maximum of 74 points, you don't beat Vogel unless someone else helps you.

True. The Sweeney Plan only works in competitive leagues, but in Stage Three, leagues are very competitive. Just running through the final standings in Heath leagues... we would have tied for first in Lookout Bush, finished second (by one point) in Washington Ghost, finished third in Pioneer Valley, second in Elizabeth River Bush, third in Blackie's, tied for second in LABR-NL — wait, that's us — finished third in Victor, third in Hot Pepper, second in Big Bamboo, second in The New Pew, second in Hennessy's, second in Hollywoods Stars, first in Artful Dodgers, tied for first in Scrooge's, first in Senior Circuit (by seven points *there's* a great league), and tied for third in the Belmar Senior League.

In AL leagues, we would have finished first in the American Dreams, third in Lone Star, second in the Dirty Dozen, third in Beizbol, second in Connecticut Valley, second in LABR-AL (what is Rotisserie Sports Hour? They got 78.5 points), first in Metropolitan, first in Red Rose, second in South Main Street, second in Garden State, third in Sour Grapefruit, first in Baker's Dozen, third in Cowtown, tied for first in Dewey Bush, first in America's Best, second in Don Zimmer, tied for first in McGoom, second in Wolverine, second in Stoverot, first in Hart-Quale, first in Ashpole, second in Earwiggers, third in Soda Jerks, second in Lonesome Glove, and third in Doghouse.

Did I name any of yours?

Uh-uh. You really think that's going to sell some books? I don't.

What else haven't we covered?

How did the Moose do?

Eighth. What else?

Can't we hear your excuses?

Don't really have any. Bill and I had a great time in Florida, and then just didn't get it done at the draft.

Didn't have a trick?

We drove all over Florida trying to think one up. The best we could think of was buy a good pitching staff — overspend on pitching — and then buy nothing but risky hitters, prospects, people like Shawn Green and Ray Durham, for about $130; and see what happens. The problem was, we bumped into another team that was doing the same thing. Green, Durham, Cordova, Delgado — we destroyed each other.

You get Delgado?

No, a third team insisted on Delgado. It was a mess. Very unsightly. Other teams were punting steals, others saves — I think we've reached the terminal phase of Stage Three in the American Dreams.

Ah, go out and win it this year; you'll feel different. Who did win?

Mark Starr and Ron Givens of Nova. With the Sweeney Plan. Not only that, as I said, another team was hell bent on the same thing. Plus they had to get the at-bats. They were forced to pay $38 for Knoblauch, $29 for Nixon; they paid $27 for Jack McDowell, $13 for Eldred, $15 for Duane Ward, and they still won.

Does anybody play it straight in your league?

At least four teams did. That's enough to cancel each other out right there.

Like my partner says, a bunch of clowns.

Serious clowns. The best kind. We done?

Let me check your notes.

You know the one thing that maybe hasn't been said about Maddux? Everybody talks about what a great fielder he is, but nobody's mentioned that after each and every pitch he takes a little hop, like he's receiving serve in tennis. You ever notice?

I don't watch tennis. Uh-oh, here's a big one. Inflation.

Too big. No room for it this year.

You sure? It's pretty important.

Hugely important. You can see it very plainly in the two freeze-list leagues in Appendix A. Inflation actually can cause overpriced freezes (look at Barry Bonds) and there are a variety of ways of figuring it: based on what you think the frozen players are going to earn this year, on what they did earn last year, on what some neutral party predicts they'll earn this year.

I'm not trying to start anything again, but wouldn't Benson maybe be better than you for that?

Absolutely. You want conservative estimates of inflation; you don't want to get into bidding wars just because there's a lot of extra money to spend. That's how it disappears. On the other hand, if you don't push the prices hard enough to hurt whoever has the best freeze list, you're giving the season away.

    Underpriced keepers have become the scourge of the game. They're great to have, but only one team can have the best ones, and that leverage is the single biggest factor in winning: more important than predicting, pricing, scouting, trading or even luck. Leagues have gotten so tough that even the sharpest owners don't have a better than one-in-six chance of winning on a level field; realizing this, many of them plan their fire sales even before the season has begun, reasoning if they play for every other year, they might win two out of six.

What's your keeper situation for this year?

Not good. Three teams fire saled.

No wonder you're bummed. Want to look at one of my lists? I've got some good ones.

Maybe next year. When I'm sure you'll have some more.

    Maybe next year I'll do an analysis of what built-in profits teams took to the draft, and how they finished.

I wish you wouldn't.

Why, in how many of your leagues did you bag it this year?

    We do get shy, don't we?

    Calculating the inflation factor is critical and it's complicated. What I would suggest readers do is simply buy my software program.

Details in the PS.

Correct. And when they do that, and enter the freezes in their league, they'll see some shockingly inflated prices for the remaining players.

    But they don't really need a software program. All they need is bids.

What do you mean?

Just make your bid prices and keeper prices add up to $3,120; it's as simple as that. If someone's got Jose Mesa for $3, and if he's the only keeper in the league, you make your bid prices add up to $3,117. Spread among 275 other players, it will ease some of the pain. But you still won't beat whoever has Mesa.

One little keeper?

One big keeper. Come on, you know that. You're putting me on.

Sometimes I have to ask questions for your new readers.

There won't be any if we don't close this up. Time to go now. Thanks for the help.

You won't let me see any of the predictions?

They haven't been done yet. That's why it's time to go.

I have to tell you something before I go.

Okay, but be quick.

My partner buys your prices. He knows they're right.

Bully for him. I've really got to move on. Would you mind?
    Why the hell did you bug me with all those questions?

It was my partner's idea. He said you've really got to push him on these prices because he doesn't seem to know how different they are.

You think I don't look at the competition? Tell your partner thanks a lot. We just wasted the entire Q&A.

No, we didn't! See, a lot of people who read your book don't even look at the numbers. Or they're like me: they pick out the ones they like. They tune out. They're missing the point.

Which is what, exactly?

Like you said at he end of last year's book... I'm sure no one paid attention because it just depresses them... Right now is an age of greatness.

It is, isn't it?
    That's the real tragedy of the last few years. Why did this colossal farce have to happen now?
    In 1994 baseball was at the all-time peak of its popularity *and* having its all-time greatest season. The owners hadn't figured out one little snag in the Basic Agreement — arbitration — otherwise what were the problems? Big markets/small markets? Total baloney. The big guys would have shared some of the loot if the *little guys* went on strike. If they suddenly had no one to play with. Revenue sharing was a smokescreen. A Jerry Reinsdorf-led faction of owners had only one thing on its mind: bust the union. Reinsdorf got all the owners together in a room, gave them a pep talk, then started passing around the Kool-Aid.
    What is it now?
    What are you pointing at your chest for? How come you're nodding your head?

That's what <u>we</u> need, a pep talk. Nobody cares about this stuff.

It's kind of hard to give one when there's still no agreement. When all these great performances have been utterly wasted. When some of the greatest performances we'll ever see were never seen. When the only place they're even recorded is in an obscure book like this.

You know what —?

That's it.

I feel a pep talk coming.

This — this right now — is Stage Four.

It exists? Stage Four exists?

It exists! It's Greg Maddux earning $68 after he earned $72. It's Albert Belle, with no speed, earning $46 in a big hitting year. It's Randy Johnson earning $58 and Jose Mesa $57 and Mike Mussina $50 when the tenth best pitcher earned, as usual, little more than $30. It's Dante Bichette returning a $24 profit on a $30 bet. It's Tony Gwynn earning $19 with his batting average alone. It's Randy Johnson earning $19 with his ratio! It's Maddux being worth $49 if he doesn't win a game. It's Barry Bonds struggling and even stumbling to a $43 season.

So where's Stage Four? I still don't see it.

Buy one of these players!

In Stage One, there really was no limit to what owners would pay. They just kept bidding until they got Eddie Murray or Jim Rice or Dale Murphy. No one had any qualms about paying $45 for any one of these players. The notion was, you had to buy one of the superstars, even if they weren't that exceptional.

People who stayed out of these fights cleaned up later on. In Stage Two, everyone tried to clean up later on, and that didn't work.

In Stage Three, the bidding for the superstars crept back up to $35, $40, in rare cases, even $45, and there it stopped. That was about as much as the best players earned in any pricing system. The risk factor caused bettors to stop short of paying quite the full amount. Things stayed like this for many years.

Then, all of a sudden, the best players got better.

It didn't happen in 1993; that was the year of the rabbit ball. The market sensed that the hitters' stats were cheap, and refused to pay more for these hitters in 1994.

I truly believe that not getting to see that particular season played out is one of the things that has hurt baseball most. To this day, we are in a kind of permanent denial over all the records that were going to be broken that season. In any event, the market was in no mood to go on spending sprees when last year finally got under way.

Last year doesn't quite make it into the archives, but considering how long the off-season was and how little time the players had to get ready, they did pretty well. More to the point, the best players continued to be far better than the best players used to be.

Stage Four may be just a temporary thing. It will last as long as the best players continue to be so extraordinary. But if they do, and if everyone else stays in Stage Three, there's your edge.

I'm getting into this. Instead of the Sweeney Plan, the Maddux Plan. I figure Maddux to earn $60 this year. He cost $36 last year. Stage Three is Stage Three: count on $38 this year, max. I top that, get him for $39. I've still got $39 more to spend on pitching before I reach $78. But I don't do that. I spend $20 divided like this: two $5 starters, two $5 relievers, and $10 spread over four of the safest pitchers I can find at the price. I stockpile starters in the reserve draft. From them I get a *starter to take the place of the $5 starter who blows up on me. Plus there's waivers. One way or the other, I get my 1000 innings, bag wins and saves, win ERA and ratio, and have $201 to sweep the hitting. That should do it. That's my Maddux Plan.*

There you go. Now I really do have to make these —

In the AL it's the Thomas Plan. I can think of at least three leagues where he won't cost more than —

Yo!

What?

I've got to make my predictions.

Right. Hey, want me to help? I've bought your program. I know how to use it. It's easy.

Thanks. And thanks for the plug. But I better do these myself. It's time for you to go home now.

How do I get there? Where do I go?

I don't know. But there's the door.

Thanks for everything. My partner says hi.

Hi.

So I'm off... But where's my...? Oh, God. Oh, Jesus...

Now what?

Didn't I see a lot of outlet stores coming through town?

Probably.

I gave my girlfriend my wallet and my credit cards are in it.

You better go find her.

I can't believe I did that.

I'm a little surprised you have a girlfriend.

Hey, I date. I date.
    But I'll tell you what: I totally agree with what that movie actor said. I don't put anything in writing. Not even, will you get some doughnuts on the way home. I get them myself.

Right. Good idea. Goodbye now.

Movie actor?

Appendix A
1995 Earnings and Predictions

American League Hitters

	earned avg			4/18 4/23 4/29 5/9 — leagues —					- touts -		$94
Name	1995	sal	+/-	BW	ADL	COW	ASH	f	AP	JH	$94
ALDRETE,M	4	0	4				1		1	2	2
ALEXANDER,M	5	0	5				1	2			
ALICEA,L	13	4	8	5	5	3	3		4	14	9
ALLANSON,A	-1										
ALOMAR,R	32	37	-6	36	36	40	43		38	32	24
ALOMAR,S	12	9	2	14	10	4	5	f	11	17	18
AMARAL,R	13	0	13	1			3		1	4	5
AMARO,R	0								R3		2
ANDERSON,B	23	27	-4	25	27	29	31		28	21	26
ANDERSON,G	24	1	23	1	2	1	6	f	2	3	1
BAERGA,C	30	35	-5	35	34	36	32	f	36	31	31
BAINES,H	21	10	11	9	10	10	14	f	16	11	17
BARBERIE,B	2	7	-5	9	6	6	7		7	9	13
BASS,K	6	0	6		1		1		2		13
BATTLE,H	0								R3		
BAUTISTA,D	0	2	-2	4	2	1	7	f	5	7	2
BECKER,R	3	4	-2	13					7	17	4
BELL,Dav	0								R2		
BELL,Juan	-1										5
BELLE,A	46	45	1	40	48	46	46	f	48	41	50
BELTRE,E	-1	0	-2		1				R3		3
BERROA,G	23	14	9	16	12	14	2	f	12	21	23
BLOWERS,M	19	5	14	7	4	3	3	f	7	17	13
BOGGS,W	19	16	3	17	13	17	15	f	18	18	25
BONILLA,B	15										24
BORDERS,P	1	4	-3	5	2	4	4		2	4	1
BORDICK,M	12	3	9	2	1	6	1		4	2	5
BRADY,D	0										
BRAGG,D	4	9	-5	7	8	13	6		4	10	-1
BRITO,B	0										
BROSIUS,S	12	1	11	1	1	1	6		2	4	8
BROWN,J	-1										0
BUECHELE,S	-1										10
BUFORD,D	-1	2	-3	1	2	3			2	8	0
BUHNER,J	28	23	5	21	27	22	25	f	26	16	19
BURNITZ,J	1								R2	3	2
CACERES,E	2										
CAMERON,M	-1										
CANSECO,J	26	36	-10	36	31	41	35	f	33	32	35
CARTER,J	20	31	-11	26	32	36	43	f	33	26	31
CEDENO,D	1										-2
CHAMBERLAIN,W	-2	1	-2		1	1			R4	3	5
CIRILLO,J	12	1	10	1	2	1	4		R2	3	1
CLARK,J	7						8		R3	8	
CLARK,T	1	0	1				1		R1	2	
CLARK,W	22	26	-4	24	27	27	32	f	29	29	29
COLE,A	5	12	-7	7	17	11	3	f	3	5	24
COLEMAN,V	27	0	26				1	27	R1		25

Name	1995	sal	+/-	BW	ADL	COW	ASH	f	AP	JH	$94
COOKSON,B	-1										
COOMER,R	4										
CORA,J	18	3	15	2	2	4	7		2	10	9
CORDOVA,M	29	15	15	14	18	12	19		17	14	
CORREIA,R	0										0
CRUZ,F	0								R3		-2
CURTIS,C	27	28	0	29	25	29	30		20	23	21
CUYLER,M	-1	1	-2	1	1				1	3	3
DALESANDRO,M	-1								R3		0
DAMON,J	8								R5		
DAVIS,C	27	20	7	19	15	26	11	f	19	26	31
DAVIS,R	2	1	1		2	1	6	f	R2		-1
DELGADO,C	-2	18	-19	19	24	10	10	f	14	14	4
DEVAREZ,Ce	0										
DEVEREAUX,M	17	7	10	8	4	10	14		1	3	-2
DIAZ,A	10						1		R3		3
DISARCINA,G	15	2	12	1	2	4			3		4
DONNELS,Ch	1										2
DUNN,S	-1								R3	3	0
DURHAM,R	14	19	-5	22	21	14	9		17	7	
EASLEY,D	0	7	-7	9	7	5	8		5	7	0
EDMONDS,J	30	6	24	7	6	5	10	f	7	5	9
EENHOORN,R	-1										0
ELSTER,K	-1										-3
ESPINOZA,A	2								R3		-1
FABREGAS,J	1						1		0		4
FELIX,J		1	-1			3			R1		17
FERMIN,F	-4	1	-5	1	2		1		3	3	14
FERNANDEZ,T	6	12	-6	15	10	11	11		8	10	18
FIELDER,C	16	25	-9	22	26	27	27		25	18	21
FLAHERTY,J	5	1	4	2		1	1		1	1	-2
FLETCHER,S	0	0	-1			1	1		R3		3
FLORA,K	0	3	-3	3	5	1			1	11	
FOX,E	-2								R3		0
FRAZIER,Lo	2										12
FRYE,J	7	3	4	4	4	1	10	f	5	11	11
FRYMAN,T	18	27	-9	24	26	30	19		27	21	18
GAETTI,G	24	4	20	5		7	1	f	5	4	15
GAGNE,G	7	6	1	8	3	6	6	f	7	11	12
GALLEGO,M	-1	4	-5	5	4	3	1		5	5	3
GARCIAPERRA,N	-1								R4		
GATES,B	6	11	-5	16	8	10	10	f	19	19	7
GIAMBI,J	5								R2		
GIBSON,K	11	5	5	6	3	7	7		9	10	22
GIL,B	1	4	-2	6	3	2	12		2	1	
GILES,B	2								R1		
GOMEZ,C	4	5	-2	8	3	5	10	f	8	8	11
GOMEZ,L	1	7	-6	14	6	1	5		15	13	14
GONZALES,R	1								R3		3
GONZALEZ,A	6	17	-11	18	17	16	16	f	11	6	-2
GONZALEZ,Ju	23	26	-2	30	23	24	35		31	25	23
GOODWIN,C	12	3	9	10					8	3	
GOODWIN,T	30	10	20	19	8	4	6		6	11	0
GREBECK,C	2						1		1	3	2
GREEN,S	15	16	-1	15	22	11	15	f	17	16	-2
GREENWELL,M	23	11	12	11	11	11	24	f	16	17	11

Appendix A — ALH

Name	1995	sal	+/-	BW	ADL	COW	ASH	f	AP	JH	$94
GREER,R	13	10	4	9	7	13	10	f	12	16	16
GRIFFEY,KJR	12	45	-33	42	51	42	51		52	41	45
GROTEWALD,J	1										
GUILLEN,O	4	5	-1	3	5	6	4		11	12	10
HALE,C	2	0	2		1				R3		1
HALL,J	-1								R3		3
HAMELIN,B	-3	22	-25	21	23	22	12	f	19	24	23
HAMILTON,D	12	16	-4	15	15	17	28	f	11	16	3
HAMMONDS,J	4	14	-10	15	16	10	10	f	12	14	13
HARE,S	0								1		-1
HARPER,B	-1	5	-6	1	9	5			R1		8
HASELMAN,B	3	0	2		1		1		R3	1	-1
HATCHER,B	-1										2
HATTEBERG	0										
HELFAND,E	-3								0		0
HENDERSON,R	28	26	2	29	26	24	27		22	22	15
HERRERA,J	0								R5		
HIATT,P	0	1	0	1	1		1		2	2	
HIGGINSON,B	6	6	0	8	3	7	4		11	17	
HOCKING,D	0	1	-1	2					2	8	2
HOILES,C	12	17	-5	17	18	16	25		17	13	12
HOLLINS,Dv	-1										2
HORN,S	-1										
HOSEY,D	7	2	5	5					9	12	
HOWARD,D	2								0		2
HUDLER,R	11	1	10			2			2	4	9
HUFF,M	0	0	-1	1					R3	5	9
HULSE,D	10	2	8	2	4	1	5		2	1	10
HUSON,J	3	0	3		1				R3		
INGRAM,R	0										0
JAHA,J	21	8	14	6	2	15	10	f	8	13	7
JAMES,C	2								2		4
JAMES,D	7								R2	6	
JAVIER,S	27	16	10	17	15	17	10	f	14	18	23
JEFFERSON,R	6	1	5		2	1	7	f	11	10	12
JETER,D	0	4	-3	3		8			R1		
JOHNSON,L	36	24	12	20	29	22	20	f	21	19	23
JORDAN,R		2	-2	2	3				2	14	10
JOSE,F	-2	10	-11	1	18	10	19	f	R1		22
JOYNER,W	22	15	8	13	17	14	18		18	19	19
KARKOVICE,R	5	3	2	4	2	3	5	f	4	2	2
KELLY,P	5	8	-4	10	5	10	7		7	10	11
KIRBY,W	2	3	-1		6	2			2	9	13
KNOBLAUCH,C	44	31	13	27	38	28	14	f	32	32	35
KNORR,R	0	2	-2	2	1	3	3		2	3	4
KREUTER,C	0	2	-2	2	2	1	1		2		-1
KRUK,John	6								R1		14
LAVALLIERE,M	1	0	1		1		1		1	2	4
LAWTON,Mat	3										
LEIUS,S	4	3	1	4	1	3	1	f	7	8	9
LEVIS,J	1	1	0		1	1			R3		0
LEYRITZ,J	7	10	-3	11	8	11	10		9	13	14
LIND,J	-1	0	-2	1			2		2	3	8
LISTACH,P	2	12	-11	10	10	17	11		5	11	2
LOCKHART,K	15										1
LOFTON,K	40	49	-9	46	55	45	55		51	49	61

Name	1995	sal	+/-	BW	ADL	COW	ASH	f	AP	JH	$94
LORETTA,Ma	1										
LYONS,Barr	4										
MAAS,K	-1	1	-2	1		1			2	6	
MACFARLANE,M	6	12	-6	15	11	11	17	f	14	12	10
MAHAY,R	0										
MALDONADO,C	7						1				1
MANTO,J	9	0	9			1			R2		
MARTIN,N	5	0	4		1				R3	5	5
MARTINEZ,An	1										
MARTINEZ,C	-1										
MARTINEZ,D	14	0	14		1				2	4	4
MARTINEZ,E	42	17	26	16	18	16	32		21	22	17
MARTINEZ,T	29	19	10	18	17	21	27		20	18	15
MARZANO,J	0										
MASTELLER	1										
MATHENY,M	2								0		-1
MATTINGLY,D	11	15	-4	16	13	16	22		17	18	14
MAY,D	0	8	-8	10	9	6	3		15	14	15
MAYNE,B	1	1	-1		1	3	2		1	1	3
MCCARTY,D	-1	1	-2	1	1	1	3		R2		2
MCGEE,W	6								R3		9
MCGINNIS,R	-1										
MCGWIRE,M	27	20	7	16	21	22	31	f	18	11	6
MCLEMORE,M	14	8	6	7	8	10	1		3	9	13
MEARES,P	14	1	13	1	1	2	1	f	1	6	6
MERCEDES,H	1										
MERULLO,M	4	0	4		1		3		R3		-1
MIESKE,M	9	3	6	3	3	3	12		5	12	9
MILLER,K	1	0	1		1						-1
MOLITOR,P	18	31	-14	28	35	31	30	f	37	29	41
MOTA,Jose	0										
MOUTON,L	8								R3		
MUNOZ,P	18	10	8	13	10	6	14		11	14	12
MURRAY,E	29	14	15	13	14	14	26	f	18	12	18
MYERS,G	7	1	5	3		1	1	f	1		0
NAEHRING,T	16	7	9	10	6	5	15		9	10	9
NEVIN,Phil	0										
NEWFIELD,M	0	2	-2	6		1			R1		-1
NEWSON,W	4						1		R3		1
NILSSON,D	12	13	-1	18	12	9	5		18	14	15
NIXON,O	33	25	7	24	29	23	26	f	19	19	26
NOKES,M	-2	5	-7	6	6	4	2	f	4	5	6
NORMAN,Les	0										
NUNALLY,J	10								R4		
OBANDO,S	1	4	-4	6	6	1	2		4	12	
OLERUD,J	13	27	-14	29	28	23	31		31	25	19
OLIVER,J	12	1	11	1	1	1	7			1	1
ORTIZ,L	1								R2	6	0
OWEN,S	1						1	f	2		12
O'LEARY,T	17	1	16	1	1	1			R3		2
O'NEILL,P	25	28	-3	24	29	31	25	f	32	22	37
PAGLIARULO,M	1								R3		
PALMEIRO,O	1										
PALMEIRO,R	37	32	5	30	36	30	27	f	34	28	33
PALMER,D	10	19	-9	19	23	16	23		22	16	13
PAQUETTE,C	8						1		R3		-3
PARRISH,L	-1	1	-2			3	1				4

Name	1995	sal	+/-	BW	ADL	COW	ASH	f	AP	JH	$94
PEMBERTON,R	1	0	0			1	3		R3		
PENA,T	5						1		0		3
PENN,S	0	1	-1		4				R2	6	
PEREZ,E	-2	4	-6	6	2	3	5		5	6	2
PEREZ,R	-1								R3		-1
PEREZ,Toma	0										
PERRY,H	7								R2		-1
PHILLIPS,T	21	14	8	12	10	19	24	f	20	17	25
PIRKL,G	0	0	-1		1				R2		4
POLONIA,L	6	18	-13	18	17	20	9		13	17	22
POZO,A	0								R2		
PUCKETT,K	30	31	-1	28	31	35	30	f	32	29	35
RAABE,Bria	0										
RAINES,T	21	17	3	15	21	16	19		20	15	17
RAMIREZ,M	34	27	7	24	30	28	20	f	29	21	17
RANDA,J	-2	0	-2		1				1	3	
REBOULET,J	6	0	6			1	1		0		3
REED,JO		0	0	1					R2		8
RHODES,Kar	-2										0
RIPKEN,B	2								0		3
RIPKEN,C	15	21	-6	19	21	22	21		26	16	24
RIVERA,R	0								R5		
RODRIGUEZ,A	4	3	0	10					R1	5	0
RODRIGUEZ,C	1						5		R3		4
RODRIGUEZ,I	18	20	-2	23	21	16	22		18	22	22
RODRIGUEZ,S	-1										
ROWLAND,R	-1	1	-2	1	1				2	3	4
SABO,C	2	12	-11	12	10	15	22	f	10	17	9
SALMON,T	39	30	9	26	30	34	20	f	32	22	22
SAMUEL,J	11	1	10	1	1	1			R2		10
SCHOFIELD,D	0								R3		7
SEITZER,K	18	6	12	7	5	7	8	f	5	11	15
SHUMPERT,T	1	7	-6	7	10	4	3	f	7	8	13
SIERRA,R	18	28	-10	26	30	27	38	f	30	24	25
SILVESTRI,D	-1								R3		-1
SINGLETON,D	-2	0	-3	1					R3		0
SMITH,MA	2								R3		0
SNOPEK,C	3								R3		
SNOW,JT	25	4	21	1	1	11	16	f	4	10	1
SOJO,L	11	0	11			1	1		2	4	7
SORRENTO,P	15	9	6	1	11	16	27		14	12	15
SPRAGUE,E	10	7	3	9	3	10	13		5	10	5
STAHOVIAK,S	5	0	5	1					2		
STAIRS,M	2								R3		
STANLEY,M	17	18	-2	19	21	15	1	f	19	19	19
STEINBACH,T	15	11	3	13	10	11	9	f	13	13	15
STEVERSON	2								R3		
STEWART,S	0								R4		
STRANGE,D	3								R3		-1
STRAWBERRY	3								R1		3
STUBBS,F	2						1			3	
STYNES,C	-1								R2		
SURHOFF,B	24	5	19	7	7	1	7		4	6	4
SWEENEY,Mi	0										
TACKETT,J		0	0	1					R3	4	1
TARTABULL,D	3	18	-15	16	17	22	34		15	16	14

Name	1995	sal	+/-	BW	ADL	COW	ASH	f	AP	JH	$94
TETTLETON,M	16	18	-2	17	15	22	26		17	9	10
THOMAS,F	37	45	-8	43	50	42	50		50	39	46
THOME,J	27	25	2	25	28	22	20	f	27	26	16
THURMAN,G	3										
TINGLEY,R	1								0		-1
TINSLEY,L	17	10	7	11	7	13	1	f	5	7	6
TOMBERLIN,A	2								R3		0
TRAMMELL,A	4	6	-2	12	2	4	5		5	10	8
TREMIE,Chr	-1										
TUCKER,M	3	7	-4	3	6	12	10		6	9	
TUCKER,Sco	-2										
TURNER,C	-1	1	-1	1	1				1	1	1
UNROE,T	0								R1		
VALENTIN,JOH	37	15	22	16	17	12	24		20	17	18
VALENTIN,JOS	10	9	1	11	10	7	1		9	10	12
VALLE,D	0								1	1	0
VAN SLYKE,A	-1	7	-8	1	6	15	19				6
VARITEK,J		0	0			1			R4		
VAUGHN,G	11	20	-9	20	17	23	29	f	12	19	17
VAUGHN,M	41	33	8	31	34	33	46	f	35	31	31
VELARDE,R	11	2	9	3	4		6		4	10	11
VENTURA,R	27	26	1	22	26	29	24		27	20	21
VINA,F	5	0	5		1				R3	4	1
VITIELLO,J	4	1	3		3				2	7	
VIZQUEL,O	20	7	13	8	5	9	4	f	4	10	11
VOIGT,J	-1	0	-1			1			R3		2
WALBECK,M	4	2	2	3	1	2	5	f	1	3	-4
WARD,T	6	2	4	3		3	3	f	R3		6
WHITAKER,L	14	6	8	9	8	1	16	f	14	11	16
WHITE,Derr	-1										
WHITE,Devo	17	25	-9	27	20	29	30	f	22	19	17
WHITEN,M	-2	23	-25	25	21	23	25		21	24	23
WIDGER,C	-1										
WILLIAMS,B	27	24	3	23	25	25	22	f	19	19	24
WILLIAMS,Geo	3										
WILLIAMS,Ger	6								R3		5
WILSON,D	11	0	11	1			5		1	1	-3
WINFIELD,D	-2	3	-5	6	2	1			5	9	8
WORTHINGTON,C	0										
YOUNG,ER	0	1	-1	1		2			R2	6	-3
ZAUN,Gregg	3										

American League Pitchers

				4/18	4/23	4/29	5/9				
	earned	avg			— leagues —				— touts —		
Name	1995	sal	+/-	BW	ADL	COW	ASH	f	AP	JH	$94
ABBOTT,J	20	8	12	10	6	8	12	f	4	15	11
ACRE,M	-4	7	-11	7	9	5	5	f	5	15	9
AGUILERA,R	39	29	10	36	23	29	34		25	24	23
AHEARNE,P	-7										
ALBERRO,J	-6	0	-6			1					
ALVAREZ,W	6	21	-15	17	23	23	13		21	19	31
ANDERSON,Bri	0	3	-3	4	2	2	10	f	2	8	4
ANDERSON,S	0										
ANDUJAR,L	5										
APPIER,K	31	22	9	20	26	20	16	f	25	28	22

Name	1995	sal	+/-	BW	ADL	COW	ASH	f	AP	JH	$94
ASSENMACHER,P	13	1	12		2		4	f	2	7	7
AUSANIO,J	-3						1		1		2
AYALA,B	20	32	-12	28	36	33	11		33	25	31
BAKER,Scot	-2										
BALDWIN,J	-13	3	-16		2	8			R1		
BANKHEAD,S	-3						1	f	R3		6
BARK,B	1										
BELCHER,T	5								R2		-15
BELINDA,S	26	0	26	1			10		1	6	1
BENES,Andy	-2										
BENITEZ,A	-2	17	-19	11	18	22	6	f	12	9	3
BENNETT,E	0								1		
BERE,J	-26	19	-45	18	20	19	10	f	17	19	22
BERGMAN,S	-8	0	-9		1				R2		0
BERTOTTI,M	-9										
BIELECKI,M	-3								R3		
BLACK,B	-5	3	-9	2	5	3			1	16	6
BLOMDAHL,B	-8										
BOEHRINGER	-15										
BOEVER,J	-11	2	-12	1	2	2	2	f	9	14	16
BOHANON,B	-7								0		-6
BOLTON,R	-9								R3		1
BONES,R	5	9	-4	7	10	10	10	f	8	15	33
BOROWSKI,J	2										
BOSIO,C	-3	7	-10	5	6	10	13		3	7	8
BOSKIE,S	2	3	-1			9	1		R3		-1
BRANDENBRG	-3										
BREWER,B	-3	5	-8	7	3	5	3		5	9	16
BRISCOE,J	-10						1	f	1	5	8
BRONKEY,J	0								1	4	2
BROWN,K	28	15	13	15	17	14	7		11	22	-1
BROWNING,T	-3	0	-3		1				R3	8	6
BUNCH,Melv	-1										
BURROWS,Te	-6										
BUTCHER,M	3	1	2	1		2	1		R3		-5
CAMPBELL,K	0	0	0	1			1		1	5	8
CARMONA,R	-6										
CARRARA,G	-11										
CASTILLO,T	20	2	19		1	4			2	7	17
CHARLTON,N	29										
CHRISTOPHER	8										
CLARK,M	2	9	-7	12	12	3	1		8	11	22
CLARK,T	5										
CLEMENS,R	12	14	-2	22	19		11		27	20	42
CONE,D	38	27	11	25	28	28	24		26	33	53
CONVERSE,J	-4								R4		-27
COOK,D	0								1		7
CORMIER,R	10	2	8	4	1	1	1		R2	15	2
CORNETT,B	-3								R2		-5
CORSI,J	11										
COX,D	-13	1	-14	1	1	1	5	f	4		12
CRABTREE,T	3										
CUMMINGS,J	-4								R2		-5
DARLING,R	-11	1	-12		1	2			1		15
DARWIN,D	-18	0	-18	1					R3	3	-5
DAVIS,T	-4	2	-7	3	1	3	1		1	8	2

Name	1995	sal	+/-	BW	ADL	COW	ASH	f	AP	JH	$94
DAVISON,Sc	-1										
DEDRICK,J	0										
DELEON,J	5	1	4		1	3			2		16
DESILVA	-1										
DETTMER,J	-1								R3		-1
DIBBLE,R	-9	0	-9		1						
DOHERTY,J	5						1	f	R2	5	-11
ECKERSLEY,D	28	22	6	25	24	16	32		22	22	24
EDDY,Chris	-2										
EDENFIELD,K	0								R4		
EICHHORN,M		0	0		1		1		R2		26
EILAND,D	-1										
ELDRED,C	2	14	-12	16	13	14	14		9	19	16
EMBREE,A	2								R3		
ERICKSON,S	10	1	9	2	1				4	7	-5
ESHELMAN,V	3						11				
FAJARDO,H	-4								R3		-7
FARRELL,J	0								R3		-5
FERMIN,Ram	-2										
FERNANDEZ,A	25	23	2	25	21	22	12		18	27	29
FERNANDEZ,S	-8	7	-15	7	9	4	10	f	9	13	7
FETTERS,M	16	21	-5	22	19	22	5	f	21	21	22
FINLEY,C	19	12	7	11	11	14	14		12	20	19
FLEMING,D	-11	3	-14			9			R2		-20
FORTUGNO,T	0										-1
FREY,Steve	-2										-4
GARDINER,M	-10	0	-11			1			R3		11
GIVENS,B	-2										
GOHR,G	4								1	4	0
GORDON,T	7	9	-2	8	9	10	3		8	15	15
GRIMSLEY,J	-8	0	-8		1		1		R3	3	4
GROOM,B	-11	0	-12			1			R3		3
GROSS,K	-7	5	-11	7	5	2	1		8	6	17
GUARDADO,E	-1								R2		-6
GUBICZA,M	24	0	24	1			1		1	4	10
GUETTERMAN	-4										
GUNDERSON	0										
GUTHRIE,M	4	1	4	1		1			R3		-3
GUZMAN,Ju	-16	10	-26	10	8	11	17	f	5	24	-4
HABYAN,Joh	1										2
HALL,D	0	15	-15	15	11	20	10	f	15	14	21
HAMMAKER,A	-6								0		1
HANEY,C	8	1	7	2			1		R3		-5
HANSON,E	22	3	19	6	4		8		7	13	7
HARIKKALA	-3										
HARKEY,M	-3										-20
HARRIS,Ge	0								R2		-7
HARRIS,GW	-13								R3		-26
HARTLEY,Mk	2										
HAWKINS,L	-8	3	-11	1	1	7	1		R2		
HAYNES,J	8								R1		
HELLING,R	-4								R2		-3
HENNEMAN,M	21	9	12	10	10	7	13		11	11	3
HENRY,Dw	2										
HENTGEN,P	-5	19	-25	17	25	16	11	f	24	20	37
HEREDIA,Wi	-1										
HERNANDEZ,R	28	34	-6	34	34	35	20	f	31	32	18

Name	1995	sal	+/-	BW	ADL	COW	ASH	f	AP	JH	$94
HERSHISER,O	30	8	22	10	9	5	4		7	12	7
HILL,Ken	5										31
HITCHCOCK,S	14	3	11	1	4	3	1		3	7	6
HOLZEMER,M	-2										
HONEYCUTT,R	15						3		R3		-6
HORSMAN,V	-2								0		0
HOWARD,Ch	2								R3		8
HOWE,S	3	9	-7	10	9	9	4	f	9	17	32
HUDSON,Joe	-1										
HUISMAN,Ri	-2										
HURTADO,E	-2								R2		
IGNASIAK,M	-4	0	-4	1			2		R3		5
JACOME,Jas	0										10
JAMES,Mike	7										
JOHNS,D	7										
JOHNSON,R	58	26	31	20	31	28	15	f	28	26	41
JOHNSTON,J	-1										
JONES,D	15	24	-10	26	20	27	22		26	21	35
JORDAN,Ric	-3										
KAMIENIECKI,S	8	5	3	6	5	3			7	8	14
KARCHNER,M	9										
KARL,Scott	5										
KEY,J	-2	25	-27	22	29	25	25		22	23	36
KEYSER,B	0										
KIEFER,M	9	3	6			9	4		R2		-4
KING,K	-2								0		-8
KLINGENBECK,S	-17								R2		2
KRIVDA,R	4								R3		
KRUEGER,B	-3								0		-12
LANGSTON,M	16	13	3	13	14	13	16	f	15	18	7
LEE,Mark	2										
LEIPER,D	1	0	1		1				R3		7
LEITER,A	16	0	16	1					1		-5
LILLIQUIST,D	-1	0	-2			1	7	f	R3		2
LIMA,J	-3	0	-3			1			R1		-6
LINTON,D	-3										-3
LIRA,F	12										
LLOYD,G	6	3	3	6	3	1	1	f	1	9	4
LOONEY,Bri	-6										
LOPEZ,A	4	0	4	1					R2		1
LORRAINE,A	2	2	1	3	1	1			R1	4	-12
LOWE,D	-2								R4		
MADDUX,Mik	16										1
MAGNANTE,M	2								R3		1
MAHOMES,P	-6	1	-7		1	1			1	7	6
MANZANILLO,J	1										15
MARQUEZ,Is	-1										
MARTINEZ,De	36	20	16	16	23	20	16	f	18	19	36
MAXCY,Bria	-8										
MCANDREW	2										
MCCASKILL,K	2	1	1		2	1			1	3	9
MCDONALD,B	7	20	-13	19	21	21	8	f	19	21	27
MCDOWELL,J	26	25	1	22	27	27	17	f	22	23	30
MCDOWELL,R	13								1	5	-9
MEACHAM,R	2	1	1	2		1	4		4	9	13
MECIR,Jim	1										

Name	1995	sal	+/-	BW	ADL	COW	ASH	f	AP	JH	$94
MELENDEZ,J	-5								R3		-3
MENHART,Pa	-3										
MESA,J	57	3	54	1	5	2	1	f	4	8	16
MILLS,A	-5	1	-6	2	1		1		3	7	3
MIRANDA,A	-5	3	-9	1	5	4			5	9	0
MOHLER,M	4								0		-1
MONTELEONE	3										9
MONTGOMERY,J	32	31	1	29	33	32	37		37	26	28
MOORE,M	-30						1		1	2	0
MOYER,J	9	2	7	1	3	1			3	3	10
MUNOZ,Osca	-2										
MURRAY,Mat	-5										
MUSSINA,M	50	30	20	28	33	29	21	f	28	27	48
MYERS,M	-2										
NAGY,C	15	16	-1	15	17	16	12		14	18	29
NELSON,J	26	2	24	3		3	4	f	3	6	7
NICHTING,C	-7										
NITKOWSKI,CJ	-9										
OGEA,C	23								R2		-4
OLIVER,D	2	9	-7	10	9	9	3		6	8	9
OLSON,G	6	3	3	6	3				R1		-9
ONTIVEROS,S	11	14	-3	10	17	15	10	f	13	18	35
OQUIST,M	-1								R2		-9
OROSCO,J	12								1	3	2
PARRA,J	-14										
PATTERSON,B	13						1		0		8
PATTERSON,J	0										
PAVLAS,D	0										
PAVLIK,R	14	3	11	1	5	3	1	f	R1	10	-14
PENA,A	-6	1	-7	1	1				R2		10
PENNINGTON,B	-3								3	2	-6
PERCIVAL,T	27	4	23	4	3	5			R1		
PEREZ,M	0	11	-11	9	11	13	8	f	8	16	22
PETTITE,A	16	1	15	1		1			R2	2	
PHOENIX,S	-4								0		0
PICHARDO,H	8	1	7	1		1			R3		4
PIERCE,Jef	-4										
PITTSLEY,J	-3								R4		
PLUNK,E	18	8	10	10	12	3	6	f	20	19	21
POOLE,J	9								R2		-6
PRIETO,A	-1										
RADINSKY,S	-2	0	-2			1	2		R1		
RADKE,B	8								R2		
RASMUSSEN,D	-4										
REYES,A	9	1	8			2					
REYES,C	2	1	1	1	2		2	f	1	6	2
RHODES,A	-7	7	-14	9	9	3	1	f	4	10	-2
RIGHETTI,D	0								R3		-12
RIGHTNOWAR	1										
RISLEY,B	11	4	7	4	4	3	3		7	9	23
RIVERA,M	0								R3		
ROA,Joe	-1										
ROBERSON,S	-5								R2		
ROBERTSON,R	2								R3		-6
ROBINSON,K	5										
RODRIGUEZ,F	-9	4	-13	5	4	3			R1		
ROGERS,J	-1										

Name	1995	sal	+/-	BW	ADL	COW	ASH	f	AP	JH	$94
ROGERS,K	35	12	23	12	10	13	1	f	9	16	20
RUFFCORN,S	-5	4	-9	7	3	3			R1	2	-7
RUSSELL,JE	20	13	6	15	14	11	20		19	10	14
RYAN,K	1	27	-25	22	27	31	8	f	29	23	22
SANDERSON,S	3						1		1		10
SANFORD,Mo	-2										
SCANLAN,B	-12	1	-13	1	1	1	1		1		8
SCHULLSTROM,E	-12	0	-12	1					R2		3
SELE,A	6	17	-12	15	18	19	10	f	12	17	18
SHAW,J	-1										
SHEPHERD,K	-3										
SHUEY,P	0	10	-10	10	14	6	12	f	R1	8	-2
SIMAS,Bill	1										
SIROTKA,M	0										
SLUSARSKI	-1										
SMITH,L	32	26	7	27	22	28	10	f	24	20	37
SMITH,Z	-1	7	-8	8	10	3	1				23
SODOWSKY,C	-1										
SPARKS,Ste	6										
SPRINGER,R	-6	0	-6			1			1	5	1
STANTON,Mk	4										6
STEVENS,D	7	3	4	1	7	1	1		R1		-5
STEWART,D	-14								3		-8
STOTTLEMYRE,T	11	3	8	5	1	3	4	f	4	7	14
SUPPAN,J	-1								R4		
TAPANI,K	4	8	-4	6	13	5	5	f	7	12	14
TAVAREZ,J	26	1	25		2		1		R1		-4
TAYLOR,S	-6										
TEWKSBURY	6	10	-4	16	4	11	16		9	13	2
THOMAS,Lar	4										
THOMAS,M	0										
TIMLIN,M	15	0	14			1	6	f	2		-1
TORRES,D	-6	0	-6		1				R2		
TORRES,Sal	-10										-10
TROMBLEY,M	-4								R3		-5
VAN POPPEL,T	6	1	5	1		1	1		R2		-12
VANEGMOND,T	-3								1		-3
VILLONE	-8	1	-9	1		2	1			2	
VIOLA,F		0	0		1				R1		-1
VOSBERG,E	12								1		0
WAKEFIELD	42										
WARD,D	-7	13	-20	9	15	14	17	f	12	18	
WARE,Jeff	-3										
WASDIN,J	3								R2		
WATKINS,S	-2										
WEGMAN,B	1	3	-2	3	4	3	3	f	3	8	10
WELLS,B	-6	0	-6		1				R2		2
WELLS,D	27	4	23	3	3	6	1	f	9	14	17
WENGERT,Do	3										
WETTELAND,J	39	38	1	37	38	40	41		42	28	37
WHITESDE,S	-4										
WHITESIDE,M	11	1	10	1		1	1		R3		-1
WICKANDER,K	5										
WICKMAN,B	6	5	1	5	3	7	1	f	7	13	24
WILLIAMS,Mit	-6						1		R3	4	-5
WILLIAMS,W	5	0	4			1	1		3	6	8

Name	1995	sal	+/-	BW	ADL	COW	ASH	f	AP	JH	$94
WILLIS,C	-5	0	-5		1				R3		-5
WITT,B	-1										-2
WOJCI'WSKI	-2										
WOLCOTT,B	2										

National League Hitters

| | | | | 4/194/23 4/29 5/9 | | | | | | | |
| | earned | avg | | — leagues — | | | | | - touts - | | |
Name	$95	sal	+/-	BW	HSS	IOC	SCN	f	AP	JH	$94
ABBOTT,Kur	14	8	6	9	7	8	5	f	12	8	7
ALFONZO,Ed	8	1	7	1		3	5		R1		
ALOU,Moise	15	32	-17	31	36	28	26	f	36	32	39
ANDREWS,Sh	2	4	-1		10	1	5		R2		
ANTHONY,Er	6	2	4	2	1	3			3	7	7
ARIAS,A	5	1	4		1	1			1	1	0
ASHLEY,Bil	4	10	-6	10	11	8	1	f	11	20	0
AUDE,Rich	2	1	1	1		3			R1		
AURILIA,R	3										
AUSMUS,Bra	15	6	9	8	4	6	9	f	8	10	6
BAGWELL,Jf	28	39	-12	39	39	40	43	f	47	41	63
BARRY,J	-1										
BATES,Jaso	10	4	5	3	5	5	7		2		
BATTLE,All	1	1	0		1	1	1		3		
BEAN,B	-1								R3		-2
BELL,David	2								AL		
BELL,Derek	35	27	7	28	28	26	28		31	27	35
BELL,Jay	11	12	-1	13	14	9	8		20	13	13
BELLIARD,R	-2								0		-1
BENARD,M	3										
BENITEZ,Ya	4								R4		
BENJAMIN,M	3						1		0	2	4
BENNETT,G	0										
BENZINGER	0	1	-1	1		2			1		9
BERRY,Sean	20	13	7	17	12	11	9		18	17	19
BERRYHILL	-1								1		6
BICHETTE,D	54	30	24	28	35	27	34		39	26	45
BIGGIO,Cra	37	29	8	27	29	31	31		35	29	40
BLAUSER,Jf	2	14	-12	15	13	13	11		12	12	7
BOGAR,Tim	4								0		-1
BONDS,Barr	43	46	-2	43	46	48	57	f	53	43	53
BONILLA,Bo	21	24	-2	23	23	25	24		24	18	24
BOONE,Bret	16	17	-2	19	19	14	10		22	20	26
BORDERS,Pa	-2										1
BRADSHAW,T	0								R2		
BRANSON,Jf	10	1	9	1	1	2	2		1	4	6
BRITO,J	0										
BROGNA,Ric	22	13	9	11	15	13	10	f	11	10	12
BROWNE,Jer	2	2	-1	1	3	3	1	f	R3		11
BRUMFIELD	12	12	0	13	12	12	4	f	4	13	9
BRUMLEY,M	-1										0
BUECHELE,S	-2	8	-10	6	8	10	9		12	10	10

Name	$95	sal	+/-	BW	HSS	IOC	SCN	f	AP	JH	$94
BUFORD,D	4										0
BULLETT,Sc	7	4	3	2	4	5	13		1	8	
BURKS,Elli	14	15	0	11	13	20	17		15	19	15
BUSCH,Mike	2										
BUTLER,Bre	22	19	2	22	19	17	20	f	23	24	30
CAMINITI,K	34	20	14	19	19	21	16	f	20	18	24
CANGELOSI	14								R3		2
CARABALLO	-1										
CARR,Chuck	6	17	-11	19	17	16	19		19	11	19
CARREON,Ma	20	1	19	1		1	1		2		4
CASTELLANO	-1	1	-2	1		3			2	3	
CASTILLA,V	34	9	24	12	8	8	10	f	1	17	9
CASTILLO,A	-2										
CASTRO,Jua	0								R4		
CEDENO,And	-1	14	-15	18	11	13	13		14	14	11
CEDENO,Rog	0								R1		
CIANFROCCO	6								R3		1
CLARK,Dave	6	4	3	5	5	1	1		4	9	15
CLARK,Phil	-1	1	-2	2	1	1			2	9	2
CLAYTON,Ro	12	15	-3	16	16	14	14		11	16	11
COLBRUNN,G	26	14	12	14	15	13	10	f	9	15	10
COLES,Darn	1						3		R3		-1
CONINE,Jef	31	24	6	25	25	23	30		25	24	31
COOPER,Sco	0	14	-14	11	12	18	18		8	13	14
CORDERO,Wi	16	26	-10	30	24	25	25		24	26	29
COUNSELL,C	0										
CROMER,Tri	-2	1	-3		1	1	1		0		0
CUMMINGS,M	1	6	-4	8	6	3			7	8	1
DAULTON,Da	9	22	-13	24	20	21	22	f	21	20	21
DAWSON,And	7	5	2	5	6	4	1		3	4	10
DECKER,Ste	1	0	0	1					1	1	
DESHIELDS	19	24	-5	24	25	24	26	f	21	23	16
DEVEREAUX	2										-2
DIAZ,Mario	0	0	-1		1				R3		4
DONNELS,Ch	1	1	0		1	1	1		R3	5	2
DUNCAN,Mar	9	9	0	8	6	12	12		7	15	15
DUNSTON,Sh	23	9	14	9	9	8	8		11	11	13
DYKSTRA,Ln	6	24	-18	22	25	25	25		27	26	13
EISENREICH	21	7	14	7	7	7	5		6	13	15
ELSTER,Kev	0										-3
ENCARNACION	-1										
EUSEBIO,To	14	4	10	3	3	5	6		8	5	9
EVERETT,Ca	11	10	2	3	12	14	10		R2	10	2
FANEYTE,Ri	-2								1		-2
FINLEY,Ste	28	16	11	15	14	20	19		15	16	17
FLETCHER,D	12	8	5	9	7	7	7		8	8	12
FLORA,K	0										
FLOYD,Clif	-2	19	-20	23	17	16	10	f	29	22	14
FOLEY,Tom	0								0		1
FONVILLE,C	10										
FORDYCE,Br	0						1				
FRANCO,Mat	0								R3		
FRAZIER,Lo	0	5	-6	3	9	4	5	f	4	9	12
GALARRAGA	33	32	1	30	30	35	33	f	40	36	42
GALLAGHER	5						1	f	R3		-1
GANT,Ron	33	24	9	18	25	28	10	f	29	18	

Name	$95	sal	+/-	BW	HSS	IOC	SCN f	AP	JH	$94
GARCIA,Car	15	13	2	14	15	9	9	21	13	17
GARCIA,Fre	-3	0	-3	1						
GARCIA,K	-1							R5		
GIANNELLI	-1									
GIBRALTER	0									
GILKEY,Ber	25	16	9	15	20	14	18	11	20	13
GIOVANOLA	-1									
GIRARDI,Jo	9	7	2	5	9	7	15	3	9	9
GOFF,J	-1							R3		-2
GONZALEZ,Lu	17	16	1	18	15	16	18	19	29	21
GRACE,Mark	32	18	14	16	17	21	18	19	17	14
GREENE,Wil	-1	9	-10	15	11			9	12	-1
GREGG,T	4									
GRISSOM,Ma	18	37	-19	35	39	37	41	45	34	33
GRUDZIELANEK	3	7	-4	10	4	7	7	6	17	
GUTIERREZ	3	2	2	1	2	2		R3	1	1
GWYNN,Chri	0	0	-1		1			R3	29	3
GWYNN,Tony	41	29	12	26	33	27	20 f	30	29	41
HAJEK,Dave	0									
HANEY,T	6							R3		0
HANSEN,Dav	3	2	1	1	4	1	1	2	4	2
HARRIS,Len	1	1	0	1	1	1		R3		7
HAYES,Char	18	15	3	15	13	16	19	17	8	17
HEMOND,Sco	-4	0	-4		1					3
HERNANDEZ,C	-3	1	-4		2	1		1	3	0
HERNANDEZ,J	8	1	8			2	1	1	4	1
HILL,Glena	29	21	8	22	24	17	16 f	18	22	23
HOLBERT,Ra	0	0	0	1				R3		0
HOLLANDSWORTH	3	5	-2	7	3	4	2	4	3	
HOLLINS,Dv	3	19	-16	16	20	20	19	15	10	2
HOWARD,Tho	14	2	12	2	3	1	1	1	4	7
HUBBARD,Mk	-1							0		
HUBBARD,Tr	4							R3		1
HULETT,Tim	0							R3		
HUNDLEY,To	14	9	5	9	8	10	5 f	10	14	10
HUNTER,B.L.	17	4	12	13				21	11	1
HUNTER,B.R.	0	4	-4	1	7	5	4 f	3	7	11
HUSKEY,But	0							R2		
HYERS,Tim	-1							R4	1	1
INGRAM,Gar	0	1	-1		2		1	R3		3
JEFFERIES	21	31	-9	30	32	30	34	35	32	30
JOHNSON,Br	3	0	3	1				1	3	3
JOHNSON,Ch	7	9	-2	11	9	7	7	5	5	2
JOHNSON,Ho	1	3	-2	4	1	4	4	R3	4	10
JOHNSON,Ma	5	1	5		1	1	1	R3		
JONES,Chip	22	15	7	14	17	14	5 f	21	13	1
JONES,Chri	9									
JORDAN,Bri	33	20	13	15	16	28	16 f	17	21	5
JORDAN,Kev	0							R2		
JUSTICE,Dv	19	30	-11	29	30	32	31	32	28	26
KARROS,Eri	34	19	15	16	20	21	26	16	14	14
KELLY,Mike	1	5	-3	3	6	5	11 f	1	6	2
KELLY,Robe	18	25	-7	24	25	27	24	26	23	24
KENT,Jeff	19	18	1	18	19	18	14	22	16	21
KING,Jeff	20	10	11	8	9	12	14	12	8	8
KINGERY,Mk	12	6	6	5	7	7	14	9	6	21

Name	$95	sal	+/-	BW	HSS	IOC	SCN	f	AP	JH	$94
KLESKO,Rya	26	17	9	19	15	16	21	f	21	19	17
KMAK,Joe	1										
KOWITZ,B	-1										
LAKER,Tim	2	1	0	1		3	1		2	5	
LAMPKIN,To	2										
LANKFORD,R	31	24	7	25	22	25	26		18	24	22
LANSING,Mk	19	9	9	8	11	9	6		9	7	12
LARKIN,Bar	42	26	16	26	24	28	22	f	28	31	26
LEDESMA,Aa	0								R3		
LEE,Manny	0								1		
LEMKE,Mark	4	5	0	2	6	6	5		2	7	9
LEONARD,Ma	0								R3		1
LEWIS,Darr	10	20	-9	18	21	20	23		15	19	18
LEWIS,Mark	10	1	9	1		1	1		R3	4	8
LIEBERTHAL	0	0	0	1					R3	1	1
LIRIANO,Ne	9	0	9		1		1		1	1	4
LIVINGSTONE	12						1		1		2
LONGMIRE,T	8								R3		1
LOPEZ,Javy	18	14	5	13	12	16	16		17	11	8
MABRY,John	12	2	10		4	2	7		R2		1
MAGADAN,Dv	14	5	9	1	8	5	7		2	4	3
MANWARING	3	3	1	2	3	3	1		2	2	2
MARSH,Tom	4								R3		0
MARTIN,Al	20	18	2	21	17	15	15		23	20	19
MAY,Derric	13										15
MCCARTY,D	0										2
MCCRACKEN	0										
MCDAVID,Ra	0								R3		0
MCGRIFF,Fr	26	38	-11	34	37	42	40	f	39	32	44
MCRAE,Bria	24	20	4	18	18	23	19		24	18	22
MEJIA,Robe	-2	6	-8	5	8	6	5	f	6	7	4
MERCED,Orl	25	10	15	8	8	13	10		7	12	14
MILLER,Orl	6	6	0	4	5	10	10	f	6	5	4
MONDESI,Ra	35	29	6	22	34	30	41		27	23	29
MORANDINI	14	4	10	3	4	5	5		3	12	12
MORDECAI,M	3								R4		1
MORMAN,Rus	2								R3		0
MORRIS,Hal	12	22	-9	23	23	19	19		25	28	32
MOUTON,Jam	13	8	4	5	8	12	14		5	5	11
MUNOZ,Noe	0										
NATAL,Bob	1								R3		1
NEVIN,Phil	-4								R1		
NEWFIELD	2										
NIEVES,Mel	5	10	-5	11	7	12	15	f	6	7	1
NOKES,Matt	0										6
OCHOA,Alex	1										
OFFERMAN,J	9	8	0	5	9	11	9		3	6	-2
OLIVA,Jose	-4	6	-10	4	4	9	12		1	2	5
OQUENDO,Jo	-2						2		R3	1	1
ORSULAK,Jo	7	3	3	1	6	3	6		5	9	10
OTERO,Rick	-2	1	-3		3				R3		
OWENS,Eric	1										
OWENS,Jayh	3								R3		0
O'BRIEN,Ch	3	1	3	1		1	1		1	1	6
PAGNOZZI,T	-3	6	-8	7	4	6	2	f	8	9	9
PARENT,Mar	9	1	8		2		1	f	1	3	3

Name	$95	sal	+/-	BW	HSS	IOC	SCN	f	AP	JH	$94
PARKER,R	1								0		-2
PATTERSON	-2	1	-3		3		1		1	3	9
PEGUES,S	3	1	2	1		1			1		2
PENA,Geron	2	14	-12	16	13	13	5	f	9	19	13
PENDLETON	20	13	7	9	16	13	22	f	9	11	6
PEREZ,Eddi	1										
PERRY,Gera	-3								R3		7
PETAGINE,R	1	3	-2	2	3	5	3	f	4		-1
PHILLIPS,J	1	9	-8	7	10	10	9		9	13	-1
PIAZZA,Mik	39	31	8	32	31	29	40		40	30	35
PLANTIER,P	7	15	-8	17	15	14	15		13		8
POLONIA,L	1										22
PRATT,Todd	-3	1	-4	1	1	2			R3		-2
PRIDE,Curt	-1	0	-2	1					R3		
PRINCE,Tom	0										0
PULLIAM,H	1										
PYE,Eddie	-1								R3		-1
READY,Rand	-2								0		3
REED,Jeff	1						1		1		-4
REED,Jody	6								R2		8
RHODES,Kar	-1						2		3	3	5
ROBERSON,K	1	1	0		2				1	1	2
ROBERTS,Bi	15	21	-7	21	20	23	17	f	18	26	25
RODRIGUZ,H	1	9	-9	8	10	10	15	f	5	8	11
SABO,Chris	0										9
SANCHEZ,Re	8	4	4	1	5	6	10	f	3	8	6
SANDERS,De	14	23	-9	25	23	21	29	f	32	23	27
SANDERS,Re	44	31	13	29	34	30	28		28	31	26
SANTANGELO	3										
SANTIAGO,B	13	8	5	7	8	8	7	f	R1	11	12
SASSER,Mac	-1	1	-2		2				0		-1
SCARSONE,S	9								R3	1	3
SCHALL,Gen	-1								R3		
SCHOFIELD	-1										7
SEFCIK,K	0										
SEGUI,Davi	21	7	14	7	8	6	10	f	1	9	6
SERVAIS,Sc	12	3	9	2	3	3	5		2	2	1
SHARPERSON	0										
SHEAFFER,D	2						4		0		-1
SHEFFIELD	24	36	-12	34	40	35	27	f	37	32	32
SHIPLEY,Cr	5	2	4	2	1	2	3		4	8	16
SIDDALL,J	0										
SILVESTRI	2										-1
SIMMS,Mike	7								R3		-1
SLAUGHT,Do	3	4	-1	1	6	4	2		5	5	6
SMITH,Dwig	3	1	2	1		2			4		9
SMITH,Ozzi	-2	6	-8	7	5	5	4		5	6	7
SNYDER,C	0								2		3
SOSA,Sammy	42	38	5	34	46	33	33		38	32	40
SPEHR,Tim	1								R3		1
SPIERS,Bil	-1	1	-1	1		1			1		4
STANKIEW'Z	-1						1	f	0		1
STINNETT,K	0	2	-2	2	2	2	1		1	1	3
STOCKER,Kv	-2	4	-7	4	4	5			4	10	6
SWEENEY,M	3										
TARASCO,To	16	11	5	10	10	12	8	f	3	14	8
TATUM,Jim	0	2	-2	1	3	3	1		3	8	

Name	$95	sal	+/-	BW	HSS	IOC	SCN f	AP	JH	$94
TAUBENSEE	11	5	7	6	4	4	2	6	5	9
TAVAREZ,Je	6							R3		-1
THOMPSON,M	2	1	1	1		2	1	1		11
THOMPSN,Ro	0	11	-11	9	13	12	8	8	11	-1
THOMPSN,Ry	6	6	0	2	7	8	2	15	11	11
TIMMONS,Oz	7	4	3	1	7	5	1	R3		
TREADWAY,J	0	0	-1	1				1		2
TUCKER,Sco	1									
VAN SLYKE	3							R1		6
VANDERWAL	8	1	7	1	1	2	2	1	7	4
VARSHO,Gar	1									0
VERAS,Quil	24	12	12	13	10	14	16	5	11	
VIZCAINO,J	14	4	9	2	6	5	4	2	7	3
WALKER,Lar	41	38	3	37	41	36	34 f	41	38	39
WALLACH,Ti	8	7	1	8	7	7	7 f	14	11	25
WALTON,Jer	11						5	R3		4
WEBSTER,Le	3	1	2		2			0		6
WEBSTER,Mi	-1	2	-3		6			R3		4
WEHNER,Joh	3							R3		0
WEISS,Walt	7	6	1	4	7	7	15	3	10	6
WHITE,Rond	26	14	12	17	13	12	16 f	24	18	4
WHITEN,Mrk	12									23
WHITMORE,D	-1	1	-3	1		3		R3	5	-1
WILKINS,Ri	0	10	-11	13	8	10	10	14	13	4
WILLIAMS,Ed	10	17	-7	18	16	17	10 f	20	18	17
WILLIAMS,Ma	26	35	-8	35	35	34	42	35	25	36
WILLIAMS,Re	-1									
WILSON,Nig	-1							R2		
WORTHINGTON	1									
YOUNG,Eric	26	9	17	13	9	4	5	8	16	17
YOUNG,Kevi	3							R3	5	-2
ZAMBRANO,E	0							2		6
ZEILE,Todd	9	17	-8	19	16	15	16	25	20	20
ZOSKY,Eddi	0	0	0		1			R3		

National League Pitchers

	earned avg			4/194/23 4/29 5/9 — leagues —				- touts -		
Name	1995	sal	+/-	BW	HSS	IOC	SCN f	AP	JH	$94
ABBOTT,Ky	0									
ACEVEDO,J	-9	0	-9			1		R1		
ADAMS,Terr	-3									
ALVAREZ,T	-8									
AQUINO,L	-5							R2		6
AROCHA,R	1	10	-9	13	7	9	8	3	5	13
ARRANDALE,M								R4		
ASHBY,A	25	11	14	10	12	12	10 f	15	17	23
ASTACIO,P	7	13	-6	14	12	13	12	15	19	8
AVERY,S	5	22	-18	24	21	22	24	21	26	16
BAILEY,C	0	0	-1	1				1		-5
BAILEY,R	-2									
BANKS,W	-17	0	-18	1				1		-4
BARBER,B	-2							R2	8	
BARTON,S	5									
BAUTISTA,J	-13	4	-17	6	3	3	3 f	2	14	7

Name	1995	sal	+/-	BW	HSS	IOC	SCN	f	AP	JH	$94
BECK,R	27	33	-6	33	39	27	48	f	36	31	31
BEDROSIAN,S	-6						2	f	1		3
BENES,Alan	-5	3	-8	6		2			R1		
BENES,Andy	1	19	-18	19	19	20	20		17	18	16
BERUMEN,A	-5	1	-6		3						
BIRKBECK	7										
BLAIR,W	4								0	4	-16
BOCHTLER,D	7										
BORBON,P	4								R2		
BORLAND,T	1	0	1			1			7	4	6
BOTTALICO,R	19	2	17	3		4	1		R1		1
BOWEN,R	-2								R3		-3
BRANTLEY,J	34	19	15	21	20	15	21		20	17	31
BREWINGTON	0										
BROCAIL,D	4								0	4	-3
BRUSKE,J	-1										
BULLINGER,J	6	6	0	3	6	9	10	f	4	8	16
BURBA,D	10								1	7	1
BURGOS,Enr	-5										
BURKETT,J	8	11	-3	13	8	12	8		8	18	12
BYRD,P	6										
CANDIOTTI,T	14	13	1	12	14	12	10		10	11	8
CARPENTER,C									R3	12	4
CARRASCO,H	1	10	-9	11	9	11	25	f	9	22	19
CARTER,A	0								R3		-1
CASIAN,L	2										-13
CASTILLO,F	23	2	21	3	1	2			R3		2
CHARLTON,N	-5	10	-15	13	10	7	11	f	12	11	
CHRISTIANSEN,	-2	3	-4	3	1	4			R3		
CLARK,T	-1								R3		
CLONTZ,B	12	14	-2	7	15	20	26		11	4	
COOKE,S		1	-1	2		2			7	7	-10
CORNELIUS	-7										
COURTRIGHT	0										
CREEK,D	3										
CUMMINGS,J	6										-5
DAAL,Omar	-5	2	-7	1	2	3	11		R3	10	1
DELEON,Jos	-3										16
DELUCIA,R	13										0
DESHAIES,J	-8										-26
DEWEY,M	1								2		1
DIPOTO,J	6	0	6	1					5	10	-8
DISHMAN,G	-3								R1		
DOUGHERTY,J	2						4		R3		
DRABEK,D	0	24	-24	23	24	26	20	f	23	28	38
DUNBAR,Mat	-7										
DYER,M	-1	0	-1			1	1		R3		0
EDENS,T	-1								R2		4
EISCHEN,J	0								R3		-3
ELLIOTT,D	0								R3	4	-1
ERICKS,Joh	-5										
ESTES,S	-2										
EVERSGERD,B	-2								R3		-1
FASSERO,J	3	20	-17	23	18	18	30		10	25	26
FERNANDZ,S	13										7
FLETCHER,P	-2										
FLORENCE,D	3										

Name	1995	sal	+/-	BW	HSS	IOC	SCN	f	AP	JH	$94
FLORIE,B	8	0	7		1				R3		3
FOSSAS,T	11								R3		2
FOSTER,K	10	7	3	8	5	8	10	f	9	8	11
FRANCO,JO	32	24	8	26	25	21	21	f	28	29	31
FRASCATORE,J	-3								R3		-4
FRASER,W	1								0		-3
FREEMAN,M	-16	10	-26	10	11	9	8		6	6	25
FREY,S	5								0	9	-4
GARCES,R	-2										
GARDNER,M	-1								R3		-1
GLAVINE,T	28	22	6	21	24	22	31	f	15	21	10
GOMEZ,P	-4								R3		1
GOODEN,D									R2		-5
GOTT,J	-2	7	-9	7	5	9	12		5		-3
GRACE,Mike	2										
GRAHE,J	-5								R3		0
GREEN,Ty	-10	0	-11		1					9	
GREENE,T	-14	3	-17	7		3	1		3	4	-3
GREER,K	-2										
GROOM,Budd	-5										3
GROTT,Matt	-3										
GUNDERSON,E	1								R3		4
GUTHRIE,M	0										-3
HABYAN,J	7						1		R3		2
HAMILTON,J	21	15	7	14	17	13	17	f	8	25	24
HAMMOND,C	13								R2	4	8
HAMPTON,M	16	6	10	8	4	6	6		1	6	1
HANCOCK,L	4										
HANSELL,G	-6								R1		
HARNISCH,P	7	13	-7	15	11	14	12		13	23	-2
HARRIS,Ge	1						1		R3		-1
HARRIS,G.A	7										-12
HARTGRAVES	4										
HARVEY,B	-2	12	-14	13	12	10			18	18	3
HENKE,T	38	22	16	19	23	23	30		24	23	22
HENNEMAN,M	8										3
HENRY,B	16	11	5	15	7	12	10	f	8	9	29
HENRY,Do	14	0	14		1						-1
HEREDIA,G	4	4	0	4	3	4	2		7	9	11
HERMANSON,D	-6						8		R2		
HERNANDEZ,JE	-5								4		14
HERNANDEZ,X	5	3	2	3	2	3	2		2	7	3
HICKERSON,B	-17						1		R2		-10
HILL,K	-6	24	-30	24	21	26	26	f	17	27	31
HOFFMAN,T	33	33	0	35	33	30	13	f	33	32	32
HOLMES,D	20	3	17	3	3	2	2		9		-9
HOOK,Chris	-3										
HOPE,J	-6								R3		-3
HUDEK,J	6	17	-11	20	17	15	10	f	25	15	20
ISRINGHAUSEN,	16								R4		
JACKSON,D	-17	11	-28	15	12	7	10		9	16	28
JACKSON,M	14	6	8	8	5	5	1		6	19	22
JACOME,J	-13	5	-18	6	4	6	3		2		10
JARVIS,K	-9								R2		-4
JOHNSTONE,J	-1								R3		-5
JONES,B	8	12	-4	14	10	11	6	f	12	17	23

Name	1995	sal	+/-	BW	HSS	IOC	SCN	f	AP	JH	$94
JONES,T	20	14	6	18	9	14	7	f	6	17	23
JUDEN,J	2								2		-4
KARP,R	0								R3		
KILE,D	-7	9	-16	10	10	8	15		5	8	-5
KONUSZWSKI	-1										
KROON,Marc	-1										
KRUEGER,Bi	-3								R3		3
LEIPER,D	5										7
LEITER,M	17	2	15	1	1	3	3		R3		7
LESKANIC,C	20								R3		-4
LEWIS,R	1								R3		-14
LIEBER,J	-10	7	-17	8	6	6	3		8	16	11
LOAIZA,E	-9	1	-10		2						
LOMON,Kevi	-4										
MADDUX,G	68	36	32	36	37	35	35	f	40	40	72
MADDUX,M	-3	0	-3			1			R2		1
MANTEI,Mat	-3										
MANZANILLO,J	-3	1	-5	1	3				4	11	15
MANZANILLO,R	0								R3		-1
MARTINEZ,PA	-9	6	-15	9	4	4			2	12	8
MARTINEZ,PJ	27	19	8	21	18	18	22		21	26	29
MARTINEZ,R	24	13	12	13	10	15	12	f	14	12	18
MATHEWS,T	12						5		R3		6
MATHEWS,TJ	9										
MAUSER,Tim	-3								R2		5
MAY,Darrel	-3										
MCCURRY,Jf	-10										
MCELROY,C	-4	4	-7	4	4	3	1		3	10	15
MCMICHAEL,G	17	11	5	13	14	7	3		21	13	21
MCMURTRY,C	-5										
MERCKER,K	3	13	-10	15	10	14	16	f	11	20	20
MICELI,D	14	9	5	12	5	10	10	f	17	18	0
MIMBS,M	3						4		R1		
MINOR,B	7								R3		-8
MINTZ,D	-6								R3		
MLICKI,Da	7								R3		
MOREL,Ramo	1										
MORGAN,M	12								R2		-23
MULHOLLAND,T	-16	7	-22	11	5	4	9		1	10	-11
MUNOZ,B	-2	4	-6	5	3	4	3		7	11	19
MUNOZ,M	-11								R3		4
MURPHY,R	-5								R3		7
MURRAY,Mat	-2										
MYERS,Mike	0										
MYERS,Rand	29	32	-3	27	39	31	36	f	27	28	19
NABHOLZ,Ch	-3										-17
NAVARRO,J	25	2	22		3	4	11		3	8	-13
NEAGLE,D	22	3	19	4	1	3			3	14	2
NEN,R	20	21	-1	23	24	16	10	f	14	18	27
NICHOLS,R	-3										
NIED,D	-7	0	-7	1					2		-1
NITKOWSKI,C	-6								R2		
NOMO,H	39	6	33	5		13	9		R2		
OLIVARES,O	-12	0	-12		1				R1		-11
OSBORNE,D	6	5	1	8	3	5	2		3	9	
OSUNA,An	1	10	-9	13	5	12	8		9	6	
PAINTER,L	2								R2		-11

Appendix A — NLP

Name	1995	sal	+/-	BW	HSS	IOC	SCN	f	AP	JH	$94
PALACIOS,V	-6								R3		5
PARK,CH	0	1	0	1		1			2		-4
PARRA,Jose	-1										
PARRETT,J	6										
PARRIS,Ste	-3										
PENA,Aleja	8										10
PENNINGTON	-3										-6
PEREZ,C	17	2	14	1	3	3	2		R2		
PEREZ,Mi	4	1	3		2	1	1		6		-4
PEREZ,Y	-1	1	-2	1	1	2	4		3	4	7
PERSON,R	6								R3		
PETKOVSEK	9										
PLESAC,Dan	8	0	7		1				R3	8	1
PORTUGAL,M	11	12	-1	12	12	13	18		7	23	14
POWELL,Jay	1										
POWELL,R	-10								R3		1
PUGH,T	6						1		R3		-10
PULSIPHER,B	6								R1		
QUANTRILL,P	1						1		2		1
RAPP,P	16	4	12	1	7	4	3	f	3	9	3
REED,R	-1										0
REED,Steve	23	1	22	1		2	1		R2		0
REKAR,Brya	-2										
REMLINGER,M	-3								R3		-6
REYNOLDS,S	19	13	7	14	12	12	10	f	9	20	22
REYNOSO,A	-7								R2		-1
RICCI,C	3										
RIJO,J	3	26	-23	26	25	27	28		24	29	21
RITZ,K	9								0		-9
RIVERA,B	-1								R3		-7
RODRIGUEZ,F	1								R2		
RODRIGUEZ,R	1								R3		1
ROGERS,K		2	-2	3		2			4		0
ROJAS,M	21	30	-10	29	28	34	10		28	30	28
ROPER,J	-7	3	-9	1	6	1			1	9	6
ROSSELLI,J	-11								R3		
RUETER,K	11	4	8	5	2	4			4	5	0
RUFFIN,B	12	15	-4	14	17	15	10	f	14	22	15
RUFFIN,J	3	6	-3	8	5	4			6	16	17
SABERHAGEN,B	7	23	-16	24	25	20	17	f	20	28	46
SAGER,A	-5								0		-10
SANDERS,S	6	3	3	4	3	3	3		6	8	0
SCHEID,R	-3								R3		3
SCHILLING,C	18	11	7	12	7	14	18		12	4	-1
SCHMIDT,Cu	-5										
SCHMIDT,J	-4								R2		
SCHOUREK,P	37	4	33	9	3	1	2		3	10	5
SCOTT,T	6	3	3	4	3	3	7		1	11	12
SEANEZ,R	-5	9	-14		8	19	10	f	1		3
SERVICE,S	5								R3		-1
SHAW,J	1	0	1	1			1		2	5	10
SLOCUMB,H	29	10	19	4	9	18	3	f	5	15	9
SMALL,A	1										-2
SMILEY,J	22	16	6	17	14	18	18	f	16	24	17
SMITH,P	-4	1	-5	1	1	1	11	f	R3	5	-10
SMOLTZ,J	24	17	7	17	15	18	21	f	17	15	10

Name	1995	sal	+/-	BW	HSS	IOC	SCN	f	AP	JH	$94
SPRINGER,D	-1										
SPRINGER,R	1										1
STANTON,M	-3	2	-5	2	3	1	1		5	12	6
STURTZE,Ta	-1										
SULLIVAN,S	-1										
SWARTZBAGH	2										
SWIFT,B	-3	15	-18	14	14	17	10		10	10	16
SWINDELL,G	2	8	-5	6	7	10	4		4		6
TABAKA,J	1								R3		0
TAPANI,Kev	-2										14
TELGHEDER	-3								R3		-4
THOBE,J	-2										
THOBE,T	-2										
THOMPSON,MA	-13								R2		-6
TORRES,S	-5	1	-6		3				R2		-10
TRACHSEL,S	-11	12	-23	12	11	13	10	f	15	15	21
URBANI,T	2								R3		-6
URBINA,U	-3								R4		
VALDES,I	33	8	25	13	8	3			7		8
VALDES,M	-9						3		R2		
VALDEZ,C	-4										
VALDEZ,S	-1										-8
VALENZUELA,F	-1								R2		8
VANLANDINGHAM	8	4	4	5		7	10	f	2	4	12
VERES,D	20	2	18	3	1	2	3		2		12
VERES,R	4								R3		0
VILLONE,R	2										
VIOLA,F	-3										-1
WADE,T	-1								R1		
WAGNER,Bil	0						2		R2		
WAGNER,P	-7	3	-10	6	1	2			6	8	-3
WALKER,Mik	1										
WALKER,Pet	-1										
WALL,D	-1										
WATSON,A	-3	2	-5	3	3	1	1		2	12	-12
WEATHERS,D	-15	1	-16	1	1	1			R3	6	-14
WELLS,Davi	9										17
WENDELL,T	-4	0	-4		1				R3		-12
WEST,D	3	3	0	5	2	1	10	f	5	13	7
WHITE,G	-4						1		R2		-2
WHITE,Ri	-3						1	f	4	4	13
WILLIAMS,Br	-10	0	-11		1		1	f	R3		-17
WILLIAMS,Mik	9								R4		-5
WILLIAMS,To	1	0	0		1						
WILSON,Gar	-1										
WILSON,P									R5		
WILSON,T	1	2	-1		6		5		R3		
WITASIK,J									R4		
WITT,B	2	2	-1	1	2	4			5	7	-2
WOHLERS,M	35	5	30	8	5	2	2		5	16	2
WOODALL,B	-2	0	-3	1			1		R2		0
WORRELL,To	38	12	26	18	13	6	15	f	22	17	18
YOUNG,A	3								R2		7

Appendix A — NLP

Appendix B
Strength and Depth of Position in 1995
American League Hitters

rk	C	OQP	AB	HR	RBI	SB	BA	$HR	$RBI	$SB	$BA	$TOT
1	SURHOFF,BJ	1B,OF	415	13	73	7	0.320	5	9	3	7	24
2	RODRIGUEZ,I		492	12	67	0	0.303	5	8	0	5	18
3	STANLEY,Mk		399	18	83	1	0.268	7	10	0	-1	17
4	STEINBACH		406	15	65	1	0.278	6	8	0	1	15
5	ALOMAR,San		203	10	35	3	0.300	4	4	1	2	12
6	HOILES,Chr		352	19	58	1	0.250	8	7	0	-3	12
7	OLIVER,Joe		337	12	51	2	0.273	5	6	1	-0	12
8	WILSON,Dan		399	9	51	2	0.278	4	6	1	1	11
9	LEYRITZ,Ji	1B	264	7	37	1	0.269	3	4	0	-1	7
10	MYERS,Greg		273	9	38	0	0.260	4	4	0	-2	7
11	MACFARLANE		364	15	51	2	0.225	6	6	1	-7	6
12	KARKOVICE		323	13	51	2	0.217	5	6	1	-7	5
13	FLAHERTY,J		354	11	40	0	0.243	4	5	0	-4	5
14	PENA,Tony		263	5	28	1	0.262	2	3	0	-1	5
15	WALBECK,Ma		393	1	44	3	0.257	0	5	1	-3	4
16	MERULLO,Ma		195	1	27	0	0.282	0	3	0	1	4
17	LYONS,Barr		64	5	16	0	0.266	2	2	0	-0	4
18	WILLIAMS,Gg		79	3	14	0	0.291	1	2	0	1	3
19	HASELMAN,B		152	5	23	0	0.243	2	3	0	-2	3
20	ZAUN,Gregg		104	3	14	1	0.260	1	2	0	-1	3
21	MATHENY,Mi		166	0	21	2	0.247	0	2	1	-2	2
22	LAVALLIERE		98	1	19	0	0.245	0	2	0	-1	1
23	TINGLEY,R		124	4	18	0	0.226	2	2	0	-2	1
24	MARTINEZ,A		191	2	25	0	0.241	1	3	0	-3	1
26	MAYNE,Bren		307	1	27	0	0.251	0	3	0	-3	1
29	FABREGAS,J		227	1	22	0	0.247	0	3	0	-2	1
	avg, top 24		267	8	40	1	0.266	3	5	1	-1	7.53

rk	1B	OQP	AB	HR	RBI	SB	BA	$HR	$RBI	$SB	$BA	$TOT
1	VAUGHN,Mo		550	39	126	11	0.300	16	15	5	5	41
2	THOMAS,Fra		493	40	111	3	0.308	16	13	1	6	37
3	PALMEIRO,R		554	39	104	3	0.310	16	12	1	8	37
4	MARTINEZ,Ti		519	31	111	0	0.293	12	13	0	4	29
5	MURRAY,Edd		436	21	82	5	0.323	8	10	2	8	29
6	MCGWIRE,Ma		317	39	90	1	0.274	16	11	0	0	27
7	SNOW,J.T.		544	24	102	2	0.289	10	12	1	3	25
8	JOYNER,Wal		465	12	83	3	0.310	5	10	1	6	22
9	CLARK,Will		454	16	92	0	0.302	6	11	0	5	22
10	JAHA,John		316	20	65	2	0.313	8	8	1	5	21
11	FIELDER,Ce		494	31	82	0	0.243	12	10	0	-6	16
12	SORRENTO,P		323	25	79	1	0.235	10	9	0	-5	15
13	MARTINEZ,D	OF	303	5	37	8	0.307	2	4	4	4	14
14	OLERUD,Joh		492	8	54	0	0.291	3	6	0	3	13
15	SAMUEL,Jua		205	12	39	6	0.263	5	5	3	-1	11
16	MATTINGLY		458	7	49	0	0.288	3	6	0	2	11
17	PERRY,Herb		162	3	23	1	0.315	1	3	0	3	7
18	COOMER,R		101	5	19	0	0.257	2	2	0	-1	4
19	STUBBS,Fra	OF	116	2	19	0	0.250	1	2	0	-1	2
	avg, top 18		399	21	75	3	0.292	8	9	1	3	21.18

rk	2B	OQP	AB	HR	RBI	SB	BA	$HR	$RBI	$SB	$BA	$TOT
1	KNOBLAUCH		538	11	63	46	0.333	4	7	21	12	44
2	ALOMAR,Rob		517	13	66	30	0.300	5	8	14	5	32
3	BAERGA,Car		557	15	90	11	0.314	6	11	5	8	30
4	CORA,Joey		427	3	39	18	0.297	1	5	8	4	18
5	LOCKHART,K		274	6	33	8	0.321	2	4	4	5	15
6	WHITAKER,L		249	14	44	4	0.293	6	5	2	2	14
7	MCLEMORE,M	OF	467	5	41	21	0.261	2	5	9	-2	14
8	DURHAM,Ray		471	7	51	18	0.257	3	6	8	-3	14
9	ALICEA,Lui		419	6	44	13	0.270	2	5	6	-1	13
10	CIRILLO,Jf	3B	328	9	39	7	0.277	4	5	3	0	12
11	HUDLER,Rex	OF	223	6	27	13	0.265	2	3	6	-1	11
12	FRYE,Jeff		313	4	29	3	0.278	2	3	1	0	7
13	GATES,Bren		524	5	56	3	0.254	2	7	1	-4	6
14	VINA,Ferna		288	3	29	6	0.257	1	3	3	-2	5
15	ALEXANDR,M		242	3	23	11	0.236	1	3	5	-4	5
16	MARTIN,Nor		160	2	17	5	0.269	1	2	2	-0	5
17	KELLY,Pat		270	4	29	8	0.237	2	3	4	-4	5
18	HUSON,Jeff	3B	161	1	19	5	0.248	0	2	2	-2	3
19	RIPKEN,B		17	2	3	0	0.412	1	0	0	1	2
20	BARBERIE,B		237	2	25	3	0.241	1	3	1	-3	2
21	CACERES,E		117	1	17	2	0.239	0	2	1	-2	2
22	LISTACH,Pa	SS	334	0	25	13	0.219	0	3	6	-7	2
23	RODRIGUEZ,C		30	0	5	0	0.333	0	1	0	1	1
24	SHUMPERT,T		47	0	3	3	0.234	0	0	1	-1	1
	avg, top 18		357	7	41	13	0.280	3	5	6	1	14.06

rk	3B	OQP	AB	HR	RBI	SB	BA	$HR	$RBI	$SB	$BA	$TOT
1	THOME,Jim		452	25	73	4	0.314	10	9	2	7	27
2	VENTURA,Ro		492	26	93	4	0.295	10	11	2	4	27
3	GAETTI,Gar		514	35	96	3	0.261	14	11	1	-3	24
4	PHILLIPS,T	OF	525	27	61	13	0.261	11	7	6	-3	21
5	BLOWERS,Mk		439	23	96	2	0.257	9	11	1	-3	19
6	BOGGS,Wade		460	5	63	1	0.324	2	7	0	9	19
7	SEITZER,Kv	1B	492	5	69	2	0.311	2	8	1	7	18
8	FRYMAN,Tra		567	15	81	4	0.275	6	10	2	0	18
9	NAEHRING,T		433	10	57	0	0.307	4	7	0	5	16
10	BONILLA,Bo	OF	237	10	46	0	0.333	4	5	0	6	15
11	BROSIUS,Sc	1B,OF	389	17	46	4	0.262	7	5	2	-2	12
12	SPRAGUE,Ed		521	18	74	0	0.244	7	9	0	-6	10
13	PALMER,Dea		119	9	24	1	0.336	4	3	0	3	10
14	MANTO,Jeff		254	17	38	0	0.256	7	4	0	-2	9
15	PAQUETTE,C	OF	283	13	49	5	0.226	5	6	2	-5	8
16	STAHOVIAK	1B	263	3	23	5	0.266	1	3	2	-1	5
17	GIAMBI,Jas	1B	176	6	25	2	0.256	2	3	1	-1	5
18	LEIUS,Scot		372	4	45	2	0.247	2	5	1	-4	4
19	STRANGE,Do		155	2	21	0	0.271	1	2	0	-0	3
20	SNOPEK,Chr		68	1	7	1	0.324	0	1	0	1	3
21	DAVIS,Russ		98	2	12	0	0.276	1	1	0	0	2
22	DONNELS,Ch		91	2	11	0	0.253	1	1	0	-1	1
24	GOMEZ,Leo		127	4	12	0	0.236	2	1	0	-2	1
25	PAGLIARULO		241	4	27	0	0.232	2	3	0	-4	1
26	ORTIZ,Luis		108	1	18	0	0.231	0	2	0	-2	1
	avg, top 18		388	15	59	3	0.278	6	7	1	1	14.86

rk	SS		OQP	AB	HR	RBI	SB	BA	$HR	$RBI	$SB	$BA	$TOT
1	VALENTN,Jn			520	27	102	20	0.298	11	12	9	5	37
2	VIZQUEL,Om			542	6	56	29	0.266	2	7	13	-2	20
3	RIPKEN,Cal			550	17	88	0	0.262	7	10	0	-2	15
4	DISARCN,Ga			362	5	41	7	0.307	2	5	3	5	15
5	MEARES,Pat			390	12	49	10	0.269	5	6	5	-1	14
6	BORDICK,Mk			428	8	44	11	0.264	3	5	5	-2	12
7	SOJO,Luis	2B		339	7	39	4	0.289	3	5	2	2	11
8	VELARDE,Ra	3,2,O		367	7	46	5	0.278	3	5	2	1	11
9	VALENTN,Js			338	11	49	16	0.219	4	6	7	-7	10
10	GAGNE,Greg			430	6	49	3	0.256	2	6	1	-3	7
11	REBOULET,J	3B		216	4	23	1	0.292	2	3	0	2	6
12	GONZALEZ,Al			367	10	42	4	0.243	4	5	2	-4	6
13	FERNANDEZ,T			384	5	45	6	0.245	2	5	3	-4	6
14	TRAMMELL,A			223	2	23	3	0.269	1	3	1	-0	4
15	GUILLEN,Oz			415	1	41	6	0.248	0	5	3	-4	4
16	GOMEZ,Chri			431	11	50	4	0.223	4	6	2	-8	4
17	RODRIGUEZ,A			142	5	19	4	0.232	2	2	2	-2	4
18	HOWARD,Dav	2B,OF		255	0	19	6	0.243	0	2	3	-3	2
19	GREBECK,Cr	3B		154	1	18	0	0.260	0	2	0	-1	2
20	ESPINOZA,A	3B,2B		143	2	17	0	0.252	1	2	0	-1	2
21	GIL,Benji			415	9	46	2	0.219	4	5	1	-9	1
22	OWEN,Spike	3B		218	1	28	3	0.229	0	3	1	-4	1
23	LORETTA,Ma			50	1	3	1	0.260	0	0	0	-0	1
24	CEDENO,Dom	3B		161	4	14	0	0.236	2	2	0	-2	1
	avg, top 18			372	8	46	8	0.262	3	5	3	-2	10.38

rk	OF		OQP	AB	HR	RBI	SB	BA	$HR	$RBI	$SB	$BA	$TOT
1	BELLE,Albe			546	50	126	5	0.317	20	15	2	9	46
2	LOFTON,Ken			481	7	53	54	0.310	3	6	24	6	40
3	SALMON,Tim			537	34	105	5	0.330	14	12	2	11	39
4	JOHNSON,Ln			607	10	57	40	0.306	4	7	18	7	36
5	RAMIREZ,Ma			484	31	107	6	0.308	12	13	3	6	34
6	NIXON,Otis			589	0	45	50	0.295	0	5	23	5	33
7	PUCKETT,Ki			538	23	99	3	0.314	9	12	1	8	30
8	GOODWIN,To			480	4	28	50	0.288	2	3	23	2	30
9	EDMONDS,Ji			558	33	107	1	0.290	13	13	0	3	30
10	CORDOVA,Ma			512	24	84	20	0.277	10	10	9	1	29
11	HENDERSN,R			407	9	54	32	0.300	4	6	14	4	28
12	BUHNER,Jay			470	40	121	0	0.262	16	14	0	-2	28
13	WILLIAMS,Be			563	18	82	8	0.307	7	10	4	7	27
14	CURTIS,Cha			586	21	67	27	0.268	8	8	12	-1	27
15	COLEMAN,Vi			455	5	29	42	0.288	2	3	19	2	27
16	JAVIER,Sta			442	8	56	36	0.278	3	7	16	1	27
17	O'NEILL,Pa			460	22	96	1	0.300	9	11	0	5	25
18	ANDERSN,Ga			374	16	69	6	0.321	6	8	3	7	24
19	GREENWELL			481	15	76	9	0.297	6	9	4	4	23
20	BERROA,Ger			546	22	88	7	0.278	9	10	3	1	23
21	ANDERSN,Br			554	16	64	26	0.262	6	8	12	-3	23
22	RAINES,Tim			502	12	67	13	0.285	5	8	6	2	21
23	CARTER,Joe			558	25	76	12	0.253	10	9	5	-4	20
24	SIERRA,Rub			479	19	86	5	0.263	8	10	2	-2	18
25	MUNOZ,Pedr			376	18	58	0	0.301	7	7	0	4	18
26	DEVEREAUX			333	10	55	6	0.306	4	6	3	4	17
27	O'LEARY,Tr			399	10	49	5	0.308	4	6	2	5	17
28	TINSLEY,Le			341	7	41	18	0.284	3	5	8	1	17
29	WHITE,Devo			427	10	53	11	0.283	4	6	5	2	17

rk	OF	OQP	AB	HR	RBI	SB	BA	$HR	$RBI	$SB	$BA	$TOT
30	TETTLETON		429	32	78	0	0.238	13	9	0	-6	16
31	GREEN,Shaw		379	15	54	1	0.288	6	6	0	2	15
32	GREER,Rust		417	13	61	3	0.271	5	7	1	-0	13
33	AMARAL,Ric		238	2	19	21	0.282	1	2	9	1	13
34	NILSSON,Dv		263	12	53	2	0.278	5	6	1	0	12
35	GOODWIN,Cu		289	1	24	22	0.263	0	3	10	-1	12
36	GRIFFEY,Ke		260	17	42	4	0.258	7	5	2	-2	12
37	HAMILTON,D		398	5	44	11	0.271	2	5	5	-0	12
38	HULSE,Davi		339	3	47	15	0.251	1	6	7	-3	10
39	DIAZ,Alex		270	3	27	18	0.248	1	3	8	-3	10
40	NUNNALLY,J		303	14	42	6	0.244	6	5	3	-4	10
41	MIESKE,Mat		267	12	48	2	0.251	5	6	1	-2	9
42	DAMON,J		188	3	23	7	0.282	1	3	3	1	8
43	MOUTON,Lyl		179	5	27	1	0.302	2	3	0	2	8
44	CLARK,Jera		109	3	15	3	0.339	1	2	1	3	7
45	MALDONADO		190	9	30	1	0.263	4	4	0	-1	7
46	JAMES,Dion		209	2	26	4	0.287	1	3	2	1	7
47	HOSEY,Dway		68	3	7	6	0.338	1	1	3	2	7
48	BASS,Kevin		295	5	32	8	0.244	2	4	4	-3	6
49	JEFFERSON,R		121	5	26	0	0.289	2	3	0	1	6
50	POLONIA,Lu		238	2	15	10	0.261	1	2	5	-1	6
51	MCGEE,Will		200	2	15	5	0.285	1	2	2	1	6
52	WARD,Turne		129	4	16	6	0.264	2	2	3	-1	6
53	HIGGINSON		410	14	43	6	0.224	6	5	3	-8	6
54	WILLIAMS,Gd		182	6	28	4	0.247	2	3	2	-2	6
55	COLE,Alex		79	1	14	1	0.342	0	2	0	2	5
56	BRAGG,Darr		145	3	12	9	0.234	1	1	4	-2	4
57	ALDRETE,Mk		149	4	24	0	0.268	2	3	0	-0	4
58	NEWSON,War		157	5	15	2	0.261	2	2	1	-1	4
59	HAMMONDS,J		178	4	23	4	0.242	2	3	2	-2	4
60	TUCKER,Mic		177	4	17	2	0.260	2	2	1	-1	3
61	LAWTON,Mat		60	1	12	1	0.317	0	1	0	1	3
62	TARTABULL		280	8	35	0	0.236	3	4	0	-4	3
63	THURMAN,G		25	0	3	5	0.320	0	0	2	0	3
64	BECKER,Ric		392	2	33	8	0.237	1	4	4	-6	3
65	FRAZIER,Lo		99	0	8	9	0.212	0	1	4	-3	2
66	SMITH,Mark		104	3	15	3	0.231	1	2	1	-2	2
67	TOMBERLIN		85	4	10	4	0.212	2	1	2	-2	2
68	STEVERSON		42	2	6	2	0.262	1	1	1	-0	2
69	STAIRS,M		88	1	17	0	0.261	0	2	0	-0	2
70	GILES,Bria		9	1	3	0	0.556	0	0	0	1	2
71	KIRBY,Wayn		188	1	14	10	0.207	0	2	5	-5	2
72	MILLER,Kei		15	1	3	0	0.333	0	0	0	0	1
73	BURNITZ,Je		7	0	0	0	0.571	0	0	0	1	1
74	PALMEIRO,O		20	0	1	0	0.350	0	0	0	1	1
75	PEMBERTON		30	0	3	0	0.300	0	0	0	0	1
76	OBANDO,She		38	0	3	1	0.263	0	0	0	-0	1
	avg, top 60		356	12	51	11	0.282	5	6	5	1	17.14

rk	DH	OQP	AB	HR	RBI	SB	BA	$HR	$RBI	$SB	$BA	$TOT
1	MARTINEZ,Ed		511	29	113	4	0.356	12	13	2	16	42
2	DAVIS,Chil		424	20	86	3	0.318	8	10	1	7	27
3	CANSECO,Jo		396	24	81	4	0.306	10	10	2	5	26
4	GONZALEZ,Ju		352	27	82	0	0.295	11	10	0	3	23
5	BAINES,Har		385	24	63	0	0.299	10	7	0	4	21
6	MOLITOR,Pa		525	15	60	12	0.270	6	7	5	-1	18

Appendix B — ALH

rk	DH	OQP	AB	HR	RBI	SB	BA	$HR	$RBI	$SB	$BA	$TOT
7	VAUGHN,Gre		392	17	59	10	0.224	7	7	5	-7	11
8	GIBSON,Kir		227	9	35	9	0.260	4	4	4	-1	11
9	KRUK,John		159	2	23	0	0.308	1	3	0	2	6
10	VITIELLO,J		130	7	21	0	0.254	3	2	0	-1	4
11	STRAWBERRY		87	3	13	0	0.276	1	2	0	0	3
12	HALE,Chip		103	2	18	0	0.262	1	2	0	-1	2
13	JAMES,Chri		82	2	8	1	0.268	1	1	0	-0	2
14	SABO,Chris		71	1	8	2	0.254	0	1	1	-1	2
15	GROTEWOLD		36	1	6	0	0.278	0	1	0	0	1
	avg, top 12		308	15	55	4	0.292	6	6	2	2	16.18

American League Pitchers

rk	Name	IP	W	Sv	ERA	Ratio	$W	$S	$ERA	$Rto	$TOT
1	JOHNSON,Ra	214	18	0	2.48	9.41	18	0	20	19	58
2	MESA,Jose	64	3	46	1.13	9.28	3	36	12	7	57
3	MUSSINA,Mk	222	19	0	3.29	9.62	19	0	13	19	50
4	WAKEFIELD	195	16	0	2.95	10.64	16	0	15	11	42
5	WETTELAND	61	1	31	2.93	7.92	1	24	5	9	39
6	AGUILERA,R	55	3	32	2.60	9.60	3	25	6	5	39
7	CONE,David	229	18	0	3.57	11.11	18	0	10	10	38
8	MARTINEZ,De	187	12	0	3.08	10.59	12	0	13	11	36
9	ROGERS,Ken	208	17	0	3.38	11.60	17	0	11	7	35
10	SMITH,Lee	49	0	37	3.47	12.22	0	29	3	1	32
11	MONTGOMERY	66	2	31	3.43	11.65	2	24	4	2	32
12	APPIER,Kev	201	15	0	3.89	10.86	15	0	6	11	31
13	HERSHISER	167	16	0	3.87	10.86	16	0	5	9	30
14	CHARLTON,N	48	2	14	1.51	7.36	2	11	8	8	29
15	BROWN,Kevi	172	10	0	3.60	10.60	10	0	8	11	28
16	HERNANDEZ,R	60	3	32	3.92	13.73	3	25	2	-2	28
17	ECKERSLEY	50	4	29	4.83	11.44	4	22	-1	2	28
18	WELLS,Davi	130	10	0	3.04	10.84	10	0	10	7	27
19	PERCIVAL,T	74	3	3	1.95	7.66	3	2	10	12	27
20	BELINDA,St	70	8	10	3.10	10.21	8	8	5	6	26
21	MCDOWELL,J	218	15	0	3.93	11.95	15	0	6	5	26
22	TAVAREZ,Ju	85	10	0	2.44	10.27	10	0	9	6	26
23	NELSON,Jef	79	7	2	2.17	9.72	7	2	10	7	26
24	FERNANDZ,A	204	12	0	3.80	11.71	12	0	7	6	25
25	GUBICZA,Ma	213	12	0	3.75	11.98	12	0	8	5	24
26	OGEA,Chad	106	8	0	3.05	10.50	8	0	8	7	23
27	HANSON,Eri	187	15	0	4.24	11.86	15	0	3	5	22
28	HENNEMAN,M	29	0	18	1.53	10.13	0	14	5	3	21
29	AYALA,Bobb	71	6	19	4.44	13.06	6	15	0	-1	20
30	ABBOTT,Jim	197	11	0	3.70	12.47	11	0	8	2	20
31	CASTILLO,T	73	1	13	3.22	10.90	1	10	5	4	20
32	RUSSELL,Jf	33	1	20	3.03	12.40	1	15	3	0	20
33	FINLEY,Chu	203	15	0	4.21	12.64	15	0	3	1	19
34	PLUNK,Eric	64	6	2	2.67	10.55	6	2	6	4	18
35	LEITER,Al	183	11	0	3.64	13.28	11	0	8	-2	16
36	FETTERS,Mk	35	0	22	3.38	15.58	0	17	2	-3	16
37	MADDUX,Mik	90	4	1	3.61	10.14	4	1	4	7	16
38	LANGSTON,M	200	15	0	4.63	12.40	15	0	-1	2	16
39	PETTITTE,A	175	12	0	4.17	12.65	12	0	3	1	16
40	NAGY,Charl	178	16	0	4.55	12.89	16	0	-0	-0	15
41	HONEYCUTT	46	5	2	2.96	9.66	5	2	4	4	15

rk	Name	IP	W	Sv	ERA	Ratio	$W	$S	$ERA	$Rto	$TOT
42	TIMLIN,Mik	42	4	5	2.14	11.79	4	4	5	1	15
43	JONES,Doug	47	0	22	5.01	13.69	0	17	-1	-1	15
44	HITCHCOCK	168	11	0	4.70	11.92	11	0	-1	4	14
45	PAVLIK,Rog	192	10	0	4.37	12.40	10	0	1	2	14
46	PATTERSN,B	53	5	0	3.04	10.29	5	0	4	4	13
47	MCDOWELL,R	85	7	4	4.02	12.71	7	3	2	0	13
48	ASSENMACHR	38	6	0	2.82	10.33	6	0	4	3	13
49	OROSCO,Jes	50	2	3	3.26	9.97	2	2	3	4	12
50	VOSBERG,E	36	5	4	3.00	12.00	5	3	3	1	12
51	CLEMENS,Ro	140	10	0	4.18	12.92	10	0	2	-0	12
52	LIRA,Felip	146	9	1	4.31	12.73	9	1	2	0	12
53	STOTTLEMYRE,T	210	14	0	4.55	13.22	14	0	-0	-2	11
54	CORSI,J	45	2	2	2.20	11.40	2	2	6	2	11
55	WHITESDE,M	53	5	3	4.08	11.38	5	2	1	2	11
56	RISLEY,Bil	60	2	1	3.13	10.89	2	1	5	4	11
57	ONTIVEROS	130	9	0	4.37	12.63	9	0	1	1	11
58	ERICKSON,S	196	13	0	4.81	12.84	13	0	-3	-0	10
59	CORMIER,Rh	115	7	0	4.07	12.68	7	0	3	0	10
60	POOLE,J	50	3	0	3.75	10.19	3	0	2	4	9
61	KARCHNER,M	32	4	0	1.69	12.66	4	0	5	0	9
62	KIEFER,Mar	50	4	0	3.44	11.60	4	0	3	2	9
63	REYES,Albe	33	1	1	2.43	9.99	1	1	4	3	9
64	MOYER,Jami	116	8	0	5.21	11.44	8	0	-4	5	9
65	HAYNES,Jim	24	2	0	2.25	8.63	2	0	3	3	8
66	KAMIEN'CKI	90	7	0	4.01	13.25	7	0	2	-1	8
67	HANEY,Chri	81	3	0	3.65	12.28	3	0	4	1	8
68	PICHARDO,H	64	8	1	4.36	13.50	8	1	1	-1	8
69	RADKE,Brad	181	11	0	5.32	12.03	11	0	-7	4	8
70	CHRISTOPHER	61	4	1	3.82	12.47	4	1	2	1	8
71	STEVENS,Dv	66	5	10	5.07	14.53	5	8	-2	-3	7
72	MCDONALD,B	80	3	0	4.16	11.81	3	0	2	2	7
73	GORDON,Tom	189	12	0	4.43	13.95	12	0	1	-6	7
74	JOHNS,D	55	5	0	4.61	11.52	5	0	-0	2	7
75	JAMES,Mike	56	3	1	3.88	12.13	3	1	2	1	7
76	TEWKSBURY	130	8	0	4.58	13.12	8	0	-0	-1	6
77	OLSON,Greg	33	3	3	4.09	12.82	3	2	1	0	6
78	ALVAREZ,Wi	175	8	0	4.32	13.58	8	0	2	-4	6
79	SPARKS,Ste	202	9	0	4.63	13.19	9	0	-1	-2	6
80	LLOYD,Grae	32	0	4	4.50	10.13	0	3	0	3	6
81	WICKMAN,Bo	80	2	1	4.05	12.38	2	1	2	1	6
82	VAN POPPEL	138	4	0	4.88	11.78	4	0	-2	4	6
83	SELE,Aaron	32	3	0	3.06	12.80	3	0	3	0	6
84	HILL,Ken	75	4	0	3.98	13.14	4	0	2	-1	5
85	ROBINSON,K	39	1	0	3.69	10.85	1	0	2	2	5
86	CLARK,T	39	2	1	3.46	12.69	2	1	2	0	5
87	BONES,Rick	200	10	0	4.63	13.52	10	0	-1	-4	5
88	ANDUJAR,L	30	2	0	3.26	11.87	2	0	2	1	5
89	BELCHER,Ti	179	10	0	4.52	13.85	10	0	0	-5	5
90	DELEON,Jos	68	5	0	5.19	11.70	5	0	-2	2	5
91	WICKANDER	23	0	1	1.93	11.96	0	1	3	1	5
92	DOHERTY,Jo	113	5	6	5.10	13.30	5	5	-3	-2	5
93	WILLIMS,Wo	54	1	0	3.69	12.07	1	0	2	1	5
94	KARL,Scott	124	6	0	4.14	13.86	6	0	2	-4	5
95	GUTHRIE,Ma	42	5	0	4.46	13.39	5	0	0	-1	4
96	LOPEZ,Albi	23	0	0	3.13	9.39	0	0	2	3	4
97	STANTON,Mk	21	1	0	3.00	10.71	1	0	2	1	4
98	THOMAS,Lar	14	0	0	1.32	9.22	0	0	2	2	4

rk	Name	IP	W	Sv	ERA	Ratio	$W	$S	$ERA	$Rto	$TOT
99	GOHR,Greg	10	1	0	0.87	10.45	1	0	2	1	4
100	TAPANI,Kev	134	6	0	4.92	12.73	6	0	-3	0	4
101	KRIVDA,Ric	75	2	0	4.54	12.07	2	0	-0	2	4
102	MOHLER,Mik	24	1	1	3.04	12.93	1	1	2	-0	4
103	BUTCHER,Mk	51	6	0	4.73	14.03	6	0	-1	-2	3
104	CRABTREE,T	32	0	0	3.09	12.09	0	0	3	1	3
105	WASDIN,J	17	1	0	4.67	8.83	1	0	-0	2	3
106	WENGERT,Do	30	1	0	3.34	12.74	1	0	2	0	3
107	ESHELMAN,V	82	6	0	4.85	13.44	6	0	-1	-2	3
108	SANDERSON	39	1	0	4.12	11.90	1	0	1	1	3
109	MONTELEONE	9	1	0	2.00	11.00	1	0	1	1	3
110	HOWE,Steve	49	6	2	4.96	15.24	6	2	-1	-4	3
111	MAGNANTE,M	45	1	0	4.23	12.29	1	0	1	1	2
112	ROBERTSN,R	52	2	0	3.83	13.76	2	0	2	-2	2
113	BOSKIE,Sha	112	7	0	5.64	12.25	7	0	-6	2	2
114	MEACHAM,Ru	60	4	2	4.98	13.73	4	2	-1	-2	2
115	MCANDREW	36	2	0	4.71	12.14	2	0	-0	1	2
116	LORRAINE,A	8	0	0	3.38	5.63	0	0	1	2	2
117	ELDRED,Cal	24	1	0	3.42	12.93	1	0	1	-0	2
118	CLARK,Mark	125	9	0	5.27	13.36	9	0	-5	-2	2
119	OLIVER,Dar	49	4	0	4.22	14.51	4	0	1	-3	2
120	MCCASKILL	81	6	2	4.89	14.44	6	2	-2	-4	2
121	WOLCOTT,B	37	3	0	4.42	13.99	3	0	0	-1	2
122	EMBREE,Ala	25	3	1	5.11	14.23	3	1	-1	-1	2
123	BOROWSKI,J	7	0	0	1.23	11.05	0	0	1	0	2
124	LEE,Ma	33	2	1	4.86	13.23	2	1	-1	-0	2
125	REYES,Carl	69	4	0	5.09	12.91	4	0	-2	-0	2
126	HARTLEY,Mk	14	1	0	5.14	10.29	1	0	-0	1	2
127	HOWARD,Chr	4	0	0	0.00	9.00	0	0	1	0	2
128	HENRY,D	9	1	5	6.23	21.81	1	4	-1	-3	2
129	MANZANILLO,J	17	0	0	2.08	14.54	0	0	2	-1	1
130	RYAN,Ken	33	0	7	4.96	15.98	0	5	-1	-3	1
131	HABYAN,Joh	33	1	0	4.13	13.22	1	0	1	-0	1
132	LEIPER,Dav	23	1	0	3.57	14.29	1	0	1	-1	1
133	MECIR,Jim	5	0	0	0.00	13.50	0	0	1	-0	1
134	SIMAS,Bill	14	1	0	2.57	16.07	1	0	2	-1	1
135	WEGMAN,Bil	71	5	2	5.35	14.01	5	2	-3	-3	1
136	RIGHTNOWAR	37	2	1	5.40	13.01	2	1	-2	-0	1
137	BARK,B	2	0	0	0.00	11.57	0	0	1	0	1
138	HALL,Darre	16	0	3	4.41	16.53	0	2	0	-2	0
139	FORTUGNO,T	39	1	0	5.59	11.41	1	0	-2	2	0
140	PAVLAS,D	6	0	0	3.18	12.71	0	0	0	0	0
141	PEREZ,Meli	69	5	0	5.58	13.11	5	0	-4	-1	0
142	RIGHETTI,D	49	3	0	4.20	15.14	3	0	1	-4	0
143	GUNDERSON	12	2	0	5.11	16.05	2	0	-0	-1	0
144	KEYSER,B	92	5	0	4.97	13.74	5	0	-2	-3	0
145	BENNETT,Er	0	0	0	0.00	0.00	0	0	0	0	0
146	HARRIS,Gen	4	0	0	4.50	11.25	0	0	0	0	0
147	CAMPBELL,K	10	0	0	4.66	12.10	0	0	-0	0	0
148	FARRELL,J	5	0	0	3.86	13.50	0	0	0	-0	0
149	DEDRICK,J	8	0	0	2.35	16.43	0	0	1	-1	0
150	THOMAS,M	1	0	0	0.00	20.25	0	0	0	-0	0
151	PATTERSN,J	3	0	0	2.70	16.20	0	0	0	-0	-0
152	RIVERA,Mar	67	5	0	5.51	13.57	5	0	-3	-2	-0
153	SHUEY,Paul	6	0	0	4.26	14.21	0	0	0	-0	-0
154	JACOME,Jas	84	4	0	5.36	13.07	4	0	-4	-1	-0

rk	Name	IP	W	Sv	ERA	Ratio	$W	$S	$ERA	$Rto	$TOT
155	COOK,Denni	58	0	2	4.53	13.89	0	2	0	-2	-0
156	EDENFIELD	13	0	0	4.26	14.21	0	0	0	-1	-0
157	BRONKEY,Jf	12	0	0	3.65	15.32	0	0	1	-1	-0
158	SIROTKA,M	34	1	0	4.19	14.68	1	0	1	-2	-0
159	ANDERSN,S	25	1	0	5.33	13.14	1	0	-1	-0	-0
160	ANDERSN,Br	100	6	0	5.87	12.64	6	0	-7	1	-0
161	SMITH,Zane	111	8	0	5.61	13.58	8	0	-6	-2	-1
162	SHAW,J	10	0	0	6.52	12.10	0	0	-1	0	-1
163	DETTMER,Jo	0	0	0	27.00	54.01	0	0	-0	-0	-1
164	DAVISON,Sc	4	0	0	6.23	16.62	0	0	-0	-1	-1
165	GUARDADO,E	91	4	2	5.12	14.19	4	2	-3	-4	-1
166	ROGERS,J	24	2	0	5.70	14.83	2	0	-2	-2	-1
167	HUDSON,Joe	46	0	1	4.11	14.87	0	1	1	-3	-1
168	DESILVA	9	1	0	7.27	15.58	1	0	-1	-1	-1
169	BUNCH,Melv	40	1	0	5.63	12.60	1	0	-2	0	-1
170	WITT,Bobby	61	3	0	4.55	14.97	3	0	-0	-4	-1
171	PRIETO,A	58	2	0	4.97	13.81	2	0	-1	-2	-1
172	OQUIST,Mik	54	2	0	4.17	15.33	2	0	1	-4	-1
173	SODOWSKY,C	23	2	0	5.01	16.20	2	0	-1	-3	-1
174	LILLIQUIST	23	2	0	6.26	14.09	2	0	-2	-1	-1
175	ROA,Joe	6	0	0	6.00	16.50	0	0	-0	-1	-1
176	MARQUEZ,Is	7	0	0	6.75	14.85	0	0	-1	-0	-1
177	SUPPAN,J	23	1	0	5.96	13.50	1	0	-2	-0	-1
178	JOHNSTON,J	4	0	0	11.25	11.25	0	0	-2	0	-1
179	SLUSARSKI	15	1	0	5.40	16.20	1	0	-1	-2	-1
180	EILAND,D	10	1	0	6.30	17.10	1	0	-1	-1	-1
181	HEREDIA,Wi	12	0	0	3.75	18.00	0	0	1	-2	-1
182	MACDONALD	46	1	0	4.86	13.99	1	0	-1	-2	-2
183	FERMIN,Ram	1	0	0	13.50	33.75	0	0	-1	-1	-2
184	HURTADO,Ed	78	5	0	5.45	14.02	5	0	-4	-3	-2
185	WATKINS,S	22	0	0	5.40	13.71	0	0	-1	-1	-2
186	KEY,Jimmy	30	1	0	5.64	13.65	1	0	-2	-1	-2
187	RADINSKY,S	38	2	1	5.45	14.92	2	1	-2	-3	-2
188	EDDY,Chris	4	0	0	7.36	22.09	0	0	-1	-1	-2
189	BENES,Andy	63	7	0	5.86	15.00	7	0	-4	-4	-2
...											
281	GROOM,Budd	41	1	1	7.52	17.93	1	1	-7	-6	-11
282	SCHULLSTROM	47	0	0	6.89	16.85	0	0	-6	-6	-12
283	SCANLAN,Bo	83	4	0	6.59	15.66	4	0	-9	-7	-12
284	BALDWIN,Ja	15	0	0	12.89	25.16	0	0	-7	-6	-13
285	HARRIS,G.W	33	0	0	8.82	18.18	0	0	-8	-6	-13
286	COX,Danny	45	1	0	7.40	18.00	1	0	-7	-7	-13
287	STEWART,Dv	81	3	0	6.89	15.56	3	0	-10	-7	-14
288	PARRA,J	62	1	0	7.59	15.32	1	0	-10	-5	-14
289	BOEHRINGER	18	0	0	13.75	23.43	0	0	-9	-6	-15
290	GUZMAN,Jua	135	4	0	6.32	14.90	4	0	-12	-8	-16
291	KLINGENBEK	80	2	0	7.12	16.15	2	0	-11	-8	-17
292	DARWIN,Dan	99	3	0	7.45	14.73	3	0	-15	-6	-18
293	BERE,Jason	138	8	0	7.19	16.80	8	0	-18	-16	-26
294	MOORE,Mike	133	5	0	7.53	16.76	5	0	-20	-15	-30
	avg,top 108	98	6	4	3.89	11.91	6	3	3	3	15.23

National League Hitters

rk	1B	OQP	AB	HR	RBI	SB	BA	$HR	$RBI	$SB	$BA	$TOT
1	PIAZZA,Mik		434	32	93	1	0.346	14	12	0	12	39
2	LOPEZ,Javy		333	14	51	0	0.315	6	7	0	5	18
3	AUSMUS,Bra		328	5	34	16	0.293	2	4	6	2	15
4	HUNDLEY,To		275	15	51	1	0.280	7	7	0	1	14
5	EUSEBIO,To		368	6	58	0	0.299	3	8	0	3	14
6	SANTIAGO,B		266	11	44	2	0.286	5	6	1	1	13
7	FLETCHER,D		350	11	45	0	0.286	5	6	0	1	12
8	SERVAIS,Sc		264	13	47	2	0.265	6	6	1	-1	12
9	TAUBENSEE		218	9	44	2	0.284	4	6	1	1	11
10	GIRARDI,Jo		462	8	55	3	0.262	4	7	1	-2	9
11	DAULTON,Da		342	9	55	3	0.249	4	7	1	-4	9
12	PARENT,Mar		265	18	38	0	0.234	8	5	0	-4	9
13	JOHNSON,Ch		315	11	39	0	0.251	5	5	0	-3	7
14	MANWARING		379	4	36	1	0.251	2	5	0	-4	3
15	O'BRIEN,Ch		198	9	23	0	0.227	4	3	0	-4	3
16	WEBSTER,Le		150	4	14	0	0.267	2	2	0	-1	3
17	JOHNSON,Br		207	3	29	0	0.251	1	4	0	-2	3
18	SLAUGHT,Do		112	0	13	0	0.304	0	2	0	1	3
19	OWENS,Jayh		45	4	12	0	0.244	2	2	0	-1	3
20	SHEAFFER,D		208	5	30	0	0.231	2	4	0	-4	2
21	LAKER,Tim		141	3	20	0	0.234	1	3	0	-2	2
22	PEREZ,Eddi		13	1	4	0	0.308	0	1	0	0	1
23	NATAL,Bob		43	2	6	0	0.233	1	1	0	-1	1
24	REED,Jeff		113	0	9	0	0.265	0	1	0	-0	1
25	DECKER,Ste		133	3	13	1	0.226	1	2	0	-3	1
	avg,top 24		243	8	35	1	0.274	4	5	0	-0	8.63

rk	1B	OQP	AB	HR	RBI	SB	BA	$HR	$RBI	$SB	$BA	$TOT
1	KARROS,Eri		551	32	105	4	0.298	14	14	1	5	34
2	GALARRAGA		554	31	106	12	0.280	14	14	4	1	33
3	GRACE,Mark		552	16	92	6	0.326	7	12	2	11	32
4	BAGWELL,Jf		448	21	87	12	0.290	9	11	4	3	28
5	MCGRIFF,Fr		528	27	93	3	0.280	12	12	1	1	26
6	COLBRUNN,G		528	23	89	11	0.277	10	12	4	0	26
7	BROGNA,Ric		495	22	76	0	0.289	10	10	0	3	22
8	JEFFERIES		480	11	56	9	0.306	5	7	3	6	21
9	SEGUI,Davi	OF	456	12	68	2	0.309	5	9	1	6	21
10	CARREON,Ma	OF	396	17	65	0	0.301	8	8	0	4	20
11	MORRIS,Hal		359	11	51	1	0.279	5	7	0	1	12
12	MABRY,John	OF	388	5	41	0	0.307	2	5	0	5	12
13	LIVINGSTONE		196	5	32	2	0.337	2	4	1	5	12
14	WILLIAMS,Ed		296	12	47	0	0.260	5	6	0	-2	10
15	SIMMS,Mike		121	9	24	1	0.256	4	3	0	-1	7
16	CIANFROCCO		118	5	31	0	0.263	2	4	0	-1	6
17	JOHNSON,Ma		221	13	28	5	0.208	6	4	2	-6	5
18	HOLLINS,Dv		205	7	25	1	0.229	3	3	0	-4	3
19	SWEENEY,M		77	2	13	1	0.273	1	2	0	-0	3
20	AUDE,Rich		109	2	19	1	0.248	1	2	0	-1	2
21	PETAGINE,R		124	3	17	0	0.234	1	2	0	-2	1
22	WORTHINGTON		18	1	2	0	0.278	0	0	0	0	1
23	PHILLIPS,J		231	9	28	1	0.195	4	4	0	-8	1
	avg,top 18		383	16	62	4	0.289	7	8	1	2	18.49

rk	2B	OQP	AB	HR	RBI	SB	BA	$HR	$RBI	$SB	$BA	$TOT
1	BIGGIO,Cra		553	22	77	33	0.302	10	10	12	6	37
2	VERAS,Quil		440	5	32	56	0.261	2	4	20	-2	24
3	DESHIELDS		425	8	37	39	0.256	4	5	14	-3	19
4	KENT,Jeff		472	20	65	3	0.278	9	8	1	0	19
5	LANSING,Mk		467	10	62	27	0.255	5	8	10	-4	19
6	GARCIA,Car		367	6	50	8	0.294	3	6	3	3	15
7	MORANDINI		494	6	49	9	0.283	3	6	3	2	14
8	LEWIS,Mark		171	3	30	0	0.339	1	4	0	5	10
9	BATES,Jaso	SS	322	8	46	3	0.267	4	6	1	-1	10
10	LIRIANO,Ne		259	5	38	2	0.286	2	5	1	1	9
11	DUNCAN,Mar	SS	265	6	36	1	0.287	3	5	0	1	9
12	HERNANDEZ,J	SS,3	245	13	40	1	0.245	6	5	0	-3	8
13	ALFONZO,Ed	3B	335	4	41	1	0.278	2	5	0	0	8
14	SANCHEZ,Re		428	3	27	6	0.278	1	4	2	1	8
15	REED,Jody		445	4	40	6	0.256	2	5	2	-3	6
16	HANEY,T		73	2	6	0	0.411	1	1	0	4	6
17	LEMKE,Mark		399	5	38	2	0.253	2	5	1	-3	4
18	PENA,Geron		101	1	8	3	0.267	0	1	1	-0	2
19	BELL,David		144	2	19	1	0.250	1	2	0	-1	2
20	BROWNE,Jer	OF	184	1	17	1	0.255	0	2	0	-1	2
	avg,top 18		348	7	40	11	0.276	3	5	4	0	12.56

rk	3B	OQP	AB	HR	RBI	SB	BA	$HR	$RBI	$SB	$BA	$TOT
1	CASTILLA,V		527	32	90	2	0.309	14	12	1	7	34
2	CAMINITI,K		526	26	94	12	0.302	12	12	4	5	34
3	WILLIAMS,Ma		283	23	65	2	0.336	10	8	1	7	26
4	JONES,Chip	OF	524	23	86	8	0.265	10	11	3	-2	22
5	BONILLA,Bo	OF	317	18	53	0	0.325	8	7	0	6	21
6	KING,Jeff	1B	445	18	87	7	0.265	8	11	2	-2	20
7	BERRY,Sean		314	14	55	3	0.318	6	7	1	5	20
8	PENDLETON		513	14	78	1	0.290	6	10	0	3	20
9	HAYES,Char		529	11	85	5	0.276	5	11	2	0	18
10	MAGADAN,Dv		348	2	51	2	0.313	1	7	1	5	14
11	BRANSON,Jf	SS	331	12	45	2	0.260	5	6	1	-2	10
12	SCARSONE,S		233	11	29	3	0.266	5	4	1	-1	9
13	ZEILE,Todd	1B	426	14	52	1	0.246	6	7	0	-5	9
14	WALLACH,Ti		327	9	38	0	0.266	4	5	0	-1	8
15	SHIPLEY,Cr		232	3	24	6	0.263	1	3	2	-1	5
16	WEHNER,Joh	OF	107	0	5	3	0.308	0	1	1	1	3
17	HANSEN,Dav		181	1	14	0	0.287	0	2	0	1	3
18	YOUNG,Kevi		181	6	22	1	0.232	3	3	0	-3	3
19	BENJAMIN,M		186	3	12	11	0.220	1	2	4	-4	3
20	ANDREWS,Sh	1B	220	8	31	1	0.214	4	4	0	-6	2
21	BUSCH,Mike		17	3	6	0	0.235	1	1	0	-0	2
22	HARRIS,Len	1B	197	2	16	10	0.208	1	2	4	-5	1
23	JOHNSON,Ho		169	7	22	1	0.195	3	3	0	-6	1
24	OWENS,Eric		2	0	1	0	1.000	0	0	0	1	1
25	DONNELS,Ch		30	0	2	0	0.300	0	0	0	0	1
	avg,top 18		352	13	54	3	0.285	6	7	1	1	15.53

rk	SS	OQP	AB	HR	RBI	SB	BA	$HR	$RBI	$SB	$BA	$TOT
1	LARKIN,Bar		496	15	66	51	0.319	7	9	18	8	42
2	DUNSTON,Sh		477	14	69	10	0.296	6	9	4	4	23
3	CORDERO,Wi	OF	514	10	49	9	0.286	5	6	3	2	16
4	BOONE,Bret		513	15	68	5	0.267	7	9	2	-2	16
5	ROBERTS,Bi	OF	296	2	25	20	0.304	1	3	7	3	15

rk	SS	OQP	AB	HR	RBI	SB	BA	$HR	$RBI	$SB	$BA	$TOT
6	VIZCAINO,J		509	3	56	8	0.287	1	7	3	2	14
7	ABBOTT,Kur		420	17	60	4	0.255	8	8	1	-3	14
8	CLAYTON,Ro		509	5	58	24	0.244	2	8	9	-6	12
9	BELL,Jay		530	13	55	2	0.262	6	7	1	-3	11
10	FONVILLE,C	2B	320	0	16	20	0.278	0	2	7	0	10
11	OFFERMAN,J		429	4	33	2	0.287	2	4	1	2	9
12	WEISS,Walt		427	1	25	15	0.260	0	3	5	-3	7
13	MILLER,Orl		324	5	36	3	0.262	2	5	1	-2	6
14	ARIAS,Alex	3B	216	3	26	1	0.269	1	3	0	-1	5
15	BOGAR,Tim	3B	145	1	21	1	0.290	0	3	0	1	4
16	AURILIA,R		19	2	4	1	0.474	1	1	0	2	3
17	GUTIERREZ		156	0	12	5	0.276	0	2	2	0	3
18	MORDECAI,M		75	3	11	0	0.280	1	1	0	0	3
19	GRUDZ'LNEK	3B	269	1	20	8	0.245	0	3	3	-3	3
20	SILVESTRI		72	2	7	2	0.264	1	1	1	-0	2
21	BLAUSER,Jf		431	12	31	8	0.211	5	4	3	-11	2
	avg,top 18		354	6	38	10	0.278	3	5	4	0	11.76

rk	OF	OQP	AB	HR	RBI	SB	BA	$HR	$RBI	$SB	$BA	$TOT
1	BICHETTE,D		579	40	128	13	0.340	18	17	5	14	54
2	SANDERS,Re		484	28	99	36	0.306	13	13	13	6	44
3	BONDS,Barr		506	33	104	31	0.294	15	14	11	4	43
4	SOSA,Sammy		564	36	119	34	0.268	16	15	12	-2	42
5	WALKER,Lar		494	36	101	16	0.306	16	13	6	6	41
6	GWYNN,Tony		535	9	90	17	0.368	4	12	6	19	41
7	MONDESI,Ra		536	26	88	27	0.285	12	11	10	2	35
8	BELL,Derek		452	8	86	27	0.334	4	11	10	10	35
9	JORDAN,Bri		490	22	81	24	0.296	10	11	9	4	33
10	GANT,Ron		410	29	88	23	0.276	13	11	8	0	33
11	LANKFORD,R		483	25	82	24	0.277	11	11	9	0	31
12	CONINE,Jef		483	25	105	2	0.302	11	14	1	5	31
13	HILL,Glena		497	24	86	25	0.264	11	11	9	-2	29
14	FINLEY,Ste		562	10	44	36	0.297	5	6	13	5	28
15	YOUNG,Eric		366	6	36	35	0.317	3	5	12	6	26
16	WHITE,Rond		474	13	57	25	0.295	6	7	9	4	26
17	KLESKO,Rya		329	23	70	5	0.310	10	9	2	5	26
18	GILKEY,Ber		480	17	69	12	0.298	8	9	4	4	25
19	MERCED,Orl	1B	487	15	83	7	0.300	7	11	2	5	25
20	SHEFFIELD		213	16	46	19	0.324	7	6	7	4	24
21	MCRAE,Bria		580	12	48	27	0.288	5	6	10	3	24
22	BUTLER,Bre		513	1	38	32	0.300	0	5	11	5	22
23	EISENREICH		377	10	55	10	0.316	5	7	4	6	21
24	MARTIN,Al		439	13	41	20	0.282	6	5	7	1	20
25	JUSTICE,Dv		411	24	78	4	0.253	11	10	1	-4	19
26	KELLY,Robe		504	7	57	19	0.278	3	7	7	1	18
27	GRISSOM,Ma		551	12	42	29	0.258	5	5	10	-4	18
28	GONZALEZ,Lu		471	13	69	6	0.276	6	9	2	0	17
29	HUNTER,B.L		321	2	28	24	0.302	1	4	9	3	17
30	TARASCO,To		438	14	40	24	0.249	6	5	9	-4	16
31	ALOU,Moise		344	14	58	4	0.273	6	8	1	-0	15
32	CANGELOSI		201	2	18	21	0.318	1	2	7	4	14
33	BURKS,Elli		278	14	49	7	0.266	6	6	2	-1	14
34	SANDERS,De		343	6	28	24	0.268	3	4	9	-1	14
35	HOWARD,Tho		281	3	26	17	0.302	1	3	6	3	14
36	MAY,Derric		206	8	41	5	0.301	4	5	2	2	13
37	MOUTON,Jam		298	4	27	25	0.262	2	4	9	-2	13

rk	OF	OQP	AB	HR	RBI	SB	BA	$HR	$RBI	$SB	$BA	$TOT
38	BRUMFIELD		402	4	26	22	0.271	2	3	8	-1	12
39	KINGERY,Mk		350	8	37	13	0.269	4	5	5	-1	12
40	WHITEN,Mrk		212	11	37	7	0.269	5	5	2	-1	12
41	EVERETT,Ca		289	12	54	2	0.260	5	7	1	-2	11
42	WALTON,Jer		162	8	22	10	0.290	4	3	4	1	11
43	LEWIS,Darr		472	1	24	32	0.250	0	3	11	-5	10
44	JONES,Chri		182	8	31	2	0.280	4	4	1	0	9
45	VANDERWAL	1B	101	5	21	1	0.347	2	3	0	3	8
46	LONGMIRE,T		104	3	19	1	0.356	1	2	0	4	8
47	TIMMONS,Oz		171	8	28	3	0.263	4	4	1	-1	7
48	PLANTIER,P		216	9	34	1	0.255	4	4	0	-2	7
49	BULLETT,Sc		150	3	22	8	0.273	1	3	3	-0	7
50	DAWSON,And		226	8	37	0	0.257	4	5	0	-2	7
51	ORSULAK,Jo		290	1	37	1	0.283	0	5	0	1	7
52	CARR,Chuck		308	2	20	25	0.227	1	3	9	-6	6
53	CLARK,Dave		196	4	24	3	0.281	2	3	1	0	6
54	TAVAREZ,Je		189	2	13	7	0.291	1	2	2	1	6
55	THOMPSN,Ry		267	7	31	3	0.251	3	4	1	-3	6
56	DYKSTRA,Ln		254	2	18	10	0.264	1	2	4	-1	6
57	ANTHONY,Er		134	5	23	2	0.269	2	3	1	-0	6
58	NIEVES,Mel		234	14	38	2	0.205	6	5	1	-7	5
59	GALLAGHER		157	1	12	0	0.318	0	2	0	3	5
60	MARSH,Tom		109	3	15	0	0.294	1	2	0	1	4
61	HUBBARD,Tr		58	3	9	2	0.310	1	1	1	1	4
62	GREGG,T		156	6	20	3	0.237	3	3	1	-2	4
63	ASHLEY,Bil		215	8	27	0	0.237	4	4	0	-3	4
64	BENITEZ,Ya		39	2	7	0	0.385	1	1	0	2	4
65	BUFORD,D		136	4	12	7	0.235	2	2	2	-2	4
66	VAN SLYKE		214	3	16	7	0.243	1	2	2	-3	3
67	PEGUES,Ste		171	6	16	1	0.246	3	2	0	-2	3
68	BENARD,M		34	1	4	1	0.382	0	1	0	2	3
69	HOLLANDSWORTH,T		103	5	13	2	0.233	2	2	1	-2	3
70	SANTANGELO		98	1	9	1	0.296	0	1	0	1	3
71	SMITH,Dwig		131	3	21	0	0.252	1	3	0	-1	3
72	LAMPKIN,To		76	1	9	2	0.276	0	1	1	0	2
73	MORMAN,Rus		72	3	7	0	0.278	1	1	0	0	2
74	NEWFIELD		55	1	7	0	0.309	0	1	0	1	2
75	THOMPSON,M		132	2	19	4	0.220	1	2	1	-3	2
76	DEVEREAUX		55	1	8	2	0.255	0	1	1	-0	2
77	CUMMINGS,M		152	2	15	1	0.243	1	2	0	-2	1
78	KELLY,Mike		137	3	17	7	0.190	1	2	2	-5	1
79	VARSHO,Gar		103	0	11	2	0.252	0	1	1	-1	1
80	BATTLE,All		118	0	2	3	0.271	0	0	1	-0	1
81	ROBERSON,K		38	4	6	0	0.184	2	1	0	-1	1
82	PULLIAM,H		5	1	3	0	0.400	0	0	0	0	1
83	POLONIA,L		53	0	2	3	0.264	0	0	1	-0	1
84	PARKER,R		29	0	4	1	0.276	0	1	0	0	1
85	RODRIGUZ,H		138	2	15	0	0.239	1	2	0	-2	1
86	OCHOA		37	0	0	1	0.297	0	0	0	0	1
87	COLES,Darn		138	3	16	0	0.225	1	2	0	-3	1
	avg,top 60		353	12	50	15	0.287	5	7	5	2	18.97

National League Pitchers

rk	PLAYER	IP	W	Sv	ERA	Ratio	$W	$S	$ERA	$Rto	$TOT
1	MADDUX,Gre	210	19	0	1.63	7.30	19	0	23	26	68
2	NOMO,Hideo	191	13	0	2.54	9.50	13	0	13	13	39
3	WORRELL,To	62	4	32	2.02	9.96	4	24	7	4	38
4	HENKE,Tom	54	1	36	1.82	9.94	1	27	6	3	38
5	SCHOUREK,P	190	18	0	3.22	9.60	18	0	7	12	37
6	WOHLERS,Ma	65	7	25	2.09	10.44	7	19	7	3	35
7	BRANTLEY,J	70	3	28	2.82	9.34	3	21	4	6	34
8	VALDES,Ism	198	13	1	3.05	9.97	13	1	9	11	33
9	HOFFMAN,Tr	53	7	31	3.88	10.46	7	23	0	3	33
10	FRANCO,Joh	52	5	29	2.44	11.32	5	22	4	1	32
11	SLOCUMB,He	65	5	32	2.89	13.64	5	24	4	-3	29
12	MYERS,Rand	56	1	38	3.88	12.45	1	28	0	-1	29
13	GLAVINE,To	199	16	0	3.08	11.23	16	0	9	4	28
14	BECK,Rod	59	5	33	4.45	12.43	5	25	-1	-1	27
15	MARTINEZ,PJ	195	14	0	3.51	10.36	14	0	4	9	27
16	ASHBY,Andy	193	12	0	2.94	11.30	12	0	10	4	25
17	NAVARRO,Ja	200	14	0	3.28	11.23	14	0	7	4	25
18	MARTINEZ,Ra	206	17	0	3.66	11.21	17	0	3	4	24
19	SMOLTZ,Joh	193	12	0	3.18	11.12	12	0	8	5	24
20	REED,Steve	84	5	3	2.14	8.79	5	2	8	8	23
21	CASTILLO,F	188	11	0	3.21	11.06	11	0	7	5	23
22	SMILEY,Joh	177	12	0	3.46	10.80	12	0	5	6	22
23	NEAGLE,Den	210	13	0	3.43	11.42	13	0	6	3	22
24	HAMILTON,J	204	6	0	3.08	10.79	6	0	9	7	21
25	ROJAS,Mel	68	1	30	4.12	13.03	1	22	-0	-2	21
26	NEN,Robb	66	0	23	3.29	11.65	0	17	2	1	20
27	LESKANIC,C	98	6	10	3.40	10.65	6	7	3	4	20
28	VERES,Davi	103	5	1	2.26	10.36	5	1	9	5	20
29	JONES,Todd	100	6	15	3.07	12.73	6	11	5	-2	20
30	HOLMES,Dar	67	6	14	3.24	11.75	6	10	3	0	20
31	BOTTALICO	88	5	1	2.46	9.44	5	1	7	7	19
32	REYNOLDS,S	189	10	0	3.47	11.08	10	0	5	5	19
33	SCHILLING	116	7	0	3.57	9.47	7	0	3	9	18
34	PEREZ,Carl	141	10	0	3.69	10.83	10	0	2	5	17
35	MCMICHAEL	81	7	2	2.79	10.71	7	1	5	3	17
36	LEITER,Mar	196	10	0	3.82	11.04	10	0	2	5	17
37	HAMPTON,Mk	151	9	0	3.35	11.35	9	0	5	3	16
38	HENRY,Butc	127	7	0	2.84	11.44	7	0	7	2	16
39	ISRINGH'SN	93	9	0	2.81	11.52	9	0	6	1	16
40	RAPP,Pat	167	14	0	3.44	12.59	14	0	5	-3	16
41	MICELI,Dan	58	4	21	4.66	13.81	4	16	-2	-3	14
42	HENRY,Doug	67	3	4	2.96	9.81	3	3	4	4	14
43	JACKSON,Mk	49	6	2	2.39	10.47	6	1	4	2	14
44	CANDIOTTI	190	7	0	3.50	11.58	7	0	5	2	14
45	DELUCIA,Ri	82	8	0	3.39	10.82	8	0	3	3	13
46	HAMMOND,Ch	161	9	0	3.80	11.40	9	0	2	3	13
47	FERNANDZ,S	65	6	0	3.34	9.60	6	0	2	5	13
48	MATHEWS,Te	83	4	3	3.38	10.56	4	2	3	4	12
49	CLONTZ,Bra	69	8	4	3.65	12.13	8	3	1	-0	12
50	RUFFIN,Bru	34	0	11	2.12	11.91	0	8	4	0	12
51	MORGAN,Mik	131	7	0	3.56	11.44	7	0	3	2	12
52	RUETER,Kir	47	5	0	3.23	8.94	5	0	2	4	11
53	FOSSAS,T	37	3	0	1.47	9.33	3	0	5	3	11

rk	PLAYER	IP	W	Sv	ERA	Ratio	$W	$S	$ERA	$Rto	$TOT
54	PORTUGAL,M	182	11	0	4.01	11.94	11	0	-0	0	11
55	BURBA,Dave	107	10	0	3.97	11.90	10	0	0	0	10
56	FOSTER,Kev	168	12	0	4.51	11.49	12	0	-4	2	10
57	RITZ,Kevin	173	11	2	4.21	12.25	11	1	-2	-1	9
58	WELLS,Davi	73	6	0	3.59	11.15	6	0	2	2	9
59	PETKOVSEK	137	6	0	4.00	11.21	6	0	0	3	9
60	WILLIAMS,Mk	88	3	0	3.29	10.98	3	0	3	3	9
61	MATHEWS,TJ	30	1	2	1.52	9.71	1	1	4	2	9
62	HENNEMAN,M	21	0	8	3.00	10.71	0	6	1	1	8
63	PENA,Aleja	31	2	0	2.61	8.42	2	0	2	3	8
64	VANLAND'HM	123	6	0	3.67	12.03	6	0	2	-0	8
65	JONES,Bobb	196	10	0	4.19	12.05	10	0	-2	-0	8
66	PLESAC,Dan	60	4	3	3.58	11.93	4	2	1	0	8
67	BURKETT,Jo	188	14	0	4.30	12.66	14	0	-3	-3	8
68	FLORIE,Bry	69	2	1	3.01	11.40	2	1	4	1	8
69	HABYAN,Joh	41	3	0	2.88	10.40	3	0	2	2	7
70	ASTACIO,Pe	104	7	0	4.24	11.42	7	0	-1	2	7
71	BIRKBECK	28	0	0	1.63	7.81	0	0	4	4	7
72	SABERHAGEN	153	7	0	4.18	11.65	7	0	-1	1	7
73	MINOR,Blas	47	4	1	3.66	10.99	4	1	1	1	7
74	MLICKI,Dav	161	9	0	4.26	11.99	9	0	-2	0	7
75	HARNISCH,P	110	2	0	3.68	11.05	2	0	2	3	7
76	BOCHTLER,D	45	4	1	3.57	11.32	4	1	1	1	7
77	HARRIS,G.A	48	2	0	2.61	11.36	2	0	4	1	7
78	BULLINGER	150	12	0	4.14	13.02	12	0	-1	-4	6
79	PUGH,Tim	98	6	0	3.84	12.08	6	0	1	-0	6
80	HUDEK,John	20	2	7	5.40	10.80	2	5	-2	1	6
81	OSBORNE,Do	113	4	0	3.81	11.59	4	0	1	1	6
82	PARRETT,J	77	4	0	3.64	11.62	4	0	1	1	6
83	CUMMINGS,J	39	3	0	3.00	11.08	3	0	2	1	6
84	SANDERS,Sc	90	5	0	4.30	11.00	5	0	-1	3	6
85	SCOTT,Tim	63	2	2	3.98	10.66	2	1	0	3	6
86	DIPOTO,Jer	79	4	2	3.78	12.13	4	1	1	-0	6
87	PERSON,Rob	12	1	0	0.75	5.25	1	0	2	3	6
88	BYRD,P	22	2	0	2.05	10.23	2	0	2	1	6
89	PULSIPHER	127	5	0	3.98	11.87	5	0	0	0	6
90	SERVICE,S	31	3	0	3.19	11.03	3	0	1	1	5
91	FREY,Steve	17	0	1	2.12	7.41	0	1	2	2	5
92	LEIPER,D	22	0	2	2.86	9.00	0	1	1	2	5
93	BARTON,S	44	4	1	4.26	11.37	4	1	-1	1	5
94	AVERY,Stev	173	7	0	4.67	11.27	7	0	-6	3	5
95	HERNANDZ,X	90	7	3	4.60	12.60	7	2	-3	-2	5
96	BROCAIL,Do	77	6	1	4.19	12.69	6	1	-1	-2	4
97	HARTGRAVES	36	2	0	3.22	11.39	2	0	2	1	4
98	VERES,Rand	49	4	1	3.88	12.58	4	1	0	-1	4
99	BORBON,Ped	32	2	2	3.09	12.94	2	1	2	-1	4
100	HEREDIA,Gi	119	5	1	4.31	11.95	5	1	-2	0	4
101	PEREZ,Mike	71	2	2	3.66	12.49	2	1	1	-1	4
102	BLAIR,Will	114	7	0	4.34	12.39	7	0	-2	-1	4
103	HANCOCK,L	14	0	0	1.93	7.71	0	0	2	2	4
104	MIMBS,Mike	137	9	1	4.15	13.30	9	1	-1	-5	3
105	YOUNG,Anth	41	3	2	3.70	13.28	3	1	1	-2	3
106	MERCKER,Ke	143	7	0	4.15	12.65	7	0	-1	-3	3
107	RUFFIN,Joh	13	0	0	1.35	10.13	0	0	2	1	3
108	WEST,David	38	3	0	3.79	12.55	3	0	0	-1	3
109	FASSERO,Jf	189	13	0	4.33	13.38	13	0	-3	-7	3
110	CREEK,D	7	0	0	0.00	6.75	0	0	2	1	3

rk PLAYER	IP	W	Sv	ERA	Ratio	$W	$S	$ERA	$Rto	$TOT
111 RIJO,Jose	69	5	0	4.17	12.78	5	0	-1	-2	3
112 FLORENCE,D	12	3	0	1.50	17.25	3	0	2	-2	3
113 RICCI,C	10	1	0	1.80	10.80	1	0	1	0	3
114 SWINDELL,G	153	10	0	4.47	12.88	10	0	-4	-4	2
115 VILLONE	26	2	1	4.21	12.27	2	1	-0	-0	2
116 SWARTZBAGH	7	0	0	0.00	9.82	0	0	2	1	2
117 GRACE,Mike	11	1	0	3.18	11.12	1	0	1	0	2
118 JUDEN,Jeff	63	2	0	4.02	12.06	2	0	-0	-0	2
119 CASIAN,L	23	1	0	1.93	14.66	1	0	3	-2	2
120 DOUGHERTY	68	8	0	4.92	13.43	8	0	-3	-3	2
21 URBANI,Tom	83	3	0	3.70	13.06	3	0	1	-3	2
22 WITT,Bobby	111	2	0	3.90	12.28	2	0	1	-1	2
23 PAINTER,Ln	45	3	1	4.37	12.90	3	1	-1	-1	2
24 SPRINGER,R	27	0	0	3.71	10.80	0	0	0	1	1
25 TABAKA,Jef	31	1	0	3.23	12.91	1	0	1	-1	1
126 RODRIGUEZ,F	11	1	0	2.53	13.50	1	0	1	-1	1
127 LEWIS,R	36	0	0	3.75	11.25	0	0	0	1	1
128 GUNDERSON	24	1	0	3.70	12.21	1	0	0	-0	1
129 FRASER,W	26	2	2	5.61	11.92	2	1	-2	0	1
130 HARRIS,Gen	19	2	0	4.26	12.79	2	0	-0	-0	1
131 DEWEY,Mark	32	1	0	3.13	13.36	1	0	2	-1	1
132 AROCHA,Ren	50	3	0	3.99	13.23	3	0	0	-2	1
133 BORLAND,To	74	1	6	3.77	14.35	1	4	1	-5	1
134 OSUNA,Anto	45	2	0	4.43	11.89	2	0	-1	0	1
135 RODRIGUEZ,R	2	0	0	0.00	0.00	0	0	0	1	1
136 WALKER,Mik	45	1	1	3.22	13.90	1	1	2	-3	1
137 CARRASCO,H	87	2	5	4.12	13.60	2	4	-1	-4	1
138 SHAW,Jeff	62	1	3	4.62	12.13	1	2	-2	-0	1
139 QUANTRILL	179	11	0	4.67	12.85	11	0	-6	-4	1
140 BENES,Andy	119	4	0	4.17	12.59	4	0	-1	-2	1
141 POWELL,Jay	8	0	0	1.08	14.04	0	0	1	-1	1
142 WILLIAMS,To	19	2	0	5.12	12.10	2	0	-1	-0	1
143 WILSON,Tre	83	3	0	3.92	13.06	3	0	0	-3	1
144 SMALL,A	6	1	0	1.42	18.47	1	0	1	-1	1
145 MOREL,Ramo	6	0	0	2.84	11.37	0	0	0	0	1
146 ABBOTT,Kyl	28	2	0	3.81	13.98	2	0	0	-2	0
147 ELLIOTT,Do	2	0	0	0.00	13.50	0	0	0	-0	0
148 BREWINGTON	75	6	0	4.54	13.50	6	0	-2	-3	0
149 PARK,Chan	4	0	0	4.50	9.00	0	0	-0	0	0
150 CARTER,And	7	0	0	6.14	7.36	0	0	-1	1	0
151 WAGNER,Bil	0	0	0	0.00	0.00	0	0	0	0	0
152 EISCHEN,Jo	20	0	0	3.10	13.28	0	0	1	-1	0
153 MYERS,Mike	2	0	0	0.00	18.00	0	0	0	-0	0
154 DRABEK,Dou	185	10	0	4.77	12.60	10	0	-7	-3	-0
155 GUTHRIE,M	20	0	0	3.66	12.81	0	0	0	-1	-0
156 MANZAN'O,R	4	0	0	4.91	12.27	0	0	-0	-0	-0
157 BRUSKE,J	10	0	1	4.50	14.40	0	1	-0	-1	-0
158 BAILEY,Cor	4	0	0	7.36	9.82	0	0	-1	0	-0
159 KARP,Ryan	2	0	0	4.50	18.00	0	0	-0	-0	-0
160 COURTRIGHT	1	0	0	9.00	18.00	0	0	-0	-0	-0
161 WILSON,Gar	14	0	0	5.02	11.30	0	0	-1	0	-1
162 SULLIVAN,S	4	0	0	4.91	14.73	0	0	-0	-0	-1
163 VALDEZ,S	66	4	0	4.75	12.89	4	0	-3	-2	-1
164 DYER,Mike	75	4	0	4.34	13.38	4	0	-1	-3	-1
165 PEREZ,York	47	2	1	5.21	12.15	2	1	-3	-0	-1
166 WADE,Terre	4	0	0	4.50	15.75	0	0	-0	-0	-1

rk	PLAYER	IP	W	Sv	ERA	Ratio	$W	$S	$ERA	$Rto	$TOT
167	VALENZUELA	90	8	0	4.98	13.45	8	0	-5	-4	-1
168	STURTZE,Ta	2	0	0	9.00	13.50	0	0	-1	-0	-1
169	WALL,D	24	3	0	5.55	14.05	3	0	-2	-2	-1
170	JOHNSTONE	5	0	0	3.86	17.36	0	0	0	-1	-1
171	WORRELL,Ti	13	1	0	4.73	14.85	1	0	-1	-1	-1
172	EDENS,Tom	3	1	0	6.00	27.00	1	0	-0	-1	-1
173	PARRA,Jose	10	0	0	4.35	13.94	0	0	-0	-1	-1
174	KROON,Marc	2	0	0	10.80	16.20	0	0	-1	-0	-1
175	GARDNER,Ma	102	5	1	4.49	13.37	5	1	-3	-4	-1
176	CLARK,Terr	4	0	0	4.91	19.64	0	0	-0	-1	-1
177	SPRINGER,D	22	0	0	4.84	12.09	0	0	-1	-0	-1
178	WALKER,Pet	18	1	0	4.58	14.77	1	0	-1	-2	-1
179	REED,R	17	0	0	5.82	11.12	0	0	-2	0	-1
180	RIVERA,R	5	0	0	5.40	18.00	0	0	-0	-1	-1
181	BOWEN,Ryan	17	2	0	3.78	18.90	2	0	0	-4	-2
182	GARCES,R	24	0	0	4.44	13.32	0	0	-1	-1	-2
183	GOTT,Jim	31	2	3	6.03	14.36	2	2	-4	-2	-2
184	CHRISTNSEN	56	1	0	4.15	13.26	1	0	-0	-2	-2
185	FLETCHER,P	13	1	0	5.40	16.20	1	0	-1	-2	-2
186	MURRAY,Mat	11	0	0	6.75	12.66	0	0	-2	-0	-2
187	REKAR,Brya	85	4	0	4.98	12.60	4	0	-4	-2	-2
188	KONUSZWSKI	0	0	0	54.01	108.01	0	0	-1	-1	-2
189	GREER,K	12	0	0	5.25	15.00	0	0	-1	-1	-2
190	THOBE,T	3	0	0	10.80	18.90	0	0	-1	-1	-2
191	ESTES,S	17	0	0	6.75	10.90	0	0	-3	1	-2
192	TAPANI,Kev	57	4	0	5.05	13.58	4	0	-3	-3	-2
193	EVERSGERD	21	0	0	5.14	13.29	0	0	-1	-1	-2
194	THOBE,J	4	0	0	9.00	20.25	0	0	-1	-1	-2
195	BARBER,Bri	29	2	0	5.22	14.42	2	0	-2	-2	-2
196	BAILEY,Rog	81	7	0	4.98	14.05	7	0	-4	-5	-2
197	WOODALL,Br	10	1	0	6.10	18.29	1	0	-1	-2	-2
198	HARVEY,Bry	0	0	0	ERR	ERR	0	0	-2	-1	-2
199	MUNOZ,Bobb	16	0	0	5.74	13.79	0	0	-2	-1	-2
...											
275	LIEBER,Jon	73	4	0	6.32	14.49	4	0	-9	-6	-10
276	MUNOZ,Mike	44	2	2	7.42	16.69	2	1	-8	-6	-11
277	TRACHSEL,S	161	7	0	5.15	14.00	7	0	-9	-9	-11
278	ROSSELLI,J	30	2	0	8.70	17.70	2	0	-8	-5	-11
279	OLIVARES,O	42	1	0	6.91	16.85	1	0	-7	-6	-12
280	THOMPSON,M	51	2	0	6.53	16.76	2	0	-7	-8	-13
281	BAUTISTA,J	101	3	0	6.44	13.05	3	0	-13	-3	-13
282	JACOME,Jas	21	0	0	10.29	20.57	0	0	-7	-6	-13
283	GREENE,Tom	34	0	0	8.29	17.38	0	0	-8	-6	-14
284	WEATHERS,D	90	4	0	5.98	15.54	4	0	-9	-10	-15
285	MULHOLLAND	149	5	0	5.80	13.77	5	0	-13	-7	-16
286	FREEMAN,Ma	95	3	0	5.89	15.50	3	0	-9	-10	-16
287	JACKSON,Da	101	2	0	5.90	15.02	2	0	-10	-9	-17
288	HICKERSON	48	3	1	8.57	18.06	3	1	-12	-9	-17
289	BANKS,Will	91	2	0	5.66	16.28	2	0	-8	-12	-17
	avg,top 108	100	6	4	3.48	11.22	6	3	3	2	14.38

Appendix B — NLP

Postscript

In addition to learning all about *Patton $ On Disk*, this is where you find out how to get the update. Buried back here, the information possibly will elude the browser's grasp in a bookstore, but getting it couldn't be simpler: just send a stamped, self-addressed envelope, preferably business-size, to:

> Patton/Lindow Associates
> Dept. U
> 13 Kempster Rd.
> Scarsdale NY 10583

About 10 days before the season starts, I'll send a new version of exact bid limits for the expected 168 best hitters and 108 best pitchers on major league rosters on opening day. There will also be a page of notes, reporting on my own observations from spring training, if I get there (the hope is to get to Arizona), or passing on what I've gleaned from others — always risky — if I don't.

For quickly and thoroughly getting prepared for the draft, the best bargain in the business remains the software program that Eric Lindow and I have been developing for years. Unfortunately, we still haven't turned out a Mac version of *Patton $ On Disk*, but if you own an IBM-compatible computer, for $35 you get a lot of everything. There are really three programs in one.

The Evaluator (EVA) gives you all facts you need to study the previous season. You get the complete stats, including secondary stats, of all 1995 hitters and pitchers. You can set the values for standard leagues or either of the two kinds of 5x5 leagues, and you can even alter the denominators yourself, emphasizing pitching or de-emphasizing stolen bases, and so forth. You can sort and double-sort to come up with all kinds of odd lists, which you can then print. The data itself is easily exported to a spreadsheet.

The Projector (PRO) contains my predictions. You can easily alter them by changing the values or the at-bats or the home runs, ERA or anything other stat in the player's data box. This is done in the Working File; you can default back to the data in the Original File with a keystroke. The denominators in the 1996 prediction formula can themselves be changed and saved, while the default denominators can always be restored.

Enter your league's freeze lists, and PRO calculates the inflation, based on the predictions.

The great thing about both EVA and PRO is the ease of intervention. Completely menu-driven, both programs can be mastered quickly (their operations are the same) and they practically beg to be tampered with so that, just fooling around for a few minutes here and there, you soon have your own personalized lists to take into the auction. If you're pressed for time, you'll have my values and bid limits to refer to, and they'll keep changing as the season nears. I'll be altering and expanding the reserve lists right up until opening day. For a nominal fee we will send an update disk.

The third program is called The Auction (AUC) and it has two uses. It can be an auction simulator that's especially helpful in showing how bad inflation is initially and how long it takes to disappear. It can be an auction manager that allows you to track every aspect of the draft itself on your laptop; at the press of a button, you see what players are left, who's got openings, and what the money situation is. You can even see who's got what in terms of projected stats.

Finally, there's a very good chance that I will be projecting pitchers — all 1134 wins and 1134 losses in each league. The difference between bids and predicted earnings for pitchers, versus those for hitters, could be interesting.

The cost of *1996 Patton $ On Disk* is $35 for first-time buyers; $25 for re-uppers. The box at the end gives ordering information. It's the same address as above, with Dept D instead of U, in order that you get the disk much sooner than, and instead of, the update. Re-uppers should note that it's not the same address as last year; even Eric has moved, albeit just a few blocks.

If you have questions, you can call Eric at (914) 472-6630. The best day to call is Tuesday, when he doesn't teach.

For reaching me, the best I can do is give you what is still the address for Patton Ink.

> Alex Patton
> Patton Ink Rm 357
> 511 Sixth Ave.
> New York NY 10011

I always enjoy getting information on leagues. Maybe next year I'll fit some round-by-round summaries into the book. If you're keeping track, try to also record who nominates and who makes the penultimate bid: both can be quite interesting. Non-freeze league prices are particularly valuable; there's a good chance the prices of your league, if it has no freezes, will be used in calculating the average salary.

Please don't order the software or send for the update at the Patton Ink address. My secretary is simply not reliable.

So that's it. The eighth book. There's been a lot to write about. Whether this coming season has more Stage Four fireworks remains to be seen. Nothing's certain in baseball, that's for sure. Roger Maris's record may not fall. The Cubs may not be hot. Most of us will settle for seeing 162 games after Cal Ripken's name.

To order *1996 Patton $ On Disk*, send a check for $35 (sorry, no credit cards) to Patton/Lindow Associates at the address below. Registered owners, send $25. First class postage is included.

Patton/Lindow Associates
Dept. D
13 Kempster Rd.
Scarsdale NY 10583

You will receive a 3.5 inch disk unless you specify a 5.25 inch disk.

Newsflash!!!! Visit our new World Wide Web site at
http://oit-unix.umass.edu/~summers/patton$/index.html